THE REGULATION OF PROSTITUTION IN CHINA

In this compelling book, Margaret L. Boittin delves into the complex world of prostitution in China and how it shapes the lives of those involved in it. Through in-depth fieldwork, Boittin provides a fascinating case study of the role of law in everyday life and its impact on female sex workers, street-level police officers, and frontline public health officials. The book offers a unique perspective on the dynamics between society and the state, revealing how the laws that govern sex work affect those on the frontlines. With clear and accessible prose, this book is a must-read for anyone interested in law, state–society relations, China, and sex work.

MARGARET L. BOITTIN is an assistant professor of law at Osgoode Hall Law School, York University, Toronto. Her articles have been published in *Law & Society Review*, *Law & Policy*, *American Political Science Review*. Boittin holds a PhD in political science from UC Berkeley and a JD from Stanford.

CAMBRIDGE STUDIES IN LAW AND SOCIETY

Founded in 1997, Cambridge Studies in Law and Society is a hub for leading scholarship in socio-legal studies. Located at the intersection of law, the humanities, and the social sciences, it publishes empirically innovative and theoretically sophisticated work on law's manifestations in everyday life: from discourses to practices, and from institutions to cultures. The series editors have longstanding expertise in the interdisciplinary study of law, and welcome contributions that place legal phenomena in national, comparative, or international perspective. Series authors come from a range of disciplines, including anthropology, history, law, literature, political science, and sociology.

A list of books in the series can be found at the back of this book.

CAMBRIDGE
STUDIES IN
LAW AND SOCIETY

THE REGULATION OF PROSTITUTION IN CHINA

Law in the Everyday Lives of Sex Workers, Police Officers, and Public Health Officials

Margaret L. Boittin
York University

CAMBRIDGE
UNIVERSITY PRESS

CAMBRIDGE
UNIVERSITY PRESS

Shaftesbury Road, Cambridge CB2 8EA, United Kingdom

One Liberty Plaza, 20th Floor, New York, NY 10006, USA

477 Williamstown Road, Port Melbourne, VIC 3207, Australia

314–321, 3rd Floor, Plot 3, Splendor Forum, Jasola District Centre, New Delhi – 110025, India

103 Penang Road, #05–06/07, Visioncrest Commercial, Singapore 238467

Cambridge University Press is part of Cambridge University Press & Assessment, a department of the University of Cambridge.

We share the University's mission to contribute to society through the pursuit of education, learning and research at the highest international levels of excellence.

www.cambridge.org
Information on this title: www.cambridge.org/9781107179226

DOI: 10.1017/9781316831946

When citing this work, please include a reference to the DOI 10.1017/9781316831946

First published 2024

A catalogue record for this publication is available from the British Library.

A Cataloging-in-Publication data record for this book is available from the Library of Congress

ISBN 978-1-107-17922-6 Hardback

A mes enfants, Emilia Simone et Gabriel Damien. Je vous aime plus que tout au monde.

CONTENTS

ACKNOWLEDGMENTS

More than anyone else, Laura Stoker helped me make this book what I wanted it to be. Its methods, organization, and writing bear her imprint in deep ways. She supported me as I plunged into unfamiliar methodological territory. She read and commented meticulously on multiple iterations of the book manuscript, providing feedback that was accurate and constructive, always delivered with infectious warmth and enthusiasm that propelled me forward. And while her intellect is great, it pales in comparison to the generosity of her spirit. Thank you, Laura, with all my heart.

My other advisors at UC Berkeley and Stanford have also provided steadfast support to me since graduate school. Kevin O'Brien has always been boundlessly generous with his time. I am lucky to have received thorough, line-by-line comments on the written work I have given him over the years. He taught me the value of focusing on "low-hanging fruit" in the research process. He is an energizing intellectual sounding board, and a consistent source of wise advice. Steven Vogel's feedback is refreshingly and immediately actionable. I am grateful for the calm demeanor with which he has always delivered it, which more than once has helped dislodge me from an intellectual rut and allowed me to move forward productively. I thank Bob Kagan for the warmth and enthusiasm that he exudes when delivering feedback. Interactions with him have always left me buoyed, with a renewed sense of excitement about my work. Amalia Kessler provides rich and thoughtful comments delivered with caring grace and impressive speed. I also benefit enormously from her incisive professionalization advice, steadfast support, and kindness. I thank Rob MacCoun for sharing his substantive expertise in many of the issues I explore, and combining careful attention to detail with larger questions about framing in his feedback.

I thank the National Science Foundation, the Charlotte W. Newcombe Doctoral Dissertation Fellowship, UC Berkeley's Graduate Division, UC Berkeley's Center for Chinese Studies, and the UC Pacific Rim Research

Program for funding my research. I am grateful to Larry Diamond for providing me with financial support and an intellectual community at Stanford's Center on Democracy, Development and the Rule of Law. Francis Fukuyama extended this support with extreme generosity and flexibility.

As a graduate student at UC Berkeley, colleagues and friends who provided me with invaluable substantive input, support, advice, and friendship include Celeste Arrington, Naazneen Barma, Jennifer Brass, Jennifer Bussell, Betsy Carter, Devin Caughey, Crystal Chang Cohen, Jennifer Choo, Thad Dunning, Brent Durbin, Jordan Gans-Morse, Matt Grossmann, Jonathan Hassid, Daniel Hidalgo, Roselyn Hsueh, Maiah Jaskoski, Jody Laporte, Amy Lerman, Danielle Lussier, Daniel Mattingly, Sara Newland, Seung-Youn Oh, Sarah Reckhow, Regine Spector, Rachel Stern, Tony Sturm, Chris Sullivan, Erica Turner, and Carsten Vala.

As I turned my dissertation into a book manuscript, I received invaluable feedback from Nicolas Bequelin, Sarah Biddulph, Kevin E. Davis, Jacques deLisle, Neil Diamant, Lawrence Friedman, Mary Gallagher, Joan Kaufman, Pierre Landry, Ji Li, Katerina Linos, Sida Liu, Samantha Majic, Andrew Mertha, Jacqueline Ross, Kim Lane Scheppele, Suzanne Scoggins, David Sklansky, Matthew Sommer, Cui Wei, and Robert Weisberg. John Grennan is an exceptional editor; thank you for your meticulous work, patience, and responsiveness. At Cambridge University Press, thank you to John Berger, Matt Gallaway, Jadyn Fauconier-Henry, as well as three anonymous book reviewers.

Thank you to Flore Nove-Josserand for designing the book cover.

Rachel Stern's input over the years has made this book better in many ways. Thank you for your support and friendship.

I thank Wang Jing for her friendship, for housing and feeding me in China for several months, for stepping in to help me navigate several delicate situations during my fieldwork, and for answering countless linguistic and cultural questions over the years. Kate Mason has been a partner-in-crime since our first exposure to China in 2001. She continues to be a wonderful source of advice and friendship. I am grateful for Denise Ho's kindness, insight and responsiveness over the years. Others who also brought great joy to me during fieldwork include Corinne Dillon, Sarah Eaton, Genia Kostka, Alex Liebman, Marc

Parich, Pam Phan, Holly Smith, and Chen Wei. Chris and Freda Murck welcomed me countless times into their Beijing home, allowing me to benefit from their wonderful hospitality and deep knowledge of China.

There are also many people in China whom I cannot name here, who went above and beyond the call of duty to make my data collection possible. I am humbled and in awe of their devotion and commitment. This is particularly the case for the sex workers who agreed to participate in my research, as well as outreach staff at various organizations working with them.

For providing an endless source of encouragement, distraction, support, and love in person, over the phone, in emails, texts, cards, and care packages, thank you to Nora Allavoine, Laure de Vulpillières, Vanessa Dillen, Anna Dreyfack, Makiko Harunari, Gaby Maradiaga Panayotti, Kate Mulvihill, Leeza Park, Letitia Stein, Jen Sugden, Laure Trebosc, and Jon Whitney.

Thank you to Sarah Reiff-Hekking for holding me accountable and keeping me on track. Thanks also to Cecilia Hyunjung Mo and Maurice Stephens.

For excellent research support, I thank Jingtian Chen, Fang Chenbo, Lingxi Huang, Lea Jia, Daniel Kim, Jiarui Li, Yi Liu, Jeffrey Kai Yiu Wong, Yu Cheng Ya, Gloria C. Yu, Jiang Yuqing, Qingyu Zheng, and Chloe Zhu. Thank you also to Caroline Brandt and Jake Grumbach.

Thank you to Jenny S. Martinez for her kindness and wisdom, and for providing the support that allowed my next project to come to life.

My colleagues are the highlight of my job at Osgoode Hall Law School. For your support and guidance, thank you to Kate Glover Berger, Amar Bhatia, Andrée Boisselle, Ruth Buchanan, Mary G. Condon, Karen Drake, Trevor C.W. Farrow, Philip Girard, Sonia Lawrence, Heidi Matthews, Adam Parachin, Bruce B. Ryder, Craig M. Scott, Dayna N. Scott, Lorne Sossin, Francois Tanguay-Renaud, Estair Van Wagner, and Sharon Wang. Benjamin L. Berger is the consummate mentor and friend. He is unfailingly responsive and calming, and an unending wealth of refreshing perspectives on and solutions to professional problems. Palma Paciocco has an impressive ability to provide razor-sharp feedback on substantive questions seemingly far removed from her own areas of research expertise. She also provides consistently astute professional advice. Above all, she is a boundlessly generous friend who knows exactly how and when to show up, time and again.

My community of friends in Toronto has enriched my daily life in countless ways throughout the years of working on the book manuscript. My interactions with them have often provided energizing counterpoints to the solitary writing process. Rainbow Writing Warriors Emily Nacol and Katherine Zubovich have provided me with years of weekly accountability, advice, celebration, and commiseration. Through their words and actions, Torrey Shanks and Ambarish Chandra always show up, as do Amélie Barras and Karim Ali. Thank you also to Brookes Brown, Bérengère Launay, Anaïs Saidy-Kanny, Fanny Sallaz, J. Barton Scott, Beatriz Vieira, and Virginie Yvars.

Miguel de Figueiredo has been by my side for this project since I started graduate school. He has helped transform many of its mountains into molehills. His intellectual curiosity, creative mind, optimism, and spontaneity are infectious, and inspiring.

My sisters Isabelle, Nathalie, and Jennifer are my rocks. They are THE BEST! They listen, observe, understand and, above all else, show up and do. This book is better because of everything they have helped me shoulder. Jennifer has provided me with support and advice over the years that combines academic expertise with great compassion. Nathalie's approaches to work, leisure, and family provide a model to which I aspire. Isabelle keeps me grounded in the practical realities of research. She also makes everything better.

I thank my maternal grandmother, Frances B. Paulu, for the effusive expressions of support she always provided in my endeavors. My interest in gender issues is no doubt tied to her own commitment to women's rights over the years. In 2001, when I told my maternal grandfather, Burton Paulu, that I wanted to go to law school, he expressed his hope that I might follow his own path by saying to me, "We'll make a PhD out of you!" He was right. My paternal grandmother, Anne-Marie Boittin *née* Morot-Raquin, always tried dutifully to keep track of my whereabouts and never failed to share kind, supportive words in times of joy and stress. Together with my paternal grandfather, Jean-Marie Boittin, she created a home for us in Burgundy that I treasure for the calm respite it provides, and for the unbridled joy it unleashes in Emilia and Gabriel's hearts and minds.

When I was growing up, my father would often inquire about our school day by asking us: "Avez-vous progressé sur la voie du savoir et de la sagesse aujourd'hui?" which translates as "Have you progressed on the path to knowledge and wisdom today?" If I have done so over the years, it is because of my parents, Jean-François and Sarah Leith Paulu Boittin. They instilled within me a deep love of learning and provided me with innumerable opportunities over the years that opened the doors and gave me the skills to carry out this project. My mother has read and edited this entire manuscript multiple times, and responded to countless questions on word choices and permutations as I neared this book's finish line. My parents model how to show up for loved ones in times of need. At multiple moments in recent years, they have upended their own lives for long stretches of time to support me, Miguel, Emilia, and Gabriel in innumerable ways on a daily basis. This time with them has been priceless. They give rides, make food, clean dishes, play games, read books, and make music. Above all, they have filled our home with more love. My biggest debt of gratitude goes to them.

1

INTRODUCTION

It was a fall afternoon in the central square of Xizhou, a red-light district in the city of Shenzhen, in southern China.[1] About two hundred female sex workers were milling around in the square near the hair salons and karaoke bars where they work. Before disappearing into these venues for the night, they were catching up with friends and snacking on grilled corn on the cob, meat skewers, and vegetable stew from neighborhood hawkers. Local government health officials were hard at work in the community, as they usually were at this time of day, and my research assistants and I worked alongside them distributing condoms and safe sex pamphlets to the sex workers in the hopes of later recruiting them to participate in a survey. All of a sudden, the women started running away from the square and into the nearby alleys, vanishing from view. When I looked around to see what was happening, I spotted a van driving slowly around the square. Men inside the van were extending their arms from its sliding door and pulling in women who had not managed to escape in time. When the van came up to me, one of the men, evidently surprised by the presence of a young white woman at the scene, hopped out to inquire about me. Only then did I realize these were undercover police officers – the man had a discreet police patch on his sweater. The neighborhood health

[1] Xizhou is a pseudonym. I use the term "red-light district" to refer to an area with a high concentration of prostitution. My use of the term is consistent with that of other scholars of sex work in China. See, e.g., Pan Suiming (潘绥铭), *Sheng Cun Yu Ti Yan (生存与体验) [Survival and Experiences]* (Beijing: Chinese Social Science Press (中国社会科学出版社), 2000); Tiantian Zheng, *Red Lights: The Lives of Sex Workers in Postsocialist China* (Minneapolis: University of Minnesota Press, 2009).

officials rushed over to vouch for me, and the officer soon lost interest and drove off with the van full of women.[2] According to one sex worker who ended up in the van, the police explained that they needed to meet their monthly arrest target for prostitution.[3] They brought the women to the local police station, confiscated their cigarettes and cash, held them overnight, and released them the next day.

Over the next two hours, the neighborhood gradually came back to life. Sex workers cautiously returned and went into their karaoke bars and hair salons, and clients trickled in shortly afterward. As night fell over Xizhou, it was back to business as usual until a group of six or seven young men crowded around the table in the square where my research assistants and I were conducting outreach. It quickly became clear that the local sex industry had sent them our way to intimidate us.

GROUP HEAD:	"What are you doing here? In the future, you're not allowed to come here."
MY RESEARCH ASSISTANT:	"We're here to do health education."
GROUP HEAD:	"Fuck health education."
MY RESEARCH ASSISTANT:	"We're with the local health bureau."
GROUP HEAD:	"Fuck the local health bureau. Finish your stuff up now. If I ever see you here again, I'm going to cream your table into pulp."[4]
MY RESEARCH ASSISTANT:	"We'll leave now."
GROUP HEAD:	"Fuck you. Get out of here. I'm going to smash all of your stuff into pulp. Don't let me see you here again."

We promptly grabbed our belongings, hailed a cab, and left for the night.[5] When we returned a few days later and recounted our experience to Wang Zhuren, the head of the local health office, he shrugged it off, using the term "youngsters" (小伙子 – *xiao huozi*) to convey that he viewed these hecklers as harmless. He was used to receiving pushback from the neighborhood sex industry when he carried out testing, training, and outreach programs to reduce HIV/AIDS in the

[2] Field Notes, November 13, 2009.
[3] Field Notes, November 17, 2009.
[4] "下次再让我看见你们砸烂你们的桌子." (*Xia ci zai rang wo kanjian nimen zalan nimen de zhouzi.*)
[5] Field Notes, November 13, 2009.

community.[6] Sex workers, madams, pimps, and managers of the venues where they work are wary of letting the state into their lives and giving it a close look at the illegal activities in which they engage, and do not want it disrupting their regular business operations.

That evening in Xizhou brings to life what this book is about: how the regulation of prostitution shapes the lives of female sex workers, street-level police officers, and frontline public health officials. It is a case study of law in everyday life in China that examines the place of law both within society and within the state, and that also brings to light how dynamics between society and the state unfold on the front lines around the law. Within society, I study how sex workers experience the laws that govern their lives. Within the state, I examine street-level police and public health officials, the individuals who are responsible for implementing the laws and policies that govern sex work in China. I observe how they contend with agency directives handed down from above, and with cross-agency tensions and local political priorities they encounter as they seek to carry out their professional responsibilities. And when sex workers (society) and law enforcement and health officials (the state) encounter each other, I examine the place of law in those dynamics: how those interactions are faithful to the law, how they flout it, and how they often sit somewhere in the middle, selectively mirroring aspects of it while holding others at bay.

Female sex workers in China are usually viewed as either scheming villains who break the law to earn easy money instead of putting in the hard work of the country's law-abiding citizens, or as innocent victims of broader socioeconomic and political trends that reduce them to engaging in illegal behavior as a last resort. The state is generally perceived as turning a blind eye to China's thriving sex industry and paying short shrift to the laws that govern it. And considering that female sex workers are among the most marginalized and stigmatized groups within China, an authoritarian state that wields prodigious power over its citizens, it makes sense to expect that whenever government officials *do* pay attention to sex workers, these interactions will exhibit the overwhelming strength of China's state and the weakness of its society.

My research, however, belies such broad-brush characterizations of prostitution in China. Instead, it brings to light the multifaceted and

[6] Field Notes, November 17, 2009.

nuanced ways in which female sex workers, police officers, and local health officials actually experience China's prostitution laws and policies. It is based on almost two years of fieldwork in which I placed myself at eye level with sex workers and the street-level bureaucrats responsible for regulating their lives, listening to how they talk about the law and observing how they behave around it amid the swirl of relationships and rules that shape their daily lives. Female sex workers certainly do cower in the face of the state: They fear its law enforcement officers and shy away from its public health programs. But they also engage with the rules and regulations that define the state's formal interventions into their lives, voice their objections, and push back against perceived injustices. Frontline police and public health officials, for their part, are no angels. They often exert control over sex workers in ways that profoundly violate these women's rights and dignity. But these officials are not only vessels of authoritarian state strength when they regulate the lives of sex workers. They also struggle to carry out their professional law enforcement and public health responsibilities as they navigate complicated power dynamics that emerge within their agencies, across agencies, and in relation to local political priorities. These challenges highlight the vulnerabilities of these street-level bureaucrats, who can be surprisingly attentive to the concerns of sex workers in the community – catering to them, treading carefully around them, or protecting them from harm. *The Regulation of Prostitution in China: Law in the Everyday Lives of Sex Workers, Police Officers, and Public Health Officials* tells the story of these experiences.

THE CASE OF PROSTITUTION IN CHINA

Prostitution is ubiquitous in contemporary China.[7] Millions of women sell sex, and millions of men buy it. It is also illegal, and this policy is a reflection of prostitution's symbolic importance in the People's Republic of China (PRC).[8] When the Chinese Communist Party

7 This book focuses on prostitution between female sex workers and male clients. Of course, the sex work landscape in China includes both heterosexual and same-sex prostitution, and men and transgender people also sell sex. Yet these other permutations of prostitution differ in a variety of ways in China, including their prevalence, their roles in society and the economy, the self-perceptions of participants, the public's views of them, and how various state actors choose to regulate them. I leave it to others to reflect upon the regulation of these other types of prostitution in China.

8 I use the terms "sex work" and "prostitution" interchangeably throughout this book in reference to the exchange of sex for money or other material goods. The term "sex work" is in fact broader than the term "prostitution" – the former includes activities such as erotic dancing and

(CCP) came to power in 1949, it portrayed prostitution as a feudal remnant of the country's colonial past.[9] It invested heavily in efforts to eradicate prostitution from society, and by the late 1950s and early 1960s, the CCP was publicly touting its success.[10] In fact, sex work continued in more disguised forms; yet for about three decades, it was remarkably less prevalent and conspicuous in Chinese society.[11] This all changed in 1978, when Deng Xiaoping introduced market-based economic reforms and opened China to the outside world, turning the PRC into a Communist-ruled country that fervently embraces capitalism. The pervasiveness of the exchange of sex for money and material goods powerfully embodies this deeply ironic ideological contradiction within Chinese society today. On a less theoretical level, prostitution has played a pivotal role in a public health crisis in China – HIV/AIDS, which expanded from high-risk groups to the population at large through sex workers, clients, and their other sexual partners.[12]

State Interests in the Sex Industry

Sex work challenges the Chinese state in three different domains: policing, public health, and commerce. From the perspective of law enforcement, it violates anti-prostitution laws. It also makes it difficult

pornography, which my study does not address, and the latter assumes some kind of vaginal, oral, or other intercourse. Samantha Majic, "'I'm Just a Woman. But I've Never Been a Victim': Re-Conceptualizing Prostitution Policy through Individual Narratives," *Journal of Women, Politics & Policy* 36, no. 4 (October 2, 2015): 383, https://doi.org/10.1080/1554477X.2015.1082889. In addition, given the type of prostitution that I examine, when I use the terms "prostitution," "sex work," "sex worker," and "client," I am referring to female sex workers and male clients.

9 Gail Hershatter, *Dangerous Pleasures: Prostitution and Modernity in Twentieth-Century Shanghai* (Berkeley: University of California Press, 1997), 7, 305; Christian Henriot, "'La Fermeture': The Abolition of Prostitution in Shanghai, 1949–58," *The China Quarterly*, no. 142 (1995): 467–68.

10 Hershatter, *Dangerous Pleasures*; Jinghao Zhou, "Chinese Prostitution: Consequences and Solutions in the Post-Mao Era," *China: An International Journal* 4, no. 2 (2006): 242; Elaine Jeffreys, *China, Sex and Prostitution* (London: Routledge Curzon, 2004), 96; Elanah Uretsky, "Mixing Business with Pleasure: Masculinity and Male Sexual Culture in Urban China in the Era of HIV/AIDS" (PhD diss., Columbia University, 2007), 6.

11 Sarah Biddulph, *Legal Reform and Administrative Detention Powers in China* (Cambridge: Cambridge University Press, 2007), 76; Jeffreys, *China, Sex and Prostitution*, 96.

12 Joan Kaufman, Arthur Kleinman, and Tony Saich, "Introduction: Social Policy and HIV/AIDS in China," in *AIDS and Social Policy in China* (Cambridge, MA: Harvard University Asia Center, 2006), 6; Yan Hong and Xiaoming Li, "Behavioral Studies of Female Sex Workers in China: A Literature Review and Recommendation for Future Research," *AIDS and Behavior* 12, no. 4 (July 2008): 623; Yan Cui, Cynthia X. Shi, and Zunyou Wu, "Epidemiology of HIV/AIDS in China: Recent Trends," *Global Health Journal* 1, no. 1 (June 1, 2017): 26–32, https://doi.org/10.1016/S2414-6447(19)30057-0; Zunyou Wu, Junfang Chen, Sarah Robbins Scott, and Jennifer M. McGoogan, "History of the HIV Epidemic in China," *Current HIV/AIDS Reports* 16, no. 6 (December 1, 2019): 458–66, https://doi.org/10.1007/s11904-019-00471-4.

to maintain order in a community, as areas with a high concentration of sex work and entertainment venues that harbor it attract large numbers of unruly and often inebriated clients. Sex workers are also at heightened risk of falling victim to crimes such as robbery, rape, and murder. And when they are coerced to engage in prostitution, it becomes an issue of sex trafficking. The country's sex industry is also associated with drug use and drug trafficking.[13] In short, prostitution and its associated activities present a variety of threats to public order and social stability that fall within the purview of police responsibilities.

The Chinese state also treats prostitution as a public health issue. Since 2003, the PRC has publicly recognized the threat that HIV/AIDS presents in the country and acknowledges the role that prostitution plays in increasing the virus' prevalence within the population. Sexual transmission is now the primary mode of HIV/AIDS infection in China, and infection rates among sex workers are as high as 10 percent in some places.[14] Public health officials monitor rates of HIV/AIDS infection among sex workers. They carry out trainings to educate these women about HIV/AIDS transmission. They promote condom use within this population and also mandate that condoms be publicly visible and available for purchase in all entertainment venues and hotels. They support voluntary counseling and treatment for HIV/AIDS patients and provide free antiretroviral treatments for them. HIV education campaigns also target the general population, in efforts to reach potential clients. Similar efforts extend to monitoring other sexually transmitted diseases such as syphilis, which also present a public health threat in China.

Lastly, the Chinese state regulates commercial aspects of the sex industry. Work culture in China revolves around a vast entertainment industry – including karaoke bars and clubs – that plays a crucial role in professional networking and business negotiations, and that represents an important contributor to economic growth. Prostitution lies at the heart of this phenomenon: Sex workers are integral to the entertainment that occurs in these spaces. The actual exchange of money for sex

[13] Jason J. Ong et al., "Sexualized Drug Use among Female Sex Workers from Eight Cities in China: A Cross-Sectional Study," *Archives of Sexual Behavior* 51, no. 5 (2022): 2689–98, https://doi.org/10.1007/s10508-021-02117-2; Katie Hail-Jares, Sugy Choi, Lin Duo, Zhi Luo, and Z. Jennifer Huang, "Occupational and Demographic Factors Associated with Drug Use among Female Sex Workers at the China–Myanmar Border," *Drug and Alcohol Dependence* 161 (April 1, 2016): 42–49, https://doi.org/10.1016/j.drugalcdep.2016.01.026.

[14] Wu et al., "History of the HIV Epidemic in China"; Kaufman, Kleinman, and Saich, "Introduction: Social Policy and HIV/AIDS in China," 6.

between clients and sex workers contributes only minimally to the economic growth that comes from the entertainment industry. Instead, it is expenditures such as food, drink, and room rentals that generate important amounts of revenue, which benefits the state through taxation of entertainment venues and their employees. Importantly, for a state where sex work is against the law, this taxation regime applies to the services that these registered businesses provide that are legal (such as food, drink, and room rentals), rather than the prostitution that they harbor; it is not a policy that officially legalizes and formally taxes the exchange of sex for money. Places with a thriving entertainment industry also provide employment opportunities for China's vast migrant population and attract investment. One study found that the national sex trade was worth 1 trillion yuan (about $157 billion) annually and another estimated that it contributes 6 to 12 percent of China's GDP.[15] In Dongguan, a city in southern China renowned for prostitution, the sex industry is estimated to generate about 10 percent of the local GDP.[16] The accuracy of these figures is not easy to verify. Yet it is undeniable that the entertainment industry is an important contributor to the local GDP throughout urban China, and that it falls apart without the promise of sex that it presents to all its patrons.

The state's three approaches to prostitution – policing, public health, and commerce – are frequently in tension with one another. Policing policies lead sex workers to shy away from the state and hide their involvement in prostitution, for fear of arrest. Yet to work effectively, health policies require sex workers to disclose that they sell sex and to proactively seek health care. Commercial regulations, meanwhile, are designed to allow the state to benefit from a thriving sex industry. Law enforcement regulations, by contrast, aim to reduce the occurrence of prostitution in society. It is these tensions that shape the daily policy implementation choices of police officers and health workers. They lie behind the many permutations that characterize how local officials interact with each other and the sex industry, and that I bring to light in this book.

[15] "Crackdown on Sex City," *The Economist*, February 14, 2014, https://perma.cc/L7ZP-P5HG; Wei Zhong, "A Close Look at China's Sex Industry," *Lianhe Zaobao*, October 2, 2000; Zheng, *Red Lights*, 66.

[16] "Crackdown on Sex City."

Tiers of Sex Workers

In this introduction thus far, I have focused on female sex workers as one group, united by a shared livelihood: exchanging sex for money or other material goods. Yet China, like every society, includes multiple markets for sex, and the characteristics of prostitution and the experience of its regulation vary widely across each market. In the lowest tier, sex workers solicit on the streets and in brothels, which are often thinly disguised as hair salons and massage parlors, and signal the services they actually provide with glowing red lights in the windows. These venues tend to lack sinks, scissors, and other tools generally found in legitimate beauty parlors. Sex is the only service provided in this lowest tier of the sex industry. In the middle tier, karaoke bar and club "hostesses" (三陪小姐 – *sanpei xiaojie*) drink, dance, and talk with guests. In addition to these services, all of which are legal, they also sell sex. In the top tier of the sex industry, "mistresses" (情妇 – *qingfu*) and "second wives" (二奶 – *ernai*) entertain businessmen and government officials.[17] Clients in this category provide housing and generous living allowances to these kept women, and may even have children with them. Neighborhoods in some cities have such a high concentration of this type of sex worker that they are called "second wife villages" (二奶村 – *ernaicun*).

These three categories encompass the major types of activities and spaces associated with female sex work in China.[18] They also reflect how actors in the sex industry talk about different types of prostitution. The women whose experiences inform this study were quick to articulate the differences between selling sex on the street/in small brothels, hustling for clients every evening at a karaoke bar, and being a kept

[17] I use the terms "second wife" and "mistress" interchangeably throughout this book: In practice, the relationship dynamics that define these two phrases are the same. This decision accords with other scholars who study this population (Suowei Xiao, "The 'Second-Wife' Phenomenon and the Relational Construction of Class-Coded Masculinities in Contemporary China," *Men and Masculinities* 14, no. 5 (December 1, 2011): 607–27, https://doi.org/10.1177/1097184X11412171; John Osburg, *Anxious Wealth: Money and Morality among China's New Rich* (Stanford, CA: Stanford University Press, 2013). It also reflects popular discourse on the phenomenon. That said, clients might object to this conflation of terms. Keeping a second wife (包二奶 – *bao ernai*) is explicitly transactional: *bao* is the verb used in the phrase "to rent a room" (包房 – *bao fang*). Use of the phrase suggests that a man does not have the qualities necessary to attract women without an explicit financial agreement. In contrast, in the phrase used for maintaining a mistress (养情妇 – *yang qingfu*), *yang* means "care," and is the verb used for caring for children or elderly parents. The term removes the transactional nature of the relationship and suggests that the woman is drawn to a client's character, rather than his wealth.

[18] Broadly speaking, these three categories also reflect how prostitution has been organized in other societies and at other historical moments. See Lena Edlund and Evelyn Korn, "A Theory of Prostitution," *The Journal of Political Economy* 110, no. 1 (2002): 187.

woman whose life revolves around the whims and wishes of one man. Clients also talk about the differences between soliciting sex on the streets/in small brothels, in karaoke venues, and maintaining a mistress or second wife. This approach to categorizing female sex workers in China also largely overlaps with how state actors who regulate the sex industry perceive these women. The police recognize a hierarchy of prostitution in their community, from streetwalkers to second wives and mistresses.[19] China's public health policies classify female sex workers according to a three-tiered hierarchy.[20] Given their focus on groups at greatest risk of HIV/AIDS, public health officials do not explicitly include mistresses and second wives in their categorization.[21]

Some may question whether prostitution encompasses this top tier of women. Second wives might reject this characterization of their situation (particularly if they have never engaged in other types of prostitution), and some of their clients would likely concur. Yet the arrangements between second wives and the men who support them fall comfortably within the bounds of the prevailing definition of prostitution as "the exchange of sex or sexual services for money or other material benefits."[22] In fact, women who move back and forth

19 Police officers I interviewed spoke about these different types of prostitution in their communities, and the police survey I developed, which received formal approval from the police bureaucracy in one Chinese city, inquired about these tiers. Law enforcement officers in China have also addressed these categories of prostitution in academic writings. See, e.g., Shen Linsong (沈林松) and Wang Zhiwen (王志文), "Maiyin Piaochang Huodong Zhong De Aizibing Chuanbo Yinhuan Ji Fangzhi Duice Chuyi" (卖淫嫖娼活动中的艾滋病传播隐患及防治对策刍议) [Comments on the HIV Risks in and Prevention Strategies Regarding Prostitution and Whoring Activities], *Journal of Hunan Public Security College (湖南公安高等专科学校学报)* 18, no. 1 (2006): 51–53.

20 These policies instruct health workers to map out the universe of prostitution spaces in a community and categorize them as "high" (高), "middle" (中), or "low" (低) tiers (层次). They define high- and middle-tier venues as nightclubs, hotels, entertainment venues, massage rooms, and bars where a sex worker is paid over 100 yuan ($15) for a sexual transaction. They define low-tier venues as spaces such as small hair salons, massage parlors, foot-washing rooms, hostels, and various areas where streetwalkers solicit and earn less than 100 yuan. Mapped on to the tiers articulated in this book, the health policy "high" category corresponds to the middle tier (hostesses), and its "middle" and "low" categories both fold in to the lowest tier (brothels and streetwalkers). Xiang-Sheng Chen, Yue-Ping Yin, and Ning Jiang, "Was the HIV Infection Burden in Female Sex Workers in China Overestimated?," *The Lancet Infectious Diseases* 13, no. 1 (January 2013): 13.

21 Mistresses and second wives present less of a public health concern as they have fewer clients. Public health outreach does access them indirectly, however. Some women move back and forth between hostessing and second wife arrangements, and thus encounter health outreach as hostesses. In addition, sex workers in all tiers of prostitution may come into contact with general population HIV/AIDS outreach.

22 Joyce Outshoorn, "Introduction: Prostitution, Women's Movements and Democratic Politics," in *The Politics of Prostitution: Women's Movements, Democratic States, and the Globalisation of Sex Commerce*, ed. Joyce Outshoorn (Cambridge: Cambridge University Press, 2004), 3.

between positions as hostesses and kept women clearly view these two arrangements on a spectrum. Other academics who study the sex industry in China also view second wives as engaging in prostitution.[23] This issue begs the question of whether marriage should then also be considered a type of sex work – a position that some feminist theorists uphold.[24] While some sex workers in China do place marriage on the spectrum of prostitution,[25] that was not the predominant view among the women whose stories inform these pages. In addition, the state does not view marriage this way and regulates it separately from prostitution.

Tiers often feature prominently in research on female sex work. The categories that scholars delineate and highlight may differ – not only due to differences across space and time but even within a given society, depending on the research question.[26] For instance, I structure my study primarily around the streetwalker/brothel worker–hostess–mistress categorization described earlier in this section of the chapter. Yet these three categories can be further dissected to reveal additional within-group distinctions,[27] and scholars such as Tiantian Zheng and Suowei Xiao have produced rich and insightful studies focused on such

[23] Pan Suiming (潘绥铭), *Cunzai Yu Huangmiu: Zhongguo Dixia "Xingchanye" Kao Cha (存在与荒谬: 中国地下"性产业"考察) [Existing in Falsehoods: An Investigation of China's Underground "Sex Industry"]* (Beijing: Qunyan Press (群言出版社), 1999); Jeffreys, *China, Sex, and Prostitution*, 168–72. Tiantian Zheng, the anthropologist and author of *Red Lights*, considers mistresses as sex workers. NPR Staff, "Corruption Blurs the Lines of China's Mistress Culture," *National Public Radio*, March 2, 2014, perma.cc/7LLU-EW84 .

[24] See, e.g., Sheila Jeffreys, *The Industrial Vagina: The Political Economy of the Global Sex Trade* (United Kingdom: Routledge, 2008), 38–61.

[25] Osburg, *Anxious Wealth*, 145.

[26] Kimberly Kay Hoang's book, *Dealing in Desire: Asian Ascendancy, Western Decline, and the Hidden Currencies of Global Sex Work*, 1st ed. (Oakland: University of California Press, 2015) is a prominent example of the centrality of tiers in recent research on the sex industry. Hoang's study does not place law at the heart of her analysis of sex work in contemporary Vietnam, and as such I do not discuss it when I turn my attention beyond China's borders. Instead, she examines how high finance, overseas remittances, and the sex industry intersect in Vietnam. In contrast to my research, differences across types of clients are central to her project. Within the entertainment industry (bars and clubs), she studies four different markets for sex distinguished by the type of client to whom they cater: local Vietnamese businessmen, overseas Vietnamese, Western businessmen, and Western budget travelers. (Although she does not focus on them, she also identifies the presence of low-tier brothels in Vietnam that appear similar to those that exist in China (Hoang, 184).) As the references to her work throughout this book make clear, aspects of her study speak to some of my findings, despite our different areas of inquiry.

[27] In the lowest tier, aspects of soliciting on the streets or in parks differ from working in a small pseudo hair salon or apartment-brothel. In the middle tier, entertainment venues vary according to the wealth of the clients to which they cater. In the top tier, the experiences of second wives differ according to the status of the men who employ them.

within-tier differences of China's sex industry.[28] While some of these within-tier differences surface in the pages that follow, they are secondary to the broader streetwalker/brothel worker–hostess–mistress categories around which I structure my study. As described in the ensuing chapters, it is largely these broader tiers that shape how sex workers experience the state in China. In short, while research on sex work may not all call for the same tier-based emphasis, a shared understanding of the deep importance of tiers weaves throughout analyses of this phenomenon.[29]

Patterns of Tier-Based Policy Implementation

Tiers of sex workers and types of state interventions provide the building blocks of this book. Part II recounts the everyday lives of female sex workers in the different tiers of prostitution. Part III focuses on the experiences and policy implementation decisions of police officers and health officials within these tiers of sex work. Unsurprisingly, many of the practices of these street-level bureaucrats diverge from the formal letter of the law, including the two predominant tier-based patterns of policy implementation that police officers and health officials adopt on the ground.

First, while all prostitution is against the law in China, low-tier female sex workers bear the brunt of the state's policing attention. In this respect, China looks remarkably similar to many other parts of the world. For instance, Elizabeth Bernstein describes how in San Francisco, Amsterdam, and Stockholm, law enforcement practices

[28] Zheng, *Red Lights*; Suowei Xiao, "China's New Concubines? The Contemporary Second-Wife Phenomenon" (ProQuest Dissertations, 2009), perma.cc/T6U2-M8ME ; Suowei Xiao (肖索未), *Yuwang Yu Zunyan: Zhuanxingqi Zhongguo De Jieceng, Xingbie Yu Qinmi Guanxi (欲望与尊严: 转型期中国的阶层, 性别与亲密关系) [Desire and Dignity: Class, Gender and Intimacy in Transitional China]* (Beijing: China Social Sciences Academic Press (社会科学文献出版社), 2018). Chinese sexologist Pan Suiming proposed an oft-cited seven-tiered hierarchy of sex workers in China that also folds into these three tiers. The seven categories are: (1) second wives and mistresses (二奶 – *ernai*); (2) short-term second wives (包婆 – *baopo*), whom clients hire for a specific event; (3) hostesses (三厅里的陪女 – *santing li de peinu*); (4) sex workers who solicit in hotels, called "doorbell girls" (叮咚小姐 – *dingdong xiaojie*); (5) women who work in brothels that masquerade as beauty salons, massage parlors, and saunas (发廊妹 – *falangmei*); (6) streetwalkers (街女 – *jienu*); and (7) women who service rural migrant men, who work mainly in construction (下工棚/住工棚 – *xiagongpeng/zhugongpeng*). When folded into the tiers around which this book is structured, categories (1) and (2) correspond to the top tier; categories (3) and (4) constitute the middle tier; and categories (5), (6), and (7) make up the low tier. Pan Suiming (潘绥铭), *Cunzai Yu Huangmiu: Zhongguo Dixia "Xingchanye" Kao Cha (存在与荒谬: 中国地下"性产业"考察) [Existing in Falsehoods: An Investigation of China's Underground "Sex Industry"]* (Beijing: Qunyan Press (群言出版社), 1999).

[29] This point comes through clearly in my subsequent discussion of contributions this book makes to the larger literature on prostitution and its regulation.

have focused on getting rid of visible evidence of prostitution – streetwalkers – while finding ways to allow it to thrive behind closed doors.[30] Prabha Kotiswaran uncovers a similar pattern in India. Prostitution is formally criminalized in the country, but Kotiswaran's fieldwork instead uncovers "indifference towards indoor sex work and extensive crackdowns on street-based sex work."[31] Indeed, "the enforcement of the anti-sex work law in Sonagachi [a red-light district in the city of Kolkata] is astonishingly similar to what Bernstein describes for San Francisco."[32] In recent years, a growing body of literature has sought to reflect upon policing practices across political regime types with an eye toward nuanced consideration of concepts such as "authoritarian" and "democratic" policing and how they emerge (or not) in different areas of law enforcement.[33] With respect to the issue of sex work, close-to-the-ground attention to tier-based implementation in China helps to illuminate similarities of policing practices across regime type.

Second, while China's sex work public health policies underscore the importance of attending to low-tier sex workers, as they are at greatest risk of HIV/AIDS, public health officials instead focus their outreach efforts disproportionally on hostesses. On one level, these street-level bureaucrats struggle to access sex workers who are most in need of health interventions, which resonates with the experiences of colleagues working in any place where prostitution is against the law. For instance, the most vulnerable sex workers everywhere hesitate to engage with the state when the threat of arrest hovers over them.[34] Yet the difficulties that Chinese health officials face in their work also point to challenges of conducting health outreach that are specific to an authoritarian regime. Transparency is not the CCP's strong suit. For Chinese health officials, this means that they have much to lose and

[30] Elizabeth Bernstein, *Temporarily Yours: Intimacy, Authenticity, and the Commerce of Sex* (Chicago: University of Chicago Press, 2007). In fact, a key part of her argument underscores how little formal policy actually matters. These cities sit on different parts of the spectrum of regulatory possibilities for prostitution (criminalization, decriminalization, and legalization), yet in practice they all converge: "The common focus of state interventions has been on eliminating the visible manifestations of poverty and deviance . . . from urban spaces, rather than the exchange of sex for money per se" (164).

[31] Prabha Kotiswaran, *Dangerous Sex, Invisible Labor: Sex Work and the Law in India* (Princeton, NJ: Princeton University Press, 2011), 229.

[32] Kotiswaran, 229.

[33] Hualing Fu and Weitseng Chen, eds., *Regime Type and Beyond: The Transformation of Police in Asia* (Cambridge: Cambridge University Press, 2023).

[34] This is one of the main reasons why the global public health community advocates for the decriminalization of prostitution worldwide. UNDP, "Risks, Rights & Health" (UNDP, 2012), perma.cc/MRZ7-NSFC.

little to gain from reporting accurate rates of HIV/AIDS among sex workers in the community if those rates are high. This political reality makes hostesses attractive targets for HIV/AIDS testing, since they bring rates down, and also lies behind other deviations from formal rules that have alarming public health consequences.

STATE–SOCIETY RELATIONS IN CHINA

Prostitution is not the lens scholars typically use to make sense of how the state and society experience and engage with one another in contemporary China. Most research on state–society relations in China focuses on citizens such as workers or peasants who may challenge the state but who also form the CCP's bedrock of legitimacy.[35] In contrast, sex workers represent what the party stands against ideologically. Indeed, when the CCP sought to eradicate prostitution after coming to power in 1949, it referred to prostitution as "a sequel to the savage and bestial system of former exploiters and power holders to ruin the spirit and the body of women and to tarnish their dignity."[36] Female sex workers are considered the dregs of Chinese society. The challenges and stigma they face can differ depending on whether they are soliciting a poor migrant man on the streets or living as a kept woman for an elite client. Yet in most cases, sex workers are poor female migrants who are both breaking the law and engaging in behavior that China's state and society condemn on moral grounds. In a country whose citizens all occupy precarious positions vis-à-vis the state, these characteristics of sex workers place them among the very weakest in society.

Logistically speaking, there is a good reason why we do not know a lot about how sex workers experience the state in China. Fieldwork is never easy in the country, and accessing individuals who engage in illegal behavior only complicates the task; all the more so when they are being asked to talk about the state. Yet there is also a substantive reason

[35] See, e.g., Mary Gallagher, *Authoritarian Legality in China: Law, Workers, and the State* (New York: Cambridge University Press, 2017); Linda Wong, "Chinese Migrant Workers: Rights Attainment Deficits, Rights Consciousness and Personal Strategies," *China Quarterly* 208 (2011); Ethan Michelson, "Justice from Above or Below? Popular Strategies for Resolving Grievances in Rural China," *China Quarterly* 193 (2008): 43–64; Kevin J. O'Brien and Lianjiang Li, *Rightful Resistance in Rural China*, 1st ed. (New York: Cambridge University Press, 2006); Diana Fu, *Mobilizing without the Masses: Control and Contention in China* (New York: Cambridge University Press, 2017).

[36] Henriot, "La Fermeture," 467. Henriot quotes an editorial from the December 1949 issue of *Xin Zhongguo Funv* (Women of New China), the official publication of the national organization for women, the All-China Women's Federation.

why more respectable members of society attract greater attention from scholars. A question that lies at the core of much research on contemporary politics and law in China is what we can learn about the stability of the CCP and possibilities for political change. It makes sense to search for answers in places that hold the most promise: among communities of individuals who seem best situated to push back against the state in ways that might leave a mark. Ordinary workers and peasants – who benefit from multiple forms of political, legal, and moral legitimacy in contemporary China – are obvious candidates.[37] Lawyers are also attractive objects of academic attention – since litigation can be a powerful source of social change, it makes sense to pay attention to these societal elites who can challenge the state through the legal system.[38] It helps that all of these high-status individuals regularly make themselves heard through protests and lawsuits. Such public manifestations of displeasure have a strong pull on researchers looking for instances of state–society contestation. In comparison, female sex workers hardly stand out as a community of interest to scholars who care about societal dissatisfaction as a source of pressure on the state. Women who sell sex in China are illegitimate in multiple ways that give the state and, by extension, students of politics and law little reason to view them as particularly threatening, a view bolstered by the observation that they only rarely voice their grievances publicly. But Joel Migdal reminds us that social forces are "often low-profile or even invisible,"[39] and female sex workers embody this characterization more than the groups that have previously been the object of research on state–society relations in China. In short, by focusing on how female sex workers experience and think about the state in China, I bring forth a story that has previously been overlooked in favor of communities that provide more low-hanging fruit to scholars who care about political change.

Yet it should come as no surprise that female sex workers have plenty to say about how they experience the state, and that it shapes their behavior in innumerable ways. Researchers who care about power, politics, and law have long seen the value in examining what Michel

[37] See, e.g., Gallagher, *Authoritarian Legality in China*; Fu, *Mobilizing without the Masses*; O'Brien and Li, *Rightful Resistance in Rural China*.

[38] See, e.g., Eva Pils, *China's Human Rights Lawyers: Advocacy and Resistance* (London: Routledge, 2014); Rachel E. Stern, *Environmental Litigation in China: A Study in Political Ambivalence* (New York: Cambridge University Press, 2013).

[39] Joel S. Migdal, "Foreword," in *The Everyday Life of the State: A State-in-Society Approach*, ed. Adam White (Seattle: University of Washington Press, 2013), xii.

de Certeau calls "tales of the unrecognized,"[40] and, in the words of James Scott, bringing to light their "hidden transcripts."[41] Likewise, Patricia Ewick and Susan Silbey urge us to seek out the "often unseen and unrecognized practices of the weak against the strong."[42] Doing so is important for understanding tensions between the state and society, because open confrontations are rare; instead, "most of the political struggle of subordinate groups is conducted in more ambiguous territory."[43] Scholars of China's upstanding citizens know this well. For instance, Diana Fu finds that labor organizations affect how individuals "think and talk about their rights in a fundamental way that constitutes a core element of political change."[44] And Rachel Stern steers us away from a search for "signs of major transitions" to instead "remain attuned to changes that leave the top leadership largely untouched," as "the steady pressure of litigation can rework the legal system from within."[45] These studies show the value of looking for subtle challenges to the state in hidden spaces, and I find the same to be true among a population that is much more marginalized in Chinese society.

More importantly, the possibility that challenges to authority that occur behind closed doors may presage larger political shifts is not necessary to justify inquiry into sex worker experiences of state power. Instead, there is intrinsic value in seeking out and bringing forth the voices of the most oppressed. Ultimately, the sex worker narratives that I share in this book deserve attention because they are too often silenced, and glossing over them contributes to the continued marginalization of this population. As Ewick and Silbey observe with respect to the expressions of resistance of ordinary people in the United States, "[r]egardless of their political significance . . . [they] stand as important in their own right . . . [t]o ignore [them] . . . because they are momentary and private is to reinscribe the relations of power they oppose."[46] This

[40] Michel De Certeau, *The Practice of Everyday Life*, trans. Steven F. Rendall, 1st US ed. (Berkeley: University of California Press, 1984). Cited in Patricia Ewick and Susan S. Silbey, *The Common Place of Law: Stories From Everyday Life* (Chicago: University of Chicago Press, 1998), 14.

[41] James C. Scott, *Domination and the Arts of Resistance: Hidden Transcripts*, 1st ed. (New Haven, CT: Yale University Press, 1990).

[42] Ewick and Silbey, *The Common Place of Law*, 1998, 188.

[43] Scott, *Domination and the Arts of Resistance*, 202.

[44] Fu, *Mobilizing without the Masses*, 142.

[45] Stern, *Environmental Litigation in China*, 2013, 234.

[46] Ewick and Silbey, *The Common Place of Law*, 1998, 14.

observation holds even greater weight with respect to female sex workers in authoritarian China today.

Turning to the state, my examination of the regulation of sex work considers separately its different interests in prostitution: policing, public health, and commercial. It also focuses on the experiences and practices of state actors responsible for implementing policies on the ground and remains attuned to how their behaviors compare to the formal letter of the law. Political scientists sometimes call this a disaggregated approach to understanding the state, an approach that eschews its reification and instead takes as a starting point the observation that "the state speaks with many, contradictory voices."[47] When I look at one issue area – prostitution – and tease out the different types of state policies and agencies that have a stake in its regulation, I am disaggregating the state horizontally. And when I examine separately the intentions of the central government and the practices of its local officials, I am disaggregating it vertically. Research on the Chinese state has long demonstrated the value in taking these dimensions seriously.

In some instances, such studies are primarily situated within the state, focused on bureaucratic politics and questions of fragmented authoritarianism.[48] I add to them a focus on the very frontlines of the state: the street-level bureaucrats (police officers and health officials) who are implementing policy on the ground.[49] Suzanne Scoggins places

[47] Rachel E. Stern and Kevin J. O'Brien, "Politics at the Boundary: Mixed Signals and the Chinese State," *Modern China* 38, no. 2 (March 1, 2012): 177, https://doi.org/10.1177/0097700411421463.

[48] See, e.g., Kenneth Lieberthal and Michel Oksenberg, *Policy Making in China: Leaders, Structures, and Processes* (Princeton, NJ: Princeton University Press, 1988); Andrew C. Mertha, *The Politics of Piracy: Intellectual Property in Contemporary China* (Ithaca, NY: Cornell University Press, 2005); Andrew C. Mertha, *China's Water Warriors: Citizen Action and Policy Change* (Ithaca, NY: Cornell University Press, 2008); Andrew Mertha, "'Fragmented Authoritarianism 2.0': Political Pluralization in the Chinese Policy Process*," *The China Quarterly* 200 (December 2009): 995–1012, https://doi.org/10.1017/S0305741009990592; Suzanne E. Scoggins, *Policing China: Street-Level Cops in the Shadow of Protest*, Studies of the Weatherhead East Asian Institute, Columbia University (Ithaca, NY: Cornell University Press, 2021).

[49] Michael Lipsky, *Street-Level Bureaucracy: Dilemmas of the Individual in Public Services* (New York: Russell Sage Foundation, 1980). Had I conducted a bureaucratic politics study in the style of Andrew Mertha's work (see previous footnote), China's Ministry of Culture (as of 2018, its Ministry of Culture and Tourism) would have featured more prominently, as it regulates many of the physical entertainment spaces that harbor prostitution. It stays on the periphery of this book because, in contrast to police officers and health officials, agents of the Ministry of Culture rarely intervene directly in the lives of sex workers.

herself there for her study of police officers in China.[50] Yet we know less about interagency dynamics at this local level of analysis, and my account of how health officials and police officers contend with one another and the economic interests of the local government around a specific issue area – prostitution – speaks to that aspect of interactions within the state. In addition, we know that China's street-level officials, like their colleagues in other parts of the world,[51] have significant discretion in their professional lives.[52] Yet we know less about what they do with that autonomy, particularly beyond the area of stability maintenance.[53] Scoggins paints a portrait of local police officers as too under-resourced and overburdened to take advantage of their discretion.[54] When it comes to regulating the sex industry, such pressures certainly weigh heavily on police officers, as well as on their health official colleagues. Yet the street-level bureaucrats I observed nevertheless – indeed, by necessity – make use of their independence to engage in numerous creative strategies to fulfill aspects of their professional responsibilities.

In other instances, studies of Chinese politics that are committed to a disaggregated view of the state are more attuned to societal experiences with the state.[55] The weight I place on how female sex workers think, talk, and act in relation to the regulations that govern their lives

[50] Scoggins, *Policing China*. Examples of other recent studies also focused on the front lines of one agency include Iza Ding's ethnography of a municipal environmental protection bureau (Iza Yue Ding, *The Performative State: Public Scrutiny and Environmental Governance in China* (Ithaca, NY: Cornell University Press, 2022), https://doi.org/10.1515/9781501760396); Zang and Musheno's study of *chengguan* officers (Xiaowei Zang and Michael Musheno, "Exploring Frontline Work in China," *Public Administration* 95, no. 3 (2017): 842–55, https://doi.org/10.1111/padm.12340; and Rui Hou's ethnographic fieldwork in the petition bureau of one district government in Beijing (Rui Hou, "Maintaining Social Stability without Solving Problems: Emotional Repression in the Chinese Petition System," *The China Quarterly* 243 (2020): 635–54, https://doi.org/10.1017/S0305741019001528).

[51] Lipsky, *Street-Level Bureaucracy*; Shannon Portillo and Danielle S. Rudes, "Construction of Justice at the Street Level," *Annual Review of Law and Social Science* 10, no. 1 (2014): 321–34, https://doi.org/10.1146/annurev-lawsocsci-102612-134046; Thomas B. Pepinsky, Jan H. Pierskalla, and Audrey Sacks, "Bureaucracy and Service Delivery," *Annual Review of Political Science* 20, no. 1 (2017): 249–68, https://doi.org/10.1146/annurev-polisci-051215-022705.

[52] See, e.g., Ching Kwan Lee and Yong Hong Zhang, "Seeing Like a Grassroots State: Producing Power and Instability in China's Bargained Authoritarianism," in *To Govern China: Evolving Practices of Power*, ed. Vivienne Shue and Patricia M. Thornton (New York: Cambridge University Press, 2017), 182.

[53] For insight into some of the strategies street-level bureaucrats adopt in the area of stability maintenance, see Lee and Zhang, "Seeing Like a Grassroots State" and Fu, *Mobilizing without the Masses*.

[54] Scoggins, *Policing China*, 96.

[55] See, e.g., Stern and O'Brien, "Politics at the Boundary"; Stern, *Environmental Litigation in China*; Fu, *Mobilizing without the Masses*.

and the street-level officials who enforce them places me squarely in this tradition. Yet as noted earlier, female sex workers are more marginalized than the societal groups other scholars interested in the state in contemporary China have studied. A close look at how health officials and police officers interact with sex workers reveals plenty of unsurprising behavior, considering the power dynamics involved – such as forced HIV/AIDS testing, arbitrary detention, physical abuse, and extraction of bribes and free sexual services. Yet it also reveals the weakness of these street-level bureaucrats. For instance, local health officials struggle to conduct outreach to the sex industry, which is averse to public health interventions. These state workers frequently find themselves trying to cajole their way into communities of sex workers, with limited alternatives when the door remains shut. And local law enforcement officers expend considerable effort on maintaining open lines of communication with members of the sex industry, requesting sex workers to lay low at certain times, urging them to reach out for assistance when they face harm, and providing them with the tools to do so. We know that on the front lines, even members of one of China's most powerful bureaucracies – the police – are weak when it comes to issues of everyday order maintenance.[56] Observing interactions between health and law enforcement officials on the one hand, and sex workers on the other, underscores just how weak these state actors are, even in relation to some of the lowest-standing members of society. These interactions bring to light the choices, strategies, and effort that the precarity of street-level bureaucrats entails, and the unexpected dependence of frontline officials upon a cooperative sex industry to fulfill their professional responsibilities.

The Dual State

A key characteristic of the state that emerges from disaggregating it to understand the regulation of prostitution in China is the street-level bureaucrat's independence and vulnerability. Yet China's patterns of prostitution-related law enforcement also speak to another approach to understanding state–society relations in the country – the dual state.[57] This concept identifies the coexistence of two systems of justice in authoritarian regimes: one for ordinary problems and another for

[56] Scoggins, *Policing China*.
[57] Ernst Fraenkel, *The Dual State: A Contribution to the Theory of Dictatorship* (New York: Oxford University Press, 1941).

political challenges.[58] With specific attention to law enforcement, the concepts of "low policing" (which concerns everyday crime control) and "high policing" (which focuses on explicitly political issues that pose a direct challenge to the state) encapsulate a similar bifurcation.[59] The policing of sex work in China generally falls under the sphere of ordinary issues and low policing, and that is the space occupied by the struggling street-level bureaucrat. Yet the CCP can also pull prostitution out of that realm and into the world of high-level politics. Specifically, when the party seeks to orchestrate the downfall of elites who challenge the CCP's legitimacy through egregious corruption, public criticism, or blatant flouting of major directives, the individual's engagement in prostitution becomes one of the allegations publicly used to cement his demise.

The recognition that dual systems of justice coexist within an authoritarian regime is immensely valuable for providing nuanced accounts of how its state and society interact.[60] And it makes sense to reflect upon the types of actions and issues that fall more easily into the worlds of the "ordinary" or the "political." For instance, private law in China is generally considered to operate relatively unfettered by the state, in contrast to the regulation of the media, religion, and ethnic affairs.[61] When I underscore that the exchange of sex for money or other material goods is present in both realms of the bifurcated state, I also draw attention to the limits inherent in sorting specific behaviors into these two realms. The line between an ordinary issue in China and a political one is often blurry,[62] and the CCP does this by design. One of

[58] See, e.g., Jothie Rajah, *Authoritarian Rule of Law: Legislation, Discourse and Legitimacy in Singapore*, Revised ed. (New York: Cambridge University Press, 2012); Sida Liu and Terence C. Halliday, *Criminal Defense in China: The Politics of Lawyers at Work* (Cambridge: Cambridge University Press, 2016), 181; Pils, *China's Human Rights Lawyers*; Kathryn Hendley, "Resisting Multiple Narratives of Law in Transition Countries: Russia and Beyond," *Law & Social Inquiry* 40, no. 2 (2015): 531–52, https://doi.org/10.1111/lsi.12132.

[59] Jean-Paul Brodeur, "High Policing and Low Policing: Remarks about the Policing of Political Activities," *Social Problems* 30, no. 5 (1983): 507–20, https://doi.org/10.2307/800268; Scoggins, *Policing China*.

[60] See, e.g., Rajah, *Authoritarian Rule of Law*; Liu and Halliday, *Criminal Defense in China*, 181; Pils, *China's Human Rights Lawyers*; Hendley, "Resisting Multiple Narratives of Law in Transition Countries." That said, some scholars question the applicability of the dual state model to China. See, e.g., Donald C. Clarke, "Is China a Dual State?," SSRN Scholarly Paper (Rochester, NY, December 15, 2022), https://doi.org/10.2139/ssrn.4317126. Clarke argues that the dual state idea is not helpful because the alleged distinction between the "ordinary" and the "political" finds no institutional expression in China.

[61] Hualing Fu, "Duality and China's Struggle for Legal Autonomy," *China Perspectives* 1, no. 116 (2019): 3–10. Broadly speaking, private law deals with interactions between private parties, and public law involves interactions with the state.

[62] Stern, *Environmental Litigation in China*, 230.

the greatest tools that an authoritarian state has at its disposal is its ability to obfuscate the boundaries of the permissible so that its citizens are left guessing as to how their actions will be received.[63] Elites who fall from grace may have forgotten that no one is immune to this defining characteristic of the regime, as the CCP turns the purchase of sex – an illegal but widespread behavior – into prime evidence of its target's misdeeds.

Human Relationships

My approach to understanding state–society relations in China – immersion in the daily lives of both state officials and members of society, including in the spaces where those lives intersect – also underscores the central role that human relationships play in these dynamics. Many studies have emphasized the importance of relationships, or *guanxi* (关系), for understanding a wide array of issues relevant to the social scientific study of China.[64] What I highlight here is less of a culturally specific, and more of a universal, reflection on connections between human beings. At the heart of state–society relations lie the actual interactions that occur between an individual who represents the state and a member of society. If we disaggregate the state and society all the way down to their smallest units of analysis, we arrive at a human-to-human exchange. This observation came alive to me powerfully when I would sit back and watch daily life unfold in Xizhou, the location of this chapter's opening anecdote. In the late afternoon, a scene would unfold where local government actors, sex workers, pimps, and other members of the community would all commingle in the central square. Middle and high school boys would be playing a basketball game on one half of the square's court, while members of the neighborhood government association (居委会 – *juweihui*) would start their own game on the court's other half. Right next to the basketball court, a group of retirees would assemble for ballroom dancing, with music blasting from their boombox. Sex workers would sit on the steps in front of their venues or huddle in small groups in the square, chatting with friends. Children returning home

[63] Stern and O'Brien, "Politics at the Boundary."

[64] See, e.g., Thomas Gold, Doug Guthrie, and David Wank, eds., *Social Connections in China: Institutions, Culture, and the Changing Nature of Guanxi* (New York: Cambridge University Press, 2002); Andrew B. Kipnis, *Producing Guanxi: Sentiment, Self, and Subculture in a North China Village* (Durham, NC: Duke University Press, 1997); Mayfair Mei-hui Yang, *Gifts, Favors, and Banquets: The Art of Social Relationships in China* (Ithaca, NY: Cornell University Press, 1994).

from school would stream through the square, stopping for snacks from the food stand vendors, and weave their way around the dancers, the basketball players, and the sex workers. These disparate groups sometimes seemed like they were leading unrelated lives while superimposed onto a shared physical space. Yet they also recognized one another's presence and would enter into dialogue with each other. When I stood outside one afternoon watching the two basketball games with Chen Ge, a pimp running a low-tier mom-and-pop brothel, Wang Zhuren, a local health official, came over from his nearby office to watch also. They struck up conversation, starting with a discussion of the pros and cons of legalizing prostitution in China, before moving on to evaluating the basketball skill levels of various players on the court – two individuals simply chitchatting on a sunny day. Both directly and indirectly, most pages of this book bear witness to such encounters. They remind us that as human beings, we share certain ways of connecting with each other that transcend the roles we might play within the state or society and, beyond that, even the impact that borders can have on our lives.

Gender

Earlier in this chapter, I mentioned two explanations for why previous studies of state–society relations in China have overlooked female sex workers – they are hard to find, and not the most likely candidates to shed light on political change. There is also a third reason: Prostitution is generally studied within disciplines and subdisciplines that place gender and sexuality at the heart of their intellectual inquiry. Sociologists and anthropologists often conduct research on this topic,[65] and political and legal scholarship on sex work is often framed in terms of gender politics and feminist legal theory – subfields that are not at the center of political science and law.[66] Social science work that situates itself primarily outside of those gender and sexuality-focused realms of academia, including inquiries into dynamics between the state and society and questions of regulation and its implementation,

[65] See, e.g., Bernstein, *Temporarily Yours*; Zheng, *Red Lights*.

[66] See, e.g., Joyce Outshoorn, ed., *The Politics of Prostitution: Women's Movements, Democratic States, and the Globalisation of Sex Commerce* (Cambridge: Cambridge University Press, 2004); Vanessa Munro and Marina Della Giusta, eds., *Demanding Sex: Critical Reflections on the Regulation of Prostitution* (Burlington, VT: Ashgate, 2008); Kotiswaran, *Dangerous Sex, Invisible Labor*; Janet Halley, Prabha Kotiswaran, Hila Shamir, and Chantal Thomas, "From the International to the Local in Feminist Legal Responses to Rape, Prostitution/Sex Work, and Sex Trafficking: Four Studies in Contemporary Governance Feminism," *Harvard Journal of Law & Gender* 29 (2006): 335.

tends not to consider that the study of prostitution can provide insight into issues other than gender and sexuality.

A number of studies prior to mine have contributed to correcting this imbalance. For instance, Elizabeth Remick situates her study of the regulation of prostitution in the early decades of the twentieth century in China around questions of statebuilding,[67] and Samantha Majic locates her research on sex worker health-service organizations in the Bay Area in the 2000s in the literature on social movements.[68] Reactions to these efforts, and to my research, show how much work remains to legitimize the study of prostitution outside the realms of gender and sexuality. On the one hand, scholars within these subfields of gender and sexuality have called out these projects for neglecting the gendered realities of prostitution in the process of emphasizing other theoretical approaches to the issue.[69] On the other hand, mainstream political science and legal academia still struggle to understand prostitution as a serious area of inquiry that can enrich those disciplines.

It is not unreasonable to expect a study of female sex workers in China to explicitly address questions of gender and the state in contemporary China. After all, the CCP demonstrates deep tension around the issue. Gender equality is one of the ideological pillars of the CCP, encapsulated in the saying "Women hold up half the sky," attributed to Mao Zedong. At the same time, the party's actual treatment of women is dismal. The state urges young, educated urban women to focus less on their careers and more on getting married, lest they become "leftover" women, doomed to a life of being single and lonely.[70] It cracks down, brutally, on its feminist activists.[71] It approaches divorce in ways that disproportionately favor

[67] Remick notes how "[f]ar from being a 'peripheral' social issue, prostitution and its regulation were at the heart of the modern statebuilding project undertaken by Chinese local governments." Elizabeth Remick, *Regulating Prostitution in China: Gender and Local Statebuilding, 1900–1937* (Stanford, CA: Stanford University Press, 2014), 2–3.

[68] Majic shows how, contrary to the literature that assumes that social movements reduce their engagement in oppositional political work as they evolve into formal institutions, the organizations that she studies continue to "foster and promote politically contentious ideas and challenge state policy," and demonstrates how they do so. Samantha Majic, *Sex Work Politics: From Protest to Service Provision* (Philadelphia: University of Pennsylvania Press, 2013), 27.

[69] For instance, Michaele L. Ferguson calls out both Majic and Remick for "largely sidestep[ping] the question of the relation between sex work and gender." Michaele L. Ferguson, "Beyond Gender Politics? Mainstreaming the Study of Sex Work," *Perspectives on Politics* 13, no. 2 (June 2015): 437, https://doi.org/10.1017/S1537592715000250.

[70] Leta Hong Fincher, *Leftover Women: The Resurgence of Gender Inequality in China* (London: Zed Books, 2014).

[71] Leta Hong Fincher, *Betraying Big Brother: The Feminist Awakening in China* (London: Verso Books, 2018).

husbands over wives.[72] And those are all women with higher standing than sex workers. This book is replete with evidence of the deeply gendered inequality that characterizes how China regulates prostitution. For instance, it is female sex workers, rather than their male clients, who bear the brunt of the regulations that outlaw prostitution, despite formal rules that hold them both responsible. Yet the problem with the expectation that a study of prostitution will address questions of gender is the double standard that it reveals. No one expects studies of elite politics in China to place gender front and center in their analyses. Perhaps they should. As of the 20th National Congress of the CCP in 2022, no woman has ever been a member of the Politburo Standing Committee, the most powerful political body in China.[73] That same event also presented an all-male Politburo (the larger and second-most powerful body), and before 2022 only six women had ever been full members of the Politburo.[74] That questions of gender are often the first to emerge in reaction to a study on the regulation of prostitution, and at best an afterthought when reflecting on CCP leadership, is indicative both of the need for more studies on sex work that do not situate themselves primarily in questions of gender and sexuality and of the importance of asking more questions about gender in spaces where such discussion is absent.[75]

[72] Ke Li, "'What He Did Was Lawful': Divorce Litigation and Gender Inequality in China," *Law & Policy* 37, no. 3 (2015): 153–79, https://doi.org/10.1111/lapo.12034; Ke Li, *Marriage Unbound: State Law, Power, and Inequality in Contemporary China* (Stanford, CA: Stanford University Press, 2022); Ethan Michelson, *Decoupling: Gender Injustice in China's Divorce Courts* (New York: Cambridge University Press, 2022); Xin He, *Divorce in China: Institutional Constraints and Gendered Outcomes* (New York: NYU Press, 2021).

[73] Alexandra Stevenson, "Leadership Changes Reveal that in China, Men Still Rule," *The New York Times*, October 23, 2022, https://perma.cc/B599-WGT8.

[74] Stevenson; Shen Lu, "Pretty Lady Cadres," *ChinaFile*, December 21, 2020, perma.cc/N375-U9VS.

[75] There has been some recent movement on this front. See, e.g., Xinhui Jiang, "Gendered Pathways to the County-Level People's Congress in China," *The China Quarterly* 249 (March 2022): 68–90, https://doi.org/10.1017/S0305741021001156; and Xinrui Feng, Yue Hou, and Mingxing Liu, "Underrepresented Outperformers: Female Legislators in the Chinese Congress," *The China Quarterly* 257 (March 2024): 59-74, https://doi.org/10.1017/S0305741023001157. Focused on China in the 1950s and 1960s, political scientist Neil Diamant's study of the Marriage Law illustrates how another topic typically excluded from mainstream political science and more often studied in fields that traditionally focus more on gender – family relations – sheds valuable light on state–society relations in Chinese history. Neil J. Diamant, *Revolutionizing the Family: Politics, Love, and Divorce in Urban and Rural China, 1949–1968*, 1st ed. (Berkeley: University of California Press, 2000).

Transnational Influences

Lastly, no account of what sex work teaches us about state–society relations in contemporary China is complete without a reflection on transnational influence, which affects both how the state regulates prostitution as a public health issue and how some sex workers experience prostitution and the state's interventions in their lives. The global public health community has shaped both the content of China's prostitution health policies (which reflect international best practices) and the health officials who administer them (and who approach the issue of sex work with transnational language and ideas). Yet street-level bureaucrats in China veer far from these transnational ideals when implementing public health policies, in ways that are harmful to both sex workers and the general public. Strikingly, the same international health community that has invested heavily in creating a domestic health infrastructure in China to its liking is noticeably disengaged from the realities of local implementation. Like many others who study how global policies intersect with local realities, I identify a deep and alarming disconnect between the intentions of transnational actors and what actually happens on the ground.[76]

Yet the news is not all bleak. Most research that examines linkages between global actors and local society is attuned to the effects of transnational ideas and practices on societal elites.[77] The international

[76] See, e.g., Mark Fathi Massoud, *Law's Fragile State: Colonial, Authoritarian, and Humanitarian Legacies in Sudan* (Cambridge: Cambridge University Press, 2013), 4, 12, 181; Sally Engle Merry, *Human Rights and Gender Violence: Translating International Law into Local Justice* (Chicago: University of Chicago Press, 2006), 3; Joel Migdal, *State in Society: Studying How States and Societies Transform and Constitute One Another*, Later Printing Used ed. (New York: Cambridge University Press, 2001), 141–42; Suli Zhu, "The Party and the Courts," in *Judicial Independence in China: Lessons for Global Rule of Law Promotion*, ed. Randall Peerenboom, 1st ed. (New York: Cambridge University Press, 2009), 65; Randall Peerenboom, "Introduction," in *Judicial Independence in China: Lessons for Global Rule of Law Promotion*, ed. Randall Peerenboom, 1st ed. (New York: Cambridge University Press, 2009), 4; David M. Trubek, "Law and Development: Forty Years after 'Scholars in Self-Estrangement,'" *University of Toronto Law Journal* 66, no.3, May 19, 2016: 301–29, https://doi.org/10.3138/UTLJ.3671; Elanah Uretsky, *Occupational Hazards: Business, Sex, and HIV in Post-Mao China* (Stanford, CA: Stanford University Press, 2016), 175; Katherine A. Mason, *Infectious Change: Reinventing Chinese Public Health after an Epidemic* (Stanford, CA: Stanford University Press, 2016), 34–35.

[77] Sidney G. Tarrow, *The New Transnational Activism* (New York: Cambridge University Press, 2005); Rachel E. Stern, "Unpacking Adaptation: The Female Inheritance Movement in Hong Kong," *Mobilization: An International Quarterly* 10, no. 3 (October 1, 2005): 421–39; Sally Engle Merry and Rachel E. Stern, "The Female Inheritance Movement in Hong Kong: Theorizing the Local/Global Interface," *Current Anthropology* 46, no. 3 (2005): 387–409; Peggy Levitt and Sally Merry, "Vernacularization on the Ground: Local Uses of Global Women's Rights in Peru, China, India and the United States," *Global Networks* 9, no. 4 (October 1, 2009): 441–61.

community seeks them out due to ease of access, which, in a country such as China, includes being located in Beijing and speaking English.[78] My focus on some of China's most downtrodden citizens expands the horizon: It reveals a smattering of poor, uneducated migrants, whose daily lives are not enmeshed in international communities, but who nevertheless speak the language of the global sex worker rights movement, and whose consciousness has been powerfully transformed by its ideas. This observation shows transnational influence taking root in places far removed from the surface where it is usually sought out.

And while I identify the transnational ideas that have made their mark on prostitution in China, one element of international concern is conspicuously absent from this book: the concept of sex trafficking. In the United States, it is difficult to talk about sex work without also talking about sex trafficking, in large part due to the abolitionist movement that has sought to reframe all prostitution as trafficking.[79] That movement has powerfully shaped not only how the US government approaches the issue of prostitution domestically but also how it engages with the issue internationally.[80] In India, for instance, global trafficking narratives play a pivotal role in shaping debates about the regulation of sex work, and the United States has influenced prostitution law reform efforts in the country.[81] Sex trafficking, in the sense of nonconsensual participation in the sex industry, certainly occurs in China, and I highlight the instances when I encountered trafficking narratives in my fieldwork. In addition, concern for trafficking and policy attention to it are on the rise in China.[82] Yet the issue does not dominate conversations about prostitution in the way it has in the United States or India. Indeed, the concept of sex trafficking rarely came up during my fieldwork, either within communities of sex workers or in interactions with state actors, as I asked about their everyday experiences with the implementation of prostitution regulations. In

[78] Stern, *Environmental Litigation in China*, 188.

[79] Elizabeth Bernstein, "The Sexual Politics of the 'New Abolitionism,'" *Differences* 18, no. 3 (December 1, 2007): 128–51, https://doi.org/10.1215/10407391-2007-013. For more on American legal discourse on sex trafficking and sex work, see Ben Chapman-Schmidt, "'Sex Trafficking' as Epistemic Violence," *Anti-Trafficking Review*, no. 12 (April 29, 2019): 172–87, https://doi.org/10.14197/atr.2012191211.

[80] Bernstein, "The Sexual Politics of the 'New Abolitionism.'"

[81] Kotiswaran, *Dangerous Sex, Invisible Labor*, 6–9.

[82] See, e.g., Bonny Ling, "Prostitution and Female Trafficking in China: Between Phenomena and Discourse," *China Perspectives*, no. 2018/1–2 (June 1, 2018): 65–74, https://doi.org/10.4000/chinaperspectives.7742.

short, my book is not about sex trafficking because that global narrative did not weave its way into the trenches of the state, society, and the regulation of prostitution in China under Hu Jintao.[83]

PROSTITUTION AND ITS REGULATION

In addition to its contributions to our understanding of state–society relations in China, this book also builds on, and informs, scholarship on sex work and its regulation. In particular, it engages with other studies on sex work in contemporary China and Chinese history, as well as sociolegal studies of sex work in other countries.

Research on contemporary China has a lot to say about female sex work. Sexologist Pan Suiming pioneered the study of sex and sexuality in China, and has carried out an abundance of studies of female sex workers since he started his research on sexual attitudes and behaviors in post-Mao China in the 1980s.[84] Anthropologist Tiantian Zheng studies the nexus of prostitution, masculinity, power, and the state through an ethnography centered around three karaoke bars (high-, middle-, and low-tier) in the city of Dalian.[85] Anthropologist Yeon Jung Yu studies how social networks influence the lives of female sex workers.[86] Sociologist Suowei Xiao examines how second wives and

83 It is beyond the scope of this book to examine why the global HIV/AIDS narrative has penetrated China's state and society deeply, while the global narrative on sex trafficking has made fewer inroads. The question could be a promising area of inquiry for a scholar of social movements. In this respect, China stands in noted contrast to India, for example. Kotiswaran notes how the "contemporary figure of the Indian sex worker is thus suspended between the two international agendas of abolition and public health control, both motivated by contradictory goals." Kotiswaran, *Dangerous Sex, Invisible Labor*, 9. (The term "abolition" here is shorthand for the position of individuals who believe that all prostitution is sex trafficking and who advocate for the abolition of all sex work.)

84 See, e.g., Pan Suiming (潘绥铭), *Cunzai Yu Huangmiu: Zhongguo Dixia "Xingchanye" Kao Cha (存在与荒谬：中国地下"性产业"考察) [Existing in Falsehoods: An Investigation of China's Underground "Sex Industry"]* (Beijing: Qunyan Press (群言出版社), 1999); Pan Suiming et al. (潘绥铭等), *Chengxian Yu Biaoding: Zhongguo "Xiao Jie" Shen Yanjiu (呈现与标定：中国"小姐"深研究) [Performing and Labeling: In-Depth Study on Female Sex Workers in China]* (Kaohsiung: Wanyou Press (万有出版社), 2005); Pan Suiming (潘绥铭), Huang Yingying (黄盈盈), and Liu Zhenying (刘振英), *Qingjing Yu Ganwu: Xinan Zhongguo Sange Hongdengqu Tansuo (情境与感悟：西南中国三个红灯区探索) [Situation and Inspiration: Study on Three Red Light Districts in Southwest China]* (Kaohsiung: Wanyou Press (万有出版社), 2005); Pan Suiming et al. (潘绥铭等), *Xiaojie: Laodong De Quanli: Zhongguo Dongnan Yanhai Yu Dongbei Chengshi De Duizhao Kaocha (小姐：劳动的权利：中国东南沿海与东北城市的对照考察) [Female Sex Workers: The Rights of Labor: Comparative Study between Southeastern and Northeastern Chinese Cities]* (Hong Kong: Hong Kong Dadao Press (香港大道出版社), 2005).

85 Zheng, *Red Lights*.

86 Yeon Jung Yu, "Positional Embodiment: How Networks Shape the Lived Experiences of the Bodies of Female Sex Workers in Post-Socialist China," *Gender, Work & Organization* 29, no. 3 (2022): 953–70, https://doi.org/10.1111/gwao.12753.

their clients enter into such relationships in search of dignity, distinction, and belonging, focused on both rural and urban women, and worker and business-elite men.[87] Sociologist Eileen Yuk-ha Tsang examines questions of intimacy, masculinity, and criminal justice through an ethnography of low-end, mid-tier, and high-end female sex workers and their clients in the southern city of Dongguan.[88] Susanne Y. P. Choi, also in sociology, has explored issues tied to agency and victimhood of female sex workers,[89] and Choi's work with Ruby Y. S. Lai examines questions of stigma.[90] Public health researchers have carried out a wealth of studies on female sex workers in China, focused largely on their health and sexual behaviors.[91] Through detailed documentary and textual analysis, political scientist and sinologist Elaine Jeffreys analyzes academic and administrative discourses on female prostitution in China to underscore their methodological and political biases, considering the policing of prostitution in China as a practice of Foucauldian governmentality.[92] Legal scholar Sarah Biddulph's study of administrative detention powers in China, rooted in a comprehensive analysis of relevant laws, policies, and other official pronouncements, includes a focus on prostitution and on custody and education centers for sex workers and clients.[93]

This overview of some of the main research on female sex workers in contemporary China reveals that the disciplines of politics and law have rarely turned their attention to contemporary prostitution in China. When they have, it has been through documentary and textual analysis, rather than through the methodologies that lie at the heart of this book: ethnography, interviews, and surveys.

Against this backdrop, I extend the study of female sex work in contemporary China to place a different question at the heart of my analysis: How is sex work regulated on the front lines? While both

[87] Xiao, "China's New Concubines?"; Xiao, *Desire and Dignity*.

[88] Eileen Yuk-ha Tsang, *China's Commercial Sexscapes: Rethinking Intimacy, Masculinity, and Criminal Justice* (Toronto: University of Toronto Press, 2019).

[89] Susanne Y. P. Choi, "State Control, Female Prostitution and HIV Prevention in China," *The China Quarterly* 205 (March 2011): 96–114.

[90] Susanne Y. P. Choi and Ruby Y. S. Lai, "Sex Work and Stigma Management in China and Hong Kong: The Role of State Policy and NGO Advocacy," *The China Quarterly* 247 (September 2021): 855–74, https://doi.org/10.1017/S0305741021000035.

[91] The public health literature on female sex workers in China is vast. See, e.g., Hong and Li, "Behavioral Studies of Female Sex Workers in China."

[92] Jeffreys, *China, Sex, and Prostitution*. Using similar methodologies, Jeffreys has also written extensively on other aspects of prostitution. See, e.g., Elaine Jeffreys, *Prostitution Scandals in China: Policing, Media and Society* (London: Routledge, 2012).

[93] Biddulph, *Legal Reform and Administrative Detention Powers in China*.

Biddulph and Jeffreys examine the formal policing policies that govern prostitution, I instead focus on the actual implementation of prostitution regulations through the experiences of both sex workers and frontline state actors. Furthermore, I examine the regulation of prostitution not only from the perspective of law enforcement but also from the angle of public health. In contrast to the public health literature on this topic, which is interested mainly in sex worker sexual behavior and disease infection rates, I focus on how health regulators carry out their responsibilities, and how sex workers experience that regulation. In addition, I place the interplay between these two state interests and a third – economic growth – at the heart of my analysis, to examine how it shapes both the behavior of street-level bureaucrats and the experiences of female sex workers.

Although I have few fellow travelers in the study of the regulation of sex work in contemporary China, I am extending a rich literature on the regulation of prostitution in Chinese history. Historian Matthew Sommer, in his analysis of the late Imperial era policies on sexuality, shows how prostitution was regulated differently based on the status of the individuals involved.[94] These distinctions were enshrined within the judicial codes of successive dynasties until the early eighteenth century, and legal case records provide ample evidence of their enforcement. In Imperial times, the law clearly articulated status differences in prostitution. In fact, the entire purpose of the policies was to maintain barriers between social strata and restrict certain practices to their proper place. In contrast, current prostitution policing policies do not formally differ according to the social standing of the individuals involved and make no official distinction between sexual transactions negotiated on the streets for a couple of yuan, and those that occur behind the closed doors of elite entertainment venues for thousands more. It is only in their implementation that these laws reinforce status distinctions. Political scientist Elizabeth Remick examines the regulation of prostitution in Late Qing and Republican China (1900–1937) and its connections to local processes of statebuilding.[95] In bringing to light different models used to control prostitution locally, Remick shows how some official class categorizations of prostitution persisted in the Republican era. For instance, police-run brothels in the city of Kunming clearly identified brothels as low, middle, or high class, where a woman's age and beauty appeared to

[94] Matthew Harvey Sommer, *Sex, Law, and Society in Late Imperial China* (Stanford, CA: Stanford University Press, 2000).
[95] Remick, *Regulating Prostitution in China*.

determine the class to which police assigned her.[96] Historian Gail Hershatter's study of the lives of female sex workers in Shanghai, starting in the late nineteenth century, also includes an examination of how prostitution is regulated, and class is central to her analysis.[97] Christian Henriot similarly devotes a section of his book to regulation, and maps out the different types of sex workers in Shanghai from the mid nineteenth to mid twentieth centuries.[98]

It is never easy to capture the voices of marginalized individuals and groups within society. Researchers who study the past face the particular challenge of how to do so when those people are no longer around to speak their truths. Remick states upfront that limitations of sources prevented her from examining sex worker experiences with the regulation of prostitution in their lives.[99] Instead, she emphasizes the perspective of the state. Sommer has more luck: The legal case records that serve as the principal source for his study include records of witness testimony that, despite not being verbatim transcripts, are "evidence of an ethnographic nature . . . [that is] as close as we will ever get to the 'voice' of the illiterate in late imperial China."[100] The use of legal case records also means that Sommer is telling a story about how sex is regulated focused on moments when individuals have formally encountered the legal system. They are, in the words of sociologists of law Richard Miller and Austin Sarat, firmly located toward the top of "the dispute pyramid."[101] What slips through the cracks is a view of how individuals experience and understand the law in their daily lives, when they are not entangled with formal legal institutions: what the sociolegal scholars Patricia Ewick and Susan S. Silbey call "the common place of law."[102] In contrast to Sommer's use of legal case records and in line with "the

[96] Remick, 163–64.
[97] Hershatter, *Dangerous Pleasures*, 1997.
[98] Christian Henriot, *Prostitution and Sexuality in Shanghai: A Social History 1849–1949* (New York: Cambridge University Press, 2001).
[99] Remick, *Regulating Prostitution in China*, 20–21.
[100] Sommer, *Sex, Law, and Society in Late Imperial China*, 26.
[101] Richard E. Miller and Austin Sarat, "Grievances, Claims, and Disputes: Assessing the Adversary Culture," *Law & Society Review* 15, no. 3/4 (1980): 525–66, https://doi.org/10.2307/3053502. The "dispute pyramid" metaphor is commonly used to understand the emergence of litigation. The base of the pyramid consists of unperceived injurious experiences. A subset of those – the next level of the pyramid – becomes perceived injurious experiences. Some of these become grievances, where a potential claimant holds someone else responsible for the perceived injury. A subset of those individuals will ask the responsible party for redress. Some of those interactions will then turn into disputes that may progress into claims in the formal legal system. The very tip of the pyramid consists in those claims that are adjudicated.
[102] Patricia Ewick and Susan S. Silbey, *The Common Place of Law: Stories from Everyday Life*, 1st ed. (Chicago: University of Chicago Press, 1998).

common place of law," Hershatter and Henriot's sources allow them to provide us with a view of law in the everyday lives of female sex workers in Shanghai, albeit not directly through their voices. Indeed, Henriot notes that he wrote his study "with the explicit purpose of retelling the history of Chinese prostitutes for themselves, though rarely by themselves and most often through the 'voice' of others."[103] And while Hershatter also notes that the historical record "is not spoken in the voice of the prostitute,"[104] she also shows how they "nevertheless left an audible trace."[105] For instance, she notes that Shanghai papers reported streetwalker arrests and court testimonies and shows how such records "let us glimpse not only the circumstances that brought these women to prostitution, but also the regulatory regimes of the local government and the way that prostitutes positioned themselves to get the most they could from the legal system."[106]

As a scholar of contemporary Chinese law and politics, I was able to hear what female sex workers have to say for themselves. Although the voices of sex workers are not the only sources I use, their words grace many pages of this book. Thus, simply by nature of the fact that I study and learn from people who are still alive, my examination of the regulation of prostitution in China is much more firmly ensconced in society than these historical projects. Of course, the use of sex worker testimony raises many questions: Which sex worker voices does a foreign, white woman hear when she is doing research in an authoritarian country where prostitution is against the law? Which are obscured? To what extent do those voices accurately reflect the lived experiences of their speakers, and how do they instead present distortions of such realities? I address these questions in the appendix of this book.

Lastly, there is a rich and multidisciplinary literature on prostitution outside of China. It includes a wealth of research on the contemporary regulation of prostitution focused on formal rules, regulations, and official policy approaches, methodologically akin to the Jeffreys and Biddulph studies of China mentioned earlier in this chapter,[107] and many historical studies of the regulation of prostitution.[108] Very little of

103 Henriot, *Prostitution and Sexuality in Shanghai*, xv.
104 Hershatter, *Dangerous Pleasures*, 1997, 4.
105 Hershatter, 26.
106 Hershatter, 26.
107 See, e.g., Munro and Della Giusta, *Demanding Sex*; Outshoorn, *The Politics of Prostitution*.
108 See, e.g., Laurie Bernstein, *Sonia's Daughters: Prostitutes and Their Regulation in Imperial Russia* (Berkeley: University of California Press, 1995); Christelle Taraud, *La prostitution coloniale: Algérie, Tunisie, Maroc (1830–1962)* (Paris: Payot, 2003); Philippa Levine, *Prostitution, Race,*

this research focuses primarily on the lived experiences of regulation among both sex workers and frontline state actors, as I do. That said, studies by Prabha Kotiswaran and Rohit De – both set in India – resonate strongly with mine, as they also place law in the everyday lives of sex workers at the heart of their research.

Like this book, Prabha Kotiswaran's legal ethnography of sex work in contemporary India is rooted in close observation of the daily lives of female sex workers.[109] By immersing herself in the two Indian sex markets of Sonagachi and Tirupati, Kotiswaran examines these markets' political economy and the place of law within them. She distinguishes between formal law and its implementation, and underscores "the layers of normative orders, including formal legal rules, social norms, and market structures that affect the bargaining potentials of various stakeholders in sex markets and the outcomes of their negotiations."[110] Yet in contrast to my approach, an explicit theoretical objective drives Kotiswaran's project: to provide a postcolonial materialist feminist theory that advances the view of sex work as a legitimate form of work (in contrast to an abolitionist perspective, which characterizes all prostitution as sexual slavery).[111] I do not disagree with Kotiswaran's perspective. In fact, readers will find ample empirical evidence in support of the "work position" in this book, with sex workers who poignantly articulate how the exchange of sex for money empowers them in their daily lives, and who can speak arrestingly about their rights and contributions to society. Yet I do not place this issue at the heart of my project, which helps explain a core difference in emphasis in our two projects. The attention I pay to the experiences of street-level police officers and health officials – aimed at bringing to light how they interact with sex workers, each other, and with the state priorities and hierarchies that weigh on them – remains largely in the background of Kotiswaran's study.[112]

Rohit De's book examines how sex workers used the Indian Constitution to challenge a newly enacted antitrafficking law in the

and Politics: Policing Venereal Disease in the British Empire (New York: Routledge, 2003), https://doi.org/10.4324/9780203881941; Alain Corbin, *Women for Hire: Prostitution and Sexuality in France after 1850* (Cambridge, MA: Harvard University Press, 1990).

109 Kotiswaran, *Dangerous Sex, Invisible Labor*.

110 Kotiswaran, 241.

111 I elaborate on these debates on prostitution in Chapter 7.

112 While Kotiswaran's fieldwork clearly included interactions with a variety of different government actors (see, e.g., Kotiswaran, *Dangerous Sex, Invisible Labor*, 17–19), my point is that their experiences of regulatory implementation are not central to her study.

1950s, the early years of the new republic.[113] His sources include the full proceedings of the Supreme Court cases he studied, such as lawyers' arguments and transcripts of witness statements. Such documents allow him to hear how some sex workers experience the state, thus bringing forth voices that, as noted earlier, are particularly elusive to historians. And while he guards against any suggestion that "this was the authentic voice of prostitutes," his research also shows how "the Constitution did allow for a voice that represented the prostitute to become visible in a public domain."[114] In contrast to my work, De's research on the place of law in the lives of sex workers is, like Sommer's research on Imperial China, firmly on the top of the dispute pyramid: He tells the story of an exceptional subset of individuals who have chosen to engage with the formal legal system, eventually making their way to the Supreme Court of India.[115] Yet sociolegal scholars must meet the law where it is. I would have found "no there, there" had I looked for the law in the everyday lives of female sex workers in contemporary China in the spaces where De found it in 1950s India. Instead, I found it in more commonplace interactions between sex workers and the state. The result is a close-to-the-ground account of the daily lives of female sex workers, as well as the police officers and health officials who regulate them that shows the centrality of questions of law and rights in places far removed from the formal legal system and its official records.

METHODS, SOURCES, AND SITES

I collected the data for this project through ethnographic observation, interviews, and surveys. I carried out the fieldwork over the course of nineteen months in 2008 and 2009, as well as shorter trips in 2005, 2011, and 2014. Hu Jintao was therefore China's leader during most of my data collection, and my concluding chapter reflects upon changes under Xi Jinping. While I was based primarily in Beijing, Shenzhen, and Guangzhou, I also spent time in Dongguan, Shanghai, Harbin, Shenyang, Changsha, and two smaller cities in Hebei and Hubei

[113] Rohit De, *A People's Constitution: The Everyday Life of Law in the Indian Republic* (Princeton, NJ: Princeton University Press, 2018). De's book also examines how other ordinary citizens use constitutional remedies against various state regulations.

[114] De, 213.

[115] This is not to say that the actions of these individuals were inconsequential for the larger population of female sex workers in India. Far from it: De notes that "this litigation prompted mobilization and associational politics outside the court and brought rights language into the everyday life of the sex trade." De, 20.

provinces, which I refer to with the pseudonyms of Fushan and Zhengti, respectively.[116] In addition, I carried out research in Hong Kong to interview people with expertise in prostitution in mainland China.

My ethnographic research led me on to the streets and into the parks, small brothels, and entertainment venues where sex workers solicit clients. It also brought me into the offices of law enforcement, health, and other government institutions, and occasionally inside a police car, riding along with officers on patrol. In Shenzhen, I carried out ethnographic observation in two red-light districts: Wanqin and Xizhou.[117] I lived in a hotel in Wanqin that catered to sex workers and clients. A local madam took me under her wing, and I spent my days in the living room of her apartment-brothel, observing sex workers and clients negotiate transactions before retreating into a bedroom. In the early evening, the madam and I would stroll around the neighborhood together. She would introduce me to others in the community and ward off clients inquiring about whether I was a Russian sex worker under her care.[118] In Xizhou, I spent my time outside in the main square, in the local government offices, and inside entertainment venues, talking to sex workers, madams, pimps, and local state officials. In Beijing, I carried out ethnographic observation in the lounge of a sex worker community organization located in the heart of a red-light district. As I became a familiar presence in that space, I connected with sex workers and observed them interact as they would come and go throughout the day – to pick up condoms, ask the staff for medical advice, or take a break. In Zhengti, I ballroom-danced with the police, and also swam and went river tubing with them. I observed police officers play mahjong together and sing karaoke with hostesses in an entertainment venue. At several of my research sites, I distributed condoms and safe-sex brochures alongside local health officials or members of sex work community groups. I absorbed the contrasting vantage points of various societal and state actors by positioning myself alongside different groups in different places. Overall, this

116 Since these towns are smaller, revealing their actual names could make it possible to identify some of my informants there.

117 Wanqin and Xizhou are pseudonyms.

118 Although the vast majority of sex workers in China are Chinese, foreign women, including from Russia, also sell sex in the country. Russian women sell sex in China's northeast, closer to the border with Russia, and also in Shenzhen. I did not focus on them in my research, nor did I encounter any during my fieldwork. Zhi Mo (至墨) and Ouyang Bin (欧阳斌), "Anfang Naxie Zai Zhongguo De Yang Jinv Men (暗访那些在中国的'洋妓女'们) [A Discrete Investigation of Foreign Prostitutes in China]," *Phoenix Weekly* (凤凰周刊), September 8, 2003, perma.cc/4LTN-R2MP.

ethnographic method provided me with front-row seats to observe regulatory dynamics around prostitution both within and across society and the state.[119] It also helped me develop rapport for in-depth interviewing. I carried out almost two hundred interviews with sex workers, clients, madams, pimps, police officers, health officials, other central and local government officials, as well as staff at both domestic and international organizations working in the areas of health, prostitution, women's rights, policing, and legal services. I also conducted a survey of 568 sex workers in one red-light district in Beijing, and a survey of 89 police officers in southern China. I discuss these research processes in greater depth in the appendices.

ORGANIZATION OF THE BOOK

Part I of the book situates prostitution and its regulation in contemporary China within three dimensions: Chinese history, key characteristics of post-Mao China, and the broader array of possible regulatory approaches to prostitution. Chapter 2 underscores the historical continuities that exist between the status-based patterns of prostitution policy implementation I observe and earlier approaches to regulating sex work in China. It also highlights how prostitution in post-Mao China reflects broader socioeconomic and political developments in the country. Chapter 3 describes the laws, policies, and institutions that govern prostitution in China, and situates them in relation to the spectrum of regulatory possibilities that societies have vis-à-vis the issue.

Part II is about the daily lives of female sex workers. Chapters 4, 5, and 6 focus on the experiences and perspectives of women in the low tier (on the streets and in small brothels), middle tier (hostesses), and upper tier (mistresses), respectively. These chapters bring forth how their lives and attitudes vary depending on the tier of sex work, and cover issues such as work conditions, health risks, perspectives on prostitution, and views of the state. Chapter 7 then examines what they have in common: similar life experiences, comparable thought processes about their engagement in prostitution, and, when they encounter sex worker grassroots organizations, a shared sense of

119 Although it is on a different topic – the Hui Muslim minority – a book on law and society in China that resonated strongly with my research from this methodological perspective is Matthew S. Erie's ethnography, *China and Islam: The Prophet, the Party, and Law* (New York: Cambridge University Press, 2016).

empowerment that comes with the consciousness of belonging to a global community of sex worker civil society.

Part III turns to the individuals behind China's prostitution policies: the state actors who implement them and the international ones who shape them. Chapter 8 examines how the police enforce anti-prostitution laws: who they punish and how. Here, it is low-tier sex workers who bear the brunt of the state. Chapter 9 maintains its focus on law enforcement, with specific attention to the extractive and protective ways that police officers interact with sex workers when they are not arresting them. These behaviors mainly affect women in the middle tier of the sex industry, and underscore the delicate balancing act that frontline police must engage in to avoid disrupting the economic benefits that a thriving sex industry brings to the local government. Chapter 10 turns to health policies, and highlights the roles and responsibilities of the global health community in shaping China's approach to prostitution as a public health issue. Chapter 11 then examines how local health officials implement these policies, including their struggles to negotiate pushback from both the sex industry and the police. It uncovers practices that stymie public health goals by overlooking women in the low tier – those most in need of health interventions – and that also harm sex workers. Chapter 12 concludes this study of law in the everyday lives of sex workers, police officers, and public health officials in China with a reflection on changes in China under Xi Jinping and policy implications.

PART I

HISTORY, CONTEMPORARY CONTEXT, AND OFFICIAL POLICIES

2

HISTORICAL CONTINUITIES AND CONTEMPORARY CONTEXT

INTRODUCTION

Sex work has presented the state with regulatory challenges throughout most of Chinese history. In Imperial China (361 BC–1912 CE), prostitution policy varied based on the status of the men and women involved.[1] In Republican China (1912–49), the regulation of sex work was formulated primarily at the local level. Some local governments sought to abolish it, but they were more likely to license and tax it, or to establish state-run brothels.[2] When the Chinese Communist Party (CCP) came to power in 1949, it moved swiftly to prohibit prostitution nationwide, and in the first few decades of the People's Republic of China (PRC), prostitution was less prevalent and more hidden. Yet the scarcity of prostitution during the Mao era is best viewed as a brief historical anomaly. Sex work reemerged in the early 1980s, in the wake of Deng Xiaoping's policy of reform and opening, and it has been integral to many of the country's major political, economic, and social developments since 1979.

1 Matthew H. Sommer, *Sex, Law, and Society in Late Imperial China* (Stanford, CA: Stanford University Press, 2000). Sommer also explores issues tied to prostitution through the lens of class in Matthew H. Sommer, *Polyandry and Wife-Selling in Qing Dynasty China: Survival Strategies and Judicial Interventions* (Oakland: University of California Press, 2015), with a focus on practices such as polyandry and wife-selling among the rural poor in Qing Dynasty China.

2 Elizabeth J. Remick, "Police-Run Brothels in Republican Kunming," *Modern China* 33, no. 4 (2007): 423–61; Elizabeth J. Remick, "Prostitution Taxes and Local State Building in Republican China," *Modern China* 29, no. 1 (2003): 38–70; Elizabeth J. Remick, *Regulating Prostitution in China: Gender and Local Statebuilding, 1900–1937* (Stanford, CA: Stanford University Press, 2014).

IMPERIAL CHINA

Prostitution policy throughout most of Imperial China varied depending on the status and gender of the concerned individuals.[3] Until 1723, no legal code explicitly banned the sale of sexual services.[4] Instead, as Matthew Harvey Sommer explains, "The legal significance of an act depended on who did it to whom."[5] There were different regulations for officials (官吏 – *guanli*), commoners (良民 – *liang min*), and people of debased status (贱民 – *jian min*). They also varied for men and women within each of these categories.

As early as the Song Dynasty (960–1279 CE), officials (*guanli*) and their sons were prohibited from frequenting brothels, patronizing prostitutes, or taking them as wives or concubines.[6] These rules were intended to reinforce status boundaries between elite men, held to the highest standards of morality, and debased-status women, who were considered sexually immoral. Perpetrators would lose their rank and degree, and receive a flogging of dozens of strokes of heavy bamboo.[7] Women who knowingly engaged in a sexual transaction with these officials were also punished. Wives of officials who engaged in illicit sex were also liable for sanctions.[8]

In contrast, male commoners (*liang min*) were permitted to engage the services of sex workers, although they too were forbidden from marrying them.[9] Commoner women did not have these types of protections: those who engaged in prostitution or any other type of sexual relationship outside of a marriage were guilty of the crime of "offenses of illicit sex (当依犯奸之律论之 – *dang yi fan jian zhi lü lun zhi*)."[10] If a commoner husband pimped his wife or concubine, the woman,

[3] Imperial China began with the Qin Dynasty in 361 BC and ended in 1912 with the founding of the Republic of China. Broadly speaking, the legal status of an individual in Imperial China, and their rights and responsibilities, fell into one of three categories: official, commoner, or person of debased/mean status. See Sommer, *Sex, Law, and Society in Late Imperial China*, 5. T'ung-tsn Ch'u wrote the classic study on this issue: *Law and Society in Traditional China* (Paris: Mouton, 1965).

[4] Sommer, *Sex, Law, and Society in Late Imperial China*, 210.

[5] Sommer, *Sex, Law, and Society in Late Imperial China*, 210.

[6] Gail Hershatter, *Dangerous Pleasures: Prostitution and Modernity in Twentieth-Century Shanghai* (Berkeley: University of California Press, 1997), 204, 474–75; Sommer, *Sex, Law, and Society in Late Imperial China*, 7, 218–21.

[7] Hershatter, *Dangerous Pleasures*, 204, 474–75; Sommer, *Sex, Law, and Society in Late Imperial China*, 7.

[8] Matthew Sommer, email message to author, August 22, 2014.

[9] Sommer, *Sex, Law, and Society in Late Imperial China*, 218.

[10] Sommer, *Sex, Law, and Society in Late Imperial China*, 54, 223.

husband, and customer would all be treated as adulterers.[11] Offenders would be subject to flogging, although women coerced into prostitution might escape punishment.[12] As an additional sanction, the married couple would be divorced – a harsh penalty for men given that marriage was an important status symbol in Imperial China, and that a man poor enough to pimp his wife would struggle to remarry.[13] The woman would be returned to her family.[14] Commoner men would also be punished for pimping their daughters.[15] It was even illegal for a commoner to coerce his domestic female slave into prostitution – an act that would result in her being freed into commoner status.[16]

Prostitution was permitted for debased-status groups (*jian min*) until the early Qing Dynasty (1644–1912).[17] This was particularly relevant for women who belonged to "music households" (乐户 – *yue hu*), who were actually *expected* to engage in prostitution.[18] This class originated in the Han Dynasty (206 BC–220 CE), as wives and daughters of executed criminals, prisoners of war, rebels, and political dissidents were forced to engage in state-supervised sexual and entertainment services.[19] These women, and any sons who were spared death along with their fathers, were registered as members of *yue hu* – and the status was hereditary.[20] Throughout the Yuan (1279–1368), Ming (1368–1644), and early Qing (1644–1912) dynasties, the Bureau of Instruction (教坊司– *jiao fang si*) had jurisdiction over the *yue hu*, and implemented policies that included registering and taxing them.[21] The law permitted sexual transactions between *yue* women and commoner men and allowed debased-status men to pimp their wives and daughters.[22] Regulations serving to demarcate this category

11 Sommer, *Sex, Law, and Society in Late Imperial China*, 55.
12 Sommer, *Sex, Law, and Society in Late Imperial China*, 55–56, 227.
13 Sommer, *Sex, Law, and Society in Late Imperial China*, 55, 226–27.
14 Sommer, *Sex, Law, and Society in Late Imperial China*, 227.
15 Sommer, *Sex, Law, and Society in Late Imperial China*, 56.
16 Sommer, *Sex, Law, and Society in Late Imperial China*, 227.
17 The *jian min* were generally slaves, serfs, and bondservants.
18 Sommer, *Sex, Law, and Society in Late Imperial China*, 7. Sommer underscores that it is a slight misnomer to describe this system as "prostitution." The term "implies paid work in a commercial sex market, and at least the possibility of female agency and choice. The sexual servitude described here was really a form of slavery, not unlike the use of sexual slaves ('comfort women') by the Japanese army during World War II. It is only in the late Ming and Qing dynasties that we see the emergence of a pervasive, private commercial sex market." (Ibid., 212)
19 Sommer, *Sex, Law, and Society in Late Imperial China*, 212.
20 Sommer, *Sex, Law, and Society in Late Imperial China*, 212.
21 Sommer, *Sex, Law, and Society in Late Imperial China*, 213.
22 Sommer, *Sex, Law, and Society in Late Imperial China*, 7, 54, 220–21, 248–50.

of individuals included sumptuary laws that required the men to wear green headgear, a practice that lives on today in the Chinese expression for being cuckold: "to wear a green hat" (戴绿帽子 – *dai lü maozi*).[23] Not all debased-status women participated in prostitution; nor were all women engaged in transactional sex members of these hereditary groups working under the auspices of the Bureau of Instruction.[24] Nevertheless, until the early Qing period, there existed a class of individuals distinct from commoners and officials who were considered below the law.[25] They were not held to what were considered moral standards of sexual behavior, and the state permitted (and in some cases forced) them to engage in prostitution.

In 1723, the Yongzheng Emperor abolished the legal category of *yue hu* and other debased-status groups, thereby elevating them to commoner status.[26] This policy is generally understood as an effort at emancipation and a reflection of socioeconomic changes that were wearing down status barriers.[27] The Yongzheng Emperor explained that these categories prevented individuals from moral reform and "self-renewal."[28] The 1723 edict, while not explicitly framed as a blanket prohibition on prostitution, effectively criminalized such practices across all social classes.[29] New regulations against pimping were enacted, which required local officials and others to play an active role in preventing prostitution.[30] Previous sanctions continued to apply – a married couple would still be divorced if the husband pimped his wife and guilty parties (husband, wife, and customer) were subject to punishments that included flogging and the cangue.[31] These policies continued into the late Qing Dynasty.[32]

It is difficult to know the extent to which individuals in Imperial China abided by the prostitution rules that applied to their specific social status or how frequently transgressions were prosecuted. That said, Sommer's analysis of legal case records provides ample evidence

23 Sommer, *Sex, Law, and Society in Late Imperial China*, 218.
24 Sommer, *Sex, Law, and Society in Late Imperial China*, 214.
25 Sommer, *Sex, Law, and Society in Late Imperial China*, 255.
26 Sommer, *Sex, Law, and Society in Late Imperial China*, 265.
27 Susan Mann, *Precious Records: Women in China's Long Eighteenth Century* (Stanford, CA: Stanford University Press, 1997), 43; Sommer, *Sex, Law, and Society in Late Imperial China*, 3.
28 Sommer, *Sex, Law, and Society in Late Imperial China*, 266.
29 Sommer, *Sex, Law, and Society in Late Imperial China*, 272–73.
30 Sommer, *Sex, Law, and Society in Late Imperial China*, 273.
31 Sommer, 274. The cangue was a portable punishment and public humiliation device that generally consisted of two pieces of flat board with a hole in the center large enough for a person's neck.
32 Matthew Sommer, email message to author, August 22, 2014.

that violations of the law did occur and that such behavior was punished, at least occasionally.[33] The 1723 reforms represented an important historical rupture, as local officials made real efforts to implement the policies that criminalized all prostitution.[34] But as Sommer's research shows, illicit forms of prostitution persisted throughout the Imperial era. By the early seventeenth century, a private enterprise-based commercial sex market had emerged separate from the state-controlled system based on hereditary penal servitude.[35] While the Yongzheng Emperor eliminated the *yue hu* system, he did not succeed in eliminating prostitution from Qing society.[36] Instead, the illicit market for commercial sex expanded to fill the void that the abolition of state-approved debased-status prostitution created.[37]

Throughout the Imperial era, it was the status of the individual that drove the state's impetus to regulate prostitution. The central concern revolved around the concept of "illicit sexual intercourse," who engaged in it, and how it "threatened the family morality and structure essential to social order."[38] The commercial aspect of the phenomenon – the exchange of money or goods for sex that commodifies a sex worker's body – was a second-order issue. As China entered the twentieth century, the focus shifted, and an individual's status no longer served as the primary concern driving the formal regulation of prostitution. Instead, objections to the sex industry and the push to regulate it became rooted in the concern that prostitution is a commodification of sex. Payment for sex (rather than promiscuity or adultery) became the problem – a distinction that continues to underlie the prohibition of prostitution in China today and in other places where sex work is against the law.

LATE QING AND REPUBLICAN CHINA

In late Qing and Republican China, prostitution policies varied at the local level.[39] In 1904–5, the central government gave local governments the authority to regulate and tax prostitution, in order to

33 Sommer, *Sex, Law, and Society in Late Imperial China.*

34 Sommer, *Sex, Law, and Society in Late Imperial China*, 289, 301.

35 Sommer, *Sex, Law, and Society in Late Imperial China*, 8, 235, 258–59.

36 Sommer, *Sex, Law, and Society in Late Imperial China*, 281.

37 Sommer, *Sex, Law, and Society in Late Imperial China*, 281.

38 Sommer, *Sex, Law, and Society in Late Imperial China*, 303. Sommer notes that a similar status concern shaped prostitution policy in ancient Rome (Ibid., 309).

39 The term "local" refers to government below the central level, either provincial or sub-provincial.

facilitate funding of provincial police forces that were established under the Late Qing Era's New Policies.[40] Three local models of prostitution policy emerged: abolition, licensing and taxation, and state-run brothels.[41]

County and municipal governments occasionally attempted to abolish prostitution. Nanjing did so when it was the capital of the Republic, from 1927 to 1937, as did localities in Hunan and Henan.[42] Policies included sudden closure of brothels and gradual license withdrawal.[43] Women might be forced to leave the town or redirected toward other forms of employment.[44] Attempts to ban prostitution were unsuccessful, however, and only pushed the activity underground.[45]

More often, localities adopted a prostitution policy that focused on regulation and taxation – registering brothels, licensing sex workers and requiring them to undergo health inspections, and taxing both the venues and the women.[46] Provincial capitals were generally the first local governments to register brothels and collect prostitution taxes, with smaller cities and towns following suit as they developed their own law enforcement institutions.[47] Localities that adopted this model frequently established organizations to facilitate women's exit from prostitution.[48] Chinese scholars refer to this system as official prostitution (公娼 – *gongchang*), which Elizabeth Remick calls the "national model."[49] This model prohibited nonregistered prostitution.

40 Remick, "Police-Run Brothels in Republican Kunming," 425; Remick, "Prostitution Taxes and Local State Building in Republican China," 45. Remick also explores the issues discussed in this section in *Regulating Prostitution in China*.

41 Remick, "Prostitution Taxes and Local State Building in Republican China," 42–43; Remick, "Police-Run Brothels in Republican Kunming," 425. Remick (2007) presents four rather than three prostitution models. Specifically, she distinguishes between a model of licensing and light taxation, and a model of heavy taxation that resulted in prostitution playing a significant role in local state-building (Remick 2003, 2007).

42 Zwia Lipkin, *Useless to the State: "Social Problems" and Social Engineering in Nationalist Nanjing, 1927–1937* (Cambridge, MA: Harvard University Press, 2006); Remick, "Prostitution Taxes and Local State Building in Republican China," 43.

43 Remick, "Police-Run Brothels in Republican Kunming," 425; Remick, "Prostitution Taxes and Local State Building in Republican China," 43.

44 Remick, "Police-Run Brothels in Republican Kunming," 425.

45 Remick, "Prostitution Taxes and Local State Building in Republican China," 43.

46 Remick, "Police-Run Brothels in Republican Kunming," 425; Remick, "Prostitution Taxes and Local State Building in Republican China," 46–47.

47 Remick, "Prostitution Taxes and Local State Building in Republican China," 45; Remick, *Regulating Prostitution in China*.

48 Remick, "Police-Run Brothels in Republican Kunming," 425.

49 Remick, "Police-Run Brothels in Republican Kunming," 425; Remick, "Prostitution Taxes and Local State Building in Republican China."

In 1913, the central government in Beijing formalized local taxation. It granted provincial governments the authority to collect prostitution taxes, and provincial governments could authorize municipal governments to administer the system.[50] The tax itself was twofold. Brothels paid a monthly licensing fee,[51] while individual sex workers also paid a monthly tax.[52] Capital cities in almost all of the main twenty-two provinces in Republican China adopted this system, as did other towns.[53] Tax revenue went toward developing the local police force and supporting healthcare and rehabilitation facilities for women.[54] Guangzhou implemented a particularly thorough version of this model. It based taxes on the volume of business, including a per-transaction tax, and a tax based on the amount spent on the banquet that clients would host as part of the transaction.[55] Guangzhou invested the revenue from these taxes in road construction, schools, universities, hospitals, and military forces.[56] Under this system, prostitution contributed actively to local state-building activities that went beyond the funding of law enforcement activities that the Qing Era prostitution policies were designed to support.[57]

State-run brothels in the cities of Kunming, Guiyang, and Chengdu represented the third model of prostitution policy in late Qing and Republican China.[58] In addition to licensing and taxing sex workers, the police in these cities created a walled-off zone for prostitution,

50 Remick, "Prostitution Taxes and Local State Building in Republican China," 45.

51 Christian Henriot, "'From a Throne of Glory to a Seat of Ignominy': Shanghai Prostitution Revisited (1849–1949)," *Modern China* 22, no. 2 (1996): 132–63; Gail Hershatter, "The Hierarchy of Shanghai Prostitution, 1870–1949," *Modern China* 15, no. 4 (1989): 463–98. Cited in Remick, "Prostitution Taxes and Local State Building in Republican China," 46.

52 Remick, "Prostitution Taxes and Local State Building in Republican China," 46.

53 Remick, 46.

54 Remick, 47.

55 Remick, "Prostitution Taxes and Local State Building in Republican China"; Remick, "Police-Run Brothels in Republican Kunming," 426.

56 Remick, "Police-Run Brothels in Republican Kunming," 453; Remick, "Prostitution Taxes and Local State Building in Republican China," 53, 58.

57 This difference leads Remick to define Guangzhou's model as a "taxation regime," distinct from the "national model." See Remick, "Police-Run Brothels in Republican Kunming," 426. While any locality could have adopted the kind of intensive system of prostitution taxation that Guangzhou developed, Remick argues that the Guangdong government had unique political incentives driving their desire for increased revenue. They had greater military expenses than other provinces, as they were frequently in conflict with the central government. In addition, provincial and municipal leaders were particularly committed to modernization, a goal that required funding costly infrastructure projects. Remick, "Prostitution Taxes and Local State Building in Republican China," 58–62.

58 Remick, "Prostitution Taxes and Local State Building in Republican China," 42; Remick, "Police-Run Brothels in Republican Kunming," 453.

called *jiyuan* (集园).[59] Police sold entrance tickets (with customers paying police rather than the women directly), claimed a percentage of sex workers' earnings, charged rent for the brothels, coordinated health inspections, and provided security.[60] Instead of regulating a privately run venue, the local government in these cases transformed brothels into state institutions, akin to fire departments, city hospitals, and slaughterhouse inspection units.[61] More important than the revenue this system provided, local governments used it to maintain social order.[62]

A BRIEF NOTE ON CONCUBINES

The state regulated concubines through a system that was separate from the one governing prostitution. Concubinage emerged as a custom among elites in the Song period (960–1279).[63] Starting with the Ming Dynasty, it had become institutionalized as a form of semi-legitimate marriage.[64] Under Qing laws, concubines were considered minor wives, a status that applied to any woman married after the first wife.[65] Unlike women engaged in prostitution, they lived at the master's residence and were subordinate to the main wife, whom they were required to obey.[66] Their status under the law was inferior to that of the first wife, who had certain legal protections against divorce.[67] In contrast, husbands had complete discretion to expel concubines from the household.[68] A concubine could, however, appeal for divorce if her husband or other household members beat her excessively, or forced her to commit adultery.[69] In Republican China, the government sought to promote monogamy and gender equality, while at the same

59 Remick explains that the two Chinese characters in the term *jiyuan* (集园) here mean "to gather together" and "garden." It is easily confused with the term *jiyuan* (妓院), or brothel, which literally means "prostitute" and "courtyard."
60 Remick, "Police-Run Brothels in Republican Kunming," 426, 432.
61 Remick, 426, 447.
62 Remick, 427, 452.
63 Lisa Tran, "The Concubine in Republican China: Social Perception and Legal Construction," *Etudes Chinoises* 28 (2008): 120.
64 Tran, 120.
65 Tran, 123; Lisa Tran, *Concubines in Court: Marriage and Monogamy in Twentieth-Century China* (Lanham, MD: Rowman & Littlefield, 2015), 7.
66 Tran, "The Concubine in Republican China," 125–26.
67 Tran, 125–26.
68 Tran, 125–26.
69 Kathryn Bernhardt, "Women and the Law: Divorce in the Republican Period," in *Civil Law in Qing and Republican China*, eds. Kathryn Bernhardt and Philip C. Huang (Stanford, CA: Stanford University Press, 1994), 210.

time providing legal protection for concubines.[70] As these goals were in tension, the state left the regulation of concubinage to the courts and made no mention of it in the civil code.[71] The courts hesitated to rule on concubinage as bigamy, given how widespread the practice was both in society and within the political leadership.[72] They instead compromised and provided concubines with additional legal rights by considering them members of the master's household.[73] The Communist Party abolished concubinage in 1950 when the first marriage law in the PRC defined the institution of marriage as monogamous.[74] Today's phenomenon of "keeping a second wife" (包二奶 – *bao ernai*) is likened to the concubinage of the past.[75]

THE PEOPLE'S REPUBLIC OF CHINA: 1949–1979

Prostitution policy in the first decades of the PRC differed from most of China's historical precedents in two important ways. First, it was uniform, with no variation by status or locality – it was banned everywhere and for everyone. Second, the ban was enforced much more successfully than previous attempts to curtail prostitution. While the CCP's claims that it had eradicated prostitution were inaccurate, both the visibility and overall scope of prostitution decreased sharply.

The CCP decried prostitution as "a sequel to the savage and bestial system of former exploiters and power holders to ruin the spirit and the body of women and to tarnish their dignity."[76] Successful eradication was of symbolic importance since prostitution was considered a feudal remnant of the country's colonial past.[77] Women who engaged in it

70 Bernhardt, 209–10.
71 Bernhardt, 210.
72 Tran, "The Concubine in Republican China," 121–22, 148; Tran, *Concubines in Court*, 53.
73 Bernhardt, "Women and the Law," 211–12; Tran, "The Concubine in Republican China," 135–36, 148; Tran, *Concubines in Court*, 53.
74 Suowei Xiao, "China's New Concubines? The Contemporary Second-Wife Phenomenon" (ProQuest Dissertations, 2009), 1, 9, perma.cc/T6U2-M8ME; Suowei Xiao (肖索未), *Yuwang Yu Zunyan: Zhuanxingqi Zhongguo De Jieceng, Xingbie Yu Qinmi Guanxi* (欲望与尊严：转型期中国的阶层，性别与亲密关系) *[Desire and Dignity : Class, Gender and Intimacy in Transitional China]* (Beijing: China Social Sciences Academic Press [社会科学文献出版社], 2018), 166, n. 1.
75 Xiao, "China's New Concubines?," 2009; Xiao, *Desire and Dignity*.
76 Christian Henriot, "'La Fermeture': The Abolition of Prostitution in Shanghai, 1949–58," *The China Quarterly* 142 (1995): 467. Henriot quotes an editorial from the December 1949 issue of *Xin Zhongguo Funü* (Women of New China), the official publication of the national organization for women, the All-China Women's Federation (ACWF).
77 Sarah Biddulph, *Legal Reform and Administrative Detention Powers in China* (Cambridge: Cambridge University Press, 2007), 70; Henriot, "La Fermeture," 467–68; Hershatter, *Dangerous Pleasures*, 305.

were perceived as proletarian victims of exploitative, wealthy business elites.[78] As Gail Hershatter explains, the Communist Party viewed its success as representing "China's emergence as a strong, healthy, and modern nation," and framed its efforts in terms of "reeducation, redemption from imperialism, and the creation of a new woman, free from her past shameful history as China was free from her national shame."[79]

Upon gaining power in 1949, the CCP promptly began a campaign to abolish prostitution, with municipalities throughout the PRC acting swiftly. Some cities closed down brothels immediately in late 1949 and early 1950, including Suzhou, Beijing, Nanjing, Hangzhou, and Tianjin.[80] Other localities, including Shanghai and Wuhan, adopted an approach of registration and gradual closure.[81] This method was meant to better manage the economic and social disruptions of a sudden crackdown.[82] Prostitution detention centers for women emerged alongside these efforts. These institutions facilitated reformed detainees' reentry into society, as they were returned to their families, married, assigned to factory employment, or sent to work on state farms in the remote provinces of Gansu, Xinjiang, or Ningxia.[83] In addition to these endeavors to redirect sex workers toward other occupations, the Communist Party developed a surveillance and control apparatus that made it increasingly difficult for anyone to engage in illicit behavior.[84] Community organizations such as resident committees collaborated closely with authorities to monitor criminal behavior, including prostitution.[85] In the years following the PRC's founding, prostitution decreased sharply in large part due to the Party's success at developing the institutions of a police state. By the late 1950s and early 1960s, the government was proclaiming that prostitution had been eradicated.[86] While the exchange of sex for money or other material benefits continued in more disguised forms, it was significantly less

[78] Henriot, "La Fermeture," 468.
[79] Hershatter, *Dangerous Pleasures*, 305.
[80] Henriot, "La Fermeture," 469; Biddulph, 71.
[81] Biddulph, 71; Henriot, "La Fermeture"; Hershatter, *Dangerous Pleasures*, 304–10.
[82] Biddulph, 71.
[83] Biddulph, 75; Hershatter, *Dangerous Pleasures*, 318–20.
[84] Henriot, "La Fermeture," 476.
[85] Biddulph, 76.
[86] Hershatter, *Dangerous Pleasures*; Jinghao Zhou, "Chinese Prostitution: Consequences and Solutions in the Post-Mao Era," *China: An International Journal* 4, no. 2 (2006): 242; Elaine Jeffreys, *China, Sex and Prostitution* (London: Routledge Curzon, 2004), 96; Elanah Uretsky, "Mixing Business with Pleasure: Masculinity and Male Sexual Culture in Urban China in the Era of HIV/AIDS" (PhD diss., Columbia University, 2007), 6.

prevalent and conspicuous than in the past.[87] The success of the 1950s campaign, in contrast to previous efforts throughout the country to abolish prostitution, speaks to the breadth and depth of the state's reach under Mao, as well as the close integration of the national and local governments at that time.[88]

PROSTITUTION IN POST-MAO CHINA

In December 1978, Deng Xiaoping launched the policy of reform and opening (改革开放 – *gaige kaifang*). As China introduced these market-based economic reforms and opening to the outside world, the extent and visibility of prostitution increased exponentially in the country.[89] Starting in the 1980s, foreigners began reporting on the presence of prostitution in cities.[90] Communist Party officials claimed it was reemerging in coastal urban areas as a result of foreign investment.[91] While researchers generally described a pattern in which prostitution spread from there into the interior and rural areas, others identified its presence outside of coastal areas soon after Deng's reforms were introduced.[92] The resurgence of prostitution reflects broader political, economic, and social developments in postsocialist China.

Poverty, Migration, and Wealth

Rural poverty in China[93] – combined with a relaxation of the household registration system (户口 – *hukou*) that had previously placed

[87] Biddulph, 76; Jeffreys, *China, Sex and Prostitution*, 96; Elaine Jeffreys, "Debating the Legal Regulation of Sex-Related Bribery and Corruption in the People's Republic of China," in *Sex and Sexuality in China*, ed. Elaine Jeffreys (London: Routledge, 2006), 171.

[88] Hershatter, *Dangerous Pleasures*, 305–6, 322.

[89] Elaine Jeffreys, *Prostitution Scandals in China: Policing, Media, and Society* (London: Routledge, 2012), 3; Jeffreys, *China, Sex and Prostitution*, 96; Elaine Jeffreys, "Introduction: Talking Sex and Sexuality in China," in *Sex and Sexuality in China*, ed. Elaine Jeffreys (London: Routledge, 2006), 14; Hershatter, *Dangerous Pleasures*, 333.

[90] Hershatter, *Dangerous Pleasures*, 327, 330–31.

[91] Hershatter, 334–35.

[92] Hershatter, 335.

[93] For an overview of poverty in China from 1978 to 2020, including a discussion of the different ways in which poverty rates have been calculated over time, see Bill Bikales, "Reflections on Poverty Reduction in China," 2021, perma.cc/WV5Y-QB54. Official data from 2007, around the time when I was conducting this research, claimed that 14.79 million people in China were living in rural poverty. United Nations Development Program, "Access for All: Basic Public Services for 1.3 Billion People," 2008, 10–11. In 2018, official data that used a higher poverty threshold identified 16.6 million people living in rural poverty. Xinhua News Agency (新华社), "China Lifts 13.86 Mln Rural Poor Out of Poverty in 2018," *Xinhua News Agency* (新华社), February 15, 2019, perma.cc/3RBS-5YC5. In early 2021, Xi Jinping announced to great fanfare that China had eradicated poverty. While questions about the metrics behind

strict restrictions on the movement of people away from the countryside – has led to massive amounts of migration to urban areas since the 1980s.[94] In 2010, official Chinese sources estimated that the population of migrant rural workers, known as "floating population" (流动人口 – *liudong renkou*), was 221 million – about 17 percent of the country's entire population.[95] About one-third of these migrants are women.[96] Referred to as "laboring sisters" (打工妹 – *dagongmei*), they are concentrated in the manufacturing sector, as well as service and domestic work.[97] They are among the lowest paid and most abused workers in the Chinese labor market,[98] and suffer from problems such as wage arrears and nonpayment of wages. Sex workers are largely drawn from this migrant population, with persistent poverty serving as a push factor into prostitution. In addition, these women's client base is made up partially of migrant men.[99]

this claim remain unanswered, China has undeniably made great progress toward reducing rural poverty in recent decades. At the same time, millions of rural Chinese citizens continue to live in difficult circumstances and migrate to urban areas, regardless of whether they are officially counted as poor. In addition, Xi Jinping's aggressive efforts at poverty alleviation may not be sustainable or cost-effective. Keith Bradsher, "Jobs, Houses, and Cows: China's Costly Drive to Erase Extreme Poverty," *The New York Times*, December 31, 2020, https://perma.cc/988D-9PDX; Lily Kuo, "China Claims to Have Eliminated Poverty, But the Figures Mask Harsh Challenges," *Washington Post*, accessed September 14, 2021, https://perma.cc/5BZJ-DS88; Scott Rozelle and Natalie Hell, *Invisible China: How the Urban-Rural Divide Threatens China's Rise*, 1st ed. (Chicago: University of Chicago Press, 2020).

94 Ching Kwan Lee, *Gender and the South China Miracle: Two Worlds of Factory Women* (Berkeley: University of California Press, 1998); C. Cindy Fan, *China on the Move: Migration, the State, and the Household* (London: Routledge, 2007); Alexsia T. Chan and Kevin J. O'Brien, "Phantom Services: Deflecting Migrant Workers in China," *The China Journal* 81 (October 22, 2018): 103–22, https://doi.org/10.1086/699215.

95 This figure increased to 290 million in 2019. Zai Liang, Zhen Li, and Zhongdong Ma, "Changing Patterns of the Floating Population in China during 2000–2010," *Population and Development Review* 40, no. 4 (December 2014): 695–716, https://doi.org/10.1111/j.1728-4457.2014.00007.x. National Bureau of Statistics (国家统计局), "2019 Nian Nongmin Gong Jiance Diaocha Baogao (2019 年农民工监测调查报告) [2019 Migrant Workers Survey Report]," 2020, perma.cc/G98B-Y9YY.

96 Julia Chuang, "Factory Girls after the Factory: Female Return Migrations in Rural China," *Gender & Society* 30, no. 3 (June 1, 2016): 467–89, https://doi.org/10.1177/0891243215621718; National Bureau of Statistics (国家统计局), "2009 Nian Nongmin Gong Jiance Diaocha Baogao (2009 年农民工监测调查报告) [2009 Migrant Workers Survey Report]."

97 Asian Development Bank, "People's Republic of China Country Gender Assessment," 2006, 22; Arianne M. Gaetano and Tamara Jacka, *On the Move: Women and Rural-to-Urban Migration in Contemporary China* (New York: Columbia University Press, 2004); Margaret Y. K. Woo, "Contesting Citizenship: Marriage and Divorce in the People's Republic of China," in *Sex and Sexuality in China*, ed. Elaine Jeffreys (London: Routledge, 2006), 63.

98 Asian Development Bank, "People's Republic of China Country Gender Assessment," 22; Tiantian Zheng, *Red Lights: The Lives of Sex Workers in Postsocialist China* (Minneapolis: University of Minnesota Press, 2009), 26.

99 Uretsky, "Mixing Business with Pleasure," 7; Lena Edlund and Evelyn Korn, "A Theory of Prostitution," *The Journal of Political Economy* 110, no. 1 (2002): 181, 206.

A second source of economic insecurity that affected China's sex industry occurred through the restructuring of state-owned enterprises (SOEs) in the 1990s. From 1995 to 2001, SOEs laid off more than 35 million workers, more than 13.3 million of whom were women.[100] According to the Asian Development Bank, only 39 percent of these women subsequently found alternate forms of legitimate employment.[101] Some of the others turned to prostitution.[102]

While poverty serves as a push factor for women who sell sex, the increasing wealth of another subset of the population – businessmen and middle-class wage earners – fuels much of the demand for prostitution. Indeed, inequality in China is rising.[103] In the 1970s, the country was one of the most economically egalitarian in the world – with a level of inequality that was close to the levels in the Nordic countries in Europe. Now, China's levels of inequality are comparable to those in the United States.[104] In 2019, China had the largest number of people in the top 10 percent of global wealth distribution (100 million individuals versus 99 million in the United States).[105] That year, the country was also home to 5.8 million millionaires, and 21,000 citizens whose individual wealth exceeded US$50 million.[106] The ranks of China's middle class are also growing rapidly. According to one study, less than 1 percent of the country was considered middle class in 2002,

[100] Xiao-yuan Dong and Lixin Colin Xu, "Labor Restructuring in China: Toward a Functioning Labor Market," *Journal of Comparative Economics* 37, no. 2 (June 2009): 287–305; Xiao-yuan Dong and Manish Pandey, "Gender and Labor Retrenchment in Chinese State Owned Enterprises: Investigation Using Firm-Level Panel Data," *China Economic Review* 23, no. 2 (June 2012): 385–95; Asian Development Bank, "People's Republic of China Country Gender Assessment," 11.

[101] Asian Development Bank, "People's Republic of China Country Gender Assessment," 11. In contrast, almost 64 percent of laid-off men found new jobs.

[102] Yingying Huang and Suiming Pan, "Job Mobility of Brothel-Based Female Sex Workers in Current Northeast China: The Process from Xiagang (Lay-Offs) to Sex Worker" (Institute of Sexuality and Gender, Renmin University of China, March 18, 2004). https://usiraq.procon.org/sourcefiles/job-mobility-of-brothel-based-female-sex-workers-in-current-northeast-china-the-process-from-xiagang-worker-lay-offs-to-sex-worker.pdf.

[103] Deborah Davis and Wang Feng, eds., *Creating Wealth and Poverty in Postsocialist China* (Stanford, CA: Stanford University Press, 2009); Sidney Leng, "Coronavirus: China's Income Inequality Could Expand in 2020 as Outbreak Rattles World's No 2 Economy," *South China Morning Post*, March 17, 2020, https://perma.cc/XD5H-KVSV; Thomas Piketty, Li Yang, and Gabriel Zucman, "Capital Accumulation, Private Property, and Rising Inequality in China, 1978–2015," *American Economic Review* 109, no. 7 (July 2019): 2469–96, https://doi.org/10.1257/aer.20170973.

[104] Piketty, Yang, and Zucman, "Capital Accumulation, Private Property, and Rising Inequality in China."

[105] Camilo Maldonado, "Credit Suisse: Top 1% Own Nearly 50% of Global Wealth and China's Wealthy Now Outnumber America's," *Forbes*, October 23, 2019, https://perma.cc/GE8M-B3XF.

[106] Credit Suisse Research, "Global Wealth Report 2020," 43, accessed October 22, 2020, perma.cc/Q8SN-TP7H.

a proportion that had increased to about 25 percent by 2018.[107] This wealth is concentrated in cities: In 2000, about 4 percent of urban households in China were middle class, a figure that rose to 68 percent in 2012, and was projected to surpass 75 percent by 2022.[108] Total household wealth has risen exponentially in the past two decades, from US$3.7 trillion in 2000 to US$78.1 trillion in 2019.[109] This economic growth is increasing consumption levels among the middle class, which is spending more on property, tourism, education, and cars.[110] It is also allowing more men to buy sex. For instance, a 2006 national survey found that 6.9 percent of men aged eighteen to forty-nine had solicited commercial sex at least once in their life.[111] This estimate was projected to reach 17 percent by 2020.[112]

A Sexual Opening

Sexual attitudes and behaviors in Chinese society have changed significantly since the adoption of market reforms in the late 1970s, and prostitution has both reflected and shaped these broader shifts. Sex and sexuality were taboo subjects under Mao, despite his own promiscuity.[113] Discussions of sex focused on reproduction rather than pleasure.[114] The one-child policy, which the CCP introduced in 1979 to help control the growth of China's population, played an important role in divorcing sex from procreation. Widespread promotion of contraception and abortions reduced fears of unwanted pregnancies, thus facilitating sexual experimentation.[115] In

107 Terry Sicular, Xiuna Yang, and Björn Gustafsson, "The Rise of China's Global Middle Class in International Perspective," IZA Institute of Labor Economics Discussion Paper Series, 2021. There are a variety of different ways of defining and calculating who is a member of the middle class. Sicular et al. discuss their methodological approach and data starting on page 4.

108 Dominic Barton, Yougang Chen, and Amy Jin, "Mapping China's Middle Class | McKinsey," *McKinsey Quarterly*, June 1, 2013, perma.cc/4XPE-AKNT. Middle class here is defined as annual household disposable income ranging from $9,000 to $34,000, in real (2010) terms.

109 Credit Suisse Research, "Global Wealth Report 2020."

110 China Power Team, "How Well-off Is China's Middle Class?," *China Power* (blog), April 26, 2017, perma.cc/U47Q-Z38D.

111 Suiming Pan, William L. Parish, and Yingying Huang, "Clients of Female Sex Workers: A Population-Based Survey of China," *Journal of Infectious Diseases* 204, no. 5 (October 31, 2011): S1211–17.

112 "Sin City – In China, Sex Work Is Being Pushed Back into the Shadows," *The Economist*, accessed October 21, 2020, https://perma.cc/3XPX-MZJ2; Suiming Pan, "The Realistic Response to China's Prostitution Problem," *Sixth Tone* (blog), November 30, 2017, perma .cc/QM47-R8LN.

113 Suiming Pan, "Transformations in the Primary Life Cycle: The Origins and Nature of China's Sexual Revolution," in *Sex and Sexuality in China*, ed. Elaine Jeffreys (London: Routledge, 2006), 27; Zhisui Li, *The Private Life of Chairman Mao: The Memoirs of Mao's Personal Physician* (New York: Random House, 1994).

114 Pan, 28–31.

115 Pan, 28–31.

China today, nonreproductive sexual behavior, including premarital and homosexual sex, has gained prevalence and acceptance.[116] Images of sex, in advertisements and the press, are ubiquitous. Public displays of affection, once taboo, are common. The sex shop industry is flourishing: The adult toys market increased from 115 billion RMB in 2011 to almost 350 billion RMB in 2018.[117] Local government agencies sponsor sex-themed exhibits and fairs. In 2009, Beijing's first sex-toy fair, somewhat euphemistically called the "Prenatal and Postnatal Care Planning Supplies (Adult Products) Exhibition" (优生优育计生用品 (成人用品) 展览会 – *yousheng youyu jisheng yongpin (chengren yongpin) zhanlanhui*), attracted over 50,000 visitors.[118] The annual Guangzhou National Sex Culture Festival celebrated its twenty-third anniversary in 2021.[119] For a few days every year, a major exhibition hall in the city overflows with a smorgasbord of products and events including sex toys, lingerie fashion shows, S&M products, lubricants, lectures on sperm donation, inflatable and silicon dolls, screenings of "how-to" sex videos, and, for good measure, displays of malformed fetuses preserved in formaldehyde.[120] Yet some boundaries still exist. Entrepreneurs in Chongqing discovered they had crossed a line when they began construction in 2009 of "Sex Park (性公园 – *xing gongyuan*)."[121] The park was forced to shut down on the orders of local officials following a proliferation of online criticisms.[122] The park's

116 Timothy Hildebrandt, *Social Organizations and the Authoritarian State in China* (Cambridge: Cambridge University Press, 2013); James Farrer, *Opening Up: Youth Sex Culture and Market Reform in Shanghai* (Chicago: University of Chicago Press, 2002).

117 Lian Mo, "China's Store-Bought Sexual Revolution," *China Daily*, July 10, 2010, perma.cc/N8A5-L8QQ; Jo McMillan, "Selling Sexual Health: China's Emerging Sex Shop Industry," in *Sex and Sexuality in China*, ed. Elaine Jeffreys (London: Routledge, 2006); Daxue Consulting, "The Adult Toys Market in China: Untapped Economic Potential," *Daxue Consulting*, March 4, 2020, perma.cc/5RHL-ZALZ.

118 City Weekend, "Beijing's First-Ever Sex Toy Fair Ends Today," April 6, 2009, perma.cc/X223-X34W.

119 "2021 Di Ershisan Jie Quanguo (Guangzhou) Xingwenhua Jie" 2021(第二十三届全国 (广州) 性文化节) [The 23rd National (Guangzhou) Sex Culture Festival 2021], Xingshang Wang (性商网), accessed April 30, 2022, perma.cc/E6S4-FZUV.

120 Robert Foyle-Hunwick, "Guys and Sex Dolls – Scenes from the Guangzhou Sexpo," *Danwei* (blog), October 16, 2012, perma.cc/6R3D-PPT5; Alex Hofford, "A Sleazy 'Sexual Culture Festival' in Guangzhou, China," *Alex Hofford Photography* (blog), November 5, 2009, perma .cc/4ZRA-ANWK.

121 Chris Buckley, "China Sex Theme Park Comes to Abrupt End," *Reuters*, May 18, 2009, https://perma.cc/9Q3Z-V5WW; Edward Wong, "Chinese City Is Chilly to a Sex Theme Park," *New York Times*, May 18, 2009, https://perma.cc/KE9F-7EAB; Yingzi Tan, "Sex Theme Park Prepares to Open," *China Daily*, May 15, 2009, perma.cc/WTQ2-C5MV.

122 Attempting this project in a different location might have met with less resistance. At the time, Bo Xilai was the mayor of Chongqing. In addition to carrying out ruthless campaigns against organized crime in the city, he also sought to revive the Cultural Revolution–era "red culture" movement, a project framed as an attempt to address declining public morality. A sex park would not be viewed in a positive light in a city seeking to project an image of moral rectitude.

developer unsuccessfully attempted to defend the project by emphasizing its ability to help adults "enjoy a harmonious sex life," thus echoing then-President Hu Jintao's "Harmonious Society" doctrine.[123]

Other markers of these shifts in sexual attitudes and behaviors include increases in divorce and sexually transmitted diseases (STDs). Although stigma against divorce remains deeply entrenched, rates have soared in recent decades. In 2003, about 1.3 million couples divorced, a number that increased to 4.15 million in 2019.[124] China's current divorce rate of 3.2 per 1,000 people is comparable to that of the United States.[125] STDs, discussed in greater depth in subsequent chapters, have proliferated with increases in unprotected sex with greater numbers of partners. Rates of syphilis, for instance, increased from 0.17 per 100,000 in 1989 to 38.37 per 100,000 in 2019.[126]

These changes have led Judith Farquhar to note that China's contemporary consumer culture "places sex at the center of just about everything."[127] These developments are frequently referred to as a "sexual revolution," though use of the term is contested.[128] Regardless of the language used to describe the change, the existence of a new space for sexual exploration is undeniable. Sociologist James Farrer describes it as "sexual opening up (性开放 – *xing kaifang*)."[129] He argues that Western and Japanese entertainment, media, and personal exchanges have played an important role in shaping such changes, with local culture influencing how these changes have been interpreted and adopted.[130]

123 See Chapter 7 for another instance in which this doctrine is appropriated in unexpected ways in Chinese society.

124 "China's Divorce Spike Is a Warning to Rest of Locked-Down World," *Bloomberg.Com*, March 31, 2020, https://perma.cc/5SKC-RNT8.

125 "Thirty More Days of Hell – Why China's Divorce Law Is So Controversial," *economist.com*, accessed October 16, 2020, https://perma.cc/EVY9-W2ZU.

126 Xiang-Sheng Chen, Xiang-Dong Gong, Guo-Jun Liang, and Guo-Cheng Zhang, "Epidemiologic Trends of Sexually Transmitted Diseases in China," *Sexually Transmitted Diseases* 27, no. 3 (March 2000): 138–42; Department of Diseases Control, National Health Commission (卫健委疾病预防控制局), "2019 Nian Quanguo Fading Chuanranbing Yiqing Gaikuang" (2019年全国法定传染病疫情概况) [The National Overview of Epidemiologic Features of Notifiable Diseases in 2019], National Health Commission (国家卫生健康委员会), April 20, 2020, perma.cc/Z4RK-G4MX.

127 Judith Farquhar, *Appetites: Food and Sex in Postsocialist China* (Durham, NC: Duke University Press, 2002), 247.

128 Elaine Jeffreys, *China, Sex and Prostitution*, 67; William L. Parish, Edward O. Laumann, and Sanyu A. Mojola, "Sexual Behavior in China: Trends and Comparisons," *Population and Development Review* 33, no. 4 (2007): 729–56; Elanah Uretsky, *Occupational Hazards: Business, Sex, and HIV in Post-Mao China* (Stanford, CA: Stanford University Press, 2016).

129 Farrer, *Opening Up*.

130 Farrer, 11–12.

During my fieldwork in China, I encountered people whose selective exposure to foreign entertainment and media led them to have skewed perceptions of Western attitudes toward sexuality. I initially encountered this a few weeks after my first move to China in 2001. During a four-hour bus ride from Shanghai to Ningbo, the businessman sitting next to me struck up a conversation and explained that he was on his way to visit his mistress. He then proceeded to underscore how pleased he was to be able to talk to me about this so openly, since I was from the West where there is much greater acceptance of extramarital affairs. More generally, throughout my fieldwork I found myself repeatedly correcting the misconception that prostitution is legal everywhere in the West. Local government officials, police officers, madams, sex workers, and clients would frequently characterize China's prostitution policies as "backwards (落后 – *luohou*)," in contrast to what they assumed was a universal legalization model in Western countries. My explanations of the overarching similarities between policing policies in China and the United States and most other Western countries never failed to surprise my interlocutors.

Another widespread belief in China is that men, but not women, have a biological and physical "need" for sex. This view – which I heard from sex workers, police officers, public health workers, and the general population – is used to justify men's solicitation of sex workers. Other scholars have also highlighted the prevalence of such attitudes. Elanah Uretsky, in her ethnography of male sexual culture in urban China, notes how the men with whom she interacted for her study argued that "their motivation for seeking multiple sexual partners stems from some sort of biological need."[131] Suowei Xiao's study of second wives underscores how "notions that men are promiscuous by nature are prevalent in public discourses."[132]

In contrast to the predominant view of marriage in the West, extramarital relationships in China are considered compatible with fulfilling one's responsibilities as a dutiful husband. Marriage in China is defined primarily in terms of duties to one's spouse, child, and parents, rather than in terms of romantic love between the couple.[133] In this conception of marriage, a good husband provides for his family by fulfilling financial and domestic duties. Emotions and romantic feelings between spouses are not part of the equation. This leaves husbands free to pursue

[131] Uretsky, *Occupational Hazards*, 119.

[132] Xiao, "China's New Concubines?," 175. See also Xiao, *Desire and Dignity*.

[133] Xiao, "China's New Concubines?," 146–47, 153–54 (see also Xiao, *Desire and Dignity*); James Farrer and Sun Zhongxin, "Extramarital Love in Shanghai," *The China Journal* 50 (July 1, 2003): 9, 19, 30; Uretsky, *Occupational Hazards*, 121.

emotional and sexual satisfaction outside the marriage. As long as they maintain their familial responsibilities, such behavior is not stigmatized as a moral transgression.

These views around men's physical needs and the nature of marriage highlight deeply rooted gendered inequalities in Chinese society. Women's sexual desires are given short shrift. It is not culturally acceptable for wives to pursue extramarital relationships. Such discrepancies are enshrined even within organizations intended to advance women's rights in China. Uretsky quotes a woman who had worked for the All-China Women's Federation (ACWF), the country's main institution for advancing women's rights, as noting that "It's natural for men to have relations with women outside their marriage (*hunwai shiqing*) and because they can distinguish their feelings from sex, it's not a big deal to have a sexual relationship outside their marriage because it doesn't threaten their marriage."[134] To hear an ACWF representative espouse tolerance of male infidelity, and assume that men, but not women, can divorce sex from emotions, demonstrates how entrenched gendered biases are within Chinese society.

The One-Child Policy and the Surplus in Men

China's one-child policy plays an important role in understanding prostitution in contemporary China, as it is indirectly responsible for gender imbalance in the population today. Enacted in 1979 in order to contain the population growth that had occurred under Mao, it was replaced in 2015 with a universal two-child policy, and a universal three-child policy in 2021.[135] Moving forward, it is likely that China will completely abolish its fertility control program.[136] Yet in the decades

[134] Uretsky, 121.

[135] Tyrene White, *China's Longest Campaign: Birth Planning in the People's Republic, 1949–2005* (Ithaca, NY: Cornell University Press, 2006); Yi Zeng and Therese Hesketh, "The Effects of China's Universal Two-Child Policy," *The Lancet* 388, no. 10054 (October 2016): 1930–38. Even when the one-child policy was in place, there existed a number of important exceptions. For instance, couples in rural areas whose first child was a girl would generally have a second child, and sometimes a third. Members of China's fifty-five ethnic minority groups were also frequently allowed to have more than one child. Wei Xing Zhu, Li Lu, and Therese Hesketh, "China's Excess Males, Sex Selective Abortion, and One Child Policy: Analysis of Data from 2005 National Intercensus Survey," *BMJ* 338, no. 2 (April 18, 2009): 920–23; "China NPC: Three-Child Policy Formally Passed into Law," *BBC News*, August 20, 2021, perma.cc/2V2B-KPA9; Yi Zeng and Therese Hesketh, "The Effects of China's Universal Two-Child Policy," *The Lancet* 388, no. 10054 (October 2016): 1930–38.

[136] Ben Westcott, "China Moves to End Two-Child Limit, Finishing Decades of Family Planning," *CNN.com*, accessed October 19, 2020, perma.cc/6RUB-6DNY; Wang Feng, Baochang Gu, and Yong Cai, "The End of China's One-Child Policy," *Studies in Family Planning* 47, no. 1 (March 2016): 83–86.

during which the one-child policy was in force, the widespread cultural preference for sons resulted in female infanticide, the abandonment of girls, higher female than male infant mortality rates due to poorer healthcare and nutrition, and the abortion of female fetuses, despite the illegality of ultrasounds.[137] While the normal range for a country's sex ratio at birth is about 105 male births for 100 female births, China's sex ratio peaked at 121 in 2005.[138] It went down to 116 in 2014, and in 2019 was estimated at 113 boys per 100 girls.[139] While China's sex ratio at birth is predicted to continue declining, it will likely not normalize for many years.[140] As a result, the number of marriage-age men is currently estimated to exceed the number of marriage-age women by thirty million,[141] which translates into 20 percent of marriage-age men remaining bachelors.[142] This phenomenon has given rise to "bachelor villages" (光棍村 – *guangguncun*), which are poor remote villages with high percentages of aging single men; the term *guanggun* literally means "bare branches," as these individuals will likely remain childless.[143] This male marriage gap will persist in coming decades.[144]

137 Asian Development Bank, "People's Republic of China Country Gender Assessment," 30–31.

138 Therese Hesketh, Li Lu, and Zhu Wei Xing, "The Consequences of Son Preference and Sex-Selective Abortion in China and Other Asian Countries," *CMAJ : Canadian Medical Association Journal* 183, no. 12 (September 6, 2011): 1374–77, https://doi.org/10.1503/cmaj.101368; S. L. Fan et al., "How Does the Two-Child Policy Affect the Sex Ratio at Birth in China? A Cross-Sectional Study," *BMC Public Health* 20, no. 1 (May 27, 2020): 789, https://doi.org/10.1186/s12889-020-08799-y.

139 Zeng and Hesketh, "The Effects of China's Universal Two-Child Policy," October 2016, 1931; Bloomberg News, "China's Two-Child Policy," *Bloomberg*, January 20, 2020, perma.cc/WR78-5CYY.

140 Zeng and Hesketh, "The Effects of China's Universal Two-Child Policy," October 2016, 1934.

141 BBC, "Chinese Birth Rate Falls to Lowest in Seven Decades," *BBC News*, January 17, 2020, perma.cc/2NAD-75ZX.

142 "1 in 5 Marriage-Age Chinese Men to Remain Bachelors within 10 Years," *People's Daily Online*, January 13, 2010, perma.cc/Z7VQ-YY8D; Andrea den Boer and Valerie M. Hudson, "The Security Risks of China's Abnormal Demographics," *The Washington Post*, April 30, 2014, https://perma.cc/J8DG-59HT.

143 Tania Branigan, "China's Village of the Bachelors: No Wives in Sight in Remote Settlement," *The Guardian*, September 2, 2011; Jessica Levine, "China's New Bachelor Class," *The Atlantic*, February 11, 2013; Rob Brooks, "China's Biggest Problem? Too Many Men," *CNN*, March 4, 2013; Robin Brant, "The Lonely Men of China's 'Bachelor Village,'" *BBC News*, August 28, 2016, perma.cc/9MRK-N3N5; Simon Denyer and Annie Gowen, "Too Many Men: China and India Battle with the Consequences of Gender Imbalance," *South China Morning Post*, April 24, 2018, https://perma.cc/8DEP-UEJG. For more on the issue of China's bachelors, see Deborah Jian Lee and Sushma Subramanian, "China's Bachelors: When Men Outnumber Women," accessed October 19, 2020, perma.cc/P3LG-HDYJ.

144 Lisa Eklund and Isabelle Attané, "Marriage Squeeze and Mate Selection in China," in *Handbook on the Family and Marriage in China*, eds. Xiaowei Zang and Lucy Xia Zhao (Cheltenham, UK: Edward Elgar, 2017), 156.

The surplus in men that arose out of the one-child policy contributes to the demand for prostitution.[145] It is also considered a threat to social stability, fueling domestic and cross-border human trafficking, the purchasing of brides, and a growing crime rate.[146] One study found that the rising imbalance in sex ratios accounts for one-sixth of the overall rise in violent and property crimes from 1988 to 2004, with each 1 percent increase in the sex ratio imbalance correlating with a 6 percent increase in crime.[147]

Interestingly, the current shortage of women and subsequent threats to social stability find echoes throughout Chinese history. Evidence of female infanticide exists as early as the Song Dynasty (960–1279), and concubinage reduced the pool of marriageable women for poorer men.[148] In the nineteenth century, overpopulation and declines in agricultural output contributed to a subsistence crisis, with a growing number of male peasants struggling to obtain the resources that would allow them to marry and raise children.[149] In some rural areas, 20 percent of adult men may have never married.[150] This population of surplus men, who were driven by desires for wives and land, eventually played important roles in the political upheavals of the late nineteenth and early twentieth centuries.[151] Political leaders in modern China may have learned from this past. Specifically, contemporary concerns for maintaining social stability, given gender imbalance and mass migration in China, are sometimes posited as explanations for the lack of effective enforcement against prostitution and the absence of political will to address the issue thoroughly.[152]

145 Edlund and Korn, 181, 205–6.

146 Valerie M. Hudson and Andrea Den Boer, "A Surplus of Men, A Deficit of Peace: Security and Sex Ratios in Asia's Largest States," *International Security* 26, no. 4 (April 1, 2002): 5–38; Eric Baculinao, "China Grapples with Legacy of Its 'Missing Girls': Disturbing Demographic Imbalance Spurs Drive to Change Age-Old Practices," *NBC News*, September 14, 2004; Lena Edlund, Hongbin Li, Junjian Yi, and Junsen Zhang, "Sex Ratios and Crime: Evidence from China," *Review of Economics and Statistics* 95, no. 5 (2013): 1520–34.

147 Edlund et al., "Sex Ratios and Crime"; Brooks, "China's Biggest Problem?"

148 Sommer, *Sex, Law, and Society in Late Imperial China*, 13.

149 Ted A. Telford, "Family and State in Qing China: Marriage in the Tongcheng Lineages, 1650–1880," in *Family Process and Political Process in Modern Chinese History*, vol. 2 (Taipei: Institute of Modern History, Academia Sinica, 1992), 924; Sommer, *Sex, Law, and Society in Late Imperial China*, 12–13.

150 Elizabeth J. Perry, *Rebels and Revolutionaries in North China, 1845–1945* (Stanford, CA: Stanford University Press, 1980), 51.

151 Sommer, *Sex, Law, and Society in Late Imperial China*, 12.

152 Petula Sik Ying Ho, Stevi Jackson, Siyang Cao, and Chi Kwok, "Sex with Chinese Characteristics: Sexuality Research in/on Twenty-First Century China," *The Journal of Sex Research* 55, no. 4–5 (2018): 502, https://doi.org/10.1080/00224499.2018.1437593.

Work Culture, Entertainment Venues, and Sex

In many places around the world, soliciting sex is considered a personal experience that is divorced from one's professional responsibilities and aspirations. It is also an action that one would likely seek to conceal from colleagues and business partners. In contemporary China, however, prostitution is central to the entertainment venues (娱乐场所 – *yulechangsuo*) – spaces such as karaoke bars and clubs – that play a crucial role in professional networking and the conducting of business across society.

This phenomenon has roots in Chinese history. Courtesan culture throughout Imperial and Republican China played an important socialization role among elites.[153] In her history of Republican Beijing, Madeleine Yue Dong notes that political and business meetings occurred in brothels, which she characterizes as the "equivalent of Western elite social and sports clubs, where a large part of real deal making took place in a relaxed atmosphere."[154] Sidney Gamble, who conducted social surveys of China in the early twentieth century, noted that "It is extremely difficult for a man to hold high official rank without spending a very large part of his time in the licensed quarter [where brothels were located], attending dinners and wasting his energy in late hours."[155]

This dynamic still holds true for businessmen and government officials in contemporary China, even under the anti-corruption campaign that Xi Jinping launched when he came to power in 2013.[156] Food, drink, and entertainment are integral to Chinese work culture. The process of hosting government officials, businessmen, and other professional contacts is called *yingchou* (应酬).[157] It involves organizing elaborate, alcohol-imbued banquets, followed by activities such as massages, hair washing, singing, dancing, and the purchase of sex. These experiences solidify *guanxi* (关系) – the personal relations network crucial to accomplishing anything in China.[158] *Yingchou* secures

153 Dorothy Ko, *Teachers of the Inner Chambers: Women and Culture in Seventeenth-Century China* (Stanford, CA: Stanford University Press, 1994), 254–56; Hershatter, *Dangerous Pleasures*, 69.

154 Madeleine Yue Dong, *Republican Beijing: The City and Its Histories* (Berkeley: University of California Press, 2003), 226.

155 Sidney D. Gamble, *Peking: A Social Survey* (New York: George H. Doran, 1921), 258, cited in Dong, *Republican Beijing*, 226.

156 Uretsky, *Occupational Hazards*, 4.

157 Katherine A. Mason, "To Your Health! Toasting, Intoxication and Gendered Critique among Banqueting Women," *The China Journal*, no. 69 (January 2013): 108–33; Katherine A. Mason, *Infectious Change: Reinventing Chinese Public Health after an Epidemic*, 1st ed. (Stanford, CA: Stanford University Press, 2016); Uretsky, *Occupational Hazards*.

158 Uretsky, "Mixing Business with Pleasure"; Thomas Gold, Doug Guthrie, and David Wank, eds., *Social Connections in China: Institutions, Culture, and the Changing Nature of Guanxi*

access, wins contracts, and facilitates career advancement. It is how professional goals are achieved, and it occupies a great deal of business peoples' and bureaucrats' time and energy.[159] In the town of Ruili in China's southwestern Yunnan province, Uretsky observed that some local government officials host visitors from 8 AM until 2 AM, sometimes six or seven days a week.[160] Katherine Mason, in her ethnography of public health institutions in the Pearl River Delta, described participating in the inspection of a hospital surveillance system. After the morning inspection, the hospital treated members of her public health work unit to over twelve hours of *yingchou*, including a banquet, foot massages, a game of *mahjong*, and a second banquet.[161] Such practices are ubiquitous across professional sectors. I participated in it as an English-language teacher in a primary school in China in the early 2000s. In addition, much of the access I obtained while conducting the research for this project on prostitution involved experiences of *yingchou* with the police, local officials, public health workers, madams, and pimps.

Prostitution is integral to the post-banquet, entertainment portion of *yingchou*. It can occur in a karaoke club where clients are also engaging in legal forms of entertainment, in hotels, or in venues that only provide sexual services. The decision to engage in prostitution as part of *yingchou* is not simply a private one – professional and social expectations come into play. Uretsky notes that many men dislike the drinking, smoking, and sexual activity required of hosting but engage in them as a display of loyalty to their superiors and the Communist Party.[162] In the *yingchou* setting, refusing sexual services becomes a public act that can cause an individual to lose face (面子 – *mianzi*).[163] Soliciting sex in this environment also serves as proof of manhood.[164]

(Cambridge: Cambridge University Press, 2002); Andrew B. Kipnis, *Producing Guanxi: Sentiment, Self, and Subculture in a North China Village* (Durham, NC: Duke University Press, 1997); Yunxiang Yan, *The Flow of Gifts: Reciprocity and Social Networks in a Chinese Village* (Stanford, CA: Stanford University Press, 1996); Mayfair Mei-hui Yang, *Gifts, Favors, and Banquets: The Art of Social Relationships in China* (Ithaca, NY: Cornell University Press, 1994); Kwang-kuo Hwang, "Face and Favor: The Chinese Power Game," *American Journal of Sociology* 92, no. 4 (January 1987): 944–74.

159 Professional men and women can both participate in it, but women are not expected to drink heavily or purchase sex.

160 Uretsky, *Occupational Hazards*, 48–49.

161 Mason, "To Your Health!" 108–9.

162 Uretsky, *Occupational Hazards*, 49–51.

163 Uretsky, 50.

164 Uretsky, 51–52. There is some evidence that the increase of women in the workforce in China is affecting the process of *yingchou* and prostitution, and leading to the "de-sexualization of banqueting." See Mason, "To Your Health!" 120. In particular, Mason notes that the

The ties between entertainment and the sex industry that characterize work culture in contemporary China are also present in other Asian societies, including Japan, South Korea, and Vietnam.[165] However, Uretsky notes an important difference between China and these other countries. In other parts of East and Southeast Asia, businessmen "work hard and then play hard" – entertainment allows men to rekindle "the 'humaneness' of their work relations."[166] In China, by contrast, a man's professional success actually depends on the skills he demonstrates as a host.[167]

The Size of the Sex Industry in China

The political, social, and economic phenomena discussed in this chapter contribute to explaining the scope and influence of the Chinese sex industry. While precise calculations regarding the size of the country's female sex worker population are unavailable, the number is thought to be in the millions.[168] Chinese Public Security sources have estimated that four to six million women are engaged in prostitution, and *China Daily*, the official English-language newspaper of the Communist Party, printed an opinion piece that estimated the size of the sex worker population as somewhere between three and ten million.[169] Nongovernmental estimates have been as large as twenty million.[170] These sources generally provide little explanation of their calculations. Official numbers might be low, given the illegality of prostitution and political sensitivity regarding its ubiquity in Chinese society. Variation could also be tied to different definitions of sex work, such as whether it includes all female service workers in entertainment venues. It is also difficult to count a population that is highly mobile and often hidden

solicitation of sex rarely followed the banquets she attended. Without denying that prostitution may have occurred in these situations, she notes instead that if it did, "it was outside the normal domain of *guanxi*-building at the work units" with which she worked.

165 Cheng Sea-ling, "Assuming Manhood: Prostitution and Patriotic Passions in Korea," *East Asia* 18, no. 4 (2000): 40–78; Anne Allison, *Nightwork: Sexuality, Pleasure, and Corporate Masculinity in a Tokyo Hostess Club* (Chicago: University of Chicago Press, 1994); Evelyne Micollier, ed., *Sexual Cultures in East Asia: The Social Construction of Sexuality and Sexual Risk in a Time of AIDS*, Routledge Curzon–IIAS Asian Studies Series (London: Routledge Curzon, 2004); Kimberly Kay Hoang, *Dealing in Desire: Asian Ascendancy, Western Decline, and the Hidden Currencies of Global Sex Work*, 1st ed. (Oakland: University of California Press, 2015).

166 Uretsky, *Occupational Hazards*, 47.

167 Uretsky, 47.

168 Tingting Shen and Joanne Csete, "HIV, Sex Work, and Law Enforcement in China," *Health and Human Rights Journal* 19, no. 2 (2017): 133–46; "Sin City."

169 Yingying Huang, "Illegal 'profession' Is Risky Business," *China Daily*, May 5, 2010.

170 Wei Zhong, "A Close Look at China's Sex Industry," *Lianhe Zaobao*, October 2, 2000.

throughout urban and rural China. Some cities are considered to have especially high concentrations of sex workers, such as Dongguan, an industrial city in the Pearl River Delta that attracts a lot of businessmen and foreign investment. Yet one is hard-pressed to identify places in China that lack a thriving sex industry.

Estimates of the size of the client population are also scarce. A nationally representative survey from 2000 found that 12.6 percent of men aged twenty-one to thirty had purchased sex in their lifetime, and that 8.8 percent of those aged thirty-one to forty had done so.[171] A survey from 2006 found that about 7 percent of men in China aged eighteen to forty-nine had purchased sex at least once in their life.[172] This proportion increased to 14 percent in 2015 and was predicted to reach 17 percent in 2020.[173] Data from China's prefectural cities found that in 2006, 10.2 percent of men aged eighteen to thirty-nine had purchased sex at least once in their lifetime, and that in 2010, 16.5 percent had done so.[174] These studies present evident sampling problems.[175] In addition, it is unclear whether the definition of commercial sex used encompasses sexual transactions that would occur in the process of the business and entertainment situations described earlier in this chapter. The sensitivity of this behavior may have also resulted in significant amounts of underreporting. In short, many men in China solicit sex, and the rates discussed here are best viewed as a lower bound.

CONCLUSION

In China, millions of women sell sex and millions of men buy it. While prostitution is present around the globe, this chapter's discussion of the political, social, and economic aspects of the post-Mao era underscore some of the dynamics of sex work that are specific to contemporary China. For instance, rural poverty and the migration it engendered fuel most of the supply of female sex workers, and the surplus in men that

171 Avraham Y. Ebenstein and Ethan Jennings, "Bare Branches, Prostitution, and HIV in China: A Demographic Analysis," in *Gender Policy and HIV in China: Catalyzing Policy Change*, The Springer Series on Demographic Methods and Population Analysis 22 (Dordrecht: Springer Netherlands, 2009), 84, https://doi.org/10.1007/978-1-4020-9900-7.

172 Pan, Parish, and Huang, "Clients of Female Sex Workers."

173 "Sin City"; Pan, "The Realistic Response to China's Prostitution Problem."

174 Huang Yingying et al., "Population-Based Sexual Behavior Surveys in China: Liuzhou Compared with Other Prefectural Cities," *AIDS and Behavior* 18, no. 2 (February 2014): 118–25, https://doi.org/10.1007/s10461-013-0645-3.

175 Pan, Parish, and Huang, "Clients of Female Sex Workers," S1214.

came in the wake of the one-child policy contributes to the demand for prostitution. In addition, increased wealth in society has provided men with more income to buy sex. And shifting conceptions of sexuality have created space for the sex industry to thrive, including in China's business culture, which is structured around prostitution.

The ubiquity of prostitution in contemporary China is particularly jarring given the sudden shift from very low levels of prostitution, most of which occurred hidden from view, that characterized the first three decades of the PRC (1949–79). With the exception of the former Soviet Union, which experienced a similarly abrupt change in the prevalence of prostitution when it opened up its markets in the 1990s, such a pattern is unusual. This chapter's survey of prostitution throughout Chinese history highlights how the main characteristics of prostitution in the Mao era – that it was very limited in scope and largely invisible – were a historical anomaly. It also underscores an important similarity between regulatory patterns in Imperial China and in the PRC after 1979. Namely, status was at the heart of how the state sought control over prostitution during the Imperial era – a pattern that is echoed in my research on state control of prostitution in contemporary China. Yet an important difference persists. Historically, status differences were officially acknowledged and enshrined within the law, which openly treated prostitution differently depending on the status of the participants. Everyone in the PRC, in contrast, is formally *equal* before the law. Inequalities in the treatment of prostitution are instead the result of how policies designed to be status-blind are actually implemented.

3

THE OFFICIAL STORY: PROSTITUTION POLICIES IN CONTEMPORARY CHINA

INTRODUCTION

What does Chinese law have to say about people who are involved in sex work and the places where it occurs? Prostitution control is a universal problem for which states have adopted a variety of policies to address the public order, public health, and commercial challenges that it presents. This chapter describes that range of regulatory possibilities. It then explains the official choices that China has made, through discussions of the policing, health, and taxation rules and institutions that the People's Republic of China (PRC) has adopted to regulate prostitution.

RANGE OF REGULATORY POSSIBILITIES

There are three general approaches regarding the legal status of prostitution in a given jurisdiction: prohibition/criminalization, decriminalization, and legalization/regulation.[1] Under the prohibition model,

[1] The term "abolition" also appears frequently and is used alternatively, and inconsistently, to describe prohibition or partial decriminalization. For more on the categorization of prostitution policies, see Janet Halley, Prabha Kotiswaran, Hila Shamir, and Chantal Thomas, "From the International to the Local in Feminist Legal Responses to Rape, Prostitution/Sex Work, and Sex Trafficking: Four Studies in Contemporary Governance Feminism," *Harvard Journal of Law & Gender* 29 (2006): 335; Marina Della Giusta, "Simulating the Impact of Regulation Changes on the Market for Prostitution Services," *European Journal of Law and Economics* 29, no. 1 (February 1, 2010): 1–14; Joyce Outshoorn, ed., *The Politics of Prostitution: Women's Movements, Democratic States, and the Globalisation of Sex Commerce* (Cambridge: Cambridge University Press, 2004); Vanessa Munro and Marina Della Giusta, eds., *Demanding Sex: Critical Reflections on the Regulation of Prostitution* (Aldershot, UK: Ashgate, 2008); Ronald John Weitzer, *Legalizing Prostitution: From Illicit Vice to Lawful Business* (New York: New York

prostitution is against the law. Decriminalization entails the removal or lack of laws that forbid prostitution. In the legalization model, the state formally recognizes prostitution as an authorized market activity. This model includes decriminalization, to which it adds interventionist business and health regulations. These are ideal types.[2] In reality, national and local government policies on prostitution often reflect a combination of these categories, depending on the type of prostitution (soliciting indoors versus outside on the streets) and the actor involved (sex worker, client, or organizer).[3]

In most jurisdictions, at least some aspects of the prostitution transaction are prohibited. Sanctions in prostitution prohibition regimes range from fines and incarceration to capital punishment.[4] Fully prohibitionist models punish sex workers, clients, and third-party organizers, and are in place in both China and most of the United States (with the exception of some counties in Nevada).[5] A number of other countries do not punish the exchange of sex for money but prohibit activities that facilitate it, such as soliciting and organizing prostitution.[6] Countries that fall within that category include England and Italy.[7] Sweden has a combined prostitution policy that

University Press, 2012); Prabha Kotiswaran, *Dangerous Sex, Invisible Labor: Sex Work and the Law in India* (Princeton, NJ: Princeton University Press, 2011), 16.

2 Elizabeth Bernstein, *Temporarily Yours: Intimacy, Authenticity, and the Commerce of Sex* (Chicago: University of Chicago Press, 2007), 230.

3 In some jurisdictions, anti-trafficking laws have recently played an increasingly prominent role in shaping the legal status of various aspects of prostitution. My research focuses on sex work, not human trafficking. As such, my discussion of the legal status of prostitution does not delve extensively into anti-trafficking laws. In brief, in places where aspects of prostitution are criminalized, anti-trafficking laws might serve to charge third-party organizers of prostitution as traffickers and could be used to treat individuals who sell sex as victims of trafficking.

4 The death penalty, when authorized, generally applies to third parties, rather than sex workers or clients.

5 In the United States, prostitution laws are determined largely by the state rather than the federal government. In Rhode Island, indoor prostitution was inadvertently decriminalized in 1980, through an amendment that was intended to speed up prostitution prosecutions in the courts. While the new law explicitly prohibited outdoor prostitution, legislators unintentionally removed certain sections that criminalized indoor prostitution. In 2009, Rhode Island recriminalized indoor prostitution. See Scott Cunningham and Manisha Shah, "Decriminalizing Indoor Prostitution: Implications for Sexual Violence and Public Health," *The Review of Economic Studies* 85, no. 3 (July 1, 2018): 1683–1715, https://doi.org/10.1093/restud/rdx065; Weitzer, *Legalizing Prostitution*, 59–61; Lynn Arditi, "How R.I. Opened the Door to Prostitution," *Providence Journal* (May 31, 2009), perma.cc/B4SF-NWCN.

6 The prohibition against solicitation means that it is against the law for someone to offer to sell sex (for the sex worker) or ask to buy it (for the client). This rule is generally used to discourage public solicitation, in an attempt to keep prostitution out of public spaces.

7 Vanessa E. Munro and Marina Della Giusta, "The Regulation of Prostitution: Contemporary Contexts and Comparative Perspectives," in *Demanding Sex: Critical Reflections on the Regulation of Prostitution*, eds. Vanessa E. Munro and Marina Della Giusta (Abingdon, UK: Ashgate, 2008), 4.

criminalizes prostitution for clients and organizers, but has decriminalized it for the sex worker. Canada has also criminalized the purchase and organization of prostitution but not the sale of sexual services. New Zealand has a fully decriminalized system for sex workers and clients, which includes the decriminalization of brothels. The regime is distinct from legalization because brothels are subject to general employment and health regulations that apply to all businesses, rather than guidelines established specifically for the sex industry.[8]

A variety of different legalization models exist. Within individual countries, subnational and local policies often shape them in important ways. In Nevada, state law allows any county with a population under 700,000 to license brothels, subject to various zoning restrictions. Under this system, prostitution is illegal in five Nevada counties and the state capital, Carson City.[9] Brothel employees must register with local authorities and undergo regular medical tests, and all prostitution occurring outside of licensed brothels is illegal. In the Netherlands, brothels are legal and subject to municipal licensing, zoning, and health and safety requirements. Unlike in Nevada, medical checkups are encouraged, but not compulsory, in order to both combat stereotypes of sex workers as vectors of disease and reduce client requests for no condom use (on the assumption that sex is safe if there is mandatory testing).[10] Streetwalking is also permitted, subject to the approval of local authorities, and can be restricted to certain places and times of day.[11] Some municipalities have officially designated areas for streetwalkers that include parking for transactions between sex workers and clients, as well as health services for sex workers.[12] In Germany, federal legislation has legalized both outdoor and indoor prostitution, including coordinating work by third-party organizers.

As state and local governments have regulatory powers over certain aspects of prostitution, laws can vary within individual countries – as

[8] Munro and Della Giusta, "The Regulation of Prostitution: Contemporary Contexts and Comparative Perspectives," 2–3.

[9] Rachel Macfarlane, Celene Fuller, Chris Wakefield, and Barbara Brents, "Sex Industry and Sex Workers in Nevada," in *The Social Health of Nevada: Leading Indicators and Quality of Life in the Silver State*, ed. Dmitri N. Shalin (UNLV: CDC Publications, January 1, 2017), 1–38. https://cdclv.unlv.edu/healthnv_2017/sexindustry.pdf.

[10] Ministry of Foreign Affairs (BZ), "Dutch Policy on Prostitution. Questions and Answers 2012" (Netherlands: Ministry of Foreign Affairs (BZ), 2012), AVT12/BZ106006, perma.cc/5GRZ-86Q9.

[11] Ministry of Foreign Affairs (BZ).

[12] Bernstein, *Temporarily Yours*, 156–61; Ministry of Foreign Affairs (BZ), "Dutch Policy on Prostitution. Questions and Answers 2012."

the example of Nevada in the United States demonstrates. Zoning laws allow municipalities to either ban prostitution completely or limit it to certain areas, depending on population size.[13] Some jurisdictions allow brothels to register as businesses while others do not.[14] Taxation systems also vary at the local level.[15] In Austria, streetwalking is legal and zoned in Vienna and one other province.[16] Brothels are legal in a number of Austrian provinces, subject to municipal authorization.[17] Under national law, prostitution is considered a form of private enterprise, which allows sex workers to enroll in Austria's social insurance system.[18]

Australia's eight states and territories illustrate the full range of regulatory possibilities for prostitution within one country. In Tasmania and South Australia, all prostitution-related activities other than the sex worker–client transaction are criminalized. New South Wales, meanwhile, has a decriminalized regime for public solicitation and brothels. While the remaining five states and territories prohibit soliciting, they have adopted varied policies to legalize brothel prostitution.[19]

Closer to mainland China, Singapore, Hong Kong, and Taiwan all have policies that allow for some forms of prostitution. In Singapore, the exchange of sex for money is not an offense, though pimping, public solicitation, and brothel management are illegal. Against this background of prohibition, a system of regulated brothels operates in designated areas of the city-state. In these areas, brothel owners and sex workers register with law enforcement. Sex workers undergo mandatory

13 Barbara Kavemann, Heike Rabe, and Claudia Fischer, "The Act Regulating the Legal Situation of Prostitutes–Implementation, Impact, Current Developments: Findings of a Study on the Impact of the German Prostitution Act, Berlin" (Berlin: Sozialwissenschaftliches FrauenForschungsInstitut an der Evangelischen Fachhochschule Freiburg, 2007), 5, perma.cc/WL8V-GBC7.

14 Kavemann, Rabe, and Fischer, 24.

15 Kavemann, Rabe, and Fischer, 42.

16 Marina Della Giusta, "Simulating the Impact of Regulation Changes on the Market for Prostitution Services," in *Demanding Sex: Critical Reflections on the Regulation of Prostitution*, ed. Vanessa Munro and Marina Della Giusta (Aldershot, UK: Ashgate, 2008), 128; Birgit Sauer, "Taxes, Rights, and Regimentation: Discourses on Prostitution in Austria," in *The Politics of Prostitution: Women's Movements, Democratic States and the Globalisation of Sex Commerce*, ed. Joyce Outshoorn (Cambridge: Cambridge University Press, 2004), 42.

17 Sauer, "Taxes, Rights and Regimentation: Discourses on Prostitution in Austria," 42.

18 Sauer, 56.

19 Barbara Sullivan, "The Women's Movement and Prostitution Politics in Australia," in *The Politics of Prostitution: Women's Movements, Democratic States and the Globalisation of Sex Commerce*, ed. Joyce Outshoorn (Cambridge: Cambridge University Press, 2004), 21; Barbara Sullivan, "When (Some) Prostitution Is Legal: The Impact of Law Reform on Sex Work in Australia," *Journal of Law and Society* 37, no. 1 (March 1, 2010): 86.

health testing and are issued yellow cards that indicate engagement in prostitution. The police consult these cards when inspecting brothels for evidence of registration with the authorities.[20] In Hong Kong, too, the exchange of sex for money is legal, while activities such as soliciting, advertising, and third-party organizing are against the law.[21] As brothels are illegal, sex workers are not allowed to work together in a shared space.[22] A common form of prostitution in Hong Kong is thus the "one-woman brothel," where a sex worker services a client alone in a small apartment.[23] In Taiwan, prostitution is legal in areas that local governments officially designate as sex-trade zones. As of 2022, local governments had yet to set up such areas since the 2011 legislation permitting their establishment.[24]

CHINA'S PROSTITUTION LAW ENFORCEMENT POLICIES

While some of its smaller neighbors are experimenting with legalized sex work, mainland China's official policies are firmly committed to the prohibition approach to regulating prostitution. All elements of sex work are against the law – it is unlawful to buy or sell sex, and organize or harbor prostitution. These rules are formally blind to both the gender and the status of the person engaging in them. On paper at least, they apply equally to sex workers (most often female) and clients (most often male), and outlaw prostitution regardless of whether it involves low-tier sex workers, hostesses, or mistresses.

20 Hui Hsien Ng, "Moral Order Underground: An Ethnography of the Geylang Sex Trade" (Master's thesis, Singapore: National University of Singapore, 2011); Shin Bin Tan and Alisha Gill, "Containing Commercial Sex to Designated Red Light Areas: An Idea Past Its Prime?," 2014, perma.cc/RQU2-KV22.

21 Amnesty International, "Harmfully Isolated: Criminalizing Sex Work in Hong Kong," 2016, 17, perma.cc/S7SV-Y68Q.

22 In practice, these restrictions that surround prostitution in Hong Kong make it difficult to engage in it in accordance with the law.

23 These spaces are called *yi lou yi feng* (一楼一凤), which literally means "one building, one phoenix."

24 "Zheng Zhidaole" (郑知道了) [Zheng Knows], *SET News* (三立新聞台), January 27, 2023, YouTube, accessed January 31, 2023, perma.cc/8STF-QVXH (starting at 6 minutes 24 seconds, commentators stated that no local government has dared to set up sex-trade zones despite the authorizing legislation ("性专区的东西法律已经通过了, 但是没有一个县市敢办")); Zhang Songyun (张松筠), "Chu Zhichi Sheli Xingzhuanqu Wai! Yanse Bufen Lanlü Zhichi Xingzhuanqu Yanse Tian Shenjie Shoudu Gongkai Zhengzhi Qingxiang Pian Dupai: Wo Shi Taiwanpai, Tianran Tai!" (除支持設立性專區外! 色不分藍綠支持性專區顏色田慎節首度公開政治傾向「偏獨派」: 我是台灣派, 天然台!) [Apart from Supporting Setting Up Sex-Trade Zones, Colorblind Support-Sex-Trade Tian Shenjie Reveals Political Orientation For the First Time: I am Pro-Taiwan, Naturally Pro-Taiwan], *Fount Media* (放言), December 27, 2022, accessed January 31, 2023, perma.cc/JL9G-WGPK.

Most aspects of prostitution pertaining to sex workers and clients are considered administrative, rather than criminal, offenses under Chinese law. It is third-party organizers – such as pimps and madams – who are generally in violation of criminal laws. Administrative offenses are generally considered more minor than criminal ones. And while police are empowered to initiate, impose, and administer *administrative* sanctions, only the courts can convict someone of a *criminal* offense.[25] This means that the police have significant discretion when it comes to punishing sex workers and clients, who are prosecuted for administrative offenses. They have less discretion when they are pursuing a criminal prosecution against third-party organizers, since these cases involve two additional agencies: the procuratorate and the courts.[26]

Defining Prostitution

Under early PRC laws and regulations, prostitution was generally understood as occurring between a female sex worker and a male client, and a number of local regulations specifically defined it as such.[27] This approach shifted in the 1990s. China's prostitution laws today apply both to male and female sex workers, and define prostitution as an act occurring between either different- or same-sex individuals.[28] Police guidelines highlight the necessity of meeting three criteria for an act to be considered prostitution. First, the act must be voluntary. Second, it must involve the sex organs of at least one of the individuals – it thus includes vaginal, anal, and oral sex, as well as masturbation. Third, the act must involve an expectation of profit in the form of money or goods.[29]

25 Sarah Biddulph, "Justice at the Margins: Notions of Justice in the Punishment of Prostitution," in *Justice: The China Experience*, ed. Flora Sapio, Susan Trevaskes, Sarah Biddulph, and Elisa Nesossi (Cambridge: Cambridge University Press, 2017), 320, https://doi.org/10.1017/9781108115919.012; Sarah Biddulph, *Legal Reform and Administrative Detention Powers in China* (Cambridge: Cambridge University Press, 2007), 8.

26 Biddulph, *Legal Reform and Administrative Detention Powers in China*, 8; Biddulph, "Justice at the Margins," 320–21; Sarah Biddulph, "Punishments in the Post Re-Education through Labour World: Questions about Minor Crime in China," in *Chinese Legal Reform and the Global Legal Order: Adoption and Adaptation*, ed. Yun Zhao and Michael H. K. Ng (Cambridge: Cambridge University Press, 2017), 27. The procuratorate is the agency responsible for investigating and prosecuting crimes in China; the courts are responsible for imposing a sentence.

27 Biddulph, *Legal Reform and Administrative Detention Powers in China*, 168.

28 Biddulph, 168.

29 Biddulph, 169.

The Policies

China's formal legal system was destroyed during Mao Zedong's reign (1949–76).[30] When Deng Xiaoping came to power in 1978, the Chinese Communist Party (CCP) committed to rebuilding it. That effort included enacting laws that governed prostitution, which was becoming more prevalent as the state introduced market-based reforms and opened up to the outside world. The first law to address prostitution in the post-Mao era was the 1979 *Criminal Law of the People's Republic of China* (中华人民共和国刑法). It focused exclusively on the actions of third parties, who could be imprisoned for a decade or more for facilitating prostitution.[31] More comprehensive rules followed shortly thereafter. In 1981, the Ministry of Public Security issued a regulation devoted entirely to prostitution, the *Notice by the Ministry of Public Security on Resolutely Prohibiting Prostitution Activities* (公安部关于坚决制止卖淫活动的通知), which also outlined sanctions against sex workers and clients.[32] Local regulations quickly appeared in its aftermath. Guangdong province passed the first such law in August 1981, entitled the *Guangdong Provincial Provisional Rules on Banning the Selling and Buying of Sex*, and other localities soon followed suit.[33]

The ensuing years have seen a proliferation of additional rules that govern sex work in China. The main body of national-level laws and regulations currently in force touching on various aspects of prostitution includes:[34]

- The 1991 *Decision of the Standing Committee of the National People's Congress on the Strict Prohibition against Prostitution and Whoring* (全国人民代表大会常务委员会关于严禁卖淫嫖娼的决定) (amended in 2009 and 2019);
- The 1991 *Decision of the Standing Committee of the National People's Congress Regarding the Severe Punishment of Criminals Who Abduct and Traffic in or Kidnap Women and Children* (全国人民代表大会常

[30] Richard Baum, "Modernization and Legal Reform in Post-Mao China: The Rebirth of Socialist Legality," *Studies in Comparative Communism* 19, no. 2 (June 1, 1986): 69–103, https://doi.org/10.1016/0039-3592(86)90007-4.

[31] Elaine Jeffreys, *Prostitution Scandals in China: Policing, Media and Society* (London: Routledge, 2012), 7.

[32] Biddulph, *Legal Reform and Administrative Detention Powers in China*, 156.

[33] Heqing Zhang, "Female Sex Sellers and Public Policy in the People's Republic of China," in *Sex and Sexuality in China*, ed. Elaine Jeffreys, Routledge Studies on China in Transition 26 (London: Routledge, 2006), 142.

[34] The dates in this list reference the year that the legislation was initially passed, rather than when it went into effect.

务委员会关于严惩拐卖、绑架妇女、儿童的犯罪分子的决定) (revised in 2009);

- The 1992 *Law of the People's Republic of China on the Protection of Women's Rights and Interests* (中华人民共和国妇女权益保障法) (amended in 2005 and 2018);
- The 2005 *Public Security Administration Punishments Law of the People's Republic of China* (中华人民共和国治安管理处罚法) (amended in 2012);
- The 1979 *Criminal Law of the People's Republic of China* (中华人民共和国刑法) (revised in 1997, and amended, most recently, in 2022);
- The 2006 *Regulation on the Administration of Entertainment Venues* (娱乐场所管理条例) (most recently revised in 2020);
- The 2013 *Measures for the Administration of Entertainment Venues* (娱乐场所管理办法) (revised in 2017);
- The 2008 *Measures for the Public Security Administration of Entertainment Venues* (娱乐场所治安管理办法).

In addition, the 1993 *Measures for the Custody and Education of Persons Engaged in Prostitution and Whoring* (卖淫嫖娼人员收容教育办法) (amended in 2011) were in force at the time I carried out the research for this project, but were abolished in 2020. Taken together, these laws regulate the behavior of sex workers, clients, individuals who organize prostitution, and venues that harbor it.

Members of the CCP are subject to additional regulations if they engage in prostitution. The 2018 *Chinese Communist Party Disciplinary Regulations* (中国共产党纪律处分条例) state that using one's position of power to have sexual intercourse or exchanging material goods for sex may result in warnings, job loss, or probation or expulsion from the Party (Article 110).[35] The 2004 *Chinese Communist Party Disciplinary Regulations*, which preceded the 2018 rules and were in force when the research for this project occurred contained similar provisions (Articles 151 and 156).

Married individuals also face additional penalties if they engage in prostitution. The 2020 *Civil Code* (中华人民共和国民法典), in the Part on Marriage and Family (婚姻家庭编), prohibits bigamy, as well as a married person's cohabitation with someone of the opposite sex who is not one's spouse (Article 1042). Bigamy and cohabitation are grounds for divorce, and the wronged spouse has the right to claim

[35] Other articles that could also apply to Party members who buy or sell sex or organize prostitution include Articles 111, 134, 135, 137, and 138.

compensation (Articles 1079 and 1091). These articles were initially introduced as part of the 2001 amendments to the 1980 Marriage Law (中华人民共和国婚姻法), and they were specifically enacted to address concerns over the growing practice of keeping mistresses and second wives in Chinese society.[36]

The Punishments

The range of possible sanctions for prostitution-related activities in China includes fines, detention, incarceration, and, until 2015, the death penalty. Sex industry actors are also the targets of campaign-style policing and public shaming.

Fines

Sex workers and clients can be fined up to 5,000 yuan ($830) when arrested for prostitution.[37] Entertainment venues that harbor prostitution activities can be fined up to 20,000 yuan ($3,265).[38] Official guidelines promote incarceration instead of fines in prostitution cases.[39] Fines are much easier for wealthy people to pay, which goes against a Communist regime's ideological concerns about inequality, and are not considered a sufficient deterrent against prostitution. In practice, however, fines are a prevalent form of sanctioning sex industry actors, as they provide a source of income for local law enforcement institutions that generally struggle with budgetary shortfalls.[40] Local police departments depend upon the local government for their funding. In practice, this results in a system where local police stations are

36 Yan Sun, *Corruption and Market In Contemporary China* (Ithaca, NY: Cornell University Press, 2004), 177–78; Xiaoqing Feng, "A Review of the Development of Marriage Law in the People's Republic of China," *University of Detroit Mercy Law Review* 79 (2002): 388–91; Clara Li, "Marriage Law Overhaul Bans 'Second Wives,'" *South China Morning Post*, April 29, 2001; Gary Sigley, "Sex, Politics and the Policing of Virtue in the People's Republic of China," in *Sex and Sexuality in China*, ed. Elaine Jeffreys (London: Routledge Studies on China in Transition, 2006), 50; John Osburg, *Anxious Wealth: Money and Morality among China's New Rich* (Stanford, CA: Stanford University Press, 2013), 10; Suowei Xiao, "The 'Second-Wife' Phenomenon and the Relational Construction of Class-Coded Masculinities in Contemporary China," *Men and Masculinities* 14, no. 5 (December 1, 2011): 609, https://doi.org/10.1177/1097184X11412171.

37 *Zhonghua Renmin Gongheguo Zhian Guanli Chufa Fa* (中华人民共和国治安管理处罚法) [Public Security Administration Punishments Law of the People's Republic of China] Art. 66 (promulgated by the Standing Comm. Nat'l People's Cong., August 28, 2005, effective March 1, 2006, amended October 26, 2012).

38 *Yule Changsuo Guanli Tiaoli* (娱乐场所管理条例) [Regulations on the Administration of Entertainment Venues] Art. 43 (promulgated by the State Council., January 29, 2006, effective March 1, 2006, revised November 29, 2020).

39 Biddulph, *Legal Reform and Administrative Detention Powers in China*, 174.

40 Biddulph, 174–76.

underfunded and rely on fines to generate income.[41] In some places, the formal budget may cover as little as one-fifth of a station's total operating costs, with more than half of police officers' salaries coming from the fines they collect.[42] As a result of this budgetary shortfall, individual police officers are sometimes required to generate a certain amount of income in fines per month.[43] In 2004, one police officer in a mid-sized city in central China had to collect 50,000 yuan ($6,000) in fines that year.[44] Others report a monthly target of 3,000 yuan ($350) per officer – double their salary – and a 200 yuan ($25) fine for failing to meet the quota.[45]

This system creates incentives for the police to favor fines over other types of sanctions. In response to growing concerns around this issue, a new system was put into place starting in the mid-1990s that aims to separate police powers of revenue collection from spending (收支两条线 – *shouzhi liangtiaoxian*), and no longer makes the police responsible for generating their own revenue.[46] Previously, the police would collect fines, deposit them into their local agency bank account, and spend these funds with limited external oversight.[47] With the reformed system, police stations and individual officers are forbidden from directly collecting fines. Instead, payment is made directly to the local government's finance department,

[41] Hualing Fu and D. W. Choy, "Policing for Profit: Fiscal Crisis and Institutionalized Corruption of Chinese Police," in *Police Corruption: Paradigms, Models and Concepts–Challenges for Developing Countries*, ed. Stanley Einstein and Amir Menachem (Huntsville, TX: Office of International Criminal Justice, 2003), 538; Hualing Fu and D. W. Choy, "Administrative Detention of Prostitutes: The Legal Aspects," in *Gender Policy and HIV in China*, vol. 22, edited by Joseph Tucker and Dudley L. Poston, The Springer Series on Demographic Methods and Population Analysis (Dordrecht: Springer Netherlands, 2009), 192–93; Kam C. Wong, *Police Reform in China* (Boca Raton, FL: CRC Press, 2012), 254, 261; Fu Hualing, "Zhou Yongkang and the Recent Police Reform in China," *Australian & New Zealand Journal of Criminology* 38, no. 2 (August 1, 2005): 241–53, https://doi.org/10.1375/acri.38.2.241; Suzanne E. Scoggins and Kevin J. O'Brien, "China's Unhappy Police," *Asian Survey* 56, no. 2 (April 1, 2016): 239, https://doi.org/10.1525/as.2016.56.2.225; Suzanne E. Scoggins, "Policing Modern China," *China Law and Society Review* 3, no. 2 (October 30, 2018): 82, https://doi.org/10.1163/25427466-00302001; Jianhua Xu, "Police Accountability and the Commodification of Policing in China: A Study of Police/Business Posters in Guangzhou," *The British Journal of Criminology* 53, no. 6 (2013): 1095–96.

[42] Fu and Choy, "Policing for Profit," 538; Fu and Choy, "Administrative Detention of Prostitutes," 192.

[43] Fu and Choy, "Policing for Profit," 541–42.

[44] Zhao Jun (赵军), "Falu Jingji Chengban Zhi Shizheng Fenxi–Yi 'Maiyin Fa' Weili (法律经济成本之实证分析-以'卖淫法'为例) [Empirical Research on the Economic Cost of China's Prostitution Laws]," *Jiangxi Gongan Zhuanke Xuexiao Xuebao* (江西公安专科学校学报) 1 (2006): 17.

[45] Fu and Choy, "Policing for Profit," 541–42.

[46] Wong, *Police Reform in China*, 325.

[47] Dali L. Yang, *Remaking the Chinese Leviathan: Market Transition and the Politics of Governance in China* (Stanford, CA: Stanford University Press, 2004), 239.

which then returns a portion of the payment to the police. This system also aims to ensure that local governments provide sufficient funding for law enforcement, thus reducing the need for the police to generate their own income. By many accounts, this system is applied inconsistently and reliance on fines continues to shape police enforcement decisions throughout China.[48]

Prostitution is an obvious target for police officers seeking to raise money through fines.[49] Its prevalence throughout China makes it easy to detect. Each arrest provides the opportunity for two fines, as both the sex worker and the client are charged separately.[50] In addition, the police encounter limited resistance from either party when they make a prostitution charge: sex workers and clients generally prefer dealing with such situations as discreetly and expediently as possible to limit the personal and professional consequences that can accompany accusations of prostitution.[51]

Detention and Incarceration Institutions

When I was carrying out the fieldwork for this project, sex workers and clients could be subject to three types of incarceration. They could be sent to administrative detention (行政拘留 – *xingzheng juliu*). They could also be incarcerated for up to fifteen days in administrative jails (拘留所 – *juliusuo*).[52] These two institutions hold individuals who have

48 Fu and Choy, "Policing for Profit," 543.

49 Gambling and traffic violations are the other two main offenses that the police in China focus on to generate fines. Gambling is easier and less costly to investigate than prostitution. Yet it is so much a part of daily life (particularly mahjong and card games), and so completely devoid of the stigma associated with prostitution, that systematically fining it, in the words of one police officer, "would make the masses dissatisfied (会让群众不满 – *hui rang qunzhong buman*)." Zhao, "中国"卖淫法"经济成本经验研究 [Zhongguo 'Maiyin Fa' Jingji Chengben Jingyan Yanjiu–Empirical Research on the Economic Cost of China's Prostitution Laws]," 5–6; Fu and Choy, "Policing for Profit," 541.

50 As discussed further in Part III, in practice the police sometimes sanction only one party – usually the sex worker – or apply different punishments to the sex worker and the client.

51 Zhao Jun (赵军), "Falu Jingji Chengben Zhi Shizheng Fenxi–Yi 'Maiyin Fa' Weili (法律经济成本之实证分析-以'卖淫法'为例) [Empirical Research on the Economic Cost of China's Prostitution Laws]," *Jiangxi Gongan Zhuanke Xuexiao Xuebao (江西公安专科学校学报)* 1 (2006): 16. Zhao, himself a former police officer, also provides a counterexample, where a client pushes back against wrongful police conduct. In 2004, new regulations in the city where Zhao was conducting his research forbade the police from investigating prostitution cases outside of their jurisdiction. When a group of law enforcement officers started arresting clients in such a manner, one client refused to abide by their demands, specifically noting that they were forbidden from crossing over to another jurisdiction. A scuffle ensued, after which the police recognized that they were in the wrong and dropped their efforts to arrest the clients.

52 *Public Security Administration Punishments Law of the People's Republic of China*, Art. 66. These institutions are distinct from criminal detention centers (看守所 – *kanshuosuo*), where individuals who are being investigated or prosecuted for violating the criminal law are held. *Juliu*

violated the *Public Security Administration Punishments Law* and are governed by the 2012 *Detention Center Measures*. Until 2020, sex workers and clients could also be detained in custody and education (C&E) institutions (收容教育 – *shourong jiaoyu*) for six months to two years.[53] Custody and education centers were longer-term prostitution incarceration institutions. They first emerged for sex workers in China in the late 1940s, as part of the PRC's campaign to rid the country of prostitution. Sex workers incarcerated in these centers were treated for sexually transmitted diseases (STDs), and given professional and moral training.[54] Upon release, they were frequently placed in the custody of families or resident committees who were responsible for reintegrating them into society.[55] These centers continued to operate until the late 1950s, when prostitution was declared officially eradicated from the country.[56] When prostitution became more prominent after 1979, authorities reestablished the C&E institutions that had been credited with ridding China of prostitution in the 1950s. These efforts began as local experiments in prostitution enforcement. The first such institution was established in 1984 in Shanghai, and the cities of Beijing, Wuhan, Dalian, and Xian soon followed.[57] Establishing these centers nationwide, for both sex workers and clients, became integral to the central government's efforts to develop comprehensive anti-prostitution measures in the 1990s.

These C&E institutions aimed to produce "law-abiding citizens who are of sound body and mind."[58] They were tasked to achieve this goal by carrying out the following three activities with inmates: providing

Suo Tiaoli (拘留所条例) [Regulation on Detention Facilities] (promulgated by the State Council, February 15, 2012, effective April 1, 2012). "Dui Hua Human Rights Journal: Is Detention Center Law Enough to Prevent Police Abuse?," accessed September 17, 2014, perma.cc/5S8P-RLG8; "Dui Hua Human Rights Journal: Detention House Rules Can't Accommodate Oversight," accessed September 17, 2014, perma.cc/MQV6-WGWS.

53 *Maiyin Piaochang Renyuan Shourong Jiaoyu Banfa* (卖淫嫖娼人员收容教育办法) [Measures for the Custody and Education of Persons Engaged in Prostitution and Whoring] Art. 9 (promulgated by the State Council, September 4, 1993, effective September 4, 1993, amended January 8, 2011, repealed March 27, 2020).

54 Biddulph, *Legal Reform and Administrative Detention Powers in China*, 75; Gail Hershatter, *Dangerous Pleasures: Prostitution and Modernity in Twentieth-Century Shanghai* (Berkeley: University of California Press, 1997), 310; Christian Henriot, *Prostitution and Sexuality in Shanghai: A Social History 1849–1949* (Cambridge: Cambridge University Press, 2001), 482.

55 Biddulph, *Legal Reform and Administrative Detention Powers in China*, 75.

56 Biddulph, 74.

57 Wang Xing (王星), "Shoujiao Sanshi Nian (收教三十年) [Detention Education for 30 Years]," *Southern Metropolis Daily* (南方都市报), July 2, 2014, perma.cc/LX44-ANQB.

58 *Shourong Jiaoyu Suo Guanli Banfa* (收容教育所管理办法) [Measures for the Administration of the Custody and Education Centers] Art. 3 (promulgated by the Ministry of Pub. Sec., April 24, 2000, effective April 24, 2000, revised June 29, 2014, repealed August 6, 2020).

them with legal and moral education, having them engage in "productive labor" (生产劳动 – *shengchan laodong*), and testing and treating them for STDs.[59] Detailed guidelines were established for sex workers, clients, and guards.[60] Inmate activities should include at least ten hours of class a week, as well as "rich and varied recreational and sports activities" (丰富多彩的文体活动 – *fengfuduocai de wenti huodong*).[61] Inmates were required to pay for their own living expenses (or have their families pay).[62] In one C&E center, sex workers were charged a monthly fee of 200 yuan ($33), in addition to a one-time payment of 700 yuan ($115) for required items such as bedding.[63] Income earned through the work they performed in custody was used to improve conditions in the center, though inmates could also be paid directly for their labor.[64] Guards were prohibited from mistreating inmates. Beatings, corporal punishment, insults, humiliation, and other abuse were all forbidden.[65]

Lastly, if a sex worker or client was a recidivist, they could be incarcerated for up to three years in reeducation through labor camps (RETL) (劳动教养 – *laodong jiaoyang*).[66] Although RETL was abolished in 2013, it was still in place when I conducted much of the

[59] *Measures for the Custody and Education of Persons Engaged in Prostitution and Whoring* (repealed March 27, 2020), Art. 2.

[60] *Measures for the Custody and Education of Persons Engaged in Prostitution and Whoring* (repealed March 27, 2020), *Shourong Jiaoyu Suo Dengji Pingding Banfa* (收容教育所等级评定办法) [Measures for Grading the Level of Custody and Education Centers] (promulgated by the Ministry of Pub. Sec., November 27, 2000, effective November 27, 2000), *Measures for the Administration of the Custody and Education Centers* (repealed August 6, 2020).

[61] *Measures for Grading the Level of Custody and Education Centers*, Art. 13.

[62] *Measures for the Custody and Education of Persons Engaged in Prostitution and Whoring* (repealed March 27, 2020), Art. 14. While the national measures place the burden of fees on inmates, at least one province – Jiangsu – reportedly abolished this policy in 2014, and covered the costs of room and board, medication, and STD testing. Wang Xing (王星), "Shoujiao Sanshi Nian (收教三十年) [Detention Education for 30 Years]."

[63] Asia Catalyst, "'Custody and Education': Arbitrary Detention for Female Sex Workers in China," December 2013, 29–30. Relative to sex worker income, this is a significant amount of money. As discussed in subsequent chapters, low-tier sex workers are most likely to be incarcerated. The low-tier sex workers whom I surveyed reported monthly earnings of about 1,600 yuan (calculated based on their self-reported monthly number of clients and payment for their most recent sexual transaction). Their first month in custody thus amounts to more than half their self-reported monthly earnings. I discuss sex worker earnings in greater depth in Part II of this book. Please see the Appendix for more information about this survey.

[64] *Measures for the Custody and Education of Persons Engaged in Prostitution and Whoring* (repealed March 27, 2020), Art. 13.

[65] *Measures for Grading the Level of Custody and Education Centers*, Art. 11.

[66] Quanguo Renmin Daibiao Dahui Changwu Weiyuanhui Guanyu Yanjin Maiyin Piaochang De Jueding (全国人民代表大会常务委员会关于严禁卖淫嫖娼的决定) [Decision of the Standing Committee of the National People's Congress on the Strict Prohibition against Prostitution and Whoring] (promulgated by the State Council, September 4, 1991, effective September 4, 1991). Fu and Choy, "Administrative Detention of Prostitutes: The Legal

fieldwork for this project. The institution thus occasionally crops up in the pages that follow as affecting the lives of sex workers and clients, even though they were much more likely to experience C&E.

The formal abolition of C&E and RETL has not actually eliminated these types of incarceration experiences: unofficial detention centers have since materialized, some former RETL centers continue to operate under a different name, and there are reports of an increase in criminal detention (刑事拘留 – *xingshi juliu*) for individuals who would previously have been sent to RETL.[67] In practice, therefore, sex workers and clients continue to face the possibility of both short- and long-term incarceration.

Criminal Law Sanctions

While the fines and incarceration described earlier all fall under the purview of administrative offenses, China's criminal law also addresses aspects of prostitution. For example, it is a crime for an individual to sell or buy sex with knowledge that they have a serious STD. Offenders can be fined and sentenced to public surveillance, criminal detention, or imprisonment for up to five years.[68] Until 2015, it was also a crime to purchase sex from a girl under the age of fourteen, which could result in fines and imprisonment for at least five years.[69] That act now falls under the crime of rape, regardless of whether or not sex was purchased.[70]

Yet it is mainly pimps, madams, and sex traffickers – rather than sex workers and clients – whose behavior falls under the purview of China's criminal law. Individuals who organize, force, induce, shelter, or introduce someone into prostitution face punishments including property confiscation, fines, public surveillance, and prison sentences ranging from a few years to life.[71] Until 2015, these actors could be sentenced to

Aspects," 191; Elaine Jeffreys, *China, Sex and Prostitution* (London: Routledge Curzon, 2004), 140.

67 Verna Yu, "How China is Using Criminal Detention in Place of Re-Education through Labour," *South China Morning Post*, April 21, 2014; Amnesty International, "China's 'Re-Education through Labour' Camps: Replacing One System of Repression with Another?," December 17, 2013, perma.cc/J8DD-CURA ; Agence France Presse, "China Province Admits Unlawful Detention Centres," February 14, 2014.

68 Zhonghua Renmin Gongheguo Xingfa (中华人民共和国刑法) [Criminal Law of the People's Republic of China] Art. 360 (promulgated by the Standing Comm. Nat'l People's Cong., July 6, 1979, revised March 14, 1997, amended December 26, 2020, effective March 1, 2021). Such STDs would include syphilis, gonorrhea, and HIV/AIDS.

69 Ibid., Art. 360.

70 Ibid., Art. 236.

71 Ibid., Arts. 358–359.

death in particularly serious prostitution cases.[72] The death penalty was rarely applied, and only in egregious instances that involved the exploitation of either children or large numbers of women.[73]

Campaign-Style Policing and Public Shaming

In addition to the sanctions specifically outlined in China's anti-prostitution regulations, law enforcement officers also engage in campaign-style policing and public shaming of sex workers and clients.

Campaign-style policing involves government agencies cooperating over a given time period to target crime in an intensified manner, through severe and swift (从重从快 – *congzhong congkuai*) punishment, and it is a key crime control tactic in contemporary China.[74] In contrast to the regular criminal justice process, campaigns require heavy punishment for the targeted populations.[75] Some of these are broad "Strike Hard" campaigns that focus on a wide range of issues. Others focus on a specific type of offense. These campaigns can last for periods ranging from a few months to several years, and they can be launched at both the national and local level.[76]

Prostitution has been targeted during both "Strike Hard" and specialized campaigns. It is the object of "Sweep Away the Yellow" campaigns (扫黄 – *saohuang*), where the color yellow refers to the sex industry, including pornography and prostitution. It is also the focus of campaigns against the "Six Evils" (六害 – *liuhai*), a category of acts deemed to undermine socialism and national stability that was created in the wake of the Tiananmen Square protests in 1989.[77] The six evils are prostitution, gambling, pornography, drugs, the sale of women and children, and profiteering from superstition.[78]

Since the first national "Strike Hard" campaign in 1983, the central government in Beijing has implemented dozens of generic and specialized anti-crime campaigns.[79] Provincial and local

[72] In 2015, the 9th Amendment to the *Criminal Law* abolished the death penalty for individuals who organize or force others into prostitution.

[73] One such execution occurred in Chongqing in 2011 under Bo Xilai, the former politician who waged an intense battle against corruption and organized crime in the city. BBC News, "China Executes 'Gangland Madam,'" *BBC News*, December 7, 2011.

[74] Susan Trevaskes, *Policing Serious Crime in China: From "Strike Hard" to "Kill Fewer"* (London: Routledge, 2010), 2; Scoggins, "Policing Modern China," 99–100.

[75] Trevaskes, *Policing Serious Crime in China*, 69.

[76] Trevaskes, 2.

[77] Biddulph, *Legal Reform and Administrative Detention Powers in China*, 136–37.

[78] Biddulph, 137.

[79] Trevaskes, *Policing Serious Crime in China*, 43.

authorities have initiated countless more.[80] National-level campaigns that included a focus on prostitution have occurred in the following years: 1983–86; 1987; 1989; 1990; 1991; 1993; 1996; 2000; 2001; 2001–3; 2010; and 2015.[81] Local anti-crime campaigns also include prostitution on a regular basis.[82] They are not exceptional events. Instead, they are a routine part of the sex industry's interactions with the state. They are also being reexamined, with officials at all levels of government questioning their efficacy.[83] Since 2003, the Communist Party has called for the incorporation of campaigns into a more professional, crime-prevention approach to policing.[84] That said, as evidenced by the anti-corruption campaign that has been a defining feature of Xi Jinping's presidency since 2012, there are no indications that campaign-style policing will disappear while he is in power.[85]

Public shaming often accompanies campaign-style policing of prostitution, but can also occur independently of such events. It takes the shape of shame parades (游街示众 – *youjie shizhong*) at public sentencing rallies, as well as other practices designed to publicly humiliate sex workers and clients and deter others from following in their footsteps. One particularly prominent public sentencing event occurred in Shenzhen in 2006. The police arrested over one hundred sex workers and clients, and paraded them down the city streets dressed in bright yellow shirts. The law enforcement officers announced individual names, birthdates, and hometowns through a loudspeaker, and publicly sentenced these sex workers and clients to fifteen days of administrative detention.[86] In 2010, the police in the southern city of Dongguan led handcuffed sex workers down crowded city streets, roped together and barefoot, and publicized their

80 Trevaskes, 18, 28, 29, 31, 34–36.

81 Trevaskes, 18, 32, 35, 36, 43; Biddulph, *Legal Reform and Administrative Detention Powers in China*, 157–64; Congressional-Executive Commission on China, "Ministry of Public Security Launches Seven-Month Nationwide 'Strike Hard' Campaign," August 11, 2010, perma.cc/7WRQ-DNWE; Jingyi Zhao (赵婧夷), "Gonganbu Youguan Bumen Bushu Gedi Yanda Shehuang Shedu Weifa Fanzui (公安部有关部门部署各地严打涉黄涉毒违法犯罪) [Deploying the National Crackdown Plan on Drug and Sex-Related Crimes by the Relative Departments of the Ministry of Public Security]," Zhongguo Zhengfu Wang (中国政府网), November 25, 2015, perma.cc/EG29-AZSQ.

82 Trevaskes, *Policing Serious Crime in China*, 28, 34–36.

83 Biddulph, *Legal Reform and Administrative Detention Powers in China*, 141–43; Trevaskes, *Policing Serious Crime in China*, 18–19.

84 Trevaskes, *Policing Serious Crime in China*, 18–19.

85 Scoggins, "Policing Modern China," 100.

86 Jonathan Watts, "Outrage at Chinese Prostitutes' Shame Parade," *The Guardian*, December 6, 2006.

identity.[87] In Zhengzhou, the police took photos of naked sex workers during arrests. They then released the images on the internet, along with these women's names.[88] In Wuhan, the local police posted notices throughout the city with the names of sex workers and clients who had been arrested for prostitution.[89] In Hangzhou, the police sent letters to the families of women in one neighborhood who were suspected of selling sex.[90] In response to the public outcry that these public shaming incidents generated, the Ministry of Public Security issued a notice in July 2010 calling for an end to prostitution shame parades.[91] They have issued similar notices in the past, namely in 1951, 1984, 1986, 1988, and 2007.[92] As of 2022, the media had not reported any new large-scale, public prostitution shaming incidents since 2010.[93]

87 Andrew Jacobs, "China Seeks End to Public Shaming of Suspects," *The New York Times*, July 27, 2010; Tan Zhihong (谭志红), "Guangdong Dongguan Jingfang Shengqian Maiyinnu Youjie Re Zhengyi (广东东莞警方绳牵卖淫女游街惹争议) [Controversy over Police from Dongguan, Guangdong Parading Prostitutes through the Streets on a Leash]," *Nanfang Daily* (南方日报), July 18, 2010, perma.cc/J5WU-BD2X.

88 Tan Zhihong (谭志红), "Guangdong Dongguan Jingfang Shengqian Maiyinnu Youjie Re Zhengyi (广东东莞警方绳牵卖淫女游街惹争议) [Controversy over Police from Dongguan, Guangdong Parading Prostitutes through the Streets on a Leash]."

89 Wang Xinzi (王欣子), "Wuhan Jingfang Jietou Tie Gaoshi Shiming Puguang Maiyin Piaochang Renyuan (武汉警方街头贴告示实名曝光卖淫嫖娼人员) [Wuhan Police Post Official Notices on the Street Revealing the Names of Individuals Who Engage in Prostitution]," *Changjiang Shangbao* (长江商报), July 17, 2010, perma.cc/RC22-7B2Q.

90 Li Yunfang (李云芳), "Hangzhou Yi Paichusuo Saohuang Xiang 'Falangnu' Jiashu Fa Gaozhixin (杭州一派出所扫黄向"发廊女"家属发告知信) [A Police Station in Hangzhou Cracks Down on Prostitution by Notifying Families of Women Who Work in Hair Salons]," *Sichuan Zaixian* (四川在线), September 6, 2010, perma.cc/2UGN-YKVA.

91 Jacobs, "China Pushes to End Public Shaming"; The New York Times, "Why Shaming Has Lost Power in China: Introduction," *The New York Times*, July 31, 2010; Li Hong Xun (李红汛) and Yin Yi (尹伊), "Gonganbu Fa Tongzhi Piping Dui Maiyin Piaochang Renyuan Youjie Shizhong (公安部发通知批评对卖淫嫖娼人员游街示众) [The Ministry of Public Security Issued a Notice Criticizing Prostitution Shame Parades]," *Dahe Bao* (大河报), July 26, 2010, perma.cc/8G5F-KYZL.

92 Dui Hua Foundation, "Dui Hua Human Rights Journal: Translation: 'Perp Walks' for Petty Thieves Should Cease," July 29, 2010, perma.cc/D4F5-BE4U; Flora Sapio, "Perp Parades," *Forgotten Archipelago* (blog), July 26, 2010, perma.cc/HT7C-6J2Q.

93 Public shaming as a prostitution-deterrence tactic is not restricted to China or other authoritarian governments with weak rule of law. That said, in other environments it tends to focus just on shaming clients, whereas in China the state has subjected both sex workers and clients to it. Naming and shaming clients lie at the heart of anti-prostitution policies in England and Wales. In dozens of locations in the United States, men arrested for soliciting prostitution attend "john schools," where they complete a course focused on the consequences of solicitation. Such programs have also been set up in the United Kingdom and Canada. Some cities in the United States also publicly share names and photos of suspected clients in newspapers, on television, on billboards, and online. Jane Scoular and Maggie O'Neill, "Legal Incursions into Supply/Demand: Criminalising and Responsibilising the Buyers and Sellers of Sex in the UK," in *Demanding Sex*, ed. Munro and Della Giusta, 17; Michael Shively et al., "Final Report on the Evaluation of the First Offender Prostitution Program," March 7, 2008; Associated Press, "Cities Shame Johns to Fight Prostitution," *SFGate*, October 14, 2012.

Official Data on Frequency of Interactions with Law Enforcement

The Ministry of Public Security reports annually on the total number of prostitution cases that it files and investigates nationwide. Those data are reproduced in the following table (Table 3.1) for the years 1997–2022. They include both the sale and purchase of sex, with two cases counted if both a sex worker and a client are arrested. These numbers tell an official

TABLE 3.1 Annual number of cases of prostitution, 1997–2022[94]

Year	Number of cases filed/ accepted (受理)	Number of cases investigated and prosecuted (查处)
1997	210,390	209,244
1998	189,972	189,452
1999	216,660	215,128
2000	225,693	222,132
2001	242,053	239,461
2002	224,976	221,930
2003	172,314	171,604
2004	142,633	141,123
2005	143,995	142,746
2006	105,724	104,474
2007	95,338	94,687
2008	87,525	86,590
2009	126,140	125,175
2010	103,215	102,407
2011	96,162	95,294
2012	94,938	94,306
2013	84,375	83,891
2014	86,729	85,887
2015	75,756	74,853
2016	82,877	80,971
2017	88,091	85,899
2018	104,599	102,202
2019	115,704	114,648
2020	103,148	101,737
2021	135,171	133,375
2022	152,130	149,454

94 Data is from the China Statistical Yearbook, Offense Cases against Public Order Handled by Public Security Organs. This category includes both the selling and purchase of sex (卖淫, 嫖娼). These yearbooks include English-language translations of the various categories of data. Starting in 2006, the yearbooks translate this category as "Prostitution or Soliciting Prostitutes." Prior years used a more jarring translation: "Prostitution or Going Whoring."

story where the annual number of prostitution cases decreased from around 200,000 to below 100,000 over the course of two decades, with an uptick in the last five years of available data.

These data do not represent the number of prostitution cases that are actually filed and investigated annually throughout China. Official statistics from the Chinese government are rarely an accurate reflection of reality. Instead, these prostitution statistics are best understood as indicative of how some government agencies choose to portray the number of prostitution cases they encounter.[95] Even if these official data were accurate, it would not make sense to compare them to the ubiquity of prostitution and conclude that the probability of police interference is low. As detailed in subsequent chapters, the police interact with sex workers in a variety of ways that would not be included in statistics on filing and investigating prostitution cases. For instance, a 2014–15 survey of 518 sex workers in three Chinese cities noted that over half (51.3 percent) had been stopped, questioned, and/or searched by the police.[96] Such interactions with law enforcement are unlikely to show up in the official figures reported in Table 3.1.

PROSTITUTION AND CHINA'S PUBLIC HEALTH POLICIES

In addition to the policing policies outlined earlier in this chapter, China's concern with HIV/AIDS drives a second type of state prostitution intervention: public health policies. The Chinese Center for Disease Control and Prevention (CDC) is primarily responsible for carrying out these activities, some of which also involve others within the National Health Commission[97] and the global public health

[95] In deciding what data to report for prostitution cases, bureaucrats need to play a delicate balancing act. On the one hand, they need to show that they are actively enforcing anti-prostitution laws. This concern would tend to drive reported numbers up. On the other hand, they do not want to appear to have a lot of prostitution. This issue would instead drive those case numbers down. These conflicting pressures lead to a Goldilocks principle guiding the decision-making process behind data reporting that needs to produce numbers that are "just right" rather than too large or too small.

[96] Asia Catalyst, "The Condom Quandary: A Study of the Impact of Law Enforcement Practices on Effective HIV Prevention among Male, Female, and Transgender Sex Workers in China," 35.

[97] When I was conducting fieldwork for this project, the China CDC was a government-affiliated organization that took direction from the MOH. A separate National Population and Family Planning Commission (NPFPC) also conducted sex worker outreach programs. In 2013, the MOH and the NPFPC merged to become the National Health and Family Planning Commission (NHFPC). In 2018, that institution was dissolved, and was replaced with the National Health Commission.

community. Within populations of sex workers (and sometimes clients), the state monitors rates of HIV/AIDS and other STDs, collects data on sexual behavior, and carries out various programs designed to reduce the spread of HIV/AIDS.[98] In contrast to official policing policies, health regulations vary based on both gender and status: They formally target (female) sex workers more than (male) clients and prioritize interventions with low- and middle-tier sex workers.

HIV/AIDS in China

Prostitution health policies emerged in China during the mid-1980s, as the state confronted its AIDS epidemic. One strand of the epidemic originated in communities of drug users in northwest and southwest China.[99] A second strand was tied to a blood contamination scandal in rural China where local governments seeking to enrich themselves through the business of blood product manufacturing encouraged inhabitants to sell their blood and used inadequate blood donation screening procedures.[100] In the past several decades, HIV/AIDS has expanded from high-risk groups to the population at large through sex workers, clients, and their other sexual partners, such that heterosexual transmission is now considered the main way in which the virus is spreading.[101]

While China remains a low-prevalence country, with about 0.09 of the world's total HIV/AIDS cases, that percentage still translates into

[98] The state also has a program in place to provide services for people who have HIV. Under the "Four Frees and One Care" policy, the Chinese government offers HIV/AIDS tests free of charge. Approved state-run health institutions are the only facilities authorized to provide them. Under this policy, AIDS patients in rural areas and individuals without insurance who live in urban areas receive anti-retroviral drugs for free. They also have access to free voluntary counseling. Pregnant women with HIV get free drugs to prevent mother-to-child transmission of the virus. AIDS orphans do not pay for school. Through this policy, the government also pledges to provide care and economic support for households with an individual who is living with HIV.

[99] Fengshi Wu, "Double-Mobilization: Transnational Advocacy Networks for China's Environment and Public Health" (PhD. diss., College Park: University of Maryland, College Park, 2005), 204.

[100] Wu, 206–7.

[101] Joan Kaufman, Arthur Kleinman, and Tony Saich, "Introduction: Social Policy and HIV/AIDS in China," in *AIDS and Social Policy in China* (Cambridge, MA: Harvard University Asia Center, 2006), 6; Yan Hong and Xiaoming Li, "Behavioral Studies of Female Sex Workers in China: A Literature Review and Recommendation for Future Research," *AIDS and Behavior* 12, no. 4 (July 2008): 623; Yan Cui, Cynthia X. Shi, and Zunyou Wu, "Epidemiology of HIV/AIDS in China: Recent Trends," *Global Health Journal* 1, no. 1 (June 1, 2017): 26–32, https://doi.org/10.1016/S2414-6447(19)30057-0; Zunyou Wu, Junfang Chen, Sarah Robbins Scott, and Jennifer M. McGoogan, "History of the HIV Epidemic in China," *Current HIV/AIDS Reports* 16, no. 6 (December 1, 2019): 458–66, https://doi.org/10.1007/s11904-019-00471-4.

one of the largest HIV epidemics in the world.[102] An estimated 1,053,000 people were living with HIV/AIDS in China at the end of 2020.[103] New case numbers increase annually – from 41,000 in 2005 to 115,000 in 2015, and 131,000 in 2019.[104] Official estimates have placed the HIV/AIDS infection rate of female sex workers at less than 1 percent over the past thirty years.[105] All of these government data are considered to underestimate the actual prevalence of HIV/AIDS, as will be discussed in Part III.

AIDS is a sensitive issue in China. It requires the state to wrestle with the presence of drug use, prostitution, and homosexuality in society. In addition, the blood donor scandal from the 1990s discussed earlier in this section revealed government corruption and incompetence that resulted in the infection of hundreds of thousands of citizens.[106] As a result, the government tightly controlled any discussion or activism pertaining to AIDS when the magnitude of the epidemic surfaced in the 1990s.[107] Only in the early 2000s did the central government begin to openly acknowledge the extent of the country's AIDS crisis.[108]

Despite this sensitivity, China allowed the global public health community to participate in shaping the country's approach to HIV/AIDS from the beginning.[109] Starting in 1988, over forty foreign states, bilateral and multilateral organizations, foundations, and non-governmental organizations have supported work on HIV/AIDS in

102 Wu et al., "History of the HIV Epidemic in China."

103 Na He, "Research Progress in the Epidemiology of HIV/AIDS in China," *China CDC Weekly* 3, no. 48 (2021): 1022–30. In 2009, when I was carrying out the fieldwork for this project, an estimated 740,000 people in China were living with HIV/AIDS. Lei Zhang, Eric Pui Fung Chow, Jun Zhang, Jun Jing, and David P Wilson, "Describing the Chinese HIV Surveillance System and the Influences of Political Structures and Social Stigma," *The Open AIDS Journal* 6 (2012): 163–68.

104 "Reported Cases of HIV in China Are Rising Rapidly," *The Economist*, January 12, 2019, https://perma.cc/CS7K-TAZK; Yan Cui, Dongmin Li, and Elizabeth Pisani, "The National HIV Surveillance Program," in *HIV/AIDS in China: Epidemiology, Prevention and Treatment*, ed. Zunyou Wu, Yu Wang, Roger Detels, Marc Bulterys, and Jennifer M. McGoogan (Singapore: Springer Singapore Pte, 2019), 37, http://ebookcentral.proquest.com/lib/york/detail.action?docID=5940511; Matthew Walsh and Danmeng Ma, "China Diagnoses 131,000 New HIV Cases This Year," *Caixin Global*, December 5, 2019, perma.cc/9P9F-YDHM.

105 Zunyou Wu et al., "Introduction," in *HIV/AIDS in China*, vii.

106 Human Rights Watch, "Locked Doors: The Human Rights of People Living with HIV/AIDS in China," September 3, 2003, 60, www.hrw.org/report/2003/09/02/locked-doors/human-rights-people-living-hiv/aids-china.

107 Wu, "Double-Mobilization," 202.

108 Wu, 209–10; Human Rights Watch, "Locked Doors," 19.

109 For focused analysis pertaining to transnational actor involvement in HIV/AIDS work in China, see Wu, "Double-Mobilization" and Yan Long, "The Contradictory Impact of Transnational AIDS Institutions on State Repression in China, 1989–2013," *American Journal of Sociology* 124, no. 2 (September 1, 2018): 309–66, https://doi.org/10.1086/698466.

China.[110] These include the World Health Organization (WHO); the World Bank; several United Nations agencies (UNAIDS, UNICEF, UNFPA); the Global Fund to Fight AIDS, Tuberculosis, and Malaria (the Global Fund); the Ford Foundation; the Gates Foundation; the Clinton Foundation; the US Centers for Disease Control; the European Union; and the development agencies of the United States, the United Kingdom, Australia, Germany, Sweden, and Norway.[111]

These international actors have provided crucial funding for HIV/AIDS work in China. In fact, prior to 2003, when the state started to prioritize the epidemic, most financial support for AIDS prevention and care came from international, rather than domestic, sources.[112] That policy change opened up the floodgates for transnational actors working in the field of HIV/AIDS, and foreign funding increased exponentially in the decade that followed. For instance, UNAIDS-coordinated funds increased from about $39 million in 2003 to $63 million in 2004.[113] Through its Global AIDS Program, the United States invested $15 million in China from 2003 to 2007.[114] From 2003 to 2012, the Global Fund contributed more than $800 million to HIV/AIDS work in China.[115] Foreign funding has decreased significantly since 2014, however, as China has reached a level of economic development where it is now ineligible for some important sources of foreign support. In fact, its HIV/AIDS efforts are now largely funded domestically, and China has itself become a source of HIV/AIDS assistance for other less developed countries.[116]

In addition to money, transnational organizations have also contributed their ideas and experience to the Chinese state and its society. For instance, technical expertise from abroad has shaped every aspect of China's HIV/AIDS health policies, including case detection and monitoring, prevention, intervention, trainings of healthcare professionals,

[110] Jiangping Sun et al., "Contributions of International Cooperation Projects to the HIV/AIDS Response in China," *International Journal of Epidemiology* 39, no. suppl 2 (January 12, 2010): ii15, https://doi.org/10.1093/ije/dyq208.

[111] For a comprehensive discussion of the transnational actors involved in HIV/AIDS work in China, see Wu, "Double-Mobilization" and Jiangping Sun et al., "International Cooperation Projects and the HIV/AIDS Response," in *HIV/AIDS in China*, 393–404.

[112] Sun et al., "Contributions of International Cooperation Projects to the HIV/AIDS Response in China," ii16; Kaufman, Kleinman, and Saich, eds., *AIDS and Social Policy in China*, 179.

[113] Wu, "Double-Mobilization," 214–15.

[114] Wu, 216.

[115] Long, "The Contradictory Impact of Transnational AIDS Institutions on State Repression in China, 1989–2013," 334.

[116] Sun et al., "International Cooperation Projects and the HIV/AIDS Response," 393.

patient care, public awareness campaigns, policy advocacy, reduction of discrimination, and civil society engagement.[117] International organizations have often worked with Chinese partners to implement pilot projects that were subsequently scaled up to become national programs. For instance, the surveillance system and the 100% Condom Use Program (100% CUP; described in fuller detail in the next section) were both developed in close collaboration with foreign actors.[118] Given the stigma attached to sex work in China, transnational actors have played a particularly important role in highlighting the importance of focusing attention and resources on this population (and other marginalized groups at high risk of HIV/AIDS). Chapters 7 and 10 delve further into these linkages between transnational actors, grassroots organizations, and state public health policies regarding prostitution.

Programs to Monitor HIV/AIDS and Encourage Safer Sex

Despite the sensitivity and delayed public recognition of the HIV/AIDS epidemic, the state has been carrying out interventions within the sex industry since the mid-1980s. Starting in 1985, China developed an HIV/AIDS case reporting system. This was mainly a passive system where doctors were required to register all diagnosed cases of the disease. That said, it also involved some active testing of female sex workers, especially those who had foreign clients or lived in provinces with higher numbers of reported HIV/AIDS cases.[119] In 1995, the state created an active national HIV/AIDS testing system called "sentinel surveillance." This system identifies specific at-risk populations. It originally included individuals seeking treatment at STD clinics, female sex workers, drug users, and long-distance truck drivers.[120] It later added a much larger number of groups: pregnant women, former blood donors, men who have sex with men (MSM), tuberculosis patients, clients of female sex workers, students, migrants, spouses of

[117] Sun et al., "Contributions of International Cooperation Projects to the HIV/AIDS Response in China."

[118] Sun et al., "International Cooperation Projects and the HIV/AIDS Response."

[119] Xinhua Sun et al., "The Development of HIV/AIDS Surveillance in China," *AIDS* 21, no. suppl 8 (December 2007): S34. In addition to testing female sex workers, this system also actively targeted foreigners intending to live in China for more than a year, and Chinese citizens returning from abroad. The first person diagnosed with HIV/AIDS in China was a tourist, and the state's early prevention efforts focused on trying to stop the disease from entering into the country. Zunyou Wu, Sheena G. Sullivan, Yu Wang, Mary Jane Rotheram-Borus, and Roger Detels, "Evolution of China's Response to HIV/AIDS," *The Lancet* 369, no. 9562 (February 2007): 680.

[120] Sun et al., "The Development of HIV/AIDS Surveillance in China," S34.

people living with HIV, individuals undergoing premarital health checks, individuals crossing China's borders, and people seeking hospital treatment.[121] It selects specific sites throughout the country – villages, counties, cities, or municipal districts – and the target population is located in each site. For sex workers, those locations include karaoke bars, hair salons, massage parlors, areas with a high concentration of streetwalkers, and, prior to their abolition in 2020, C&E centers. Once a year, health officials sample individuals from each site for anonymous HIV/AIDS testing.[122] In 1995, forty-two such sites were established in twenty-three different provinces.[123] In 2006, 393 national sites existed in all thirty-one provinces, with an additional 370 provincial-level sites that follow the same protocol as the national system.[124] By 2009, when I was carrying out the fieldwork for this project, a total of 600 national sentinel surveillance sites had been established.[125] Of those, 161 (27 percent) targeted female sex workers.[126] In 2015, there were 1,867 surveillance sites, with 509 (27 percent) focused on female sex workers.[127] In the late 2000s, a handful of sites (in 2009, 8 out of 600) specifically targeted clients of female sex workers.[128] Other sites focused on two male populations thought to regularly purchase sex: long-distance truck drivers and migrants. Of the 1,867 sites that were identified in 2015, 57 (3 percent) focused on the former and 87 (5 percent) targeted the latter.[129] Surveillance site numbers appear to have remained comparable since

121 Sun et al., S34; Ministry of Health of the People's Republic of China, "China 2010 UNGASS Country Progress Report," April 2, 2010, 65.

122 Zhang et al., "Describing the Chinese HIV Surveillance System and the Influences of Political Structures and Social Stigma," 165. Wen Lin et al., "Is the HIV Sentinel Surveillance System Adequate in China? Findings from an Evaluation of the National HIV Sentinel Surveillance System," *Western Pacific Surveillance and Response Journal* 3, no. 4 (2012): 81. Until 2005, this testing occurred semi-annually at each site.

123 Sun et al., "The Development of HIV/AIDS Surveillance in China," S34.

124 Sun et al., S35. The term "province" here refers to the twenty-two provinces (省), five autonomous regions (自治区) (Xinjiang, Inner Mongolia, Tibet, Ningxia, and Guangxi), and four municipalities (直辖市) (Beijing, Tianjin, Shanghai, and Chongqing), which together constitute the highest-level administrative divisions in China (省级行政区).

125 Lin et al., "Is the HIV Sentinel Surveillance System Adequate in China?," 79.

126 Cui, Li, and Pisani, "The National HIV Surveillance Program," 29.

127 Ge Lin et al. 葛琳等, "2010–2015 Nian Zhongguo Aizibing Shaodian Jiance Renqun HIV, Meidu He HCV Ganran Zhuangkuang Fenxi" (2010–2015年中国艾滋病哨点监测人群HIV、梅毒和HCV感染状况分析) [Population Specific Sentinel Surveillance for HIV Infection, Syphilis and HCV Infection in China, During 2010–2015], *Jibing Jiance* (疾病监测) *[Disease Surveillance]* 32, no. 2 (2017): 111–17.

128 Lin et al., "Is the HIV Sentinel Surveillance System Adequate in China?," 79.

129 Ge Lin et al., "Population Specific Sentinel Surveillance for HIV Infection, Syphilis and HCV Infection in China, During 2010–2015," 112–13.

then.[130] Since 2000, case reporting and sentinel surveillance have been supplemented with behavioral surveillance surveys (BSS), which ask participants to report on various HIV-related behaviors. For sex workers, the BSS includes questions on frequency of condom use and number of sexual partners. In 2008, BSS surveys were conducted at 155 sites, with 87 of them (56 percent) targeting female sex workers.[131] Since then, BSS surveys have been integrated into the sentinel surveillance system at all sites.[132] This combination of case reporting with sentinel and behavioral surveillance forms a comprehensive HIV surveillance system articulated in two key government documents: the *Standards for HIV Surveillance and HIV/AIDS* and the *STD Comprehensive Surveillance Guidelines*.[133]

The HIV/AIDS risk profiles of individual sex workers differ based on a variety of factors tied to conditions of work, such as number of clients and expectations around condom use. In recognition of these differences, the official guidelines for conducting sentinel surveillance adopt a tier-based categorization of sex workers.[134] After mapping out the universe of prostitution venues in a community, health workers are instructed to categorize them into "high" (高 – *gao*), "middle" (中 – *zhong*), or "low" (低 – *di*) tiers (层次 – *cengci*).[135] At least

130 National Health Commission (国家卫生健康委员会), "Dui Shisanjie Quanguo Renda Yici Huiyi Di 4342 Hao Jianyi De Dafu" (对十三届全国人大一次会议第4342号建议的答复) [Reply to Proposal No. 4342 of the First Session of the Thirteenth National People's Congress] (September 27, 2018), perma.cc/N9RH-HJ7J.

131 Lin et al., "Is the HIV Sentinel Surveillance System Adequate in China?," 79.

132 Lin et al., "Is the HIV Sentinel Surveillance System Adequate in China?"; National Center for AIDS/STD Control and Prevention (性病艾滋病预防控制中心), "Quanguo Aizibing Shaodian Jiance Shishi Fangan Caozuo Shouce (全国艾滋病哨点监测实施方案操作手册) [Guidebook for Monitoring on the Implementation of National AIDS Checkpoints]" (2017), perma.cc/Y4K2-N5DC; National Center for AIDS/STD Control and Prevention (性病艾滋病预防控制中心), "Quanguo Aizibing Shaodian Jiance Shishi Fangan (Shixing) Caozuo Shouce (全国艾滋病哨点监测实施方案(试行)操作手册) [Guidebook for Monitoring on the Implementation of National AIDS Checkpoints (for Trial Implementation)]" (2009), perma.cc/X8DA-2DY2.

133 Chinese Ministry of Health (dissolved), "Quanguo Aizibing Jiance Gongzuo Guifan (全国艾滋病监测工作规范) [Standards for HIV Surveillance and HIV/AIDS]" (Chinese Ministry of Health (dissolved), March 20, 2002), www.moh.gov.cn/mohyzs/pzcxx/200804/32066.shtml; Chinese Center for Disease Control and Prevention, "Aizibing Xingbing Zonghe Jiance Zhinan Ji Fangan (Shizing) 艾滋病性病综合监测指南及方案(试行) [STD Comprehensive Surveillance Guidelines (For Trial Implementation)]," April 2002, www.hfcdc.ah.cn/include/downloand.php?ID=247.

134 National Center for AIDS/STD Control and Prevention (性病艾滋病预防控制中心), Quanguo Aizibing Shaodian Jiance Shishi Fangan Caozuo Shouce (全国艾滋病哨点监测实施方案操作手册) [Guidebook for Monitoring on the Implementation of National AIDS Checkpoints].

135 The guidelines do not explain the criteria to be used for classifying spaces into each of these tiers.

10 percent of the sample must come from the low tier, and at least 40 percent of the sample must come from middle-tier prostitution venues, as rates of HIV/AIDS are likely higher for sex workers in these spaces.[136]

China's public health institutions also carry out behavioral change programs designed to reduce the incidence of HIV/AIDS and other STDs by educating sex workers about safe sex, disease transmission, and condom use.[137] Systematic efforts at developing these interventions started in 2001 with pilot projects of the 100% Condom Use Program (100% CUP). The goals of this program are to ensure that sex workers and clients use condoms every time they engage in a high-risk sexual relationship and that clients who refuse to wear a condom will not find sex workers willing to have unprotected sex.[138] Over the last two decades, the central government has publicly endorsed such behavioral interventions and supported their adoption nationwide.[139] For instance, the Ministry of Health (MOH) released a notice in 2004 that called for CDCs at all levels of government to establish an intervention task force for groups at high risk of contracting HIV/AIDS, including sex workers.[140] In 2005, it issued *Guidelines for High-Risk Group Behavioral Interventions*, which outline the responsibilities of

136 In each surveillance site, a total of 400 sex workers must be tested, a number which is reduced to 250 if the HIV/AIDS prevalence rate from the previous surveillance round exceeds 10 percent. National Center for AIDS/STD Control and Prevention (性病艾滋病预防控制中心), Quanguo Aizibing Shaodian Jiance Shishi Fangan Caozuo Shouce (全国艾滋病哨点监测实施方案操作手册) [Guidebook for Monitoring on the Implementation of National AIDS Checkpoints].

137 HIV/AIDS was the impetus for health interventions among sex workers in China. That said, other diseases that also present important health risks are more common, including syphilis, hepatitis C, gonorrhea, and chlamydia. Sentinel surveillance also includes testing such other STDs, which serve as surrogate markers as risk of HIV rises along with increased rates of STDs. They can also increase one's vulnerability to contracting HIV.

138 Wiwat Rojanapithayakorn, "The 100% Condom Use Programme in Asia," *Reproductive Health Matters* 14, no. 28 (2006): 42.

139 Elaine Jeffreys and Gang Su, "China's 100 Per Cent Condom Use Program: Customising the Thai Experience," *Asian Studies Review* 35, no. 3 (2011): 325; Tony Saich, "Social Policy Development in the Era of Economic Reform," in *AIDS and Social Policy in China*, 42; Rojanapithayakorn, "The 100% Condom Use Programme in Asia," 45–46.

140 National Health and Family Planning Commission (国家卫生和计划生育委员会), "Weishengbu Bangongting Guanyu Zai Geji Jibing Yufang Kongzhi Zhongxin (Weisheng Fangyi Zhan) Jianli Gaowei Renqun Ganyu Gongzuodui De Tongzhi (卫生部办公厅关于在各级疾病预防控制中心(卫生防疫站)建立高危人群干预工作队的通知) [General Office of Ministry of Health's Notice for Setting up Intervention Working Group for High-Risk People at Health and Epidemic Prevention Centers at Every Administrative Level]," August 20, 2004, www.moh.gov.cn/mohbgt/pw10409/200804/27106.shtml. The other target groups are individuals who have an STD, MSM, intravenous drug users (IDU), migrant workers, individuals who actively seek HIV testing and counseling, individuals who have tested positive for HIV, and their spouses or sexual partners.

CDCs nationwide for conducting such activities.[141] These guidelines underscore the importance of using peer educators to reach these populations (e.g., training sex workers to do outreach to other sex workers). They also outline the health services the state should make available, the necessity of providing easy access to and information about condoms, and the types of educational materials to distribute. Elements of the 100% CUP pilot projects also made their way into the 2006 *Regulation on the Prevention and Treatment of HIV/AIDS*. Under this regulation, managers of public places (公共场所 – *gonggong changsuo*) must provide access to condoms, with provincial governments granted decision-making authority as to which public places should do so.[142] The regulations also empower local health agencies to penalize public places that do not distribute condoms through warnings, fines, and a temporary suspension of activity until condom access is established. Noncomplying public places can also have their business license revoked.[143]

Although they do not specifically address prostitution, the state's attempts to increase HIV/AIDS awareness in the general population serve as an additional source of information on safe sex and transmission of HIV/AIDS for sex workers and clients. These efforts include regular media coverage of Chinese leaders meeting with individuals who have tested positive for HIV, and large-scale safe sex and AIDS awareness public service announcements with major celebrities such as actors Jackie Chan, Pu Cunxin, and Zhang Ziyi, singer Peng Liyuan (in 2007, before her husband, Xi Jinping, became China's leader), and basketball players Yao Ming and Magic Johnson.[144]

These surveillance and behavioral outreach programs show how China's formal public health policies focus much more on female sex

141 General Office of the Ministry of Health, "Gaoweixian Xingwei Ganyu Gongzuo Zhidao Fangan (Shixing) 高危行为干预工作指导方案 (试行) [Guidelines for Intervention Works on High-Risk Behaviors (For Trial Implementation)]," June 9, 2005, www.china.com.cn/chinese/PI-c/885526.htm.

142 *Aizibing Fangzhi Tiaoli* (艾滋病防治条例) [Regulation on the Prevention and Treatment of HIV/AIDS] Art. 29 (promulgated by the State Council, January 18, 2006, effective March 6, 2006, revised March 2, 2019). The category "public places" (*gonggongchangsuo*–公共场所) includes all of the types of places that harbor prostitution in China. *Gonggong Changsuo Weisheng Guanli Tiaoli* (公共场所卫生管理条例) [Regulations on the Administration of Sanitation at Public Places] Art. 2 (promulgated by the State Council, April 1, 1987, effective April 1, 1987, amended April 23, 2019).

143 *Regulation on the Prevention and Treatment of HIV/AIDS*, Art. 61.

144 Peng Liyuan has continued her HIV/AIDS advocacy since she became first lady of China, for instance, as the WHO's Goodwill Ambassador for Tuberculosis and HIV/AIDS. Hong Hu, Guy Taylor, and Qingfeng Chen, "HIV Education: Raising Awareness and Increasing Knowledge," in *HIV/AIDS in China*, 236.

workers than male clients. This disproportionate focus on women mirrors public health HIV/AIDS programs worldwide.[145] While I discuss elements of this imbalance in Part III, my point at this juncture is simply to underscore that when it comes to prostitution, it is the women who sell sex, rather than the men who buy it, who are the main targets of China's official prostitution health regulations.

TAXING CHINA'S ENTERTAINMENT INDUSTRY

In addition to policies aimed at prohibiting prostitution and reducing the spread of HIV/AIDS, the Chinese government has also enacted policies that allow it to benefit financially from the sex industry. More specifically, the state enriches itself through taxation of entertainment venues and their employees. To be clear, these are not policies that officially claim to be taxing brothels and sex workers, as happens in regulatory regimes of legalized prostitution (or as occurred in some places in Republican China).[146] Instead, these are the taxes applied to venues that are registered with the state as businesses that provide services that are legal in China, such as entertainment (singing and dancing), food, drink, haircuts, and massages, as well as to their personnel.

Acknowledging Prostitution at Entertainment Venues

The Chinese state recognizes that entertainment venues may serve as gateways to the purchase of sex. Indeed, a spokesperson for the State Council Legislative Affairs Office (国务院法制办 – *guowuyuan fazhiban*) noted in 2006 that "As everyone knows, entertainment venues have a dual nature. On the one hand, they can enrich people's cultural life; on the other hand, these types of venues can quite easily propagate prostitution, gambling, drugs and other such illegal activities."[147]

To address the sale of sex at entertainment venues, the Chinese government enacted the *Regulation on the Administration of*

145 Elanah Uretsky, *Occupational Hazards: Business, Sex, and HIV in Post-Mao China* (Stanford, CA: Stanford University Press, 2016), 209; Shari L. Dworkin, *Men at Risk: Masculinity, Heterosexuality, and HIV Prevention* (New York: New York University Press, 2015); UNAIDS, "Blind Spot: Reaching Out to Men and Boys Addressing a Blind Spot in the Response to HIV," 2017, perma.cc/9QSB-2XDV.

146 Elizabeth Remick, *Regulating Prostitution in China: Gender and Local Statebuilding, 1900–1937* (Stanford, CA: Stanford University Press, 2014).

147 Legislative Affairs Office of the State Council, "Guowuyuan Fazhiban Jiaokewen Fazhisi Youguan Fuze Tongzhi Jiu 'Yule Changsuo Guanli Tiaoli' De Youguan Wenti Da 'Zhengfu

Entertainment Venues in 2006, which includes extremely detailed rules designed to deter the occurrence of sex work at these places. For instance, they specifically forbid entertainment venues and their employees from facilitating or engaging in prostitution.[148] Venues must remain closed between 2 and 8 AM.[149] They are required to install video monitoring equipment that records continuously in the entrance, exit, and main venue passageways.[150] The doors to private rooms within these spaces may not have locks on them.[151] Doors and windows of each room must be at least partially transparent, so that the entire room is visible from the outside.[152] No objects that would obstruct one's view (such as screens or partitions) may be placed within a room.[153] With the exception of a toilet, no separate room may be installed within a private room.[154] Lights in these rooms must be on at all times during business hours, and dimmable light systems are forbidden.[155] These efforts to signal distance between entertainment venues and the prostitution that many of them harbor extend even to the clothes that employees in entertainment venues are required to wear, which must be modest and "may not be harmful to public morals" (不得有伤风化 – *bude youshang fenghua*).[156] Hostess uniforms are generally matching traditional Chinese *qipao* (旗袍) dresses, or Western-style ball gowns reminiscent of 1980s American prom dresses. The outfits for massage parlor and hair salon employees are completely desexualized and resemble medical professional scrubs. All of these rules governing the physical presentation of entertainment venues and their employees are designed to signal propriety, order, and legality. This is a far cry from the prostitution they actually harbor,

Fazhi Xinxi Wang' Jizhe Wen 国务院法制办教科文卫法制司有关负责同志就《娱乐场所管理条例》的有关问题答《政府法制信息网》记者问 [Legislative Affairs Office of the State Council's Reply for the Reporter from Government Legal Information Website on Questions Regarding the Regulation on the Administration of Entertainment Venues]," December 4, 2006, perma.cc/UX6W-DZZX.

148 *Regulation on the Administration of Entertainment Venues*, Art. 14.

149 *Regulation on the Administration of Entertainment Venues*, Art. 28.

150 *Regulation on the Administration of Entertainment Venues*, Art. 15. *Yule Changsuo Zhian Guanli Banfa* (娱乐场所治安管理办法) [Measures for the Public Security of Entertainment Venues] Arts. 12–14 (promulgated by the Ministry of Public Security, April 21, 2008, effective October 1, 2008).

151 *Regulation on the Administration of Entertainment Venues*, Art. 16.

152 *Regulation on the Administration of Entertainment Venues*, Art. 16. *Measures for the Public Security of Entertainment Venues*, Art. 9.

153 *Regulation on the Administration of Entertainment Venues*, Art. 16. *Measures for the Public Security of Entertainment Venues*, Art. 8.

154 *Measures for the Public Security of Entertainment Venues*, Art. 8.

155 Ibid., Art. 11.

156 Ibid., Art. 21. *Regulation on the Administration of Entertainment Venues*, Art. 27.

and whose availability lies at the heart of their ability to attract clients, and thus generate revenue from the legal entertainment activities they provide.

Taxing Entertainment Venues and Their Personnel

By signaling through its regulations that it expects entertainment venues to prohibit prostitution, the state strengthens its case to treat (and tax) them as standard legal businesses. Prior to 2017, the business tax applied to these spaces ranged from 5 to 20 percent of revenue earned.[157] Those regulations were subsequently repealed, and businesses have since been subject to value-added tax regulations, ranging from 3 to 6 percent, as well as the enterprise income tax, which in practice ranges from 5 to 25 percent.[158] Business owners must also pay taxes in areas such as urban maintenance and construction, education, cultural construction, real estate, and urban land use.

Individual proprietors of entertainment businesses, as well as venue employees, are subject to personal income tax (PIT) regulations, with rates ranging from 3 to 45 percent.[159] In some places, local governments have established a fixed amount of taxes that venue employees are required to pay – an approach called presumptive taxation. In Beijing, for instance, employees at beauty salons, bathhouses, massage parlors, and entertainment venues pay between 50 and 500 yuan per month in PIT.[160] Other cities that have issued similar rules include

[157] *Zhonghua Renmin Gongheguo Yingyeshui Zanxing Tiaoli* (中华人民共和国营业税暂行条例) [Provisional Regulations of the People's Republic of China on Business Tax] Annex (promulgated by the State Council, December 13, 1993, revised November 5, 2008, repealed November 19, 2017).

[158] *Yingyeshui Gaizheng Zengzhishui Shidian Shishi Banfa* (营业税改征增值税试点实施办法) [Measures for Implementing the Pilot Program of Replacing Business Tax with Value-Added Tax] Arts. 15, 16 (promulgated by the Ministry of Fin. and St. Admin. of Tax'n, December 12, 2013, effective January 1, 2014); *Zhonghua Renmin Gongheguo Qiye Suodeshui Fa* (中华人民共和国企业所得税法) [Enterprise Income Tax Law of the People's Republic of China] (promulgated by the Standing Comm. Nat'l People's Cong., March 16, 2007, effective January 1, 2008, amended December 29, 2018). Wei Cui, "What Is a 'Small and Micro-Profit Enterprise' in China?," *Centre for Asian Legal Studies Peter A. Allard School of Law at the University of British Columbia* (blog), December 5, 2019, perma.cc/3T6M-H3KS.

[159] *Zhonghua Renmin Gongheguo Geren Suodeshui Fa* (中华人民共和国个人所得税法) [Individual Income Tax Law of the People's Republic of China] (promulgated by the Standing Comm. Nat'l People's Cong., September 10, 1980, amended August 31, 2018, effective January 1, 2019).

[160] *Beijing Shi Difang Shuiwuju Duiyu Benshi Yule Yinshi Fuwuye Bufen Congye Renyuan Shixing Dinge Zhengshou Geren Suodeshui De Zanxing Banfa Buchong Guiding De Tongzhi* (北京市地方税务局关于对本市娱乐、饮食服务业部分从业人员实行定额征收个人所得税的暂行办法补充规定的通知) [Notice of the Supplementary Regulations for Beijing Local Taxation Bureau's Provisional Measures on Collecting Personal Income Tax from Entertainment and

Shenzhen, Hainan, Putian, Shenyang, and Nanjing.[161] Local officials have spoken candidly about how these regulations are intended to target hostess earnings, and have acknowledged the fine line the rules walk between legality (payment for singing, dancing, and drinking) and illegality (payment for sex).[162] For that reason, these measures have generated controversy, particularly when localities first started enacting them.[163]

While this overview of relevant tax regulations provides an explanation of the formal policies through which the state can extract rents around the sex industry, actual taxation practices may differ by locality and type of venue. For instance, small businesses such as those that harbor prostitution might pay a lump sum that combines all the different taxes already discussed.[164] Furthermore, informal, nonrule-based tax collection is also

Food Service Industry Employees] (promulgated by the Beijing Local Taxation Bureau, July 25, 2000, effective October 1, 2000).

161 Fu and Choy, "Policing for Profit," 542; *Guanyu Chongxin Fabu "Guanyu Tezhong Xiaofei Hangye Linshi Shoupin Fuwu Renyuan Geren Suodeshui Zhengshou Guanli De Zanxing Guiding" Wenjian De Jueding* (关于重新发布《特种消费行业临时受聘服务人员个人所得税征收管理的暂行规定》文件的决定) [Decision on Reissuing the Interim Provisions on the Collection of Individual Income Tax from Temporarily Employed Service Providers in the Special Services Industries] (promulgated by the Shenzhen Local Tax'n Bureau, November 6, 2003, effective November 6, 2003); Lu Yansi (陆妍思), "Xiang Anmou Nu Zhengshui De Shishi Feifei (向按摩女征税的是是非非) [Pros and Cons on Taxing Massage Parlor Girls]," *Xin Kuai Bao (新快报)*, November 20, 2002, perma.cc/DAJ6-CZVE; Xu Yuanfeng (徐元锋), "Shenyang Fenji Guanli Yule Changsuo (沈阳分级管理娱乐场所) [Classification Management of the Entertainment Venues in Shenyang]," *Renminwang (人民网)*, April 20, 2006, perma.cc/97A4-7QSJ; Pang Jingcheng (庞京城) and Shen Deli (沈德理), "Zhifa Tongyi Yu Guanli Youxiao: Ruhe Renshi Dui Yule (Baogua Shehuang) Changsuo Congye Renyuan De Shoushui Wenti (执法统一与管理有效:如何认识对娱乐(包括涉黄)场所从业人员的收税问题) [Effective and Unified Law Enforcement: How to Recognize the Problem of Taxing Employees in Entertainment Venues (Sex-Related Industries Included)]," in *The 8th (2013) Annual Conference of Chinese Society for Management Modernization – Session Essays on A Study of Management Cases* (Beijing: Chinese Society for Management Modernization, 2013). Pan Suiming notes that in 1998, over forty-three cities had enacted such policies. Suiming Pan, *Cun Zai Yu Huang Miu: Zhongguo Di Xia "Xing Chan Ye" Kao Cha [Existing in Falsehoods: An Investigation of China's Underground Sex Industry]* (Beijing: Qunyan, 1999).

162 Fang Lin (方琳), "Shilun Xiandai Gonggong Zhengce De Jiazhi Chongtu (试论现代公共政策的价值冲突) [On Value Confrontation in Modern Public Policy]," *Administrative Management in China (中国行政管理)* 12 (1998): 66–69.

163 Lu Yansi (陆妍思), "Xiang Anmou Nu Zhengshui De Shishi Feifei (向按摩女征税的是是非非) [Pros and Cons on Taxing Massage Parlor Girls]," *Xin Kuai Bao (新快报)*; Legal Daily (法制日報), "Ping Lun: Xiang Anmo Xiaojie Deng Shoushui Yu Zongrong Seqing Bingbu Xianggan (评论: 向按摩小姐等收税与纵容色情并不相干) [Commentary-It's Pointless in Comparing Taxing Parlor Girls to Indulging Sex Business]," *Sohu.Com (搜狐)*, December 24, 2002, perma.cc/96SN-NAZN.

164 Correspondence with Wei Cui, December 2020. *Geti Gongshanghu Shuishou Dingqi Dinge Zhengshou Guanli Banfa* (个体工商户税收定期定额征收管理办法) [Measures for the Administration of Regular and Fixed-Amount Taxation on Self-Employed Industrial and Commercial Households] (promulgated by the St. Admin. of Tax'n, August 30, 2006, effective January 1, 2007, amended June 15, 2018).

widespread.[165] Regardless of the specific taxation practices affecting individual businesses and their employees, the takeaways are twofold. First, entertainment venues are likely paying taxes,[166] with some variation in their level of compliance with various tax regulations. Second, despite the existence of targeted presumptive taxation rules in some localities, the vast majority of entertainment venue employees do not pay income tax: More likely, they are among the estimated 98 percent of Chinese citizens who do not pay their taxes.[167] When it comes to China's entertainment industry, it is venues, rather than individuals, that generate the bulk of tax revenue.

CONCLUSION

Policymakers in post-Mao China have had their hands full when it comes to figuring out the formal rules the PRC needs to address the various effects that prostitution has on Chinese politics, economics, and society. They have chosen, first, to outlaw all aspects of the phenomenon – selling sex, purchasing it, and organizing sexual transactions. This decision is consistent with the political ideology of the CCP: Socialism is not theoretically compatible with the commodification of the human body that prostitution represents.[168] It is also generally aligned with how prostitution is regulated in most places around the world, even though prohibition models vary across

165 Wei Cui, "Administrative Decentralization and Tax Compliance: A Transactional Cost Perspective," *The University of Toronto Law Journal* 65, no. 3 (2015): 186–238.

166 For instance, the city of Dongguan generated over 30 billion yuan in tax revenues in 2013, and 3.6 billion yuan of that was estimated to come from the entertainment industry. "Anti-Vice Crackdown on China's 'Sin City' Takes Extra Toll as Economy Slows," *Reuters*, April 3, 2014, https://perma.cc/PH4F-334S.

167 "Why Only 2% of Chinese Pay Any Income Tax," *The Economist*, December 1, 2018, https://perma.cc/HX7H-F52M.

168 Of course, the CCP pursues plenty of policies that appear theoretically at odds with socialist and communist ideologies, such as its active embrace of capitalism. My point here is simply that the PRC's official prostitution laws do not currently fall into the category of ideological contradictions that characterize the regime. For more reflections on the inconsistencies between socialism and prostitution in China, see Tiantian Zheng, "The Plight of Sex Workers in China: From Criminalisation and Abuse to Activism," *Made in China Journal* (blog), April 18, 2019, perma.cc/8W6L-U996; Eric Fish, "The Lives of Sex Workers in Modern China (Interview with Zhang Lijia)," *Asia Society* (blog), February 7, 2017, perma.cc/E6Y2-6AUU; Liqun Cao and Steven Stack, "Exploring Terra Incognita: Family Values and Prostitution Acceptance in China," *Journal of Criminal Justice* 38, no. 4 (July 1, 2010): 531–37, https://doi.org/10.1016/j.jcrimjus.2010.04.023; Hershatter, *Dangerous Pleasures*, 361; Gary Sigley and Elaine Jeffreys, "On 'Sex' and 'Sexuality' in China: A Conversation with Pan Suiming," *Bulletin of Concerned Asian Scholars* 31, no. 1 (March 1999): 55, https://doi.org/10.1080/14672715.1999.10415730; Tiantian Zheng, *Red Lights: The Lives of Sex Workers in Postsocialist China* (Minneapolis: University of Minnesota Press, 2009), 66; Zhang, "Female Sex Sellers and Public Policy in the People's Republic of China," 155–156.

jurisdictions with respect to which aspects of the prostitution transaction are against the law. Second, China's leaders have thought carefully about the intersection between sex work and public health policies. In the context of the country's HIV/AIDS epidemic, the PRC has developed a comprehensive system of health policies designed to monitor rates of HIV/AIDS and reduce the spread of the disease, in which sex workers feature as prominent targets for interventions. These rules were designed in collaboration with the global public health community and are generally considered to align with international best practices.[169] Lastly, PRC lawmakers have developed official policies that allow the state to reap the financial benefits of an active sex industry. Keenly aware that the simultaneous pursuit of policies that prohibit prostitution and tax it sends a mixed message about the state's priorities, they have approached this task in two steps. They openly recognize the close ties that exist between prostitution and entertainment venues, and create rules designed to signal that they are eliminating sex work from these spaces. This approach paves the way for the state to tax entertainment venues and their employees.

This chapter examined the policies that tell the "official story" of how the Chinese state regulates prostitution. The lived experiences of the sex workers, health officials, and police officers who negotiate the boundaries of the law are at the heart of the remaining chapters of this book.

[169] Fan Lu et al., "Evolution of HIV/AIDS Policy," in *HIV/AIDS in China*.

PART II

SOCIETY

4

ON THE STREETS AND IN THE BROTHELS

INTRODUCTION

In China, selling sex in the lowest tier of prostitution is both difficult and dangerous. Women who do so solicit either on the streets or in small brothels located in apartments or in businesses that masquerade as hair salons or massage parlors. In all of these spaces, work conditions are grueling and take their toll on sex workers' health. The threat of violence and even death at the hands of clients, madams, and pimps looms large. The beliefs and attitudes of women who sell sex on the streets and in brothels reflect these challenging experiences. They are critical of prostitution and of themselves for engaging in it, and oppose proposals to legalize it. They also view the state with suspicion and do not feel comfortable seeking assistance from the police when doing so would reveal that they engage in prostitution. Within Chinese society, the lives of low-tier sex workers elicit both disgust and pity.

SETTING THE SCENE

On the Streets

Beijing's Xicheng Park is widely known as a place to solicit prostitution.[1] It is a small space – about half a square mile – tucked behind a subway station, with banks, hotels, and hospitals towering

[1] As noted in the introductory chapter, I use pseudonyms for specific locations within cities such as parks, and also for my informants.

over it. Both female and male sex workers loiter there at all times of day.[2] They share the space with retirees, who use it to practice *tai qi* and various dance routines. During my fieldwork, I talked to several women who frequently solicited sex work in the park. Xiao Huang from Hunan province is divorced, childless, and had been working in this park for four years.[3] Ling Ling was a farmer from rural Jiangsu province before coming to Beijing to work as a housekeeper. When that job fell through, a friend introduced her to the sex industry.[4] She is married, and her husband is a migrant worker in Shanghai. Su Yin was a farmer in Sichuan before moving to Beijing to support her two children and deadbeat husband back home – she characterized him as the "type of man who is completely dependent on his wife, failed to live up to expectations, and doesn't want to work."[5] Wen Ling has been married for twenty years, and has a nineteen-year-old son who is a sophomore in college in Beijing. She waited tables and cleaned houses for three years before losing those jobs and entering the sex trade.[6]

The women in Xicheng Park work independently, without pimps or madams. When a client solicits one of them, she first talks to him to get a sense of whether he seems dangerous. If not, they will either have sex in the park bushes, or go back to his or her home. These women estimate that their clients range in age from twenty to eighty. The sex workers are always on the lookout for undercover cops. If they think they see one, they start walking and try blending in with passersby. When Shu Li was soliciting in Xicheng Park one night, she witnessed the police arrest her friend who was having sex with a client, and later learned that they had incarcerated that friend for several months. The officers had invited a reporter to join them, and he was taking photos. Shu Li did not know whether the incident made it into the press.[7] Yet now, in addition to concerns about being arrested, the Xicheng Park sex workers fear public humiliation through the media.[8]

2 Despite sharing the same solicitation space, these two groups rarely interacted with each other. The female sex workers were scared and suspicious of the men, and uncomfortable at being in such close proximity to homosexuality.
3 Sex Worker Interview 6, August 20, 2009.
4 Sex Worker Interview 5, August 20, 2009.
5 Sex Worker Interview 4, August 20, 2009.
6 Sex Worker Interview 7, August 20, 2009.
7 I did not find any evidence that it did.
8 Sex Worker Interview 3, August 20, 2009.

In Brothels

Xiao Li works for Mei Jie, a madam who runs a brothel out of her apartment in Shenzhen. Xiao Li did not like studying and had bad grades, so after graduating from middle school in Sichuan, she decided to move to Shenzhen, following in her older brother's footsteps.[9] She arrived in 2007 and spent two years working in a factory. She found it too tiring, so she quit and returned to Sichuan to work as a waitress in a hot pot restaurant. When she returned to Shenzhen to visit her friends, one of them was selling sex and introduced her to Mei Jie. Xiao Li started to work for Mei Jie in August 2009, four months before I met her. Xiao Li did not tell me her age, but her graduation year suggests that she was probably sixteen or seventeen years old when I interviewed her. She prefers selling sex over working in a factory, saying that it is less tiring because of the time she has to rest between the six to fourteen clients she sees per day. These clients usually pay 150 yuan per transaction – 50 for Mei Jie, and 100 ($15) for herself, which is enough to cover her lunches from local restaurants for a week.

Mei Jie's brothel is located in the heart of Wanqin, one of Shenzhen's most active inner-city red-light districts. Although it is a fairly sleepy place during the day, it comes to life in the early evening. This is especially the case on weekends, when a wave of clients from nearby Hong Kong joins the ranks of local men wandering in and out of the karaoke bars, massage parlors, hair salons, and other venues that provide prostitution services in the neighborhood. The apartment where Mei Jie maintains a brothel is in a building in a narrow alleyway that often has sex workers soliciting on the street. It has six rooms – three bedrooms, a living room that doubles as a dining room, a kitchen, and a bathroom. The living room has two couches, a table, a small desk with a computer, and a bed set off behind a curtain. In between clients, Xiao Li and her two colleagues spend most of their time online at the computer. The living room also serves as their bedroom – the three of them sleep on the couches or the bed at night.

One of the bedrooms is Mei Jie's, which she shares with her husband, Lao Guo. They have an extremely tense relationship and frequently yell at each other. She accuses him of being a lazy partner who gambles away all her hard-won income (albeit earned from the sexual labor of others). In Mei Jie's defense, her husband does seem to spend most of his days sitting in their living room and watching television. On some

[9] Interview 186, November 5, 2009.

weekends and holidays, they share their bedroom with their seven-year-old son, Dou Dou. They send him to a private boarding school nearby in order to limit his exposure to the sex industry. Tuition there costs 10,000 yuan per semester ($1,600), a fact that she never ceases to reiterate to Dou Dou. Mei Jie wants Lao Guo to rent an apartment by the school so that he can live with Dou Dou and help him with his schoolwork, but Lao Guo does not want to. My heart goes out to this child. When I asked him how often he comes home, he choked up and through tears said that his parents only bring him home when they miss him, and that he only misses his mom, not his father. Although I do not know exactly how much he understands about what prostitution entails, he has at least some awareness of the phenomenon occurring in his midst. When Mei Jie and I were talking about where I might locate more sex workers to interview, Dou Dou piped in, eager to be helpful, and listed all sorts of places in the neighborhood where he knew they could be found. His mom became visibly flustered at what this display of knowledge said about the world to which she was exposing her son.

Children were a common part of the landscape in mom-and-pop brothels like Mei Jie's. At one such place in Xizhou, a neighborhood in outer Shenzhen, the owner's eight-year-old daughter picked up some of the American condoms in round packaging that I had brought with me as gifts to interviewees and asked me what they were. As I racked my brain to come up with an age-appropriate explanation of a condom in Chinese, one of my research assistants told her they were stickers. However, when she saw those wrapped in familiar square packaging, she triumphantly declared, "I know what *these* are! They're condoms!" (这个我知道是套子 – *Zhege wo zhidao shi taozi*).[10]

The second bedroom in Mei Jie's apartment is rented out to Yang Ge. He is essentially a permanent, residential client in the brothel. He comes in from his home in Hong Kong, lives in the apartment a few days each week, has his own key, and seems to have unlimited access to Mei Jie's girls. He appears to be an integral member of this odd community, frequently hanging out in the living room, and joining us out for lunches and dinners.

The third bedroom is for sexual transactions with all of the other clients who come to the apartment. I rarely interacted with them. Mei Jie asked me to stay behind the living room curtain divider when they

[10] Field notes, November 12, 2009.

came, so as not to startle them. They usually passed through quickly. I would hear them enter the apartment, choose a girl, have sex, exit the room to take a shower, go back in to get dressed, and leave. In one case, a new client came in and noticed me sitting behind the curtain. At first, he thought I was also a sex worker. When Mei Jie explained that I was a researcher, he sat down and started talking to me about himself, his wife, and his children, as though we were meeting at a dinner party rather than in a brothel where he had come to purchase sex.[11]

The police loom large in this world. In the early mornings, whenever I walked by the neighborhood police station, a handful of sex workers and clients were sitting behind its glass doors. I arrived at Mei Jie's one afternoon to find her all out of sorts: The police had stormed into two apartment brothels just a few doors down from hers the night before, and arrested the sex workers, clients, and madams. Later that day, one of those sex workers came by Mei Jie's apartment. She told us that she had been caught in the act, dragged into the room next door, and slapped and kicked in order to force her to admit to prostitution.[12]

These descriptions of Xicheng Park and Mei Jie's brothel highlight two important and related differences between the experiences of outdoor and indoor low-tier sex workers. First, streetwalkers usually have greater independence, as they tend not to have pimps or madams monitoring their lives. When women work in indoor spaces, they do so under the watchful eyes of gatekeepers.[13] Second, sex workers who solicit outside are more likely to find themselves in isolated situations, further away from colleagues and bosses who can keep tabs on them. When these differences matter in subsequent sections of this chapter, I highlight them. With the exception of the oldest and least-educated women discussed later in this chapter, women move easily back and forth between these outdoor and indoor spaces, and there is no clear hierarchy between them.[14] Shu Li's circumstances illustrate this: When I met her, she was a twenty-three-year-old streetwalker who also had experience working in several brothels masquerading as hair salons, but had settled on outdoor prostitution "because it is more free."[15] For the most part, sex workers experience similar conditions in these two

[11] Field Notes, November 2, 2009.
[12] Field Notes, November 7, 2009.
[13] Gatekeepers are individuals such as madams, pimps, and entertainment venue managers.
[14] In contrast, the boundaries between low-tier, middle-tier, and elite prostitution are relatively rigid, and there are clear status differences between each tier. Chapter 7 discusses this in greater depth.
[15] Sex Worker Interview 3, August 20, 2009.

spaces: They interact with clients for the briefest of moments, provide them with nothing but sex, and work in squalid conditions for a pittance.

AGE AND EDUCATION

The vulnerability of women who work in spaces such as Xicheng Park and Mei Jie's brothel is immediately apparent in their demographic characteristics. They are the oldest of sex workers and the least educated. As part of my research, I conducted a survey of 568 sex workers in Beijing.[16] The mean reported age of low-tier sex workers in the survey was thirty-three, with a range from nineteen to fifty-one years old. In contrast, the mean reported age of middle-tier sex workers was thirty with a range from seventeen to forty-six years old.[17] Women in the bottom tier of prostitution also start selling sex later on in life – at the age of thirty, in contrast to twenty-seven for hostesses.[18] The women of Xicheng Park illustrate this pattern. Xiao Huang was forty when I met her and had started selling sex when she was thirty-six.[19] Su Yin told me she was forty-two, but had the weathered appearance of a sixty-year-old and had been engaging in prostitution for the previous two years.[20] Wen Ling was forty-two years old.[21] Sex workers in the low tier also report fewer years of formal schooling than their hostess and mistress colleagues.[22] Within this lowest stratum of the sex industry, the oldest

[16] Please see the Appendix for more details about the survey.

[17] A t-test rejects the null hypothesis that the distributions of ages of low- and middle-tier sex workers are the same with a p-value of 0.001. Other studies consistently find comparable, if not larger, age differences. Xiang-Sheng Chen et al., "HIV Prevalence Varies between Female Sex Workers from Different Types of Venues in Southern China," *Sexually Transmitted Diseases* 39, no. 11 (November 2012): 868–70, https://doi.org/10.1097/OLQ.0b013e318264c3ba; Huso Yi et al., "A Profile of HIV Risk Factors in the Context of Sex Work Environments among Migrant Female Sex Workers in Beijing, China," *Psychology, Health & Medicine* 15, no. 2 (March 2010): 172–87, https://doi.org/10.1080/13548501003623914; Yanli Guo et al., "Risk Behaviours and Prevalences of HIV and Sexually Transmitted Infections among Female Sex Workers in Various Venues in Changzhou, China," *International Journal of STD & AIDS* 28, no. 11 (October 1, 2017): 1135–42, https://doi.org/10.1177/0956462416689763.

[18] A t-test rejects the null hypothesis that the distributions of ages at which low- and middle-tier sex workers started selling sex are the same with a p-value of 0.003.

[19] Sex Worker Interview 6, August 20, 2009.

[20] Sex Worker Interview 4, August 20, 2009.

[21] Sex Worker Interview 7, August 20, 2009.

[22] Yi et al., "A Profile of HIV Risk Factors in the Context of Sex Work Environments among Migrant Female Sex Workers in Beijing, China"; Yan Li et al., "Difference in Risk Behaviors and STD Prevalence between Street-Based and Establishment-Based FSWs in Guangdong Province, China," *AIDS and Behavior* 16, no. 4 (May 2012): 943–51, https://doi.org/10.1007/s10461-011-0102-0; Guo et al., "Risk Behaviours and Prevalences of HIV and Sexually Transmitted Infections among Female Sex Workers in Various Venues in Changzhou, China."

and least educated women are more likely to solicit outside on the streets than inside brothels: Such demographic characteristics make them unattractive candidates to pimps or madams who manage brothels, which means that in some cases, their only option is to work independently.

WORK

Work conditions for low-tier sex workers are difficult. They are paid the least, have the greatest number of clients, and are the most likely to experience abuse at the hands of clients and madams. The one positive aspect of their work environment pertains to how sex workers respond to these pressures: Their relationships to each other are characterized by support and solidarity rather than competition.

Numbers

Low-tier sex workers in my survey reported a monthly mode of three to five clients, with an average payment for their most recent sexual transaction of 424 yuan ($64), ranging from 0 to 1,000 yuan. For reasons tied to stigma, sex workers appear to underreport the number of clients they have and inflate their earnings.[23] My observation of women who work on the streets and in brothels suggests that in reality, they tend to have several clients a day rather than several a month, and are paid 30 to 300 yuan for sex. These are women who have sex with many more clients than hostesses and second wives. They are also paid much less. Surveyed middle-tier sex workers reported a monthly mode of one to two clients, and my ethnographic work suggested they might actually have closer to four or five clients a week. The average reported payment for their most recent sexual transaction was 648 yuan ($103), with a range from 0 to 3,000 yuan. My fieldwork suggested an average payment might actually be closer to 200 to 500 yuan.[24] Second wives receive at least several thousand yuan per month from their one exclusive client.[25]

[23] I discuss these reasons more fully in Chapter 7.

[24] These differences in earnings reported in the survey are statistically significant. A t-test rejects the null hypothesis that the distributions of reported payments by low- and middle-tier sex workers are the same with a p-value of 0.000.

[25] In general, sex work was the sole professional activity for most women in this study, regardless of their tier. They were not cobbling together income from a variety of different types of employment, or engaging in prostitution on an occasional basis in order to make ends meet. For instance, only one of the low-tier survey participants reported currently working in another

Abuse

Sex workers across all tiers of prostitution experience workplace abuse, which can happen at the hands of clients, madams, and pimps.[26] Yet women in the low tier are particularly vulnerable to mistreatment. Their low levels of income limit their ability to refuse any opportunity to sell sex, and their high numbers of clients increase their exposure to dangerous situations. In addition, those who work independently on the streets do not benefit from the protection that gatekeepers can provide.

Shu Li once went home with a client who locked her up in his apartment for several hours after he did not ejaculate when they had sex and refused to pay her.[27] Wen Ling once had a client who tied her up back-to-back with another sex worker, both naked, and attached bells to their nipples with clips.[28] A client drove Li Ting to a desolate forest outside of Beijing. He raped her and stole her rings, cell phone, and camera. In an odd show of sympathy, he returned Li Ting's keys to her before abandoning her, expressing concern about how she would get back into her house. "I was so scared that for one week I didn't leave my house, and my whole entire body wouldn't stop shaking," she recollected.[29] Fei Wen was once working in a massage parlor brothel when a client beat up a colleague of hers in the back room, raped her, and paid her in counterfeit money before leaving. Although she heard the noise, she did not intervene, thinking the man had asked her friend to participate in sexual role play.[30] Ming Jia's friend went home with a client who tried to rob her. She escaped onto his balcony. He grabbed a knife, smashed through the glass door leading to the balcony, and stabbed her multiple times. She jumped off the balcony and survived the fall with only a broken leg.[31] Xiu Mei described multiple encounters with clients who beat her and left without paying.[32]

industry, as a (legitimate) hair dresser. Similarly, the surveyed women working in karaoke venues rarely worked in other fields. Two of them cut hair. One was a student. Two worked in an office. Fifteen worked in small shops.

26 The descriptions of abuse in this section beg the question of whether sex workers report these types of experiences to the police, which I touch upon in a subsequent section of this chapter, "Views of the State." Chapters 8 and 9 also address interactions between sex workers and the police.

27 Sex Worker Interview 3, August 20, 2009.

28 Sex Worker Interview 7, August 20, 2009.

29 Sex Worker Interview 2, August 24, 2009.

30 Sex Worker Interview 3, August 24, 2009.

31 Sex Worker Interview 4, August 24, 2009.

32 Sex Worker Interview 5, August 24, 2009.

Although madams and pimps can protect sex workers from some abusive clients,[33] they can also harm the women under their care and control. Ming Jia described a brothel in her neighborhood where the pimp brought in several young girls from his hometown and kept them under his strict control, forcing them to work from 9 AM until midnight every day.[34] Xiu Mei described a similar practice, where women who spend their days under the complete control of madams and pimps who yell and beat them are completely helpless: "They are in a new environment, they don't know anything, they can't do anything, and they have no place to go."[35]

Jia Qing's testimony also illustrates this type of experience.[36] She is from Hebei province. She stopped attending school after sixth grade and worked in the fields. After her parents divorced, she lived with her father, stepmother, and stepsister. Her stepmother did not like her and would frequently forbid her from socializing with other people. When Jia Qing was fifteen, she decided to run away. She joined Xiao Xue, a nineteen-year-old acquaintance, and Xiao Xue's boyfriend in Shijiazhuang, the capital of Hebei. Xiao Xue told Jia Qing that they could find work for her in a restaurant that would also feed and house her. She trusted Xiao Xue because their mothers had been close friends. When Xiao Xue brought her to Shijiazhuang, however, things took a turn for the worse. Instead of setting Jia Qing up with a legitimate job at a restaurant, Xiao Xue brought her to work in a brothel. Jia Qing was not given a proper living space and had to sleep on the floor of the brothel. Xiao Xue also denied Jia Qing proper food – giving her just one steamed bun (馒头 – *mantou*) per day. If she tried to eat more than one, Xiao Xue and her boyfriend would get really angry. As Jia Qing told me her story, her hatred toward Xiao Xue was palpable. She would pause every few sentences, and repeat: "Xiao Xue was so horrible to us" (小雪对我们特别差 – *Xiao Xue dui women tebie cha*). When Xiao Xue and her boyfriend told Jia Qing she would have to sell sex, she tried to escape, but could not. They beat her and broke her nose. When she

33 For instance, they can turn away clients or intervene to assist a sex worker whom a client is mistreating. Huso Yi et al., "Occupational Safety and HIV Risk among Female Sex Workers in China: A Mixed-Methods Analysis of Sex-Work Harms and Mommies," *Global Public Health* 7, no. 8 (2012): 840–55, https://doi.org/10.1080/17441692.2012.662991.

34 Sex Worker Interview 4, August 24, 2009.

35 Sex Worker Interview 5, August 24, 2009.

36 When I met Jia Qing, she was working as a hostess in a middle-tier venue. As I discuss in Chapter 7, there is limited movement across tiers. Yet as Jia Qing was initially forced into prostitution, her trajectory differs from that of her peers with more agency.

started selling sex, they took all her earnings. She thought about going to the police, but Xiao Xue preempted her. "Go ahead, give them a call, report [it] to the police. You're a sex worker. They'll also arrest you," recounted Jia Qing. Xiao Xue also said that she had told everyone in their home village that Jia Qing was now "working as a whore" (做妓女 – *zuo jinü*), and that everyone was "cursing her for being a whore" (都骂我是妓女 – *dou ma wo shi jinü*). Jia Qing eventually did escape, and when I interviewed her she was working in a karaoke venue in Beijing.[37] She has never dared to return to her hometown.

Of course, madams and pimps in the middle tier of the sex industry can also abuse the women under their control. Yet it is indoor sex workers in the low tier who are the most vulnerable. The brothels where they work are small and most often controlled by one madam or pimp. In contrast, middle-tier entertainment venues usually have several madams working with different groups of sex workers. This arrangement can protect women from the most egregious types of abuse, as madams are more likely to refrain from extreme behavior knowing that other gatekeepers could intervene and potentially lure dissatisfied sex workers into their fold.

Low-tier sex workers are also targets for murder. In Zhengti, the town where I shadowed law enforcement officers, the police told me about a murder case against a pimp who ran a brothel with six sex workers. He kept them under horrific conditions, with one woman even starving to death. In order to hide the body, the pimp chopped it up into pieces that he threw away in the trash. Someone came across the woman's arm and reported it to the police. The police already had the woman's fingerprints on record from a previous minor encounter with law enforcement, which allowed them to identify her, find out where she had worked, trace the crime back to the pimp, and free the other women.[38] Middle-tier sex workers can also become murder victims – a client stabbed the twenty-three-year-old hostess friend of one informant to death.[39] Yet it is women in the lowest tier who are most at risk.

Solidarity

While work conditions on the streets and in small brothels are extremely challenging, the main positive aspect of selling sex in the

[37] Sex Worker Interview 5, August 22, 2009.

[38] Field Notes, August 5, 2009. Field Notes, August 7, 2009. Field Notes, August 10, 2009.

[39] Sex Worker Interview 1, August 26, 2009. Other informants also shared sex worker murder stories. Interview 173, September 4, 2009. Interview 66, April 17, 2009.

low tier of prostitution is the solidarity and support that exists between the women. The sex workers in Xicheng Park described a dynamic where they watch out for one another, share information about perverted (变态 – *biantai*) or dangerous clients, and warn each other when the police come.[40] Shu Li described a situation where she got into a car with a client. As they drove away, her friend called her and warned her that a police car was following them. When she asked the client to let her out, he refused, so she opened the door while the car was moving to escape. He tried pulling her back in, telling her that he was a police officer, but she managed to free herself from his grasp and get away.[41] Fei Wen described how she would take newcomers under her wing and give them advice on how to avoid being arrested by the police.[42] The camaraderie between the women working for Mei Jie was similarly palpable. Instead of treating each other as competitors vying for the preferential attention of clients or Mei Jie, these women were close friends who spent all of their free time together, walking around the neighborhood arm in arm, or surfing the internet to stay up-to-date on the personal lives of various Chinese pop stars. Women in the low tier of the sex industry experience the most extreme work conditions, and this shared adversity may serve to foster supportive and close relationships. This dynamic contrasts sharply with the competition that characterizes interactions among middle-tier hostesses, a difference explored further in Chapter 5.

HEALTH

Low-tier sex workers' older age, lower education levels, and challenging work conditions are often linked to negative health outcomes. They are less likely to care for their health and know less about HIV/AIDS than their higher-status colleagues. These differences translate into higher rates of HIV/AIDS for women in this category of prostitution.

Women in the low tier of sex work are less likely to have regular health checkups. Of the surveyed women in the lower tier, only 53 percent had received a checkup in the past year. In contrast, 67 percent of women in the middle tier had done so.[43] Of the respondents who had

40 Sex Worker Interview 4, August 24, 2009.
41 Sex Worker Interview 3, August 20, 2009.
42 Sex Worker Interview 3, August 24, 2009.
43 A two tailed *t*-test is significant with a *p*-value of 0.08. A Mann–Whitney rank sum test is significant with a *p*-value of 0.08.

received at least one checkup, those in the low tier had fewer, on average, than their middle-tier colleagues (1.3 in the past year versus 1.6).[44] Sex workers sometimes avoid state-certified medical services because they are afraid of incurring sanctions for engaging in prostitution.[45] They do have access to underground healthcare clinics, however, many of which provide services in red-light districts. Staff at these clinics provide questionable care. For example, Xiao Li quoted one doctor at a clinic who told her that as long as she washed herself with a specific product after sex, she could safely have intercourse without a condom. He also explained to her that she could avoid HIV/AIDS infection by learning to recognize the visual signs that a client has a sexually transmitted disease (STD).

Low-tier sex workers are also less likely to get tested for HIV/AIDS than their counterparts in other tiers of prostitution.[46] In my sex worker survey, 22 percent of women in the low tier reported having been tested for HIV/AIDS, in contrast to 26 percent for hostesses. These differences are substantively small and not statistically significant.[47] However, I also conducted a field experiment that demonstrated surveyed women in the low tier were less willing to get an HIV/AIDS test than women in the middle tier. As shown in Figure 4.1, when provided with the opportunity to receive a token gift (worth $1) after receiving a free HIV/AIDS test, women in the low tier were barely responsive to it.[48]

While only 26 percent of women in the low tier requested an HIV/AIDS test in response to the promise of receiving the gift, a full 60 percent of women in the middle tier of the sex industry did so.[49]

Women who sell sex on the streets and in brothels are also the group that is least knowledgeable about HIV/AIDS. In my survey, 92 percent of sex workers in the low tier had heard of HIV/AIDS, versus 99 percent

[44] Neither a *t*-test nor a Mann–Whitney test of this difference is statistically significant.

[45] I elaborate on this point in the "Views of the State" section later in the chapter. See also Margaret Boittin, "Using Incentives to Increase HIV/AIDS Testing by Sex Workers: Evidence from a Randomized Field Experiment in China," *Law & Policy* 40, no. 4 (2018): 398–402, https://doi.org/10.1111/lapo.12114.

[46] Yi et al., "A Profile of HIV Risk Factors in the Context of Sex Work Environments among Migrant Female Sex Workers in Beijing, China"; Susanne Y. P. Choi and Eleanor Holroyd, "The Influence of Power, Poverty and Agency in the Negotiation of Condom Use for Female Sex Workers in Mainland China," *Culture, Health & Sexuality* 9, no. 5 (2007): 489–503; The Global Fund, "The Global Fund to Fight AIDS, Tuberculosis and Malaria Sixth Call for Proposals Guidelines," 2006; Yan Hong et al., "HIV Testing Behaviors among Female Sex Workers in Southwest China," *AIDS and Behavior* 16, no. 1 (January 2012): 44–52, https://doi.org/10.1007/s10461-011-9960-8.

[47] Neither a *t*-test nor a Mann–Whitney test of this difference is statistically significant.

[48] Boittin, "Using Incentives to Increase HIV/AIDS Testing by Sex Workers."

[49] Boittin.

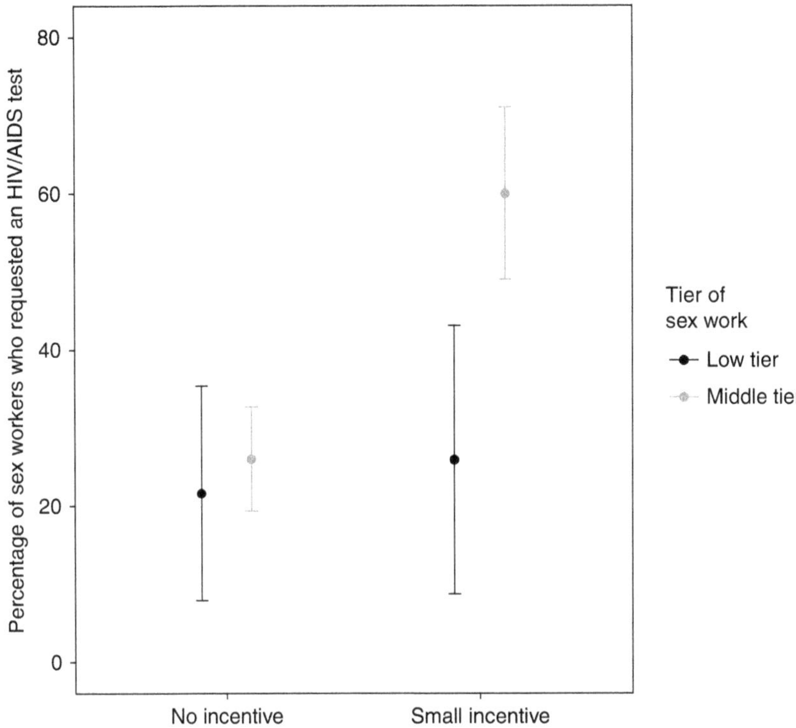

Figure 4.1 Low-tier sex workers barely respond to small incentive for HIV/AIDS test

in the middle tier.[50] Although these rates of general knowledge are high, they do not appear to translate into behavior that systematically protects low-tier sex workers from HIV/AIDS infection. When Xiao Huang feels like a client is unhealthy, she asks him to wear a condom, unless he is a repeat customer.[51] Wen Ling makes this decision based on whether or not a client's genitals look diseased.[52] When Shu Li's clients refuse to wear a condom, she will wash herself after sex.[53] Some women lack even the most basic safe-sex knowledge: Despite being married, Su Yin had never even heard of condoms before coming to Beijing – intrauterine devices were the only contraceptive method she had been exposed to in her rural hometown.[54] Xiao Li charges an additional

[50] These differences are statistically significant.
[51] Sex Worker Interview 6, August 20, 2009.
[52] Sex Worker Interview 7, August 20, 2009.
[53] Sex Worker Interview 3, August 20, 2009.
[54] Sex Worker Interview 4, August 20, 2009.

"rinse fee" (冲洗费 – *chongxi fei*) of 30–50 yuan ($5–$8) for clients who do not want to wear a condom – she uses the money to purchase the product she learned about at the underground clinic. Her madam, Mei Jie, appears similarly uninformed (or perhaps simply uninterested in prioritizing the health of her sex workers). When I provided Xiao Li with a voucher for a free health checkup at a legitimate local hospital, which included an optional HIV test, Mei Jie grabbed it from her. "I'll take that," she declared. "Young girls don't need to see the doctor. This is for old women like me."[55]

Unsurprisingly, these unsafe behaviors and low levels of knowledge appear to result in higher rates of HIV/AIDS infection for low-tier sex workers.[56] The range of infection rates varies significantly across studies. For example, a study conducted in six cities in southern China found an HIV prevalence rate of 1.37 percent for streetwalkers and 0.07 percent for middle-tier sex workers in karaoke venues.[57] In the Yunnan province city of Kaiyuan, researchers found an HIV infection rate of 25.8 percent for streetwalkers and 5.9 percent for hostesses. Even with these variations across China's provinces, researchers consistently identify higher infection rates for women who solicit in low-tier spaces.

PERSPECTIVES ON PROSTITUTION

The strenuous work environment and its effects on the health of sex workers shape the attitudes of women in the low tier. In comparison to their middle-tier and elite colleagues, these individuals are most critical of both prostitution in general and of themselves for engaging in it.

Low-tier sex workers have the most negative views of prostitution. As shown in Figure 4.2, women from my survey who sell sex on the streets and in brothels are more likely to consider prostitution as harmful (不利 – *buli*), rather than beneficial (有利 – *youli*), for both themselves and their clients.

55 Interview 188, November 5, 2009.

56 Haibo Wang et al., "Prevalence and Predictors of HIV Infection among Female Sex Workers in Kaiyuan City, Yunnan Province, China," *International Journal of Infectious Diseases* 13, no. 2 (2009): 162–69; Xiangsheng Chen, Yue-Ping Yin, and Ning Jiang, "Was the HIV Infection Burden in Female Sex Workers in China Overestimated?," *The Lancet Infectious Diseases* 13, no. 1 (2013): 13, https://doi.org/10.1016/S1473-3099(12)70298-0; Chen et al., "HIV Prevalence Varies between Female Sex Workers from Different Types of Venues in Southern China"; Bang-Yong Zhu et al., "Epidemiology of Sexually Transmitted Infections, HIV, and Related High-Risk Behaviors among Female Sex Workers in Guangxi Autonomous Region, China," *Japanese Journal of Infectious Diseases* 65, no. 1 (2012): 75–78.

57 Chen et al., "HIV Prevalence Varies between Female Sex Workers from Different Types of Venues in Southern China."

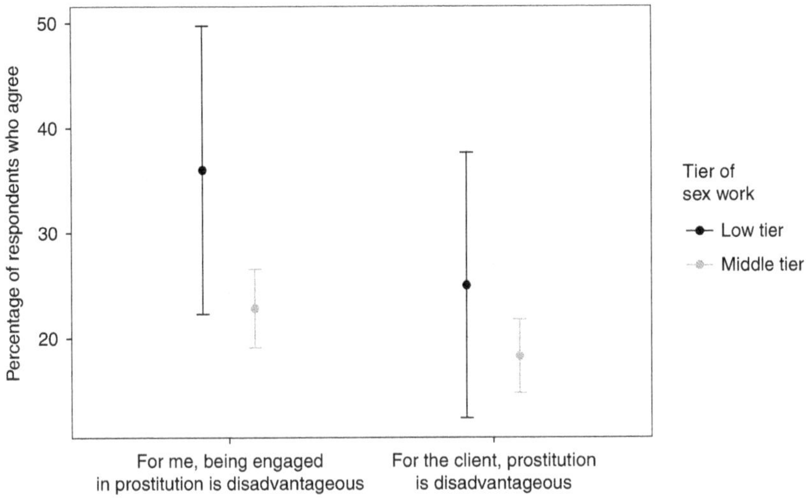

Figure 4.2 Low-tier sex workers view prostitution as more harmful than hostesses do

While 36 percent of low-tier survey respondents consider that prostitution is more harmful than beneficial to themselves, only 23 percent of hostesses hold such beliefs.[58] Similarly, while 25 percent of surveyed streetwalkers and women working in brothels emphasize the disadvantages of prostitution over its benefits for clients, only 18 percent of women in the middle tier espouse such beliefs.[59] These tier-based differences around perspectives on clients extend to how respondents think about their own husbands. While only 15 percent of women in the low tier claimed that they would accept it if their husband solicited a sex worker (可以接受 – *keyi jieshou*), a full 30 percent of hostesses stated that they would accept such behavior.[60] When presented with this question, a woman who sells sex on the street or in a brothel is likely thinking only about how she would feel if her husband purchased sex. In contrast, a hostess might be thinking more broadly about the other services she provides – singing, dancing, and drinking. This difference might contribute to understanding the greater expression of opposition of women in the low tier.

[58] The *t*-test is significant with a *p*-value of 0.04. The Mann–Whitney test is significant with a *p*-value of 0.04.

[59] A *t*-test is not significant with a *p*-value of 0.26. The Mann–Whitney test is not significant with a *p*-value of 0.26.

[60] The *t*-test is significant with a *p*-value of 0.02. The Mann–Whitney test is significant with a *p*-value of 0.02.

For streetwalkers and brothel sex workers, criticisms of prostitution extend to their own engagement in it. These women are most likely to blame themselves for selling sex and not having skills that would allow them to engage in more reputable work. Xiao Fen attributed her engagement in prostitution to her poor study habits in school. She explained that her grades were bad because she did not like to work, so she failed out of school and thus did not receive training that would have allowed her to seek employment in another sector.[61] Ming Jia similarly held herself accountable for her circumstances: "People such as myself who are in this class (阶层 – *jieceng*), we're uneducated (没有文化 – *meiyou wenhua*), we don't have any skills. The only thing we can do is sell sex behind closed doors."[62] Several women expressed responsibility for their actions by emphasizing their active decision to go down the "path" (路 – *lu*) of prostitution. "I went down this path because there was nothing else I could do . . . I have no other skills," explained Su Yin.[63] Ling Ling concurred: "When I had just arrived in Beijing, there wasn't anything else for me to do, so I took this path."[64] Li Ting more bluntly emphasized her actions as erroneous: "I don't have any other abilities, which is why I went down this wrong path (走错路 – *zou cuolu*)."[65] It can be heart-wrenching to hear these sex workers blame themselves. Xiu Mei, for example, explained, "In doing this, I feel like I've really let myself sink to the bottom. I feel so terrible."[66] Such self-loathing is widespread in this tier of prostitution and is often accompanied by total resignation. Su Yin declared that "Ever since I was young, I was destined to a life of misery."[67] Ling Ling had given up on caring for her health because in her words, "If there's a problem, I don't care" (如果有问题, 也无所谓 – *ruguo you wenti, ye wusuowei*).[68]

VIEWS OF THE STATE

Low-tier sex workers' negative perspectives on prostitution and on themselves carry over to their overall attitudes toward the state, as women in this tier of the sex industry are both most critical and least

[61] Sex Worker Interview 2, May 11, 2009.
[62] Sex Worker Interview 4, August 24, 2009.
[63] Sex Worker Interview 4, August 20, 2009.
[64] Sex Worker Interview 5, August 20, 2009.
[65] Sex Worker Interview 2, August 24, 2009.
[66] Sex Worker Interview 5, August 24, 2009.
[67] Sex Worker Interview 4, August 20, 2009.
[68] Sex Worker Interview 5, August 24, 2009.

trusting of the state. They also display the greatest level of knowledge of the legal regime that governs prostitution in China and are the most opposed to legalization proposals. These bleaker attitudes reflect the harsher experiences that women who solicit on the streets and in brothels have when they interact with the state, which are discussed in Part III of this book.

Distrust of the Government and the Police

Sex workers in the low tier express more skepticism toward the state than women in other tiers do. As displayed in Figure 4.3, women in the low tier from my survey have lower levels of trust in the central government, local government, and the police than middle-tier hostesses have.

On average, trust in the central government is 9 percentage points lower for women in the low tier, trust in the local government is 11 percentage points lower, and trust in the police is 8 percentage points lower.[69] In conversations, streetwalkers and brothel workers

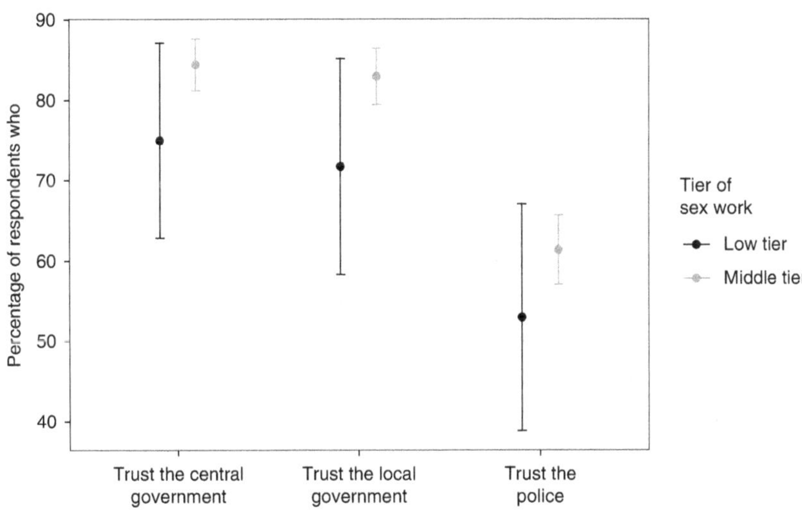

Figure 4.3 Low-tier sex workers have lower levels of trust in the state than hostesses have

[69] For trust in the central government, the *t*-test is significant with a *p*-value of 0.08. The Mann–Whitney test is significant with a *p*-value of 0.08. For trust in the local government, the *t*-test is significant with a *p*-value of 0.06, and the Mann–Whitney test is significant with a *p*-value of 0.06. Trust in the police is not statistically significant ($p = 0.24$), though the 8 percentage point difference is substantively significant. In addition, if I do not collapse the answer scale into

frequently expressed visceral fear and hatred toward the police. Mei Mei explained how she "trusts all sorts of different people, but not the police. The police are the worst crooks out there (警察是骗子的骗子 – *jingcha shi pianzi de pianzi*)."[70] Shu Li told me she "despises" (恨 – *hen*) them.[71] Ling Ling described feeling "terrified" (害怕 – *haipa*) when she sees them.[72] Mei Mei and Li Ting characterized them as "fierce" (凶 – *xiong*) and "extremely unreasonable" (变态 – *biantai*).[73]

Sex workers in the low tier also signal distrust of the police through their greater stated reticence toward seeking police assistance if a client were to commit a crime against them. Women in the low tier repeatedly said that they "dare not" (不敢 – *bugan*), "cannot" (不能 – *buneng*), or "will not" (不会 – *buhui*) report clients' violence against them to the police.[74] Figure 4.4 shows how sex workers would respond to being robbed by a client or being raped by one.

There is an 18 percentage point difference between the willingness of a low-tier sex worker to report being robbed by a client (64 percent) versus a middle-tier hostess (82 percent).[75] Similarly, 67 percent of women in the low tier state that they would report being raped by a client, in contrast to 81 percent of hostesses.[76] If a woman who solicits on the streets or in brothels reports these types of crimes to the police, she automatically reveals her own status as a lawbreaker and thus increases

"trust" and "not trust" (it is collapsed in Figure 4.3, with "trust" including "trust a lot" and "trust" and "not trust" including "not really trust" and "not trust at all"), the *p*-value is significant (0.06 for the *t*-test and the Mann–Whitney test).

70 Sex Worker Interview 1, August 24, 2009.

71 Sex Worker Interview 3, August 20, 2009.

72 Sex Worker Interview 5, August 20, 2009.

73 Sex Worker Interview 1, August 24, 2009. Sex Worker Interview 2, August 24, 2009. The word "变态" is used frequently in China and can take on a number of different meanings, generally referring to something out of the ordinary. Earlier on, when a sex worker used it to describe a client, I translated it as "perverted," as it likely referred to specific sexual demands a client made of a sex worker that she perceived of as not normal. Here, used to describe the police, it does not refer to sexual demands, but rather actions that she perceives to be beyond the scope of regular police behavior.

74 Sex Worker Interview 3, August 20, 2009; Sex Worker Interview 4, August 20, 2009; Sex Worker Interview 5, August 20, 2009; Sex Worker Interview 7, August 20, 2009; Sex Worker Interview 2, August 24, 2009.

75 Both the *t*-test and the Mann–Whitney test are significant with a *p*-value of 0.002.

76 Both the *t*-test and the Mann–Whitney test are significant with a *p*-value of 0.01. The high overall percentages of respondents in both tiers of prostitution who expressed a willingness to report to the police if they were robbed or raped by a client may be due to the hypothetical nature of these questions. In reality, the percentage of sex workers who actually report being victims of such crimes is likely much lower. My focus here is not on the overall percentages, but rather on the differences in responses between women in the low tier and the middle tier. Across tiers, the differences between how sex workers respond to hypotheticals versus how they actually behave should remain constant.

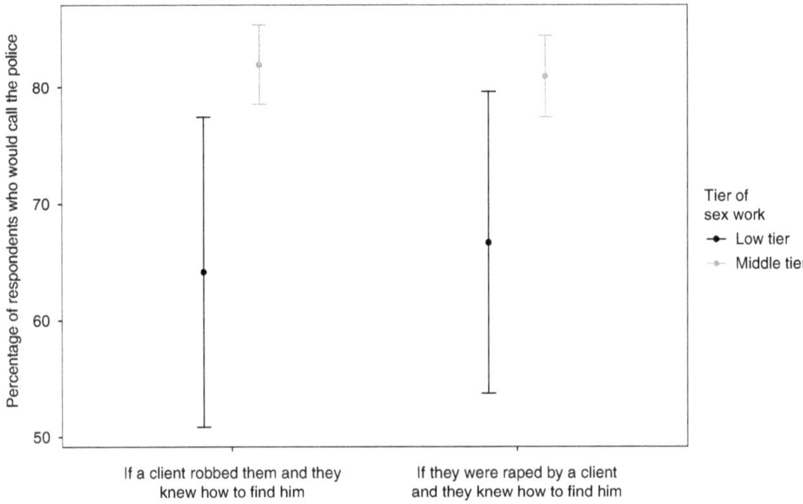

Figure 4.4 Low-tier sex workers express less willingness than hostesses to seek police assistance with crimes committed by clients

her own risk of arrest for engaging in prostitution. By contrast, a hostess can report such crimes and claim that she was engaging in legal activities, such as drinking, singing, and dancing. This potential cover story may explain the greater willingness of women in the middle tier to say that they would reach out to the police in these circumstances. In fact, when presented with hypothetical harms that do not place a sex worker in the context of her engagement in prostitution, these tier-based differences disappear. As shown in Figure 4.5, low- and middle-tier sex workers from my survey are equally likely to claim that they would report harm that does not necessarily expose their involvement in prostitution.

When presented with a hypothetical conflict with neighbors that they could not resolve on their own, 81 percent of low-tier sex workers and 83 percent of middle-tier hostesses expressed willingness to call the police. Similarly, about 80 percent of sex workers (76 percent in the low tier and 81 percent in the middle tier) said they would report being robbed to the police – in this hypothetical, the criminal was not identified as a client. Willingness to report was highest in response to a scenario where the respondent's valuables were stolen, with 93 percent of sex workers (94 percent in the low tier and 93 percent in the middle tier) stating that they would seek out police assistance in this case.[77]

[77] There are no tier-based statistically significant differences for these three variables.

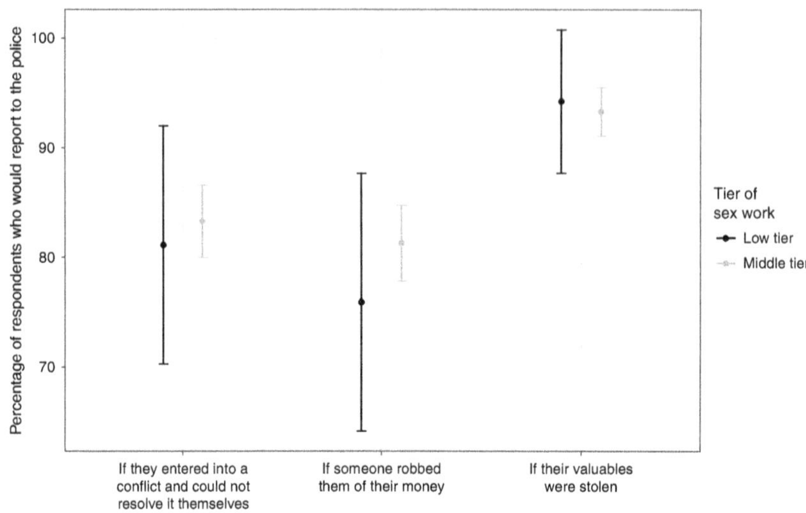

Figure 4.5 Low-tier sex workers and hostesses are equally likely to report harm unrelated to prostitution

Greater disengagement from politics accompanies these lower levels of trust in the state. Figure 4.6 shows that women who work on the streets and in brothels are less likely to believe that politics is important or express an interest in it.

While 77 percent of hostesses believe in the importance of politics, only 55 percent of women in the low tier do.[78] While 67 percent of women in the middle tier are interested in politics, only 50 percent of streetwalkers and women in brothels are.[79]

This greater distrust of the state has important implications for the health outcomes discussed earlier in this chapter: Lower rates of health checkups and HIV/AIDS testing among women in the low tier appear connected to fears that interactions with state health officials might result in an actual arrest for prostitution. Li Ting mentioned how "Every time I go get tested . . . I worry that the hospital worker will know that I am a sex worker . . . and report me to the police."[80] Xiu Mei echoed a similar concern: "I don't want any trouble . . . Sometimes I don't feel good, but I am not willing to get tested. It's because I'm

[78] Both the *t*-test and the Mann–Whitney test are significant with a *p*-value of 0.0005.

[79] These differences are significant with both the *t*-test and the Mann–Whitney test having a *p*-value of 0.01.

[80] Sex Worker Interview 2, August 24, 2009.

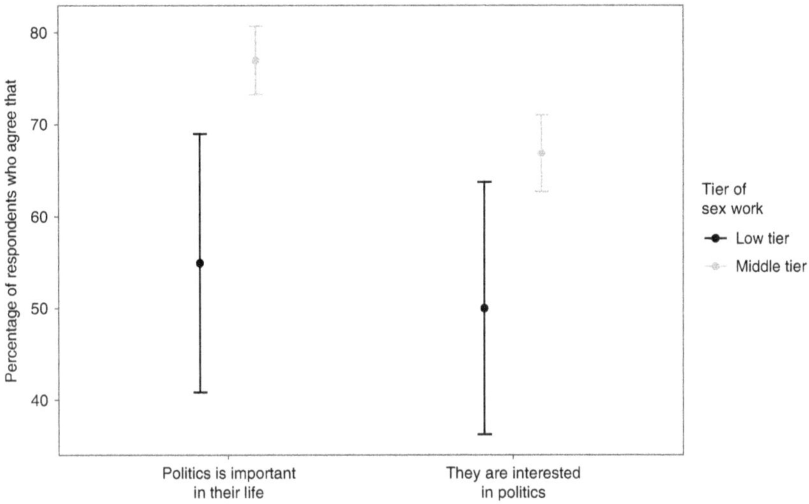

Figure 4.6 Low-tier sex workers are less engaged in politics than hostesses

scared to get tested, if they find out I am a sex worker."[81] While underground health clinics are popular among sex workers for this reason, HIV/AIDS testing in China is generally available only at official state health institutions. Research on individuals in the United States who have broken the law finds that they often shy away from any involvement with the state.[82] Rather than avoid only those agencies and institutions they have directly interacted with in the past, they also avoid other institutions that could provide them with much-needed access to healthcare, education, or other social services. The most oppressed and marginalized of sex workers in China appear to behave similarly: In response to fears of the police, they also stay away from agencies that could provide them with healthcare.

Views on Prostitution Policies

Low-tier sex workers' more negative experiences with prostitution also shape their knowledge of and attitudes toward prostitution policies.

[81] Sex Worker Interview 5, August 24, 2009.

[82] Vesla M. Weaver and Amy E. Lerman, "Political Consequences of the Carceral State," *American Political Science Review* 104, no. 4 (2010); Alice Goffman, "On the Run: Wanted Men in a Philadelphia Ghetto," *American Sociological Review* 74, no. 3 (2009); Alice Goffman, *On the Run: Fugitive Life in an American City* (Chicago: University of Chicago Press, 2014); Dina R. Rose and Todd R. Clear, "Incarceration, Social Capital, and Crime: Implications for Social Disorganization Theory," *Criminology* 36, no. 3 (1998): 441–480.

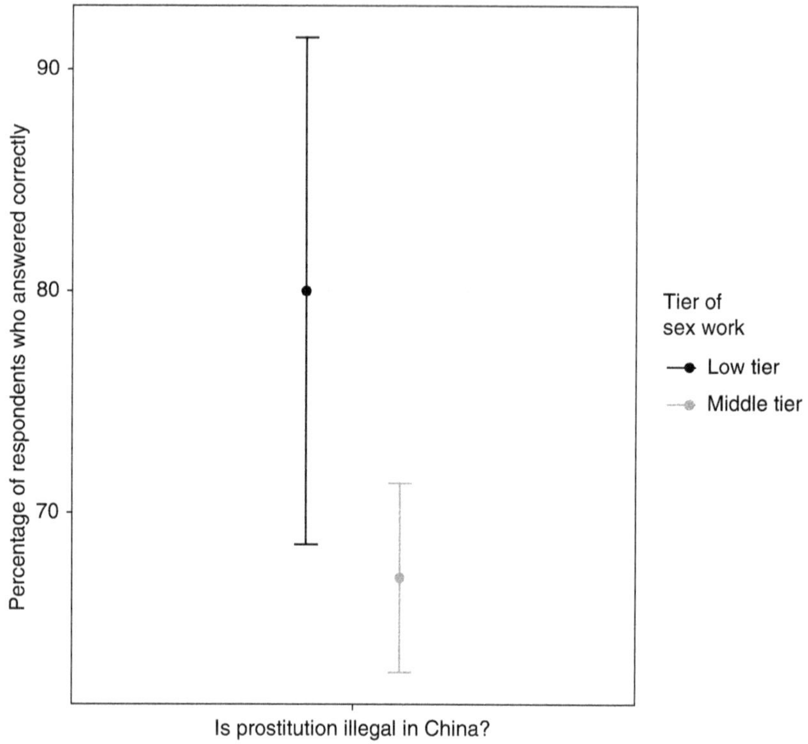

Figure 4.7 Low-tier sex workers have more knowledge of legal status of prostitution than hostesses have

These women are both more likely to know that prostitution is against the law and more likely to oppose a policy that would legalize it. As displayed in Figure 4.7, low-tier sex workers in my survey are 13 percentage points more likely to correctly identify that prostitution is against the law.

While 80 percent of surveyed women in the lowest tier of prostitution know that sex work is illegal, only 67 percent of middle-tier hostesses do.[83] This difference in legal knowledge also came through in the details that the women shared in interviews, where those in the low tier expressed more knowledge – and less misinformation – about sequencing, amounts, and lengths of different types of punishments, as well as the types of evidence required by law to prove that prostitution has

[83] These differences are statistically significant. The p-value for the t-test and the Mann–Whitney test is 0.06.

occurred. For instance, Su Yin underscored how, legally, police are only able to make an arrest for prostitution if they "catch participants in the act, in which case we can be fined several thousand yuan and incarcerated for half a year."[84] Wen Ling also rattled off the various possible punishments, and then noted, "If they have not caught you in the act, then whatever you do, just don't let them force you to admit [that you sell sex]."[85] Middle-tier sex workers whom I interviewed lacked such detailed knowledge of sanctions for selling sex and appropriate arrest procedures, and occasionally told me that prostitution is legal in China.[86] These differences are likely tied to the increased risks of arrest that women face when they solicit on the streets and in brothels, which makes the legal status of prostitution more salient in their lives.[87]

Sex workers in the low tier also express greater opposition to the legalization of prostitution than women in the middle tier. Figure 4.8 displays these differences.

In the low tier, 57 percent of sex workers in my survey support legalizing sex work. In contrast, a full 80 percent of hostesses do so.[88] Women in the low tier were more likely to express opinions such as "The government should not permit prostitution," and "If I were a government leader, I would not allow prostitution to occur."[89] These lower levels of support among women who solicit on the streets and in brothels appear to be tied to the greater harm that they experience as sex workers. For these women, prostitution is synonymous with the harsh working conditions, violence, and abuse they have encountered when selling sex. Women in the low tier view the idea that sex work could occur in ways that are respectful and healthy as either an abstract notion far removed from their daily lives or an outright impossibility. They reject the legalization of prostitution because such a policy would signal state approval of the phenomenon and official endorsement of the harm it causes. In their opinion, sex work should be illegal because it is inevitably detrimental to the women who engage in it.

[84] Sex Worker Interview 4, August 20, 2009.
[85] Sex Worker Interview 7, August 20, 2009.
[86] Sex Worker Interview 5, August 18, 2009; Sex Worker Interview 1, August 23, 2009.
[87] Chapters 8 and 9 on the policing of prostitution address this point further.
[88] These results include only those survey respondents who were in the control group ($N = 93$) for an endorsement experiment that treated individuals with different prompts about the legalization of prostitution. These differences are not statistically significant. The p-value for the t-test and the Mann–Whitney is 0.51. That said, the 13 percentage point difference is substantively significant. In addition, if instead of collapsing the answer scale into "support" and "oppose," as is done here, I conduct the analysis using the answer scale without collapsing the response scale, the p-value is significant (0.06 for the t-test and the Mann–Whitney test).
[89] Sex Worker Interview 4, August 20, 2009. Sex Worker Interview 4, August 24, 2009.

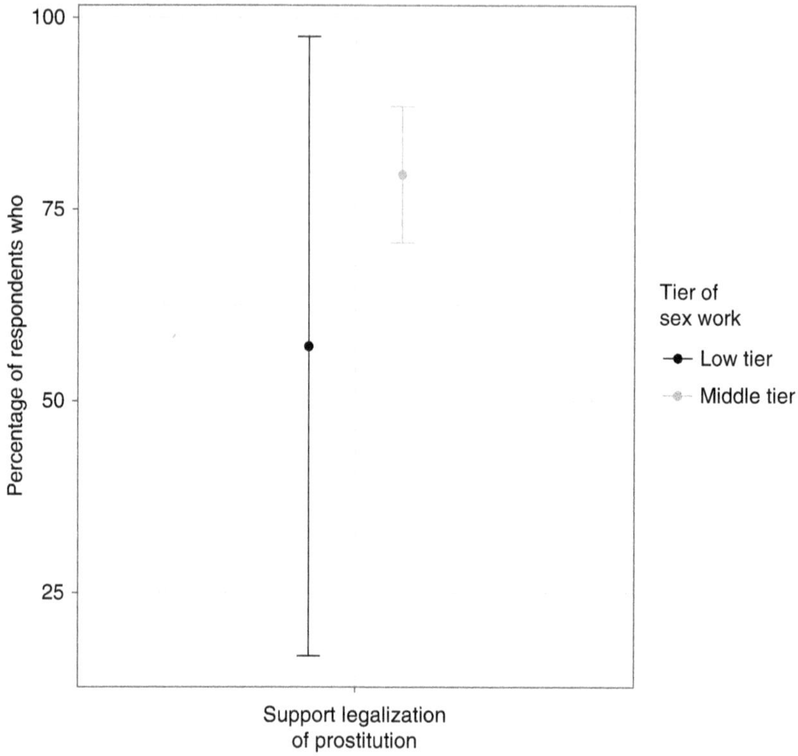

Figure 4.8 Low-tier sex workers are more opposed to legalizing prostitution than hostesses are

OUTSIDERS' PERSPECTIVES

Public opinion in China toward sex workers who solicit on the streets and in brothels alternates between disgust and pity.[90] Disgust is rooted in the perception that low-tier sex workers are engaging in the crudest type of prostitution: They sell sex in exchange for money, without providing other types of services

[90] I use the terms "public opinion" and "general public" to describe the overall tenor of narratives tied to low-tier sex workers in Chinese society as a whole. Ideally, this type of discussion would include a general population survey that inquires specifically about attitudes toward different types of sex workers. The World Values Survey includes a question that asks whether prostitution is ever justified and, in China in 2018, 82.5 percent of respondents said that it was never justified. Yet I am unaware of large-scale, representative surveys that systematically compare attitudes toward different types of sex workers. Absent such data, I draw instead on my observations on this question over the course of my fieldwork, in combination with media portrayals and other academic research.

(singing, drinking, dancing, and companionship) that could make the prostitution aspect of their interactions with clients appear less essential to the relationship. Their often grimy places of work, high number of clients, lower knowledge of HIV/AIDS, and more limited use of condoms all contribute to a perception of them as "dirty" women.[91] For instance, throughout my fieldwork, I struck up conversations about prostitution with cab drivers taking me to and from interviews and research sites. I usually started such discussions by mentioning that a friend of mine would be coming to visit and that he wanted to know where he could find sex workers. I would then ask more specifically about low-tier brothels and middle-tier entertainment venues. Repeatedly, they would tell me that my friend should steer clear of the brothels, because they were "unsanitary" (不卫生 – *bu weisheng*).[92]

Conditions of low-tier sex work also engender feelings of sympathy from the general public, who view the poverty and difficult life circumstances these women face as factors outside of their control that have led them to sell sex. In this view, "Their lives were already tragic (悲惨 – *beican*) [before selling sex], and just became more tragic once they crossed the threshold into a brothel."[93] They are society's "weakest" (最弱者 – *zui ruozhe*) and "most helpless" (最无助 – *zui wuzhu*) group, and have "lost all hope" (无望 – *wu wang*) in life.[94] This framing of women who solicit on the streets and in brothels as victims of forces beyond their control absolves them of blame. They are portrayed as acutely aware that prostitution is "disgraceful" (很丢人的 – *hen diu ren de*) and "shameful" (见不得人 – *jianbuderen*) but are sacrificing themselves to support their family.[95]

91 Yingying Huang et al., "HIV/AIDS Risk among Brothel-Based Female Sex Workers in China: Assessing the Terms, Content, and Knowledge of Sex Work," *Sexually Transmitted Diseases* 31, no. 11 (November 2004): 695–700.

92 See, for instance, Field Notes, April 1, 2009.

93 "Shanghai Pudong Diqu Mouzhen Falang Xingfuwu Zhuangkuang Diaocha" 上海浦东地区某镇发廊性服务状况调查 [Investigation on Sex Service Work Conditions in a Township in Shanghai Pudong District] (original article by Gu Zexu 顾则徐), Tianya Luntan 天涯论坛 [Tianya Forum], accessed November 16, 2021, http://bbs.tianya.cn/post-no01-86555-1.shtml (webpage discontinued).

94 Ibid.

95 "Butong Leixing Maiyingnü De Xinli Tezheng" (不同类型卖淫女的心理特征) [The Psychological Characteristics of Different Types of Female Sex Workers], *Daofeng 1927 (刀锋1927) on Wangyi Hao (网易号) [NetEase Accounts]*, February 8, 2021, perma.cc/E778-9ASA (original webpage discontinued).

CONCLUSION

Sex workers who solicit outdoors at places like Xicheng Park or in small brothels located in places such as Mei Jie's apartment, hair salons, or massage parlors have been dealt a rough hand in life. They are the oldest and least educated of sex workers in China – in some cases, illiterate women in their sixties. These demographics severely restrict their professional opportunities, providing them with limited alternatives in the face of challenging work conditions. They receive a constant flow of clients who pay them poorly for sex, regularly abuse them, and sometimes kill them. Those who work indoors have madams and pimps who can alleviate some of these difficulties. Outside, streetwalkers work independently, and thus do not benefit from such protection. Still, these gatekeepers at indoor brothels can treat the women under their control in horrific ways; sex workers are thus sometimes better off on their own. The only silver lining to emerge from all the adversity that characterizes their daily lives is the solidarity that exists between women who sell sex in this lowest tier of prostitution.

The vulnerabilities of low-tier sex workers have alarming consequences for their health. It is terrifying to hear them talk about visually assessing a client's health when deciding whether or not to use a condom or relying on a rinsing product after sex to guard against HIV infection. And it is disheartening to hear stories of madams and doctors at underground health clinics providing them with inaccurate health information. These are women with low levels of knowledge, high numbers of clients, and limited power to push back against their demands. It comes as no surprise, then, that rates of HIV/AIDS are highest for women who solicit in the lowest tier of prostitution.

How do low-tier sex workers make sense of all these challenges? They have a lot to say about prostitution and the state that regulates it, most of which is negative. Their opposition to prostitution and its legalization speaks volumes about their lives in the sex industry. They blame themselves for selling sex and express self-loathing for doing so. Their high levels of legal knowledge reflect their frequent interactions with law enforcement, and their low levels of trust in the state, including expressions of visceral fear of the police, show us how sex workers experience those encounters. The circumstances of low-tier sex workers also shape how outsiders view them – with a combination of disgust and pity.

5

IN THE CLUBS

INTRODUCTION

The life of a hostess is exhausting. In addition to selling sex, women in this tier of the sex industry spend hours every evening engaging in their other professional responsibilities, which include drinking, dancing, and singing with clients. They face intense competition from their peers. Their work environment exposes them to health risks not only from HIV/AIDS and other sexually transmitted diseases but also from the alcohol and tobacco they consume as part of their work. Although these conditions are taxing, they also provide middle-tier sex workers with more agency than their colleagues who work on the streets or in brothels, and lead to these women having more positive perspectives on prostitution than do their lower-tier colleagues. Hostesses tend to be assertive and reject any portrayal of their engagement in the sex industry as a story of victimhood. They also exhibit more trust in government institutions, an attitude that, on rare occasions, can even lead them to make public demands of the state. This work environment, autonomy, and willingness to take initiative contribute to public perceptions that tend to criticize hostesses as lazy and dishonorable.

SETTING THE SCENE

Ying Yi works in a karaoke venue in Beijing.[1] She is from northeastern China. She says she is twenty-seven years old, has been living in Beijing

[1] Sex Worker Interview 4, August 23, 2009.

for seven years, and started hostessing soon after arriving there. Relative to many of her peers, she is younger and has more years of experience in the sex industry. Hostesses I surveyed reported a mean age of thirty, ranging from seventeen to forty-six.[2] On average, they had started selling sex at age twenty-seven and had been engaged in prostitution for 2.4 years.

Ying Yi came to Beijing with her first husband, who was a drug addict. While her family disapproved of him and she wanted to leave him, she struggled to make a clean break before eventually divorcing him. She remarried a few years later but divorced her second husband also. She does not have any children. In her hometown, she had opened a "real" hair salon (one that only provides hair care and not sexual services) and also sold clothing. When she moved to Beijing, she initially found work at a legitimate beauty parlor. She could not stand having to take orders from the boss, however, who she felt bullied her. It was too stark a reminder that she used to be in charge of her own hair salon. She soon left to become a hostess at a karaoke bar.

Like many hostesses, Ying Yi's day starts around noon, when she wakes up. She will often go out for lunch with friends, who also tend to work in entertainment venues. She might then go shopping and may spend some time catching up with friends on the phone. Around 3 PM, she heads home and gets ready for work. She prepares her hair, nails, and makeup, unless she got them done at a beauty salon that afternoon. She also changes into tight, revealing clothing. Some of her colleagues at other venues are required to wear specific uniforms,[3] but most of the time the managers at her karaoke bar allow hostesses to wear what they want. Ying Yi then heads out the door, grabs a bowl of noodles at a neighborhood restaurant, and walks to her venue, which is called "Golden Age" (金色年代 – *jinse niandai*).

About 200 hostesses work at Golden Age, each managed by one of the venue's fifteen madams and ready at any moment to entertain clients who book one of the space's sixty private karaoke rooms. When Ying Yi arrives, she heads to one of several back rooms and settles in on a couch, where she and other hostesses who are supervised by her madam wait for clients. Groups of men – often work colleagues or friends – will start arriving together in the late afternoon and rent private karaoke rooms. The windowless rooms at Golden Age have

2 Please see the Appendix for more details about the survey.
3 The uniform is often a Chinese *qipao* dress, as discussed in Chapter 3.

dark red velvet wallpaper, plush couches, and a disco ball hanging from the ceiling. The karaoke equipment is located in one of the corners, and a screen hangs on a wall opposite the couches.

Once the clients are settled in their room, a waiter takes drink orders. A madam comes in to greet them, and, if they are regular customers, takes the time to catch up with them. She then rounds up her hostesses. If Ying Yi is among them, she walks into the room with about a dozen other women. They all line up in front of the clients, who either each pick one or more women for themselves or defer to the host of their group to select them. The remaining women all file back out. When Ying Yi first started this work, she "didn't understand it at all, and it felt really strange to just stand there in a line waiting for clients to order you." The word she used for "order" (点 – *dian*) is the same one used for ordering food in a restaurant. Other hostesses also use this meal analogy to describe the selection process and echo similar feelings about it. In Jing Fen's words, "It feels like being at the market (菜市场 – *cai shichang*). We stand in the room as if we were produce vendors at the market. If the client doesn't choose you, then you need to discreetly be on your way. The rejection really makes your heart ache. After a while, you get used to it."[4] Ying Yi might spend the entire evening without the opportunity to host a client. Since all of her income comes directly from clients, this means she could spend ten to twelve hours at a karaoke bar without getting paid for any of that time.

If Ying Yi does spark a customer's fancy, she steps out of the line and spends the rest of the evening by his side. The more he likes her, the larger her tip, and the greater the likelihood that he will pay her even more for sex. She encourages him to spend a lot on drinks and food. She drinks with him, yet tries to limit her own consumption of alcohol. She sings songs with him, and they might dance together in the room as well. She lets his hands wander over her body enough to suggest that she is open to selling sex to him, while simultaneously playing hard to get, in order to increase his desire for her. At the end of the evening, if he expresses an interest and seems safe, she takes him back to her apartment for sex, for which her clients usually pay her a couple hundred yuan.[5] If either Ying Yi or her client is not interested in sex, he still usually tips her for the time she has spent by his side at the venue – the going rate at Golden Age is 100 yuan ($15). That said, a disgruntled client – who is dissatisfied with her service or upset that

[4] Sex Worker Interview 2, August 16, 2009.

[5] Hostesses and clients do not usually have sex on the premises of entertainment venues. They are more likely to go to the home of the hostess or client, or to a hotel.

she turned him down for sex – might simply leave without paying. While his friends, madams, or venue staff might gently prod the client to pay, Ying Yi sometimes ends up wasting hours entertaining a client who decides not to compensate her. Her workday ends around 3 or 4 AM, when she walks back home and crawls into bed.

WORK

Hostesses have fewer clients than sex workers in the lowest tier and are paid more per sexual transaction. Yet they also experience a type of workplace stress that is especially pronounced in the middle tier of the sex industry: competition with peers.

Numbers

Hostesses are usually paid 200–500 yuan ($30–$75) per sexual transaction and have four or five such clients per week. In contrast to streetwalkers and women who solicit in brothels, for whom prostitution is their only source of income, hostesses also earn money from the tips (小费 – *xiaofei*) that customers give them for the hours they spend drinking, dancing, and singing together in entertainment venues. Ying Yi, for example, estimated that her combined income from sex and hostess tips amounted to about 5,000 yuan per month ($800). A standard hostess tip for an evening ranges from 100 to 300 yuan ($15–$45); each venue sets the expected amount based on the overall quality of the space and the services it provides. In fact, when I asked hostesses to describe the different venues in which they had worked, they would regularly use the tip amount to characterize it, using phrases such as "we are a 100 venue" (我们是一百场 – *women shi yibai chang*) or "I first worked at a 200 karaoke bar for 6 months" (我在第一个歌厅200场工作了半年 – *wo zai diyige geting 200 chang gongzuole bannian*).[6] The experience that Ying Yi describes of spending hours entertaining a client and not being compensated happens on a regular basis. Venues do not pay their hostesses a salary, and while there is a strong norm in favor of tipping, it is not required. When talking about the more unpleasant work situations they have encountered, sex workers frequently shared stories about not getting paid for their hostessing work.[7] These were not necessarily the most

[6] Sex Worker Interview 3, August 21, 2009; Sex Worker Interview 4, August 22, 2009.
[7] Sex Worker Interview 2, August 18, 2009; Sex Worker Interview 2, August 17, 2009; Sex Worker Interview 1, August 17, 2009; Sex Worker Interview 4, August 15, 2009; Sex Worker Interview 3, August 15, 2009; Sex Worker Interview 2, August 26, 2009.

dangerous or harmful situations that these women had encountered in the workplace. Yet they often weighed heavily on sex workers because of the moral injury they caused, by signaling complete disregard for these women's labor.

Competition among Hostesses

From the perspective of streetwalkers and women who solicit in brothels, hostesses' greater pay and smaller number of clients both seem attractive. Yet the fierce workplace competition between hostesses in entertainment venues is less enviable. Wei Wei, one of the hostesses I interviewed, described the competition by saying, "After all, there are lots of wolves, and not a lot of meat (狼多肉少 – *langduoroushao*). It's a common phenomenon."[8] Ting Ting concurred: "There is so much infighting (勾心斗角 – *gouxindoujiao*). You'll have three women hosting a rich and generous client. Hostesses will all fight for him, and discretely badmouth and backstab each other in front of him."[9] Xia Ting underscored how hostesses do not tell each other which clients pay them for sex. Since clients often purchase sex from several different hostesses, a sex worker risks incurring the wrath of those colleagues who are also selling him sex.[10]

A number of differences between the work environments of women who solicit in the low and middle tiers of prostitution help explain the greater presence of competition among hostesses. The extreme conditions that women experience when selling sex on the streets and in brothels may help foster greater bonds of support among these lower-tier sex workers. In addition, the process of clients selecting a sex worker in the middle tier lends itself particularly well to competition. Hostesses line up next to each other, making the comparison between them extremely obvious. Throughout the evening, especially if several women are entertaining one man, they are engaged in an actual

[8] Sex Worker Interview 5, August 18, 2009.
[9] Sex Worker Interview 2, August 23, 2009.
[10] Sex Worker Interview 1, August 17, 2009. Zheng, in her ethnography of hostesses in Dalian, also identifies the prevalence of competition among her research subjects. Tiantian Zheng, *Red Lights: The Lives of Sex Workers in Postsocialist China* (Minneapolis: University of Minnesota Press, 2009). Yet the hostess environment does not necessarily create a competitive environment among sex workers. Hoang, in her ethnography of hostess bars in Ho Chi Minh City, Vietnam, notes how, "[i]n contrast to findings in previous studies that describe sex work as … rife with competition, the vast majority of the workers in my study believed in and succeeded in creating a collaborative work environment." Kimberly Kay Hoang, *Dealing in Desire: Asian Ascendancy, Western Decline, and the Hidden Currencies of Global Sex Work*, 1st ed. (Oakland: University of California Press, 2015), 125.

competition to curry his favor. On the streets, meanwhile, a client will walk directly up to one woman. In a brothel, he might look at several women who would be sitting on couches or chairs when he enters and select one, but the process is not ritualized in a way that objectifies them so starkly: They do not file into the room and stand side by side waiting for him to pick one. In addition, there are fewer women from whom to choose in any given brothel. Brothel madams bring in sex workers according to consumer demand. Consequently, once a sex worker is working at a brothel, she can reasonably depend upon her madam to assure her a regular stream of clients, thus eliminating direct competition.

HEALTH

HIV/AIDS is less of a danger for hostesses than for streetwalkers and women who solicit in brothels. Infection rates are lower for hostesses because they have fewer sexual partners, more general awareness of HIV/AIDS, and are more likely to receive health checkups. Of the women I surveyed, 99 percent of hostesses had heard of HIV/AIDS, and 67 percent of them had received a checkup in the previous year. That said, the sexual behavior of hostesses and their clients is far from safe and poses serious public health concerns in China. Even though rates of condom use appear higher in the middle tier of sex work, hostess testimony still underscores a prevalence of unsafe sexual practices.[11] These are due to an unequal power dynamic, where a hostess who refuses a client's request to have sex without a condom will simply lose that customer. As hostess Xiao Han explained to me, "There are clients who will only have sex without a condom, so in order to earn money, we have no choice but to not use one."[12] Asked about the risks hostesses incur in such cases, Qing Lai actually downplayed them, and instead highlighted the greater gamble that the client is taking: "As long as [the client] gives money, if he says not to wear [a condom], then we don't wear one. We have more sexual partners than them, so if they aren't scared, that's up to them."[13] Similar to low-tier sex workers, hostesses described how

[11] China Sex Worker Organization Network Forum (CSWONF), "Zhong Guo Di Dang (Di Shou Ru) Nu Xing Xing Gong Zuo Zhe Ai Zi Bing Fang Zhi Xian Zhuang Yan Jiu Bao Gao (中国低档(低收入)女性性工作者艾滋病防治现状研究报告) [Research on HIV/AIDS Prevention and Intervention among Chinese Low-Tier (Low-Income) Female Sex Workers]," 2013, 20.

[12] Sex Worker Interview 6, August 16, 2009.

[13] Sex Worker Interview 2, August 26, 2009.

they "look at the client's penis to decide whether or not he has a sexually transmitted disease."[14] They also said they wash after sex as an alternative to using a condom, wear one only if the client seems like he might not be a good person, and agree not to use one in exchange for higher payment.[15]

Alcohol consumption is an integral aspect of hostessing, one that presents a health risk that is particularly acute in this tier of the sex industry. Clients expect hostesses to drink with them: "Singing and drinking is at the heart [of what we do]" (以唱歌喝酒为主 – *yi changge hejiu weizhu*), explained Xiao Ting.[16] Sex workers repeatedly described situations when they were forced to drink excessively.[17] Xiao Yun talked about clients who "don't treat us like human beings, and force us to drink" (不把小姐当人, 逼小姐喝酒 – *bu ba xiaojie dangren, bi xiaojie hejiu*).[18] Women who cannot hold their alcohol are at a serious disadvantage, and often describe this issue as a problem that they are working to remedy. Fang Ting explained that "I still can't hold my liquor, so I have fewer clients than others."[19] Xiao Yang was similarly apologetic: "I can't hold my liquor, but I am slowly learning how to. In a few months I should be a bit better at it."[20] A common strategy that hostesses use to meet the drinking demands of their clients is to excuse themselves for a few minutes so that they can go to the restroom and force themselves to throw up so that they can continue drinking.[21] This pressure to drink excessively in the workplace contributes to alcoholism among some hostesses, who describe drinking themselves to sleep at home, alone, after a night's work.[22] Smoking is also a common habit among hostesses, often developed on the job to respond to client urgings.[23] Similarly, the entertainment venue environment can also expose sex workers to drug use.[24]

14 Sex Worker Interview 7, August 20, 2009.
15 Sex Worker Interview 2, August 21, 2009; Sex Worker Interview 4, August 23, 2009; Sex Worker Interview 6, August 16, 2009.
16 Sex Worker Interview 2, August 21, 2009.
17 Sex Worker Interview 1, August 15, 2009; Sex Worker Interview 3, August 22, 2009; Sex Worker Interview 4, August 17, 2009; Sex Worker Interview 4, August 16, 2009; Sex Worker Interview 2, August 17, 2009; Sex Worker Interview 2, August 15, 2009.
18 Sex Worker Interview 1, August 15, 2009.
19 Sex Worker Interview 2, August 22, 2009.
20 Sex Worker Interview 2, August 18, 2009.
21 Sex Worker Interview 3, August 15, 2009.
22 Sex Worker Interview 2, August 23, 2009.
23 Xia Wan et al., "Smoking among Young Rural to Urban Migrant Women in China: A Cross-Sectional Survey," *PLOS ONE* 6, no. 8 (August 4, 2011): e23028, https://doi.org/10.1371/journal.pone.0023028.
24 Sheldon X. Zhang and Ko-lin Chin, "A People's War: China's Struggle to Contain Its Illicit Drug Problem," Foreign Policy at Brookings, 2016, 3, perma.cc/HM5Z-KUSM; Ko-lin Chin

PERSPECTIVES ON PROSTITUTION

Hostessing is challenging and exposes the women involved in it to significant health risks. Its difficulties lead some hostesses to talk in profoundly dark terms about the personal transformations they have experienced. Comparing hostessing to a "dyeing vat" (染缸 – *rangang*), Bing Bing described it as a completely corrupting environment "which can only dye people black; it can't dye them white. It destroys people."[25] Some hostesses described physical reactions to simply entering their place of work. Xiao Yuan, who generally projected great confidence, revealed a more vulnerable side of herself when she explained that "As soon as I enter a venue, I get a splitting headache, and I always have to force myself to cross the threshold."[26] Wei Wei experiences a similarly unpleasant physical response: "The moment I walk through the iron gate [of the venue], my head starts to hurt."[27]

Yet by and large, hostesses have more positive perspectives on prostitution than do lower-tier sex workers. More than three-quarters of surveyed hostesses feel that prostitution is overall beneficial to themselves, rather than harmful, and more than four-fifths think that it is beneficial to clients. Hostesses are twice as likely to tolerate their own husband soliciting sex than women in the low tier (30 percent of middle-tier respondents versus 15 percent of low-tier sex workers). Hostesses repeatedly emphasize how "normal" (正常 – *zhengchang*) prostitution is when they express positive views toward it. "This is such a normal thing, it's just no big deal," explained Xiao Ai.[28] They also present it as a personal choice that two individuals make, based on "mutual consent" (你情我愿 – *ni qing wo yuan*).[29]

Hostesses' more positive views toward prostitution go hand-in-hand with their greater rights awareness and agency, and lower levels of personal blame, in response to experiences of client abuse. For example, some hostesses argue that abuse is unfair because, as human beings, they have certain basic rights unrelated to their lawbreaking behavior.[30]

and Sheldon X. Zhang, *The Chinese Heroin Trade: Cross-Border Drug Trafficking in Southeast Asia and beyond* (New York: New York University Press, 2015), 248.

25 Sex Worker Interview 2, August 15, 2009.

26 Sex Worker Interview 3, August 18, 2009.

27 Sex Worker Interview 5, August 18, 2009.

28 Sex Worker Interview 1, August 21, 2009.

29 Sex Worker Interview 7, August 20, 2009; Sex Worker Interview 2, August 22, 2009; Sex Worker Interview 3, August 20, 2009.

30 A version of this paragraph and the next first appeared in Margaret L. Boittin, "New Perspectives from the Oldest Profession: Abuse and the Legal Consciousness of Sex Workers in China," *Law & Society Review* 47, no. 2 (2013): 245–78.

This argument rests on a conception of self that emphasizes a dual identity: as sex workers engaged in an illegal activity, and human beings who have an existence separate from prostitution. This duality exhibits itself in the way that Xia Fen coped with being raped. A regular client of hers invited her and some of his friends to a hotel restaurant. They stayed out late and suggested that she spend the night with them at the hotel. Although he promised Xia Fen that they would not touch her, he subsequently forced her to have sex with him, as did one of his friends. After they raped her, the client asked her how much money she wanted. "Thinking about it makes me so furious ... I didn't want any money," Xia Fen said, "I just told him I never wanted to see him again."[31] By refusing payment from the rapist, she drew a clear distinction between client behavior that is appropriate and that which is unacceptable; between her identity as a sex worker and as a human being with basic rights.

Relatedly, some hostesses opposed the idea that a client can do whatever he wants because he is paying. "Some clients will take liberties with you, grope your chest and private parts ... They assume that since they paid you 100 yuan [$15], they can grope away to their heart's content," complained Xiao Ting.[32] Xiu Qing expressed a similar attitude: "Some people mistakenly assume that since they've spent money, they can do as they please."[33] In rejecting the view that they have fully abandoned themselves to a client because he is paying for their time, these women recognize the existence of an identity that is separate from their involvement in prostitution. Other hostesses articulated the notion of dual identities more directly, specifically underscoring their humanity through use of the term "human" (人). "When a client wrongs you, and doesn't respect you ... it makes you feel really uncomfortable in your heart. We're all humans, but instead [that kind of behavior] makes you feel like you have a lower rank," explained Wei Wei.[34] "Some clients just don't perceive sex workers to be humans, they force sex workers to drink alcohol ... and beat them," complained Zi Han.[35] She articulated this notion in a particularly powerful manner: "Even though we are sex workers, we are also human ... we also have ... rights."[36] These opinions illustrate how some hostesses

[31] Sex Worker Interview 6, August 22, 2009.
[32] Sex Worker Interview 2, August 21, 2009.
[33] Sex Worker Interview 3, August 23, 2009.
[34] Sex Worker Interview 5, August 18, 2009.
[35] Sex Worker Interview 1, August 16, 2009.
[36] Sex Worker Interview 1, August 16, 2009.

recognize that, as human beings, they have certain rights that engaging in illegal activities cannot take away from them, and use this language in reflecting upon abuses. They are appealing to a profound conception of humanity that arises in reaction to their experiences of abuse.[37]

Hostesses also reject the notion that they are victims and emphasize that they have agency. Jing Ming, a kindergarten teacher prior to working in the sex industry, simply transferred her leadership skills from the classroom into the bedroom: "Dealing with clients (哄客人 – *hong keren*) is just like dealing with children (哄小孩 – *hong xiaohai*).[38] No matter how old they are, when men find themselves in front of a woman, they still just act like kids."[39] These women tend to diminish their experiences of abuse and instead emphasize how they can inflict harm upon others. "We are really badass. We're the ones to bully clients," asserted Wei Ting.[40] "I am really fierce," explained Xiao Hong. "Usually I am the one to beat a client. I'll just give him a beating and whack him in the face. I've beaten a bunch of clients, including with a beer bottle," she continued.[41]

These women also underscore the freedom that comes from selling sex. Financial independence is central to this feeling of liberation. Many hostesses viewed prostitution as a way to have an income so as to "not depend on men," and remarked upon how "gratifying it is" to earn money.[42] They spoke of the economic aspects of prostitution in ways that signaled control and ownership over their decision to sell sex. In the words of Ting Ting, "I am no slave to money. I am its master."[43] Other than financial independence, middle-tier sex workers also viewed their daily routine as liberating. It allows for greater

[37] Researchers have identified sex workers expressing similar attitudes in other places. Kotiswaran, recounting the experiences and perspectives of a sex worker in Kolkata, India, noted how "[j]ust because she was selling her body for a short time did not mean that a customer could do whatever he wanted. She was also a human being and had some *izzat* [self-respect]." Prabha Kotiswaran, *Dangerous Sex, Invisible Labor: Sex Work and the Law in India* (Princeton, NJ: Princeton University Press, 2011), 154.

[38] The verb 哄 means "to coax someone to do something through manipulation and/or flattery."

[39] Sex Worker Interview 6, August 23, 2009. Jing Ming's opinion echoes that of sex workers in other countries as well. Bernstein reproduced the following quote from Amanda, a San Francisco–based sex worker who taught preschool for years: "Even though there's no nap time, both jobs are really about connecting nonverbally. And in both cases, you often have to repeatedly set boundaries and clean up the mess." Elizabeth Bernstein, *Temporarily Yours: Intimacy, Authenticity, and the Commerce of Sex* (Chicago: University of Chicago Press, 2007), 97.

[40] Sex Worker Interview 4, August 18, 2009.

[41] Sex Worker Interview 3, August 17, 2009.

[42] Sex Worker Interview 2, August 16, 2009; Sex Worker Interview 3, August 15, 2009.

[43] Sex Worker Interview 2, August 23, 2009.

flexibility than working in a restaurant or factory – the jobs that are often alternatives to prostitution for unskilled female workers. Aside from increased salaries, Yu Han underscored how "There are no restrictions when you do this job, no rules, you have more freedom. It's not like a regular job where you get a salary at the end of the month. Here, you can see the money you earn every day."[44] Sexual freedom is another such manifestation of independence: "One really strange and fun thing about this profession is that before I was engaged in it, I would just make love the normal way with my partner. Now, when I go out [with clients] we do things like watch [pornographic] films, there are so many different ways to make love!" explained Jing Ming.[45] Sexual independence came through clearly in her pricing strategy. In a blurring of the boundaries between prostitution and sexual needs and desires, she explained: "If I like the client, I'll go with him regardless of money. We women also have our own needs, we need to have a sex life as well!"[46]

VIEWS OF THE STATE

Hostesses' more positive attitudes toward prostitution and greater assertiveness in their interactions with clients extend to their views of the state. Compared to lower-tier sex workers, hostesses have higher levels of trust in the state. They also express more support for legalizing prostitution. Their increased confidence has even translated into them making public demands of the state.

Trust in the State

Hostesses have more trust in state agencies than do streetwalkers and women who solicit in brothels. Of the surveyed sex workers, 84 percent of hostesses said they trust the central government (versus 75 percent in the low tier), and 83 percent trust the local government (versus 72 percent in the low tier).[47] Women in the middle tier are also more likely to consider politics to be important (78 percent of hostesses versus 55 percent of women in the low tier) and express an interest in it (67 percent of hostesses versus 50 percent of women in the low tier).[48]

[44] Sex Worker Interview 5, August 16, 2009.
[45] Sex Worker Interview 6, August 23, 2009.
[46] Sex Worker Interview 6, August 23, 2009.
[47] See Chapter 4, Figure 4.3.
[48] See Chapter 4, Figure 4.6.

This increased trust in the state comes through in the ways that middle-tier sex workers interact with health agencies. While women in the lowest tier have lower rates of health checkups and HIV/AIDS testing, hostesses are more willing to reach out to health agencies and express more confidence in them.[49] Wei Wei gets a health checkup every three months: "Good health is a basic necessity. You can't enjoy the money you earn if you are not around to spend it."[50] Her peers emphasized similar arguments about the importance of staying healthy in explaining why they go to the doctor, despite concerns about the costs of testing and some nervousness around possible bad health news.[51]

Hostesses also have greater trust in the police than do low-tier sex workers. Surveyed hostesses were 8 percentage points more likely than women in the low tier to express trust in the police (61 versus 53 percent).[52] They were 18 percentage points more likely to express a willingness to report a robbery by a client (82 versus 64 percent), and 14 percentage points more likely to say they would report a rape by a client (81 versus 67 percent).[53] Hostesses speak openly about having close relationships with the police and their willingness to call on them for help when they encounter an unruly client.[54] Bing Bing estimated that in her venue, hostesses will reach out to the police about four or five times a year. Generally, it happens when a conflict arises with a client:

> Clients are not all of very high quality (不是每个客人素质那么好 – *bushi meige keren suzhi name hao*). If they have had too much to drink and want to harass a hostess, if an argument happens and they start beating

[49] Margaret Boittin, "Using Incentives to Increase HIV/AIDS Testing by Sex Workers: Evidence from a Randomized Field Experiment in China," *Law & Policy* 40, no. 4 (2018): 398–423, https://doi.org/10.1111/lapo.12114.

[50] Sex Worker Interview 5, August 18, 2009.

[51] Sex Worker Interview 2, August 22, 2009; Sex Worker Interview 7, August 20, 2009; Sex Worker Interview 4, August 20, 2009; Sex Worker Interview 3, August 20, 2009; Sex Worker Interview 4, August 17, 2009. The presence of madams in the lives of all hostesses does not necessarily explain these higher rates of checkups and HIV/AIDS testing. Madams, pimps, and entertainment venue managers may encourage or require sex workers to seek out various forms of healthcare, but they are also known to dissuade or prevent them from doing so. Chapter 11 discusses the complex relationships that gatekeepers have with state health authorities and some of their concerns with encouraging sex workers to engage with them. See also Huso Yi et al., "Occupational Safety and HIV Risk among Female Sex Workers in China: A Mixed-Methods Analysis of Sex-Work Harms and Mommies," *Global Public Health* 7, no. 8 (2012): 851, https://doi.org/10.1080/17441692.2012.662991.

[52] See Chapter 4, Figure 4.3.

[53] See Chapter 4, Figure 4.4.

[54] Sex Worker Interview 4, August 15, 2009; Sex Worker Interview 5, August 16, 2009.

the girl, if she has a bad disposition (脾气不好 – *piqi buhao*) then she'll report it to the police.[55]

Some hostesses also described instances when they called the police to complain about clients who did not tip them for their (non-prostitution) entertainment venue services. Xiao Hua described a situation in which her colleague's client refused to tip. She called a police officer she knew, who told the client: "If you want to play, you have to play nicely, and you should pay for what you're getting."[56] Chapter 9 discusses police attempts to forge close relationships with middle-tier sex workers, as part of their duty to maintain law and order in the neighborhood. Hostesses appear to be aware of these efforts, and responsive to them: They express confidence that the police will answer their calls for help, "because the police are worried about public order problems"[57] and "they want us to work in a safe and comfortable environment."[58]

Knowledge of and Attitudes toward the Law

Hostesses are less likely than low-tier sex workers to know that prostitution is against the law. Of the sex workers I surveyed, 67 percent of hostesses were aware that China prohibits prostitution versus 80 percent of women in the low tier. This difference appears tied to the reduced likelihood for hostesses of actually being arrested, as discussed in Chapters 4 and 8. Hostesses are also more likely to express support for legalized prostitution: 80 percent of surveyed middle-tier sex workers support legalization, in contrast to 57 percent of low-tier sex workers. Hostesses argue that legalized prostitution would bring improvements to their safety, health, and general well-being. "The advantage of legalization is that if you have a problem [you can get help], and you won't get locked up," explained Xiao Xiang.[59] "There's no need to be scared [to report if prostitution is legal], there won't be any psychological obstacles [to reporting harm]," said Wen Ting.[60] Fang Qing, a madam and former sex worker, argued that legalization would make prostitution more orderly: "It is much better if prostitution can be out in the open. It's so messy when it's underground. [If it's legal] it can be regulated, which is better."[61]

55 Sex Worker Interview 2, August 16, 2009.
56 Sex Worker Interview 3, August 15, 2009.
57 Madam Interview, August 15, 2009.
58 Sex Worker Interview 2, August 15, 2009.
59 Sex Worker Interview 4, August 22, 2009.
60 Sex Worker Interview 4, August 25, 2009.
61 Madam Interview 1, August 26, 2009.

Streetwalkers and brothel workers who oppose legalized prostitution emphasize the inherent harm that sex work engenders, including violence and exploitation. Hostesses who support legalization, on the other hand, are less likely to have experienced the darkest forms of abuse that can occur in the sex industry. Their better work conditions lead them to distinguish between prostitution per se – the actual exchange of sex for money or other material benefits – and some of the injustices associated with it. This makes them less likely to view the abolition of prostitution as the only way to address its harms and instead opens them up to the idea that regulatory reform could improve their experience.

Making Public Demands of the State

Hostesses' assertiveness, combined with their greater trust in the state, even led in one instance to an actual demonstration against the state, an event that is extremely sensitive in contemporary China. In January 2007, more than 2,000 hostesses and other entertainment venue employees protested in front of the Shenzhen City Government building.[62] This event occurred six weeks after a series of harsh crackdowns in Shazui, a Shenzhen red-light district that attracts thousands of businessmen from Hong Kong and elsewhere in China, had temporarily shut down its entertainment venues, leaving thousands of migrants unemployed. Protesters clamored for their rights to live (生存 – *shengcun*), eat, and work. It was a short-lived protest, quashed within a few hours, as special security forces loaded participants onto buses headed toward detention centers. It was also not explicitly about prostitution. As employees in legally registered entertainment venues, at face value they were simply asking for those spaces to be reopened so that they could continue to earn a living. Yet it is nonetheless a significant event because it provides evidence of hostesses' attitudes translating into actions.

OUTSIDERS' PERSPECTIVES

Hostesses do not repulse the general public, but they also do not elicit a lot of sympathy, as public opinion toward middle-tier sex workers

[62] EastSouthWestNorth, "Shenzhen Sex Worker Protest 2006," 2006, perma.cc/XH2R-TFLQ. Parts of this paragraph first appeared in Boittin, "New Perspectives from the Oldest Profession."

tends to be disdainful and disapproving.[63] Media depictions and societal understanding of sex workers in the lowest tier often portray an isolated and lonely woman providing sexual services to several clients a day in a dirty room, a situation that engenders disgust but also compassion. Depictions of hostesses, meanwhile, show women seducing a man by singing, dancing, and drinking with him in an entertainment venue. These improved work conditions highlight middle-tier sex workers' greater agency, and with that comes increased blame. For instance, Tiantian Zheng's ethnography of hostesses in the northern city of Dalian describes how "hostesses are portrayed as evil and dangerous 'foxes' in the state and popular media."[64] One commentator used the alternative opportunities that hostesses shun – ranging from white-collar jobs to manual labor to begging on the streets – as evidence that they lack all "human dignity" (人格 – *renge*) and "honor" (尊严 – *zunyan*) and are "unworthy of sympathy" (不值得人同情 – *bu zhide ren tongqing*).[65] Laziness is also a recurring descriptor of hostesses.[66] In the words of one commentator, "They are lazy, like to enjoy the good things in life without expending any effort, and want to earn easy money."[67] In short, these are women who are understood to be making poor choices that demonstrate their lack of moral rectitude as they pursue what outsiders consider an easy way to earn money.

CONCLUSION

Many aspects of a hostess's life are unenviable. To start with, her ability to earn money is contingent upon a humiliating ritual wherein she lines up alongside her colleagues and endures the uncomfortable gaze and commentary of clients comparing her appearance to that of her peers.

[63] As noted in Chapter 4, I use the terms "general public" and "public opinion" in reference to the dominant societal narrative about hostesses in China. Ideally, this discussion would include data from a general population survey, but I am unaware of any representative surveys of the general population in China that specifically examine different attitudes toward sex workers in different tiers of prostitution. Instead, I draw on my fieldwork observations of public opinion, as well as media portrayals and other academic research on hostesses.

[64] Zheng, *Red Lights*, 24.

[65] Do*** (豆***), "Ruhe Kandai Sanpeinu Ne? (如何看待三陪女呢?) [How Do People Perceive Escort Girls?]," *Iask* 爱问知识人, 2007, perma.cc/N8PM-3UX6.

[66] Tiantian Zheng, "Commodifying Romance and Searching for Love: Rural Migrant Bar Hostesses' Moral Vision in Post-Mao Dalian," *Modern China* 34, no. 4 (October 2008): 456, https://doi.org/10.1177/0097700408319493.

[67] Lucky Xue Molin (薛墨麟), "Ruhe Kandai KTV Li Peijiu De Nuren (如何看待ktv里陪酒的女人) [How Do You See Women Who are Hostesses in KTVs?]," *Zhihu* (知乎), April 16, 2020, perma.cc/KQ5L-WBYP.

When she is down on her luck, she might be paraded into an entertainment venue room dozens of times over the course of one evening, with nothing to show for it at the end of the night other than a bruised ego. When she does strike someone's fancy, the hard work begins. She makes small talk, sings, and dances with her client. She urges him to drink, a process that usually requires that she also consume excessive amounts of alcohol. She might smoke with him and do drugs. In a dark space with music blaring and lights pulsing, she spends hours on these activities trying to make just one client feel like he is the center of her universe, all for the promise of a few hundred yuan in tips, and possibly more if he solicits her for sex. In that case, she exposes herself to even more health risks: If she wants to get paid for sex, her client calls the shots on whether or not he will wear a condom.

The assertiveness and empowerment that hostesses display under these difficult conditions are remarkable. They talk about the power they have over their clients and the financial and sexual independence they get from their work. They express clear views on the boundaries beyond which they deem a client's behavior inappropriate; in so doing, they exhibit a strong sense of self and personal dignity. They have relatively positive views of prostitution and tend to support its legalization. Their confidence extends to their perceptions of and engagement with the state. They even trust – and seek help from – the police, and are not averse to seeking care from health agencies. Hostesses have even gone as far as to publicly challenge the state's actions. Such evidence of agency in the lives of hostesses does not ingratiate them with the general public. While society responds sympathetically to the total destitution and expressions of deep shame that are often characteristic of low-tier sex workers, it views women in the middle tier as having more personal responsibility for their actions, and judges them harshly for that.

6

IN THE HOME

INTRODUCTION

Second wives or mistresses – who form the highest tier of sex work in China – are often rural migrant women whose demographics overlap with those of hostesses.[1] This type of prostitution also attracts poorer and less educated women from urban areas, as well as university students.[2] Women in this tier of the sex industry live comfortably, and as their clients rarely reside with them full time, they have a lot of independence. Their daily routines are leisurely and include a combination of sexual, domestic, social, and emotional responsibilities that straddle public and private domains. Yet they also experience substantial isolation and are limited in their ability to push back against emotional abuse from clients. Although they rarely encounter physical abuse, they sometimes fall prey to murder at the hands of clients or legal wives who want these women gone. Compared to their colleagues in lower tiers, this work environment presents relatively limited threats to their health. Yet even though elite sex workers have very few sexual

[1] "Second wives" are sex workers who are engaged in a long-term, exclusive relationship with a man who is already legally married to another woman. As discussed in the introductory chapter and in accordance with scholarly and popular discourse, I use the term interchangeably with "mistress."

[2] Suowei Xiao, "China's New Concubines? The Contemporary Second-Wife Phenomenon" (ProQuest Dissertations, 2009), https://perma.cc/T6U2-M8ME; Suowei Xiao, "The 'Second-Wife' Phenomenon and the Relational Construction of Class-Coded Masculinities in Contemporary China," *Men and Masculinities* 14, no.5 (December 1, 2011): 607–627, https://journals.sagepub.com/doi/10.1177/1097184X11412171; Suowei Xiao (肖索未), *Yuwang Yu Zunyan: Zhuanxingqi Zhongguo De Jieceng, Xingbie Yu Qinmi Guanxi (欲望与尊严: 转型期中国的阶层, 性别与亲密关系) [Desire and Dignity: Class, Gender and Intimacy in Transitional China]* (Beijing: China Social Sciences Academic Press 社会科学文献出版社, 2018).

partners, they remain vulnerable to sexually transmitted disease (STD) infection through their clients. They also tend to drink and smoke in response to client demands, habits that often carry over from their experiences as hostesses. Emotions play a key role in the relationships between elite sex workers and their clients. The presence of these feelings shapes how second wives and mistresses think and talk about their work and, by extension, about their client's legal wife. Although elite sex workers generally deny that they are engaging in prostitution, the ever-looming presence of a client's legal wife serves as a constant reminder that they are participating in illegal behavior that the state condemns. Still, they are less likely than low- or middle-tier sex workers to be punished for breaking the law. For this reason, their criticisms of the state are more muted, and based on abstract reflections on the role it plays in their lives, rather than reflecting genuine concerns that they themselves might be arrested. When they do experience the state firsthand, it is usually because their client is a government official or because they serve as whistleblowers who denounce corruption they have witnessed. Second wives and mistresses are the sex workers who elicit the greatest amount of criticism in Chinese society – not only from the general population but also from legal wives, as well as former clients who are investigated for corruption.[3]

Taken together, these characteristics of the lives of elite sex workers underscore both the power and precariousness of their circumstances. Due to the intensity of their client interactions, they have greater power over their clients than do hostesses, streetwalkers, or brothel workers. At the same time, their entire livelihood depends on one person, which places them in an extremely vulnerable position vis-à-vis their client. For women in the low and middle tiers of the sex industry, the impact of one failed client interaction is limited. For second wives and mistresses, it can leave them destitute in an instant.

[3] I draw on Suowei Xiao's (2009, 2011, 2018) research on second wives for this chapter. Her 2009 work is her dissertation, written in English. Her 2018 work is her book, based on her dissertation, written in Chinese. When I quote Xiao's research, I draw from her English (2009) work. When Xiao's 2018 book provides the same or a similar quote in Chinese, I then also provide reference to her 2018 work. My direct exposure to this tier of the sex industry came through women working in the low and middle tiers, including a handful of hostesses who had also worked as second wives. Yet I did not have the opportunity to observe mistresses over the course of their daily lives as I had done with sex workers in the lower tiers. Xiao's research is in part structured around class differences between second wives (from rural or urban areas) and clients (workers or business elites). The distinctions she highlights are insightful and nuanced. I do not dwell on them extensively in this chapter because, while recognizing the status differences that exist within each of the three tiers of sex work around which this project is structured, my focus is instead on between-tier differences.

SETTING THE SCENE

Rural Second Wives

Ah-Fang is from rural Guizhou.[4] She has a primary school education and migrated at age nineteen to Guangzhou, where she first held jobs at various factories. She fell in love with another migrant, but the relationship ended traumatically when he was sentenced to seven years in jail for involvement in a gang. When she was twenty-four, she met "Bird (鸟–*niao*)," the man who would subsequently become her client, one evening when she was out with friends. A few months after they had met, Ah-Fang was detained for failing to renew her temporary residence permit. Bird bailed her out, took her back to his apartment in Guangzhou, and offered to pay her the amount she earned as a factory worker – a few hundred yuan a month – if she quit her job and instead became his second wife.

Bird was a forty-year-old businessman who lived with his wife and two sons in the city of Chaozhou, about 400 kilometers east of Guangzhou. He sold accessories made in Chaozhou to vendors in Guangzhou and neighboring cities, earning enough to support both his family and Ah-Fang. From the outset, he had been clear with Ah-Fang about the nature of their relationship, and was upfront about having no intention of leaving his wife. He put Ah-Fang up in a two-bedroom apartment in Guangzhou, which was the nicest place she had ever lived.

On a daily basis, Ah-Fang's life was lonely. The apartment she shared with Bird was in a part of the city that was closer to his networks and further away from her community. She took advantage of this physical distance to cut herself off from her social circles, as she did not want word to get back to people in her hometown that she was a second wife: "My situation is not something glorious. I do not want people to gossip behind my back. [This neighborhood] is a small community. Any news will be spread out quickly. They will point their fingers at you behind your back, especially those housewives who have nothing to do. They just gossip. I hate that."[5] Ah-Fang was right to suspect that her neighbors might be talking about her behind her back. One of them mentioned that "Ah-Fang must be a second wife. She stays at

[4] Ah Fang's story is the subject of Chapter 4 of Xiao, "China's New Concubines?," 2009 (in English) and Chapter 4 of Xiao, *Desire and Dignity*, 2018 (in Chinese).

[5] Xiao, "China's New Concubines?," 111. See also Xiao, *Desire and Dignity*, 87.

home every day and does not work. Who supports her? The [man from Chaozhou] is much older, probably twice her age. Chaozhou men are traditional. They only marry women from the same region."[6] Although Ah-Fang occasionally reached out to her fellow Guizhou migrant friends, for example when she had an abortion, she relied almost exclusively on Bird for emotional support in her life. Ah-Fang rarely left her neighborhood – every few months she would go shopping in downtown Guangzhou and once a year she would return to her hometown to visit her family. She would occasionally leave the apartment to play mahjong with some acquaintances in the neighborhood or do some small paid needlework with neighbors. More often, she would spend the day at home – doing housework, watching television, and waiting for Bird to return home to be with her.

Urban Second Wives

Like Ah-Fang, Lucy also became a second wife after a bad breakup.[7] She is from a working-class family in Guangzhou, and her education included some training as a graphic designer. Prior to earning income as a mistress, she had opened a small accessories store and had also occasionally held office jobs. She was twenty-six years old and had been in a second wife relationship with her client, a Hong Kong architect, for three years. Every month, he gives her an allowance of about 10,000 yuan (about $1,500). Lucy notes that while it is not as much as some of her colleagues receive, "It covers my basic living expenses – rent, meals, taxi, and some shopping. If I want something big, I ask him for more money."[8] He spends about two weekends a month with her in her apartment, located in the most expensive area of downtown Guangzhou.

When her client is not in town, Lucy usually wakes up around noon. She spends several hours each day on her appearance, including going to beauty salons, getting facials, and getting her hair done. She grabs a quick lunch, and then goes shopping and has coffee in the afternoon with female friends, some of whom are also second wives. She often goes out to dinner with these and other acquaintances as well. She has much more social interaction than second wives like Ah-Fang, who as

6 Xiao, "China's New Concubines?," 112. See also Xiao, *Desire and Dignity*, 89.
7 Xiao, "China's New Concubines?," 65. See also Xiao, *Desire and Dignity*, 46–47.
8 Xiao, "China's New Concubines?," 66. See also Xiao, *Desire and Dignity*, 47.

a migrant knows fewer people in the city. Lucy is able to speak openly about her relationship with her friends who are in similar circumstances and whom she has known for years. That said, she still hides her second wife status from her family.

When Lucy's client is in town, she is at his beck and call, and drops everything to cater to his needs and desires. She makes a big show of leaving her eighth-floor apartment, which has no elevator, for the express purpose of buying him his favorite snacks. When they go shopping together, she prioritizes his preferences over hers – choosing, for example, to buy the coat that he liked for her over the one she favored. He has a temper and is controlling. He once called her from Hong Kong while she was out celebrating her female friend's birthday and demanded that she leave, saying that he did not want her to be out drinking at a bar late at night without him. She generally hesitates to push back against his rage, out of fear that he will leave her. Over the years, his anger has worn on her:

> My friends told me that my temper has been getting worse over the years. I used to be a mild and pleasant person, but now I am very easily irritated. I've been with [my] boyfriend for too long and have taken too much of his abuse. Sometimes when I lose my temper at someone else, I feel very strange about myself – how come I act like that?[9]

Lucy eventually got tired of her client's abuse, left him, moved to Shenzhen, and was seeing a single man whom she was considering marrying.

Becoming a Second Wife

Unlike Ah-Fang, who appears to have moved directly from a factory job to a second wife relationship, most migrant women transition from a hostess position to a second-wife arrangement.[10] In fact, they tend to meet their long-term clients at their entertainment venue.[11] Clients return regularly to a venue when they take a liking to a hostess, shower her with gifts, and gradually woo her into an exclusive relationship

[9] Xiao, "China's New Concubines?," 78. See also Xiao, *Desire and Dignity*, 52.

[10] John Osburg, *Anxious Wealth: Money and Morality among China's New Rich* (Stanford, CA: Stanford University Press, 2013), 146–47.

[11] Sex Worker Interview 3, August 18, 2009. Brendan Hong, "China's Concubine Culture Lives On in Mistress Villages," *The Daily Beast* (blog), April 14, 2014, https://perma.cc/75V7-ZBHD; James Palmer, "How Young Women in China Become Mistresses," *Aeon*, October 10, 2013, perma.cc/9EBM-27YK.

complete with a rented apartment and monthly stipend.[12] This was the case for Shanshan, who migrated from rural Sichuan to its capital, Chengdu, when she was seventeen. She worked as a hostess in a karaoke bar there, and then moved to Beijing to pursue similar work. In Beijing, Wu was a repeat client of hers who worked at a state-run oil company. He put Shanshan up in an apartment that cost more than 2.5 million yuan ($410,000), gave her a monthly allowance of about 20,000 yuan ($3,260), and provided her with expensive gifts.[13] Others share similar stories of the paths that migrant women take from hostessing to becoming a second wife.[14] The transition is not always seamless, as hostesses who want to make it sometimes encounter obstacles from within their karaoke venue. For example, Mei Lin had worked in a venue that prohibited its sex workers from becoming kept women. As she explained it:

> When a hostess becomes kept (包养 – *baoyang*), she won't come to work anymore. The client also won't often come to the venue. The venue loses the revenue it would get from things like room rental and drinks. That is a lot of money. So in order to keep clients, they don't let the hostesses randomly take off with them. They're scared they'll develop too close a connection, and become kept women.[15]

In an attempt to control and prevent the development of these relationships, any client who wanted to purchase sex from a hostess working in that venue was required to make those arrangements through her madam rather than directly with the sex worker.

Urban women such as Lucy, as well as university students, do not generally sell sex in entertainment venues prior to becoming kept women. Instead, they might meet clients while out in bars or clubs, online, or through specialized agencies devoted to such matchmaking.[16] Their social status tends to be slightly higher than that of migrant second wives such as Ah-Fang. In the case of Lucy and her friends, their status as urban residents gives them a more cosmopolitan identity, although they tend to come from poor and uneducated backgrounds. In the case of university students, their socioeconomic

[12] Hong, "China's Concubine Culture Lives On in Mistress Villages"; Palmer, "How Young Women in China Become Mistresses."
[13] Palmer, "How Young Women in China Become Mistresses."
[14] Hong, "China's Concubine Culture Lives On in Mistress Villages."
[15] Sex Worker Interview 3, August 22, 2009.
[16] Dan Levin, "China's New Wealth Spurs a Market for Mistresses," *The New York Times*, August 9, 2011, https://perma.cc/Y7U5-W9EC.

background is often similar to that of migrant second wives: They are often young women from poor rural areas. Yet they are very much in demand.[17] On weekend evenings, the gates by the entrances of university campuses throughout the country are lined with sleek cars that whisk college students away to their clients.[18] These are women whose education, in addition to their youth and attractiveness, presents assets to the men who choose to support them. Despite their different educational backgrounds, shared experiences with poverty often drive both urbanites and rural migrants to become second wives.

WORK

Second wives and mistresses are paid more than hostesses and low-tier sex workers. Their day-to-day living conditions are comfortable. While streetwalkers and women who work in small brothels provide services that are almost entirely private, hostesses offer ones that allow their clients to publicly display their masculinity. Elite sex workers, meanwhile, straddle the private and public lives of their clients. Privately, they provide men with sex, household labor such as meals and laundry, and emotional support. Publicly, they enhance their client's social status by signaling his wealth and desirability. Yet some darkness lies behind daily routines that on the surface appear quite leisurely – including isolation, emotional abuse, and occasional threats to their lives when relationships with clients sour or legal wives seek revenge.

Numbers

Second wife relationships can last for anywhere from a few months to many years.[19] Monthly income from a client ranges from a few thousand to tens of thousands of yuan. In some cases, these relationships allow women to become financially independent from all the money and gifts they have amassed over the years. They might have significant savings, be running their own business, and have property under their name.[20] Such wealth would allow them to leave the sex industry. In other cases, their earnings are insufficient to lead to any significant changes in economic status, and they might return to hostessing. That

17 Osburg, *Anxious Wealth*, 69; 169.
18 Osburg, 67; He Hui Feng 何慧峰, "Da Xue Sheng Dang 'Er Nai' Kai Chu Xue Ji Re Zheng Yi 大学生当'二奶'开除学籍惹争议 [College Student Dismissed for Being a 'Second Wife' Aroused Controversy]," *South China Morning Post*, August 7, 2010.
19 Xiao, "China's New Concubines?," 28. See also Xiao, *Desire and Dignity*, 24.
20 Palmer, "How Young Women in China Become Mistresses."

happened to Xiao Yuan, who as a seventeen-year-old hostess met a long-term client a few days after she started her first job at an entertainment venue in Beijing.[21] He put her up in a three-bedroom apartment that his employer had given him. He allowed her to rent out the other two rooms. As a monthly stipend, he let her keep the 1,600 yuan ($250) she received in rent. Two years into their relationship, he let her go, and she returned to hostessing.

In Private: Sex, Domestic Labor, and Emotional Support

In the privacy of the home, second wives are sources of sexual and domestic services for their clients, as well as emotional support. These women often provide their clients with more sex (and different types of sex) than they get from their legal wives. As Ah-Run notes: "We are compatible in almost every aspect of life, including sexual life."[22] More surprising is that sex is actually relatively infrequent in some of these relationships. Ah-Fei and her client Ah-Dong, who had been supporting her for three and a half years, sometimes went for several months without having sex.[23] Although she had worried this signaled the end of their relationship, he had recently bought her an apartment, continued to pay her, and regularly came to see her. Other second wives also reported that their clients only occasionally had sex with them.[24]

Second wives also provide their clients with domestic labor. Ah-Cai spends ten to fifteen days a month living in Guangzhou with his second wife, Ah-Run, when he comes to town for work.[25] She keeps the apartment clean, washes his clothes, and cooks for him, all services that Ah-Cai recognizes as valuable: "My old woman is very useful. . . . She knows how to take care of people."[26] Second wives often learn to cook their client's favorite meals and encourage them to eat healthily.[27]

On the one hand, this is an economically wise arrangement, as clients end up saving money on services they need to pay for on business trips. Yet as Xiao notes, when second wives provide these services that could instead be delivered through a purely commercial and impersonal third party, they engage in "emotion work" that makes their client feel

[21] Sex Worker Interview 3, August 18, 2009.
[22] Xiao, "China's New Concubines?," 43. See also Xiao, *Desire and Dignity*, 100.
[23] Xiao, "China's New Concubines?," 32. See also Xiao, *Desire and Dignity*, 27.
[24] Xiao, "China's New Concubines?," 33. See also Xiao, *Desire and Dignity*, 28.
[25] Xiao, "China's New Concubines?," 41. See also Xiao, *Desire and Dignity*, 30.
[26] Xiao, "China's New Concubines?," 41. See also Xiao, *Desire and Dignity*, 30, 96, 99.
[27] Xiao, "China's New Concubines?," 42, 49. See also Xiao, *Desire and Dignity*, 31.

cared for.[28] More generally, second wives constantly signal deference and respect for their clients, and set aside their own feelings. Ah-Ying described intense boredom at having to field her client's calls, during which he would talk endlessly about his business, a topic that she found excruciatingly tedious. Yet she would feign interest in order to make him feel good about himself.[29] These acts of subordination differ from the behavior of a client's legal wife. For instance, Lao Wang described how his legal wife "blam[ed] me for not being capable and hardworking enough . . . I had a lot of pressure at home where I felt very repressed and disrespected."[30] In contrast, his second wife "always welcomed me when I visited her. She cooked meals for me, held faith in me, and never pushed me for anything. She thought I was a very good man . . . I felt very comfortable and relaxed at this woman's place."[31]

In Public: Status Work

While sex, domestic labor, and emotional support are all private services that a second wife provides to her client, she also serves a public function. When she accompanies her client to social events, she helps secure his status in the eyes of his friends and colleagues. Second wives are mindful to project an image of femininity and sophistication that sets them apart from the more sexualized hostesses who might also be present at the events where they accompany their clients. Younger second wives must be careful to avoid looking as though they could be their client's granddaughter, and the older ones must not appear too dowdy. All of them must disguise any evidence of coming from rural backgrounds.[32] They also need to signal that they hold their client in high regard. Ah-Xue described remaining physically close to her client throughout the evening, pouring beer for him, drinking for him, and toasting other guests.[33] Ah-Run noted the pride she felt when her client's friends mentioned that he had found a "'virtuous-wife-and-good-mother' type of woman," who contrasted from the "shallow and noisy" type that others had.[34]

28 Arlie Russell Hochschild, *The Managed Heart: Commercialization of Human Feeling* (Berkeley: University of California Press, 1983).
29 Xiao, "China's New Concubines?," 52. See also Xiao, *Desire and Dignity*, 38–39.
30 Xiao, "China's New Concubines?," 45–46. See also Xiao, *Desire and Dignity*, 33–34.
31 Xiao, "China's New Concubines?," 45–46. See also Xiao, *Desire and Dignity*, 34.
32 Xiao, "China's New Concubines?," 55–56. See also Xiao, *Desire and Dignity*, 40.
33 Xiao, "China's New Concubines?," 56. See also Xiao, *Desire and Dignity*, 41.
34 Xiao, "China's New Concubines?," 46–47. See also Xiao, *Desire and Dignity*, 100.

In addition to bringing second wives to social events, men also talk openly about these women to their colleagues and friends in order to enhance their status. At a professional dinner, conversation about the latest Apple iPhone led one client to mention that he had to buy one for his second wife, and then he held up his phone as he spoke to show the incoming messages she was sending him about the new iPhone.[35] Men bond over the demands that their second wives make of them in order to signal their wealth and desirability. In some cases, the only reason a man keeps a second wife is to enhance his public image. Ah-Ying had a client in his sixties who was impotent, and they never had sex over the course of their year together. When she asked him why he kept her, he explained that he wanted to communicate to his friends, all of whom also had second wives, that he too had qualities that made him attractive to young women – virility, charm, wealth, and success.[36]

Isolation

Being a kept woman can be an isolating and lonely experience, both physically and emotionally. Physical isolation occurs when women quit their jobs and withdraw from their social circles once they become kept women. Their daily routines suddenly revolve almost entirely around one person, whose needs they must privilege over their own. In addition, the client is not living with them full time, which leaves the second wife with a lot of time on her own. Physical isolation can occur in response to a client's demands, and it can also be self-imposed. Client motivations for requesting that a second wife stop working are twofold: They want to signal that they have sufficient wealth to fully support her, and they also want to keep her away from situations where she would be spending time with other men who could pose a threat to him. The latter is of particular concern for hostesses who become second wives, given the nature of their entertainment venue responsibilities. When second wives willingly choose to distance themselves from their social networks, it is often out of a sense of shame and fear that their family might find out. Ah-Fang's situation, discussed earlier in this chapter, illustrates isolation motivated both by the client and the second wife.[37]

35 Hong, "China's Concubine Culture Lives On in Mistress Villages."
36 Xiao, "China's New Concubines?," 55. See also Xiao, *Desire and Dignity*, 39.
37 Xiao, "China's New Concubines?," 108–114. See also Xiao, *Desire and Dignity*, 87–89.

Not all second wives live in physical isolation. Some, like Lucy, spend a great deal of time socializing with friends, many of whom are also second wives. This is particularly the case when they live in "second wife villages" (二奶村 – *ernaicun*), areas with high concentrations of second wives. Yet even second wives in these situations cannot escape feelings of loneliness, especially when their long-term personal aspirations include marriage, as is frequently the case. Second wives have placed themselves in a situation that in many ways resembles marriage, yet that lacks several of the characteristics of marriage that they find desirable, such as monogamy and permanence. However, they cannot pursue that type of relationship while simultaneously serving as a second wife. The constant reminders they receive of this void in their lives, combined with the fact that they are actively preventing themselves from addressing it by being kept women, can leave second wives feeling adrift and lonely. Ah-Fang expressed feelings of paralysis: "Thinking about the future only makes me worry, gets [me] upset and desperate, so I just stop bothering myself. It is useless to think."[38]

Emotional Abuse

In addition to loneliness, second wives are also vulnerable to emotional abuse. Out of fear of alienating their client, they tend to passively absorb any mistreatment directed at them. Ah-Run described this process with her client:

> He is a nice guy except for his big temper. He wants things done at his command. If not, he will lose his temper. For example, if he wants to have lunch at eleven and I cannot get ready by then, he will shout at me, 'How come you are so late!' I will not shout back. Fighting with him will do no good, but make him more angry. I tell myself that he is just like that. He does not mean it although he appears rude. So I just keep silent or say something blaming myself or comforting him.[39]

Ah-Fei described similar outbursts from her client, Ah-Dong. When she complained that he came to see her less often, he accused her of being an ungrateful "bitch" who had been "fucked by so many men."[40] Although his words stung, she kept her feelings to herself, in order to

[38] Xiao, "China's New Concubines?," 120. See also Xiao, *Desire and Dignity*, 93.
[39] Xiao, "China's New Concubines?," 43. See also Xiao, *Desire and Dignity*, 32.
[40] Xiao, "China's New Concubines?," 51. See also Xiao, *Desire and Dignity*, 37–38.

avoid escalating the tension between them. Lucy described how, in response to her client's outbursts, her financial dependence upon him leads her to "hold my breath, keep myself silent, and swallow his words. It is really hard."[41]

Physical Violence and Murder

Second wives are less vulnerable to physical harm and violence than women in the bottom two tiers of the sex industry. Since they do not place themselves in intimate situations with strangers, they are relatively shielded from random acts of violence. They are, however, at risk of domestic violence, including murder. An official in Hubei province, for instance, was arrested following the death of his mistress. She was pregnant with twins, and he was accused of strangling her to death and throwing the body into a river after she demanded either marriage or a payment of $300,000.[42] In 2006, an official in Beijing paid his driver to strangle his mistress. The following year, a bureaucrat in the city of Jinan rigged a bomb on to his second wife's car. In 2011, another Beijing official had his mistress murdered and chopped into pieces.[43] In addition, stories of physical violence and murder at the hands of vengeful wives occasionally emerge in the media. Zhang Yufen, known as "the mistress killer" (二奶杀手 – *ernai shahou*), trains legal wives to beat up their husbands' mistresses (Zhang has apparently not actually been involved in any murders of mistresses).[44] Although such violent incidents occur relatively rarely, their horrific details provide insight into second wife relationships that go awry.

HEALTH

Work conditions in the top tier of the sex industry present fewer health risks than in the lowest and middle tiers. With only one sexual partner at any given time, second wives are less exposed to sexually transmitted diseases than hostesses, streetwalkers, and brothel workers. That said, they are still vulnerable to STD infections through their clients. Unlike women in the low and middle tiers of the sex industry, a second wife cannot ask her client to wear a condom. If she frames the request as a way

41 Xiao, "China's New Concubines?," 51. See also Xiao, *Desire and Dignity*, 38.
42 Dan Levin, "China's New Wealth Spurs a Market for Mistresses," *The New York Times*, August 9, 2011, https://perma.cc/Y7U5-W9EC.
43 Palmer, "How Young Women in China Become Mistresses."
44 Jiayang Fan, "China's Mistress-Dispellers," *The New Yorker*, June 19, 2017, https://perma.cc/W7QJ-275C.

to protect his health, she is signaling either that she has an STD from a previous relationship or that she is having sex with other men while he is supporting her. If she instead underscores concerns about the possibility that he might transmit an STD to her, he could be offended by her suggestion that he might not be healthy. Either way, the request is likely to result in the client terminating the relationship. One might expect clients of sex workers in the top tier to be at low risk of STD infection – they are generally businessmen and government officials, and are thus among the most educated in Chinese society. Yet, as discussed in Chapter 2, *yingchou*, the process of hosting professional contacts, is integral to work culture in China, and prostitution is a central component of that experience. As a result, these men are actually at significant risk of having STDs, and their behavior poses a threat to their legal wives, second wives, and any other sexual partners.[45] The risks that elite sex workers take when they have unprotected sex with their clients are thus serious.

In addition to concerns tied to HIV/AIDS and other STDs, the professional responsibilities of second wives also lead them to engage in other behaviors harmful to their health. Like hostesses, women in this tier of the sex industry are likely to smoke and drink excessively when they accompany their clients to social events. Ah-Fei sometimes spent weeks going out every night with her client Ah-Dong and his friends, returning home drunk in the early hours of the morning.[46] There is no elevator in her apartment, and twice she fell down the stairs after an alcohol-imbued night. While second wives do not engage in these entertainment activities as frequently as hostesses, this part of the job still takes its toll on their health.

EMOTIONS

The key distinguishing feature of elite prostitution, when compared to sex work in the low and middle tiers, is the central role that emotions play in relationships between second wives and clients. Both second wives and clients talk about fondness and love for each another, and when they decide to have a child, they perceive of this decision as evidence of the feelings that bond them together. These emotions

[45] Elanah Uretsky, *Occupational Hazards: Business, Sex, and HIV in Post-Mao China* (Stanford, CA: Stanford University Press, 2016), 3; Elanah Uretsky, "'Mobile Men with Money': The Socio-Cultural and Politico-Economic Context of 'High-Risk' Behaviour among Wealthy Businessmen and Government Officials in Urban China," *Culture, Health & Sexuality* 10, no. 8 (November 2008): 804.

[46] Xiao, "China's New Concubines?," 54. See also Xiao, *Desire and Dignity*, 41.

highlight the presence of counterintuitive narratives for both parties in the relationship: first, that a sex worker demands her client be faithful, and second, that a client believes that his relationship with a second wife actually allows him to be a more dutiful husband to his legal wife.

Language of Feelings

Second wives and clients use the term "have feelings for" (有感情 – *you ganqing* and 有感觉 – *you ganjue*) to describe the presence of emotions in their relationship. In describing her relationship to Ah-Cai, Ah-Run notes: "I felt like I was in love again."[47] Ah-Ping talked about how much she missed her client when they were apart.[48] Ah-Lan described how "I love [my client] Xiaomao because I feel I can rely on him."[49] Clients similarly express fondness for their second wife.[50] Xiaoshen talked about his love for his second wife, and how "I was willing to do anything for [her] . . . I was ready to go up to the sky and steal the moon for her if she ever asked."[51] Ah-Ping described how her client "was so crazy about me."[52] In response to one of her client's angry outbursts, Lucy asked, "[i]f he loves me as he claims to, how could he treat me like that?"[53] To be clear, not all second wives express these emotions for their clients. In some cases, they explicitly deny such feelings.[54] Although Lucy believed that her client loved her, she made clear that the feeling was not mutual: She was "way too good for him."[55] Ah-Fang also denied that she was in love with Bird, though in her case the observation was neutral, rather than grounded in an expression of superiority.[56] Yet, by and large, language of emotions plays an important role in how second wives and their clients discuss their relationships, much more so than in the lower two tiers of the sex industry.

The sincerity of these feelings, or their denial, is hard to gauge. Sex workers may emphasize love for a client for purely strategic reasons – to make him feel like she is attracted to his personality, character, and appearance, rather than his wealth. These women may also be trying to convince themselves that money is not driving the relationship. As

[47] Xiao, "China's New Concubines?," 129. See also Xiao, *Desire and Dignity*, 96.
[48] Xiao, "China's New Concubines?," 129–30. See also Xiao, *Desire and Dignity*, 123–24.
[49] Xiao, "China's New Concubines?," 142.
[50] Xiao, "China's New Concubines?," 145. See also Xiao, *Desire and Dignity*, 124, 142.
[51] Xiao, "China's New Concubines?," 146.
[52] Xiao, "China's New Concubines?," 128. See also Xiao, *Desire and Dignity*, 119–120.
[53] Xiao, "China's New Concubines?," 79. See also Xiao, *Desire and Dignity*, 53.
[54] Xiao, "China's New Concubines?," 96. See also Xiao, *Desire and Dignity*, 73, 82, 85.
[55] Xiao, "China's New Concubines?," 80. See also Xiao, *Desire and Dignity*, 53.
[56] Xiao, "China's New Concubines?," 96, 120. See also Xiao, *Desire and Dignity*, 93.

discussed in Chapter 7, many women in all tiers of the sex industry deny that what they are doing is prostitution, and emphasizing their emotional connection to the client helps them to sustain that perception. At the same time that some women may be expressing emotions that they are not actually feeling, other women, such as Lucy and Ah-Fang, may be concealing those same emotions. When a second wife recognizes that she is attached to her client, she places herself in an extremely vulnerable position of hoping that he will leave his legal wife for her, which rarely happens.

Children as Evidence of Love

While some of these expressions of love may be insincere, the decision of a second wife and her client to have a child is concrete evidence that a strong emotional bond exists between the two of them. The birth of a second wife's child is rarely the result of an unplanned pregnancy and an unwillingness to terminate it; as a result of the one-child policy, abortion is not stigmatized in China the way it is in some other societies. When a second wife and her client choose to become parents, they both face uphill battles, as does the child. The decision complicates a client's efforts to shield his legal wife from the knowledge of his second wife. It also increases the second wife's marginalization. She faces judgment for engaging in prostitution, an activity she can no longer hide from her family because of her need for childcare assistance. In addition, she is criticized for having a child out of wedlock, a major transgression of social boundaries in China. The child starts out life with a significant disadvantage: He or she cannot easily get a legal household registration, which opens up the door to major social services such as education and healthcare.[57] Given all of these challenges, it is difficult to view the decision to have a child as anything other than an emotional one. As Li Ya, who had a one-year-old daughter with her client, noted, her relationship "is built on deep love … [t]hat's why I have dared to have a baby."[58]

Expectations of Fidelity

Evidence of some second wives' emotional attachment to their client comes through in their expectation of his fidelity. Wen expressed surprise upon learning that her client also kept other women: "I knew

[57] Xiao, "China's New Concubines?," 131. See also Xiao, *Desire and Dignity*, 122.
[58] Xiao, "China's New Concubines?," 133. See also Xiao, *Desire and Dignity*, 123.

he had to have a wife. . . . I'm not stupid. But I thought I was his *ernai* [second wife], that he loved me. Then I found that he kept three others around the city. I was his 'fifth woman,' not his second."[59] Lucy claimed to demand loyalty from her client, a request that she framed as an issue of basic respect: "I am young, pretty, and treat him well. I deserve him being faithful to me. If he were to cheat on me, it would be degrading to me."[60] Yet, in practice, a second wife is limited in her ability to control her client's behavior: If she threatens to leave, she runs the risk of losing her sole source of income. In addition, the demand is rife with contradictions. The fact that a married man supports a second wife shows a track record of infidelity. When the second wife meets her client as a hostess at an entertainment venue, she has further evidence that he has likely paid for sex in the past. More generally, given that second wives are in a line of work where they are surrounded by married men who purchase sex, they have more reason to question male fidelity than most other women in China. When women such as Lucy request fidelity from their clients, or when they express surprise or dismay upon learning of other women in their clients' lives, the dissonance with their own life experiences is jarring.

The Dutiful Husband

When clients talk about their feelings toward their second wives, they highlight another counterintuitive observation: They believe that having an extramarital affair is compatible with being a dutiful husband and family member. In their eyes, their marital responsibilities include adequate financial support for their family, and participation in childcare and household chores. They do not involve being faithful, physically present beyond fulfilling their basic responsibilities, or emotionally invested in their wife.[61] Their relationship with their second wife exists within the realm of individual desire, which they view as completely separate from the moral obligations they have toward their spouse. Chen Yu, a man who had been in several long-term extramarital relationships, explained: "I was a decent husband and father, generally speaking. I took care of the family finances, sent our son to a good private school, and stayed at home for all the important holidays."[62]

[59] Palmer, "How Young Women in China Become Mistresses."
[60] Xiao, "China's New Concubines?," 80. See also Xiao, *Desire and Dignity*, 53.
[61] Osburg, *Anxious Wealth*, 67; Xiao, *China's New Concubines?*, 154. See also Xiao, *Desire and Dignity*, 155.
[62] Xiao, "China's New Concubines?," 153. See also Xiao, *Desire and Dignity*, 155.

Zheng Meng spent three nights a week with his second wife, but pointed to the fact that he spent weekends and holidays at home as evidence of his dutiful behavior.[63]

According to this view of marriage, a client's decision to remain married to his legal wife is in fact the ultimate evidence that he is behaving in a morally upright manner. Bird told Ah-Fang that he would not get divorced because his wife had earned her keep: She gave birth to two boys, worked hard, and cared for her in-laws.[64] Lao Wang had similar praise to bestow upon his wife, who is "a good person, kind and warm-hearted, and is devoted to our family and our son."[65] He emphasized how he would still be married to her had she not insisted on getting divorced upon learning of his second wife, explaining: "I would still be fulfilling my duty as a husband and a father."[66] Chen Yu's wife also wanted a divorce, but Chen Yu persuaded her to stay married: "I didn't really care if we divorced or not. It actually was not wise for her to divorce me. ... At her age (mid-30s), it would not be easy to get remarried, especially to a man as responsible as I am."[67] Chen Yu's observation about the difficulty of divorce and remarriage for women is accurate. Yet it obscures the effect that divorce can have on the husband, including the way it can emasculate him by portraying him as unable to properly balance his familial duties and extramarital relationships. When his wife is a respectable woman who has treated him well, divorce reflects poorly on the husband, who is viewed as lacking a sense of responsibility toward his family.[68]

Second wives concur with this view that their clients are upstanding citizens, without acknowledging how keeping a second wife might taint others' views of him. Ah-Run praised her client in strong terms: "He provides the best for his family. When he is home, he does almost all the housework, cooking, sweeping the floor, taking the kids to school, etc. He calls his family every day when he is here to make sure everything is

[63] Xiao, 154. See also Xiao, *Desire and Dignity*, 155. Clients also reconcile their marital responsibilities with their decision to solicit sex in the lowest and middle tiers of the sex industry: sex, singing, drinking, and dancing are all activities that exist purely within the realm of personal enjoyment. Yet the ability to also do so in relation to keeping a second wife is most striking, given the intensity and length of relationships with second wives, and overlap with dynamics of a legal marriage.

[64] Xiao, "China's New Concubines?," 117–18. See also Xiao, *Desire and Dignity*, 91–92.

[65] Xiao, "China's New Concubines?," 152. See also Xiao, *Desire and Dignity*, 157.

[66] Xiao, "China's New Concubines?," 152. See also Xiao, *Desire and Dignity*, 157.

[67] Xiao, "China's New Concubines?," 153. See also Xiao, *Desire and Dignity*, 155.

[68] Osburg, *Anxious Wealth*, 72.

fine back home. . . . He is such a good man, responsible and caring."[69] On the one hand, a view of marriage that reconciles being a dutiful husband with having a second wife reflects a social and cultural perspective that differs from the norm that predominates in Western countries. Yet clients' first wives, while often resigned to accepting their husband's infidelity, rarely embrace it, as discussed later in this chapter. The harm it often causes them, and their resistance to it, highlights how the "dutiful husband perspective" neglects the preferences of the first wife and serves more to convince the client and the second wife of the acceptability of their actions.

PERSPECTIVES ON THEIR OCCUPATION

Much as second wives talk about the role that emotions play in their relationship with a client, they also recognize that they are engaged in compensated work. Lucy stated this explicitly after describing various gifts that her client had given her: "But you know I am not getting economic resources from him for free. I am paying with my body, time, youth, and emotions. I am actually the party that pays more. Even though he is away most of the time and cannot control me, I have to accompany him and make him happy at least twice a month."[70] In sharing their perspectives on this work, second wives generally express satisfaction with their daily lives and their decision to be kept by a man, despite the isolation, emotional abuse, and threats to health and safety that sometimes characterize their experiences. When compared with both hostesses and women in the lowest tier of prostitution, elite sex workers have the most positive attitudes toward their work, which they find provides them with "personal dignity, distinction, and belonging" in society.[71] The client provides them with the ability to pursue an otherwise unaffordable "modern, urban, consumerist" lifestyle, and they gain "a home where they obtained a sense of security, belonging, understanding, caring and even some fun."[72] They earn "recognition and respect from their peers," and achieve a "more dignified life with a physical and emotional space that makes them feel at home in urban areas."[73]

69 Xiao, "China's New Concubines?," 142. See also Xiao, *Desire and Dignity*, 101.
70 Xiao, "China's New Concubines?," 77. See also Xiao, *Desire and Dignity*, 51–52.
71 Xiao, "China's New Concubines?," 8. See also Xiao, *Desire and Dignity*, 21, 59.
72 Xiao, 73; 117. See also Xiao, *Desire and Dignity*, 60, 86.
73 Xiao, 8. See also Xiao, *Desire and Dignity*, 59, 91.

Attitudes toward Legal Wives

In reflecting upon her work, a second wife has to contend with her client's legal wife. A woman who engages in prostitution in the low or middle tiers of the sex industry can easily avoid thinking about a client's personal life. She only has fleeting interactions with him. Even if he shares information about his marital status, the legal wife is only an abstract figure in the background whose existence can quickly be forgotten. The same cannot be said about elite sex work: The second wife's role in the man's life is defined entirely in relation and in contrast to the legitimate spouse. Given the long-term nature of the illicit relationship, the second wife tends to learn a lot about the spouse. She is acutely aware that the client is constantly comparing them, given the overlapping roles they play in his life. They both provide him with sexual and domestic services, as well as emotional support. In cases where a client and a second wife have a child together, it means both the first wife and the second wife are parenting a client's children. As second wives cannot easily ignore a legal wife, they instead appear to either blame her for her husband's extramarital affair or express guilt for interfering in the marriage. Second wives express blame when they criticize a legal wife for not being able to hold on to her husband.[74] They express guilt when, like Ah-Run, they liken their own behavior to "stealing her husband."[75] In fact, Ah-Run sought to assuage her remorse by going out of her way to assemble gifts for Ah-Liang to give on his behalf when he returned to his legal family. Regardless of whether mistresses focus on blame or guilt, the legal wife's presence looms large in their daily lives.

VIEWS OF THE STATE

The background presence of a client's legal wife serves as a reminder that second wives are engaged in behavior that is against the law. Yet, as described in Part III, the state rarely targets them for engaging in prostitution. Because of their limited experiences with state interventions that aim to regulate their lives, most women in this tier of the sex industry have relatively little to say about the state. They do not feel its presence with the same immediacy as do low-tier sex workers and

[74] Osburg, *Anxious Wealth*, 167.
[75] Xiao, "China's New Concubines?," 155. See also Xiao, *Desire and Dignity*, 101.

hostesses. Consequently, when second wives talk about their daily lives, the state does not feature prominently in their narratives.

Yet mistresses do in fact experience the state directly. For one thing, their clients are often government officials. Even if they perceive of the state as largely irrelevant and unthreatening, second wives whose clients work for the state are actually embedded within it. Mistresses are also occasionally involved in their clients' business dealings, including representing their clients at illicit business meetings and receiving bribes on their behalf.[76] This type of professional responsibility is unique to sex workers in the top tier, and it can translate into opportunities for second wives to launch their own businesses. For example, Wen runs a multimillion dollar property business that flourished through her client's connections.[77] Li Zhen, a former Tax Bureau chief of Hebei Province tried and executed for corruption in 2003, admitted to using his connections to secure government construction contracts for his mistress.[78]

Second wives' embeddedness in state affairs – either as mistresses to government officials or even in some cases through active participation in their clients' work – undoubtedly contributes to their lack of concern about the state, as they feel a sense of protection and immunity. This embeddedness also gives them the greatest power they have over their clients, because they gain information that allows them to serve as whistleblowers who expose the corruption of former clients. In 2013, Yi Junqing, the head of the Compilation and Translation Bureau, was fired for "lifestyle behavioral problems" after his mistress publicized their relationship online. She had discovered that he was in multiple extramarital relationships and had also grown frustrated with his empty promises to help her secure a job at his agency.[79] In Heilongjiang, civil servant Sun Dejiang's infidelities were exposed by his mistress, who was also a reporter.[80] Tian Hanwen, a local official in Henan province, was expelled from the Communist Party after his mistress posted a sex video of them. She had grown frustrated that he had never

76 Osburg, *Anxious Wealth*, 176.
77 Palmer, "How Young Women in China Become Mistresses."
78 Osburg, *Anxious Wealth*, 176.
79 François Bougon and Brice Pedroletti, "Chine: Le Marxiste En Chef Tombe Pour Un Scandale Sexuel," *Le Monde*, January 19, 2013, perma.cc/BZ65-J6ZJ.
80 Oiwan Lam, "Mistresses – China's New Corruption Warriors," *Global Voices* (blog), November 27, 2012, perma.cc/D3SM-GHVW.

followed through on his promise to help her find a job.[81] A deputy director of the State Archives Administration, Fan Yue, was exposed by the young TV host who was his mistress when she found out that he was married.[82] Liu Zhihua, a former vice mayor of Beijing, was turned in for corruption by his mistress.[83] Li Zhen – the former Tax Bureau chief of Hebei province mentioned earlier in this section who was executed for graft – was hiding from the authorities until his mistress told them where to find him.[84] Liu Tienan, a former deputy director of the National Reform and Development Commission, China's main economic-planning institution, lost his job following an investigation that his mistress instigated by contacting a journalist.[85] An anti-corruption official in Dongguan noted that in over 80 percent of corruption cases they investigate, mistresses played an important role in exposing the case.[86] The phenomenon is prevalent enough that it even has a specific name, "mistress-driven anti-corruption" (二奶反腐 – *ernai fanfu*), and has graced the editorial pages of the Communist Party's mouthpiece newspaper, the *People's Daily*. The *People's Daily* article warns against relying on such sources in combatting corruption, given the less-than-noble motivations often underlying such whistleblowers' decisions to report their clients' misdeeds, and the fact that they too can be involved in the corruption they are denouncing.[87]

Although the vast majority of second wives will never act as whistleblowers, it is a significant way that some elite sex workers encounter the state. Rather than living in fear of the state and seeking to avoid it, these women instead experience it on their own terms when they choose to address an issue unrelated to their participation in the sex industry: the corrupt actions of their clients.

81 Xinhua, "Online Sex Video Leads to Dismissal of Chinese Official," *Xinhua*, August 6, 2011, www.wantchinatimes.com/news-subclass-cnt.aspx?id=20110806000032&cid=1303.

82 Lijia Zhang, "China's Corrupt Officials Have More to Fear from Jilted Lover than Crackdown," *South China Morning Post*, August 16, 2013, perma.cc/JLC4-NRZC; Jia Lynn Yang, "Jilted Mistresses Expose Chinese Officials' Corruption," *The Washington Post*, July 25, 2013, perma.cc/2K2E-QHQH.

83 John Osburg, "Tough Love: Money and Mistresses in the Middle Kingdom," *Foreign Affairs*, June 12, 2014, perma.cc/92QJ-2QGH.

84 Osburg.

85 Josh Chin, "Mistress-Driven Anticorruption: Study Says 15 percent of Accusers Are Lovers," *WSJ.Com* (blog), October 17, 2013, perma.cc/T57S-77BC.

86 Sky Canaves, "Mistresses Enlisted in the Fight against Corruption," *WSJ Blogs – China Real Time Report* (blog), June 26, 2008, perma.cc/WYF2-DN2Y.

87 Chin, "Mistress-Driven Anticorruption"; Megha Rajagopalan and Yan Huang, "China's Spurned Mistresses Can't Be Relied on to Bust Graft," *Reuters*, May 29, 2013, perma.cc/77T8-6RJX.

OUTSIDERS' PERSPECTIVES

Mistresses are in the tier of sex work that elicits the least amount of sympathy within Chinese society. Legal wives place more blame on second wives than on their husbands. They also sometimes take active steps to break off the extramarital affair, by hiring a "mistress dispeller" to sever the relationship with the second wife. When exposed, clients also place all the blame for a relationship on their mistress, and Chinese public opinion generally views second wives much more harshly than clients or other types of sex workers.

The Legal Wife

Although a husband will generally try to hide his extramarital affair from his legal wife, she is likely to suspect that something is going on. In the words of one second wife: "I'm not sure if she knows about me. But I would be suspicious if my husband spent a couple nights out of the house every week."[88] Upon learning about a husband's relationship with a second wife, a legal wife generally places more blame on the woman. This was the case for Fang Li, who was more upset toward the second wife than her husband, whom she still loved.[89] Although the second wife can pose a threat to the legal wife, she can also be the weaker party: The legitimate spouse sometimes rightfully underscores her own greater staying power and points out that a second wife can be more easily discarded once the husband tires of her.[90]

Faced with suspicions or evidence that her husband is keeping a second wife, most legal wives choose to turn a blind eye rather than take action.[91] As noted earlier in this chapter, divorce is stigmatized in China, and the remarriage prospects for a Chinese divorcée in her thirties or above are slim. These women are often economically dependent on their husbands, with limited opportunities to maintain their current quality of life, and frequently decide that resigned acceptance is the best course of action for their economic stability and their children's well-being. In the words of one woman, reflecting on the many acquaintances she knew in this situation: "Most [legal wives] quietly tolerate it and focus on their children. Others get lost in

[88] Xiao, "China's New Concubines?," 173.
[89] Xiao, "China's New Concubines?," 172.
[90] Osburg, *Anxious Wealth*, 168.
[91] Xiao, "China's New Concubines?," 173; Osburg, *Anxious Wealth*, 167. See also Xiao, *Desire and Dignity*, 134, 152.

shopping or playing mahjong."[92] In the cases when a legal wife does initiate divorce, she is likely to have high education levels and socioeconomic status.[93]

Instead of passively accepting the relationship, or seeking a divorce, a legal wife sometimes tries to separate her husband and the second wife, and win him back to a committed monogamous relationship. The desire for this outcome has given rise to the recent emergence of professional "mistress dispellers" (小三劝退师 – *xiaosan quantuishi*) in China. One goal of their work is to break up the illegal relationship by focusing on the second wife. An investigation team, which might include a psychotherapist and a lawyer, first conducts background research on her. "Once we figure out what type of mistress she is – in it for money, love or sex – we draw up a plan," explained the director of one mistress dispeller organization.[94] A team member will then try to get to know the second wife, by moving into her apartment building or becoming a regular presence in her life, for example by going to the same gym.[95] Mistress dispellers use a variety of strategies to drive off the second wife. They might convince her to break off the relationship, perhaps by sharing unsavory details about the husband's life.[96] Although they deny it, mistress dispellers also use seduction and violence as tactics.[97]

The second goal of mistress dispellers' work is to increase the legal wife's desirability in her husband's eyes. They might recommend that she buy him gifts, write romantic messages to him, or wear seductive clothes.[98] They might also suggest playing hard to get. To justify this tactic, the head of one mistress dispeller agency explained: "Chinese women think that if you treat men well, they'll love you more. But often, we men love the people who hurt us the most."[99] Discretion is a significant aspect of their work, as they strive to prevent the husband from learning about their efforts to reconnect him with his legal wife.

Mistress dispelling services are only accessible to the wealthiest of Chinese wives. The base fee can start at 300,000 yuan (about $45,000),

92 Osburg, *Anxious Wealth*, 167.
93 Xiao, "China's New Concubines?," 173–174.
94 Emily Feng and Charlotte Yang, "China's Cheating Husbands Fuel an Industry of 'Mistress Dispellers,'" *The New York Times*, July 29, 2016, sec. Asia Pacific, perma.cc/H7QQ-Y9L3.
95 Feng and Yang.
96 Fan, "China's Mistress-Dispellers."
97 Feng and Yang, "China's Cheating Husbands Fuel an Industry of 'Mistress Dispellers'"; Fan, "China's Mistress-Dispellers."
98 Fan, "China's Mistress-Dispellers."
99 Feng and Yang, "China's Cheating Husbands Fuel an Industry of 'Mistress Dispellers.'"

excluding expenses.[100] Yet demand for them is high. One agency reported serving about 10,000 clients annually, and another reported almost 200 inquiries on any given day.[101] As of 2016, one agency had branches in fifty-nine different cities in the country.[102] This demand highlights the extent to which legal wives object to the presence of a second wife. Although they are likely also displeased with the idea that their husband is paying for sex from low- and middle-tier sex workers, it is the second wife who elicits the strongest negative reaction.[103] As noted in Chapter 2, the idea that men, but not women, have a biological need for sex is widespread, and straight-up exchange of sex for money is thus more easily tolerated. It is the intensity of the second wife relationship, and its overlap with many of the defining characteristics of marriage, that makes it harder for a legal wife to accept and justify.

The Client

Clients accused of corruption frequently blame their second wife for their behavior. In the courtroom, investigated officials regularly defend their actions by portraying themselves as weak men driven to corruption in order to try to satisfy their insatiable mistresses. Li Zhen, the former Hebei official whose mistress helped the authorities find him, noted that "[a]s soon as [women] become your plaything you become their slave."[104] He further declared that "[i]n this world, only the kiss of a woman will send you to your doom," a warning he sought to "tell all the men of the world."[105] His public blaming of his second wife is total: "Without her, I wouldn't have committed crimes; I wouldn't have committed such big crimes, and I definitely wouldn't be [facing] death!"[106] A former official in the transportation bureau in Chongqing defended his involvement in corruption as follows: "I knelt down before [my mistress] in my office, but she still wouldn't let me go. I was just too weak. She wanted to bleed me dry."[107] These are

100 Feng and Yang; Fan, "China's Mistress-Dispellers."
101 Feng and Yang, "China's Cheating Husbands Fuel an Industry of 'Mistress Dispellers.'"
102 Feng and Yang.
103 Zhao Jun (赵军), *Chengfa De Bianjie: Maiyin Xingshi Zhengce Shizheng Yanjiu (惩罚的边界：卖淫刑事政策实证研究) [The Limit for Punishment: The Positive Research on Prostitution Criminal Policy]* (China Legal Publishing House, 2007), 164–68, www.chinamaxx.net/showbook?dxNumber=11948339&d=824FA35C0D356EFFAF3717B64482C52F.
104 Osburg, *Anxious Wealth*, 176.
105 Osburg, 178.
106 Osburg, 178.
107 Osburg, 176.

confessions of accused men. The officials making them are in an extremely vulnerable position, desperate to say whatever might alleviate their sentences, regardless of what they actually believe. In addition, the state has approved release of their testimony to the public, which suggests it endorses a message focused on vilifying the second wife.

The Public

Public opinion largely echoes the perspectives of legal wives and husbands in holding second wives responsible for the behavior of the men in extramarital relationships, and is quick to judge these women as predatory schemers responsible for moral decline in contemporary China. One media commentator called mistresses the "fertilizer" of corrupt officials, noting that these men "increase the speed and power of their corrupt activities" in response to the demands of their mistress.[108] A website that the lawyer Zheng Baichun created to inform second wives of their legal rights created an outpouring of criticism for portraying these women as victims, rather than villains.[109] Movies and television shows portray them as homewreckers.[110] Female entrepreneurs, who have succeeded professionally without becoming involved in the sex industry, view second wives as "simply lazy, lacking in ability . . . and of low quality."[111] Scholars and intellectuals portray them as symbols of a societal shift away from ideals of gender equality that were central to the emergence of modern China and part of a crisis in values that plagues the country.[112] Low-tier sex workers tend to garner sympathy due to their poverty and the hardships they experience on a daily basis in their work environment. Second wives, meanwhile, are perceived as power-hungry opportunists who are paid to live in comfortable homes, spend money on luxury items, and travel to exotic places with their clients.

CONCLUSION

Second wives live in a world of simultaneous precariousness and power. Their precariousness comes from their total dependence on one man.

[108] Osburg, 175.
[109] Osburg, 181.
[110] Osburg, 143–44.
[111] Osburg, 148–49.
[112] Osburg, 143–44.

Unlike women in the lower tiers of the sex industry who solicit on the streets, in brothels, or in entertainment venues, for second wives, finding another client can be a complicated, drawn-out process. Their vulnerability also comes from the state of limbo inherent in a mistress arrangement. They know the relationship is temporary, and while they often yearn for marriage, as kept women they cannot take steps toward that goal. Their power, meanwhile, comes from the emotional dependence their clients sometimes have on them. Smitten men will go to great lengths to keep their second wives happy and shower them with countless gifts to do so. It also comes from the knowledge that second wives sometimes gain of their client's business activities, which provides these women with tools that can be used to help orchestrate his professional downfall when a relationship sours. This combination of vulnerability and strength presents a picture of second wives that belies the harsh reception they receive in Chinese public opinion.

7

PERSPECTIVES AND EXPERIENCES SHARED ACROSS TIERS OF PROSTITUTION

INTRODUCTION

The daily lives of low-tier sex workers, hostesses, and second wives in China differ in important ways. Yet despite relatively fixed boundaries between tiers of prostitution, these women do not exist in unrelated, independent silos. After all, their source of income comes from the same activity: exchanging sex for money or other material goods. This chapter first highlights how movement across tiers of sex work is limited, and how low-tier sex workers and hostesses express a preference for the work conditions in their own tier, rather than voice a desire to move up in the pecking order. It then examines narratives that these women have in common across all three tiers. Lastly, it discusses how sex workers who cross paths with grassroots organizations develop a shared consciousness of their membership in a global community of sex work civil society, and appropriate its language and symbols in their own lives.

BOUNDARIES BETWEEN TIERS

Sex workers rarely hold simultaneous positions in several different tiers. Among the more than 500 sex workers I surveyed, only six reported working concurrently in both a middle-tier and a low-tier venue.[1] Movement between tiers over time also appears limited: Only nine surveyed women had moved from a low-tier to a middle-tier space, and

[1] Please see the Appendix for more details about the survey

none reported transitioning in the other direction. Borders are more porous between the middle and top tiers: Clients sometimes recruit hostesses to become second wives, and these women might revert back to hostessing if the relationship falls apart.

PERSPECTIVES ON SEX WORK HIERARCHY

Viewed from the higher ranks of the sex industry, the status differences between low-tier sex workers, hostesses, and second wives seem clear. The further removed a woman is from a straightforward exchange of sex for money, the higher her social standing. Second wives and hostesses speak in disparaging terms of their lower-tier counterparts. Ah-Run, who had been a second wife for three years, describes her situation as follows: "I am not a prostitute. I can't do it (have sex) with just any man."[2] As Suowei Xiao notes of this statement, "Ah-Run drew a clear boundary between [her] particular arrangement and those that she saw as less acceptable."[3] This is a distinction that the other mistresses in her study make as well.[4] Hostesses I interviewed also tended to be condescending toward sex workers in the low tier. They portray low-tier prostitution as both easier – because it does not require an ability to sing, dance, or provide nonsexual entertainment for clients – and also more dangerous. Song Qin characterized prostitution in hair salons and on the street as easy money: "In hair and massage salons, they have sex right away, the money comes quickly. After a few minutes, they get to pocket 100 *kuai* [$15] and then can just do it again."[5] Ying Yi explained, "in bathhouses and hair salons who knows what kind of person you'll encounter. You do any client who comes in, you haven't built

2 Suowei Xiao, "China's New Concubines? The Contemporary Second-Wife Phenomenon" (ProQuest Dissertations, 2009), 129, perma.cc/T6U2-M8ME.

3 Xiao, 129. The process that Ah-Run and the other sex workers in this section are engaging in is called "boundary work" in sociology. See Thomas F. Gieryn, "Boundary-Work and the Demarcation of Science from Non-Science: Strains and Interests in Professional Ideologies of Scientists," *American Sociological Review* 48, no. 6 (1983): 781–95, https://doi.org/10.2307/2095325. For discussion of the concept in contemporary China, see Sida Liu, "Boundary Work and Exchange: The Formation of a Professional Service Market," *Symbolic Interaction* 38, no. 1 (2015): 1–21, https://doi.org/10.1002/symb.137; Lily Liang, "No Room for Respectability: Boundary Work in Interaction at a Shanghai Rental," *Symbolic Interaction* 41, no. 2 (2018): 185–209, https://doi.org/10.1002/symb.325.

4 Xiao, "China's New Concubines?," 2009, 155. See also Suowei Xiao (肖索未), *Yuwang Yu Zunyan: Zhuanxingqi Zhongguo De Jieceng, Xingbie Yu Qinmi Guanxi* (欲望与尊严: 转型期中国的阶层, 性别与亲密关系) *[Desire and Dignity : Class, Gender and Intimacy in Transitional China]* (Beijing: China Social Sciences Academic Press (社会科学文献出版社), 2018), 97.

5 Sex Worker Interview 3, August 26, 2009. The term "kuai" is colloquial for "yuan."

erstanding."[6] Xiao Ting concurred, noting er the place, it isn't like hair salons and t venues you can acquire a lot of know- ing mentioned how "in hair salons, in a dozen clients … that is really asized how low-tier prostitution "is a bit , but your life is even more important."[9] ed the superiority of hostessing:

> If you have worked in a hair salon or bathhouse, you can't pull off venue work. In hair salons, it's direct sexual services. The exchange is over quickly, and it's easy. In entertainment venues, by contrast, you have to host for three hours, you need to drink and sing. It's so exhausting (太苦 – *tai ku*). Women in hair salons and bathhouses can't pull off venue work.[10]

Mei Lin was among the harshest, telling me that "those girls [in low-end sex work] are really cheap, that is no way to earn money."[11]

Yet instead of accepting this pecking order and expressing a desire to move up in the hierarchy, women in the lower two tiers instead emphasize the benefits of their respective work environments. Sex workers I interviewed in the lowest tier portrayed hostesses' required activities as burdensome and unhealthy. They emphasized the

6 Sex Worker Interview 4, August 23, 2009.

7 Sex Worker Interview 2, August 21, 2009.

8 Sex Worker Interview 4, August 18, 2009.

9 Sex Worker Interview 2, August 15, 2009.

10 Sex Worker Interview 1, August 23, 2009.

11 Sex Worker Interview 3, August 22, 2009. Disdain for lower-tier sex workers is not limited to China. Talking about middle-class sex workers in the San Francisco Bay Area, Bernstein found that

> "[t]here is a crucial … distinction that is enforced between 'professional sex workers' and those who walk the streets. It is not just the distinction between trained professional and unskilled labor that is at stake here, but a fierce reluctance to hover anywhere near (let alone to cross!) the class divide … a more general sensibility which placed certain kinds of sex work … socially beneath them."

Elizabeth Bernstein, *Temporarily Yours: Intimacy, Authenticity, and the Commerce of Sex* (Chicago: University of Chicago Press, 2007), 86. The distinctions that sex workers make about different tiers echo patterns found within other groups of marginalized individuals. Examining poor urban residents living on Los Angeles' Skid Row, Forrest Stuart notes how they "internalize and reproduce the negative stereotypes of the urban poor, which stimulated internal differentiation and mutual distancing as residents constructed rigid moral dichotomies between themselves and their neighbors." See Forrest Stuart, "Becoming 'Copwise': Policing, Culture, and the Collateral Consequences of Street-Level Criminalization," *Law & Society Review* 50, no. 2 (2016): 295–96, https://doi.org/10.1111/lasr.12201.

disadvantages of having to spend more time with a clien[illegible] tainment venue, along with the health threats of havin[illegible] smoke, and occasionally use drugs when working as a hos[illegible] Mei described her middle-tier colleagues' experiences as follows: [illegible] have to drink with the client. You're always drinking, drinking mo[illegible] Clients will feel you up, feel you up all over your body. They'll force you to drink, get you completely drunk. In the entertainment venue you'll have to work three hours, sometimes five hours. It won't last more than forty minutes in a hair salon."[12]

Li Ting similarly presented her participation in hair salon prostitution as a conscious choice against hostessing: "I thought about working in an entertainment venue, but working there is too complicated. Drinking alcohol is harmful to your body. Also, they have ecstasy there. If you leave the room to go to the bathroom, they might put drugs into your glass. You won't even know, and then you'll get addicted. Entertainment venues are too complicated."[13] Su Yin admitted to being personally unfamiliar with entertainment venues, before sharing with me how her understanding was that "in those places . . . you'll drink a lot of alcohol, it will make your stomach hurt, and people there are a little perverted (变态 – *biantai*)."[14] Xiao Huang also highlighted her aversion to alcohol as a reason she preferred soliciting on the street.[15] Wen Ling underscored the increased independence she has as a sex worker who solicits in a public park: "Streetwalkers have more freedom. [Hostesses] have a lot of restrictions at work."[16] She went on to discuss the strict work hours and percentage of work earnings that she would be required to give her madam if she worked in an entertainment venue. Hostesses, meanwhile, highlight the benefits of their circumstances compared to second wives. Jia Qing discussed the loss of independence that comes with being a kept woman.[17] Xiao Yuan concurred, describing the difficulties of managing a long-term partner's jealousy and fear that she might be engaging in other relationships.[18]

There is some truth to the advantages these women highlight about their respective work environments. Yet by most external measures,

12 Sex Worker Interview 5, August 24, 2009.
13 Sex Worker Interview 2, August 24, 2009.
14 Sex Worker Interview 4, August 20, 2009.
15 Sex Worker Interview 6, August 20, 2009.
16 Sex Worker Interview 7, August 20, 2009.
17 Sex Worker Interview 4, August 22, 2009.
18 Sex Worker Interview 3, August 18, 2009.

quality of life increases as one moves up the hierarchy of the sex industry. One interpretation of the case sex workers make for their own circumstances is that when they interact with me, a foreign researcher, they seek to disguise the shame and embarrassment they feel for working in a lower tier. Yet given the relationships I forged with some sex workers over time, and other types of personal reflections they shared with me in interviews, this explanation rings hollow.[19] More likely, these women were providing me with insight into a much deeper internalization of their lot in life, and evidence of the human ability to come to terms with disappointing circumstances in ways that still allow individuals to hold their head up high.

SHARED NARRATIVES

Despite the lines that sex workers draw between the different types of prostitution in which they engage, and the differences across tiers highlighted in Chapters 4–6, these women also have many shared perspectives. Women in all three tiers of the sex industry recount similar narratives around their entry into prostitution, reasons for selling sex, and the temporary nature of their engagement in it. Other similarities include complicated family dynamics and denial that their work is prostitution. They express similar opinions about the benefits of prostitution and share an ambivalence about its morality. Finally, while the previous chapters underscore differences in their perspectives on the state, sex workers' overall attitudes toward the state are more negative than the views that the general population holds.

Gradual Transition into Prostitution

Across all three tiers, entry into the sex industry is rarely a premeditated or immediate process, with a young woman in rural China migrating to an urban area with the specific intent to sell sex. Most of these women do not engage in prostitution prior to leaving their hometown. Of the sex workers in my survey, only forty-three (8 percent) had sold sex before arriving in Beijing. They also rarely enter sex work immediately upon settling in their new environment. Instead, they gradually make

[19] Please see the Appendix for a more in-depth discussion of how I carried out the research for this project.

their way into prostitution after other plans fail to work out or they realize they can earn more money selling sex.[20]

Most women who end up in the sex industry first make a decision to migrate from their rural hometown to an urban area in search of better economic opportunities. My survey participants all worked in a red-light district in Beijing, but only three (less than 1 percent) were originally from that city. The others came from twenty-two different provinces throughout China, as shown in Figure 7.1.

The narratives of sex workers in Chapters 4–6 tell similar migratory stories. Upon arrival in the city, these women tend to find jobs in factories, restaurants, stores, or domestic service.[21] Work hours and conditions in these sectors are grueling, with average monthly salaries of a couple hundred yuan – only a fraction of the several thousand yuan per month that the lowest-paid sex workers earn.[22] Jing Ming went from earning 600 yuan per month as a nanny/housekeeper (阿姨 – *ayi*) to 3,400 yuan in her first month selling sex in a karaoke venue. She remembered the figure "very clearly," because it was so much more than she had ever earned in a month before.[23] Ting Ting earned 1,000 yuan a month cutting hair at a legitimate hair salon in her hometown in Hubei province, and saw her monthly income increase tenfold to 10,000 yuan as a hostess.[24] As these women become integrated into communities of other migrant workers, they hear about and meet peers who have left similar jobs and are now earning much more in the sex industry. This opportunity to rub elbows with sex workers reveals the benefits of prostitution compared to other types of employment: better pay, fewer hours, and more flexibility. It also helps normalize the exchange of sex for money. Exposure and familiarity can quickly transform an act that appears appalling in the abstract into one that seems instead like a perfectly acceptable and reasonable source of livelihood.

[20] The pattern described here applies to women who have agency as it pertains to their engagement in prostitution. It does not reflect the experience of women who are forced and trafficked into the sex industry.

[21] The migration and employment pattern described here does not apply to those second wives who are university students, as they move to an urban area because they have been accepted to university there, or to those urban women who sometimes become second wives in their hometown.

[22] See Chapter 4 for more information on low-tier sex workers' earnings. See also Ye Zhang, Joe Young, and Virginia A. Hulme, "Hope for China's Migrant Women Workers," *China Business Review* 29, no. 3 (2002): 30–37; Min Liu, "Chinese Migrant Women in the Sex Industry: Exploring Their Paths to Prostitution," *Feminist Criminology* 7, no. 4 (2012): 327–49.

[23] Sex Worker Interview 6, August 23, 2009.

[24] Sex Worker Interview 2, August 23, 2009.

Figure 7.1 Home provinces of sex workers surveyed in Beijing

From this initial contact, a migrant woman who is considering prostitution will often then move one step closer by observing the sex industry from the sidelines and shadowing a sex worker friend. When I asked my informants how they entered the sex industry, they repeatedly explained that "someone/a friend introduced me to it" (有人/朋友介绍的 – *youren/pengyou jieshaode*).[25] In the middle tier, this process involves engaging in the legitimate hostessing activities that occur in an entertainment venue: singing, drinking, and dancing with clients. In the lower tier, this could entail spending time in massage parlors or parks where soliciting occurs and observing dynamics between sex workers and clients. This process is easiest for second wives, particularly when they start out as hostesses who meet their clients while working in an entertainment venue.

It is from these positions that a woman will then launch herself into prostitution. Xiao Wen's story illustrates this gradual transition nicely. She describes her entry into prostitution as having happened by chance (偶然的机会 – *ouran de jihui*), rather than as a strategized move.[26] When she first arrived in Beijing, she worked as a manual laborer (做工程 – *zuo gongcheng*) and met the girlfriend of a project manager who was a sex worker. She told her what she did because "we are both northerners, and tell it like it is (豪爽直接 – *haoshuang zhijie*)." She took Xiao Wen to a small entertainment venue, and that evening Xiao Wen earned 300 yuan ($40) as a legitimate hostess for three clients. She felt like it was "a really easy way to earn money, and so started doing it." Xiu Mei described how she worked in a supermarket for a low salary when she first arrived in Beijing.[27] She was in touch with friends from her village who were also in Beijing, and they had good things to say about their experiences in prostitution. Based on those recommendations, Xiu Mei ended up following in their footsteps and selling sex in a low-tier hair salon. Xiao Yuan, meanwhile, came to Beijing to help her aunt care for the daughter she had in a second wife arrangement.[28] Her aunt used to work in an entertainment venue, and when her former colleagues came to visit, Xiao Yuan saw how much they earned. She convinced her aunt to let her work there as well.

[25] Sex Worker Interview 1, August 17, 2009.
[26] Sex Worker Interview 2, August 17, 2009.
[27] Sex Worker Interview 5, August 24, 2009.
[28] Sex Worker Interview 3, August 18, 2009.

Reasons for Selling Sex

Across all three tiers, sex workers repeatedly underscore the economic benefits of prostitution as the driving force behind their decision to engage in it. This explanation comes across most succinctly in a saying popular in Chinese culture that some of my respondents shared with me: In contemporary society, people "mock poverty, not prostitution" (笑贫不笑娼 – *xiao pin buxiao chang*).[29] Sex workers I interviewed repeatedly underscored their poor backgrounds when describing to me how they ended up selling sex. Sometimes, job loss leads to a transition into prostitution. Both Xiao Wen and Xia Ting started selling sex after losing jobs at state-owned enterprises in their hometowns.[30] Other times, divorce or a breakup is the precipitating factor. Xiao Yang first migrated to Beijing after her divorce, and then turned to the sex industry after her second marriage also failed.[31] Xia Fen needed a source of income when her husband divorced her.[32] Often, the necessity of caring for children, siblings, or elderly parents weighs on this population. Qing Lai, who was originally a victim of sex trafficking, later willingly continued to engage in prostitution in order to support her family back home:

> At first, I wanted to go back home. But then I decided not to go home so that I could earn money. I have siblings. One is in university, and the other in high school. Our family needs money. My father beats my mother so much that she is basically an invalid. I continue doing this for my brother and sister, and to be a dutiful (孝顺 – *xiaoshun*) daughter to my mother.[33]

Qing Yu also spoke powerfully of her decision as a form of sacrifice for her family:

> I want my child to have some savings. Regardless of how I make my money, it helps my child, who won't have to overcome financial obstacles to get an education. It's money his mother earned. It can all be spent, no matter how I made it. How I earned those bills isn't written on them (钱上也没写那钱是怎么挣的 – *qian shang ye mei xie na qian shi zenme zheng de*).[34]

29 Sex Worker Interview 3, August 18, 2009.
30 Sex Worker Interview 1, August 17, 2009; Sex Worker Interview 2, August 17, 2009.
31 Sex Worker Interview 2, August 18, 2009.
32 Sex Worker Interview 1, August 22, 2009.
33 Sex Worker Interview 2, August 26, 2009.
34 Sex Worker Interview 1, August 26, 2009.

Ming Jia talked about the anxiety she felt at not being able to provide adequately for her child: "He didn't have good things to eat, and other people's children had enough to eat, so I decided to do this."[35] Financial stability also permeates second wives' explanations for why they became kept women.[36] Ah-Fang, whose story I discuss in Chapter 6, had worked in several different factory jobs when she first arrived in Guangzhou. After a traumatic breakup – her boyfriend was sentenced to seven years in jail for involvement in a gang – she met a businessman who took a liking to her. He bailed her out from a detention center where she had been incarcerated for failing to renew her temporary residence permit. Tired of the meager wages and physical labor of her factory job, she subsequently agreed to become his second wife.[37]

Rhetoric of Temporariness and Future Aspirations

Low-tier sex workers, hostesses, and second wives consistently presented their engagement in prostitution as a short-term commitment. They described plans to work for a few more months, or one to two years at most, save some money, return to their hometown to buy a house for their family, and open up a small store, restaurant, or legitimate beauty salon. Some spoke of going back home to raise their children. Those without husbands spoke of wanting to marry. They referred to these future plans as wanting to "live a normal life" (过正常的生活 – *guo zhengchang de shenghuo*), in contrast to their current "abnormal" (不正常 – *bu zhengchang*) situation.[38] Xiao Wen had been working as a hostess for a year and a half when I interviewed her, and was planning to continue for no more than one year. She would quit once she had saved up 30,000 yuan to pay for her child's education.[39] Xia Ying planned to return home permanently in a few months, after two and a half years in an entertainment venue, to reunite with her child.[40] Xiao Ai had been selling sex for two years but underscored that "this isn't a permanent job," and planned to either return

35 Sex Worker Interview 4, August 24, 2009.

36 Xiao, in her study of second wives, argues that in addition to economic motivations, men and women enter into these relationships "in an attempt to search for personal dignity, distinction, and belonging as they navigate through emerging patterns of social stratification in postsocialist China." Xiao, "China's New Concubines?," 2009, 8. See also Xiao, *Desire and Dignity*, 25. While these emotions are important, I view them as intrinsically tied to financial considerations: It is the increased wealth that comes with selling sex that serves to remedy the feelings of inferiority that Xiao highlights.

37 Xiao, "China's New Concubines?," 107–8. See also Xiao, *Desire and Dignity*, 86.

38 Sex Worker Interview 2, August 18, 2009.

39 Sex Worker Interview 2, August 17, 2009.

40 Sex Worker Interview 3, August 16, 2009.

home or stay in Beijing to work at a business – either selling clothes or food.[41] Xiang Ting had been in the sex industry for three years – one as a sex worker, and two as a madam – but emphasized that she was "working here temporarily" and planned to transition into opening a day care, tea shop, or makeup store.[42] Ming Jia had been soliciting on the streets for three years and, in two months, planned to move back home to Anhui to reunite with her husband and ten-year-old.[43] Second wives also spoke of their relationships as provisional, and rarely hoped or expected to marry their current partner.[44] Ah-Fang wanted to "have some fun" before returning home to the countryside and to a life that she knew would be much more taxing.[45]

This rhetoric of temporariness does not accord with reality. While sex workers I surveyed had been selling sex for an average of 2.4 years, ranging from three days to twenty years, women with more years of prostitution experience spoke no differently of the timing of their long-term plans than those who had recently started: They consistently explained that they would transition out of sex work in a few months, or a year or two at most. On one level, this rhetoric reflects concern about and awareness of a market for prostitution that tends to privilege younger sex workers. Yet sex work can actually be a viable long-term source of income: The stated age of the women whom I interviewed and surveyed ranged from seventeen to fifty-one. When my informants emphasized the temporary nature of their work, they were not primarily highlighting the greater appeal of younger women and fears of age-related loss of income. Instead, I interpreted these remarks as a way for sex workers to diminish the gravity of a perceived moral transgression. It seemed to be done not so much for my benefit or that of others who might judge them, but rather as a coping strategy that made it easier for them to grapple with their current life circumstances. Prostitution seems more acceptable when viewed as a short-term phase in one's life, rather than a permanent state of being and a defining characteristic of one's professional identity.

In Denial

In addition to emphasizing the temporary nature of their decision, sex workers also seek to diminish any potential or perceived moral impropriety

41 Sex Worker Interview 1, August 21, 2009.
42 Madam Interview 1, August 15, 2009.
43 Sex Worker Interview 4, August 24, 2009.
44 Xiao, "China's New Concubines?," 2009, 90, 117. See also Xiao, *Desire and Dignity*, 59, 91–92.
45 Xiao, "China's New Concubines?," 103. See also Xiao, *Desire and Dignity*, 86, 93.

of their behavior by denying that what they are doing is prostitution. Regardless of the venues where they worked, the women I interviewed consistently defined themselves in contrast to their image of an actual "prostitute" (妓女 – *jinü*) – someone who is paid for a one-time sexual encounter with a complete stranger and who establishes no personal rapport with a client. The formal term for prostitution in Chinese is *maiyin piaochang* (卖淫嫖娼), and it translates as "selling lewdness and visiting a prostitute." It sounds extremely derogatory and is alienating to sex workers. Instead, low- and middle-tier sex workers refer to themselves as *xiaojie* (小姐), which translates literally as "miss." Second wives often refer to themselves using the term "girlfriend" (女朋友 – *nüpengyou*). These linguistic differentiations are not just euphemisms, where interlocutors share an understanding of the issue at hand and use terms that soften its edges. Rather, women in all three tiers would explain to me that what they were doing was actually different from the terms *jinü* and *maiyin*. Their clients were all "friends" (朋友 – *pengyou*) and "close acquaintances" (熟人 – *shuren*). A repeat client quickly became a "partner" (对象 – *duixiang*), a "boyfriend" (男朋友 – *nanpengyou*), or a "hubby" (老公 – *laogong*).

These women's interpretation of their source of livelihood is most understandable coming from second wives, whose daily lives are the furthest removed from common perceptions of prostitution. As noted in the earlier discussion of how sex workers in the different tiers perceive of each other, Ah-Run explicitly states that as a second wife she is "not a prostitute."[46] Kept women repeatedly emphasize the emotional elements of their relationship and the presence of "feelings" as evidence that they are not selling sex.[47]

Hostesses' denial of prostitution is also easy to understand, given the additional services they provide to clients – drinking, dancing, and singing. Jia Qing, who refused to return to her hometown because she worried that rumors might be circulating there about her life as a sex worker, made the following request when I asked her about potential government support for sex workers: "People shouldn't say that a *xiaojie* is a whore (鸡 – *ji*).[48] Many *xiaojie* are not whores. I wish [the government] could tell everyone that a *xiaojie* is different from a whore. That way, people in my village

[46] Xiao, "China's New Concubines?," 129.
[47] See Chapter 6 for a fuller discussion of this point.
[48] The term she uses, *ji* (鸡), is different from the character in *jinü* (妓). It is slang for "whore," and means "chicken."

wouldn't call me a whore."[49] Similarly, Bing Bing explained: "I would be terrified of straight-up prostituting myself; that is really horrible."[50] Zi Han noted: "On television shows that take place in ancient China, everyone despises the brothel prostitutes. People nowadays imagine that *xiaojie* are that type of prostitute."[51] Xiao Yang explained that in her venue, she had "never seen any prostitution, only heard about it."[52] Yet she then went on to say that "when a client wants to leave with you (出台 – *chutai*), he'll generally say, 'I like you, why don't you come home with me? I won't treat you poorly.'"[53] In her mind, what she had described was unrelated to the concept of prostitution. Bing Bing also distinguished between the activities in which she and her peers engage as hostesses and prostitution. "There's no [prostitution] here. But there are people who make friends and find partners," she notes.[54] Xiao Wen saw the connection more clearly, yet also made a distinction:

> There's no prostitution here in the sense of a client openly saying he needs a specific type of person, but there are people who go out (出去 – *chuqu*) with clients. Usually they'll go out with familiar clients who they have hosted eight to ten times, once they understand him, and it's like they are friends. They leave with you (出台 – *chutai*) once they've built a foundation of mutual understanding. People don't go straight from hosting someone (坐台 – *zuotai*) to leaving with them (出台 – *chutai*). There are no straight-up sexual transactions.[55]

The most surprising denial comes from women who solicit on the streets and in brothels. When these women refer to their clients as "friends," they are expressing their conviction that even a couple of minutes of conversation prior to a sexual transaction is evidence that they are engaging in a relationship that is distinct from prostitution. Fei Wen, who solicits in a hair salon, explained that her clients are "close acquaintances, good friends."[56] Ming Jia also used the term "close acquaintance" in describing the individuals with whom she has sex.[57] Mei Mei explained that she only gives "special

[49] Sex Worker Interview 5, August 22, 2009.
[50] Sex Worker Interview 2, August 15, 2009.
[51] Sex Worker Interview 1, August 16, 2009.
[52] Sex Worker Interview 2, August 18, 2009.
[53] Sex Worker Interview 2, August 18, 2009.
[54] Sex Worker Interview 2, August 15, 2009.
[55] Sex Worker Interview 2, August 17, 2009.
[56] Sex Worker Interview 3, August 24, 2009.
[57] Sex Worker Interview 4, August 24, 2009.

services" (特殊服务 – *teshu fuwu*), a euphemism for sex, to "particularly good customers . . . who I feel good about . . . they are just helping me out a bit."[58]

While sex workers in all tiers recognized the existence of prostitution, they rarely identified with it personally.[59] Instead, they defined their situations as different from an impersonal, purely physical and fleeting exchange of sex for money.[60] This coping strategy helps explain why the most sensitive questions in my sex worker survey were not about sexual experiences, marital status, entry into prostitution, or violence and abuse at the hands of clients, madams, and the police. Sex workers spoke freely on such issues. In contrast, they were extremely reluctant to answer questions about numbers of clients and the amount of money they earned per sexual transaction. When we first piloted the survey in several red-light districts in Shenzhen, we struggled to recruit participants. Mei Jie, the madam who took me under her wing in that city, suggested that we remove those questions. Word was spreading that we were asking about numbers of clients and payment, which was dissuading sex workers from

58 Sex Worker Interview 1, August 24, 2009. Sex workers in other environments have also been found to express denial about their activities. Joanna Phoenix, who focused on sex workers in Great Britain, captured the genuine surprise of one woman coming to terms with her profession: "It hit me when I was 19 that I was actually a prostitute. I didn't really think about it before – it was just work. But then it hit me. I was actually selling myself . . . I was a prostitute." See Joanna Phoenix, "Prostitute Identities: Men, Money and Violence," *The British Journal of Criminology* 40, no. 1 (2000): 44.

59 Some clients also appear to distance themselves from the idea that they are purchasing sex, preferring instead to believe that sex workers have a nonpecuniary attraction to them. John Osburg, *Anxious Wealth: Money and Morality among China's New Rich* (Stanford, CA: Stanford University Press, 2013), 72–74.

60 There are parallels between this coping strategy and what Bernstein, focused on sex work in the San Francisco Bay Area, calls "bounded authenticity." Bernstein describes this concept as follows:

> "In contrast to the quick, impersonal 'sexual release' associated with the street-level sex trade, much of the new variety of sexual labor resides in the provision of what I call 'bounded authenticity' – the sale and purchase of authentic emotional and physical connection . . . [E]vidence of middle-class sex workers' efforts to manufacture authenticity resided in their descriptions of trying to simulate – or even produce – genuine desire, pleasure, and erotic interest for their clients. Whereas in some cases this involved mere 'surface acting' . . . it could also involve the emotional and physical labor of manufacturing authentic (if fleeting) libidinal and emotional ties with clients."

Bernstein, *Temporarily Yours*, 103. What I observe differs from Bernstein's characterization of "bounded authenticity" in two ways. First, for Bernstein, "bounded authenticity" is a characteristic of the middle tier of the sex industry, in contrast to low-tier sex work. In contrast, low-tier sex workers in my research also talk about what they are doing with the language of authentic connection. Second, rather than coming across as a new type of sexual labor in which sex workers engage for their clients, in my study this language is simply how sex workers justify – for themselves – what they do.

participating, even though they were free to not respond.[61] When asked to quantify the number of sexual transactions they have, and the amount of money they receive for each one, women like Mei Mei, Bing Bing, and Zi Han have no choice but to momentarily confront the stark reality that they in fact do generate income from the exchange of sex for money, just like in the brothels of ancient China depicted in television shows. In their own eyes, this would make them common whores. Presented with this blunt portrayal of their actions, they prefer to disclose lower numbers of clients to create an impression of minimal engagement in prostitution. Similarly, they report inflated fees per transaction, in order to project an image of high self-worth. If they are going to acknowledge that they sell sex, they want to make it seem like they place great value on themselves.

Complicated Family Dynamics

Low-tier sex workers, hostesses, and second wives may deny that they are engaging in prostitution. Yet at the same time, they also behave in ways that show awareness of their boundary-transgressing behavior, such as shielding their families from knowledge of their source of income. Both shame and a consciousness of the social stigma that surrounds prostitution result in complicated family dynamics for sex workers.

Sex workers in China are often married. This was the case for about 60 percent of my survey respondents, in both the low and middle tiers of the sex industry.[62] These marital rates might seem high, particularly as prostitution and marriage are sometimes considered incompatible.[63] Yet this assumption does not hold in the context of China's sex industry.

In rare cases, the husbands of the women I interviewed were actively aware that their wives engage in prostitution.[64] Song Ling lives with her husband in Beijing. He knows that she sells sex. He gets particularly

[61] In Beijing, where we eventually carried out the survey, we recruited participants through a community outreach center. It was a trusted presence in the red-light district, which seemed to reduce the effect of specific questions on actual turnout and willingness to participate.

[62] Others have also identified high rates of marriage among Chinese sex workers. Suiming Pan (潘绥铭), *Sheng Cun Yu Ti Yan (生存与体验) [Survival and Experiences]* (Beijing: Chinese Social Science Press (中国社会科学出版社), 2000), 107–14; 127–28. Second wives are less likely to have a legal spouse. It would be difficult to conceal his existence from their client, who would generally object to such an arrangement.

[63] Economists Lena Edlund and Evelyn Korn, for example, posit that "a woman cannot be both a prostitute and a wife." They rely on this observation to explain the following puzzle: Why is prostitution so well paid, when it is a profession that is low-skill, labor intensive, and dominated by women? Their answer is that "prostitution must pay better than other jobs to compensate for the opportunity cost of forgone marriage market earnings." See Lena Edlund and Evelyn Korn, "A Theory of Prostitution," *The Journal of Political Economy* 110, no. 1 (2002): 181–214.

[64] A husband could also pimp his wife. I did not encounter any such situation in my research.

upset when she comes home late from her hostess work, so she tries to return early. She also reminds him that she does this work to earn money so that they can have a better life in the future.[65] Qing Yu grew up in Inner Mongolia – her parents met and remained there when both of them had been sent to the countryside during the Cultural Revolution. She moved to Beijing to find work, ended up selling sex, and met her husband because he was the driver for one of her regular clients. They returned to Inner Mongolia when they got married but moved back to Beijing after a few years in order to improve their employment prospects. They initially left their now eight-year-old daughter behind with her mother. Now, the three of them share a home, along with her husband's child from his first marriage. Yet Qing Yu also rents a separate apartment where she entertains clients, since selling sex in their home "would be a bad influence on our children." Her rental apartment is her primary residence. Every week or two, she returns to her family, "to live the life of a married couple, and see my kids" (过过夫妻生活, 看看孩子 – *guoguo fuqi shenghuo, kankan haizi*). Despite what her living arrangement and profession might suggest, she is very committed to her marriage:

> Whatever you do, don't get emotionally invested in a client. When we are done with work for the day and go back home, we return to our normal life (过我们的正常生活 – *guo womende zhengchang shenghuo*), with our husbands and kids. When you have a problem, the only person who is really going to help you is your own husband. A client is just a client. You can't reject your husband and kids for a client and take off with him. That is the principle that I follow.

Qing Yu has been arrested for prostitution several times. On one such occasion, the police contacted her husband and told him that they would release her immediately for 5,000 yuan ($800). Her husband was eager to pay but she refused: "I know how difficult it is for me to earn this money, it's really hard work." Instead, she opted to spend seven days in administrative detention.[66]

More commonly, sex workers can balance marriage and prostitution not because they have husbands who tolerate it but because of how easy it is to hide their daily activities from their spouses – telling them that they have jobs as waitresses or service personnel (服务员 – *fuwuyuan*). As migrants, these women often live hundreds of miles from their

[65] Sex Worker Interview 1, August 23, 2009.
[66] Sex Worker Interview 1, August 26, 2009.

husbands.[67] Only 15 percent of the surveyed married sex workers were currently living with their husbands. The other couples typically only see each other once annually, to celebrate Chinese New Year in their hometown. Under such circumstances, a husband would not be exposed to direct evidence that his wife was selling sex. Indirect signs might still abound, especially with respect to her income, which would seem high for a service worker. Ming Jia explained a strategy she and her colleagues use to address this issue: "We accumulate a lot of money, and every month just bring out 1,000 yuan ($160) and say that it is earnings from our regular job. Then, when there's a real problem we take out more, and just say that someone else lent it to us."[68] While some men might have suspicions about their wives' actual work, such hints may be easier to ignore than to confront.

In addition to hiding their sex work from their spouses, women in all three tiers of prostitution also conceal it from other family members and friends back home. Informants repeatedly underscored that they did not tell people because the profession is "disgraceful" (不光彩 – *buguang-cai*), because people back home are "close-minded" (封建 – *fengjian*, which translates literally into "feudal"), and they would "lose face in a big way" (丢脸丢大了 – *diu lian diu da le*).[69] Yu Han's words were among the most poignant: "No one knows back home. If they did, they would drown me in their spit" (他们的唾沫星子都会把人淹死 – *tamen de tuomo xingzi dou hui ba ren yansi*).[70] Ling Ling's description was also memorable – she would be "butchered alive" if people back home knew that she solicited on the streets (要不回家要被宰的 – *yao bu hui jia yao bei zai de*).[71] Feelings of guilt vis-à-vis their loved ones accompanied these descriptions of how families would respond to knowledge that my informants were engaging in prostitution. Ming Jia, who explained that she sells sex "behind [her] husband's back," emphasized feeling that she is betraying her husband (觉得自己对不住老公 – *juede ziji duibuzhu laogong*).[72] Such sentiments of guilt exist in tension with sex worker denial that they are engaging in prostitution,

67 A common migratory pattern in China – not restricted to sex workers – is for spouses to migrate to different cities, or for one spouse to stay in the couple's hometown and the other to leave for work.

68 Sex Worker Interview 4, August 24, 2009.

69 Sex Worker Interview 2, August 17, 2009; Sex Worker Interview 2, August 21, 2009; Sex Worker Interview 4, August 16, 2009; Sex Worker Interview 5, August 24, 2009; Sex Worker Interview 6, August 23, 2009; Sex Worker Interview 4, August 20, 2009.

70 Sex Worker Interview 5, August 16, 2009.

71 Sex Worker Interview 5, August 20, 2009.

72 Sex Worker Interview 4, August 24, 2008.

and underscore their recognition of the moral ambiguity of their source of livelihood, regardless of how they choose to label it.

The feelings of self-reproach that women such as Ming Jia articulate are particularly intense when sex workers talk about their children. Of the women I surveyed, 60 percent had at least one child. Of those, twenty-five respondents had two children, three had three children, and one respondent had five children.[73] These children generally stay in their parents' hometown, raised either by their father or their grandparents. The guilt these women express about their children is often twofold. In addition to concerns about bringing shame upon their children, sex workers also regret not raising them. "I really worry about her," said Xia Fei about her sixteen-year-old daughter. "I feel deep regret toward her (觉得很对不住孩子 – *juede hen duibuzhu haizi*). She is lacking a mother. Ever since she was small I was away working, and wasn't taking care of her."[74]

There are of course exceptions to this general pattern of dissimulation. When second wives have a child, they tend to open up to their families and ask for assistance with childcare.[75] This was the case in Xiao Yuan's family, discussed earlier in this chapter. Her aunt was a second wife who needed help after she had a child with her client. Xiao Yuan came to Beijing to assist with childcare before transitioning into hostessing herself.[76] Another case where a sex worker was open with her family about her work involved Zhang Xiaojie, a madam who lived in Hubei province with her two sisters who worked as hostesses, and their mother. Zhang Xiaojie's five-year-old son was autistic, and attended a costly special education school in Beijing – the monthly fees were about 10,000 yuan ($1,600). Zhang Xiaojie took me home to her luxury apartment one afternoon, and throughout our conversation on her life in the sex industry, her mother sat in the corner of the living room, silently sewing insoles for shoes. She had a huge pile of them, which she sold at a local market – a pastime that she engaged in out of habit, rather than financial necessity. The mother knew that her three daughters made a significant amount of money in the sex industry but still chose to work herself. I only encountered one situation in which an informant's role in the sex industry was actually a source of pride that

[73] As discussed in Chapter 2, these would not necessarily have constituted violations of the one-child policy. That said, it is rare to encounter a Chinese citizen with five children.
[74] Sex Worker Interview 3, August 21, 2009.
[75] Xiao, "China's New Concubines?," 2009, 131.
[76] Sex Worker Interview 3, August 18, 2009.

the entire family celebrated. This was the case because it was a male madam. Wang Ge had started working as a waiter at an entertainment venue, and his interpersonal skills dealing with both clients and hostesses led the venue boss to suggest that he be promoted to a role supervising hostesses.[77] As he explained: "My parents and friends all know I do this. My parents are quite supportive. When I first started they were worried about me. They weren't supportive, and worried about how disorderly (乱 – *luan*) hostesses are. But when I started earning a lot of money, they started being supportive of me."[78] The different standard to which Wang Ge is held is likely tied to the fact that, unlike women in his position, there would be no suspicions of him selling sex. When he introduced his fiancée to his parents, he did not tell them that she was a hostess. It would have been embarrassing. Judging from this decision, Wang Ge is unlikely to have been praised had he been a daughter.

Moral Ambiguity and the Benefits of Prostitution

When sex workers talk about their family, they simultaneously express feelings of guilt for engaging in stigmatized behavior while also underscoring how their desire to help pull their family out of poverty led them to sell sex in the first place. These tensions translate into very divided views on the morality of prostitution, which do not appear to correlate with a sex worker's specific tier of prostitution. When asked to rank the types of harm that prostitution causes in society, 40 percent of sex worker survey respondents identify it primarily as a moral harm – less than the number who view it primarily as a threat to public health (46 percent) and much more than the number who view it mainly as a threat to public order (13 percent).[79] When asked for an overall assessment of prostitution, 43 percent of respondents find that selling sex is "very good" or "good," and 57 percent of sex workers think that it is appropriate for men to solicit sex.[80]

Although they are divided with respect to questions of morality, sex workers of all types share a rhetoric about prostitution that emphasizes

[77] While the more appropriate English translation here might be "pimp," he self-identified as a madam (*mami*). The Chinese term for pimp (*laoban*), which means "boss," does not accurately reflect the specific responsibilities of a venue *mami* – the person who manages a group of hostesses, greets venue guests when they arrive, and maintains relationships with them.

[78] Madam 2 Interview, August 21, 2009.

[79] The total of these responses is slightly less than 100 due to rounding error.

[80] Responses to these two questions do not vary according to whether respondents are low-tier sex workers or hostesses.

its advantages.[81] Women I surveyed found that the benefits of prostitution outweigh its harms, both for themselves (75 percent of respondents) and for clients (81 percent of respondents). Sex workers also underscore the benefits of prostitution for the Chinese state, through its contributions to the economy and society.[82]

Sex workers display a keen awareness of the importance of prostitution to the local economy. Xiao Hua explained that "prostitution has solved part of the unemployment problem."[83] Responses to the survey suggest that this belief is widespread. Most sex workers (76 percent) believe that prostitution reduces rural unemployment. When asked to elaborate on sex work's contributions to the economy, they highlighted two points. The first, which mostly pertains to middle-tier sex work, is that "entertainment venues promote economic development."[84] Clients purchase sex, rent rooms, and buy alcohol in these venues.[85] Second, sex workers in all tiers, though particularly hostesses and second wives, stimulate the economy through their spending habits. As one respondent explained, "[We] earn money and then spend it, thus contributing to clothing, food, and housing markets."[86] As evidence of the economic importance of sex worker consumption habits, Yu Han recounted the impact of shutting down the sex industry: "I heard that during SARS, [this red light district] shut down. Everyone went home. Everyone withdrew their money from the banks, the Beijing banks collapsed ... The economic impact of sex workers is very significant."[87] Certainly, the impact of millions of migrants suddenly withdrawing their savings would affect the local economy. Regardless of whether the sex worker population of one red-light district single handedly caused the local banking system to collapse, sex workers' beliefs about this economic connection are significant.

In terms of sex work's contributions to society, most surveyed sex workers (83 percent) believe that prostitution has contributed to reducing the number of rapes in China. This idea came up unsolicited in my

[81] As noted in Chapter 4, women in the lowest tier have a more negative assessment of prostitution than their higher-tier counterparts. That said, their overall emphasis is still on the beneficial aspects of selling sex.

[82] The following five paragraphs are adapted from Margaret L. Boittin, "New Perspectives from the Oldest Profession: Abuse and the Legal Consciousness of Sex Workers in China," *Law & Society Review* 47, no. 2 (2013): 245–78.

[83] Sex Worker Interview 3, August 15, 2009.

[84] Sex Worker Interview 6, August 23, 2009.

[85] Sex Worker Interview 6, August 23, 2009.

[86] Sex Worker Interview 6, August 23, 2009.

[87] Sex Worker Interview 5, August 16, 2009.

interviews as well. "When there wasn't any prostitution, there was a lot of rape. Now there is much less rape" explained Su Yin.[88] The idea underlying this belief appears to be that prior to 1979, a man who "needed" sex had to rape a woman, since prostitution was not readily available. Now that prostitution and a market economy have reemerged, this man will purchase sex instead: "Thanks to us, men do not have to risk committing the crime of rape; they spend a couple hundred [yuan] and satisfy their needs," noted Wen Ling.[89] Sex workers were not the only informants to present this belief to me as a given – the theory seems to be part of popular culture and came up repeatedly over the course of my fieldwork.

Sex workers also speak of their role as service providers who ultimately help their clients' families. "Sometimes, a man wants to go out and drink," explained Song Ling. "His wife won't do that with him. When my boyfriend is in a bad mood, his wife tells him to go out and have fun. Then he comes to find me. The next day, he is in a much better mood."[90] As for how sex workers situate themselves vis-à-vis clients' families, one might expect them to acknowledge the belief that sex workers are "home wreckers" or to avoid the issue entirely. Respondents did recognize (and criticize) the widely held belief that they are more to blame than the unfaithful husbands who purchase sex from them.[91] Yet only rarely did they directly express guilt in relation to their clients' families. Fang Ting, a sex worker who divorced her husband after he repeatedly solicited sex from hostesses and later took on a second wife, was one of the rare women who did. When asked about her attitude toward clients, she shifted the conversation toward their families: "From the bottom of my heart, I never meant to destroy other people's families. I've also been hurt in life [and wouldn't want to inflict it on others]."[92] Ah-Run, a kept woman, also expressed guilt toward her client's legal spouse: "'It's like stealing her husband,'" she noted.[93] That sex workers would instead view prostitution as actively beneficial to a healthy marriage is more counterintuitive. Yet interviewees repeatedly told me that since older Chinese women are not interested in sex, sex workers fill a void in family relations. "Nowadays, women get old quickly. But a fifty-year-old man is full of vitality ... He doesn't have

88 Sex Worker Interview 4, August 20, 2009.
89 Sex Worker Interview 7, August 20, 2009.
90 Sex Worker Interview 1, August 23, 2009.
91 Sex Worker Interview 3, August 26, 2008.
92 Sex Worker Interview 2, August 22, 2009.
93 Xiao, "China's New Concubines?," 2009, 155. See also Xiao, *Desire and Dignity*, 101.

a sex life with his wife, so he relies on prostitution to satisfy his physiological needs," explained Mei Lin.[94] "After a wife gives birth, her vagina becomes flabby, it isn't as tight as a sex worker's. So it isn't comfortable for her to make love, and the quality is bad," explained Xiao Yuan.[95]

Underlying these discussions of a wife's lack of sexual desire is the idea that sex workers fulfill a harmonizing role in a married couple's life. "We can harmonize people's sex lives," explained Lai Lai.[96] "It's better for the government not to crack down, because that is the only way things will be harmonious," explained Wei Wei.[97] "Some families are unharmonious, [because] men have needs," emphasized Wen Ling.[98] This use of the term "harmony" (和谐 – *hexie*) carries a great deal of political significance and illustrates how sex workers view themselves as active participants in the larger project of constructing the modern Chinese nation. The doctrine of "Harmonious Society," which Hu Jintao introduced in 2005 as a guiding principle of Communist Party policies, was generally viewed as a catch-all propaganda slogan to justify any number of political decisions. It has been the subject of a fair amount of derision within some intellectual circles in China – a censured website is said to "have been harmonized" (被和谐 – *bei hexie*); a popular political satire cartoon features "river crabs" (河蟹), a homonym of the word "harmony." Yet, sex workers were not using the term ironically. Instead, it came across as a sincere explanation of sex workers' contribution to the well-being of the Chinese family and society. While most people use the term "Harmonious Society" in jest nowadays, here is a population using it earnestly, although it is probably one of the last groups that Hu would have wanted adopting it.

Whether discussing their contributions to economic development, public safety, or the family, sex workers view themselves as actively helping to construct a better modern China. Shu Li called for the taxation of prostitution, so that she could give something back to her country.[99] Wei Ting likened sex workers to soldiers, even adopting a slogan with great symbolic significance to describe their work: "We are in service of the country, in service of society (我们也是为国家, 社会服务 – *women ye shi*

94 Sex Worker Interview 3, August 22, 2009.
95 Sex Worker Interview 3, August 18, 2009.
96 Sex Worker Interview 1, August 18, 2009.
97 Sex Worker Interview 5, August 18, 2009.
98 Sex Worker Interview 7, August 20, 2009.
99 Sex Worker Interview 3, August 20, 2009.

wei guojia, shehui fuwu). Just like the country cares for our soldiers, we also work for the benefit of the country."[100] This is very powerful rhetoric – most Chinese people hearing it would recognize it as an echo of the popular slogan "in service of the people" (为人民服务 – *wei renmin fuwu*). It was the title of a speech that Mao Zedong wrote in 1944 to commemorate the death of a soldier and has since become a concept central to the Chinese Communist Party (CCP). It is displayed prominently at the headquarters of the CCP and the State Council. The military uses the slogan in ceremonial troop inspections. In daily life, this language of service has come to be associated with discussions of undesirable jobs. It is used following two sayings that express the notion that no job should be considered too lowly: "Regardless of your profession, you can become an expert in it" (三百六十行，行行出状元 – *san bai liushi hang, hang hang chu zhuangyuan*), and "A profession is not what distinguishes the lowly from the noble" (职业不分高低贵贱 – *zhiye bufen gaodi guiqian*). Used with the service rhetoric, these sayings express the idea that any job provides valuable contributions to society. While usually a reference to menial work such as street cleaning, sex workers have appropriated these slogans to legitimize prostitution. Just as they have adopted the concept of "Harmonious Society" to describe their contributions to the Chinese family, so too are they framing their role in national political and militaristic terms.[101]

Criticism of the State

In addition to making the case that they help strengthen the Chinese state, sex workers also criticize it and underscore how it treats them unfairly. Chapters 4–6 underscore differences between low-tier sex

100 Sex Worker Interview 4, August 18, 2009.

101 Kimberly Kay Hoang's study of sex work in Vietnam unearths a similar rhetoric connecting sex workers to state strength:

> "Chu Xanh [a wealthy Vietnamese businessman who had helped Hoang gain access to one of the bars where she conducted her research] informed me that he felt an obligation to take care of some of the workers' family members because the women were making huge sacrifices not merely for their own families but also for the nation. He went on: 'These poor girls leave everything behind to come to the city to take care of their families, [but] they are the ones who really move money into this country in a way that no one sees. We have to do the right thing and take care of our families."

Kimberly Kay Hoang, *Dealing in Desire: Asian Ascendancy, Western Decline, and the Hidden Currencies of Global Sex Work*, 1st ed. (Oakland: University of California Press, 2015), 169.

workers, hostesses, and second wives when it comes to knowledge and attitudes about the state and its prostitution policies. Yet regardless of where sex workers stand on these issues in relation to each other, their views of the state are more negative than the views held by the general population. They also share a critical attitude toward the policies that regulate their behavior and how those rules are implemented. These views underscore the extent to which this population is politically engaged.

Compared to the general population in China, sex workers have low levels of trust in the government and the police. In my survey of sex workers, 84 percent of respondents expressed trust in the central government, and 82 percent expressed trust in the local government. Trust in the police was much lower – only 60 percent of respondents claimed to trust them. In absolute terms, these numbers may seem high. Yet as shown in Figure 7.2, which compares responses from the sex worker

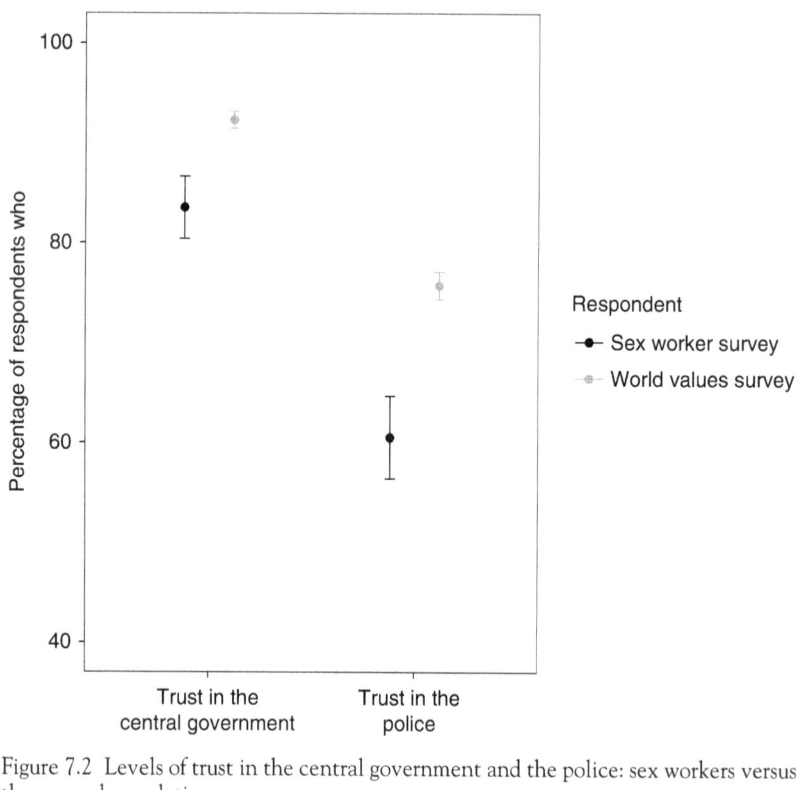

Figure 7.2 Levels of trust in the central government and the police: sex workers versus the general population

survey to the World Values Survey of the Chinese population as a whole, they are much lower than the general population's levels of trust.[102]

The World Values Survey shows that 92 percent of the Chinese population trusts the central government, which is 8.8 percentage points more than sex workers' level of trust.[103] It also shows that the general population is 15.2 percentage points more likely to trust the police than sex workers are.

As for government policies regarding prostitution, sex workers find them unjust. When asked their opinions of prostitution policies toward sex workers, 61 percent of surveyed women find that they are unfair. In contrast, only 43 percent of respondents find these policies to be unfair toward clients. Sex workers also find them ineffective. Most survey respondents (67 percent) noted that the primary goal of the policies is to reduce prostitution. Yet when then asked to rank the effectiveness of the policies in achieving that goal on a 1–10 scale, the average response was 5.3.

Sex workers also tend to take politics seriously. In my survey, 75 percent of respondents noted that politics is important, and 65 percent stated that they were interested in it. These rates are significantly higher than those of the general population, as shown in Figure 7.3.

This figure compares average responses from the sex worker survey to the World Values Survey of Chinese society as a whole. Sex workers are 25.5 percentage points more likely than the general population to think that politics is important and 9.3 percentage points more likely to express an interest in politics. The differences displayed in Figure 7.3 reflect the state's many intrusions into the daily lives of sex workers (see Part III of this book for an in-depth discussion of these intrusions).

GROUP CONSCIOUSNESS AND THE GLOBAL COMMUNITY OF SEX WORK CIVIL SOCIETY

When discussing people who play a positive role in their lives, most sex workers mention various friends and family members, as well as some of the individuals they encounter in the workplace (colleagues, madams, and clients). Yet in rare cases, these women encounter grassroots

[102] The Appendix provides additional information on how responses from these two surveys were compared.

[103] The World Values Survey does not ask respondents about trust in the local government in China.

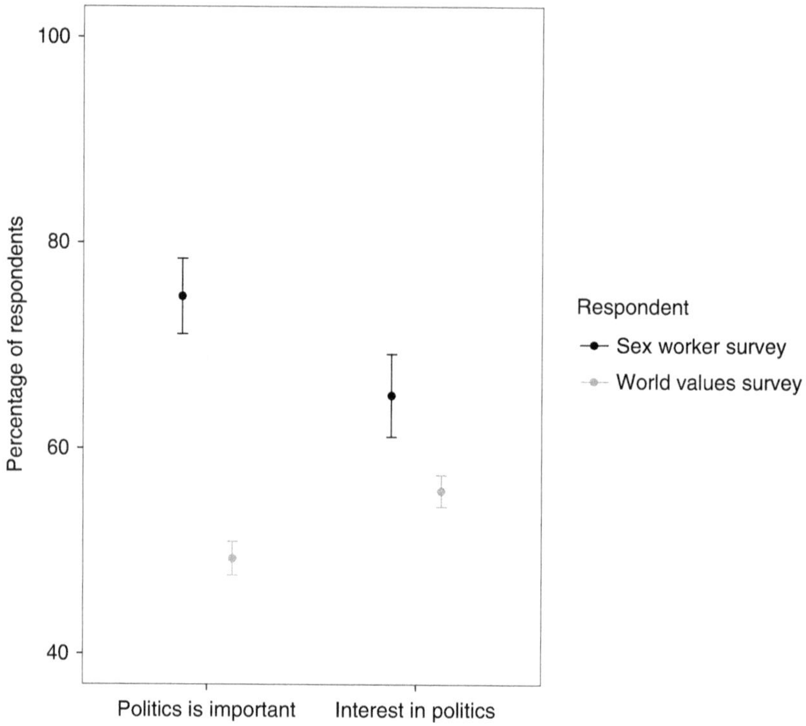

Figure 7.3 Importance of and interest in politics: sex workers versus the general population

organizations devoted to supporting sex workers.[104] Such groups, backed by international organizations and inspired by counterparts abroad, focus on health outreach, legal education, and community building. They mainly interact with sex workers in the low and middle tiers of the sex industry.[105] Through their work, these organizations

[104] I use the terms "grassroots organization," "nongovernmental organization (NGO)," and "civil society organization" interchangeably here. Following other scholars, I define civil society as "composed of a diverse array of organizations with voluntary membership and some degree of operational autonomy from the state, defined as the ability to set a self-determined agenda." See Diana Fu, *Mobilizing without the Masses: Control and Contention in China* (New York: Cambridge University Press, 2017), 26. While there is a rich literature on civil society in China (see, e.g., Fu, 1–26), a more in-depth discussion of it is beyond the scope of this chapter.

[105] These organizations are less likely to prioritize second wives for two reasons. From a public health perspective, sex workers in the top tier present less of a concern around HIV/AIDS because they have fewer sexual partners. From the perspective of rights awareness work and community building, second wives are the sex workers who are most reluctant to identify with prostitution, which means they are unlikely to perceive of these activities as relevant to their lives.

introduce some of China's most downtrodden members of society to transnational ideas that help them develop a shared sense of community and belonging, an experience that can be profoundly transformative.

Female Sex Worker Nongovernmental Organizations

A handful of grassroots organizations in China are devoted to supporting female sex workers.[106] They are located throughout the country, including in larger cities such as Beijing, Tianjin, Qingdao, Wuhan, and Guangzhou, and smaller cities such as Jiaozhou (in Shandong province), Jiangyou and Panzhihua (both in Sichuan province), and Gejiu and Ruili (both in Yunnan province). For the most part, these organizations are structured very loosely. I visited one in Guangzhou that a former sex worker who is HIV-positive ran out of her bare-bones apartment. She and her boyfriend raised funds for their work through an online clothing business.[107] Another nongovernmental organization (NGO) was trying to start a sex worker outreach center attached to a car washing business that would help generate income.[108] The most structured organization I encountered was the center where I served as a participant observer in Beijing, which was affiliated with a major domestic HIV/AIDS NGO. It operated out of a rented room in a building in a red-light district. Its program manager was a young university graduate who ran the center jointly with a peer educator who was a former sex worker. Most of these groups are members of the China Sex Worker Organization Network Forum (CSWONF), which supports and connects its members through a variety of different activities.[109]

These local groups receive financial and training support from international organizations. For instance, the United Nations Population Fund (UNFPA) and the Joint United Nations Programme on HIV/AIDS (UNAIDS) support the CSWONF group, which also has relationships with two transnational sex worker organizations (the Asia-Pacific

[106] There are also groups that work with male sex workers. As noted in the introductory chapter, male sex work is beyond the scope of this project.

[107] Interview 83, May 6, 2009.

[108] Interview 18, October 2, 2008; Interview 32, October 19, 2008.

[109] For instance, it has organized trainings and managed a collaborative report documenting the effects of a nationwide prostitution crackdown on sex workers and HIV/AIDS in China. China Sex Worker Organization Network Forum, "Research on the Impact of 2010 Crackdown on Sex Work and HIV Interventions in China (2010年严打对性工作与艾滋病防治影响研究)" (China Sex Worker Organization Network Forum (中国性工作者机构网络平台), 2011).

Network of Sex Workers and the Global Network of Sex Work Projects).[110] Many of the major international organizations that have worked closely on HIV/AIDS in China, such as the World Health Organization and the Global Fund, have supported the grassroots organizations' public health projects.[111] Other foreign organizations, including the Hong Kong group Ziteng and the Dutch organization Mama Cash, have worked with these Chinese NGOs on sex worker rights.[112]

NGO Activities

These grassroots organizations provide sex workers with health services, legal education, and spaces for community building. For health services, groups that do not have a physical space to welcome sex workers spend most of their time distributing condoms to women working in nearby prostitution venues, networking with local pimps and madams to secure access to sex workers, and carrying out workshops about safe sex practices. Organizations that have a physical space perform these tasks and also serve as drop-in centers for sex workers seeking these types of services. The Beijing community center where I was a participant observer even had a volunteer doctor on site a few days a week, who would provide free health consultations to sex workers.

In addition to health outreach, a number of these organizations run legal education and advocacy projects. For example, the Beijing center carried out rights awareness trainings to advise sex workers on interactions with law enforcement. A lawyer who conducts them explained that "We teach them about their rights if they are arrested, and we do trainings for how they can protect themselves. For example, if [sex workers] are arrested, the police have to prove that sexual relations occurred, and that money was exchanged."[113] This same lawyer was also careful to recognize the practical limitations of these types of rights trainings, since the police "often . . . don't have that proof, they just see condoms and use that as proof."[114] The advocacy events that these centers organize promote the legalization or decriminalization of

[110] Joan Kaufman, "HIV, Sex Work, and Civil Society in China," *Journal of Infectious Diseases* 204, no. suppl 5 (January 12, 2011): S1221, https://doi.org/10.1093/infdis/jir538.

[111] See Chapter 3 for more discussion of these international organizations and their roles in supporting HIV/AIDS work in China.

[112] In addition to working directly with sex worker grassroots groups, transnational organizations have also played a crucial role in working with Chinese state actors to create a (tenuous) space for these NGOs to operate. I discuss this point further in Chapter 10.

[113] Interview 23, October 9, 2008.

[114] Interview 23, October 9, 2008.

prostitution in China. For example, the Beijing center has facilitated informal discussions on the advantages of legalizing prostitution and organized a small celebration for International Sex Worker Rights Day (March 3). Such events are usually discreet. Most sex worker NGOs try to avoid drawing attention to themselves, out of concern that otherwise state authorities will interfere with their work.

The third type of activity in which sex worker groups are involved is community building, which can occur when grassroots organizations provide a physical space, distinct from the workplace, where sex workers are able to convene.[115] As illustrated throughout this book, the daily life of a sex worker can be chaotic and isolating. Clients make sexual demands of her, madams place revenue requirements on her, and other sex workers can be a source of competition. Sex worker outreach centers provide women with respite from these pressures and a forum where they can reflect upon their lives. Qing Yu explained to me that "[t]his center is so nice. It lets us speak truthfully, and honestly. With clients, we just lie all the time. But here, we can talk about our experiences, and let loose."[116] In describing the benefits of these centers, Xiu Mei talked about how "[s]ome of the girls we work with are good, but there is also a lot of competition. You don't dare say anything ... If you haven't been a sex worker, you can't understand the pressure. That is why you need to have a place like this to pour out your heart."[117] Jing Fen concurred, discussing how at the Beijing center "You can share the problems that weigh on your heart here, and get advice. There is always someone here to speak with you ... There is a feeling of mutual trust here."[118] Zi Han talked about how "When you come here, no one will divulge your identity, no one will look down on you."[119] Yi Chun acknowledged the community-building benefits of the center along with the health and rights knowledge it provides to sex workers when she explained how it "helps to ease the pressure we feel, and increases our knowledge of safety and our human rights consciousness."[120]

115 Samantha Majic describes a similar role for the San Francisco Bay Area nonprofit organizations catering to sex workers. See Samantha Majic, *Sex Work Politics: From Protest to Service Provision* (Philadelphia: University of Pennsylvania Press, 2013).
116 Sex Worker Interview 1, August 26, 2009.
117 Sex Worker Interview 5, August 24, 2009.
118 Sex Worker Interview 2, August 16, 2009.
119 Sex Worker Interview 1, August 16, 2009.
120 Sex Worker Interview 1, August 17, 2009.

Policy discussions about improving the lives of sex workers often focus on regulatory issues and, in particular, whether and how the legalization of prostitution would benefit these women. While these debates are valuable, such regulatory reform is complicated to design and implement. Much less attention is directed toward this seemingly more mundane approach to providing meaningful support to sex workers: fostering a shared sense of community. Yet China's grassroots organizations show that such efforts have undeniably positive effects on sex workers, and they are much more immediately beneficial and simpler to enact. In a world with such a pressing need to meaningfully address the many struggles that sex workers face, the value of community-building outreach merits greater attention than it currently receives.

Changing Sex Worker Consciousness

Exposure to organized civil society and its links to global communities of sex workers changes the way that sex workers think and talk about themselves and their work. For instance, one of the most striking aspects of Yi Chun's comment on the community center in the previous section is her use of the term "human rights consciousness" (人权意识 – *renquan yishi*). Yi Chun was a familiar face at the center – she regularly attended its workshops, had become close to staff members, and would come in and make herself comfortable on the communal couches when business at her neighboring entertainment venue was slow. The language she used and concepts she embraced illustrate the impact of these experiences on her. She was part of a small subset of women who have adopted the terms "sex work" and "sex worker" (性工作(者) – *xing gongzuo(zhe)*) to talk about her work and herself.[121] While sex workers who have not encountered transnational ideas about prostitution refer to themselves with the euphemism *xiaojie* ("miss"), those who have been exposed to these ideas use the term *xing gongzuozhe* (sex worker). By doing so, they signal their exposure to the global community of sex worker rights activists, and their belief that prostitution can be a job that someone might engage in by choice or by circumstance and that it is not inherently coercive.[122]

121 Sex Worker Interview 2, August 16, 2009; Sex Worker Interview 6, August 25, 2009. These terms are literal translations of the English "sex" (*xing*) and "work/er" (*gongzuo/zhe*).

122 The terms "sex work" and "sex worker" first emerged in the United States in the 1970s, and were popularized through the writings of sex worker rights advocate Carol Leigh. See Majic, *Sex Work Politics*, 15. They are value-laden within global feminist debates on prostitution.

Wang Yue's story illustrates the personal transformations that occur when a sex worker who was previously isolated learns that she belongs to a broader community that gives her a voice and tools to interpret her identity. Wang Yue is in her forties. She was a teenager when she entered the sex trade as a hostess at an entertainment venue and, over the years, has had a fairly typical experience in the business. Clients have raped and cheated her, and the police have arrested and abused her. She has also been a madam. She is now married and has a ten-year-old son. She has a long-term partner, and occasionally continues to entertain clients. Wang Yue was introduced to the world of sex worker civil society by chance a few years before I met her in 2008. One of her neighbors in Beijing volunteered for an HIV/AIDS NGO, and when Wang Yue heard that they distributed condoms to women in local brothels, she offered to help. When the organization decided to establish an outreach center, they recognized her potential as a peer educator who could help access other sex workers. She soon found herself co-coordinating outreach. The NGO, with its connections to the global HIV/AIDS community, started sending her to international conferences on sex worker rights and inviting her to speak at high-level HIV/AIDS conferences in China.

The transformation Wang Yue experienced was profound. Her first contact with the global network of sex worker activists occurred when she was sent to Malaysia to attend an international sex worker conference. "At the beginning, I was too embarrassed to say that I was a sex worker," she recalled. By the end of the conference, when she realized that she was part of an international movement and was surrounded by sex workers who were forthcoming about engaging in prostitution, she was inspired to speak up. She brought this newfound confidence back with her to China, where she attended a high-level meeting of the Global Fund that included prominent foreign and domestic government officials. At the meeting, she identified as a sex worker. She also openly denounced China's 100% Condom Use Program described in

Proponents of the term "sex work" place themselves in opposition to advocates for the abolition of prostitution. The latter believe that prostitution is always sexual slavery that reduces women to commodities and forms the basis of female oppression in society and therefore cannot be called "work." (Writings in this vein include Kathleen Barry, *Female Sexual Slavery* (New York: New York University Press, 1984) and Catharine A. MacKinnon, *Toward a Feminist Theory of the State* (Cambridge, MA: Harvard University Press, 1989).) Globally, advocates for the legalization of prostitution have embraced the term "sex work." As discussed in Chapter 10, the public health sector has done so as well, as the term "sex worker" carries less stigma than the word "prostitute."

Chapter 3. She explained its practical limitations: that sex workers will, for the most part, readily accept a client's offer to pay more for sex without a condom, and that most sex workers have boyfriends with whom they will not use a condom.[123] Wang Yue spoke to me in a very impassioned manner about the personal transformations she has undergone through her interactions with the international sex work community. "[What I had before] was not a life. . .My life had no meaning. Now, my life has meaning (意义 – *yiyi*), it is so rewarding (太充实 – *tai chongshi*)," she explained. "Before, I just worked to earn money. Now, I work in service of other sex workers (我为他们服务—*wo wei tamen fuwu*). Now, I have a goal (目标 – *mubiao*). My goal is to legalize prostitution."[124]

For the most part, members of sex work grassroots organizations in China try to keep a low profile and support their community without attracting the attention of the state. Yet one woman has chosen instead to make her activities and grievances public. Ye Haiyan founded a sex worker outreach organization in Wuhan called the China Grassroots Women's Rights Center. She is a prominent figure in China, whose efforts to raise awareness about sex workers in China and advocate for the legalization of prostitution have propelled her into the public sphere.

In 2010, Ye Haiyan and her NGO organized a protest in Wuhan in favor of legalizing prostitution. On several main thoroughfares in the city, participants held up placards calling for the abolition of laws criminalizing prostitution and the end of discrimination against sex workers. They asked passersby to sign a petition in support of their cause and rallied some of them to join their protest.[125] Ye Haiyan subsequently posted videos of the event on the internet, as well as a photograph of herself carrying a sign that read, "Legalize sex work, decriminalize prostitution! Sex work is also work!"[126] Transnational

[123] Interview 24, October 13, 2008.

[124] Interview 24, October 13, 2008.

[125] Tania Branigan, "Chinese Sex Workers Protest against Crackdown," *The Guardian*, August 3, 2010, perma.cc/SQD9-CDCE; Elaine Chow, "First Sex Workers Protest in China Demands Legalization of Prostitution," *Shanghaiist*, August 4, 2010, perma.cc/2R7P-VBJ7; John Kennedy, "China: Sex Workers Demand Legalization, Organizer Detained," Global Voices, August 1, 2010, perma.cc/EZ9V-CJGJ; Associated Press, "Police Detain China Activist for Sex Worker Rights," *The San Diego Union-Tribune*, August 2, 2010, perma.cc/6F8D-5Y8P.

[126] Branigan, "Chinese Sex Workers Protest against Crackdown"; Chow, "First Sex Workers Protest in China Demands Legalization of Prostitution"; Kennedy, "China: Sex Workers Demand Legalization, Organizer Detained"; Associated Press, "Police Detain China Activist for Sex Worker Rights."

influence on this event came through in the red umbrellas that the protesters carried on a sunny July afternoon. Although Chinese women often carry umbrellas to protect their skin from the sun, these red ones were chosen because they are the international symbol for sex worker rights.[127] In the aftermath of the protest, Ye Haiyan was detained for several days and instructed to leave Wuhan. The event and its aftermath garnered considerable attention both domestically and internationally.[128]

Two years later, Ye Haiyan engaged in another controversial effort to raise awareness about sex worker rights. For two days, she provided sexual services free of charge to migrant workers. She generated significant amounts of attention to the campaign by describing it on the microblog Weibo.[129] In 2013, she merged her prostitution advocacy work with the issue of child abuse. In response to a case involving a primary school principal in Hainan accused of raping six girls, Ye Haiyan and others posed in front of his school, holding up a sign that read, "Principal: If you want to get a room, come find me. Let the primary school kids go" (校长:开放找我. 放过小学生 – *xiaozhang: kaifang zhaowo. Fangguo xiaoxuesheng*), along with her name and the phone number for a national hotline for women.[130] The campaign caught on, resulting in a slew of internet users posing with similar signs.[131] The widespread attention that Ye Haiyan garnered once again drew backlash from the state. Upon her return from Hainan, thugs attacked her at her home in Guangxi province, allegedly hired by the state. The police then charged her with assault, detained her for

[127] First used at the 2001 Venice Biennale in an art installation and protest to raise awareness about sex work, the color red was chosen to represent beauty, and the umbrella represents protection from abuse.

[128] Branigan, "Chinese Sex Workers Protest against Crackdown"; Chow, "First Sex Workers Protest in China Demands Legalization of Prostitution"; Kennedy, "China: Sex Workers Demand Legalization, Organizer Detained"; Associated Press, "Police Detain China Activist for Sex Worker Rights." This protest, and Ye Haiyan's activism more generally, is qualitatively different from the hostess protest described in Chapter 5. The former was explicitly about the rights of sex workers and the legalization of prostitution and grew out of the activism of Ye Haiyan and her grassroots organization. The latter was disguised behind the legality of entertainment venues and hostessing, involved a variety of nonhostess employees of entertainment venues, and was a reaction to the closure of the venues. It did not involve sex work grassroots organizations.

[129] The Economist, "Old Profession, New Debate: One Woman's Controversial Campaign to Legalise Prostitution," *The Economist*, October 27, 2012, perma.cc/8XNE-DUSU.

[130] Amy Li, "China Activists Launch Campaign against Paedophiles: 'Call Me, Not Schoolchildren,'" May 30, 2013, https://perma.cc/QD3U-QBHR; Mimi Lau, "School Sexual Abuse Protester Ye Haiyan Beaten up in Her Own Home," *South China Morning Post*, May 31, 2013, https://perma.cc/3U24-FRCC.

[131] Lau, "School Sexual Abuse Protester Ye Haiyan Beaten Up in Her Own Home."

thirteen days, and forced her to leave the town.[132] Since then, local state actors have repeatedly harassed and pushed Ye Haiyan and her daughter out of towns where they have sought to settle down.[133]

Of the millions of sex workers in China, only a handful have the opportunity to experience the changes in consciousness that come from interacting with grassroots organizations. Very few grassroots groups focus on female sex workers in China, and their reach is limited. The CCP is often suspicious of NGOs, wary that an independent civil society can pose a threat to the stability of the state. This political reality limits the extent to which NGOs can thrive in the country, particularly when they are committed to working with illegal populations such as sex workers.[134] I knew of less than a dozen such groups when I was carrying out this research, in the Hu Jintao era. Since then, their ranks have thinned. When Xi Jinping came to power in 2013, the political environment for NGOs became even more hostile.[135] One of the many casualties of this changed environment has been the most prominent and well-organized Chinese sex worker NGO, which by 2014 had ceased most of its activities due to political pressure.

Academics and policymakers often care about NGOs in China (and in other authoritarian regimes) because of the insight they can provide into possibilities for political change.[136] An active civil society might say something about the state's inability to control challenges to its power and could presage regime change. A weak or nonexistent civil

[132] The protest and its aftermath are the subject of a widely acclaimed documentary, "Hooligan Sparrow," whose director, Nanfu Wang, shadowed Ye Haiyan and her family through their ordeal. *Hooligan Sparrow (流氓燕)*, Documentary, 2016, perma.cc/WBL8-RGJC.

[133] Mimi Lau, "Activist Ye Haiyan Evicted from Home by Guangdong Police," *South China Morning Post*, July 7, 2013, https://perma.cc/U3GW-ER93. Over the years, Ye Haiyan has also engaged in a variety of activities considered subversive that do not pertain directly to the issue of prostitution. For instance, in 2011 she posed nude in a photograph with artist Ai Weiwei, and the piece resulted in the artist being investigated for pornography. Jonathan Watts, "Ai Weiwei Investigated over Nude Art," *The Guardian*, November 18, 2011, perma.cc/DV6D-ENVZ.

[134] For instance, another group at high risk of HIV/AIDS that engages in illegal behavior is intravenous drug users, and they also have very few civil society organizations advocating for them. In contrast, grassroots organizations working with gay men, also considered at high risk of HIV/AIDS, have proliferated in China. Homosexuality, while stigmatized, is not against the law, and thus faces fewer obstacles than organizations that support populations that are both socially stigmatized and illegal.

[135] Josh Chin, "China Poised to Approve Crackdown on Foreign NGOs," *Wall Street Journal*, April 26, 2016, sec. World, perma.cc/AV5Y-AZLV.

[136] As Timothy Hildebrandt notes, "The literature covering the main debates of NGOs in China, and in other authoritarian polities, undersell the actions of these organizations and treat their very existence as little more than an axiomatic means to another end (e.g., political change)." Timothy Hildebrandt, *Social Organizations and the Authoritarian State in China* (New York: Cambridge University Press, 2013), 2.

society might instead signal the regime's strength and suggest limited possibilities for political change in the foreseeable future.[137] By that metric, the small number of sex worker grassroots groups in China is barely worth our attention – China's sex workers are unlikely to challenge the CCP's hold on power anytime soon. Yet the problem with this approach is that it pays little heed to the role that sex work grassroots organizations play for the women who come into contact with them. As this chapter demonstrates, these interactions can be transformational for individual human beings. They merit attention in their own right, regardless of what they say about the political stability of a regime.

When we examine sex work grassroots organizations and their impact on individual sex workers, we also gain novel insight into processes of transnational influence in China. Indeed, most research on the relationship between international actors and civil society focuses on the effects of transnational ideas and practices on societal elites.[138] This attention to elites follows from the observation that, due to ease of access, international actors seek out civil society partners from a small group of "charismatic, English-speaking Chinese activists or Beijing-based INGOs [international nongovernmental organizations]."[139] Sex workers such as Wang Yue, in contrast, are usually poor, uneducated migrants from rural China. By showing that they adopt the language and ideas of the global sex worker rights movement, my research identifies transnational influence occurring within a previously unexamined and unexpected subset of the population. In contrast to elites, sex workers are far removed from international networks. Some of them hardly speak Mandarin, let alone English.[140] To hear a Chinese sex worker describe her work

137 These are not the only explanations for the existence of a strong or weak organized civil society in an authoritarian country. A more thorough discussion of such questions is beyond the scope of this chapter.

138 Sidney G. Tarrow, *The New Transnational Activism* (New York: Cambridge University Press, 2005); Rachel E. Stern, "Unpacking Adaptation: The Female Inheritance Movement in Hong Kong," *Mobilization: An International Quarterly* 10, no. 3 (October 1, 2005): 421–39; Sally Engle Merry and Rachel E. Stern, "The Female Inheritance Movement in Hong Kong: Theorizing the Local/Global Interface," *Current Anthropology* 46, no. 3 (2005): 387–409; Peggy Levitt and Sally Merry, "Vernacularization on the Ground: Local Uses of Global Women's Rights in Peru, China, India, and the United States," *Global Networks* 9, no. 4 (October 1, 2009): 441–61.

139 Rachel E. Stern, *Environmental Litigation in China: A Study in Political Ambivalence* (Cambridge: Cambridge University Press, 2013), 188.

140 While Mandarin is the official language of China, dozens of dialects continue to thrive in the country. Mandarin is taught in schools, but older generations and individuals who have only had a few years of education often do not master standard Mandarin.

conditions using phrases such as "human rights" or "legalization of sex work" is to witness transnational ideas taking root within obscure corners of Chinese society.

CONCLUSION

The shared experiences and perspectives of women who solicit sex in the low, middle, and top tiers of the sex industry are illuminating. Their gradual transition into prostitution, based on conscious and informed decision-making processes, belies the narrative of anti-trafficking activists who equate all prostitution with sex trafficking and who portray all women in the sex industry as innocent, duped victims. At the same time, my informants' emphasis on the temporary nature of their engagement in prostitution and discussions of alternative plans for the future underscore their discomfort with the fact that they sell sex. They have agency, but that does not mean this is their dream job. Their shared sense of unease at their source of income also comes through in their refusal to characterize their work as prostitution. It is one thing to hear such arguments coming from a second wife, who is in a long-term relationship with one client; it is much more striking to hear that same logic from a woman who solicits on the streets or in brothels. It is also startling to hear some of sex workers' shared narratives about prostitution's societal and political contributions. For instance, these women talk about playing an actively beneficial role in a marriage, since they are providing sex to married men whose wives do not satisfy their sexual desires. They have even appropriated Hu Jintao's slogan of "Harmonious Society" to describe that role – saying that they can "harmonize" the families of their clients – and, more generally, characterize their engagement in prostitution as done in service to their country. Such rhetoric shows sex workers using political slogans that the state has created to convey certain values among its citizens.[141] It is powerful to observe sex workers engage in that process because it shows a marginalized subset of China's population appropriating tools intended to encourage state-sanctioned behavior and using them to justify their illegal (and publicly scorned) source of livelihood.

Lastly, it is eye-opening to observe grassroots organizations help sex workers create a shared sense of identity and a consciousness of

[141] Jianlin Song and James Paul Gee, "Slogans with Chinese Characteristics: The Political Functions of a Discourse Form," *Discourse & Society* 31, no. 2 (March 1, 2020): 201–17, https://doi.org/10.1177/0957926519880033.

belonging to a large and global community of sex work civil society. The mere existence of these groups is surprising: Most observers of China are much more accustomed to encountering grassroots groups in domains such as the environment and labor – areas that are not necessarily politically controversial – than in illegal and stigmatized communities such as sex work. And while it is easy to dismiss China's sex worker civil society for seeming so small, piecemeal, and haphazard, that assessment disappears in the presence of its activists. Drop-in centers provide meaningful respite for the women who can access them. Women who refer to themselves using the Chinese translations of the terms "sex work" and "sex worker" project a strong sense of empowerment and confidence in themselves. In one case described in this chapter, that group consciousness led a few women to organize and participate in a protest in Wuhan calling for the legalization of prostitution in China. These are powerful manifestations of changes that can occur when women in any tier of prostitution encounter the grassroots community of sex work civil society.

PART III

THE STATE

8

PATTERNS OF PUNISHMENT

INTRODUCTION

China's anti-prostitution regulations outlaw the exchange of sex for money or other material goods in all of its forms, and for all individuals who engage in it. Yet in practice, police enforcement primarily targets low-tier sex workers. Of the array of possible sanctions, these women are more likely to be incarcerated than fined, and they are placed in institutions with a rehabilitative mission that, in practice, is not met. In addition, law enforcement officials often engage in illegal and abusive practices when arresting sex workers. Clients are not completely immune from punishment, but they are less likely to be arrested than are the women they solicit. The major exception to that pattern involves high-profile men whose actions have crossed the Chinese Communist Party (CCP). Their cases are taken out of the hands of street-level police officers and into the world of elite politics, with prostitution charges used to help secure their downfall.

POLICE TARGETING OF LOW-TIER SEX WORKERS

When I asked Qing Yu, a woman who had been selling sex in the low tier for eleven years, whether she had ever been arrested for prostitution, she laughed at the seeming naiveté of my question and responded: "When you're constantly walking alongside the river, how can you avoid getting your feet wet?" (常在河边走，怎能不湿脚呢？*Chang zai hebian zou, zenneng bu shi jiao ne?*).[1] As a low-tier sex worker, Qing Yu is exactly the kind of person whom the police target when they enforce anti-prostitution regulations. One of her arrests occurred in Beijing in 2008, when she brought a client back to her apartment one evening at around 10 PM. He got undressed and was taking a shower while she tidied up her room. All of a sudden, she heard someone knocking on her door. She figured it was the police because the other sex workers to whom she lent her apartment all had keys to let themselves in. Sure enough, the people outside identified as law enforcement, kept pounding on the door and threatened to force it open, so she quickly told her client to get out of the shower and get dressed. When she opened the door, she saw that two of the law enforcement agents were plainclothes officers, and a third was an auxiliary police officer (协警 – *xiejing*). They told Qing Yu that a neighbor reported that she often came home with men. They then brought her and the client to the local police station. They separated the two of them, made them squat, interrogated them, and took their testimony.[2] The client was fairly young – twenty-seven years old – and inexperienced with evading law enforcement. Instead of denying that they were engaging in prostitution, he admitted everything, including the agreed-upon price for their sexual transaction, and both Qing Yu and the client spent the night at the police station. The next day, they were first moved to the district detention center for a few hours and then transported to a larger detention center just outside of Beijing. They were both incarcerated there for seven days, for what she called "failed attempt at prostitution" (卖淫未遂 – *maiyin weisui*). Qing Yu moved to another apartment after that incident, but a few months later had another police encounter. This time, she and her client told each other their real names. If they were caught, this measure would make it easier for them to disprove an accusation of prostitution.[3] On this occasion, a law enforcement agent knocked on her door, and when Qing Yu opened it, the officer saw the client wearing only his boxers. They told the officer that they were friends and shared their real names. The law enforcement agent accused Qing Yu of lying and started insulting her. When he checked their ID cards and saw that the client was fifty-nine years old, he commented on how she would apparently do

1 Sex Worker Interview 1, August 26, 2009.

2 Making detainees squat (蹲着–*dunzhe*) is a form of humiliation and torture that Chinese law enforcement uses.

3 Police officers will ask suspected sex workers and clients to identify their partner by name, and use a failure to do so as evidence of prostitution.

anything for money, even sleep with old guys (老头 – *laotou*). He proceeded to go through everything in her apartment and confiscated all her CDs. When he found her condoms, he asked how many she used each day and demanded she tell him her total number of sexual partners. He then warned her that if he came across her again in this situation, he would lock her up for six months.[4]

Qing Yu's testimony illustrates a broadly entrenched pattern where the police systematically target low-tier sex workers for arrest. As shown in Figure 8.1, low-tier sex workers from my survey in Beijing were more than twice as likely to report frequent police inspection than hostesses were (35 percent versus 16 percent).[5]

They were also four times more likely to report being arrested by the police (17 percent versus 4 percent).[6] Of women who had been arrested, most had only been arrested once (71 percent). Another 21 percent had been arrested twice, and two participants had been arrested three times.

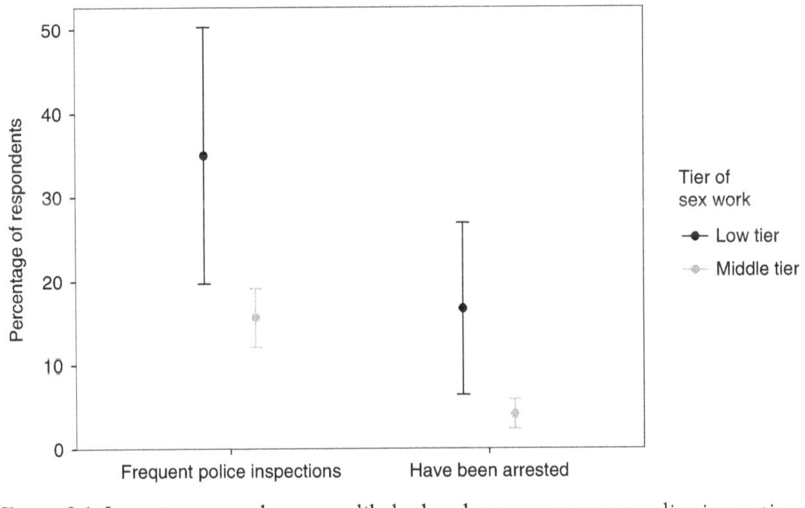

Figure 8.1 Low-tier sex workers more likely than hostesses to report police inspections and arrests

[4] Sex Worker Interview 1, August 26, 2009.

[5] Please see Appendix C for more details about the survey. The question asked was: "In the past year, how many times did the police come to your place of work?" I defined "frequent" as once a week, two to three times a month, several times a week, or came every day. I defined "infrequent" as never came, more or less once a month, a few times a year, or once a year. This difference is statistically significant. A Fisher's exact test yields a p-value of .004.

[6] This difference is statistically significant. The p-value for a Fisher's exact is .001.

Police testimony corroborates the data from the sex worker survey. The police I surveyed in Lianshu acknowledged the occurrence of prostitution in both low- and middle-tier spaces.[7] Yet when asked to identify the venues where they are most likely to arrest sex workers and clients, they mainly (68 percent) identified a focus on low-tier venues.[8] They also identified low-tier venues as most likely punished for harboring prostitution activities, with 85 percent of respondents highlighting those businesses.[9]

Others conducting research on prostitution in China have also observed that law enforcement focuses on low-tier sex workers. Scholars based in Beijing and Shanghai have underscored this pattern.[10] Susanne Y. P. Choi, focused on southwestern China, observes that local governments selectively enforce national orders on prostitution.[11] As a result, "the most vulnerable section of the sex industry, such as drug-using sex workers and streetwalkers, often become the prime target of police arrests."[12] In its report on sex worker custody and education (C&E), the organization Asia Catalyst notes that "low-tier sex workers are the most likely to be targeted" in law enforcement operations such as "strike hard" and "anti-vice" campaigns.[13] A survey of 348 sex workers in Beijing in 2008 found that women in the low tier were two to four times more likely to have been arrested than middle-tier sex workers.[14] A study of the effects of anti-prostitution campaigns in twelve cities in 2010 noted that these campaigns disproportionately affected low-tier sex workers.[15] Taken together, these sources of data provide

7 Please see Appendix D for more details about the police survey. The question asked was: "The following places are all spaces where sex workers might work. According to you, and in this city, which are the three types of venues where sex workers are most likely to be found?"

8 The question asked was: "In your city, in which venues are sex workers and clients often caught?"

9 The question asked was: "Which of the following three businesses are most frequently punished?"

10 Interview 64, April 16, 2009. Interview 59, April 3, 2009. Interview 67, April 17, 2009.

11 Susanne Y. P. Choi, "State Control, Female Prostitution and HIV Prevention in China," *The China Quarterly* 205 (March 2011): 96–114.

12 Choi, 102.

13 Asia Catalyst, "'Custody and Education': Arbitrary Detention for Female Sex Workers in China," December 2013, 15.

14 Huso Yi et al., "A Profile of HIV Risk Factors in the Context of Sex Work Environments among Migrant Female Sex Workers in Beijing, China," *Psychology, Health & Medicine* 15, no. 2 (March 1, 2010): 172–87.

15 Cai Lingping (蔡凌萍), "Research on the Impact of 2010 Crackdown on Sex Work and HIV Interventions in China (2010年严打对性工作与艾滋病防治影响研究)" (The China Sex Worker Organization Network Forum (中国性工作者机构网络平台), 2011), 20, perma.cc/2TUH-C4SY.

strong evidence of a policing pattern focused on low-tier sex workers, rather than hostesses or second wives.

Frontline law enforcement officers are not in a position to simply ignore the presence of prostitution in the community: They experience dual pressures to enforce the law from both the state above and society below.[16] From above, they must respond to pressures such as "rules, regulations, and directives"[17] to enforce anti-prostitution policies. Indeed, police officers I surveyed reported that external pressures, rather than intrinsic motivation, drive their decision to make arrests for prostitution in their communities. They identified two main instigators of increased crackdowns over the course of a year: orders from above (43 percent of respondents), and important national or local events (41 percent of respondents).[18] Only 4 percent of respondents said that it was their personal decision to crack down.[19] In another question from this survey, police officers' ranking of factors that drive their own personal enforcement decisions tell a similar story. The two highest-ranked reasons are that they are responding to orders from higher-ranked authorities (a mean of 7 on a 10-point scale), and that a crackdown has been declared (a mean of 7.3 on a 10-point scale). A police officer's personal decision to enforce has the second-lowest ranking (a mean of 5.7 on a 10-point scale).[20] These pressures from above sometimes take the form of quotas, either to raise certain amounts of money through fines or meet a certain number of arrests. Such quotas are against the law,[21] but both interviewed and surveyed

[16] Michael Lipsky, *Street-Level Bureaucracy: Dilemmas of the Individual in Public Services* (New York: Russell Sage Foundation, 1980), 14; 28.

[17] Lipsky, 14.

[18] Such events include major national holidays, high-profile political meetings, and international sports gatherings such as the Olympics.

[19] The question was: "If the intensity of crackdowns varies over the course of a year, what are the reasons for this?"

[20] The question was: "How important are the following reasons in driving your own decision to crack down on prostitution?"

[21] Elaine Jeffreys, "Exposing Police Corruption and Malfeasance: China's Virgin Prostitute Cases," *The China Journal* 63 (January 1, 2010): 127–49, https://doi.org/10.1086/tcj.63.20749197; Hualing Fu and D. W. Choy, "Administrative Detention of Prostitutes: The Legal Aspects," in *Gender Policy and HIV in China*, vol. 22, edited by Joseph Tucker and Dudley L. Poston, The Springer Series on Demographic Methods and Population Analysis (Dordrecht: Springer Netherlands, 2009), 189–99; Chen Fei (陈菲) and Wu Jing (吴晶), "Zhongyang Zhengfa Wei Chutai Shouge Qieshi Fangzhi Yuanjia Cuoan De Zhidao Yijian (中央政法委出台首个切实防止冤假错案的指导意见) [The First Guideline on Effective Prevention of Wrongful Convictions Published by the Committee of Political and Legal Affairs]," *The Xinhua News Agency (新华社)*, August 13, 2013, perma.cc/Q5PW-RXER; Chris Buckley, "China Aims to Abolish Goals for Arrests and Convictions," *The New York Times*, January 21, 2015, perma.cc/D2PD-VRFB; Guangdong People's Procuratorate (广东省人民

police officers openly recognize their prevalence. Survey respondents ranked police department target requirements as a significant factor behind strict enforcement against prostitution (a mean of 6.5 on a 10-point scale). In the city of Zhengti in 2009, one district's police station had to meet a 20,000 yuan annual target for fines, and another had to meet a 40,000 yuan target.[22] While the police can focus on a variety of different activities when seeking to generate income from fines, arresting sex workers and clients provides an attractive source of such revenue.[23] These targets can also take the form of a quota for number of sex worker arrests.[24]

The police also experience pressure from below, when society asks them to rid the community of prostitution. One law enforcement officer I interviewed emphasized the role that "social forces" (社会力量 – *shehui liliang*) played in pressuring the police to enforce prostitution laws.[25] When I shadowed him in the community, he drove me down a long street that was lined with small brothels that were poorly disguised as hair salons and massage parlors. He then took me to another avenue a few blocks away. It was prostitution-free, but the officer explained to me that a few years earlier, the venues on the other block had all moved from this location. The former red-light district was right by a prestigious high school, and parents had mounted a successful campaign to clean up the neighborhood.[26] Informants in other cities mentioned similar occurrences, as did pimps and sex workers explaining that they had been arrested or experienced police pressure in response to neighbor complaints.[27] These instances of responsiveness to public opinion challenge a preconceived notion that policing in an authoritarian regime does not take public opinion into account, and aligns with

检察院), "Guo Sheng Kun: Cong Zhongyang Zhengfa Danwei Zuoqi! Yanjin Xiada Pibu Lü Qisu Lü Jiean Lü Deng Zhibiao (郭声琨: 从中央政法单位做起! 严禁下达批捕率起诉率结案率等指标) [Guo Shengkun: Central Political and Legal Affairs Authorities to Lead by Example! Quotas for Criminal Detention, Arrests, Prosecutions, Convictions and Case Closures are Strictly Forbidden]," *Yangguang Jianwu Wang* (阳光检务网), April 16, 2019, perma.cc/VGG5-XH9L.

22 Field Notes, August 8, 2009; Field Notes, August 9, 2009.

23 See Chapter 3 for more discussion of why prostitution is an obvious target for police officers who need to raise money through fines.

24 Interview 99, August 6, 2009. Sex Worker Interview 3, August 18, 2009. Sex Worker Interview 3, August 15, 2009.

25 Interview 44, October 28, 2008.

26 Field Notes, August 8, 2009.

27 Interview 62b, April 16, 2009. Interview 68, April 17, 2009. Boss Interview, August 26, 2009. Sex Worker Interview 4, August 24, 2009. Sex Worker Interview 1, August 24, 2009. Sex Worker Interview 6, August 23, 2009. Sex Worker Interview 3, August 20, 2009.

research showing that law enforcement in China "has long engaged in efforts to reach out to the masses."[28]

Police officers address these dual sources of pressure (from above and below) by focusing on arresting sex workers in the low tier. They are the easiest to locate and identify, as they are in spaces that primarily provide sexual services. In contrast, hostesses in entertainment venues are simultaneously engaging in legitimate activities such as drinking and dancing. And second wives' daily routines are not easily distinguishable from those of upstanding citizens. Low-tier sex workers are also easier to arrest than hostesses.[29] Owners and managers of entertainment venues shield middle-tier sex workers from immediate police interference, providing some protection that low-tier sex workers do not have. Furthermore, arrests of low-tier sex workers leave untouched the entertainment industry with hostesses at its core, thus avoiding the possibility of significant harm to the local economy. This approach focusing on the lowest tier of sex work also allows the police to avoid the perils that come with challenging China's elite, many of whom have second wives. Finally, the immediate visual impact of arresting sex workers is greatest when it targets women in the low tier. Police physically remove them from streets and barbershops, rather than from behind the closed doors of entertainment venues (for hostesses) or residential apartments (for mistresses). It creates neighborhoods that appear free from vice, thus sending signals to both the state above and society below that the police are addressing their concerns about prostitution.

ILLEGAL AND ABUSIVE POLICE ARREST PRACTICES

As recounted by sex workers, police officers engage in a number of illegal and abusive practices, sometimes relying on auxiliary police officers in order to protect themselves from direct accusations of wrongdoing. Their problematic behavior includes posing as clients, abusing sex workers

[28] Suzanne E. Scoggins, "Policing Modern China," *China Law and Society Review* 3, no. 2 (October 30, 2018): 103, https://doi.org/10.1163/25427466-00302001. Scoggins also mentions such efforts under Xi Jinping. Suzanne E. Scoggins, *Policing China: Street-Level Cops in the Shadow of Protest*, Studies of the Weatherhead East Asian Institute, Columbia University (Ithaca, NY: Cornell University Press, 2021), 121–22; 136–37.

[29] This focus on the easiest cases is one that Scoggins notes more generally among the police: "Crunched for time, police instead focus on 'easy cases' in which they can get the person or persons involved to admit guilt, and meanwhile try to ignore everything else." Scoggins, *Policing China*, 97.

verbally and physically, forcing confessions, and extorting bribes. These actions can occur without any evidence that prostitution has occurred, such as when police arrest streetwalkers for simply standing in areas known for prostitution.[30]

Auxiliary Police Officers

The police outsource some aspects of their enforcement activities to auxiliary police officers (协警 – *xiejing*, also called 联防 – *lianfang* or 保安队员 – *baoan duiyuan*). This is an informal position, rather than a specific rank within law enforcement, and individuals who serve in this capacity are not official police officers.[31] Police stations in China are chronically underfunded and short on manpower, and hiring auxiliary officers for a fraction of the cost of employing a formal police officer helps address these issues.[32] The practice also allows law enforcement officials to delegate some illegal and abusive aspects of their work to these auxiliary officers, in order to avoid personal responsibility for violating the law. If things go wrong, the auxiliary police can be blamed and quickly fired.[33] One foreign informant who interacted with auxiliary officers in his work described them as "hired thugs."[34] In Zhengti, the police station for the largest district was staffed with forty-eight official police officers – trained civil servants who have graduated from police academies and are paid several thousand yuan a month – and 100 unofficial agents, untrained employees who are paid only a few hundred yuan per month.[35] In Wanqin, one of the Shenzhen red-light districts where I conducted fieldwork, auxiliary officers would drive around the neighborhood on officially labeled "public security patrol" scooters (治安巡逻 – *zhian xunluo*), in plain clothes and looking distinctly unofficial.[36] In Xizhou, one such officer strolled around the neighborhood wearing army fatigues and a red and yellow "public security patrol" armband.[37] Xiao Yuan, a sex worker I interviewed whose boyfriend worked as an auxiliary officer, explained that one of his jobs was to assist with

[30] Sex Worker Interview 7, August 20, 2009.

[31] For more on auxiliary police officers, see Scoggins, "Policing Modern China," 95–96; Scoggins, *Policing China*.

[32] Scoggins, *Policing China*, 43–65.

[33] Scoggins, 54.

[34] Interview 48, October 30, 2008.

[35] Interview 102, August 9, 2009.

[36] Field Notes, November 2, 2009. Field Notes, November 5, 2009.

[37] Field Notes, November 7, 2009.

prostitution arrests. He would first identify a suspected sex worker in the community. He would then spend hours monitoring her, and when a client arrived, he would contact an official police officer to join him. The auxiliary officer would burst onto the scene first, often picking the lock to do so. The official officer would follow him in and start the formal investigation into prostitution.[38]

Posing as Clients

Police agents sometimes pose as clients. As recounted in Chapter 4, Shu Li, who works at Xicheng Park in Beijing, once got in the car with a client who came to the park.[39] He revealed himself to be a police officer, but she managed to exit the car before getting arrested. In some cases, these undercover agents will solicit a sex worker, have intercourse, and then return later to arrest the woman.[40] Shu Li once encountered a client who gave her money and then wanted to leave without actually having sex. This seemed suspicious to her, so she tried to return the money. He changed his mind and penetrated her a few times, left, and then returned shortly after with a uniformed police officer to arrest her. One time in Li Ting's brothel, an undercover agent had sex with her colleague, left, and immediately returned with another agent to arrest the woman, who had not had time to get dressed.[41]

Harsh and Abusive Treatment

Sex workers who have experienced police interventions report harsh and abusive treatment. Law enforcement agents exceed the legal time limits for interrogating and investigating sex workers prior to detaining them. According to the Public Security Administration Punishment Law, this initial process must not exceed twenty-four hours.[42] Yong Qing recounted an instance when the police detained her colleague for seventy-two hours until her pimp intervened for her release.[43] Xiao Yuan described the police forward-dating her arrest to cover up

[38] Sex Worker Interview 3, August 18, 2009. By the time I interviewed her, her partner had stopped working as an auxiliary police officer. He quit after the police sent him to do a drug bust that resulted in a drug trafficker putting a gun to his head.

[39] Sex Worker Interview 3, August 20, 2009.

[40] Sex Worker Interview 5, August 24, 2009. Sex Worker Interview 4, August 20, 2009.

[41] Sex Worker Interview 2, August 24, 2009.

[42] *Public Security Administration Punishments Law of the People's Republic of China* (中华人民共和国治安管理处罚法) Art.83 (promulgated by the Standing Comm. Nat'l People's Cong., August 28, 2005, effective March 1, 2006).

[43] Sex Worker Interview 6, August 25, 2009.

extending her interrogation time beyond legal limits.[44] During one roundup, Song Qin was locked up for hours without access to food, water, or a restroom; a similarly mistreated colleague sharing her cell was reduced to defecating in it.[45] Police sometimes abuse sex workers to extract confessions. Li Ting was working in a hair salon when the police brought her in for questioning, even though they had not caught her with a client. They interrogated and threatened her, eventually transitioning from verbal abuse to violence in order to extract a forced confession.[46] Other interviewees also described the police extorting confessions from them.[47] Yong Qing was soliciting on the street with five other sex workers when the police brought them into the station, and auxiliary officers beat them and forced them to admit to prostitution.[48] Li Ting described being undressed while in police custody in Beijing, made to stand outside in the winter, and doused in cold water.[49] Xiao Yuan similarly described how police stripped her down to her underwear in the winter, wrapped her up with rope, attached her to the ceiling in the bathroom so that only her toes touched the ground, and doused her with cold water.[50] The cold water method was successful in extracting confessions from both women. In one instance of police abuse, a group of sex workers in Beijing encountered an agent on their way into public restrooms. He asked for their temporary residence cards, which he promptly tore to shreds.[51] This incident occurred in the early 2000s, when a procedure called "custody and repatriation" allowed the police to detain people without valid residence permits and return them to their hometown. This repatriation would entail total humiliation, as local police would be informed of these women's involvement in prostitution and report it back to their families.[52]

Police officers also extort bribes from sex workers. When I spoke to Yong Qing in August 2009, she had already been arrested three times that year. She had twice been required to pay her arresting officer 3,000 yuan ($480) for her release and knew the money was going straight into his pocket because he did not give her a receipt.[53] Other sex workers described similar situations and identified payments as bribes when they

44 Sex Worker Interview 3, August 18, 2009.
45 Sex Worker Interview 3, August 26, 2009.
46 Sex Worker Interview 2, August 24, 2009.
47 Sex Worker Interview 7, August 20, 2009.
48 Sex Worker Interview 6, August 25, 2009.
49 Sex Worker Interview 2, August 24, 2009.
50 Sex Worker Interview 3, August 18, 2009.
51 Sex Worker Interview 3, August 17, 2009.
52 Custody and repatriation was abolished in 2003.
53 Sex Worker Interview 6, August 25, 2009.

occurred immediately after arrest and prior to having their case officially registered at the police station.[54] Auxiliary police officers are often the ones responsible for demanding bribes. For instance, an auxiliary officer who was the boyfriend of one of my sex worker informants was responsible for negotiating her release price when she was arrested and actually accepting the bribe. After the sex worker paid the bribe, the officers involved in her arrest would all go out together to spend the money on a meal and divide the remaining amount among themselves.[55]

The police officers with whom I interacted did not corroborate the occurrence of such abuse. When I would gently raise the issue of police misconduct toward a sex worker, my interlocutor would usually respond with an evasive "this is very sensitive" (很敏感 – *hen mingan*) or "I'm unsure about that" (搞不清楚 – *gao bu qingchu*).[56] That said, the roundup of sex workers that I witnessed in Xizhou proceeded without any evidence of prostitution.[57] In addition, a number of the public shaming events described in Chapter 3 bolster the plausibility of the claims these women shared with me. For instance, the internet was awash in photos of sex workers roped together, barefoot and naked, at the Dongguan public shaming event. Similarly, the photos of naked sex workers that Zhengzhou police officers took while arresting them and shared online were widely available. The frequency of these practices is also difficult to ascertain, though sex workers generally talked about them as being the norm, rather than the exception.

SANCTIONS: INCARCERATION AND THE DEMISE OF SOCIALIST IDEALS OF REHABILITATION

When I was doing my fieldwork, sex workers who were incarcerated were sent to custody and education (C&E) institutions (收容教育所 – *shourong jiaoyusuo*), an administrative punishment under police control.[58] These centers, originally designed in the 1940s to rehabilitate women who sell sex, had drifted far from their reform-minded roots

[54] Sex Worker Interview 5, August 24, 2009.

[55] Sex Worker Interview 3, August 18, 2009.

[56] Interview 99, August 6, 2009. For more on the difficulty of engaging police officers on the topics of misconduct and corruption, see Scoggins, *Policing China*, 38–42.

[57] I describe this episode at the beginning of Chapter 1. Police officers drove slowly around the central square in Xizhou, pulled sex workers who were standing outside into their van, and brought the women to the local police station. Field Notes, November 13, 2009 and November 17, 2009.

[58] I discuss administrative sanctions (versus criminal sanctions) in Chapter 3 and also later on in this chapter.

over the decades. They had essentially become punitive spaces, a shift that the institution's founders bemoaned.[59] As these facilities lost their reform emphasis, they also dwindled in both numbers and inmates. In addition, they were facing calls for their abolishment, which came to pass in 2019. That said, the end of custody and education did not spell the end of sex worker incarceration. Instead, sex workers in China today are simply incarcerated in nonspecialized penal institutions.

The Inmates

Although nothing in the content of the regulations called for such an emphasis, C&E institutions (*shourong*) in the early twenty-first century held mostly low-tier sex workers.[60] Discussing a Shenzhen center, a public health worker said inmates were "young [women], do not have a lot of experience with prostitution, and do lower-class types of prostitution."[61] A researcher familiar with dozens of *shourong* in the country emphasized the presence of older women and explained that "the people at the *shourong* are the streetwalkers, the old and ugly ones, the lowest of the low in the hierarchy of sex workers."[62] Another informant, who had volunteered at *shourong* in both Tianjin and Beijing, noticed clusters at both ends of the age spectrum: "The women [there] are all the lower-class sex workers ... [they are] very innocent and naïve. They are either young (eighteen) or old (over thirty). ... The women who end up there are not educated, they are poor, and from the countryside. They don't have any income."[63]

The incarcerated women's lives of poverty became especially apparent to one of my informants who volunteered at a C&E institution every Thursday, the day when family members were permitted to visit. In particular, she described how heartrending (特别可怜 – *tebie kelian*) it was to interact with poor migrant husbands and parents who came to see their wives and daughters, and who expressed deep guilt and powerlessness for their inability to provide a life for them where they would not have to sell sex. Custody and education inmates also have high rates of STDs. Under Chinese law, police are supposed to test

59 Interviews 69 and 70, April 18, 2009.
60 Incarceration was also the most common form of sanction for low-tier sex workers I surveyed. In the survey, only one low-tier sex worker was fined, and four were incarcerated. The remaining surveyed low-tier sex workers who had been arrested (another four women) did not report a sanction.
61 Interview 81, May 4, 2009.
62 Interview 59, May 4, 2009.
63 Interview 68, April 17, 2009.

suspected sex workers for STDs when they are arrested and incarcerate them in a *shourong* if they test positive.[64] This policy leads to a higher rate of STDs among C&E inmates than among the sex worker population as a whole.[65]

Reformatory Aspirations versus Punitive and Exploitative Reality

By the early twenty-first century, conditions in C&E institutions had drifted far from the reformatory aims enshrined within the policies regulating the centers. Notably, the role labor played in these centers shifted. Originally, labor requirements at the centers were just one of several activities (including education) integral to training women to reenter the work force. At the time of my research, however, at least some of these institutions appeared to simply operate as labor camps. Inmates at a center in Shenzhen allegedly produced plastic flowers all day.[66] In Tianjin, they assembled cardboard boxes for a local company.[67] In another city, production demands at a local factory were said to drive decisions about whether to fine or incarcerate sex workers.[68] Labor in these centers was forced and unpaid.[69]

More generally, testimonies of women incarcerated within C&E centers made these places sound indistinguishable from traditional correctional facilities. The arrest and incarceration experience of Mei

64 Interview 69, April 18, 2009, Interview 64, April 16, 2009. "Weishengbu Gonganbu Guanyu Dui Maiyin Piaochang Renyuan Qiangzhi Jinxing Xingbing Jiancha Zhiliao Youguan Wenti De Tongzhi (卫生部、公安部关于对卖淫嫖娼人员强制进行性病检查治疗有关问题的通知) [Notice of the Ministry of Health and the Ministry of Public Security of Issues Concerning Compulsory STD Inspection and Treatment of Persons Engaging in Prostitution], Para. 2 (Promulgated by the Ministry of Health and the Ministry of Public Security, December 16, 1991)" (1991). Compulsory testing continues to be a part of police procedure since the abolition of C&E, and is used to determine whether the sex worker or the client can be charged with the criminal offense of selling or buying sex while knowing that one has a venereal disease. Luo Congran 罗聪冉 and Wu Jie 武杰, "Li Yundi Piaochang Beiju Yansheng Pufa Xiaoketang: Ruohe Rending Zhengju? Huiyou Hezhong Yingxiang? (李云迪嫖娼被拘衍生普法小课堂：如何认定证据？会有何种影响?) [A Popular Law Class on Li Yundi's Detention over Prostitution: How to Evaluate Evidence? What Are the Consequences?]," *Legal Daily* 法治日报, October 21, 2021, perma.cc/KTE5-MBTY.

65 These patterns of high rates of poverty and STDs among C&E inmates have historical precursors. In Shanghai in the late 1940s, limited space in the city's first detention center led police to focus on sex workers who were homeless, living on the streets, and soliciting on the streets or in other public places. In the Beijing facility in 1950, out of the 1,303 incarcerated women 1,259 tested positive for an STD. See Sarah Biddulph, *Legal Reform and Administrative Detention Powers in China* (Cambridge: Cambridge University Press, 2007), 74–75.

66 Interview 96, January 19, 2009.

67 Interview 68, April 17, 2009.

68 Interview 69, April 18, 2009. A similar pattern also exists for incarceration decisions in other, non-sex work-specific detention centers. Interview 96, January 19, 2009.

69 Interview 190, March 26, 2009. Interview 68, April 17, 2009.

Mei, a woman from Sichuan who sells sex in a foot massage parlor, illustrates this observation clearly.[70] Mei Mei had just started selling sex twenty days earlier when the police caught her and a client in the back room of the venue. They told her that if she signed a confession, she would be detained for five days and then released. She agreed, and instead found herself transferred from short-term detention to a C&E center for six months. Upon arrival, she was given a blood test and a full physical. They were mandatory, and she had to pay for them herself. The police shared her test results with her. Inmates who had STDs were kept together, separate from those who did not. The center provided them with only minimal supplies, and they had to purchase most daily necessities themselves. She found the food they served inedible, and thus spent her own money to buy better meals. In all, Mei Mei estimated spending about 10,000 yuan ($1,600) while incarcerated.[71] Despite C&E's rehabilitative mission, the institution where she was incarcerated did not provide her with either classes or trainings.[72] Instead, inmates were forced to sit on small stools (做板凳 – *zuo bandeng*), sew vests, and watch television.[73] While Mei Mei said that the guards at the short-term detention facility in Beijing treated her well, she characterized the behavior of those in long-term detention as worlds apart (天壤之别 – *tianrangzhibie*). They yelled and shouted obscenities at her. They inflicted physical punishments on inmates, such as forcing them to stand for hours on end until Mei Mei's legs would collapse beneath her. Only Mei Mei's skill at negotiating with the guards enabled her to avoid beatings.[74]

C&E Founders' Views

Custody and education inmates were not the only individuals to highlight the absence of meaningful training, services, and support that would allow sex workers to find other employment upon leaving the facility. Some of the most damning critiques of the system came from the people who created and managed it. I interviewed the founders of

[70] Sex Worker Interview 1, August 24, 2009.

[71] Others also described having to spend several thousand yuan while incarcerated. Sex Worker Interview 3, August 24, 2009.

[72] Other interviewees did describe attending courses. Interview 68, April 17, 2009. Sex Worker Interview 3, August 24, 2009.

[73] Another interviewee also described being forced to sit on stools. Sex Worker Interview 3, August 24, 2009. This is a practice used on inmates in China that is very uncomfortable. The stools are small, women must sit on them with their backs straight, they are not allowed to stretch their legs, and sometimes must sit on them for hours.

[74] Other interviewees also shared testimony of guards treating the women poorly. Interview 68, April 17, 2009.

the male and female C&E centers established in Shanghai in the 1980s, who spearheaded the municipal and nationwide reemergence of the institutions in response to the resurgence of visible prostitution at that time. Their two centers served as models for the national system. Wang Yi, the founder of the center for men, was intimately involved in the entire legal and policymaking process at the local and central government levels. Both he and Hong Xiu Ying, the head of the center for women, noted the gulf between the centers' original design and the practices that actually prevailed by the time I met with them. Their testimonies are striking because they underscore a genuine commitment to reform in the early stages of the project. Hong Xiu Ying described how the centers "used to have education, competitions, health exercises ... It was a school, [which provided participants with] a very rich life."[75] In fact, the terminology used within the institution underscores these goals. Incarcerated sex workers and clients were called "students/trainees" (学员 – *xueyuan*). Staff were called "instructors" (辅导员 – *fudaoyuan*). As evidence of their success, Hong Xiu Ying discussed the high attendance at an alumni reunion they organized, and talked more generally about all her former students who would come back to visit her and bring her gifts. She showed me a stack of cards that she had received over the years from former sex workers, thanking her for everything she had done for them.

Wang Yi and Hong Xiu Ying even served as matchmakers for incarcerated men and women, arranging marriages between single men and single women who had completed their time in custody.[76] Historical precursors of these institutions played a similar matchmaking role. Gail Hershatter, in her history of prostitution in Shanghai, notes that during the early years of the PRC the staff of reform institutions "regarded it as part of their work to see that married women were reunited with their spouses and unmarried women were married off."[77] Elizabeth Remick notes that institutions in Republican China took on a similar responsibility for matchmaking.[78] There is no evidence to suggest such pairings

[75] Interview 70, April 18, 2009.

[76] Interviews 69 and 70, April 18, 2009.

[77] Gail Hershatter, *Dangerous Pleasures: Prostitution and Modernity in Twentieth-Century Shanghai* (Berkeley: University of California Press, 1997), 319.

[78] Elizabeth J. Remick, "Police-Run Brothels in Republican Kunming," *Modern China* 33, no. 4 (2007): 440; Elizabeth J. Remick, "Prostitution Taxes and Local State Building in Republican China," *Modern China* 29, no. 1 (2003): 47. Matthew H. Sommer notes that from the late Ming until the end of the Qing dynasties, an official matchmaker would play a similar role for women held in custody, usually when they were convicted of either adultery or prostitution. See

occurred in the last few decades of C&E institutions before they were abolished in 2019.

During our interview, both Wang Yi and Hong Xiu Ying talked about prostitution in ways that were understanding and empathetic. Wang Yi viewed it as "just a profession" (职业 – *zhiye*) and talked about it as a special, victimless crime which, unlike drug use or drug trafficking, does not harm two willing participants. He was also open to multiple explanations for why people engage in prostitution, including life circumstances, a bad relationship with parents, laziness, peer pressure, or an unhappy marriage. Clients might purchase sex to satisfy their physical needs, spend their excess income (有钱没有地方用 – *youqian meiyou difang yong*), or find an outlet to deal with work pressure. Others might be bad people (本来是坏人 – *benlai shi huairen*) or just think about things differently (想法不一样 – *xiangfa buyiyang*).[79]

Dwindling Numbers and Calls for Abolition

As C&E institutions departed from their original reform-oriented mission, the number of centers and inmates began to decline and they faced calls for their abolition. Following a steady increase throughout the 1990s, numbers of C&E centers began to fall. In 1992, there were 111 such institutions nationwide. The number rose to 150 in 1995, 160 in 1996, 183 in 1999, and more than 200 in 2005.[80] Yet by 2014, the Ministry of Public Security reported that there were somewhere between 90 and 116 C&E institutions remaining in China.[81] The heads of the Shanghai C&E institutions corroborated those most

Sommer, *Sex, Law, and Society in Late Imperial China* (Stanford, CA: Stanford University Press, 2000), 282.

79 Interview 69, April 18, 2009.

80 Biddulph, *Legal Reform and Administrative Detention Powers in China*, 165; Wang Xing (王星), "Shoujiao Sanshi Nian (收教三十年) [Detention Education for 30 Years]," *Southern Metropolis Daily* (南方都市报), July 2, 2014, perma.cc/TNZ4-TFYY.

81 "Dui Hua Human Rights Journal: MPS: China Has 116 Custody and Education Centers Nationwide," accessed September 8, 2014, perma.cc/Y689-85QD. Interestingly, this estimate comes from requests through China's 2008 Open Government Information (OGI) reform, which requires a vast number of agencies at all levels of government to respond to information-disclosure requests from the public. Lawyer Zhao Yunheng's OGI request yielded the 116 count from the national-level MPS (Ministry of Public Security). The lower boundary of ninety institutions resulted from a separate inquiry, in which the newspaper *Southern Metropolis Daily* contacted each provincial-level public security agency in China with OGI requests, and reporters followed up with visits to those provincial agencies that did not respond. See Greg Distelhorst, "The Power of Empty Promises: Quasi-Democratic Institutions and Activism in China," *Comparative Political Studies* 50, no. 4 (March 1, 2017): 464–98, https://doi.org/10.1177/0010414015617960 and Wang Xing (王星), "Shoujiao Sanshi Nian (收教三十年) [Detention Education for 30 Years]."

recent numbers, estimating in 2009 that about 100 such institutions were in operation nationwide.[82]

The number of individuals incarcerated in these institutions also declined in the last years of C&E's existence. According to official data, C&E institutions housed 20,000 individuals in 1992, 40,000 in 1999, but only 28,000 in 2002.[83] Taking the 1999 figures, 40,000 inmates spread across 183 institutions means an average of 219 per center. But in 2014, law enforcement officials in several provinces reported that there were about ten to twenty individuals incarcerated in a typical C&E institution.[84] Accurate data from the Shanghai women's center substantiated these official reports. When it opened in 1984, the institution housed eighty-six sex workers, and the numbers increased steadily until 1998, when the population reached a peak of about 1,900 in a space intended for no more than 1,800 women. That number began shrinking in 2002, and by 2009, the Shanghai women's C&E housed only about 100 women.[85]

Calls for the abolition of C&E gained increasing prominence in China in the early 2000s.[86] Legal arguments against the system underscored the absence of due process in C&E procedures, which permit the police to bypass the legal system and deprive accused sex workers of their personal freedom without oversight by the procuratorate or the courts.[87] Custody and education critics highlighted Article 37 of China's constitution, which states that citizens shall

[82] Interview 69, April 18, 2009.

[83] Wang Xing (王星), "Shoujiao Sanshi Nian (收教三十年) [Detention Education for 30 Years]"; Zhan Wei (詹伟), "Zhongguo Dui Maiyin Piaochang Renyuan Shourong Jiaoyu Zhidu De Yanjiu Baogao (中国对卖淫嫖娼人员收容教育制度的研究报告) [A Study on China's Custody and Education System for Prostitutes]," in *Xianzhi Dui Renshen Ziyou De Xianzhi–Zhongguo Xingzhengxing Xianzhi Renshen Ziyou Falu Chufen De Fazhi Jianshe* (限制对人身自由的限制-中国行政性限制人身自由法律处分的法治建设) *[To Refrain From the Restrictions of Personal Freedom]*, ed. Guo Jianan (郭建安) and Zheng Xiaze (郑霞泽) (Beijing: China Law Press (法律出版社), 2005), 416–66; Asia Catalyst, "'Custody and Education': Arbitrary Detention for Female Sex Workers in China," 19.

[84] Wang Xing (王星), "Shoujiao Sanshi Nian (收教三十年) [Detention Education for 30 Years]."

[85] Interview 70, April 18, 2009.

[86] "Dui Hua Human Rights Journal: Detained Actor Spotlights Custody and Education, Censors Intervene," accessed September 8, 2014, perma.cc/Y4AN-T7JU.

[87] Haibo He, "Why Should Custody and Education Be Abolished?," *Peking University Law Journal* 4, no. 1 (2016): 1–44, www.tandfonline.com/doi/full/10.1080/20517483.2016.1174426. Chapter 3 also discusses this point: Most aspects of prostitution are considered administrative, rather than criminal, offenses under Chinese law, which means that the police are empowered to initiate, impose, and administer most sanctions against sex workers and clients, including custody and education. Also as noted in Chapter 3, the procuratorate is the agency responsible for investigating and prosecuting crimes in China; the courts are responsible for imposing a sentence.

only be deprived of their freedom "pursuant to statute and legal process"; Article 8 of the Legislation Law, which notes that restrictions on freedom "shall only be governed by law"; and Article 10 of the Administrative Penalty Law, which does not allow for punishments through administrative rules and regulations that restrict "freedom of the person."[88] Public debate on the issue included a petition delivered to the National People's Congress in May 2014, which more than 100 legal experts, scholars, and officials endorsed.[89] One month later, the front page of the *Procuratorate Daily*, which is the official newspaper of the Supreme People's Procuratorate, published an article entitled "What Is the Legal Basis for 'Custody and Education'?"[90] The government quickly forbade other media outlets from republishing the article.[91] While others also published critiques of the C&E system, this article may have caught censors' attention because it concluded with a call to go beyond abolishing C&E and create a mechanism for constitutional review to provide citizens with more systematic and effective ways of challenging the constitutionality of laws in China more generally.[92] Public debate on this issue continued after this incident, eventually leading to the abolition of C&E in 2019.[93]

88 *Constitution of the People's Republic of China* (中华人民共和国宪法) (promulgated by the Standing Comm. Nat'l People's Cong., December 4, 1982, effective December 4, 1986). *Legislation Law of the People's Republic of China* (中华人民共和国立法法) (promulgated by the Standing Comm. Nat'l People's Cong., March 15, 2000, effective July 1, 2000). *Administrative Penalty Law of the People's Republic of China* (中华人民共和国行政处罚法) (promulgated by the Standing Comm. Nat'l People's Cong., March 17, 1996, effective October 1, 1996).

89 Signatories included Guo Daohui, who was deputy director of the research center for the NPC's Legislative Affairs Work Committee; Du Guang, former librarian of the Central Party School; Cao Haiqing, at the Central Institute for Correctional Police; and Wang Ying, an elite Chinese businesswoman. See Didi Kirsten Tatlow, "Petition Seeks Closure of Extrajudicial Detention Centers," *Sinosphere Blog*, May 5, 2014, perma.cc/F8TT-793Q.

90 Xiao Rong (肖荣), "'Shourong Jiaoyu' Falu Yiju Hezai? ('收容教育'法律依据何在?) [What Is the Legal Basis for 'Custody and Education' ?]," *Procuratorate Daily* (检察日报), June 4, 2014, sec. 01, perma.cc/36V9-MNMU.

91 Anne Henochowicz, "Minitrue: Legal Basis for Custody and Education," China Digital Times (CDT), June 6, 2014, perma.cc/ULF6-EZCY.

92 "Dui Hua Human Rights Journal: Detained Actor Spotlights Custody and Education, Censors Intervene."

93 Gao Yu Yang (高语阳), Dong Xin (董鑫), and Zhao Meng (赵萌), "San Wei Lushi Daibiao Weiyuan Jianyi Feizhi Maiyin Piaochang Shourong Jiaoyu (三位律师代表委员建议废止'卖淫嫖娼收容教育') [Three Lawyer Representatives Recommend to Abolish Custody and Education of Prostitutes and Clients of Prostitutes]," *Beijing Youth Daily* (北京青年报), March 10, 2018, perma.cc/K8EL-B4P7.

Sex Worker Incarceration Continues

The abolition of C&E did not end sex worker incarceration. Instead, it put a formal end to the rehabilitative approach to regulating prostitution that had already become fully punitive in practice. Even before C&E was abolished, some of these institutions were physically merged with non-specialized detention centers (拘留所 – *juliusuo* and 看守所 – *kanshousuo*), with sex workers treated like other detainees.[94] Sex workers were also sometimes sent to regular detention centers despite the availability of space in C&E facilities. In fact, the sex workers I spoke to rarely distinguished between different types of institutions. Instead, they used the terms *juliu* (administrative detention), *shourong* (custody and education), and *laojiao* (labor camps) interchangeably to refer to an incarceration experience, without necessarily knowing the official type of institution where they were held.[95] Rather than indicating that sex workers are ignorant about their interactions with law enforcement, this linguistic fluidity highlights the blurring of institutional boundaries that occurs when sex workers are incarcerated. And while the regulations allowing law enforcement to send sex workers to C&E centers are now defunct, reports in recent years note an increased use of Article 360 of China's Criminal Law, which makes it a crime to sell or buy sex while knowing that one has a venereal disease. Violators of this law can receive up to five years imprisonment.[96]

PUNISHING HOSTESSES AND SECOND WIVES

Although law enforcement officials expend most of their enforcement energy on women in the low tier of the sex industry, they do occasionally target hostesses and second wives.[97] When hostesses are arrested, they report paying a fine with greater frequency than low-tier sex workers do. Hostesses are more likely to have the money to pay a fine, which means they might choose to do so if given a choice between a fine and imprisonment, and police are more likely to focus on hostesses if they are seeking to raise revenue. Of the sex workers I surveyed who reported being arrested, 24 percent of hostesses were fined (five women) versus only 11 percent of low-tier sex workers (one woman). In line with the observation that low-tier sex workers are poor candidates for fines

[94] Wang Xing (王星), "Shoujiao Sanshi Nian (收教三十年) [Detention Education for 30 Years]."

[95] Chapter 3 provides more discussion of *juliu* and *laojiao*.

[96] Shen Tingting, "A Rare Rights Victory in China," The Diplomat, accessed April 21, 2020, perma.cc/NE7P-8863.

[97] Chapter 9 discusses the circumstances where middle-tier sex workers encounter law enforcement.

because they are unable to afford them, the one low-tier sex worker who reported being fined paid 500 yuan ($81), while hostesses who were fined paid an average of 1,660 yuan ($268). Yet even when sex workers can afford to pay a fine, they sometimes prefer to spend time in detention rather than lose several thousand yuan. This was Qing Yu's reasoning when she opted for seven days of incarceration rather than paying a 5,000 yuan fine.[98] Other respondents echoed a similar logic. When the police came to Qing Lai's brothel in Beijing, a number of her colleagues panicked and paid them 3,000 yuan for immediate release. Qing Lai adopted a different approach: "I didn't have any money then, and I also wasn't in any particular rush. I wasn't scared. The worst-case scenario was that they would lock me up, so I didn't hand over any money. They incarcerated me overnight, and then let me go the next day."[99]

On rare occasions, second wives also become entangled with law enforcement. But in these cases, prostitution is not the basis for their arrest or conviction. Instead, they get caught up in corruption investigations, described later in this chapter, that primarily target their clients. This tends to happen when sex workers are active participants in their client's corrupt activities, rather than passive recipients of the fruits of the corruption. In the late 1990s, Cheng Kejie, who was deputy chairman of the Standing Committee of the National People's Congress (NPC), and his mistress, Li Ping, were investigated for corruption activities that included accepting over $3 million in bribes. Cheng was sentenced to death and executed in 2000, and Li Ping was sentenced to life imprisonment.[100] In January 2011, the mistress of an official in Guangdong Province (who was himself sentenced to death for bribery scandals involving $4.5 million) was imprisoned in connection with property and gifts he had given her.[101] In 2014, Luo Fei, mistress of a Ministry of Railways official, Zhang Shuguang, was sentenced to five years' imprisonment for accepting bribes that exceeded $250,000. Zhang was given a suspended death sentence for accepting over $7 million in bribes, which was later reduced to life imprisonment.[102] In 2016, Xu

98 Sex Worker Interview 1, August 26, 2009.
99 Sex Worker Interview 2, August 26, 2009.
100 Yan Sun, *Corruption and Market in Contemporary China* (Ithaca, NY: Cornell University Press, 2004), 63.
101 Dan Levin, "China's New Wealth Spurs a Market for Mistresses," *The New York Times*, August 9, 2011, perma.cc/Y7U5-W9EC.
102 Sun Liangzi 孙良滋, "Zhang Shuguang Qingfu Luofei Beijianyi Jianxing Cengyin Shouhui Panxing Wunian (张曙光情妇罗菲被建议减刑 曾因受贿判刑五年) [Reduced Sentence Recommended for Luo Fei, Mistress of Zhang Shuguang, Who Had Been Sentenced for Five Years for Accepting Bribery]," *Caixin News* 财新新闻, August 25, 2017, https://perma

Qiulin, mistress of Guangdong Party Secretary Chen Hongping, was sentenced to six years' imprisonment for offering over $500,000 in bribes; Chen was given a suspended death sentence for corruption, including accepting millions of dollars in bribes.[103] In 2018, the mistress of Yang Chenglin, the party secretary and chairman of the Bank of Inner Mongolia, was sentenced to five years imprisonment for accepting about $1.3 million in bribes; Yang was given a suspended death sentence for his corrupt activities.[104]

TARGETING CLIENTS

As Qing Yu's story at the beginning of this chapter shows, clients are not completely immune to arrest. And just as low-tier sex workers are the ones most at risk of attracting the unwanted attention of street-level law enforcement officers, their clients are also more vulnerable to being caught for soliciting sex. My police informants in Zhengti noted that anyone with social stature (地位 – *diwei*) would avoid soliciting sex in low-tier venues because of their increased risk of being caught.[105] Cab drivers, who are generally familiar with the local geography of prostitution and frequently have arrangements to bring customers to specific brothels, consistently warned me of the arrest dangers tied to soliciting in hair salons.[106] Yet, by and large, clients are punished less frequently than the women from whom they purchase sex. They are also more likely to be fined than incarcerated. The major exception to this disproportionate focus on sex workers is among China's elite,

.cc/9YL4-KEC9; "Chinese Rail Official's Mistress Jailed over Bribery," BBC News, March 12, 2014, perma.cc/J5GX-UBY6.

103 Huang Xiaoqing 黄晓晴, "Chen Hongping Qingfu Shousheng (陈弘平情妇受审) [Chen Hongping's Mistress on Trial]," *Yangcheng Evening News* 羊城晚报, June 17, 2015, perma.cc/6Z5E-GGKZ, Dong Liu 董柳, "Guangdong Jieyang Fubaiwo An De Shenmi Nvzi Xu 'Xiaowan' Huoxing (广东揭阳腐败窝案的神秘女子'许小婉'获刑) ["Xu Xiaowan" – Mysterious Woman in Guangdong Jieyang Corruption Case Receives Sentence]," *Yangcheng Evening News* 羊城晚报, April 26, 2016, perma.cc/26NY-NSBH; "'Xu Xiaowan' Fan Xinghuizui Huoxing Liunian ('许小婉'犯行贿罪获刑6年) ["Xu Xiaowan" Convicted for 6 Years for Accepting Bribery]," *Legal Systems Times* 法制时报, April 27, 2016.

104 Ergege Yule 二哥哥娱乐, "Tashi Shean Liuyiduo De Zhengtingji Jutan, Beipan Sihuan, Erzi Pan Shijiunian, Qingfu Huoxing Wunian 他是涉案6亿多的正厅级巨贪, 被判死缓, 儿子判19年, 情妇获刑5年 [He Is a Department-Level Corrupt Official Involved In a 600 Million CNY Case, Received Suspended Death Sentence; Son Received 19-Year Sentence, and Mistress 5-Year Sentence]," *Ergege Yule* 二哥哥娱乐 *on Wangyi Hao* 网易号 *[NetEast Accounts]* (blog), June 22, 2021, www.163.com/dy/article/GD2L33I805373JOH.html.

105 Field Notes, August 6, 2009.

106 I would frequently start such conversations by explaining that an out-of-town friend of mine was coming to visit soon and had asked me to inquire about where he should go to "look for girls." Field Notes March 27, 2009, March 31, 2009, and April 1, 2009.

where it is the clients who are targeted rather than the women whom they solicit. When this happens, the state's primary concern is to orchestrate a powerful man's downfall. In these cases, accusations of prostitution are usually folded into a broader investigation into his other corrupt and illegal activities that allows the state to undermine his moral standing in society.

Clients: Fewer Arrests, More Fines

Sex workers I surveyed reported that the police were more likely to punish them than their clients. Of arrested sex workers, 23 percent reported receiving no punishment. In contrast, 57 percent of them noted that their clients received no punishment. Sex workers' descriptions of arrest experiences echo this imbalance, with multiple accounts of being arrested when no client was present.[107] When clients are punished, they are more likely to be fined, while sex workers are more often incarcerated.[108] Across the country, C&E institutions were reported to include only a handful of male clients as compared to hundreds of female sex workers.[109] Sex workers I surveyed confirmed this imbalance: 50 percent of those arrested were incarcerated, in contrast to only 15 percent of their clients. Police officers I surveyed acknowledged this difference. Asked to rate the frequency of various punishments on a scale of 1 to 10, on average they rated the frequency of fines as 7.8 for sex workers and 8.5 for clients. This pattern of client fines and sex worker incarceration is one that other law enforcement officers have also recognized.[110] It allows the police to balance the dual pressures they face of both generating income through fines and

107 See, e.g., arrest stories recounted earlier in this chapter from Sex Worker Interview 3, August 17, 2009; Sex Worker Interview 2, August 24, 2009; Sex Worker Interview 6, August 25, 2009.

108 Interview 64, April 16, 2009. The Dui Hua Foundation, "Custody and Education Worse than Reeducation through Labor?," *Dui Hua Human Rights Journal* (blog), December 26, 2013, perma.cc/5BUT-NH4L; Hu Xiujie (胡秀洁), "Wanshan Woguo Seqing Wenti Lifa Han Zhifa De Sikao (完善我国色情问题立法和执法的思考) [Reflections on How to Improve the Legalization and Law Enforcement of the Sex Industry]," *Journal of Zhangzhou Normal University (漳州师范学院学报)* 2 (2011): 25–30.

109 Scott Burris and Guomei Xia, "The 'Risk Environment' for Commercial Sex Work in China: Considering the Role of Law and Law Enforcement Practices," in *Gender Policy and HIV in China*, vol. 22, The Springer Series on Demographic Methods and Population Analysis (Springer, 2009), 184; Dui Hua Foundation, "Reference Materials"; Hu Xiujie (胡秀洁), "Wanshan Woguo Seqing Wenti Lifa Han Zhifa De Sikao (完善我国色情问题立法和执法的思考) [Reflections on How to Improve the Legalization and Law Enforcement of the Sex Industry]." Interview 92, June 16, 2009. Interview 64, April 16, 2009.

110 Burris and Xia, "The 'Risk Environment' for Commercial Sex Work in China: Considering the Role of Law and Law Enforcement Practices," 184.

displaying an adherence to a policy that officially privileges incarceration over fines.[111]

Incarcerated Men

While men are less likely to be incarcerated for prostitution-related crimes than women, they are not completely immune to such experiences. I met one client, Tang Ming, who agreed to share his incarceration experience with me.[112] The most striking aspect of the conversation was his sense of entitlement. Rather than recognizing that he had violated the law and must suffer the consequences, he instead blamed the state for not properly communicating the range of sanctions a client might face. This attitude stood in sharp contrast to sex workers' more nuanced responses to comparable situations: They might object to being arrested and criticize state prostitution policies, but they rarely refused to acknowledge the ways in which they were personally responsible for the harm that had befallen them. Granted, I knowingly interacted with sex workers much more frequently than clients over the course of my fieldwork.[113] In addition, clients who feel shame or guilt might not be willing to share their experiences with others, especially a foreign woman. Even if Tang Ming did recognize his personal responsibility, he might hesitate to express it to me. That said, his reaction was very much at odds with the reality that he had, in fact, violated the law. His ignorance about being vulnerable to incarceration also speaks to how the police in China are much more likely to fine clients than imprison them.

When he was arrested, Tang Ming was an unmarried university graduate in his late twenties. He declined to provide details about his employment. He had been released just a few weeks prior to our interview. As we met over coffee in Beijing, I felt less like I was conducting an interview and more like I was attending a lecture about the indignity of being incarcerated for six months for having purchased sex. While he was aware of the possibility that he could be fined and spend a few days in detention for soliciting sex, he had not

111 As discussed in Chapter 3, official guidelines promote incarceration instead of fines for prostitution cases because fines are easier for the wealthy to pay, which goes against the CCP's ideological concerns about inequality. In addition, fines are not considered a sufficient deterrent against prostitution.

112 Interview 42, October 23, 2008.

113 I say "knowingly" because, given how common it is to purchase sex in China, some of the male informants whom I interviewed or observed not as clients, but based on their professional identity, had also likely solicited sex workers but did not share that information with me.

known that he could be incarcerated for up to two years. His indignation stemmed from the belief that the state should publicize more information about the existence of C&E centers for clients, which he claimed no one knows about and are not covered in the media. These feelings of injustice had led him to thoroughly investigate all relevant laws regulating prostitution in China, and their names, verbatim quotes, and article numbers rolled off his tongue as he argued his case.

Tang Ming was caught having sex in a small brothel run out of an apartment in Beijing in 2008.[114] Along with several other sex workers and clients, he was first taken to a short-term detention facility and then transferred to the Beijing C&E center. This building was divided into two sections, where sex workers were all incarcerated in the section to the left of the main entrance, and clients were all incarcerated in the section to the right.[115] Every morning, male inmates woke up at 6 or 6:30, showered, and had breakfast. They then studied for a few hours, an activity which included reading books and being shown moral and legal instructional videos. Lunch followed, along with a nap, more studying, and another shower. Twice a day, the guards would take attendance. Tang Ming did not mention engaging in any manual labor tasks. This omission is interesting, because women in C&E custody often described being forced to engage in manual labor.[116]

While Tang Ming provided the only testimony of client incarceration that I collected, others have also chronicled similar experiences. One account comes from a foreign woman living in China, who anonymously blogged about her Chinese husband's experience of arrest for prostitution in a massage parlor in Beijing in 2009.[117] When her husband failed to return home after work one day, she enlisted his colleague to help find him. After filing a police report and contacting various hospitals in Beijing, she was summoned to the police station where her husband was being detained, and told that he had been arrested for participating in prostitution and would be released within

[114] This occurred in the run-up to the 2008 Summer Olympics in Beijing, when the state was cracking down on prostitution more aggressively in anticipation of the global spotlight shining on China.

[115] Another informant who had been inside the Beijing C&E facility described the same physical separation as this client, with women on the left and men on the right. Interview 68, April 17, 2009.

[116] Interview 68, April 17, 2009.

[117] In chronicling the experience, her stated goal was to publicly document the corruption and bribery in which she found herself enmeshed through her attempts to have him released. Anonymous, "Wednesday-Day 27," *Beijing Haze* (blog), August 28, 2009.

twelve to twenty-four hours. Instead, he was sentenced to fourteen days of detention and transferred to a facility in the outskirts of Beijing. A formal letter documenting his sentence was sent to the address of his household registration, where his parents lived in the city of Wuhan. During his second week of incarceration, he was sentenced to six months of C&E in a Beijing facility. Neither his wife nor other family members were granted permission to visit him. They dropped off clothing and money for him, and also mailed him letters, all of which he acknowledged receiving. He was permitted to make three calls – the first of which he used to contact his work colleague rather than his wife, out of fear that she would be too upset to take steps to help him. During his incarceration, he was assigned to fix computers at the center. Throughout this process, the client's wife and family paid bribes to try to facilitate his early release. The outcome of their efforts is not documented in the blog, which ends with the client still incarcerated.

In contrast to the population of sex workers in C&E centers, incarcerated clients come from a variety of different socioeconomic backgrounds. As discussed in Chapter 1, wealthier clients solicit across all three tiers of prostitution. Even though it is common knowledge among clients that risk of arrest is higher in low-tier spaces, men who can afford to purchase sex in the low, middle, and top tiers might gravitate toward streetwalkers and brothel workers when they seek a quick exchange of sex for money. Sometimes, they pay a steep price for doing so. The incarcerated men whose cases are discussed in this section – a university graduate and a man married to a foreigner – are among China's elite. An informant who volunteered at the Beijing C&E center confirmed the socioeconomic diversity of its client population: "You have all sorts of people there. Plain peasants, workers, university professors, and business owners. The institution actually had a calligraphy competition, and you could admire the calligraphy hanging on bulletin boards in there. ... There were some really talented people there, skilled at music, calligraphy, writing articles, etc."[118] In this person's experience, men end up in C&E centers "just because of bad luck." Indeed, the likelihood that a client would be both arrested and then denied the opportunity to pay a fine rather than be incarcerated is so slim that, as Tang Ming's reaction demonstrates, it is simply not on most men's radar screens.

[118] Interview 68, April 17, 2009.

Targeting Elite Clients

For law enforcement officials focusing on prostitution, clients are generally an afterthought. Yet clients can become the object of the state's attention when they are members of the elite whose actions have crossed the CCP. When the Chinese state goes after prominent men who purchase sex, it usually has decided to orchestrate their downfall for political reasons. In these cases, prostitution is removed from the realm of "low policing" (street-level police officers and everyday crime control) and brought into the world of "high policing" (CCP political priorities, perceived threats to the state, and official corruption investigations).[119] The purchase of sex is typically just one of many legal transgressions that surface over the course of an investigation. These are rarely cases where evidence of prostitution is necessary for the state to prove wrongdoing or increase the severity of sanctions it applies to an individual. The targeted person has usually engaged in a number of other activities that constitute egregious violations of the law. Instead, public allegations of prostitution allow the state to destroy their target's moral standing in society. Indeed, despite its prevalence, prostitution continues to hold deep symbolism in China as a phenomenon that is fundamentally incompatible with the communist ideology upon which the People's Republic of China rests. When the CCP chooses to highlight an elite man's participation in prostitution, it is engaging in the PRC's time-honored populist practice of orchestrating a prominent man's complete public downfall as both a lawbreaker and a morally depraved individual.[120]

Most reported corruption investigations against officials include a prostitution-related charge. Political scientist Yan Sun notes that most officials at or above the deputy provincial governor level who have been accused of graft were also found to shelter one or several mistresses.[121] The group that formulated revisions to the *Marriage Law* in 2001 collected statistics showing that 95 percent of officials disciplined for corruption had mistresses.[122] Other studies have found that

[119] Jean-Paul Brodeur, "High Policing and Low Policing: Remarks about the Policing of Political Activities," *Social Problems* 30, no. 5 (1983): 507–20, https://doi.org/10.2307/800268; Scoggins, *Policing China*.

[120] Sida Liu and Terence C. Halliday, *Criminal Defense in China: The Politics of Lawyers at Work* (Cambridge: Cambridge University Press, 2016), 134.

[121] Sun, *Corruption and Market in Contemporary China*, 33.

[122] Sun, 177. Other official sources corroborate such findings. For instance, the Discipline Inspection Commission and the All-China Women's Federation have conducted studies that find a similarly high prevalence of second wives among officials investigated for corruption. In 2000, the Deputy Procurator-General noted that almost all of the ministerial-level

almost all high-ranking officials who accept bribes or embezzle public funds have mistresses, receive sexual favors in exchange for various benefits, or engage in more traditional forms of prostitution.[123]

High-Profile Cases of Elite Clients

Accusations of prostitution feature prominently in some of the most egregious corruption investigations against Chinese elites. Liu Zhijun was China's Minister of Railways in 2011 when a high-speed train collision on the route from Beijing to Fuzhou resulted in 40 deaths and about 200 injuries.[124] Although Chinese media were instructed to downplay the incident, both the crash and the botched rescue and investigation efforts that followed generated a great deal of public outrage.[125] Ultimately, it became clear that corruption permeated the high-speed rail construction project, resulting in problems that contributed to the crash. Liu Zhijun became the target of an anti-corruption investigation and was expelled from the CCP for "severe violations of discipline," "primary leadership responsibilities for the serious corruption problem within the railway system," and "sexual misconduct."[126] On the count of sexual misconduct, Liu was reported to have eighteen mistresses.[127]

Bo Xilai, a former member of the Central Politburo and a Party secretary in Chongqing, was sentenced to life imprisonment in 2013 for a wide variety of corruption-related offenses. The Party began publicly investigating him in the aftermath of the scandal that started with the death of Neil Heywood, a British citizen with ties to Bo's wife, Gu Kailai. The crime eventually led Chongqing Police Chief Wang Lijun to seek refuge in the US Consulate in Chengdu and to share evidence that Gu and Bo were involved in Heywood's poisoning. The list of corruption accusations included in the official announcement of Bo Xilai's ouster included the offense of "engaging in improper sexual relations with

cases they were investigating involved an element of sexual abuse of power. In 2007, the Procuratorate noted that 90 percent of senior officials charged with corruption in previous years had mistresses. Sun, 177; Elaine Jeffreys, "Debating the Legal Regulation of Sex-Related Bribery and Corruption in the People's Republic of China," in *Sex and Sexuality in China*, ed. Elaine Jeffreys (London: Routledge, 2006), 161–62; Levin, "China's New Wealth Spurs a Market for Mistresses."

123 Brendan Hong, "China's Concubine Culture Lives On in Mistress Villages," *The Daily Beast* (blog), April 14, 2014, perma.cc/E7SP-3FN7; Elaine Jeffreys, "Debating the Legal Regulation of Sex-Related Bribery and Corruption in the People's Republic of China," in *Sex and Sexuality in China*, ed. Elaine Jeffreys (London: Routledge, 2006), 160.

124 Evan Osnos, "Boss Rail," *The New Yorker*, October 15, 2012.

125 Osnos.

126 Osnos.

127 Levin, "China's New Wealth Spurs a Market for Mistresses."

several women," and in court he testified to being unfaithful to his wife.[128]

In 2013, Lei Zhengfu, an official from Chongqing, was sentenced to thirteen years in prison for bribery. The case broke when a sex tape with Lei and his mistress, Zhao Hongxia, was posted online. The tape, filmed in 2007, was part of an elaborate extortion racket that led to the downfall of several other Chongqing officials. The head of a construction company had hired Zhao and several other women to seduce Lei and other officials who were allocating land for construction and to videotape their sexual interactions. When business relations between Lei and the company soured in 2009, the construction company boss threatened Lei with the tape. Lei sought protection from Bo Xilai, the then Chongqing Party chief, who dispatched Wang Lijun (the Chongqing police chief mentioned in the previous paragraph) to investigate the matter. At the time, the mistress was detained for thirty days, and the company head was incarcerated for a year. The scandal reemerged in 2013 with the release of the tape, which precipitated an investigation into Lei's other corrupt behaviors and also led to the subsequent downfall of twenty-one other Chongqing officials.[129]

Lower-ranked officials are also targets for such investigations. In 2011, the former vice mayor of the city of Hangzhou was executed for bribery and embezzlement of $30 million. He was also reported to have had dozens of mistresses.[130] In 2013, Huang Sheng, a former deputy provincial governor of Shandong, was tried for accepting 12.23 million yuan in bribes (about $2 million), and allegedly had forty-six second wives.[131] In 2012, Qi Fang, former head of the police in the town of Wusu in northern Xinjiang province, was fired for keeping two sisters as

[128] Josh Chin, "Chinese Officials Ousted over Alleged Sexual Exploits," *The Wall Street Journal*, January 25, 2013, https://perma.cc/AR5R-PMBD; Pinhui Zhuang, "I Was Unfaithful to Wife Gu Kailai, Bo Xilai Admits in Court," *South China Morning Post*, August 25, 2013, https://perma.cc/2M5L-GRUC.

[129] Keith Zhai, "Chongqing 21 Sentenced over Sex Scandal," *South China Morning Post*, May 8, 2013, https://perma.cc/C7FZ-PLEP; Chris Luo, "Chongqing Authority to Examine Official's Alleged Sex Romp," *South China Morning Post*, November 21, 2012, https://perma.cc/PC5P-C7WV; Keith Zhai, "Chongqing Cadre Lei Zhengfu, Taped Having Sex, Is Jailed 13 Years for Bribery," *South China Morning Post*, June 29, 2013, perma.cc/E8FD-67E4; Huifeng He, "Chongqing Official Wu Hong Latest to Become Embroiled in Sex Scandal," *South China Morning Post*, December 5, 2012, https://perma.cc/QJH7-5TJK; Sophie Beach, "Chongqing Sex Scandal May Implicate Wang Lijun," *China Digital Times*, November 25, 2012, perma.cc/Z85P-4QLQ; Keith Bradsher, "China's Anticorruption Commission Investigates Senior Official," *The New York Times*, December 5, 2012, perma.cc/DJ3Z-WNDC.

[130] Levin, "China's New Wealth Spurs a Market for Mistresses."

[131] Liz Carter, "China's Latest Corruption Target Allegedly Embezzled Millions and Kept 46 Mistresses; Where's the Shock?," *Tea Leaf Nation*, April 9, 2013, perma.cc/5BTN-Z4M7.

mistresses, women whom he had also hired to work in his agency. Neither sister appeared to have any previous experience or training in law enforcement.[132] Xu Jie, former deputy head of the State Bureau for Letters and Visits, was expelled from the CCP in 2014 for graft and adultery.[133] Tao Yi, a former senior tax officer in Guangxi province, was fired in 2013 after an unofficial contract that he had with his mistress was leaked online. The contract stipulated that the parties would meet at least weekly and would not engage in any other extramarital affairs. If either party violated that agreement or caused any "mental distress," they would pay the other 10,000 yuan ($1,600). Tao's mistress would not interfere with his family or work life, and he would be responsible for her living expenses. Termination of the relationship would require formal written notice.[134] By the time these and other cases end up on the dockets of the Discipline Inspection Commission or the courts, their primary focus is not necessarily on the sex lives of specific individuals. Instead, it may be on issues such as the amount of money embezzled or accepted as bribes. Yet, reports on these individuals frequently list the number of mistresses they harbored and provide details about their participation in other types of prostitution. By prominently featuring an attack on the official's moral core – both their purchase of sex and their use of state funds to do so – the CCP orchestrates a comprehensive public takedown from which their target is unlikely to recover.

Government officials are not the only elites whom the state accuses of prostitution to bring about their fall from grace. For instance, when criminal defense lawyer Li Zhuang was being tried in Chongqing for the crime of lawyer's perjury in a 2009–11 case that garnered a lot of attention in China, the procuratorate, police, and media jointly conspired to put forth a baseless allegation that Li Zhuang had engaged in prostitution.[135] In 2020, Tsinghua University law professor Xu Zhangrun, an outspoken critic of Xi Jinping, was detained for allegedly soliciting sex. While in detention, Tsinghua University fired him due to both the prostitution accusations and his anti-Xi writings.[136] World-

132 "Pictured: The Twin 'Mistresses' at the Centre of Xinjiang Police Official Scandal," *South China Morning Post*, December 10, 2012, https://perma.cc/P6ZQ-8G8H.

133 "Communist Party Expels Xu Jie, Former Petitions Bureau Deputy, over 'Bribery and Adultery,'" *Reuters*, June 27, 2014, https://perma.cc/3S64-468A.

134 Tom Phillips, "Chinese Official Shamed over Adultery 'Contract' That Fines Bad Behaviour," *The Telegraph*, November 18, 2013, https://perma.cc/E9L9-WGPG.

135 Liu and Halliday, *Criminal Defense in China*, 122–43.

136 Yew Lun Tian, "Chinese Professor Who Criticized Xi Seeks to Overturn Prostitution Charge, Lawyer Says," *Reuters*, July 29, 2020, sec. China, perma.cc/SJ5H-SM4D.

renowned pianist Li Yundi, who is a major celebrity in China, was detained in 2021 for soliciting sex, and subsequently expelled from the China Musicians Association – a move that severely limits his ability to pursue professional opportunities domestically.[137] By engaging in prostitution, he had failed to abide by a recent crackdown on China's cultural sector which called upon celebrities to behave morally in both their public and private lives.[138] Contrary to Li Zhuang and Xu Zhangrun, the charges against Li Yundi do not appear to be trumped up. This last case serves to underscore the heightened imperative under Xi Jinping for all high-status individuals – not only those whose professional pursuits challenge the state's legitimacy – to project moral rectitude. Indeed, there is no evidence that, prior to this incident, Li Yundi was considered a political opponent of the CCP.

Once the CCP publicizes a high-status man's purchase of sex, it causes irreversible harm to his career, regardless of the veracity of the claim. While the cases discussed here are among the most prominent, many other members of the elite have experienced similar fates. Indeed, the combined legal, moral, and public takedown of elite men whose actions have made them *personae non gratae* in the eyes of the state is one of the oldest tricks in the PRC's book to permanently tarnish a high-profile individual's image and warn others of the perils of following a similar path, and this practice shows no signs of letting up under Xi Jinping.

CONCLUSION

There are a few things people need to keep in mind if they are worried about being punished for prostitution in China. For starters, their likelihood of getting into trouble is much higher if they are a female sex worker instead of a male client.[139] A sex worker is most at risk if she solicits on the streets and in brothels, less at risk if she is a hostess, and pretty much off the state's radar if she is a second wife. Clients are

137 Emma Graham-Harrison and Vincent Ni, "China's 'Piano Prince' Li Yundi Detained for Allegedly Hiring Sex Worker," *The Guardian*, October 22, 2021, sec. World news, perma.cc/67QT-L9LX.

138 Vincent Ni and Helen Davidson, "China's Cultural Crackdown: Few Areas Untouched as Xi Reshapes Society," *The Guardian*, September 10, 2021, sec. World news, perma.cc/56G5-XVFK; Helen Davidson and Vincent Ni, "Chinese Celebrities Warned over Morality in Cultural Crackdown," *The Guardian*, September 8, 2021, sec. World news, perma.cc/K5MA-R764.

139 As noted previously, I do not examine male sex work or female clients in this book.

similarly better off staying away from women in the low tier, and are least likely to encounter the authorities if they maintain a mistress. Regarding punishment, incarceration is a real possibility for low-tier sex workers. For everyone else, fines are the more likely sanction. That said, it would be a mistake for a man to purchase sex with the assumption that he can pay his way out of any trouble with the police. A safer way for clients to avoid incarceration would be to stay away from sex workers in the low tier.

The takeaway here is as old as time: Although rules about engaging in prostitution in China appear to be gender-neutral and blind to social status, in reality it is poor women who lose the most – the ones the state punishes more frequently and harshly than anyone else who sells or purchases sex. There does appear to be one exception to this observation. When China's most prominent men get under the CCP's skin, their dissolute sex lives quickly become part of the official narrative of their downfall, while the women whom they were paying for sex receive less attention. These cases involving elite men are primarily about politics and use prostitution accusations as a tool to discredit elites whose bigger mistake was to challenge the CCP's legitimacy through egregious corruption, public criticism of the regime, or other blatant flouting of major party directives. Thus, although these cases show the fall from grace of elite men who purchase sex, they do little to counter the broader observation that when the state's primary object of attention is the offense of prostitution, it is poorer female sex workers who pay the steepest price.

Frontline police officers in China have their own problems. They are underfunded, overworked, and largely left to their own devices when it comes to the control of everyday crime.[140] This reality shapes all aspects of their approach to order maintenance in their communities, and elucidates why, when it comes to prostitution, they target low-tier sex workers. These women are the easiest to arrest, and these arrests provide an immediate visual signal to police officers' superiors that frontline police officials are doing their job and to community members that law enforcement is responsive to societal demands for neighborhoods that appear vice-free. While these professional woes might elicit some sympathy for the figure of the street-level law enforcement agent in China, they do not excuse the egregious treatment of sex workers in

[140] I discuss this observation further in Chapter 9. See Scoggins, *Policing China*. In a nutshell, "[i]n China, the world of everyday policing limps along as overworked, underpaid, and poorly trained officers struggle to get through another week." Scoggins, 113.

which some police officers engage. The list of abuses is long. It includes having sexual intercourse with sex workers and then arresting them; depriving sex workers of access to food, water, and basic sanitation while in detention; extreme verbal abuse; forced confessions; extortion of bribes; public humiliation; beatings; and torture. Sex workers describe such abuse as a pervasive element of their interactions with law enforcement agents, who are unsurprisingly more evasive when they are asked about it. Regardless of its frequency, this behavior is unacceptable and deeply troubling.

Lastly, no account of how the Chinese state punishes its citizens who engage in prostitution is complete without an examination of C&E centers. These spaces, their rehabilitative ideals, actual practices, and ultimate demise in 2019 embody the CCP's struggles to adapt to deep societal changes over time while staying true to the ideology in which it is rooted. These institutions emerged from the theory that prostitution was an exploitative phenomenon whose existence was anathema to communist ideals, and that the state could intervene to redirect its participants toward activities worthy of upstanding individuals. Yet with prostitution flourishing in China, and C&E centers taking in only a very small percentage of its poorest female sex workers and failing to improve their post-incarceration lives, those ideals have taken a serious beating. So serious, in fact, that C&E has been abolished, and the formal rules that govern sex work in China no longer bear any trace of the ideals around which they were initially created.

9

THE WEAK YET SAVVY STREET-LEVEL POLICE OFFICER

INTRODUCTION

By focusing their enforcement efforts on low-tier sex workers, the police help create a space for the middle tier of China's sex industry – entertainment venues and their hostesses – to thrive. In this context, frontline officers are usually characterized as "turning a blind eye" to prostitution.[1] Yet such a description is incomplete: It implies police passivity and lack of engagement with prostitution when they are not busy arresting people for selling or purchasing sex. By observing dynamics on the ground, I find instead that law enforcement officers engage actively and in myriad ways with the sex industry when they are not focused on arresting sex workers. Some of their actions, such as bribery and extortion of sexual services, are purely extractive interactions where the police abuse their power. Yet other police behavior, while still self-serving, also benefits sex workers – such as warning them about upcoming crackdowns and providing them with tools for protection from dangerous clients. Frontline police officers expend considerable effort carrying out these activities. Making sense of police actions in this context requires shifting our framework from exclusively viewing police as powerful figures in relation to sex workers to also viewing them as street-level bureaucrats who are accountable to the local government

[1] Eileen M. Otis, "The Dignity of Working Women: Service, Sex, and the Labor Politics of Localization in China's City of Eternal Spring," *American Behavioral Scientist* 52, no. 3 (November 1, 2008): 357–58, https://doi.org/10.1177/0002764208325309; Susanne Y. P. Choi, "State Control, Female Prostitution and HIV Prevention in China," *The China Quarterly* 205 (March 2011): 96–114.

where they work and the vast police bureaucracy of which they are at the forefront. This approach provides a different perspective on street-level police officers, underscoring their weakness within China's bureaucratic system rather than their strength in relation to the sex workers they arrest and abuse. Their vulnerability vis-à-vis the state even affects how they engage with sex workers (some of the country's most marginalized citizens) and underscores conditions under which the job security of frontline police officers in fact depends on a cooperative local sex industry.

COEXISTENCE OF THE STATE AND THE SEX INDUSTRY

It is hard to miss the fact that police officers all across China provide a space for prostitution to occur in their communities. Indeed, police and other government offices are often in jarringly close proximity to spaces where prostitution occurs. In Wanqin, one of the Shenzhen red-light districts where I carried out fieldwork, a main street cuts through the center of the neighborhood, with small alleyways branching off from it. Walking down this main street, one passes by a karaoke bar where several hostesses stand outside every day and recruit customers from noon until the early hours of the morning. A few steps further down, the next building houses most of Wanqin's local government offices (社区工作站 – *shequ gongzuo zhan*), including letters and petitions (信访 – *xinfang*), family planning, and the police. One door down is the hotel where my research assistants and I stayed, and which mainly hosts sex workers and clients from neighboring karaoke venues. We would periodically bump into them in the elevator and corridors. One night, the hotel manager pounded loudly on the door of the room opposite my research assistants' room, waking them up. "Do you want a whore?" (你要不要鸡 – *ni yaobuyao ji?*), she asked the guest, who proceeded to decline the offer.[2] The rest of the main street alternates between karaoke bars, restaurants, and small shops. Every time local government officials in Wanqin look out their office windows, they can see hostesses, clients, and entertainment venues. More tucked away from view, a few streetwalkers often linger in the alleyways that branch off the main street. The alleyways also host a handful of pseudo–hair salons with low-tier sex workers, as well as apartment-brothels such as

[2] Field Notes, October 31, 2009.

Mei Jie's, where I spent long hours observing sex workers interact with each other, their clients, and Mei Jie, their madam.

This physical coexistence between the sex industry and the state is similarly jarring in Xizhou, my field site on the outskirts of Shenzhen. That red-light district is centered around a main square, with surrounding alleyways that are home to dozens of spaces that harbor prostitution. While a major road borders one side of the square, the neighborhood itself is pedestrian. Karaoke venues and small restaurants line two sides of the square. A large building occupies most of the fourth side of the square, which houses a karaoke venue on the first floor. The local government offices take up the second floor of this very same building. Strikingly, the sex industry and the local government in Xizhou actually share the same space. From their perch, local officials not only witness sex workers and clients coming and going at various times of day throughout the neighborhood but also feel the thumping of the music in the entertainment venue below them, reverberating on the floor when it starts to play in the late afternoon.

I saw versions of this coexistence of the state and the sex industry in cities throughout China. In Beijing, I lived across the street from an entertainment venue. The neighboring building to its immediate right housed the city's urban management bureau (城管 – *chengguan*).[3] In Guangzhou, I went to several dozen police stations and systematically sought out the entertainment venue closest to each one; they were usually within sight of each other. Shanghai, Shenyang, and Harbin presented similar patterns. In Zhengti, my police contact showed me around the grounds of a state-owned hotel that included a stand-alone building with a big sign that said "spa" in English. I have spent a lot of time inside businesses that provide sexual services in China. For the most part, they attempt to deemphasize the occurrence of prostitution in their spaces and use discretion in signaling it. Karaoke venues point to their audiovisual equipment as evidence of the legitimate services available on their premises, and pseudo–hair salons are sparsely furnished, sterile-looking spaces. This "spa" in Zhengti was different. The rooms were decorated entirely in dark reds and pinks and outfitted with private saunas and Jacuzzis. A round bed was positioned in the middle of each room, covered in plush pillows. The ceiling above each bed was

[3] The *chengguan* are not part of the police bureaucracy. They were created in order to manage low-level crime in cities. Suzanne E. Scoggins, *Policing China: Street-Level Cops in the Shadow of Protest*, Studies of the Weatherhead East Asian Institute, Columbia University (Ithaca, NY: Cornell University Press, 2021), 23–24. Prostitution is not part of their official responsibilities.

covered in mirrors, with a sex swing hanging down from it.[4] This space was unapologetically a haven for prostitution.

At least some of this physical proximity is against the law. The national regulations governing entertainment venues include zoning restrictions that explicitly forbid these businesses from being located at or around (周围 – *zhouwei*) any state or government units.[5] The exact interpretation of "around" varies by province but usually encompasses those situations already described of entertainment venues on the premises of or adjacent to government buildings, and also tends to require a minimum distance of 30–200 meters between these two types of places.[6] With these laws in mind, this chapter's descriptions of the physical proximity of spaces of prostitution and spaces of the state provide a powerful image of the reality of the nonenforcement of prostitution laws in China.[7] Namely, this is not about a handful of discreet lawbreakers who manage to escape the vigilant gaze of frontline police officers. Rather, spaces that harbor prostitution are located just a stone's throw away from the offices of state agents who are formally

4 Field Notes, August 9, 2009.

5 *Yule Changsuo Guanli Banfa* (娱乐场所管理办法) [Measures for the Administration of Entertainment Venues] Art. 6.6 (promulgated by the St. Coun., January 25, 2013, effective March 11, 2013).

6 *Yule Changsuo Guanli Banfa* (娱乐场所管理办法) [Measures for the Administration of Entertainment Venues] Art. 6 (promulgated by the St. Coun., January 25, 2013, effective March 11, 2013). *Beijing Shi Wenhuaju Xingzheng Xuke Shixiang He Xingzheng Xuke Chengxu* (北京市文化局行政许可事项和行政许可程序) [Beijing Municipal Bureau of Culture Administrative Licensing Items and Procedures] (promulgated by the Beijing Municipal Bureau of Culture, October 28, 2009, effective October 28, 2009), para. 2(5). *Yule Changsuo Xingzheng Shenpi Gongzuo Zhidao Yijian* (娱乐场所行政审批工作指导意见) [Guiding Opinions on the Administrative Approval of Entertainment Venues] (promulgated by the Jiangsu Provincial Department of Culture, July 1, 2013, effective August 8, 2013), para. 1(1).

7 My use of the term "nonenforcement" overlaps with a variety of concepts in the political science literature. For instance, *forbearance* is nonenforcement of the law that is both intentional and revocable, and is distinct from *weak enforcement*, where a state lacks the institutional capacity to enforce. Alisha C. Holland, "Forbearance," *American Political Science Review* 110, no. 2 (May 2016): 232–46, https://doi.org/10.1017/S0003055416000083. *Selective policy implementation* refers to the choices that local officials make with respect to which policies they do or do not enforce, decisions that are generally driven by central government incentive structures. Kevin J. O'Brien and Lianjiang Li, "Selective Policy Implementation in Rural China," *Comparative Politics* 31, no. 2 (January 1, 1999): 167–86. The nonenforcement that I observe in the middle tier of the sex industry involves elements of all three of these concepts: it is revocable; at the same time, the police lack the institutional capacity to definitively crack down on all prostitution in China; relatedly, they are constantly making decisions about which policies to enforce against whom. I use the term "nonenforcement" because I am mainly interested in simply noting the absence of enforcement and then bringing to light the other activities that occur in that space and what they allow us to say about frontline police officers. While I discuss the political economic drivers of this nonenforcement, I am not primarily interested in discussing the extent to which it is forbearance versus weak institutional capacity. Lastly, "nonenforcement" is not equivalent here to "de facto legalization." As described in Chapter 8 and also later on in this chapter, the threat of enforcement is ever-present in the low and middle tiers of the sex industry.

empowered to intervene but are visibly not always doing so. Given this reality, it is not surprising that 52 percent of police officers I surveyed stated that current prostitution policies were ineffective and that 34 percent support legalizing prostitution – they are reminded every day of the prevalence of sex work in their surroundings.[8] As one police officer told me, "there's just no way" (没办法 – *mei banfa*) to control prostitution.[9]

FRONTLINE POLICE OFFICERS AND THE LOCAL POLITICAL ECONOMY OF PROSTITUTION

The inherent tension between prostitution's illegality and its benefits to the local economy comes to a head in the middle tier of the sex industry. And the coexistence between the police and the sex industry described in the previous section, which does allow for some low-tier prostitution to slip through the cracks but mainly concerns the middle tier of the sex industry, makes clear that the local state's economic interests have the upper hand. These economic gains do not come directly from the exchange of money for sex that occurs between clients and hostesses. Instead, they come from the vast entertainment industry built around prostitution, which is integral to work culture in China.[10] They include clients' spending on food, drinks, and room rentals in entertainment venues; the contributions to the local economy of migrant workers who work in these businesses; and investment in the local economy, including foreign investment, which is attracted to places with a thriving entertainment sector. Estimates of the dollar amounts attached to all of these activities are hard to come by. One study found that China's sex trade was worth 1 trillion yuan (about $157 billion) annually.[11] In the city of Dongguan, the thriving sex industry is estimated to generate about 10 percent of the local GDP.[12] Although these figures are hard to verify, it is clear that the entertainment industry plays a key role in the local GDP throughout urban China. Without the possibility of sex at its heart, the entire industry would crumble, with important economic ramifications.

[8] Please see the Appendix for more discussion of the police survey.
[9] Field Notes, August 10, 2009.
[10] See Chapter 2 for more discussion of the relationship between China's work culture, entertainment venues, and prostitution.
[11] "Crackdown on Sex City," *The Economist*, February 14, 2014, https://perma.cc/L7ZP-P5HG.
[12] "Crackdown on Sex City."

Local governments cannot afford to lose this source of revenue. The legitimacy of the Chinese Communist Party rests on economic growth,[13] and the state has institutionalized the importance of this goal through its cadre evaluation system.[14] Local government officials are promoted, punished, and fired based on their ability to meet the performance measures put forth in this system, and local economic development, assessed through a number of different variables, is one of the two key factors taken into account when local cadres are evaluated by their superiors.[15] The second major factor is "stability maintenance" (维稳 – *weiwen*).[16] While the sex industry can pose challenges to law and order, the Communist Party does not consider it a major threat to political stability when compared to protests and other forms of dissent. In fact, as noted in Chapter 2, prostitution arguably contributes to the goal of stability maintenance when considering how it helps address the sexual desires of China's "surplus of men" and provides employment opportunities in entertainment industry venues for hostesses and other service personnel.

This local political economic reality establishes the boundaries within which frontline police officers must operate with respect to anti-prostitution enforcement in their communities. While they must respect those limits, they must also carry out responsibilities expected of them as the lowest-ranking members of China's law enforcement hierarchy. Indeed, street-level law enforcement agents are simultaneously accountable to two sources of authority: the local government

[13] Dingxin Zhao, "The Mandate of Heaven and Performance Legitimation in Historical and Contemporary China," *American Behavioral Scientist* 53, no. 3 (November 1, 2009): 425, https://doi.org/10.1177/0002764209338800; André Laliberté and Marc Lanteigne, "The Issue of Challenges to the Legitimacy of CCP Rule," in *The Chinese Party-State in the 21st Century: Adaptation and the Reinvention of Legitimacy*, ed. André Laliberté and Marc Lanteigne, 1st ed. (London: Routledge, 2011), 4; Bruce Gilley, "Legitimacy and Institutional Change: The Case of China," *Comparative Political Studies* 41, no. 3 (March 1, 2008): 274, https://doi.org/10.1177/0010414007308020; Teresa Wright, *Accepting Authoritarianism: State-Society Relations in China's Reform Era* (Stanford, CA: Stanford University Press, 2010), 38.

[14] Much has been written about the cadre evaluation system. See, e.g., Pierre F. Landry, *Decentralized Authoritarianism in China: The Communist Party's Control of Local Elites in the Post-Mao Era* (Cambridge: Cambridge University Press, 2008), www.library.yorku.ca/eresolver/?id=1247241; Maria Edin, "State Capacity and Local Agent Control in China: CCP Cadre Management from a Township Perspective," *The China Quarterly* 173 (March 2003): 35–52, https://doi.org/10.1017/S0009443903000044; Victor Shih, Christopher Adolph, and Mingxing Liu, "Getting Ahead in the Communist Party: Explaining the Advancement of Central Committee Members in China," *American Political Science Review* 106, no. 01 (February 2012): 166–87, https://doi.org/10.1017/S0003055411000566.

[15] Scoggins, *Policing China*, 5.

[16] Scoggins, 5; Xie Yue, "The Political Logic of Weiwen in Contemporary China," *Issues & Studies* 48, no. 3 (September 2012): 1–41.

where they work, and the Ministry of Public Security (MPS) in whose bureaucracy they are embedded. These power dynamics are well-known to people who think about the state in China.[17] As pertains specifically to how they play out in policing, Suzanne Scoggins quotes police informants talking about having "two bosses," and noting that '[t]he center wants to manage local police, but this is very difficult . . . The truth is that we police must also follow the local government."[18] This happens because local governments control police funding and also wield power over police station leadership appointments.[19] Scoggins explains that these two sources of pressure on police officers either align or conflict with each other depending on the type of crime.[20] Given the importance of middle-tier prostitution to their economies, local governments have a strong interest in preventing the police from enforcing laws against prostitution in ways that harm economic growth. While China's policing agency does not share that goal, prostitution generally does not constitute a threat to its main priority: protest control. In fact, when asked to rank threats that prostitution poses to society, police officers I surveyed were most likely to identify it as a moral threat (危害社会道德 – *weihai shehui daode*) (44 percent), followed by a public health threat (危害公共健康 – *weihai gonggong jiankang*) (36 percent), and only lastly as a social order problem (危害社会秩序 – *weihai shehui zhixu*) (20 percent). Local police officers generally do not experience pressure from the MPS to act counter to local governments' economy-driven preferences around the issue of prostitution. Indeed, for the police the issue of prostitution usually falls into the realm of everyday crime where they experience only limited oversight from within the policing hierarchy, provided it does not get out of hand.[21]

[17] The literature on fragmented authoritarianism in the Chinese bureaucracy, and much that has come in its aftermath, is built around the reality of shared power between the local and central government. See, e.g., Kenneth Lieberthal and Michel Oksenberg, *Policy Making in China: Leaders, Structures, and Processes* (Princeton, NJ: Princeton University Press, 1988); Kenneth G. Lieberthal and David M. Lampton, eds., *Bureaucracy, Politics, and Decision Making in Post-Mao China* (Berkeley: University of California Press, 1992); Andrew C. Mertha, *China's Water Warriors: Citizen Action and Policy Change*, 1st ed. (Ithaca, NY: Cornell University Press, 2008); Andrew Mertha, "'Fragmented Authoritarianism 2.0': Political Pluralization in the Chinese Policy Process," *The China Quarterly* 200 (December 2009): 995–1012, https://doi.org/10.1017/S0305741009990592.

[18] Scoggins, *Policing China*, 91.

[19] Scoggins, 100.

[20] Scoggins, 91–112.

[21] For more on limited oversight for everyday crime control, though not specifically around prostitution, see Scoggins, 91–112.

Unfortunately for frontline police officers, the boundary beyond which the characteristics of prostitution in a given community become unacceptable to higher-ranked police officials is fluid.[22] For instance, a crackdown against prostitution announced at the national, provincial, or municipal level is likely to turn what was previously a tolerable amount of prostitution in the neighborhood into a problem. And while it is generally accepted that frontline officers receive bribes from the local sex industry, that behavior could become objectionable in the context of an anti-corruption campaign, or when it looks less like petty bribery between individual police officers and sex industry actors, and more like heavy-handed police participation in the management of the local sex industry.

What frontline officers do know is that at any time they can be subject to an intervention from the higher ranks of their agency. That intervention process, called supervision (监督 – *jiandu*), is institutionalized at all levels of the MPS to assess police behavior and compliance with laws and regulations. It is usually instigated by provincial-level authorities, though central government officials also do so.[23] In describing supervision, Scoggins notes that "When possible, the ministry will bypass station leaders because officials (perhaps rightly) do not fully trust reports originating at the local level. Sometimes, this entails conducting unannounced inspections."[24] Entertainment venues that harbor prostitution are subject to such raids.[25] In fact, a police chief in Zhengti described a raid in the neighborhood under his jurisdiction just a few weeks prior to our conversation.[26] The national MPS had orchestrated the event, in collaboration with the provincial police bureau. At the beginning of the raid, provincial police officials arrived at the district police station and confiscated each police officer's cell phone. This move aimed to prevent any individual officers from warning their sex industry contacts of an impending crackdown. Simultaneously, two plainclothes police officers had been dispatched to the targeted

22 Stern and O'Brien discuss how mixed signals from the Chinese state muddy the waters for individuals in society seeking to gauge the acceptability of various types of pushback against the state. Rachel E. Stern and Kevin J. O'Brien, "Politics at the Boundary: Mixed Signals and the Chinese State," *Modern China* 38, no. 2 (March 1, 2012): 174–98, https://doi.org/10.1177/0097700411421463. Moving boundaries can similarly confuse frontline police officers' understanding of what their higher-ups within the state expect of them.

23 Scoggins, *Policing China*, 73.

24 Scoggins, 73.

25 Entertainment venues are also targeted in the supervision of the local police in the context of drug raids. Scoggins, 101.

26 Field Notes, August 7, 2009.

entertainment venue in Zhengti, masquerading as clients. After these officers confirmed that prostitution was occurring in the space, uniformed officers rushed in to make arrests. In the interim, a number of sex workers and clients were able to escape – the police chief believed that someone had been able to issue a warning despite the cell phone confiscations. In the end, only two prostitution arrests were made.[27]

Gatekeepers and sex workers in Beijing also spoke of being on the receiving end of such inspections.[28] One venue boss in Beijing explained that her local police contacts would warn her as soon as they got wind of police officers coming in from outside the jurisdiction to inspect entertainment venues.[29] She also described an experience where a client came to her venue in a car with a license plate from the northern province of Jilin and asked for sex workers. This made her suspicious, and she claimed that the women in her venue did not provide sexual services. She later learned that he was an undercover police officer from that province who was participating in a supervision exercise.[30]

Frontline officers are members of one of China's most powerful state agencies,[31] and their abusive behavior toward the sex workers they arrest, described in Chapter 8, shows them wielding that power with impunity. At the same time, however, the police are actually quite weak in relation to the state bureaucracies to which they are accountable and that create the framework for how they enforce prostitution regulations. This observation confirms, with specific attention to the issue of sex work, one of Scoggins' major findings about frontline police officers in China: When it comes to everyday crime control (and in contrast to protest response), the police bureaucracy is weak.[32] This explains why most anti-prostitution enforcement efforts of street-level police officers target low-tier sex workers, as described in Chapter 8. This approach contributes to controlling prostitution so that it stays

27 Law enforcement officers in a different district of Zhengti recounted experiencing a similar incident in the recent past as well. Field Notes, August 9, 2009.

28 Sex Worker Survey Respondent 127 and 407, question 81. Boss Interview, August 26, 2009. Gatekeepers are individuals such as madams, pimps, and entertainment venue managers.

29 Boss Interview, August 26, 2009.

30 In her research on prostitution in Dalian, Zheng also uncovers instances of cross-jurisdictional raids on prostitution. Tiantian Zheng, *Red Lights: The Lives of Sex Workers in Postsocialist China* (Minneapolis: University of Minnesota Press, 2009), 71.

31 Scoggins, *Policing China*, 13; Suzanne E. Scoggins, "Policing Modern China," *China Law and Society Review* 3, no. 2 (October 30, 2018): 80, 90, https://doi.org/10.1163/25427466-00302001.

32 Scoggins, *Policing China*.

within acceptable boundaries instead of descending into mayhem that would attract the unwanted attention of policing authorities higher up in the MPS hierarchy. It also provides space for the entertainment industry built around middle-tier sex work to thrive, in deference to the local government's focus on economic development.

POLICE ACTIVITY IN THE SHADOW OF NONENFORCEMENT

What happens in China's spaces of nonenforcement of prostitution laws? It will come as no surprise to learn that frontline officers take advantage of them for personal gain. For instance, they collect bribes from entertainment venue managers in their jurisdiction.[33] While none of my police officer contacts discussed such bribes, the sex workers, madams, and venue managers I interviewed described these payoffs as an institutionalized norm in the sex industry.[34] Police officers also go to entertainment venues as clients.[35] In Zhengti, the police officers I was shadowing took me to a karaoke venue one evening after dinner. We got settled in our private room, and a few minutes later, about fifteen hostesses streamed in and lined up in front of us. Their madam accompanied them and greeted our group like old friends. One of the police officers chose a hostess for himself and a second one for his colleague. For the rest of the evening, while I was not busy singing or dancing with other members of our party, I observed these two women entertain their clients. While I do not know whether that specific evening involved prostitution, it is common for police officers to solicit sex. Indeed, although I was not able to ask police officers directly about their own behavior, a full 27 percent of police I surveyed stated that they found it appropriate to purchase sex (in contrast, only 18 percent stated that it was appropriate to sell it). In addition, more than half of

[33] Interview 28, October 16, 2008; Interview 59, April 3, 2009; Interview 6, September 10, 2008; Sex Worker Interview 1, August 16, 2009; Sex Worker Interview 1, August 23, 2009; Madam Interview 1, August 21, 2009; Boss Interview 1, August 26, 2009.

[34] This observation is in line with Scoggins' discussion of the prevalence of taking bribes and accepting gifts among police officers more generally. Scoggins, *Policing China*, 39.

[35] Police officers who are off duty and not in police uniform are allowed to engage in the legal activities available at entertainment venues (for instance, drinking, dancing, and singing). Yet they are not allowed to participate in activities at entertainment venues in connection with their work. *Gongan Jiguan Renmin Jingcha Guanli Tiaoling* (公安机关人民警察纪律条令) [Ordinance on Disciplines for the People's Police of the Public Security Organs] (promulgated by the Ministry of Supervision, the Ministry of Human Res. & Soc. Sec. and the Ministry of Pub. Sec., April 21, 2010, effective June 1, 2010).

the hostesses I surveyed (53 percent) reported having had a police officer as a client in the previous six months, as did 38 percent of low-tier sex workers.[36] When police do solicit sex, they frequently refuse to pay. Qing Lai recounted one such instance where a police officer who did not pay after having sex with her said: "You just try reporting me to the police . . . I am the police."[37] Law enforcement officers make some efforts to avoid detection when they solicit sex: For example, they avoid doing so in the neighborhoods where they work.[38] Such separation between their personal and professional lives allows them to maintain some anonymity and reduce the likelihood of being easily identified and possibly sanctioned by higher-ups.

Yet frontline police officers cannot afford to use this space of non-enforcement solely for extractive purposes. Indeed, if prostitution does get out of hand in their community, their own livelihood is on the line. While they cannot predict or prevent all circumstances that might upset the status quo of limited interference with the local sex industry, the key to avoiding trouble is communication. More specifically, street-level law enforcement agents invest heavily in sharing information with the local sex industry by developing one-on-one relationships, holding meetings, and creating and advocating for the use of tools that both allow them to communicate important information to the local sex industry and also encourage sex workers and gatekeepers to seek them out if they encounter unruly or dangerous clients. These mutually beneficial exchanges of information help keep all parties out of trouble.

One-on-One Relationships and Meetings with the Local Sex Industry

Street-level police officers invest significant time and effort to stay in frequent contact with entertainment venue managers, pimps, madams, and sex workers. The police share news about upcoming crackdowns, increased scrutiny of the neighborhood, or crime spikes that could put sex workers in harm's way, urging members of the sex industry to lay low until these moments pass.

In some cases, this communication occurs through personal relationships between the police and actors in the sex industry. A venue manager might have one specific law enforcement contact who will alert him or her about upcoming prostitution crackdowns. As Bing Bing, a sex worker in

[36] Please see the Appendix for more details about the sex worker survey.

[37] Sex Worker Interview 2, August 26, 2009.

[38] Boss Interview, August 26, 2009; Sex Worker Interview 3, August 24, 2009; Madam Interview, August 21, 2009.

Beijing, explained, "The manager has an informant [in law enforcement], who will warn him before [inspections] (老板局里有人, 会提前告诉 – *laoban juli youren, hui tiqian gaosu*)."[39] One manager explained how her contact warns them during these events to only allow known clients into her space to avoid infiltration from undercover police officers.[40] Personal lines of communication can also be established directly between sex workers and the police. As Xiao Yang noted, "The police are pretty good, they protect us, tell us when not to go out [with clients], and tell us which places aren't safe, where people have been murdered."[41] Fei Wen described how the police will stop by the venues and warn them about robbers and escaped criminals who are thought to be in the neighborhood.[42] Wen Ling explained that auxiliary police officers sometimes come in and tell them to lay low at certain times,[43] and sex worker survey respondents acknowledged getting police warnings both directly or through pimps.[44]

In addition to these one-on-one relationships, local law enforcement officials also hold meetings for venue managers where they convey public order and safety information. Upon returning to their venues, the managers then organize meetings with the women working there to pass on that same information. Ting Ting described the process as follows:

> The boss and the manager often have meetings (去开会 – *qu kaihui*) [with law enforcement]. After their meeting, they have a meeting with us. The meetings happen twice a month. Sometimes the meeting is at the local police station. Yesterday, they went to the city police station. The manager told us that [there would be a crackdown] because of the sixtieth anniversary [of the People's Republic of China].[45] The police were going to inspect for pornography, gambling, and drugs.[46] They gave us a safety warning, and said that it is forbidden to do those things in the venue. We'll get fired if the manager discovers us doing any of that, and if it's serious, they may even send us to the police station. The managers do that to protect themselves. If the police find these things occurring, they'll not only fine the manager, but also shut down the venue.[47]

39 Sex Worker Interview 2, August 15, 2009.
40 Boss Interview, August 26, 2009.
41 Sex Worker Interview 2, August 18, 2009.
42 Sex Worker Interview 3, August 24, 2009.
43 Sex Worker Interview 7, August 20, 2009.
44 Sex Worker Survey Respondents 118 and 407, question 81.
45 The 60th anniversary of the founding of the PRC occurred on October 1, 2009. As often occurs in the lead-up to major national holidays and events, social order and stability concerns were heightened in the months preceding the celebrations.
46 These three vices (黄赌毒 – *huang du du*) are often discussed together in relation to entertainment venues. Pornography is understood to encompass prostitution.
47 Sex Worker Interview 2, August 23, 2009.

Jing Ming described a similar system: "The boss and madam get called in for meetings and told about crackdowns. Then they'll come back, and tell us . . . to all be careful, be attentive, and avoid conflicts with clients."[48] A number of other sex workers and madams spoke of these meetings.[49] In some cases, sex workers are called in to participate in them directly. Fei Wen recognized the delicate nature of these events:

> Even the devil (恶魔 – *emo*) still has to attend meetings.[50] . . . The most recent meeting I attended was last year. They had us go to the local government offices, and asked us to cooperate with their efforts to maintain public order. Another time we had a meeting at the police station close by, everyone in the venues had to go. They warned us about thieves and swindlers, and told us to be very careful.[51]

Gatekeepers also spoke to me about these meetings. One manager explained that "since there's a crackdown (严打 – *yanda*) going on now, they constantly call us and send us text messages, and have us come in for meetings."[52] She had attended three or four meetings in the previous month at the district police station. She explained that the police hold these events because it is in their interest to avoid troubles that would reflect poorly upon their capacity to maintain order in the neighborhood. One madam described monthly meetings with all the entertainment venue bosses and managers, who then organize a separate meeting for venue madams.[53] At one such gathering, they received warnings to be on the lookout for raids initiated from outside the jurisdiction, as one had just occurred in the district next door.

Tools to Connect with the Police

In addition to creating systems to transmit information to gatekeepers and sex workers, police officers also make sure these individuals can contact them directly. For instance, they publicize the local police station's phone number in entertainment venues and urge people to avoid using the national emergency hotline (110). When someone makes an emergency call to 110, it is officially recorded and automatically becomes part of the statistics that are used to assess crime levels in

48 Sex Worker Interview 6, August 23, 2009.
49 Sex Worker Interview 2, August 18, 2009; Madam Interview, August 15, 2009.
50 Fei Wen is using the term "devil" here to refer to sex workers, madams and pimps, since they are engaged in immoral/illegal activities.
51 Sex Worker Interview 3, August 24, 2009.
52 Boss Interview, August 26, 2009.
53 Madam Interview, August 21, 2009.

Figure 9.1 Entertainment venue placard forbidding pornography, drugs, gambling, and prostitution[54]

a neighborhood. Local law enforcement has no control over those data because the call goes through several levels of the MPS before it is routed to the local police station.[55] When an individual calls the local police number, however, the police can avoid creating a formal record. This creates an incentive for them to reduce the number of calls made to 110. Entertainment venue regulations require these businesses to post placards throughout the space – including in the private rooms – that state that pornography, drugs, gambling, and prostitution are forbidden (see Figure 9.1).[56] The phone number these placards provide for reporting the occurrence of any of these activities is the 110 national hotline number.

Yet what I observed in entertainment venues was that a sticker had frequently been placed on these placards that covered up the "110" number and instead listed the number for the local police station. The manager of one of those venues in Beijing told me that the local police had made the change: "The police all stick their own local (片区 – *pianqu*) phone number [on the placard]. They don't want us to call 110."[57] The manager said that at a recent meeting at the district police station, the police specifically told them that they do not like it when people at

[54] The sign reads: "It is strictly forbidden to engage in illegal criminal activities such as drug use, drug trafficking, gambling, prostitution, etc. To report, call: 110."

[55] *110 Jiechu Jing Gongzuo Guize* (110接处警工作规则) [Handling Policing Affairs by 110 Hotline] Arts. 10, 13, 26 (promulgated by the Min. of Public Security, April 30, 2003, effective April 30, 2003). Scoggins, *Policing China*, 157.

[56] *Yule Changsuo Guanli Tiaoli* (娱乐场所管理条例) [Measures for the Administration of Entertainment Venues] Art. 30 (promulgated by the State Council, January 18, 2006, effective March 6, 2006).

[57] Boss Interview, August 26, 2009.

the venues call 110. "That is not beneficial to anyone," the police told the manager, before elaborating on how doing so creates an official record of the problem, reflects poorly on the police for being incapable of maintaining control over the area under their jurisdiction, and could harm the police professionally.[58] To be clear, these signs request that viewers report any knowledge of drug abuse, gambling, or prostitution. They do not instruct gatekeepers, clients, or sex workers to call if they are in imminent danger. Yet in practice, they serve as a general notice to call the local number in case of any problems in the venue. And while I was particularly attuned to this practice in entertainment venues, it appears to be part of a broader effort to systematically steer members of the local community (not just in entertainment venues) away from the national police emergency hotline and toward the neighborhood police phone number so that local police officers can reduce the number of cases officially recorded in their jurisdictions.[59]

Local police officers also install alarms in entertainment venues so that sex workers or gatekeepers who face an imminent threat do not even need to make a call to the police. Instead, they can simply push the alarm button. In Zhengti, law enforcement officers in several districts had set up this system specifically in response to an increase in violence against sex workers in several areas in the city. In one district, every entertainment venue has these alarms, which provide a silent signal that goes directly to the district police station and lets them know to dispatch agents to the venue immediately. In another district, the police installed alarms that, when activated, emit loud noises and flashing lights, to both scare away the perpetrator and serve as a call for help from anyone in the vicinity. The police in Zhengti had purchased and installed a total of 800 of these two different warning systems in three of the city's districts, at a cost of 300 yuan ($50) per alarm.[60] This represented an informal crime control strategy rather than an officially approved program. As one police officer described, it is "done but not spoken about" (做不说 – *zuo bu shuo*), because of the sensitivity of a system designed to protect sex workers

58 Boss Interview, August 26, 2009.

59 Scoggins, *Policing China*, 76. In Guanghzou, for instance, the police were accused of creating a system to actually fine migrant workers if they called the 110 emergency hotline during the 2010 Asian Games rather than the local number. Jianhua Xu, "Police Accountability and the Commodification of Policing in China: A Study of Police/Business Posters in Guangzhou," *The British Journal of Criminology* 53, no. 6 (2013): 1106–7.

60 Field Notes, August 5, 6, 7, and 9, 2009.

rather than punish them.[61] If it were publicized, he explained, it would attract a lot of unwanted attention. In his words, "It is as close as we can get to saying that we will help out, without legalizing prostitution."[62] I did not encounter police-installed alarm systems in other cities – which was more likely a reflection of the better access to police I had in Zhengti than an indication of the city's uniqueness.

Setting aside any claims to generalizability, the fact that frontline police officers in Zhengti took the initiative to implement this off-the-books crime control strategy provides evidence of their ability to police in ways that are innovative and even controversial. We rarely observe such experimentation among frontline police officers in China. Indeed, Scoggins notes that the MPS adopts a decentralized approach to managing many frontline officers' activities, which in theory opens up spaces for local-level experimentation.[63] Yet Scoggins also finds that local police are too weak, overworked, and underfunded to benefit from the discretion that decentralized control provides.[64] Without disputing this reality for most street-level police agents in China, it is still worth searching for, and highlighting, those instances when the police do find creative ways to solve pressing problems in the community. Doing so underscores the precarity of their position within the Chinese state: Despite limited resources and support, they expend great effort to manage problems that could get them into trouble, going so far as to implement policies that appear to keep lawbreakers safe rather than punishing them for engaging in illegal activities.

CONCLUSION

Frontline police officers' behavior toward the middle tier of the sex industry highlights their weaknesses, and shows us how they are at the mercy of both the local government that surrounds them and the police hierarchy that towers over them. This vulnerability affects how they engage with hostesses and entertainment venue personnel in their communities. In particular, it requires them to establish relationships and systems that allow them to communicate information easily to the

61 Field Notes, August 9, 2009.
62 Field Notes, August 9, 2009.
63 Scoggins, *Policing China*, 12–13, 96, 109–10, 124–25.
64 She notes, for instance, that "[i]n interview after interview, police say they have neither the time nor the desire to make use of discretionary power, and they are not interested in thinking up new techniques or methods for dealing with cases." Scoggins, 96.

sex industry and to make themselves immediately accessible to sex workers in search of assistance.

These arrangements are striking because their success requires collaboration between law enforcement and members of the sex industry. For instance, when local police officers share information about crackdowns with neighborhood entertainment venues, sex workers need to absorb that information and lie low so that the police can avoid problems with their superiors. When law enforcement officers provide local phone numbers and install alarms in entertainment venues, sex workers need to use those tools for the police to reap their benefits. Granted, it is in the interest of sex workers to follow such guidance and call the police for help – what keeps the police out of trouble with their superiors also keeps sex workers out of the state's punitive grip and safe from dangerous clients. Nevertheless, it is remarkable that the good standing of some frontline police officers within the state bureaucracy depends on cooperation from members of the sex industry, and that in this context the police cannot rely exclusively on brute force and coercion to elicit their desired outcomes.

Police officers' vulnerability is not inconsistent with their often brutal treatment of sex workers documented in Chapter 8, but it does contrast sharply with that portrayal of them. Given the power imbalance inherent in these relationships, it is extremely jarring to envision these collaborative moments that police officers, madams, and sex workers described to me, where members of China's law enforcement agency summon madams and sex workers to local police stations for meetings on upcoming prostitution crackdowns and crime in the neighborhood, and even go to local entertainment venues to install protective alarm systems. Through these activities, the police are acknowledging the illegal activities in which members of the sex industry engage. Yet instead of punishing them for breaking the law, law enforcement officers provide them with information and assistance to keep them safe.

Lastly, it bears noting how much effort and creativity goes into these arrangements between the police and the sex industry. Frontline police officers across China are stretched thin and under-resourced, which makes their daily work lives a constant struggle. While this reality gives them ample reason to simply scrape by, it has not prevented them from sometimes delivering beyond the bare minimum, and establishing ingenious methods of engaging with their communities in ways that benefit everyone involved.

10

CHINA'S SEX WORKER HEALTH POLICIES: THE INFLUENCE OF TRANSNATIONAL ACTORS AND THEIR LIMITATIONS

INTRODUCTION

While the policing of prostitution in China is a story of domestic law and politics, the public health approach to regulating sex work in China starts in the international global health community. It then makes its way into central government health institutions in Beijing, and trickles down into the lives of local state health workers and the sex workers in their community. These transnational roots matter. They have shaped both the content of sex work health policies and the public health officials who manage their administration. Indeed, the approach that China's health policies and officials endorse for gauging the prevalence of HIV/AIDS and reducing its occurrence among sex workers, and the language these authorities use, reflect best practices in the global public health community. Yet the obstacles that Chinese health agents encounter result in practices that fall short of these ideals and harm sex workers. That often grim reality is the subject of Chapter 11. What I highlight in this chapter is how the global public health community working in China to support the creation of HIV/AIDS policies seems disengaged from what actually happens on the ground.

TRANSNATIONAL IMPRINT ON CHINA'S APPROACH TO THE PUBLIC HEALTH REGULATION OF SEX WORK

In the face of considerable resistance, the global public health community has molded China's sex work–related health policies to reflect international best practices. That influence shows up not only in the substance of the health rules that affect sex workers but also in the ways that China's elite public health agents talk, write, and think about prostitution.

Transnational Influence on the Substance of State Health Policies

International best practices to reduce the prevalence of HIV/AIDS among sex workers emphasize three steps. First, sex workers need to be tested for HIV/AIDS. Second, they need to share accurate information about their sexual behavior. At the most basic level, this requires that they acknowledge selling sex, and report both how many clients they have and how frequently they use condoms. Third, sex workers need to make behavioral changes, such as taking regular HIV/AIDS tests and using condoms consistently.

The global health community has developed a twofold model to carry out these steps that involves collecting quantitative data on sex workers while respecting sex workers' rights.[1] The data-gathering component includes counting sex workers in the community and collecting information about their health and sexual behavior. The "health and rights" approach emphasizes the importance of carrying out these activities in ways that are not coercive, in order to provide an accurate overall picture of HIV/AIDS in China and increase the likelihood that individual sex workers will make behavioral changes that could help reduce the incidence of HIV/AIDS.[2] For instance, if health officials force a sex worker to get an HIV/AIDS test, she is likely to have negative associations with testing and shy away from voluntarily testing in the future. To gain a better understanding of the disease, public health officials are better off creating an environment where a sex worker willingly tests on a regular basis. Similarly, it is possible to compel a sex worker to attend training on safe sexual behaviors, but she is much more likely to assimilate the information and implement behavioral changes if her participation is not coerced. And when state officials want to collect data on sex worker condom use and number of clients, they are much more likely to receive truthful answers from sex workers who are voluntarily taking part in such surveys. The transnational community has

[1] UNAIDS, "Intensifying HIV Prevention: A UNAIDS Policy Position Paper," 2005, perma.cc/3ZNK-LE76; UNAIDS, *UNAIDS Guidance Note on HIV and Sex Work* (UNAIDS, 2012), perma.cc/2FFH-HB5B; UNAIDS, "HIV and Sex Work," Human Rights Fact Sheet Series, 2021, perma.cc/CW7K-22U4.

[2] Chapter 11 provides examples of how health officials coerce sex workers to participate in data collection and outreach activities.

identified civil society engagement as crucial to achieving quantitative public health targets in ways that respect sex worker rights.[3] The grassroots community can play a key role in HIV/AIDS outreach and prevention because sex workers often shy away from the state and are more likely to trust peer educators (current or former sex workers) and nongovernmental organizations (NGOs).

China's sex work health policies embody this dual quantitative and rights-based approach to regulating HIV/AIDS. As described in Chapter 3, the state has established an HIV/AIDS monitoring system that identifies certain villages, counties, cities, and municipal districts throughout China as surveillance sites, a subset of which are designated as sex worker surveillance sites. At these locations, local health officials are required to identify all spaces where prostitution occurs, categorize them by tier of sex work, and randomly sample venues and sex workers at these venues for HIV/AIDS testing. They also survey these women to collect data on their behaviors that put them at risk of HIV/AIDS. These same policies that lay out a quantitative approach to understanding HIV/AIDS also carefully spell out the importance of implementing these measures in ways that respect the targeted individuals' rights. For instance, China's *Regulation on the Prevention and Treatment of HIV/AIDS* emphasizes the state's responsibility to adhere to the HIV voluntary counseling and testing system, as do surveillance system implementation guidelines.[4] The policies also highlight that peer educators and grassroots organizations have a role to play in this process.[5]

In working with the Chinese state to develop comprehensive HIV/AIDS policies, the global public health community faced considerable resistance to including a focus on sex workers and other stigmatized

[3] World Health Organization et al., *Implementing Comprehensive HIV/STI Programmes with Sex Workers: Practical Approaches from Collaborative Interventions* (Geneva: World Health Organization, 2013), perma.cc/N54C-5YB4. As noted in Chapter 7, civil society is "composed of a diverse array of organizations with voluntary membership and some degree of operational autonomy from the state, defined as the ability to set a self-determined agenda." Diana Fu, *Mobilizing without the Masses: Control and Contention in China* (New York: Cambridge University Press, 2017), 26.

[4] *Aizibing Fangzhi Tiaoli* (艾滋病防治条例) [Regulation on the Prevention and Treatment of HIV/AIDS] Art. 23 (promulgated by the St. Council, January 29, 2006, effective March 1, 2006, revised March 2, 2019). National Center for AIDS/STD Control and Prevention (性病艾滋病预防控制中心), "Quanguo Aizibing Shaodian Jiance Shishi Fangan Caozuo Shouce (全国艾滋病哨点监测实施方案操作手册) [Guidebook for Monitoring on the Implementation of National AIDS Checkpoints]," 2017, perma.cc/Q79M-M93F.

[5] *Gaowei Xingwei Ganyu Gongzuo Zhidao Fangan (Shixing)* (高危行为干预工作指导方案(试行)) [Guidelines for Intervention Work on High-Risk Behavior (For Trial Implementation)] (promulgated by the Ministry of Health (dissolved), May 20, 2005, effective May 20, 2005).

populations, let alone doing so in nonpunitive ways that respect sex worker rights.[6] The idea of collaborating with and providing services to a population of lawbreakers presented a challenge to state officials who were creating the health policies. Transnational actors addressed these concerns with financial incentives. They conditioned millions of dollars of international HIV/AIDS funding to China on the state, allocating some of these funds to support grassroots organizations that work with marginalized groups such as sex workers and including them in state HIV/AIDS governance processes.[7] International actors also invested heavily in "soft support": international trainings, study tours, conferences, and meetings that introduced Chinese officials to HIV/AIDS health strategies adopted in other countries.[8] For instance, the director of the HIV/AIDS division of the Chinese Center for Disease Control and Prevention (CDC) has said that open discussion about HIV/AIDS outreach to high-risk populations such as sex workers in China dates back to a particular workshop held in 1997 that brought together academics, government officials, as well as representatives from the World Health Organization, the United Nations, and the World Bank.[9] As one Chinese employee of the United Nations Population Fund (UNFPA) explained:

> Female sex worker projects are sensitive. In the beginning … the national government was not very accepting [of them]. But … the World Health Organization started to provide seed funds at the local level and organize international study tours to Australia and Thailand. People here learned about good projects from other countries … Then, they set up pilot sites for that here in China.[10]

[6] Chapter 3 provides background information on transnational involvement in China's HIV/AIDS policies more generally.

[7] This was the case, for instance, for some of the grants that the Global Fund to Fight AIDS, Tuberculosis and Malaria (the Global Fund) provided to China. Sharon Lafraniere, "In Grant Dispute, AIDS Funds Frozen for China," *The New York Times*, May 20, 2011, perma.cc/4EER-6E6S.

[8] Rachel Stern explores the importance of soft support in relation to the efforts of international organizations to foster the development of civil society, in *Environmental Litigation in China: A Study in Political Ambivalence* (New York: Cambridge University Press, 2013), 179–210. As shown here, these types of activities are also central to influencing the state. Jiangping Sun et al., "Contributions of International Cooperation Projects to the HIV/AIDS Response in China," *International Journal of Epidemiology* 39, no. suppl 2 (December 1, 2010): ii14–ii20, https://doi.org/10.1093/ije/dyq208; Zunyou Wu, Sheena G. Sullivan, Yu Wang, Mary Jane Rotheram-Borus, and Roger Detels, "Evolution of China's Response to HIV/AIDS," *The Lancet* 369, no. 9562 (February 2007): 679–90.

[9] Wu et al., "Evolution of China's Response to HIV/AIDS," 680.

[10] Interview 104, August 12, 2009.

These events gradually created a space where Chinese officials recognized the importance of including sex workers in their programs and have been pivotal in aligning the country's HIV/AIDS policies with international best practices.[11]

Transnational Influence on the Language of China's Health Policies and Officials

This transnational influence extends beyond the content of China's sex worker health policies and also shapes how the country's public health officials think, write, and talk about prostitution. Indeed, my conversations with state health officials and analysis of government health documents provided constant reminders of foreign influence on China's domestic health system. My interlocutors systematically used Chinese translations of global health terms for prostitution (rather than domestic Chinese ones) and used those same terms in written documents. Health officials' linguistic choices stand in marked contrast to choices made by law enforcement officers – as discussed later in this chapter.

Mandarin Chinese has a number of terms traditionally used to discuss the phenomenon of prostitution. The most formal one, used in official documents such as national laws against prostitution, is *maiyin piaochang* (卖淫嫖娼). This literally means "selling lewdness" (in reference to the sex worker) and "visiting a prostitute" (in reference to the client), and it sounds extremely derogatory. A *maiyin nü* (卖淫女) is a "woman who sells lewdness" and a *piaoke* (嫖客) is a "guest who visits prostitutes." The Chinese government translation of *maiyin piaochang*, as it appears in its English-language version of the regulations, is equally off-putting: The main anti-prostitution law, for example, is entitled *Decision of the Standing Committee of the National People's Congress on Prohibiting Prostitution and Whoring*. Less pejorative terms for clients of sex workers include *keren* (客人), which means "guest," and *guke* (顾客), which means "customer" or "client." *Anchang* (暗娼) means "secret/underground prostitute," *jinü* (妓女) translates roughly as "prostitute," and *biaozi* (婊子) corresponds to "whore." The term used most frequently in everyday life to refer to sex workers is *xiaojie* (小姐). Literally, it means "miss," or "young lady," but it is widely employed as a euphemism for sex worker. It is the term that most clearly put my subjects at ease when I interviewed them. For example, I would ask "When did you start being

[11] Wu et al., "Evolution of China's Response to HIV/AIDS," 681.

a *xiaojie* (当小姐)?" It is also the term clients often use when looking for sex workers – *zhao xiaojie* (找小姐).

The terms for prostitution that have taken root within Chinese state public health circles, meanwhile, are "sex work" and "sex worker" (性工作 – *xing gongzuo*, and 性工作者 – *xing gongzuozhe*). These are literal translations: *xing* (性) means sex, and *gongzuo/gongzuozhe* (工作/工作者) means work/worker. Like sex workers who use this language after interacting with the transnational sex worker rights movement, China's health officials have followed the lead of the global public health community to use terms that carry less stigma than the word "prostitute." This linguistic choice to remove judgment from the exchange of sex for money reflects the public health community's primary focus on disease prevention and healthcare, which is better achieved when not condemning individuals engaged in sex work.[12]

Chinese public health workers have absorbed the linguistic practices of their foreign counterparts. The terms *xing gongzuo* (sex work) and *xing gongzuozhe* (sex worker) permeated my interviews with public health officials throughout the country. In fact, over the course of interviews I was conducting in Chinese, my interlocutors would sometimes even favor English-language abbreviations for sex workers – "FSW" (female sex worker) and "CSW" (commercial sex worker). For example, I once asked about prostitution in a certain city, and my interviewee responded, "*Shenyang* FSW *hen duo*" ("In Shenyang, there are lots of FSWs").[13] Such lapses into English did not occur for my benefit; I also heard health officials use these abbreviations while talking among themselves.[14] My informants and I were particularly grateful for this shorthand when we met for an interview in a coffee shop or other public place; we both welcomed the opportunity to dissimulate the subject of our conversation by using three-letter English abbreviations unknown to the people around us. Public health workers also use these terms in writing: "*xing gongzuo*" and "FSW" are ubiquitous in public health research reports, Chinese journal articles, and internal CDC data on HIV/AIDS infection rates.[15]

12 This approach to prostitution is called "harm reduction." It takes as a given the existence of prostitution in society (rather than trying to eliminate it), and from there focuses on minimizing the harmful aspects of the phenomenon.

13 Interview 26, October 15, 2008.

14 Nor did they happen only in reference to female sex workers. State health workers also frequently referred to three other groups using English-language abbreviations: MSM (men-who-have-sex-with-men), MB (money boy, a term used to refer to a male sex worker), and IDU (intravenous drug users).

15 Data on file with author.

There are limits to Chinese officials' use of these foreign public health terms, however. In particular, the phrase *xing gongzuo* is noticeably absent from official laws, regulations, and policy documents pertaining to health and prostitution. These types of pronouncements favor terms like *anchang* (secret/underground prostitute), which emphasizes the illicit nature of prostitution, as well as the disparaging phrase *maiyin piaochang* (selling lewdness/visiting a prostitute).[16] Absence of the term "sex work" in these more official documents suggests awareness within state health circles of the political sensitivity of adopting a foreign term that destigmatizes an illegal and morally condemned activity in China, and a sense within this community that there are boundaries beyond which its use may be unacceptable.

In contrast to the linguistic practices that occur in public health circles, in the sphere of law enforcement, where the international community has not played a prominent role, the traditional Mandarin Chinese terminology still prevails in discussions of prostitution. I never once heard a police officer say the terms *xing gongzuo/xing gongzuozhe*, except in response to my own use of the words, which I quickly learned to avoid. I became well-aware that the terms had not made their way into common usage based on the many blank stares I received early in my fieldwork when I used them in casual conversations with nonspecialists. I also feared that my use of such language would alienate a police officer if they happened to be familiar with it, given its associations with a more tolerant perspective on prostitution. The research center I worked with on my police survey confirmed these instincts in our process of developing question wording and piloting with law enforcement agents.[17] The terms that police officers use most frequently to talk about sex work are *maiyin piaochang* for prostitution, *xiaojie* for sex workers, and *keren/guke* for clients.

That said, some law enforcement leaders in China have acknowledged the derogatory tone of the terms police use to discuss prostitution and

[16] For example, this is the case for the *Performance Assessment Screening Criteria for Disease Control and Prevention*, as well as the 2006 *Regulations on AIDS Prevention and Treatment*. See Ministry of Health, People's Republic of China (dissolved), "2012 Jibing Yufang Kongzhi Gongzuo Jixiao Pinggu Biaozhun (疾病预防控制工作绩效评估标准 (2012年版)) [2012 Performance Assessment Screening Criteria for Disease Control and Prevention]," January 7, 2013, perma .cc/R236-KYNP; *Aizibing Fangzhi Tiaoli* (艾滋病防治条例) [Regulation on the Prevention and Treatment of HIV/AIDS] (promulgated by the State Council, January 18, 2006, effective March 6, 2006).

[17] Please see the Appendix for more details about the police survey.

have taken steps to address the issue. In December 2010, the Ministry of Public Security (MPS) issued directives calling for the police to use more polite language in reference to sex workers. Liu Shaowu, then head of the MPS's Security Management Bureau, was quoted in the *Beijing News* as saying, "'Women who sell lewdness (卖淫女—*maiyin nü*),' as we have been calling them, should be termed 'women who have lost their way' (失足妇女—*shizu funü*) from now on. . .We ought to show respect to this special group of people."[18] Unlike "sex work" (*xing gongzuo*), the term "women who have lost their way" is not a translation of an English phrase. While it is less disdainful than its predecessor, the new term continues to contain a strong moral bent. A woman who has lost her way has veered off her intended path, an image that places blame on her and emphasizes how prostitution is an unacceptable activity. Since 2010, the term "women who have lost their way" has made its way into official government documents, though "women who sell lewdness" continues to be far more prevalent.[19] Regardless of the extent to which this linguistic change has taken root, Liu Shaowu's pronouncement shows how the police – an agency that is much less subject to transnational influence than China's public health system – is also thinking carefully about language around prostitution. In this process, the police have made a conscious choice to adopt a term that is recognizably drawn from Mandarin Chinese rather than based on foreign sources. It represents an improvement, perhaps, but continues to perpetuate an attitude about prostitution that is more judgmental than the phrase *xing gongzuo* (sex work).

DISENGAGEMENT ON THE GROUND

The transnational public health community has invested heavily in shaping sex worker health policies in China to reflect international best

[18] Southern Weekly, "Gongan Bu: 'Maiyin Nu' Ke Gai Jiao 'Shizu Funu' (公安部: '卖淫女'可改叫'失足妇女') [The Ministry of Public Security: 'Prostitutes' Should Be Termed 'Women Who Have Lost Their Way']," *Southern Weekly*, December 13, 2010, perma.cc/42LH-4WK3; Kenneth Tan, "The World's Oldest Profession Gets a New Name in China and a Thumbs up from Li Yinhe," Shanghaiist, December 18, 2010, perma.cc/CV38-Z43V; Wang Junrong, "Gaicheng Shizu Funu Shi Dui Teshu Renqun De Zunzhong (改称"失足妇女"是对特殊人群的尊重) [To be Renamed as 'Women Who Have Lost Their Way' Is to Show Respect for the Special Group]," *Eastday*, n.d., perma.cc/Y4KU-CBZ9.

[19] For instance, a search for the term "失足妇女" ("women who have lost their way") in the PKULaw database, which is one of the most comprehensive databases of PRC laws, regulations, and cases, included 311 counts of the term in administrative penalty decisions from 2010 to 2022. In contrast, the term "卖淫女" ("woman who sells lewdness") came up 12,145 times.

practices, and the content of the state's rules and the terminology it uses provide plenty of evidence that this engagement has made its mark. At the same time, however, representatives of the global public health community in China are noticeably disengaged from the on-the-ground realities of the implementation practices their institutions have shaped.

Often isolated in the Beijing offices of embassies and international organizations, transnational public health professionals are easily deceived, and impressed, by the limited exposure they do get to sex worker outreach – exposure that has been carefully curated by the Chinese state. One of my informants was an HIV/AIDS expert at a foreign development agency that has donated millions of dollars to China for HIV/AIDS work. He was also a member of the Global Fund Country Coordinating Mechanism – the organization's governance body in China, responsible for overseeing all Global Fund grants in the country. I was struck by the disconnect between his rosy portrayal of state-run sex worker outreach and my own fieldwork observations, which were much bleaker.[20] For example, he noted how "in general, CDCs work well with entertainment venues," a remark that seemed at odds with the fraught dynamics I observed between these two entities.[21] He then launched into a story about how well-informed Chinese sex workers are about HIV/AIDS. On a site visit for a program his agency was supporting, he described how the sex workers he spoke with (via an interpreter) told him that they knew about HIV/AIDS and even showed him condoms they kept in their pockets. When he asked whether they used them even if clients offered to pay them more for sex without a condom, he indicated that they told him they always wear them because they understand how important it is to protect themselves from AIDS. His takeaway from the visit was that "there is a lot of awareness and self-preservation [within sex worker communities]. The CDC will counsel them, talk to madams, and encourage them to get check-ups."[22]

These comments are not consistent with my findings, however. As evidence that the sex workers he spoke with were accurately reflecting their actual behaviors, this international expert noted that he had been allowed to speak to them without the presence of a government representative. But he did not reflect upon the many reasons why these sex

[20] See Chapter 11 for more discussion of my bleaker observations.
[21] Interview 94, August 4, 2009.
[22] Interview 94, August 4, 2009.

workers might not be speaking truthfully, including his status as both a foreigner and a stranger, pressure from their madams or the local CDC, and the possibility that the interpreter was a state informant. He also failed to acknowledge the possibility that the site he was touring might not be representative of sex worker outreach in the country and might instead have been selected as a best-case example. I heard similarly glowing reports about CDC sex worker outreach from very well-respected foreign leaders of two other major Beijing-based international institutions working on HIV/AIDS in China.[23] These remarks were also based on official visits of model pilot sites. Yet rather than recognize that they might have been exposed to an exceptional program carefully curated for them, my interlocutors instead talked as though these sites were representative of outreach programs available throughout China.

Just as they appear quick to embrace as reality the model sex worker intervention programs that the state presents to them, transnational public health actors in Beijing also accept the data that Chinese state actors provide to them. The global public health community systematically attaches numerical reporting requirements to the HIV/AIDS grants they disburse in China. Consequently, the state regularly provides its foreign partners with data on rates of HIV/AIDS infection, testing, condom use, number of participants attending trainings, and other quantifiable aspects of their programs. Some transnational actors I interviewed expressed confidence in the numbers they have received. For example, the foreign expert discussed in the previous two paragraphs noted, "I don't usually worry about the validity of the data. This is because the Chinese, like the Global Fund, are both target-driven. There are enough checks and balances."[24] In fact, he should be concerned about the validity of the data he receives. His observation underscores how some key foreign decision makers are unaware of on-the-ground practices that result in data on sex worker HIV/AIDS infection rates and outreach that are an inaccurate reflection of reality (described in Chapter 11). Others are more skeptical of the quality of the data. Reflecting beyond the specific issue of sex work and HIV/AIDS, Mason notes how few "Western health officials and scientists . . . were under any illusions they received 'true' numbers . . . [and] felt they had no choice but to accept the fact that post-SARS statistics were still

23 Interview 38, October 22, 2008; Interview 130, August 19, 2009.

24 Interview 94, August 4, 2009. See also Interview 105, August 13, 2009 and Interview 130, August 19, 2009.

significantly lacking in accuracy."[25] The foreigners whose views Mason brings forth are more attuned to the realities of data production in China. Yet they are also resigned. And regardless of whether transnational actors express acceptance or resignation, they are not questioning the decision to place numbers at the heart of the model. Instead, they reinforce the centrality of quantification through continued support and requests for numerical accountability.

Likewise, while the transnational public health community has pushed for China to engage with civil society organizations to design and implement sex worker public health policies, in this area too it appears disengaged from the actual on-the-ground processes that have unfolded in response to the millions of dollars their organizations have spent in support of this goal. In 2010, there were about a dozen grassroots organizations working with female sex workers in China. For the most part, they operated on shoestring budgets and were constantly scrambling to fundraise in unconventional ways, such as running an online clothing store or a car wash business.[26] While these grassroots groups could point to some financial support from international organizations, it was clear they were not the primary recipients of the generous amounts of transnational public health funding earmarked for community groups.

Instead, most of that funding was going to organizations with much closer links to the state. In some cases, local CDCs created groups that they called NGOs in order to be eligible for international grants that included civil society requirements. The district CDC in one city where I carried out fieldwork hired an independent consultant to distribute condoms to sex workers at local entertainment venues and called the arrangement an NGO for the purposes of an international grant they were receiving.[27] The state also accessed more funding when China's CDC changed the Global Fund's proposed definition of civil society in 2006. As a result of this modification, only 15 percent of Global Fund civil society

[25] Katherine A. Mason, *Infectious Change: Reinventing Chinese Public Health after an Epidemic* (Stanford, CA: Stanford University Press, 2016), 100. See also Katherine A. Mason, "The Correct Secret: Discretion and Hypertransparency in Chinese Biosecurity," *Focaal*, no. 75 (January 1, 2016): 53. www.berghahnjournals.com/view/journals/focaal/2016/75/fcl750104.xml.

[26] Chapter 7 provides more information on these grassroots organizations.

[27] Timothy Hildebrandt notes a similar situation with government officials creating gay groups in order to be eligible for international funding, and recounts a widely circulated story of a CDC official in Heilongjiang Province who, in order for his institution to be eligible for HIV/AIDS funds, had his niece start a gay group. See Hildebrandt, *Social Organizations and the Authoritarian State in China* (New York: Cambridge University Press, 2013), 126.

funding for China went to NGOs, while 20 percent went to government-organized NGOs (GONGOs), such as the All-China Women's Federation, and the rest went to research institutions, most of which are affiliated with government organizations.[28] Most egregiously, a Global Fund audit in 2010 found that China had failed to give a pledged 35 percent of a $238 million grant to community-based organizations, including groups working with sex workers and intravenous drug users.[29] Instead, NGOs received only 11 percent of this grant.[30] The transnational community did respond to this particular misallocation of funds: The Global Fund froze its payments to China and only resumed them once the government agreed to allocate more of the grant to NGOs and create a separate entity to supervise the process.[31] Yet it is unclear whether these measures actually benefited grassroots organizations. I found no such evidence in the immediate aftermath of the audit, and by 2014 China was no longer receiving any Global Fund grants as it had transitioned from receiving Global Fund support to being a donor to the organization.[32]

When the Chinese state fails to disburse funds that the transnational community allocated toward fostering a vibrant civil society, or when it redirects that money to government-affiliated institutions, it strengthens the state at the expense of society. Such actions are problematic not only because they distort and violate grant conditions, but more importantly because they fail to advance the public health goal of strengthening sex worker civil society: to improve health outcomes by empowering society, rather than the state, to provide outreach and support to sex workers. China's efforts to repurpose transnational resources intended to strengthen civil society to instead advance state power extend beyond the issue of sex work and characterize HIV/AIDS policy in China more generally. This is an important concern but one that lies beyond the scope of this book.[33] My point here is to underscore how the global public health community that has actively promoted sex

28 Hildebrandt, 128.

29 Lafraniere, "In Grant Dispute, AIDS Funds Frozen for China."

30 China requires that such foreign HIV/AIDS funds be funneled through the state prior to their allocation to grassroots organizations. Hildebrandt, *Social Organizations and the Authoritarian State in China*, 125–28. Such a restriction facilitates divergence from the grantors' intentions since it prevents them from disbursing funds directly to their preferred recipients.

31 Lafraniere, "In Grant Dispute, AIDS Funds Frozen for China"; Gillian Wong, "Global Fund Lifts China Grant Freeze," *Associated Press*, August 23, 2011, perma.cc/4GPM-44BQ.

32 The Global Fund, "Government Donors-China," *The Global Fund* (blog), accessed November 23, 2019, perma.cc/SM9R-PS4D.

33 See, for instance, Yan Long, "The Contradictory Impact of Transnational AIDS Institutions on State Repression in China, 1989–2013," *American Journal of Sociology* 124, no. 2 (September 1, 2018): 309–66, https://doi.org/10.1086/698466.

worker civil society's role in China's response to HIV/AIDS remains remarkably disconnected from how those efforts are taking shape on the ground.

Why the Disconnect?

Why is the transnational community not keeping a closer eye on what is actually happening on the ground in China? This disengagement seems at odds with the amount of effort and funds it has invested in shaping sex worker health policies and supporting their local implementation. There is a rich academic literature on how global policies intersect with local realities, which overwhelmingly identifies a deep disconnect between the intentions of transnational actors who have developed policies and the actual impact of local implementation.[34] And while I leave it to others to focus their research more systematically on the search for answers, I offer some explanations here regarding my specific case study – prostitution in China.

First, even the best-intentioned and most diligent foreign public health expert in Beijing encounters significant state-erected barriers to gaining direct access to local citizens.[35] As an unthreatening graduate student operating under the radar, I was relatively free to observe and ask about conditions on the ground.[36] The Chinese state keeps much closer tabs on employees of foreign embassies, international organizations, and global foundations. These individuals cannot easily show up unannounced to monitor the sex work programs they support, and they are unlikely to receive honest answers to probing questions about implementation that might reveal weaknesses that could threaten current or future funding. Moreover, barriers to proper

[34] See, e.g., Mark Fathi Massoud, *Law's Fragile State: Colonial, Authoritarian, and Humanitarian Legacies in Sudan* (Cambridge: Cambridge University Press, 2013), 4, 12, 181; Sally Engle Merry, *Human Rights and Gender Violence: Translating International Law into Local Justice* (Chicago: University of Chicago Press, 2006), 3; Joel Migdal, *State in Society: Studying How States and Societies Transform and Constitute One Another* (Cambridge: Cambridge University Press, 2001), 141–42; Suli Zhu, "The Party and the Courts," in *Judicial Independence in China: Lessons for Global Rule of Law Promotion*, ed. Randall Peerenboom, 1st ed. (Cambridge: Cambridge University Press, 2009), 65; Randall Peerenboom, "Introduction," in *Judicial Independence in China: Lessons for Global Rule of Law Promotion*, ed. Randall Peerenboom, 1st ed. (Cambridge: Cambridge University Press, 2009), 4; David M. Trubek, "Law and Development: Forty Years after 'Scholars in Self-Estrangement,'" *University of Toronto Law Journal*, May 19, 2016, https://doi.org/10.3138/UTLJ.3671; Elanah Uretsky, *Occupational Hazards: Business, Sex, and HIV in Post-Mao China* (Stanford, CA: Stanford University Press, 2016), 175; Mason, *Infectious Change*, 34–35.

[35] Mason notes how "it was impossible . . . for any foreign organization . . . to gain access to local people directly in China." Mason, *Infectious Change*, 34.

[36] I discuss my research experience in the Appendix.

implementation of the international model are numerous and complicated.[37] The motivated transnational employee would need to invest substantial time and effort in order to grasp the intricacies of local Chinese politics and society that present obstacles to the model.

In addition, the transnational community tends to diminish the significance of local implementation challenges it encounters, favoring a macrolevel narrative emphasizing that some sort of foreign involvement is better than none.[38] This perspective assumes that over time, a transnational presence advocating for accurate data collection and respect for individual rights among sex workers in China will gradually nudge local partners to work toward achieving those goals, even if there are bumps along the way. The problem with this approach is that it does not engage seriously with concerns that the internationally developed public health model could be at the root of unintended harm when implemented locally, as I describe in Chapter 11. It takes for granted that the overall benefits of transnational interventions will outweigh any problems they might contribute to, and that the global community might detect by keeping its eyes and ears close to the ground.

Lastly, the global health community's efforts to stay at arm's length of the realities of local implementation can be seen as an act of self-preservation. If foreign global health experts acquire an in-depth understanding of how their sex worker health models are carried out on the ground and obtain convincing evidence of serious problems, their responsibility to question the model and consider changing it increases. It is difficult and bothersome to challenge the model. In addition, doing so raises a question that is deeply disruptive to the global health community: whether universal best practices are even a reasonable approach to disease prevention and monitoring. If not, the transnational community of health experts needs to rethink the fundamental assumptions upon which it has built a lot of its work.[39] Global public health researchers also stand to lose professionally if they learn too much about what occurs on the ground in China. If they obtain incontrovertible evidence that the data are inaccurate or have been collected in violation of professional ethical standards, they cannot use

[37] I address these barriers in Chapter 11.

[38] An abundance of literature reflects on this issue. For one discussion of this, tied to international humanitarian aid, see David Keen, "Opinion | When 'Do No Harm' Hurts," *The New York Times*, November 6, 2013, sec. Opinion, perma.cc/VWF8-7QW2.

[39] Much of the medical anthropology research in the field of global health raises this issue. See, e.g., Paul Farmer, Arthur Kleinman, Jim Kim, and Matthew Basilico, eds., *Reimagining Global Health: An Introduction* (Berkeley: University of California Press, 2013), 218–81, 429.

the information in their research in good conscience.[40] The easier path is to avoid poking around too much in the first place.

CONCLUSION

This chapter has taken the reader momentarily away from the trenches of regulatory implementation and the voices of frontline state officials and sex workers that are woven through the rest of the book. Instead, it shines a light on how the global public health community has influenced China's sex worker health policies and the state officials who implement them. International actors encountered significant resistance in the process of encouraging the Chinese state to focus on the issue of sex worker health. They also made important inroads. Most notably, China's tier-based approach to sex worker public health outreach is modeled after transnational best practices, as is the outreach and testing model that combines quantitative targets with respect for sex workers' individual rights. This transnational influence also comes through in the language that China's public health officials use, as they talk and write about prostitution in ways that show that they have absorbed the nonjudgmental terms that the global public health community uses to discuss the issue.

Yet while the transnational public health community has been closely engaged with shaping sex worker health policy and the language that health officials use to reflect on prostitution, these same international actors are disengaged from the realities of implementation of the sex worker health and rights model they introduced in China. They accept the version of sex worker health outreach that the Chinese state shows them, along with the data it gives them and its expanded definition of civil society, which includes government organizations. They might acknowledge some issues with the data or move to implement sanctions in response to egregious misallocation of funds.[41] Yet if they have doubts about how the state is carrying out their global model of sex worker health and rights, they have not acted on them in any meaningful way.

40 See, e.g., Mason, *Infectious Change*, 126–28.

41 As noted earlier, the Global Fund froze its payments to China in 2010 in response to the state's misallocation of a Global Fund grant. Lafraniere, "In Grant Dispute, AIDS Funds Frozen for China"; Gillian Wong, "Global Fund Lifts China Grant Freeze," *Associated Press*, August 23, 2011, perma.cc/P7EJ-GRFS.

In short, a variety of different factors push transnational public health experts away from gathering detailed knowledge of how sex work health policies are implemented locally in China. The reasons may vary across individuals – ranging from understandable (resistance from the Chinese state, complicated local context) to questionable (unexamined faith in the model, prioritization of professional advancement over well-being of sex workers).

Yet regardless of what has kept the global health community from closely examining the realities of how their programs are implemented locally, it was always clear that establishing a rights-based and quantitative program among sex workers in China was going to be challenging. Authoritarian regimes provide only limited protections of citizens' rights, and provide even fewer protections for marginalized individuals engaging in illegal actions, such as sex workers. A program that rests on respect for the rights of sex workers is in tension with the very nature of the Chinese state. The global health community might like to think that the quantitative pillar of its model is scientific and thus apolitical, making it universally applicable and immune to the vagaries of different political systems. Indeed, numerical data is often perceived to "offer a particularly reliable form of truth."[42] Yet this view overlooks how the global health indicators that the transnational community has created in the comfort of its facilities in places such as Geneva and New York "do not stand outside regimes of power and governance but exist within them, both in their creation and in their ongoing functioning. They are a blending of science and politics, of technical expertise and political influence."[43] These tensions do not necessarily mean that rights-based programs are doomed to fail in China. But it does make it difficult to absolve the global health community of responsibility for the implementation problems I describe in Chapter 11, as trouble on the ground was predictable. Elucidating the barriers to implementing the policies on the frontlines, explaining the politics behind these obstacles, and documenting the harmful public health consequences of poor implementation is the subject of Chapter 11.

[42] Sally Engle Merry, *The Seductions of Quantification: Measuring Human Rights, Gender Violence, and Sex Trafficking*, 1st ed. (Chicago: University of Chicago Press, 2016), 26.

[43] Merry, 21.

11

STREET-LEVEL HEALTH OFFICIALS

INTRODUCTION

Local health officials are responsible for implementing China's surveillance and behavioral outreach health policies for understanding the prevalence of HIV/AIDS and reducing its occurrence among sex workers. These policies set out clear guidelines for targeting certain types and numbers of sex workers for HIV/AIDS testing and outreach, with the goal of obtaining an accurate understanding of the overall sex worker population and reaching out to the individuals who present the greatest concerns to public health. They are also designed to protect the individual rights of sex workers, a prerequisite for obtaining higher quality data and increasing the likelihood that public health interventions will yield safer sexual behaviors.[1] Yet frontline health workers often deviate from these rules, as obstacles within China's health bureaucracy complicate proper policy implementation. Local health officials must also contend with two powerful entities that are predisposed to oppose their work: the sex industry and the police. Taken together, these challenges lead health agents to focus their testing and outreach efforts on hostesses instead of low-tier sex workers – even though women in the low tier are most in need of health interventions – and result in other irregularities in policy implementation with grave public health consequences.

[1] Chapters 3 and 10 discuss these policies in greater depth.

CHALLENGES WITHIN CHINA'S HEALTH BUREAUCRACY

China's Ministry of Health (known since 2018 as the National Health Commission) is a politically weak agency with limited authority, even at its highest levels.[2] The party secretaries of Guangdong province and Beijing, for example, rank higher in the Communist Party's leadership hierarchy than the national health minister.[3] Within this health bureaucracy, the Chinese Center for Disease Control and Prevention (CDC) is particularly weak. It has limited power to enforce its directives, both within the agency's hierarchy and in the broader community.[4] The CDC operates at national, provincial, municipal, district, and community levels, yet a higher-ranked CDC is not empowered to enforce public health policies within a lower-ranked one. Its downward oversight powers are limited to technical direction, such as offering scientific training and assistance with initiatives.[5] It is the Ministry of Health at the same administrative level as a CDC bureau that has legal and financial power over it.[6] For example,

[2] Tony Saich, "Is SARS China's Chernobyl or Much Ado about Nothing?," in *SARS in China: Prelude to Pandemic?*, ed. Arthur Kleinman and James L. Watson (Stanford, CA: Stanford University Press, 2006), 93. Interview 108, August 14, 2009, noting that "the Ministry of Health does not have the most influence in the government." Interview 38, October 22, 2008. As noted in Chapter 3, in 2013 the Ministry of Health merged with the National Population and Family Planning Commission to become the National Health and Family Planning Commission. In 2018, that institution was replaced with the National Health Commission.

[3] Saich, 93. This has continued to be the case since the Ministry of Health became the National Health Commission. As of 2023, the party secretaries of Guangdong and Beijing were among the twenty-five members of the Politburo of the Chinese Communist Party, and the head of the National Health Commission was a member of the CCP's Central Committee, which ranks below the Politburo.

[4] Interview 64, April 16, 2009; Interview 38, October 22, 2008; Zhou Yu (周羽 & Liao Kaidi 廖开迪), "Zhong Nanshan: Yao Tigao Woguo Jikong Zhongxing De Diwei" (钟南山: 要提高我国疾控中心的地位) [Zhong Nanshan: We Need to Elevate the Position of Our CDCs], *Yangguang News (央广网)*, February 27, 2020, perma.cc/4P94-5XRB.

[5] Katherine A. Mason, *Infectious Change: Reinventing Chinese Public Health after an Epidemic* (Stanford, CA: Stanford University Press, 2016), 216.

[6] Katherine A. Mason, "Becoming Modern after SARS. Battling the H1N1 Pandemic and the Politics of Backwardness in China's Pearl River Delta," *Behemoth* 3, no. 3 (December 2010): 16; Katherine A. Mason, *Infectious Change: Reinventing Chinese Public Health after an Epidemic* (Stanford, CA: Stanford University Press, 2016). In describing what this institutional feature of the CDC meant for disease containment efforts around H1N1 (swine flu), Mason notes the following:

> "The Ministry of Health put out general directives, but provincial and city leaders tended to make their own decisions about how to respond to those directives. The success of any national effort was ultimately reliant on the cooperation of the local CDCs, and the leaders of those CDCs had a considerable amount of latitude as to how they wished to carry out any particular project."

a municipal health bureau has power over a municipal CDC.[7] Similarly, a local CDC that identifies violations of public health directives in its community is not empowered to sanction rule-breakers directly.[8] CDC employees throughout the agency's hierarchy explained to me how crippling this inability to enforce is. Any time they detect rule violations, whether by CDC bureaus lower down in the hierarchy or by community members breaking public health rules, they need to contact other units within the Ministry of Health to address the issue.[9] This process is complex, labor-intensive, and usually fails to effect change.[10] Consequently, most CDC employees who identify policy implementation problems do not engage with the enforcement process and resign themselves to accepting these violations of public health rules. CDC officials also lack the authority to compel community participation in its interventions.[11] Instead, as described later in this chapter, they must cajole their way into accessing their target population.[12]

Mason, "Becoming Modern after SARS. Battling the H1N1 Pandemic and the Politics of Backwardness in China's Pearl River Delta," 17.

7 This combination of vertical power dynamics (within one same institution, from one administrative level down to the next) and horizontal ones (across institutions at the same administrative level) in Chinese politics is referred to as the *tiao-kuai* system.

8 Mason, "Becoming Modern after SARS," 16. The reasons for this decision to limit the CDC's enforcement powers are difficult to establish with certainty. By some accounts, it was a conscious organizational choice designed to increase people's willingness to interact with the CDC, without fear that the CDC be able to sanction them for violations.

9 Field Notes, October 20, 2009. *Chuanranbing Fangzhifa* (传染病防治法) [Law on Prevention and Treatment of Infectious Diseases] Art. 68 (promulgated by the Standing Comm. Nat'l People's Cong., February 21, 1989, rev'd August 28, 2004, amended June 29, 2013).

10 Field Notes, October 20, 2009.

11 Cui Junjie (崔俊杰), "Gonggong Xingzheng Renwu Quxiang De Jibing Yufang Kongzhi Tixi Gaige" (公共行政任务取向的疾病预防控制体系改革) [Public Administrative Oriented Reforms of the Disease Prevention and Control System], *Administrative Law Review (行政法学研究)* no. 5 (2020):102–16, 107. Zhou Yu (周羽) & Liao Kaidi (廖开迪), "Zhong Nanshan: Yao Tigao Woguo Jikong Zhongxing De Diwei" (钟南山: 要提高我国疾控中心的地位) [Zhong Nanshan: We Need to Elevate the Position of Our CDCs], *Yangguang News (央广网)*, February 27, 2020, perma.cc/4P94-5XRB.

12 The characteristics of China's health infrastructure discussed in this section continue to plague it today and are at the root of its failure to successfully address COVID-19. Zhou Yu (周羽) & Liao Kaidi (廖开迪), "Zhong Nanshan: Yao Tigao Woguo Jikong Zhongxing De Diwei" (钟南山: 要提高我国疾控中心的地位) [Zhong Nanshan: We Need to Elevate the Position of Our CDCs], *Yangguang News (央广网)*, February 27, 2020, perma.cc/4P94-5XRB. Junfang Xu, Yu Shi, Feng Cheng, and Wannian Liang, "China's Public Health System: Time for Improvement," *The Lancet Public Health* 6, no. 12 (December 2021): e869–70, https://doi.org/10.1016/S2468-2667(21)00250-4. Jennifer Bouey, "China's Health System Reform and Global Health Strategy in the Context of COVID-19" (RAND Corporation, 2020), https://doi.org/10.7249/CTA321-1. In 2021, the Chinese government created a new national agency, the National Administration of Disease Prevention and Control, that is absorbing the China CDC. I discuss it further in Chapter 12.

A SEX INDUSTRY RELUCTANT TO COOPERATE

Adding to challenges within China's health bureaucracy, local health officials must also contend with sex workers and gatekeepers who do not want inquiries that could attract police attention or alienate clients.[26]

Sex workers seek to avoid drawing the attention of the state upon themselves. As discussed in Part II of this book, low- and middle-tier sex workers are hesitant to proactively seek out healthcare.[27] Encountering health officials in their place of work is even more disconcerting to them and thus often met with suspicion. Since their work environment associates them with prostitution in ways that showing up at a health clinic does not, they fear that welcoming health officials into their space amounts to recognizing their involvement in prostitution and might result in police sanctions. For instance, one CDC official noted how the sex workers he encounters when conducting outreach and testing "are worried . . . It is difficult. They do not know what the purpose of the CDC is, they do not know if we have a relationship with the police."[28] Another public health official noted how "sex workers do not want to accept" local CDC outreach.[29] As sex worker Mei Mei noted, "accepting [the CDC's] interventions would mean admitting I do that [sell sex], so I refuse them to save face."[30]

Gatekeepers, similarly, worry about opening up their business to health workers who could report on the presence of prostitution in their venue. These fears obstructed and ultimately thwarted my efforts to survey sex workers in Xizhou, the red-light district on the outskirts of Shenzhen where I conducted fieldwork. Local health officials who supported the survey reached out to venue managers for assistance. The first manager they contacted set us up in a few private karaoke rooms, and my research assistants began surveying hostesses. An hour later, the manager returned. He was extremely polite and apologetic but explained that his boss had just called and told him we had to leave. They were worried that we were going to report that there was

[26] Gatekeepers are individuals such as madams, pimps, and entertainment venue managers.

[27] In my sex worker survey, 22 percent of low-tier sex workers and 26 percent of middle-tier sex workers reported having been tested for HIV/AIDS in the past year; 53 percent of low-tier sex workers and 67 percent of middle-tier sex workers had received a health checkup in the past year. (As will be described later in this chapter, health officials do not reach out to mistresses and second wives.)

[28] Interview 57, March 26, 2009.

[29] Interview 104, August 12, 2009.

[30] Sex Worker Interview 1, August 24, 2009.

prostitution in their karaoke bar.[31] The second manager that local health agents contacted in the neighborhood also let us in to conduct surveys. As my research assistants got settled in a room, he stuck his head in and asked if we were the same group that had been working in a neighboring venue. He returned a few minutes later and requested that we put our bags in the opposite corner of the room. When he then asked to inspect the pens my assistants were using, unscrewed them, and meticulously scrutinized each part, we realized he was concerned that we were journalists recording what was happening in the venue. He also inspected our questionnaire. He came back about ten minutes later, told us that he was busy (我有事 – *wo you shi*), and kicked us out.[32]

Gatekeepers also worry that providing health workers access to their venues will deter clients from patronizing their business. One might think that gatekeepers would be eager for the opportunity to monitor HIV/AIDS and other STDs, increase knowledge of HIV transmission, and encourage behavioral changes among women engaged in prostitution. Healthier sex workers could be economically beneficial to businesses that harbor prostitution activities, helping the venue attract more clients with evidence of STD-free women. Yet venue gatekeepers worry instead that opening up their spaces to public health workers will project a message that the venue's sex workers may have HIV/AIDS, which would send clients running. Awareness of HIV/AIDS among the general population in China (including among clients) varies widely.[33] Knowing that a venue has been inspected in relation to HIV/AIDS can be enough to deter men from even crossing its threshold. The industry benefits more from an environment where the presence of HIV/AIDS is simply not suggested at all, rather than one where its existence has been

31 Field Notes, November 17, 2009.

32 Field Notes, November 19, 2009.

33 Horizon Market Research and Futures Group Europe, "2001 Behavioural Surveillance Survey in Yunnan and Sichuan. Adult Male Report," Horizon Market Research (Beijing, 2002). Zhu Guang Rong, Cheng Ye Ji, and Xing Hua Yang, "Relationship between Migration and HIV Risky Behavior: A Comparative Study of Returning Migrants and Non Migrants Based on Rural Out-of-School Youth in Jilin, China," *Biomedical and Environmental Sciences* 28, no. 6 (2015): 429–36, https://doi.org/10.3967/bes2015.060. Bo Yang, Zheng Wu, Christoph M. Schimmele, and Shuzhuo Li, "HIV Knowledge among Male Labor Migrants in China," *BMC Public Health* 15, no. 1 (December 2015): 323, https://doi.org/10.1186/s12889-015-1653-1. Ye Zhenmiao et al. (叶振淼等), "Wenzhou Shi Nongcun Diqu ≥ 60 Sui Laonian Nanxing Piaoke Aizibing Zhishi Ji Xingxingwei Tezheng Diaocha" (温州市农村地区≥60 岁老年男性嫖客艾滋病知识及性行为特征调查) [HIV/AIDS–Related Knowledge and Sexual Behavior Characteristics among Elderly Male Clients Aged 60 Years and Above in Rural Areas of Wenzhou City]," *Practical Preventive Medicine* （实用预防医学） 27, no. 1 (2020): 38–41, https://doi.org/10.3969/j.issn.1006-3110.2020.01.010.

acknowledged and then declared absent from the premises through state health inspections. As one CDC-affiliated researcher explained:

> The bosses (老板 – *laoban*) don't want anything that will interfere with their business. If they think that what you are doing will harm their business, then they won't let you in. Health is important, but it is not as important as bringing in business. They think that having outreach, health information etc. in their venues will have a negative effect on business. It will make it look like there is a health problem in their venue, that their girls are not clean ... They think that if you come to their place and do HIV work, then it means there is a problem with the place.[34]

This concern also emerged when I was setting up my sex worker survey in Beijing.[35] One nongovernmental organization (NGO) staff member who was working with us asked me whether the HIV/AIDS test that we were providing as part of the study was optional. After I clarified that participants were under no obligation to get tested, she explained that she was asking me this question because she did not want to upset the neighborhood venue managers, who objected to the testing because they did not want any rumors spreading about any of their sex workers possibly having HIV/AIDS.[36] Knowledge of health activities makes clients aware of the possibility of HIV/AIDS infections in the venue. Complete absence of such interventions takes the issue entirely off the minds of those same business patrons.

Facing resistance from sex workers and gatekeepers and, as noted in the previous section, lacking the authority to require participation, local health officials instead invest significant efforts in persuasion. Simply explaining the purpose of their work to sex workers and gatekeepers often helps to open doors. Local CDC officials emphasize that their sole focus is on health and that they are not empowered to sanction sex workers or businesses tied to prostitution. In the words of one provincial CDC leader, "We explain to the bosses that all we care about is disease prevention. We aren't taking a moral approach to this, rather we are just focused on saving lives."[37] Their efforts include educating gatekeepers about the spread of HIV/AIDS. By explaining how HIV/AIDS can be transmitted to the nonpaying sexual partners of both sex workers and clients, CDC workers emphasize the benefits of

[34] Interview 64, April 16, 2009.
[35] Please see the Appendix for more details about the sex worker survey.
[36] Field Notes, November 30, 2009.
[37] Interview 49, November 3, 2008.

health outreach among sex workers on public health in Chinese society as a whole.[38] Appeals to the overall well-being of China's general population, paired with reassurances that interventions will occur discreetly and away from the gaze of clients, are often sufficient to garner the support of gatekeepers.

These local health agents' efforts to gain access to spaces that harbor prostitution can be extremely successful, and evolve from a relationship of suspicion to one of enthusiastic collaboration. I experienced the results of fruitful interactions between state health actors and the sex industry in the southern city of Dongguan, where I met with officials from the municipal CDC. Following an afternoon of exploratory conversations, the CDC officials invited me to dinner at an entertainment venue with both a restaurant and a karaoke bar. The facility's owner joined us, and mealtime dynamics provided evidence of warm familiarity between her and my meal hosts.[39] The CDC employees evidently knew her personally, starting out the dinner conversation by sharing information about her background. This owner had a fascinating rags-to-riches story. Now in her fifties, she was born into poverty in Hong Kong, where she first earned money as a waste picker, going through trash and selling salvageable items. She then moved on to smuggling used cars to mainland China, and was now the owner of several middle-tier entertainment spaces in Dongguan. At the end of the dinner, one of the CDC officials explained that we wanted to conduct a survey of sex workers and asked whether she would help provide access. She immediately made a phone call, and in a matter of minutes, I was in the lobby of the hotel meeting with two madams who worked at the karaoke venue attached to the restaurant, discussing implementation details such as the number of women we wanted to interview.[40] The CDC had directly inquired about sex worker access, and the owner readily agreed, without denying the presence of prostitution on the premises.

I also witnessed failed attempts at persuasion. This occurred most notably in Xizhou, where, as noted earlier in the chapter, managers of two middle-tier venues thwarted our efforts to survey sex workers. To negotiate access to the first venue, the local health official,

38 Interview 49, November 3, 2008.

39 Others have also documented closeness between Chinese CDC officials and the managers and employees of the places where the CDC carries out monitoring activities and inspections. Mason, *Infectious Change*.

40 Field Notes, October 20, 2009. I ended up not pursuing the opportunity to carry out the survey in Dongguan.

Wang Zhuren, called the manager into his office and explained that we wanted to distribute condoms, conduct health education, and interview hostesses. In the moment, the manager agreed and also said he would reach out to other bosses in the neighborhood to do the same for us.[41] When we later returned to Wang Zhuren's office to explain that we had been asked to leave the entertainment venue, he was impassive. The following day, he called the manager of the second venue into his office. This time, he explained that while in the past the Chinese government had been completely opposed to prostitution, there was now more openness around the issue, so he could feel comfortable letting us work in his karaoke bar.[42] This entreaty was no more successful than the first, and spelled the end of my efforts to survey sex workers in Xizhou. It also provides a powerful illustration of local health officials' limited enforcement power. When we reported our first mishap to Wang Zhuren, I had expected him to pick up the phone, call the manager back, and take him to task for his behavior. His decision to move on to a second manager, who also refused to help us, underscores a dynamic where entertainment venue gatekeepers feel empowered to push back against local health officials and where these state agents accept that response, at least in some instances.

CONTENDING WITH THE POLICE

In the course of carrying out their professional responsibilities, local health officials must contend not only with the obstacles that actors in the sex industry present to them but also with resistance from the police. These two agencies' prostitution policies conflict with one another: Policing policies that outlaw prostitution are inherently in tension with health policies that seek to reduce the spread of HIV/AIDS. In China as in other places where prostitution is illegal, sex workers minimize their visibility, deny their involvement in the sex industry, and avoid engaging with the state.[43] Yet health workers need access to sex workers in order to conduct testing and outreach, and these officials also need to create an environment where sex workers

[41] Field Notes, November 17, 2009.

[42] Field Notes, November 19, 2009.

[43] Open Society Foundations, "10 Reasons to Decriminalize Sex Work" (Open Society Foundations, 2015), perma.cc/XV2P-47YN.

feel comfortable acknowledging that they sell sex.[44] One China CDC employee explained to me that the "public health community does not want these [crackdowns on prostitution] because then they can't find female sex workers."[45] Another one acknowledged how health worker preferences conflict with law enforcement, as these crackdowns are "necessary for the police."[46]

Health workers in China must take this inherent tension seriously when considering how they will gain access to sex workers. They are at a disadvantage in relation to the police when seeking to advance their prostitution policy goals, because within China's state bureaucracy, health officials are weaker than the police. As I explained earlier in this chapter, the country's health agency is weak. And as discussed in previous chapters, law enforcement officers are members of one of China's most powerful state agencies.[47] Local health officials are stymied by the greater clout of their police colleagues when they attempt to carry out sex worker outreach and testing. A national CDC employee explained to me that they had limited female sex worker

[44] Tensions between health and law enforcement actors are not specific to China. Rather, they present obstacles for reducing HIV/AIDS among illegal populations in a wide range of countries and political systems. The challenges that these conflicting policies present explain why globally, the public health community endorses decriminalization as the regulatory model that best advances its goals. International organizations and foundations such as UNAIDS, UNFPA, the World Health Organization, the Open Society Foundation, and Human Rights Watch have all issued policy recommendations that advocate for this policy as a means of reducing transmission of HIV. Human Rights Watch, "Sex Workers at Risk: Condoms as Evidence of Prostitution in Four US Cities," July 2012; Svati P. Shah, "Trafficking and the Conflation with Sex Work: Implications for HIV Control and Prevention," Working Paper for the Third Meeting of the Technical Advisory Group of the Global Commission on HIV and the Law, 2011, perma.cc/Q5LB-3XNK; Nada Al-Riahi, "Prostitution in the Arab World: A Legal Study of Arab Legislation," Working Paper Prepared for the Middle East and North Africa Regional Consultation of the Global Commission on HIV and the Law, 2011, perma.cc/FNG4-M6MX; UNDP, "Risks, Rights & Health" (UNDP, 2012), perma.cc/5QEP-WVCY; World Health Organization, UNFPA, and UNAIDS, "Prevention and Treatment of HIV and Other Sexually Transmitted Infections for Sex Workers in Low and Middle-Income Countries," December 2012, perma.cc/P4SC-5VVS; UNAIDS, "UNAIDS Guidance Note on HIV and Sex Work" (UNAIDS, 2012), perma.cc/583C-YSBE; Open Society Foundations, "10 Reasons to Decriminalize Sex Work" (Open Society Foundations, 2015), perma.cc/XV2P-47YN; Matthew Chersich, "Preventing HIV among Sex Workers in Sub-Saharan Africa: A Literature Review" (WHO, 2011), perma.cc/T49G-GYYD; Anand Grover, "Report of the Special Rapporteur on the Right of Everyone to the Enjoyment of the Highest Attainable Standard of Physical and Mental Health" (UN Human Rights Council, 2010), perma.cc/A77J-WZMY; UNAIDS, "International Guidelines on HIV/AIDS and Human Rights" (UNAIDS, 2006), perma.cc/3BNZ-UUD9.

[45] Interview 26, October 15, 2008.

[46] Interview 26, October 15, 2008.

[47] Suzanne E. Scoggins, *Policing China: Street-Level Cops in the Shadow of Protest*, Studies of the Weatherhead East Asian Institute, Columbia University (Ithaca, NY: Cornell University Press, 2021), 13; Suzanne E. Scoggins, "Policing Modern China," *China Law and Society Review* 3, no. 2 (October 30, 2018): 80, 90, https://doi.org/10.1163/25427466-00302001.

projects in Shenzhen because the police there are "hard to work with" and restrict CDC access to entertainment venues.[48] One public health informant had colleagues who were arrested while doing sex worker outreach in a small town in Liaoning province – the police there had never heard of any state-sponsored programs to reach out to sex workers.[49] An HIV/AIDS rights activist provided examples of local law enforcement officers trailing CDC staff and arresting groups of sex workers after they had taken part in health outreach activities. The police explained that these women had essentially admitted to engaging in prostitution through their participation in the event.[50] Another interviewee recounted instances when sex workers were arrested for accepting free condoms from an outreach program.[51] A doctor in the southern city of Liuzhou described how police once "confiscated all the condoms I sent to a beauty parlor and used them as evidence against its owner."[52] The police have also spoken out publicly against CDC-sponsored health events for sex workers. For instance, local media coverage of a safe sex lecture that the city of Harbin CDC had organized for sex workers included a quote from a local police officer who noted that "the lectures could prove embarrassing to public security authorities."[53] A public health researcher noted that the "CDC usually has contacts with the police, but the relationship is not smooth. The police are aware of what they are doing, but they also have to crack down."[54]

This tension affected my own fieldwork plans. As noted earlier in this chapter, I explored the possibility of conducting a sex worker survey in Dongguan and received initial support from that city's CDC. A few weeks after my initial CDC meeting in Dongguan, the central government threatened to give Dongguan the worst possible crime rating if the

48 Interview 26, October 15, 2008.

49 Interview 58, April 2, 2009.

50 Interview 32, October 19, 2008.

51 Interview 38, October 22, 2008.

52 Xinhua News Agency (新华社), "Anti-AIDS Campaign Spotlights Sex Workers," *China.Org.Cn* (中国网), May 5, 2005, perma.cc/GM57-GXVB. The police in China are allowed to use the presence of condoms as evidence when arresting individuals for prostitution. This policy conflicts with public health guidelines that encourage condom use, since fears that presence of condoms could be used to prove criminal behavior can discourage sex workers from carrying and using them. Asia Catalyst, "The Condom Quandary: A Study of the Impact of Law Enforcement Practices on Effective HIV Prevention among Male, Female, and Transgender Sex Workers in China," July 2016, perma.cc/G9PF-AGRZ; Human Rights Watch, "Sex Workers at Risk."

53 Xinhua News Agency, "Safe-Sex Education for Prostitutes Stirs Debate," *China.Org.Cn* (中国网), October 16, 2006, perma.cc/H268-FEHP.

54 Interview 97, January 19, 2009.

local government did not crack down more harshly on the local sex industry. The police began conducting raids throughout the city.[55] As a result, the Dongguan CDC temporarily ceased all public health outreach with sex workers and would not assist me in accessing venues.

Public health policies officially address this tension in ways that defer to law enforcement and make clear that they do not change the criminalized status of prostitution. These health policies seek to reconcile the two regulatory approaches, frame them as complimentary, and underscore the continued importance of cracking down on prostitution as integral to efforts to reduce HIV/AIDS. For example, the 2006 State Council Notice on China's AIDS action plan states that "relevant departments in all regions shall . . . enforce the HIV prevention and treatment in accordance with law and policy, and crack down on . . . the illegal behavior of commercial sex."[56] Central-government health officials also underscore that health outreach does not constitute an endorsement of prostitution.[57] These types of pronouncements recognize the hierarchy that exists between these two agencies, with health officials being very careful to state that they are not challenging policing policies.

Given these power relations, the burden lies on health officials to navigate the tension between these two regulatory approaches to prostitution in ways that do not clash directly with the police. No publicly available official directives appear to provide guidance on how to do so. Instead, in their day-to-day work, local health actors are often left to manage dynamics with the police on their own. They do so by alternatively ignoring the police, engaging them on a personal level to not interfere with public health efforts, and actively leaning on them to carry out outreach.

55 Fiona Tam, "Party Chief Vows to Crack down But Excessive Measures Will Be Avoided," *South China Morning Post*, November 26, 2009, https://perma.cc/H268-FEHP; Fiona Tam, "Crackdown Fails to Scare Dongguan's Sex-Trade Veterans," *South China Morning Post*, November 26, 2009, https://perma.cc/FA8J-ZJ3B.

56 The 2011–15 Action Plan contains a similar statement. General Office of the State Council (国务院办公厅), "Zhongguo Ezhi Yu Fangzhi Aizibing Xingdong Jihua 2006-2010 (中国遏制与防治艾滋病行动计划（2006-2010年）) [China's Action Plan for Containment and Prevention of HIV/AIDS (2006–2010)]," 2006, perma.cc/G4ZY-8KLK; General Office of the State Council (国务院办公厅), "Zhongguo Ezhi Yu Fangzhi Aizibing Shierwu Xingdong Jihua (中国遏制与防治艾滋病'十二五'行动计划) [China's '12th Five-Year' Action Plan for Containment and Prevention of HIV/AIDS (2011–2015)]," 2012, perma.cc/YK58-QZLW.

57 Elaine Jeffreys, *Prostitution Scandals in China: Policing, Media, and Society* (New York: Routledge, 2012), 141–45.

Ignoring the Police

In some communities, the CDC plows ahead with its sex worker surveillance and outreach projects without alerting law enforcement of its plans. In describing this approach, a doctor with the city of Beijing CDC noted that "it is better not to contact the police."[58] Informants in Shenzhen and Zhengti described a similar strategy.[59] The rationale for this approach is that preemptively reaching out may cause more trouble than necessary, and that it is simpler to proceed under the radar rather than announce their intentions beforehand and possibly attract unwanted attention. The health workers who described this strategy worked in large cities, where their activities could feasibly blend into the larger chaos of urban daily life.

Engaging the Police to Not Interfere

A second approach that health officials adopt is to request that the police not interfere when the CDC is conducting outreach. This requires convincing law enforcement of the importance of health outreach with sex workers. When first presented with the idea of nonpunitive, state-sponsored interventions with sex workers, local law enforcement agents generally reject it as tantamount to legalizing prostitution. A CDC doctor in one town explained, "When we first met with the police, the head was not receptive to our work. He didn't see how this was any different from legalization."[60] CDC officials working in a number of different places described a similar initial reaction, noting how "at the beginning, the local police could not understand"[61] and how "the police were worried our work signaled that prostitution was legal."[62] One health official told me how at one of these meetings, two police representatives stood up and said, "No way . . . If we know they sell sex, we have to arrest."[63]

Public health officials respond to the concerns of their law enforcement colleagues by emphasizing that creating a space for health outreach does not preclude punishing individuals who are caught selling sex.[64] Over time, this engagement has borne fruit: CDC employees

[58] Interview 55, April 1, 2009.
[59] Interview 81, May 4, 2009; Interview 75, April 28, 2009; Interview 98, August 6, 2009.
[60] Interview 100b, August 7, 2009.
[61] Interview 26, October 15, 2008.
[62] Interview 49, November 3, 2008. See also: Interview 34, October 20, 2008; Interview 190, March 26, 2009; Interview 44, October 28, 2008.
[63] Interview 46, October 30, 2008.
[64] Interview 46, October 30, 2008.

consistently portray their relations with the police as having shifted since sex worker health outreach began in China, with extremely tense relations giving way to a more accepting environment. A doctor at one local CDC noted this evolution:

> We have a good working relationship with the police. At first, we did not . . . But the head of the police attended some of our workshops, and eventually came to see the utility of what we were doing. Once he was on board, he spread the word among the police at a big meeting. Now, we work well with the police.[65]

Another CDC employee explained, "At the beginning, the local police did not understand what we were doing. There was conflict between the health providers and the police. But with information, we made them aware. Now our relationship is smooth."[66] A number of other health officials described a similar progression over time, where the police now give them more space to carry out testing and outreach free from interference.[67]

Engaging the Police to Assist with Health Interventions

A third way that health officials carry out public health surveillance and outreach is to actively lean on the police for assistance. This approach, like the previous one, also involves actively engaging with law enforcement. One way in which this occurred in the recent past was through custody and education centers: Before they were abolished in 2020, they all served as CDC surveillance sites.[68] Health officials also seek out opportunities to test and conduct outreach with sex workers when they are first arrested for prostitution. I learned about this in the Shenzhen red-light district of Wanqin, where most evenings, the local police would arrest a handful of sex workers, detain them overnight, and release them the following morning. A contact in the neighborhood had observed health officials conduct sex worker testing and outreach at the police station in the morning prior to their release. She suggested that I ask the police to allow me to carry out my survey

[65] Interview 100b, August 7, 2009.

[66] Interview 26, October 15, 2008.

[67] Interview 26, October 15, 2008; Interview 190, March 26, 2009; Interview 44, October 28, 2008; Interview 49, November 3, 2008; Interview 104, August 12, 2009.

[68] Interview 26, October 15, 2008. In fact, until 2003, they served as the only source of surveillance data on sex worker HIV/AIDS infection rates. Jia et al., "Sources of Data for Improved Surveillance of HIV/AIDS in China."

with these detained sex workers, an option I declined to pursue.[69] Health officials also seek out police assistance in noncarceral settings. One health official described how "in a lot of places, the CDC contacts the police, who go into venues and force sex workers to participate in trainings."[70] A member of a sex worker health and rights NGO described a pattern where a police officer would be posted at the entrance of a venue until the hostesses inside all agreed to cooperate with the CDC and get tested.[71] In Shanghai, the CDC routinely conducts outreach through the police. Law enforcement officers go to a venue with health officials, tell the hostesses to collaborate with the outreach and testing, and let them know that they will not be arrested.[72]

Personal Relationships with the Police

Strong personal relationships with the police are essential for local health officials who engage them not to interfere and rely on them when conducting outreach and testing.[73] When I asked one national CDC official to identify the most successful testing and outreach projects and the reasons for their success, he cited a city in western China where the police chief and the head of the municipal CDC's HIV/AIDS division were brothers.[74] Others consistently underscored similar factors, for example, noting that "the personal contacts between the CDC and the police are important."[75] I also witnessed the benefits of close personal ties across agencies: in Zhengti, my main police contact took me to lunch with his law enforcement colleague and their high school friend, a doctor with the local CDC's HIV/AIDS division. During the meal, the three of them had a thoughtful conversation that acknowledged how their lifelong friendship helped shape a model local surveillance program.[76]

[69] It would have been unethical. In addition, sex workers might hesitate to answer questions truthfully in that setting.
[70] Interview 58, April 2, 2009.
[71] Interview 77, April 30, 2009.
[72] Interview 64, April 16, 2009.
[73] As noted in Chapter 2, personal relations (*guanxi*) are crucial for accomplishing anything in China.
[74] Interview 190, March 26, 2009.
[75] Interview 97, January 19, 2009.
[76] Interview 100b, August 7, 2009.

IMPLEMENTATION IRREGULARITIES

Faced with problems within the Chinese state's health apparatus, combined with an uncooperative sex industry and unwelcoming police officers, it is no wonder that local health officials' policy implementation practices seldom go according to plan. Surveillance guidelines instruct local health officials to map out the universe of prostitution spaces in their community and categorize them according to tier of prostitution (low, middle, and high). On the basis of this categorization, the officials should then randomly sample the spaces where they will conduct testing, ensuring that at least 10 percent of the sample comes from the low tier and 40 percent comes from the middle tier. Sex workers from each space should also be sampled randomly. Each year, officials must test 400 sex workers in the community for one round of surveillance.[77] Sex workers should not be coerced to participate in this process. Behavioral outreach (such as education on safe sex and condom use) in communities of sex workers should be carried out in a similarly thorough and systematic manner, in ways that respect individual rights, and with a focus on those women at highest risk of HIV/AIDS. However, as the following pages show, local health officials do not follow these rules.

Weak Mapping Processes

Despite clearly articulated guidelines, local health officials do not carry out the processes of mapping prostitution spaces in their community in a rigorous manner. An employee involved in sex worker surveillance at a Shenzhen CDC recognized that "mapping for female sex workers is not done well, it is hard to know whether it is representative."[78] A doctor working at a district CDC in Beijing was similarly skeptical of the quality of the maps his office develops, noting that "they are not quite right."[79] He explained that his district's CDC acquired an official list of all legally registered entertainment venues to map out the district. This means, however, that their map included every entertainment venue in the district, regardless of whether it actually harbored

[77] This number is reduced to 250 at surveillance sites that, in the previous surveillance round, had an HIV/AIDS prevalence rate that exceeded 10 percent. National Center for AIDS/STD Control and Prevention (性病艾滋病预防控制中心), "Quanguo Aizibing Shaodian Jiance Shishi Fangan Caozuo Shouce (全国艾滋病哨点监测实施方案操作手册) [Guidebook for Monitoring on the Implementation of National AIDS Checkpoints]" (2017), perma.cc/6WZ6-CKM9.

[78] Interview 75, April 28, 2009.

[79] Interview 55, April 1, 2009.

prostitution activities. The map also excluded unregistered venues and public areas such as parks and alleyways where streetwalkers gather. One Chinese researcher who collaborates closely with the Shanghai CDC expressed great skepticism about map quality.[80] Of Shanghai's sixteen districts, only two responded to her requests to see their maps. She interpreted this lack of responsiveness as an indication that these district CDCs either had not carried out the mapping exercise or had conducted it in such a cursory manner that they did not want to share the end result. Of the two maps she had received, one was done "really poorly, it seemed sloppy."[81] The second district had done its map more thoroughly, specifying where they had obtained information for each venue – such as asking cab drivers or going themselves.[82] Yet when the research team sought to verify the accuracy of this more detailed and better-sourced map, they discovered that "it just did not correspond to reality."[83] A foreign employee at an international health organization who has worked with and observed CDC sex worker outreach projects throughout China was complimentary of some of the maps he had seen for pilot projects in a handful of counties.[84] Yet he recognized that these were exceptions to a mapping process that is rarely comprehensive. Most of the time, when local health officials use these maps to carry out surveillance, they are relying on information that provides an imprecise and inaccurate reflection of the actual universe of spaces that provide prostitution services in any given location.

Community Testing and Outreach Focused on the Middle Tier

Instead of adhering to official guidelines regarding public health surveillance of both low-tier and middle-tier sex workers and focusing outreach efforts on low-tier sex workers who are at highest risk of HIV/AIDS, local health officials gravitate toward middle-tier hostesses. Nothing in this chapter's earlier discussion of the sex industry's wariness of health officials suggests that hostesses are easy targets. Instead, local health officials view them as the least bad option when compared to low-tier sex workers and second wives in the upper tier. First, hostesses are physically located in entertainment venues, which gives

80 Interview 67, April 17, 2009.
81 Interview 67, April 17, 2009.
82 Interviewees who work with the CDC in other locations also mentioned the informative role that cab drivers play in helping to map the sex industry. Interview 97, January 19, 2009. I also found cab drivers to be extremely knowledgeable about the local geography of prostitution.
83 Interview 67, April 17, 2009.
84 Interview 130, August 19, 2009.

health workers an easily identifiable physical space where they can find these testing and outreach targets. And since most such venues are legally registered, officials can consult government registries to assist them in identifying these spaces in their community. In addition, the legitimacy that this registration confers, along with the legal entertainment services the spaces offer (food, drink, singing, and dancing) means that while individuals in the venues may not welcome health workers with open arms, they are unlikely to scatter immediately upon a state actor's approach. Second, hostesses all have gatekeepers who are one step removed from the illegality of sexual transactions and are thus more approachable. Gatekeepers are also less transient than the women under their supervision, which facilitates repeat visits to venues. And hostesses are unlikely to resist gatekeeper instructions to cooperate with health officials. Third, one middle-tier venue often has dozens of hostesses, if not more. Consequently, they present the most efficient option for health officials who must meet numerical targets for sex worker testing and outreach. In short, the easiest way for local health officials to carry out sex worker testing and outreach is to develop relationships with entertainment venues and their gatekeepers. Eliciting cooperation from a sizeable subset of the population of low-tier sex workers requires significantly more effort because they work independently or in much smaller groups than hostesses. And since low-tier sex workers and their gatekeepers cannot hide behind their provision of legitimate entertainment services, they are more wary of local health officials.[85]

This misplaced focus on middle-tier sex workers is well documented. A sex work health and rights activist who works with groups throughout China remarked that "people do not do outreach with streetwalkers."[86] The head of a domestic network of sex worker activists who works closely with the Shanghai CDC explained to me that in his experience, "The CDC does entertainment venues, but no one does streetwalkers."[87] An employee of an international organization who works on the 100% Condom Use Program (100% CUP) with national and local CDC branches evaluated it as follows: "The question of its success depends on how you define 100% CUP. If it is in EEs [entertainment establishments]

[85] Recruiting mistresses and second wives for testing and outreach would also be complicated, as it would require health workers to mill about urban areas with high concentrations of mistresses. Health officials are not required to target elite sex workers as they are not considered at highest risk of HIV/AIDS.

[86] Interview 95, January 15, 2009.

[87] Interview 63, April 16, 2009.

with a *mami* [madam], that is one thing . . . [But] street-based sex workers are very under-researched . . . That is where the 100% CUP program is weak."[88] State health actors also acknowledge this problem. One of them explained that "The commercial sex workers who need the outreach on AIDS education are the lowest-class ones – the ones in far away, obscure places. But people do not want to go there to do outreach. It is easy to go to venues such as nightclubs, but much more complicated to get access to those other women."[89] A staff member at a CDC in Shenzhen told me that "We do female sex work surveillance, but we do not have a good program."[90] She then proceeded to describe an implementation system focused entirely on entertainment venues. And a national-level CDC employee noted that the agency "mostly does entertainment center outreach stuff" in their prostitution programs.[91] CDC officials have even acknowledged these shortcomings in prominent publications. In 2013, researchers at the National Center for STD Control, part of the CDC, published a letter in the medical journal *The Lancet Infectious Diseases* in which they noted that low-tier sex workers are less well represented in China's HIV/AIDS surveillance program than hostesses.[92]

Surveillance Sampling Issues

Compounding this problematic focus on hostesses are unsystematic methods for sampling them, which lead to inadequate information on middle-tier sex workers in the community. Instead of randomly sampling from an accurate mapping of entertainment venues, local CDC officials instead select venues based on convenience. A CDC employee who works in the national office and monitors sex worker surveillance sites throughout the country recognized a clear disconnect between the sampling guidelines they issue and the local CDC practices he observes nationwide, including in places as far-flung as Jilin, Gansu, Guizhou, Hainan, and Xinjiang. He explained how "the outreach is designed, at the national level, to be random sampling, but in practice, at the local level it ends up being convenience

[88] Interview 108, August 14, 2009.
[89] Interview 58, April 2, 2009. Nightclubs are a venue-type similar to karaoke bars.
[90] Interview 75, April 28, 2009.
[91] Interview 172, September 2, 2009.
[92] Xiang-Sheng Chen, Yue-Ping Yin, and Ning Jiang, "Was the HIV Infection Burden in Female Sex Workers in China Overestimated?," *The Lancet Infectious Diseases* 13, no. 1 (January 2013): 13.

sampling."[93] A Shenzhen CDC official corroborated this remark when he explained that they "just go to wherever they can get access."[94] Local health officials also adjust their sampling strategies with an eye to achieving rates of HIV/AIDS that will not cause trouble within the state hierarchy. When those rates appear too high, they increase the sample size hoping to bring their HIV/AIDS estimates down; conversely, when they reach more desirable rates, they prematurely wrap up the surveillance process.[95]

The process of sampling women within these spaces is also flawed. Indeed, it is implemented in such a way that it can include women who are not actually sex workers. For the purposes of its testing and outreach, the CDC assumes that all women who work in an entertainment venue sell sex. While health officials could of course try to avoid inclusion of non-sex workers in their sample by asking upfront, respondents are unlikely to admit to selling sex when a stranger from a government agency asks. Cognizant of this issue, the CDC surveillance survey instrument does not even have a question that allows the respondent to self-identify as a sex worker.[96] Instead, when a health worker arrives at a venue, they recruit anyone present for testing. A sex work activist who has observed this process noted how "a lot of [those tested] are not commercial sex workers, but get included in the statistics anyway."[97]

Cutting Corners in Behavioral Outreach

Local health officials also sometimes adopt a liberal interpretation of HIV/AIDS behavioral outreach programs. CDC guidelines explain that these safe sex education workshops should include health education, trainings on client interactions, and condom distribution.[98] In

[93] Interview 57, March 26, 2009.
[94] Interview 81, May 4, 2009.
[95] Interview 57, March 26, 2009.
[96] National Center for AIDS/STD Control and Prevention (性病艾滋病预防控制中心), "Quanguo Aizibing Shaodian Jiance Shishi Fangan Caozuo Shouce (全国艾滋病哨点监测实施方案操作手册) [Guidebook for Monitoring on the Implementation of National AIDS Checkpoints]" (National Center for AIDS/STD Control and Prevention (性病艾滋病预防控制中心), 2012), perma.cc/H3WW-2MCM.
[97] Interview 77, April 30, 2009.
[98] *Gaowei Xingwei Ganyu Gongzuo Zhidao Fangan (Shixing)* (高危行为干预工作指导方案 (试行)) [Guidelines for Intervention Works on High-Risk Behaviors (For Trial Implementation)] (promulgated by the Ministry of Health (dissolved), May 20, 2005, effective May 20, 2005). National Center for AIDS/STD Control and Prevention (性病艾滋病预防控制中心), "Yixing Xingchuanbo Gaowei Renqun Yufang Aizibing Ganyu Gongzuo Zhinan" (异性性传播高危人群预防艾滋病干预工作指南) [Working Guidelines on Intervention on High-Risk

practice, local health officials often only distribute condoms, and report such actions as behavioral outreach. In Shenzhen, for example, a local health official invited me to observe her weekly round of sex worker outreach. She presented the project as integral to implementing national guidelines and showed me data on the number of women they had reached through their efforts, which they reported to higher-level officials. I prepared myself for a long night of educational workshops on HIV/AIDS transmission and negotiating condom use with clients. Instead, when I met up with the health official in a park by a red-light district in the early evening, she made a phone call, and a few minutes later a madam appeared. My contact handed her a large bag of condoms, and we all went our separate ways. The next day back at her office, I pushed to clarify my understanding of their outreach program, and learned that the previous night's delivery of 500 condoms went down in the books as outreach with 500 sex workers. A CDC-affiliated researcher witnessed a similar practice in Shanghai: "They just deliver condoms in a box," she said of that city's local health officials.[99] Of course, it is unreasonable to equate the number of condoms distributed to a gatekeeper with the number of sex workers reached. In addition, as demonstrated by the CDC guidelines' emphasis on educating sex workers and providing them with skills to negotiate condom use with clients, effecting behavioral change to reduce HIV/AIDS transmission requires much more than simply handing out condoms.

Coercion

Lastly, health officials routinely coerce sex workers to get tested for HIV/AIDS and participate in outreach activities, thus disregarding rules on implementing these policies in ways that respect the individual rights of sex workers. The most egregious coercion occurs when health workers collaborate with the police to test incarcerated sex workers for HIV/AIDS. As noted earlier in this chapter, sex worker sentinel surveillance in China initially occurred exclusively in detention centers. I also recounted instances when health workers conducted testing and outreach with sex workers who had been incarcerated overnight.[100]

Populations for HIV/AIDS Heterosexual Sex Transmission], China CDC (中国疾病预防控制中心), May 2016, perma.cc/X8UB-SZHD.

99 Interview 64, April 16, 2009. See also Interview 108, August 14, 2009; Interview 172, September 1, 2009.

100 When they engage in these practices, local health officials are veering away from their predominant focus on hostesses in the middle tier. As discussed in Chapter 8, incarcerated sex workers are more likely to come from the low tier.

And when CDC officials carry out work in entertainment venues, they sometimes enlist police officers to assist with hostess compliance. Sex workers who are incarcerated, or have police officers hovering around their place of work, are not able to decline requests to take an HIV/AIDS test, nor can they refuse to answer questions about their sexual behavior[101] or to participate in other public health interventions. When health officials rely on gatekeepers to recruit sex workers for testing and outreach, they are also enabling coercive behavior: The cost to sex workers of disregarding the instructions of their madams, pimps, or venue managers is job loss.[102] In addition, health officials sometimes abuse their authority in their direct interactions with sex workers.[103] For instance, when they carry out surveillance, they are supposed to obtain the informed consent of each sex worker.[104] Instead, they largely gloss over this step when they draw the blood of the person in front of them. In fact, the surveillance implementation guidelines enable this practice: They recommend that health workers "not overemphasize informed consent" (不能过度强调征求同意 – *buneng guodu qiangdiao zhengqiu tongyi*) in their interactions with sex workers to avoid low participation rates.[105]

Public Health Consequences

The public health consequences of the implementation practices described in this chapter are grave. Outreach that largely bypasses low-tier sex workers in favor of hostesses compromises the goal of reducing the spread of HIV/AIDS in China: It deprives the sex workers at highest risk of HIV/AIDS of interventions that could improve their health, the health of their clients, and the health of the population at large (especially clients' other sexual partners, including their wives). Furthermore, coercing sex workers to participate in such trainings undermines their efficacy.

In addition, local health officials' surveillance practices result in inaccurate data on sex worker HIV/AIDS rates and sexual behavior.

101 They are, however, free to provide inaccurate answers to such questions.

102 Interview 26, October 15, 2008; Interview 57, March 26, 2009.

103 Interview 104, August 12, 2009; Interview 77, April 30, 2009; Interview 26, October 15, 2008; Interview 57, March 26, 2009.

104 National Center for AIDS/STD Control and Prevention (性病艾滋病预防控制中心), "Quanguo Aizibing Shaodian Jiance Shishi Fangan Caozuo Shouce (全国艾滋病哨点监测实施方案操作手册) [Guidebook for Monitoring on the Implementation of National HIV/AIDS Checkpoints]," 2017, perma.cc/U4U6-5KJ6.

105 National Center for AIDS/STD Control and Prevention (性病艾滋病预防控制中心). For more reflection on informed consent in public health research in China, see Mason, *Infectious Change*, 136–37.

More specifically, the data is thought to underrepresent actual rates of HIV/AIDS within China's sex worker population. When the CDC carries out surveillance testing, its overemphasis on hostesses and its recruitment practices that can lead to non-sex workers being included in the testing contribute to underestimation of infection rates. When the CDC tests incarcerated sex workers, it is more likely capturing a snapshot of women in the low tier. Yet these women could be more recent entrants into the sex industry who were arrested due to their inexperience with evading law enforcement, which would suggest that their rates of HIV/AIDS infection might be lower than their more seasoned low-tier colleagues. Chinese public health officials have openly acknowledged their concerns about the underestimation of HIV/AIDS rates. For instance, they note that "Although surveillance shows that the rate of HIV infection in CSWs [commercial sex workers] is low, there may be a large proportion of the population that goes undetected, which would mean that the rate of HIV infection in CSWs, in actuality, may be significantly higher."[106]

This issue extends beyond sex workers: It constitutes part of a larger problem of bias and lack of representation within HIV/AIDS surveillance data in China more generally, especially in regard to other key populations who are at elevated risk for infection. National CDC researchers have noted that "[s]urveillance systems in most regions of China suffer from lack of coverage of key populations [and] quality control problems."[107] They recognize how "surveillance approaches often capture only a small fraction of the total population of some subgroups and there is no assurance that biases in coverage will remain constant over time."[108] They acknowledge how, as a result, "surveillance data can be misleading or can fail to capture significant pockets of infection," which can increase the spread of HIV in China.[109] They attest to the challenges to sampling groups such as sex workers, intravenous drug users, and men-who-have-sex-with-men in a representative manner, as well as the difficulties in obtaining truthful answers about their sexual behaviors.[110] The occurrence of these practices for a variety of populations who are at high risk of HIV/AIDS underscores just how much of a threat this approach to implementation presents to Chinese society.

106 Wang and Wang, "HIV/AIDS Epidemic and the Development of Comprehensive Surveillance System in China with Challenges," 3499.
107 Jia et al., "Sources of Data for Improved Surveillance of HIV/AIDS in China," 7.
108 Jia et al., "Sources of Data for Improved Surveillance of HIV/AIDS in China," 7.
109 Jia et al., "Sources of Data for Improved Surveillance of HIV/AIDS in China," 7.
110 Jia et al., "Sources of Data for Improved Surveillance of HIV/AIDS in China," 7.

CONCLUSION

Given the three sources of often conflicting constraints that weigh on local health officials – constraints from the health bureaucracy, the sex industry, and the police – it is not surprising that these officials implement sex worker testing and outreach in ways that deviate from formal policies. For example, their community outreach and testing work largely focuses on middle-tier sex workers. It is only when they turn their attention to incarcerated sex workers that they are more likely to engage with women in the low tier. The public health consequences of largely glossing over streetwalkers and women in small brothels are alarming. To make matters worse, coercion is integral to how health officials implement these policies. This tactic violates the individual rights of sex workers and reduces the likelihood that they will engage in long-term behavioral changes beneficial to their health. Coercion is most extreme when health officials interact with incarcerated sex workers. It is also integral to how health officials carry out community sex worker outreach, working with gatekeepers and the police. These practices all undermine the global public health community's belief that numerical data represents an apolitical truth, which I discussed in Chapter 10. Indeed, China's local health officials work in an authoritarian system that incentivizes them to distort and massage data to reflect a desired rate of HIV/AIDS, or number of sex workers trained, rather than the on-the-ground reality.

Why does the central government tolerate this less-than-perfect approach to monitoring and reducing the spread of HIV/AIDS? After all, ever since 2003, the issue of HIV/AIDS has been an official state priority.[111] Exploring this question in detail and in relation to the many other issues vying for the CCP's attention is beyond the scope of this book. Yet I suspect that part of the answer is that the CCP considers the status quo on HIV/AIDS to be "good enough." The central government would have a problem on its hands if rates of HIV/AIDS in the general

[111] See Chapter 3 for more discussion of this. Even throughout COVID-19, the PRC has continued to prioritize the issue of HIV/AIDS. See, e.g., "Li Keqiang Dui Aizibing Fangzhi Gongzuo Zuochu Zhongyao Pishi" (李克强对艾滋病防治工作作出重要批示) [Premier Li Keqiang Issues Major Comments on HIV Prevention and Treatment Work], *Xinhua News Agency* (新华社), November 30, 2021, perma.cc/5XGX-SMLK; *"Shisi Wu" Guomin Jiankang Guihua* ("十四五"国民健康规划) [The 14th Five Year Plan on National Health Planning] (promulgated by the Gen. Office of the St. Council, April 27, 2022, effective April 27, 2022); "Xi Jinping Jiangshu De Gushi: Renlei Mianlin De Gongtong Tiaozhan" (习近平讲述的故事:人类面临的共同挑战) [Story Told by Xi Jinping: Common Challenges Faced by Humankind]," *Xinhua News Agency* (新华社), December 1, 2021, https://perma.cc/JZ6X-M8NU.

population were straining its public health infrastructure, with possible downstream effects on regime stability. But imperfect as it may be, the current approach to testing and outreach is keeping that threat at bay. That sex workers bear the brunt of it, through poor health outcomes and the state's disregard for their human dignity, is of limited concern to an authoritarian regime that cares little for its most marginalized citizens.

12

CONCLUSION

This book is about the regulation of prostitution in contemporary China. Using ethnographic observation, along with interviews and surveys, I have explored the daily lives and perceptions of female sex workers living in an authoritarian regime where prostitution is against the law. I have also examined the practices and experiences of frontline state officials who implement China's prostitution policies, and the legal, political, economic, and social realities that shape their behavior. Sex workers' everyday lives and experiences with the state vary based on their tier of prostitution. These tiers differentiate between women who solicit on the streets and in small brothels (the lowest tier), those who work as hostesses in entertainment venues (the middle tier), and mistresses and second wives (the top tier). In addition, three main types of state priorities converge around the issue of prostitution: maintaining law and order; improving public health; and sustaining economic growth. With these distinctions in mind, I have structured my analysis in this book around tiers of sex work and types of state intervention.

Work conditions in the lowest tier of prostitution are grueling. These women either work outside (usually independently), in small brothels run out of private apartments or in businesses that masquerade as hair salons or massage parlors, where they remain under the watchful eyes of madams or pimps. Low-tier sex workers have many clients, who pay them a pittance and sometimes abuse them in horrific ways. These are women who are robbed, beaten, raped, and sometimes even murdered while plying their trade. Their gatekeepers – if they have them – might protect them from harm, but can also be an additional source of emotional and physical abuse. As the oldest and least educated of sex workers, their alternative employment options are limited. These demographics, in combination with their work environment, have serious consequences for the health of low-tier sex workers. They know little about safe sex. They might decide not to wear a condom if they think their client looks healthy and sometimes use a scientifically dubious rinsing product to ward off HIV/AIDS and other sexually transmitted diseases. If they insist on condom use, they might be paid less or lose the client. Furthermore, they shy away from medical checkups and HIV/AIDS tests, fearful that such interactions with state health officials might lead to their arrest for prostitution. Unsurprisingly, rates of HIV/AIDS infection are highest in this tier of prostitution. The experiences that shape the daily lives of women in the low tier lead to critical views on sex work and self-blame for engaging in it. They have high levels of knowledge of the legal regime governing prostitution, likely tied to the frequency of their brushes with law enforcement, which also appear to inform their low levels of trust in the police and the government more generally. One might expect these negative interactions with the state to translate into opposition to its current prostitution policies and support for their reform. Instead, low-tier sex workers are skeptical that legalizing prostitution could meaningfully alleviate the harsh realities of selling sex on the streets and in small brothels, and are more likely than their higher-status colleagues to support the current policy of criminalization. Streetwalkers and brothel workers do recognize one quality of life in the lowest tier of prostitution: the solidarity that it fosters among women who work in it.

Selling sex in China's middle tier of prostitution involves long and stressful hours. Women in this tier work as hostesses in karaoke bars and clubs, where clients come with colleagues and friends. A madam at these venues will usher her sex workers into the rented room, where they line up and wait for each client to make their choice. If they make it past this selection process, which they frequently characterize as humiliating, they spend the next few hours drinking, singing, and dancing with clients, and often end the evening by selling them sex. There are always many more hostesses than clients in this competitive environment, and the hostess lineup process is an obvious exercise in side-by-side physical comparison. When one client selects several hostesses in one evening, they are often competing for his attention throughout the night, each hoping to ultimately be chosen to sell him sex.

Hostesses are paid more than low-tier sex workers per sexual transaction and receive tips for singing, dancing, and drinking with clients. They also have fewer clients, more knowledge of HIV/AIDS, and a greater willingness to get health checkups – which helps explain their lower rates of HIV/AIDS infection. Yet middle-tier prostitution still presents significant health risks. As in the low tier, condom use is not systematic – after spending hours entertaining a client, a sex worker may lose him if she insists on using protection. Hostessing also presents additional health risks – women at karaoke bars and clubs may consume excessive amounts of alcohol in the process of entertaining clients, smoke with them, and do drugs.

Yet when hostesses talk about prostitution, it is their sense of empowerment and agency that stands out. They emphasize the benefits of sex work – higher income and more flexibility than restaurant or factory work, the main alternatives available to them – and support its legalization. They establish clear boundaries around appropriate client behavior, which allows them to articulate a sense of self that exists independently of their engagement in prostitution: When clients cross a line, hostesses perceive those actions as violating their identity as human beings, separate from their work. Hostesses also express greater trust in the central and local government, as well as the police, who sometimes help them dispatch unruly clients. On rare occasions, these women even publicly push back against the state. Such confidence makes sense when considering that middle-tier sex workers are less likely to be arrested for prostitution than their low-tier counterparts.

Second wives and mistresses have comfortable lives that belie the precarity of their work. Like their colleagues in the low and middle tiers of the sex industry, many of them are rural migrant women, but this higher tier also draws from poorer and less educated urban women and includes some university students. Their demographics often overlap with those of hostesses, and some women move back and forth between these two tiers of prostitution. The second wife's daily responsibilities are relatively predictable and not especially onerous, which likely explains why these women have more positive perspectives about their work than women in other tiers. A second wife's client provides her with housing. When he is there, she provides him with sexual services, as well as domestic ones. She keeps the house clean, and shops and cooks for him. She also accompanies him to social events, where her presence serves to boost his status among his friends and colleagues. He is often away – at work, or with his legal wife and family (who may live in a different city or province). When her client is gone, she has a lot of leisure time and independence. The health risks of these routines are limited: Second wives have fewer sexual partners than their lower-tier colleagues and spend less time drinking and smoking than hostesses.

Yet this is a lifestyle that often leaves the mistress feeling isolated. She does not have the built-in social networks of hostesses in entertainment venues, or of streetwalkers and sex workers in small brothels. Her client may seek to control her social interactions, out of fear that she might be tempted to violate the commitment to monogamy that she made when she agreed to be a kept woman. Even without direct client pressure, she might withdraw from her social circles out of shame for entering into this type of relationship. The arrangement also places her in a position of vulnerability, as her financial stability depends entirely on her relationship with one individual. When it dissolves, she stands to instantly lose both her home and her source of income. Emotions are central to the ways in which mistresses and clients talk about their relationship. Women use the presence of feelings for their client to justify their decision to become kept women, and clients use it to contrast with their marital relationship, which they often view as an obligation lacking in affection. The emotional hold second wives have on their clients can be an important source of power that allows them to extract significant wealth from them. These women usually do not have much to say about the state, as it rarely intervenes in their lives. When they do engage with it, it is because their client might be a government official, or when they serve as whistleblowers denouncing corruption to which they have been exposed in the course of relationships with Chinese elites.

Public opinion in China is attuned to the different work environments across tiers of sex work. It vacillates between disgust and profound sympathy for women who solicit on the streets and in small brothels. Hostesses evoke a very different response: The image of these women cavorting with men in karaoke bars and clubs, instead of engaging in upstanding forms of labor, tends to elicit disapproval and disdain. Similarly, mistresses and second wives rarely elicit much pity. Instead, they receive endless amounts of blame for contributing to the moral decline of Chinese society.

Despite very real differences in their work environments and daily lives, sex workers in the different tiers of prostitution share a number of experiences and perspectives. Many have migrated from rural to urban areas in search of better economic opportunities. They often first find employment in factories and restaurants, and become exposed to prostitution by talking to friends or acquaintances who earn significantly more in the sex industry. The transition to selling sex is made easier by the fact that sex workers in each tier overwhelmingly deny that they engage in prostitution, as they believe that "actual" prostitution is a one-time sexual encounter with a stranger with whom one establishes no personal rapport. In contrast, they emphasize the personal relationships they have with their clients. For mistresses and second wives, this comes through in the central role that emotions play in the narratives they tell about their relationship with their client. Hostesses underscore the connections they develop with clients as they get to know them over the course of an evening spent drinking, singing, and dancing, and often mention waiting to sell sex until they have hosted the client several times at their entertainment venue. The claim that they are not engaging in prostitution is most striking when it comes from low-tier sex workers. From the outside, they are participating in exactly the types of transactions from which mistresses and hostesses seek to distinguish themselves. But streetwalkers and women who solicit in small brothels see things differently – they talk about clients as friends and acquaintances with whom they establish a good connection when negotiating a sexual transaction.

This denial coexists with a variety of other shared views that highlight sex worker recognition of the moral gray zone of the actions from which they derive their source of livelihood. They hide their work from their family and friends. They justify their decision to sell sex on financial grounds, and emphasize the temporary nature of this work as a stepping stone toward a more respectable situation. They make the case that their work is undervalued and explain how it contributes to economic growth, societal and familial well-being, and state strength. The sense of shared identity that comes from reliance on the same source of income is at its strongest when they come into contact with sex work grassroots organizations. These groups provide sex workers with sources of support and can also introduce them to transnational sex work civil society networks. While interactions with these groups are rare due to their small numbers, they can provide sex workers with experiences of community and belonging that can be profoundly transformative.

The state is never far from the lives of sex workers in China. It might make itself more or less present in their daily routines and engage with them in ways that are more or less direct. Yet through the laws and policies it creates to regulate prostitution and the choices its frontline officials make about how to implement them, the state influences virtually every aspect of sex workers' lives as it contends with the implications of prostitution on policing, health, and economic growth in China.

Exchanging sex for money or other material goods is always against the law in China, regardless of who engages in it. Yet in practice, it is streetwalkers and women who solicit in small brothels who bear the brunt of anti-prostitution policies. Police officers target them for arrest more often than they target hostesses, and stay even farther away from mistresses and second wives. Low-tier sex workers are also subject to the harshest punishments: They are more likely to be incarcerated, while their middle-tier colleagues are more likely to be fined. And any time a sex worker is arrested, she is vulnerable to police abuse – frontline police officers sometimes treat sex workers brutally.

Until 2019, incarceration for prostitution in China usually occurred in the country's custody and education centers. These spaces held great symbolic importance: They were designed in the PRC's early years to rehabilitate women who sold sex and emerged from the belief that a communist political system could eradicate the exchange of sex for money or other material goods from its society. As prostitution continued to thrive in contemporary China, these centers morphed into mere punitive institutions. Their abolition in 2019 signaled official resignation to one aspect of the gulf that separates the ideology upon which the Chinese Communist Party (CCP) built its legitimacy and the country's social, political, and economic reality. Since then, sex workers have simply been incarcerated in nonspecialized institutions.

Clients are mostly absent from this law enforcement picture. When they do encounter the police, they are more likely to be fined than incarcerated. There is, however, an important instance when clients take center stage: when they are elites who cross the CCP. In such situations, the state unearths their target's sexual transgressions along with a variety of other illegal activities in order to orchestrate his public downfall. When this happens, the policing of prostitution leaves the realm of street-level law enforcement officers and enters the purview of government corruption investigations.

In deciding how to approach prostitution in their community, street-level police officers balance a variety of different and sometimes conflicting pressures. On one level, they need to enforce anti-prostitution laws. They experience pressures from the policing hierarchy above them to do so: The threat of arrest serves to deter some individuals from buying or selling sex, leads others to do so out of the public eye, and signals more broadly that the law matters in China. They also enforce in response to societal pressures to rid the community of the eyesore of sex work. For these reasons, enforcement contributes to maintaining law and order in the country.

On another level, however, frontline law enforcement officers need the local economy to thrive. Indeed, they are beholden to the priorities of the local government, which controls the police budget and local leadership appointments. Those priorities include economic growth – the legitimacy of the CCP rests on it, and it factors into the professional advancement of local government officials. Since the entertainment industry, with prostitution at its heart, plays an important role in local economic growth, frontline police interfere with it at their own peril. It does not help matters that local police officers are underfunded, overworked, and mostly left to their own devices when it comes to issues other than protest control. Under these circumstances, it makes sense for the police to arrest low-tier sex workers, while giving hostesses and mistresses more leeway. Yet unfortunately for the police, their interactions with the sex industry do not end there. In addition, they need to manage the threats to law and order that accompany a thriving middle tier of prostitution without systematically enforcing laws against prostitution. They do so by establishing relationships and systems that allow them to easily communicate information to individuals in the sex industry and by making themselves readily available to sex workers who need assistance. These practices underscore the precarious position of street-level police officers, which can result in nimble and attentive interactions with sex workers and gatekeepers.

Local health officials struggle even more than their law enforcement colleagues to fulfill their responsibilities vis-à-vis prostitution. They are tasked with implementing policies to both accurately determine the prevalence of HIV/AIDS among sex workers and to effectively reduce its occurrence in ways that respect individual sex workers' rights. Achieving these goals would require attending to low-tier sex workers, who present the greatest public health risks, and gaining their consent and trust. Instead, health workers focus mainly on hostesses, who are much easier to reach. They also coerce sex workers to participate in interventions and engage in other practices that veer away from the rules. The implications of these choices are grave: They result in incorrect data on sex worker HIV/AIDS infection rates and sexual behavior, deprive those sex workers most in need of valuable interventions, and constitute serious rights violations of some of China's most vulnerable citizens. As with the police, many of these misdirected practices are the result of local health officials' efforts to contend with the pressures and barriers that emanate from a variety of state and societal forces. In fact, they have it decidedly worse than their law enforcement colleagues, who, with greater power and a prostitution mandate that conflicts with that of health officials, serve as one more obstacle around which health officials must navigate. Another obstacle is that sex workers and their gatekeepers are predisposed to push back against any state health interference in their lives. This challenge is especially hard to overcome given that local health officials have few formal powers to enforce health directives in the face of recalcitrant members of the community. In fact, this weakness extends throughout the hierarchy of the Chinese Center for Disease Control and Prevention, such that even when its higher-level officials detect a frontline officer engaging in problematic implementation, they cannot easily require more compliant behavior. It does not help that when it comes to HIV/AIDS, there is only one politically salient issue: reporting local infection rates that, regardless of their accuracy, are neither alarmingly high nor unbelievably low. It is to this number that frontline health officials and the local government are ultimately held accountable when it comes to sex worker health interventions, and this imperative compromises other public health objectives.

Lastly, any analysis of the Chinese state's approach to regulating sex worker health must account for its transnational roots. The global health community has shaped the content of China's sex work health policies in important ways. In the face of considerable resistance, it pushed to include nonpunitive outreach to sex workers when working with Chinese officials to develop the country's HIV/AIDS policies. And the core of China's sex worker outreach model – which includes both quantification and respect for sex workers' individual rights – reflects international best practices. Transnational public health actors have also influenced how China's elite public health officials talk, write, and think about sex work. Significant funding and support in the form of trainings and international exchanges have been crucial aspects of this process. Yet global health community representatives in China are noticeably disengaged from the problematic on-the-ground implementation practices that veer far from their ideals, are a disservice to public health goals, and harm sex workers. They largely accept the misleading version of sex worker outreach and data that the state presents to them, without keeping a close eye on the realities thus obscured. Granted, it is challenging to secure the type of access that would allow global health actors to peer behind the curated information that the state provides to them. Yet even without such access, it makes sense to anticipate trouble on the ground. Any program that includes both quantitative benchmarks and rights-based implementation practices with sex workers is bound to encounter obstacles in an authoritarian regime that seriously restricts the rights of even its most law-abiding citizens. And while the global public health community might seek reassurance in the idea that a request for numbers is rooted in scientific truth, this approach disconcertingly glosses over the inescapable political realities in which the production of these data is embedded.

THE XI JINPING ERA

I conducted most of the fieldwork for this book when Hu Jintao was in power. He led China from 2002 until 2012, presiding over a time of relative political openness. Elements of that environment shaped the regulatory portrait I have painted in these pages. For instance, under Hu Jintao, the state's heightened transparency about HIV/AIDS and willingness to engage with the global public health community to address it shaped how China designed its system to regulate the health of sex workers. Similarly, Hu Jintao created a space for grassroots organizations in China, allowing for the emergence of groups working with sex workers to improve their health, increase their rights awareness, and help them develop a sense of belonging to a larger community of sex workers.

When Xi Jinping came to power in 2013, he ushered in a much more repressive era. Characteristics of his regime that could reasonably be expected to reshape how sex workers have experienced the state and how local state officials have implemented prostitution policies in the past decade include a far-reaching campaign against corruption and indiscipline in the CCP, police reforms, and more stringent restrictions on the ability of foreign organizations and domestic nongovernmental groups to operate in China. Similarly, the repercussions of COVID-19 on the CCP's approach to public health also merit attention with respect to possible impacts upon the regulation of sex work. I hope that the curiosity of others might be piqued to examine the regulation of prostitution under Xi Jinping through the experiences of sex workers and frontline bureaucrats; in the meantime, I offer some reflections on what they might find.

Anti-Corruption Efforts

The campaign that Xi Jinping has undertaken against corruption and indiscipline in the CCP in the process of consolidating power is unprecedented in scope in the PRC.[1] Both high-level officials and local civil servants have fallen victim to it and, with the creation of the National Supervision Commission in 2018, its reach extends beyond members of the party to include anyone who performs a public duty – such as doctors, professors, and managers of state-owned enterprises.[2] When someone is targeted for a corruption investigation, their sex life frequently features in the narrative of their misdeeds.

Even though the anti-corruption campaign does not appear to have reduced the prevalence of prostitution in China,[3] it may have led some officials and prominent citizens to adjust their behavior. Matthew S. Erie noted that in 2017, in response to the anti-corruption campaign, the cars of PRC officials were no longer visible in front of entertainment venues and that karaoke bars with sex workers had been shut down.[4] Elanah Uretsky also remarked upon the closure of entertainment venues that relied on business from government officials, as well as the plummeting sales of luxury alcohol brands favored by Chinese elites.[5] Yet even if some Chinese elites (mainly government officials) are staying away from spaces where middle-tier prostitution occurs, enough other elites (more often nonstate employees such as businessmen) are continuing to patronize them, such that these spaces continue

1 Susan L. Shirk, "China in Xi's 'New Era': The Return to Personalistic Rule," *Journal of Democracy* 29, no. 2 (April 10, 2018): 22–36, https://doi.org/10.1353/jod.2018.0022.

2 Shirk; Fu Hualing, "Understanding the Evolving Relationship between the Party and the Law: The Case of China's National Supervision Commission," SSRN Scholarly Paper (Rochester, NY, December 6, 2020), https://doi.org/10.2139/ssrn.3743636.

3 See, e.g., Eileen Yuk-ha Tsang, *China's Commercial Sexscapes: Rethinking Intimacy, Masculinity, and Criminal Justice* (Toronto: University of Toronto Press, 2019); Guojun He and Wenwei Peng, "Guns and Roses: Police Complicity in Organized Prostitution," *Journal of Public Economics* 207 (March 2022): 104599, https://doi.org/10.1016/j.jpubeco.2022.104599.

4 Matthew S. Erie, "Anticorruption as Transnational Law: The Foreign Corrupt Practices Act, PRC Law, and Party Rules in China," *The American Journal of Comparative Law* 67, no. 2 (July 31, 2019): 233–79, https://doi.org/10.1093/ajcl/avz018.

5 Elanah Uretsky, *Occupational Hazards: Business, Sex, and HIV in Post-Mao China* (Stanford, CA: Stanford University Press, 2016), 4.

to thrive under Xi Jinping.[6] Furthermore, the individuals who are avoiding entertainment venues have probably not renounced the activities in which they previously engaged in such spaces. Instead, they are likely finding alternative and less conspicuous ways of fulfilling not only their sexual needs but also their professional networking ones.[7]

The example of Vietnam provides an instructive comparison when reflecting upon the capacity of state officials to adapt their combined sexual and professional behaviors to prevailing political pressures. According to Kimberly Kay Hoang's study of the sex industry in Vietnam from 2006 to 2010, officials and businessmen in that country used entertainment venues in ways similar to their counterparts in China.[8] Several years later, political pressures and a stagnating economy resulted in the high-profile arrest of some sex workers and clients, creating an environment in which elites then avoided such spaces. In the words of one of Hoang's informants, "It's too risky now. They will do anything to charge us for corruption, even if that means catching us naked in hotel rooms with sex workers."[9] Instead, government officials and businessmen started hosting private parties with madams and sex workers in their own homes.[10] As Hoang notes, Vietnam has not "eliminated the informal economy crucial to brokering business deals. Instead, new players must find new spaces of leisure and entertainment and invent new strategies to build informal relationships of trust."[11] I suspect that similar adaptations have occurred under Xi Jinping. The sex industry in China is likely adjusting to new political circumstances in ways that continue to allow for the three tiers of prostitution described in this book and the various functions they play within Chinese society.

Police Reforms

Xi Jinping's consolidation of power could also be expected to affect how frontline police officers enforce laws against prostitution and the other ways in which they engaged with the sex industry under Hu Jintao – including the collection of bribes and development of relationships

[6] James Palmer, "The Bro Code," *ChinaFile*, February 4, 2015, perma.cc/HMC4-3F9L; Tsang, *China's Commercial Sexscapes*.

[7] Uretsky, *Occupational Hazards*, 4.

[8] Kimberly Kay Hoang, *Dealing in Desire: Asian Ascendancy, Western Decline, and the Hidden Currencies of Global Sex Work*, 1st ed. (Oakland: University of California Press, 2015).

[9] Hoang, 177.

[10] Hoang, 177.

[11] Hoang, 178.

that allowed them to both communicate important order maintenance information to sex workers and their gatekeepers and also protect them from harm. After all, such behavior falls within the scope of corruption and CCP indiscipline, and Xi Jinping was quick to focus on the Ministry of Public Security (MPS) when he became China's leader. First, he purged Zhou Yongkang, former head of the MPS and member of the Politburo Standing Committee, known as China's security czar, expelling him from the party and having him sentenced to life in prison for corruption.[12] Xi Jinping also purged some of Zhou's prominent colleagues.[13] Beyond this shake-up of the elite, Xi issued ambitious police reforms in 2015 that signaled his attention to the institution more broadly.[14] Despite the potential of these reforms to shift the everyday crime control practices of street-level police officers tied to issues such as prostitution, the available evidence suggests that such changes are not occurring. Instead, regime stability issues such as protest control are garnering the most attention.[15] For instance, Suzanne E. Scoggins notes that the reforms do not directly address local police corruption or the need to articulate specific steps to eliminate misconduct of frontline officers, nor have MPS officials implemented any such interpretation of the reforms.[16] Furthermore, street-level police officers remain underfunded, with no apparent increase in supervision from higher up within the police hierarchy.[17] With neither additional support to actually implement policies appropriately nor better monitoring of their behavior, police officers under Xi Jinping have little ability or reason to alter their approach to prostitution in their communities.

Restrictions on Foreign and Grassroots Organizations

Xi Jinping is much more suspicious of foreign organizations than his predecessor was. China's Foreign NGO law, which took effect in 2017, has shifted oversight of international organizations from the Ministry of Civil Affairs to the MPS, and has greatly increased the bureaucratic

[12] Suzanne E. Scoggins, "Authoritarian Policing under Xi Jinping," *Journal of Chinese Political Science* (July 23, 2022): 12, https://doi.org/10.1007/s11366-022-09825-z; "Profile: China's Fallen Security Chief Zhou Yongkang," *BBC News*, July 29, 2014, sec. China, perma.cc/8NT8-EGJX.

[13] Scoggins, "Authoritarian Policing under Xi Jinping," 12.

[14] Scoggins, "Authoritarian Policing under Xi Jinping."

[15] Scoggins.

[16] Scoggins, 12.

[17] Scoggins, 13, 18.

hurdles they must overcome in order to work in China.[18] Relations between China and the West have soured since Xi came to power, with wide-ranging consequences across most areas, including the types of collaborations that played pivotal roles in developing HIV/AIDS and sex work public health programs under Hu Jintao. For instance, the US Centers for Disease Control and Prevention went from about fifty staff members at its Beijing office in the 2010s to just a handful by 2020.[19] This wariness of international influence extends to domestic grassroots groups: In 2013, the CCP issued a communiqué that criticized civil society as a "Western value" that poses a threat to China.[20] The party has followed up with harsh crackdowns on a variety of different types of grassroots organizations and activists, and the Foreign NGO Law makes it difficult for such groups to receive international funding.[21] Although these shifts have been transformative on many levels,[22] I would expect them to have a relatively minimal impact on the lives of sex workers. China's public health infrastructure is now much more developed than it was when Hu Jintao came to power, and it no longer relies on foreign expertise or funding as it did when it was developing its HIV/AIDS program.[23] It has the technical knowledge and resources to carry out sex worker HIV/AIDS testing and outreach regardless of the current state of China's foreign relations. And sex worker civil society was already a small, marginalized, and bare-bones community under Hu Jintao – the increased restrictions of recent years have had a much greater impact in areas where such organizations previously thrived, such as the environment.[24]

COVID-19

Of course, COVID-19 upended many characteristics of sex work and its regulation in China. Its visibility and prevalence temporarily dropped.

[18] Joan Kaufman, "Civil Society Involvement in National HIV/AIDS Programs," in *HIV/AIDS in China: Epidemiology, Prevention and Treatment*, ed. Zunyou Wu et al. (Singapore: Springer, 2020), 438, https://doi.org/10.1007/978-981-13-8518-6_22.

[19] Deborah Seligsohn, "The Rise and Fall of the US-China Health Relationship," *Asian Perspective* 45, no. 1 (2021): 203–24, https://doi.org/10.1353/apr.2021.0023.

[20] Samson Yuen, "Friend or Foe?: The Diminishing Space of China's Civil Society," *China Perspectives; Wanchai*, no. 3 (2015): 51.

[21] Yuen, "Friend or Foe?"; Anthony J. Spires, "Regulation as Political Control: China's First Charity Law and Its Implications for Civil Society," *Nonprofit and Voluntary Sector Quarterly* 49, no.3 (October 25, 2019): 581, https://doi.org/10.1177/0899764019883939; Kaufman, "Civil Society Involvement in National HIV/AIDS Programs."

[22] Seligsohn, "The Rise and Fall of the US-China Health Relationship."

[23] Seligsohn.

[24] Yuen, "Friend or Foe?"

With every lockdown (of which there were many under China's "zero-Covid" policy), the businesses that harbor sex work would close their doors. The use of online apps to communicate with clients and provide online sexual services, peripheral to prostitution in the Hu Jintao era but on the rise under Xi Jinping,[25] increased. Backed by the full force of the state, frontline police and public health officials directed much of their attention to enforcing policies aimed at containing the pandemic and monitoring its spread. In that process, health surveillance, outreach, monitoring, and healthcare focused on other issues – including HIV/AIDS – have suffered.[26]

Some of these shifts could have longer-term impacts on prostitution and the choices the state makes with respect to its policing and public health regulation, and merit further attention over the next few years. The most likely source of possible changes to the regulatory dynamics that characterized sex work under Hu Jintao is China's overhaul of its public health bureaucracy. This was announced in 2021, in response to concerns that the previous structure impeded rapid flow of information about COVID-19 from local to national authorities.[27] The health bureaucracy's weakness lies at the root of its problematic health practices vis-à-vis sex workers, and a more empowered health agency with better funding and more qualified staff at all levels of the bureaucracy might not need to tiptoe around entertainment venues and local police officers to implement surveillance and outreach. Indeed, according to public health professionals, these same problems are at the root of China's failed handling of COVID-19: the CDC's lack of enforcement power, low budget, and small and weakly skilled staff.[28] Whether the 2021 reforms will successfully address these concerns, and, if so, how

[25] Tsang, *China's Commercial Sexscapes*, 150.

[26] Xueying Yang et al., "HIV Service Interruptions during the COVID-19 Pandemic in China: The Role of COVID-19 Challenges and Institutional Response from Healthcare Professional's Perspective," *AIDS and Behavior* 26, no. 4 (April 1, 2022): 1270–78, https://doi.org/10.1007/s10461-021-03484-6; Lingen Shi et al., "The Impact of COVID-19 Pandemic on HIV Care Continuum in Jiangsu, China," *BMC Infectious Diseases* 21 (August 7, 2021): 1–9, https://doi.org/10.1186/s12879-021-06490-0.

[27] Dennis Normile, "China Overhauls Its Public Health Bureaucracy," *Science* 372, no. 6544 (May 21, 2021): 779, https://doi.org/10.1126/science.372.6544.779.

[28] Junfang Xu, Yu Shi, Feng Cheng, and Wannian Liang, "China's Public Health System: Time for Improvement," *The Lancet Public Health* 6, no. 12 (December 1, 2021): e869–e870, https://doi.org/10.1016/S2468-2667(21)00250-4; Jennifer Bouey, "China's Health System Reform and Global Health Strategy in the Context of COVID-19" (RAND Corporation, 2020), https://doi.org/10.7249/CTA321-1; Zhou Yu (周羽) and Liao Kaidi (廖开迪), "Zhong Nanshan: Yao Tigao Woguo Jikong Zhongxing De Diwei (钟南山: 要提高我国疾控中心的地位) [Zhong Nanshan: We Need to Elevate the Position of Our CDCs]," *Yangguang News* (央广网), February 27, 2020, perma.cc/H5J6-KYRT.

they might affect the specific issue of sex work, are open questions. Yet it is worth approaching the idea that these public health reforms will lead to meaningful improvements with a healthy dose of skepticism. That would require monumental shifts not only within the health bureaucracy but also throughout the political system that, instead of rewarding transparency, continues to create incentives for local level officials to hide or distort problems in their communities.

All in all, the changes that have accompanied Xi Jinping's reign have been seismic in many areas of Chinese politics, law, economics, and society, with wide-ranging implications both domestically and across the globe. On the margins, they have touched sex work in China. Some elites have adjusted their choices of where to buy sex, eager to avoid falling victim to Xi Jinping's anti-corruption campaign. Sex workers hoping to create organized communities of support and advocacy and to seek international assistance in that process are likely to encounter even greater resistance nowadays. And COVID-19 put a temporary hold on the normal routines of sex workers, police officers, and health officials, and spurred institutional reforms that could affect sex worker public health outreach.

Furthermore, China has experienced increased hostility to research under Xi Jinping, and the study of prostitution, and sexuality more generally, has not escaped this more constrained academic climate.[29] Most notably, prominent sexologist Pan Suiming received an administrative penalty for reportedly "swindling State scientific research funds," including "failure to provide invoices of payments to sex workers during interviews."[30] He was demoted, and forced to retire early.[31] Yet, while it may be more difficult to conduct research on sex work under Xi Jinping, there is little reason to suspect that the lives of low-tier sex workers, hostesses, and mistresses have changed in ways that fundamentally alter the types of experiences and attitudes recounted in this book. Similarly, when it comes to prostitution in their communities, the behavior of frontline police officers and health officials, the challenges they face, and their approaches to addressing them likely resonate with their approaches to regulating sex work under Hu Jintao. In thinking about China today, it is easy to focus on the country's many

[29] Petula Sik Ying Ho et al., "Sex With Chinese Characteristics: Sexuality Research in/on 21st-Century China," *The Journal of Sex Research* 55, no. 4–5 (2018): 493, https://doi.org/10.1080/00224499.2018.1437593.

[30] Wanli Yang, "Sexologist Punished for Swindling Research Funds," *China Daily*, October 29, 2014, perma.cc/2GUQ-RNTF.

[31] Yang.

changes since the early years of the twenty-first century. Yet by keeping our eyes and ears close to the ground and observing how citizens and representatives of the state carry out their daily lives, we might uncover significant evidence of continuity that larger narratives of change belie.

POLICY IMPLICATIONS

A natural question to ask while reading (and writing) a book on how female sex workers and state officials experience the regulation of prostitution in China is what the regulations *should* be in the country, based on the empirical data I collected and have encountered in the studies of others. Of the three ideal types of prostitution policies described in Chapter 3 – prohibition, decriminalization, and legalization – none is a silver bullet.[32] As Michaele Ferguson observes, "Regardless of whether they aim at abolition, decriminalization, or legalization, sex work policies all have the effect of benefiting some sex workers while harming others."[33] Yet considering the respective characteristics of these policies in light of the attributes of prostitution on the ground in China, I support legalization, which is also the opinion of the majority of sex workers whose voices inform this study.

Sex workers clearly display agency in the experience of engaging in prostitution. A policy of legalization acknowledges that agency. At the same time, it provides the state with space to address many aspects of prostitution that sex workers find harmful. It facilitates safer working conditions and allows for better access to healthcare and other social services. In contrast, the ubiquity of prostitution in the country belies China's current abolitionist policy. And while a decriminalization approach might keep sex workers out of trouble with law enforcement, it does not provide them with other forms of supports and services.

Models of legalized prostitution vary widely around the world. There is no one-size-fits-all model, because thoughtful approaches to legalization are responsive to the realities of national and local variations in politics, economics, and society. For the legalization of sex work to succeed in China, the policy development process would need to involve careful consultation with all local stakeholders – including sex workers – and adapt to local circumstances. As my research highlights, it would also require thinking carefully about actual implementation practices, which

[32] See Chapter 3 for more discussion of these three approaches to the legal status of prostitution.
[33] Michaele L. Ferguson, "Beyond Gender Politics? Mainstreaming the Study of Sex Work," *Perspectives on Politics* 13, no. 2 (June 2015): 442, https://doi.org/10.1017/S1537592715000250.

in China today diverge in significant ways from the formal rules. Any changes to the official regulations are similarly unlikely to have their intended effects on the lives of sex workers, police officers, and health officials if they assume that on-the-ground practices will neatly mirror the content of the policies instead of contending seriously with the many obstacles to implementation that local realities present. An empirically informed approach to legalizing sex work in China should also recognize the presence of a variety of markets for sex in the country and the different challenges they present within society and for the state. Writing about India's sex industry, Prabha Kotiswaran challenges the assumption "that one national level law can realize its goals in highly disparate settings" and instead proposes "regulatory models tailored for specific sex markets."[34] Michaele Ferguson makes a similar point when she cautions against policies "that treat all sex work as the same (e.g., as street walking), and those that treat all sex workers as the same (e.g., as coerced or trafficked)."[35] Similarly, a policy of legalizing prostitution in China should vary in accordance with the different experiences of female sex workers in China's tiers of prostitution. For instance, it might make sense to learn from how the Netherlands, Germany, and Austria have legalized prostitution, adopting different rules for brothel prostitution and streetwalking, and using zoning restrictions to further manage sex work in the community.

There is no harm in reflecting upon alternative prostitution rules and approaches to developing them in China today. Yet doing so is of limited practical utility because it is ideology, rather than empirical data, that shapes prostitution policy decisions in the country. All prostitution is against the law in China because the CCP's political ideology defines itself against prostitution's existence. Any policy reform that involves legalizing or decriminalizing sex work inherently challenges the belief system upon which the CCP came to power, and the symbolism that accompanied the party's claim, upon coming to power, that it had eradicated this feudal remnant of the country's colonial past. Of course, the party is certainly capable of rhetorical contortions to accommodate this type of ideological tension. After all, while capitalism is theoretically antithetical to communism, the CCP has opened up its membership to entrepreneurs. Nevertheless, an official regulatory change away from the prohibition of prostitution would

34 Prabha Kotiswaran, *Dangerous Sex, Invisible Labor: Sex Work and the Law in India* (Princeton, NJ: Princeton University Press, 2011), 247.

35 Ferguson, "Beyond Gender Politics?," 442.

draw unwanted attention as one more political, economic, and societal contradiction coexisting in China today.

China's ideological obstacles to prostitution policy reform are specific to its political system. Yet scholars of sex work more attuned to Western and democratic states are no strangers to ideology-based challenges to prostitution policy. In that environment, the issue is often framed as one of "morality politics" – a concept whose characteristics include "being ruled by ideology," "resistant to facts," and a sense that "the symbolism of policy formulation is seen as more important than policy implementation."[36] While these descriptions resonate strongly with the CCP's approach to sex work policy, "morality politics" is not a term commonly used to reflect on contemporary China. Indeed, many of the other issues often subsumed under that category in the Western and Judeo-Christian world – such as abortion, contraception, gambling, same-sex marriage, and capital punishment – do not present the same ideological obstacles in China as prostitution. For instance, the CCP has actively endorsed abortion and contraception since the 1970s, in its efforts to curb population growth. Yet when it comes to the possibility of meaningful changes to how the state governs sex work, the initial response to questions about what empirically informed regulations should look like is the same in any place that prohibits prostitution. Ideology is the primary obstacle to overcome. Until that happens, it is unrealistic to expect that sex work might be legalized in China.

In the meantime, I have a much more modest proposal that transnational actors could pursue to improve the quality of life of some of China's female sex workers: support more nongovernmental centers in the country's red-light districts. These centers would provide sex workers with spaces to convene, find respite from their workplaces, develop more consciousness of sex worker rights, seek healthcare, and obtain other types of support. Implementing such a plan would not be without obstacles, including Xi Jinping's hostility toward civil society, the many difficulties that international organizations encounter on the ground in China, and the particular sensitivity of working with a population of individuals engaged in an illegal activity. Yet creative, discreet ways of supporting the development of such spaces are available. Based upon

[36] Hendrik Wagenaar and Sietske Altink, "Prostitution as Morality Politics or Why It Is Exceedingly Difficult to Design and Sustain Effective Prostitution Policy," *Sexuality Research and Social Policy* 9, no. 3 (September 2012): 279–92, https://doi.org/10.1007/s13178-012-0095-0.

the transformational impact they can have on sex workers who cross their paths, they are well worth the effort of pursuing.

A FINAL WORD

Lastly, if the reader comes away with one lasting impression from this book on law in the everyday lives of sex workers, police officers, and public health officials in China, my hope is that it is centered around an understanding of and empathy for the sex workers who are at its heart and, by extension, those who preceded them and those who have since succeeded them – not only in China, but everywhere. At best, they are overlooked. Indeed, it takes effort to be aware and remind ourselves of their existence, much of which unfolds behind closed doors and in hidden, liminal, or marginal parts of our communities. At worst, they are scorned – blamed for making poor choices, criticized for being lazy, and held responsible for breaking up marriages, destroying families, and weakening the social fabric underlying communities of "upstanding" citizens. These individuals, however, deserve so much more. As a society, we can approach the decision to engage in sex work and the experiences of those who do so with respect, empathy, humility, and a desire to learn. We need to develop a greater recognition of the diversity inherent in prostitution and the wide variety of circumstances and perspectives of people who sell sex. Most importantly, we should not reduce people who sell sex to their participation in prostitution. They are multifaceted individuals who deserve to be viewed in their full humanity. This book aims to further that goal.

APPENDIX A

ABOUT THE RESEARCH

When I talk about this project, people often ask me how I was able to carry it out. Two different lines of inquiry are embedded in that question. The first is logistical, focused on the process of accessing the people whose stories fill this book's pages. The second concern is more personal, focused on what the experience was like for me. Both elements of the question recognize the challenges inherent in conducting fieldwork on any topic in an authoritarian country such as China. They also acknowledge the added difficulties of studying a phenomenon such as prostitution, which is illegal, politically sensitive, and morally transgressive. The response that I usually provide in public settings is a pithy "It took blood, sweat, and tears," followed by a few words on spending a long time in the field and being persistent. That answer is not inaccurate. Yet it fails to convey the intensity of my fieldwork experience. In this appendix, I elaborate on both logistical and personal aspects of my experience conducting research on prostitution in China during the Hu Jintao era. This discussion is important: It could be valuable to others seeking insight into how they might approach the study of similar phenomena in comparable settings; it allows me to highlight some of the limitations of my methodological approaches; and it provides a reflection on the toll this type of work can take on the researcher – information that is often excluded from accounts of fieldwork.

That said, I am uncomfortable with the question of how I carried out this research because it makes me the locus of attention. This is a book about individual human beings in difficult life circumstances. On a daily basis, they struggle with significant challenges, and their futures are likely bleak. I accompanied some of them temporarily on their paths. In the process, as ethnographers do, I internalized aspects of their lives.[1] But it

[1] Matthew Desmond, for instance, describes ethnography as "what you do when you try to understand people by allowing their lives to mold your own as fully and genuinely as possible. You do this by . . . observing and experiencing what they do . . . .until you think like they think,

was not my life. In situations that were deeply uncomfortable, I would remind myself that I was in fact free to leave, even if doing so might be offensive or have a negative impact on my research.[2] The coping strategy I used was to instead focus on the fact that the specific encounter that felt uneasy would be coming to a close, usually in a matter of hours. I also knew that my immersive fieldwork had a concrete end date, after which I would physically leave behind all of the people and spaces shaping my understanding of sex work in China. I would then continue to make sense of that world within the offices and conference rooms of Western academic institutions, thousands of miles away. The people whose life stories have left an imprint upon every page of this book do not have that luxury.

ACCESSING PLACES AND PEOPLE

In the summer of 2005, I carried out preliminary research for this project in Beijing. I spent those weeks meeting with members of various grassroots and international organizations working in the fields of women's rights, law, and public health. I became familiar with the HIV/AIDS work that public health agencies, grassroots groups, and international organizations were doing in China tied to prostitution. As I discuss in Chapter 3, China began to prioritize its HIV/AIDS crisis in the early 2000s. This relative openness around the epidemic created opportunities for individuals working in those organizations to engage with the issue of prostitution and also made it possible for them to welcome a foreign researcher's inquiries on that subject. By the end of that trip, I was reasonably confident that I would be able to carry out a qualitative project on the regulation of prostitution in China, whose empirical core would come from interviews with members of the HIV/AIDS public health community focused on prostitution. When I returned to China three years later, in summer 2008, to begin my fieldwork, I reconnected with that community. I also cast my net wider, both in terms of the types of individuals I contacted and the research

and feel something like they feel." Matthew Desmond, *Evicted: Poverty and Profit in the American City*, 1st ed. (New York: Crown Publishers, 2016), 317–318. Kimberly Kay Hoang, referencing Erving Goffman, discusses carrying out fieldwork that "enables the researcher to feel as her participants feel." Kimberly Kay Hoang, *Dealing in Desire: Asian Ascendancy, Western Decline, and the Hidden Currencies of Global Sex Work*, 1st ed. (Oakland, CA: University of California Press, 2015), 193.

2 Reflecting on this issue of exit, Hoang notes how "I always knew that I could hit the eject button at any moment and put an end to my research." Hoang, *Dealing in Desire*, 23.

methods I used. In December 2009, after nineteen months of fieldwork in China, I had conducted almost 200 interviews in cities throughout the country. Interviewees included sex workers, madams, pimps, clients, staff of domestic and international nongovernmental organizations, and local- and central-government officials working in policing, health, and other state agencies. Furthermore, I had surveyed 568 sex workers in a red-light district in Beijing, and eighty-nine police officers in a city in southern China. Finally, and of greatest value in terms of the insights it provided, I had carried out ethnographic observation in communities of sex workers, public health officials, and police officers.

The Places

I started my fieldwork in Beijing because of the city's high concentration of individuals and organizations that could serve as potential informants and points of entry. From there, opportunities to connect with sex workers, public health officials, or police officers led me to Shenzhen, Guangzhou, Dongguan, Shanghai, Harbin, Shenyang, Changsha, as well as two smaller cities in the provinces of Hebei and Hubei (which I refer to with the pseudonyms Fushan and Zhengti, respectively).[3] I also interviewed individuals in Hong Kong who have expertise pertaining to prostitution in mainland China.

As is often the case for fieldwork-intensive projects in China, this was the only approach that opened doors to populations that are difficult to access and that established the trusting connections necessary for collecting rich data. Yet this process also presents challenges around issues of representativeness and generalizability. How might findings based on the experiences, attitudes, and opinions of people located in these cities inform our understanding of the regulation of prostitution elsewhere in China?

It helps that these cities vary considerably based on their geographic locations, population sizes, and levels of wealth. While Changsha, Harbin, and Zhengti are all inland, the others are all coastal cities, spread out from north to south. The smallest cities I observed were Fushan and Zhengti, with populations around 1.5 million each.[4] By contrast, Shanghai (27 million) and Beijing (21 million) are the two most populous cities in the country. I learned about sex work in China's

[3] I use pseudonyms when referencing these two smaller cities in order to protect the identities of my informants there.

[4] China has more than 100 cities with a population over 1 million, so Fushan and Zhengti are not considered especially large in the Chinese context.

wealthiest cities (Shanghai, Beijing, Shenzhen, and Guangzhou), as well as in cities with average levels of wealth (Fushan and Zhengti). Rural areas are largely missing from this picture, as are the country's poorest cities and those located in western China. I did catch some glimpses of them: through the eyes of the many sex workers I encountered who had migrated from rural China; from the abject poverty that characterizes the lives of streetwalkers in even the wealthiest of Chinese cities; and in stories of public health officials, researchers, and staff of organizations who had firsthand experiences in those places. I hope future research on the regulation of prostitution in China will train a more sustained gaze on these places.

Yet when it comes to the urban China I came to know, mine is a story of similarities, rather than differences, across space. I did not expect this to be the case. In fact, I had planned to focus primarily on explaining variation in levels of enforcement of prostitution regulations at the local level. For instance, when I asked about prostitution policing patterns, knowledgeable experts systematically painted a picture of high levels of efficient policing in Beijing, which they contrasted with lax enforcement in the southern cities of Dongguan, Guangzhou, and Shenzhen.[5] This expectation – differences in enforcement – guided the way I approached my first few months of fieldwork. Yet I struggled to identify concrete manifestations of it. Instead, streetwalkers in Beijing described their daily lives in ways that sounded very similar to those in Shenzhen. Police officers in northern cities talked about the challenges they face around prostitution using the same terms as their colleagues in southern cities. Public health officials everywhere discussed the difficulties of accessing sex workers and contending with law enforcement. As I listened and observed, I realized that the much more salient story was one of shared experiences of similar individuals across locations.

The People

Prostitution is a difficult topic of inquiry because it is about sex, which people can feel uncomfortable discussing. In places where sex work is against the law, its illegality shrouds it in an additional layer of sensitivity. Carrying out such research in an authoritarian country, where all words and actions are subject to the arbitrary power of an unchecked state, only complicates the process further. Why, then, did the people

[5] I interviewed several researchers and policy experts who made these claims. See, e.g., Interview 44, October 28, 2008; Interview 23, October 9, 2008; Interview 92, June 16, 2009; Interview 84, May 6, 2009; Interview 41, October 23, 2008.

whose experiences inform this book agree to talk with me, invite me into parts of their lives, put me in touch with their colleagues and friends, and vouch for me in their communities? The answers to this question are tied to how respondents perceived me and how I framed my interest in prostitution in China.

First, prostitution is not the worst offender on the spectrum of politically sensitive topics in China. That honor goes to issues that the state perceives as most threatening to its stability, such as protests and dissidents. The ubiquity of the exchange of sex for money does not reflect positively on China. It provides evidence of widespread, seemingly uncontrolled criminal behavior within society. It is also a jarring reminder of the disconnect between the communist political ideology upon which the People's Republic of China (PRC) was founded and the unbridled capitalism that has taken its place. Yet the presence of sex work does not distinguish China from other countries; it does not provide obvious fodder for outsiders to shame China for egregious violations of citizens' rights, or an inability to govern according to the norms and standards of Western democratic nations. In short, inquiries about prostitution do not raise the loudest alarm bells in China, an observation that likely factored into many of my respondents' decisions to engage with me on the issue and sometimes welcome me into their lives.[6]

Against that backdrop, a number of characteristics tied to my identity likely also nudged people to open up. As a white foreigner, it was immediately apparent to most people who saw me that I was not a member of their community. The recognition that I was a complete outsider – and that any information shared with me could not easily make its way back to an informant's colleagues, friends, and family – may have created a sense of security with my interlocutors. Sex workers did not need to worry that talking to me might result in people in their hometown learning that they engage in prostitution, and police officers and other government officials could criticize state policies knowing that such pronouncements would not make their way back to colleagues and superiors.[7] Respondents would also gravitate toward me because the novelty of a foreigner inquiring about prostitution in

[6] Given the increased repression that China has witnessed under Xi Jinping (2012–present), individuals might be more reluctant to engage with a researcher carrying out this type of project now. The perception widely shared among scholars is that the research environment under Xi is more restricted, and my personal experience, based on other projects I have pursued in recent years, confirms this assessment.

[7] The informed consent procedures I followed may have also reassured interviewees and encouraged them to engage with me. I received approval to carry out this study from the UC Berkeley

their community piqued their curiosity. In addition, widely held assumptions in China about greater sexual permissiveness in the West likely played to my advantage. When talking about sex, prostitution, and extramarital relationships, my interlocutors often contrasted "backwards" (落后 – *luohou*) China with a more "open" (开放 – *kaifang*) West. These views also translated into regulatory misconceptions: The great majority of people in China with whom I spoke about my research – members of the sex industry, government officials, and the general population – thought that sex work was legal in most Western countries, including the United States. Projected onto me, these assumptions likely meant that respondents felt I would not judge them for behaviors and attitudes that are highly stigmatized in their communities – such as buying or selling sex, engaging in extramarital affairs, or supporting legalized prostitution.

My elevated social status also likely worked in my favor: While society undervalues the sex workers, madams, and street-level officials whose stories inform this book, I was showing them that they mattered in the eyes of a researcher from a prestigious American institution. Being a woman was particularly helpful for connecting with female sex workers who cater to male clients, as it largely removed ambiguities around my interest in their lives: They were not trying to solicit me, and I was not trying to solicit them. It also facilitated conversations on a variety of personal matters, such as sexual experiences. In short, I came across not only as unthreatening but also as a desirable person with whom to engage, and this combination appeared to be at the heart of respondents' willingness to engage with me.

Strategic motivations might also have factored into an individual's decision to interact with me. Some respondents clearly felt that my presence by their side enhanced their status in the community. Mei Jie, the madam in Shenzhen who welcomed me into her life, very deliberately broadcast our association throughout her neighborhood. In the early evenings – the time of day that would guarantee maximum visibility in the community – we would leave her brothel, and she would link arms with me as we strolled methodically up and down the local streets and alleyways, stopping to chat with everyone she knew.

Office for the Protection of Human Subjects, CHPS Protocol #2008-9-15. In line with this approval, I assured all interviewees that any and all information they shared with me was confidential. When they were members of a vulnerable population (such as sex workers, madams, and pimps), I also confirmed that I would not be collecting any identifying information from them.

She always introduced me as a foreign researcher whom she was helping – she told this to her bank teller, the cell phone booth manager, nearby restaurant owners, and, my personal favorite, the local kung fu teacher who pulled his phone out to entertain me with videos of himself splitting bricks and performing various other complex martial arts moves. She rightly underscored how this process was for my benefit, as it made me a known entity in the community who had her stamp of approval. But it also enhanced her status, signaling to the outside world that she was sufficiently important to warrant the attention of an academic from the United States. Similarly, when a former law enforcement officer brought me back to his hometown and introduced me to his colleagues still on the local police force, other professional contacts, childhood friends, and family members, he was showing them that he had achieved a high status in his new career, which included forging connections with foreign researchers who were willing to travel halfway across China to benefit from his professional expertise.

Respondents also availed themselves of the concrete skills that I could provide, including English tutoring, editing, and translation, and advice for applying to foreign universities. Sex workers sometimes reached out to me for health advice, and I always responded to those requests with contact information for an organization that treated sex workers without bias and that was staffed by health professionals. As sex workers often assumed that prostitution is legal in most places outside of China, they also occasionally inquired about job prospects in the sex industry in other countries. I would correct their misconception, and also explain that I had only cursory familiarity with prostitution work conditions elsewhere. Lastly, some people appeared motivated to engage with me out of a shared commitment to the issues I was investigating. Grassroots organizations working with sex workers were eager for a platform that might amplify awareness of their concerns. Individual sex workers were sometimes committed to increasing knowledge about their experiences and grievances and those of their peers. Chinese Center for Disease Control and Prevention (CDC) officials who were trained medical and public health professionals – those working in Beijing, at the provincial level, and in major cities – are themselves researchers, and were happy to engage with another academic and share knowledge and data collection experiences.

The way that I framed my research for any given contact also shaped the access I received to people and the information they shared with me, and I adapted my narrative accordingly. When presenting my project to the sex worker community, I focused on the dearth of accurate information about sex workers in China and my desire to help remedy that situation by learning about their daily lives, experiences, thoughts, and opinions. To dispel concerns that I might seek to vilify sex work, or China, I discussed how sex workers in many other parts of the world experienced a variety of different struggles in their lives, and explained that I was curious to understand whether this was also the case in China. When talking to public health officials, I explained that I wanted to understand how China approaches the issue of sex work from the perspective of public health and that I hoped to learn about their personal experiences in that domain.

The framing stakes felt highest when I reached out to the police and other government officials who were not working in public health, as they were the most suspicious of my motivations. In these interactions, I explained that I wanted to understand how China managed the issue of prostitution. I noted that in the United States, where prostitution is against the law in most places, it was nevertheless quite prevalent and authorities really struggled to reduce its occurrence. I then mentioned China's stated achievement, under Mao, of ridding the country of prostitution, and how so few states had ever claimed a similar accomplishment. I told them I wanted to understand the regulation of prostitution in a place that had a more successful official record than the United States. I then underscored how I was particularly interested in learning about what it was like to be responsible for maintaining order around prostitution in the local community, and how in other countries, I heard that police officers and local officials experienced a great deal of pressure and stress managing this issue along with all their other professional duties. This approach was usually quick to disarm the skepticism I would initially encounter. When I started these conversations by praising elements of China's record, I usually elicited harsh assessments of the country's actual accomplishments, as respondents sought to dispel the myths I had referenced. Similarly, my inquiries into the struggles of frontline officers paved the way for thoughtful and critical engagement with the issues of sex work, crime control, and the challenges of policing in China.

While I tailored how I presented my project to each individual or community with whom I was engaging, I approached each person with a mindset of genuine humility and respect. On one level, this is a moral commitment – a decision about how one chooses to be in society. It was not always easy. I am predisposed to sympathize with sex workers, yet

I encountered plenty of circumstances that required concerted mental and emotional effort to stay in that space. I was inclined to be more skeptical of the police and state actors, but I sought to set aside their institutional affiliations and to think of them as human beings trying to navigate life in an authoritarian country for themselves and their loved ones. Yet on another level, my openness was also a beneficial professional commitment – it was a way of thinking that would yield the richest findings. It provided me with a wide field of vision as I inquired about, absorbed and interpreted what I was seeing and hearing. It also yielded rich data when interlocutors responded to it by drawing me into their lives.

Lastly, a broader observation underlies this entire reflection on how I connected with the people who made this book possible. Throughout my fieldwork, I was interacting with people who are rarely asked to talk about themselves. When I respectfully inquired into their lives, and expressed genuine curiosity about their experiences and opinions, I was placing value on aspects of their identity that are generally disregarded, yet about which they had much to say. More often than not, when an interview neared its end and I expressed heartfelt gratitude for everything my respondent had shared with me, she or he would in turn thank me for listening and providing them with a space to take a step back and reflect upon their lives. Many of my interlocutors commented on the therapeutic benefits of our interactions, a reaction that other ethnographers have also heard from their informants.[8] The sincere interest I showed in listening to their untold stories provided the momentum for people to consider engaging with me, reflect upon who they perceived me to be, and hear me out in my attempts to draw them in.

THE LOGISTICS: INTERVIEWS, SURVEYS, AND ETHNOGRAPHIC OBSERVATION

The access I secured provided me with opportunities to carry out interviews, surveys, and ethnographic observation. Appendix B provides a complete list of the interviews, including type of respondent and location. Appendices C and D provide additional information on the surveys. My focus here is to share more information on the process of carrying out these three types of data collection.

[8] For instance, Hoang mentions how clients she spoke with found their conversations to be "cathartic and therapeutic." Hoang, *Dealing in Desire*, 192. Similarly, Desmond underscores the psychological benefits that likely help explain why some people opened up to him, with some of them calling him their "shrink." Desmond, *Evicted*, 318.

Interviews

When I started my fieldwork in Beijing, I reached out to individuals and organizations conducting research or working in the fields of public health, women's rights, or rule of law to solicit interviews. I also reached out to colleagues and foreign journalists for suggestions of people to contact. From those various entry points, I relied mainly on snowball sampling to recruit interviewees, asking informants for recommendations of people to contact who were knowledgeable about prostitution, public health, or law enforcement. More than once in these early stages, a recommendation would come up that, based on my respondent's description, or some further investigation, seemed irrelevant. I would set it aside but return to the contact if their name came up a second time from another source. Some of my richest sources of access and information came from these individuals I had initially ignored, and I quickly learned to follow up with anyone whose name came my way. I continued to carry out interviews until their content started to sound repetitive and no longer provided me with new information.

The interviews I conducted ranged in length from thirty minutes to six hours, with most lasting between ninety minutes and two hours. They took place in coffee shops, tea houses, restaurants, respondent homes, brothels, karaoke venues, parks, offices, community centers, and taxi cabs. I would defer to my respondent's proposed interview location, in order to increase their level of comfort during our interactions.[9] When I was arranging to meet someone for the first time, I learned to specify that I was not ethnically Chinese, in case this affected their willingness to meet with me or their decision of where to meet.[10] For the most part, these were one-on-one interviews. While they often occurred in public spaces, these were also settings where both the interviewee and I felt comfortable that we were away from prying ears. Appendix B specifies those instances when I interviewed several people together.[11]

[9] The only respondents who invited me into their homes were individuals whom I had met previously, or who came recommended by a trusted colleague, friend, or other informant. These invitations did not feel like potentially dangerous situations where a stranger was proposing that we meet in an isolated location.

[10] Early on in my field research, I met with a visibly flustered civil society activist who, upon seeing me in the café where we had planned to meet, quickly ushered me into his organization's office nearby in order to avoid attracting unwanted attention. While I had introduced myself as a foreign researcher in our previous exchanges, he had assumed that I was ethnically Chinese.

[11] These situations would occur at the behest of the interviewees. When I showed up to unexpectedly find several people waiting to talk with me, I would usually suggest separate interviews, and oftentimes respondents had no objections.

I adopted a semi-structured approach to my interviews.[12] I had multiple interview guides that were tailored to the type of person I was interviewing. Prior to any meeting, I adapted the relevant guide to the specific individual based on any additional information I had already received about them. In the process of the actual interview, I let the flow of the conversation determine the order in which I posed questions. I also followed up with new questions based on my respondents' answers, and removed specific questions or entire lines of inquiry when it became apparent that they were either irrelevant or inappropriate. Over the course of each interview, I would regularly skim my interview guide in order to keep my inquiries on track.[13] I carried out all of my interviews with Chinese respondents in Mandarin Chinese.[14] When interviewing foreigners in China, we spoke in either English or French. I took handwritten notes, primarily in English but frequently interspersed with Chinese, and I strove to approximate a word-for-word translation/transcription of our conversation. As soon as possible after the actual interview, and always on the same day, I typed up all of my notes. I did not make audio or video recordings of any of my interviews, as I could not guarantee that my data would be completely secure from agents of the Chinese state. While I felt confident that state officials would not be able to identify a respondent based on interview notes, I worried they might be able to ascertain an informant's identity if they secured an audio recording of our conversation. Similarly, I was concerned that respondents might withhold information if I recorded the interview, and that even the act of requesting to record might alienate an already cautious interviewee.

When I interviewed sex workers I had recruited through the outreach community organization I partnered with in Beijing, I usually had a research assistant with me who made a second handwritten transcription of the interview, entirely in Chinese, which she also typed up that same day. This process provided me with more direct quotes for my data analysis and writing, since I cannot take handwritten notes in Chinese

[12] In Herbert J. Rubin and Irene S. Rubin, *Qualitative Interviewing: The Art of Hearing Data*, 3rd ed. (Thousand Oaks, CA: SAGE, 2011), the authors describe their approach as "responsive interviewing." Their discussion of what this entails resonates closely with how I carried out my interviews.

[13] I learned to condense all my questions on to one page so that I could do this as seamlessly as possible and avoid interrupting the flow of the conversation.

[14] Mandarin is the official language of the PRC. Yet individuals who have received less formal education and come from areas of the country where other dialects dominate in daily life might not speak it fluently. Some of the sex workers I interviewed fell into this category, but they always spoke enough Mandarin for us to have an intelligible conversation.

as fast as a native speaker can.[15] My research assistant was a young, female university student who was an unobtrusive presence during the interviews. If she affected my respondents, it did not come through in any obvious ways in either their demeanor or in the content that they shared with me, when compared with interviews I conducted without her.[16]

Surveys

I experienced many false starts with the sex worker and police officer surveys. When it involves face-to-face (rather than online) interactions, this method of data collection in China often catches the attention of prying eyes.[17] Interviews and participant observation can be carried out more discreetly. Furthermore, the data collected from those interactions – handwritten notes – are often perceived as relatively harmless. Surveys seem much more official. Answers are recorded from many people on standardized forms that produce aggregate numbers, which can feel more threatening to state officials than a sheet of handwritten notes. And since surveys involve recruiting sizeable numbers of participants, they can be difficult to conduct under the radar. In addition, formal approval is required to survey state actors such as the police, who would refuse to participate without the authorization of their superiors.

The sex worker survey false starts occurred in the two Shenzhen neighborhoods I refer to as Wanqin and Xizhou. A public health contact who had previously carried out research there recommended these locations, and invested considerable time and effort to introduce me to local community members and facilitate survey implementation. While survey enumerators were able to complete several dozen surveys

[15] I did not use any qualitative data software to analyze my interview and participant observation transcripts and notes. I read and reread them, and also organized specific sections of them thematically (for instance, "health," "policing," "low-tier sex work," etc.) by copying and pasting them into other documents.

[16] I did not have a research assistant for the other interviews I conducted for this book. The outreach community center was an ideal environment to carry out interviews with a research assistant: I was familiar with the space, it was safe for a research assistant, and she could easily leave if an interviewee expressed a preference to speak to me alone (which never happened). After conducting a few of them, I felt confident about their quality. I had less control over all aspects of interviews that took place elsewhere, with both sex workers and non-sex workers. I worried about possibly endangering my research assistant, alienating my informants, and compromising the quality of the information they might choose to share with me, particularly if they were government officials. This uncertainty led me to conduct them on my own. Lastly, it would have been logistically complicated and expensive to have a research assistant accompany me on all my interviews throughout China.

[17] It would not have been possible to reach sex workers or police officers through an online survey.

in these locations, the recruitment process was extremely laborious and became more difficult over time. We depended upon entertainment venue managers to open their doors to us, and they had limited incentives to do so. While a handful were willing to take a chance on us, we were never close to recruiting the several hundred sex workers I was hoping to survey.

We did have success in Beijing, largely due to help from the sex worker outreach organization I partnered with. For several years, this group had made itself a familiar presence in the community. Its staff members had good relationships with venue managers, madams, and pimps, who are generally long-term fixtures in the neighborhood. As described in Chapter 11, gatekeepers generally hesitate to open up their spaces to outsiders, due to the illegal nature of some of the activities they harbor.[18] Center staff worked to explain that they were not a government agency, and that their only motivation was improving sex workers' health. They further emphasized that venues would benefit from sex workers having tools to protect themselves from sexually transmitted diseases and other health risks. Over time, as it became evident that venues providing access to center staff were not attracting the authorities' unwanted attention, gatekeepers grew to trust the center and support its work. To be clear, most of the individual sex workers who participated in the survey had limited or no previous direct interactions with the center. They were transient migrants, and as such they were often not very familiar with the neighborhood and what it had to offer. They also number in the thousands when considering just those venues within a 100-meter radius of the center – too many for staff to connect with systematically. Yet the endorsement of their gatekeepers and colleagues – who assured sex workers that the survey was safe and confidential – was sufficient to assuage any concerns of the close to 600 sex workers who participated in it. It also helped that we could use the center's space to administer it: Gatekeepers who were supportive but did not want us at their place of work could encourage sex workers to participate at the center, and sex workers who wanted to take part unbeknownst to their colleagues and employers could seek us out there.

I carried out the survey of police officers through a research center that has extensive experience conducting police trainings throughout China. I worked closely with the center for months to design what we thought would be a survey of several hundred law enforcement officers,

[18] Gatekeepers are individuals such as madams, pimps, and entertainment venue managers.

randomly sampled from all police stations in a major Chinese city. Ultimately, it turned into a much more modest endeavor: The research center surveyed eighty-nine police officers in that city who participated in its trainings. While the research center made impressive inroads to secure local police agency approval for the larger project, the authorities ultimately deemed it too sensitive.

Ethnography

Most pages of this book bear the traces of my interviews and survey data. Yet at its heart, this project is an ethnography of the sex industry in China.[19] It is ethnographic in the sense that it involved participant observation, understood as "immersion in a community, a cohort, a locale, or a cluster of related subject positions ... [t]he premise is that one must be 'neck-deep' in a research context to generate knowledge based on that context."[20] Viewed from this lens, I can identify specific parts of my fieldwork that involved time spent observing the everyday lives of the people I was studying, and I describe the main ones in this section.[21] Just as importantly, I situate my research in a second understanding of ethnography, as "a *sensibility* that goes beyond face-to-face contact. It is an approach that cares – with the possible emotional engagement that implies – to glean the meanings that the people under study attribute to their social and political reality."[22] I carried this sensibility with me throughout this project, and it guided all aspects of my data collection – the participant observation, interviews, and surveys – as well as my data analysis and writing processes.

The participant observation elements of my fieldwork took place primarily at four sites. In Beijing, I was a regular presence at a sex worker outreach center from October 2008 to December 2009. I spent full days there for a total of about three months, mainly in the summer and fall of 2009. Outside of those more concentrated periods of time, I would stop by for a few hours on a regular basis, and stayed in touch with my main points of contact there via text, email, and phone. I also reconnected in

[19] Edward Schatz reflects upon how, "whenever ethnographic techniques are subsumed by different, nonethnographic sensibilities or techniques ... their character changes fundamentally." Edward Schatz, ed., *Political Ethnography: What Immersion Contributes to the Study of Power* (Chicago, IL: University of Chicago Press, 2009), 9. My project does the opposite, with ethnography subsuming interview and survey methods.

[20] Schatz, 5.

[21] As with interviews, I took detailed notes throughout the day and every evening to record my experiences of participant observation.

[22] Schatz, *Political Ethnography*, 5.

person during my return trips to Beijing in 2011 and 2014. While at the center, I spent most of my time talking to sex workers and staff members, participating in activities that staff organized to raise awareness about sex worker health and rights, and observing interactions among sex workers and between sex workers and staff members. I also carried out interviews of sex workers and staff in that space, and managed most aspects of the Beijing sex worker survey there. In addition, I accompanied the center's outreach workers to entertainment venues and outdoor spaces where sex workers congregated.

I also carried out participant observation in Wanqin and Xizhou, the two red-light districts in Shenzhen where I sought to survey sex workers. I first developed sex work community connections in those two neighborhoods through a public health contact during the spring of 2009. I returned in October and November 2009, living in a hotel in Wanqin that catered mostly to clients and sex workers. I describe these two red-light districts in Chapter 9. In Wanqin, I spent my days in Mei Jie's apartment-brothel, talking to Mei Jie, her sex workers, and occasionally to her clients. I also walked around the neighborhood with her, which helped me make connections with other members of the sex work community. In Xizhou, I spent my days outside in the main square, in the local government offices, and inside entertainment venues, talking to sex workers, madams, pimps, and neighborhood officials. In both places, three research assistants – young Chinese female undergraduate students – joined me when it was time to attempt implementing the survey. In Xizhou, we set up a table in the main square and spent time each day distributing sex education pamphlets and condoms. While the purpose was to recruit survey respondents, the experience provided an opportunity for local health officials, sex workers, pimps, madams, and unaffiliated community members to congregate, and I benefited from observing the ensuing interactions and conversations.

At my fourth site of more protracted participant observation, I spent time in a world of frontline police officers. This occurred in the summer of 2009, in the city that I refer to with the pseudonym of "Zhengti." A former police officer from there invited me to join him on a trip back to his hometown, where he returned regularly not only to see his family but also because, in his new line of work, he benefited from continuing to keep a pulse on his former colleagues' work. I felt like a stealth researcher in the town: My contact introduced me as a foreign friend who wanted to learn more about what his life as a police officer in

Zhengti had been like, and he initiated substantive conversations of interest to me so that I did not appear too inquisitive.

My days in Zhengti were long and action-packed. My contact spent hours driving me around, showing me the areas with high concentrations of sex workers, describing to me the changes he had observed over the years pertaining to the geography of prostitution in the city, and recounting specific instances of anti-prostitution enforcement he had engaged in when he had been an officer. He took me to police stations throughout Zhengti, showed me around, and introduced me to his former colleagues. They, in turn, took us around various neighborhoods as they provided my contact with community updates since his departure. We were wined and dined during lunch and dinner banquets. I sang karaoke and danced with Zhengti detectives and police station heads, and watched them play late-night games of mahjong. As discussed in Chapter 9, I observed hostesses entertain these law enforcement officers at a karaoke bar. I spent a day with a madam, who hosted us in her home and then took us to the brothel where she worked, on the grounds of a hotel and entertainment complex. My contact and his colleagues also took me on trips to river tube and swim in tributaries of the Yangtze River.

During these gatherings, my contact would initiate conversations about how work was going, and from there steer inquiries toward prostitution. When full group conversations would break up into smaller ones, I had the opportunity to inquire independently about issues of interest to me. In downtime between meetings and activities, my contact would debrief with me; repeat, elaborate, and contextualize information gleaned earlier; answer my questions; and prep me for our next encounter. Whenever the activities involved social events with other police officers, he brought along Lawyer Lu, a former female police officer colleague of his who had since left the force and now practiced law. Her presence balanced out situations when I would have been the only woman, and I appreciated the additional company – especially during late night, alcohol-imbued events. Lawyer Lu also served as a constant source of additional information, to whom I could turn to follow up on and clarify what I saw and heard. When we went on social day trips, my contact's young son came along, and his former colleagues also brought along their children.

In addition to these four sites, I also engaged in shorter instances of participant observation in the cities where I carried out my fieldwork. For instance, I attended a full-day retreat with sex work grassroots organizations; spent time in their offices scattered across the country; hung out with hostesses at karaoke bars; observed dynamics between sex workers, clients, and other passersby at a park known for soliciting prostitution; and attended meetings and observed activities at CDCs, hospitals, police stations, and law enforcement agencies.

Ethnography as a method also permeated my interviews and surveys. Much of what I learned in the process of conducting interviews is not reflected in the answers my informants gave to the questions I posed during the official part of a given interview. I viewed all the exchanges I had with an informant – both before the actual interview began and after it ended and I had closed my notebook – as potentially valuable sources of data. I paid careful attention to the interview location, particularly if it was a respondent's home or workplace, or a familiar public space where they appeared to have ties to people passing by. I observed their interactions with others and how they introduced me. I took note not just of what they said to me but also of what they chose not to share with me, and carefully observed nonverbal cues and body language.

I also approached my experiences of developing and conducting surveys of sex workers and the police as an ethnographer. I uncovered as much about sex work and its regulation from the processes of trying to collect survey data as I did from the actual survey data I eventually gathered, and I include many of those insights in this book. For instance, when I piloted the surveys with sex workers and police officers, I received feedback on question wording, areas of inquiry to avoid, and others that I should add. Through this process, I learned that asking sex workers about their earnings and number of clients was particularly sensitive, and that I should not hesitate to ask police officers to critically assess the policies they were responsible for enforcing. In addition to improving the quality of the data I was able to collect through the survey, piloting processes also served as valuable fora to hear sex workers and police officers reflect more broadly on their experiences with the regulation of prostitution.

Similarly, when seeking to carry out a survey of sex workers in collaboration with the Dongguan CDC, I observed the closeness of CDC officials' relationship with the entertainment industry when we dined at a restaurant attached to a venue and discussed study logistics with the owner. When the CDC later declined to proceed with the survey, citing a political corruption scandal in Dongguan that had attracted the unwanted attention of Beijing and a subsequent crackdown on the city's entertainment industry, my project suddenly became the casualty of one of the rare occasions when the central government paid heed to what is usually considered a local issue. In Wanqin, I witnessed the local government's deep indifference to the issue of prostitution when an official asked to see a copy of the survey I hoped to administer, skimmed it (complete with a series of questions on sex worker experiences with the police), and sent me on my way with his stamp of approval. I also witnessed local officials' powerlessness in Xizhou. Entertainment venues in that neighborhood repeatedly pushed us out of their spaces, in direct defiance of requests for cooperation from Wang Zhuren, the local health official supporting our work. Ultimately, it was in Beijing that we succeeded in carrying out the survey, where, as described earlier in this chapter, I attribute our success to the role of the sex worker outreach organization.

I was one step removed from law enforcement officers when I carried out the police survey, as the research center I partnered with was responsible for all interactions with survey participants. Yet once again, the survey development process was hugely informative. Most notably, the center had initially expected that they would have the opportunity to survey police officers from every police station in one major city. As the survey included questions on respondent experiences enforcing prostitution regulations in their neighborhood, I also sought to collect data on the prevalence of sex work in the area under each police station's jurisdiction. Working from a list of the roughly 200 police stations in the city, a research assistant and I spent days driving to police stations, walking around them to ascertain the prevalence of entertainment venues and sex workers in the vicinity, and striking up conversations with locals we encountered to supplement our assessment. Although that specific survey opportunity fell through, the mapping process helped me situate prostitution spatially in the broader community and allowed me to hear about how locals who are unaffiliated with the sex industry perceive it. These failed attempts at carrying out surveys of sex workers and police officers still ended up being rich experiences of participant observation, making the months of additional time in the field worthwhile.

BOUNDARIES AND LIMITATIONS

I have addressed issues of geographic representativeness of my work earlier in this chapter, noting that my research sites reflect the diversity of urban areas in the country, but that rural China makes only peripheral appearances. Questions of representativeness also arise with respect to the people: Whose stories are absent, and why should I believe what I heard and saw?

The voices of the most vulnerable girls and women involved in prostitution in China are largely missing from these pages: They are victims of sex trafficking whose freedom of movement is restricted, which made them inaccessible to me. I received glimpses into that world through a handful of sex workers who had previously been trafficked into prostitution. Yet for the most part, this is a story about women who have agency with respect to their engagement in prostitution. Sex trafficking, and human trafficking more generally, is beyond the scope of this study.

When it comes to the people with whom I did interact, I needed to be attuned to stories left unspoken and voices that mislead. Had I been in another country, researching a different topic, I could have addressed these issues through fact-checking.[23] In a handful of instances, events my informants discussed had received media coverage or were mentioned in reports or academic articles. Occasionally, several respondents had witnessed or participated in the same event, and I could compare their recollections. But for the most part, I would have placed informants at risk by reaching out to others in their community to corroborate their stories, and could also have brought unwanted attention to myself. Logistically, connecting with individuals who could substantiate my respondents' claims would have been complicated. Even keeping in touch with my respondents over time was challenging – especially sex workers, who move around frequently and for whom I seldom had contact information. Yet while I was rarely able to verify specific testimonies, I was constantly situating what I heard and observed in one context in relation to my other sources of information. On one level, I triangulated among actors within the sex industry – for instance, reflecting on what a police officer was (and was not) saying and comparing that to his colleagues' testimonies and the testimonies of sex workers. On a second level, I weighed types of data in relation to each other – comparing what I saw with what I heard in interviews and observed in survey data. I approached the survey data – and the police survey in particular – with the greatest skepticism. I sampled in a way that limits my ability to make broader claims of representativeness, and

[23] See, e.g., Desmond, *Evicted*, 327, where the author describes the verification process he adopted in his ethnography of evictions in Milwaukee.

I discounted survey data when it was difficult to reconcile with my interviews and participant observation.

TRIBULATIONS

On a personal level, this fieldwork was challenging.[24] On rare occasions, I was in harm's way. More often, I was anxious about the possibility of trouble. And I frequently felt uncomfortable, awkward, and sad. It was depressing to be on the receiving end of so many stories of hardship, to witness it in the surroundings of informants, and then to relive those interactions once I had left China, as I read and reread interview and participant observation notes, analyzed survey data, and wrote and rewrote dissertation and book chapters.

In relative terms, China was a safe place for me to carry out this research. It is a country with very low levels of crime. It is even safer for many foreigners than Chinese citizens: The negative publicity that would accompany any serious harm caused to a foreign national – particularly a white woman – would increase the risks to a perpetrator. I only experienced trouble once, when a few young men surrounded me and my research assistants in Xizhou and threatened to destroy our belongings if we did not leave promptly.[25] I do not have a clear sense of the actual level of danger we were facing. I was alarmed in the moment, and we left immediately. Yet when we continued data collection in the days following the incident, working indoors and only during daytime hours, we experienced no more direct confrontation. That said, we ultimately struggled to recruit participants in Xizhou, and it seems possible that behind the scenes, potential respondents and gatekeepers were being urged not to engage with us.

That tense incident had only a limited impact on my research. Yet it occurred against the backdrop of another violent encounter that played a defining role in shaping the ultimate contours of this project. Initially, I set out to compare the regulation of prostitution in Russia and China: two countries that saw sharp decreases in sex work when the Communist Party took power, only to see it resurge when the countries implemented market reforms. One day, when I was shadowing a sex

24 For a reflection on my fieldwork focused specifically on the experience of being out of place as a researcher studying the sex industry in China, please see Margaret L. Boittin, "Out of Place Studying China's Sex Industry," in *Out of Place: Fieldwork and Positionality in Law and Society*, ed. Lynette J. Chua and Mark Fathi Massoud (Cambridge University Press, 2024), www.cambridge.org/core/books/out-of-place/DF0793FDF8D5F2638980268A06FF0145.

25 I describe this episode in the book's introduction.

worker outreach organization during preliminary fieldwork in St. Petersburg, Russia, we encountered a drunk police officer who interrupted our conservation with a sex worker, brandished a gun, and punched her in the stomach. He then tried to drag her into his car, but when she broke free of his grasp, he gave up and drove off.

To be clear, the most salient element of the situation was the horrific violence this woman experienced. The perpetrator's identity – an agent of the state whose professional responsibilities include protecting people from harm – exacerbated it, while also confirming some of the egregious behavior in which law enforcement officers are reputed to engage. Only the sex worker suffered physical harm, and she was at greatest risk of being shot. Yet the incident also underscored my own heightened vulnerability in an environment with high crime rates, where I was physically indistinguishable from my research subjects, and where white foreigners are not afforded a privileged status. That trip, combined with subsequent research in the far eastern city of Vladivostok, established the limits of the research I could carry out on the sex industry in Russia. As in China, doors to the public health sector and nongovernmental organizations in Russia opened easily, and in both countries access to law enforcement presented more obstacles.[26] Yet I struggled to identify an approach in Russia where I could safely observe the daily lives of sex workers, their dynamics with clients, and their interactions with the state – as I had already been doing in China. Rather than contend with very different data sources across two countries, I set Russia aside.

Those were the only two times I was aware of being in harm's way during my fieldwork. Both instances took me by surprise, and on a daily basis I did not worry that individuals acting in a private capacity might try to hurt me. One concern that did weigh on me – and that took up gradually more headspace as I spent more time in the field – was that I might encounter trouble at the hands of the Chinese state. I was increasingly anxious, with moments that bordered on paranoia. At one point, when I noticed that the watch I had left on my bedside table no longer worked, I concluded that someone must have entered my apartment and tinkered with the battery to send me a signal that the state was tracking my every move. When I prepared to leave China with all

[26] Lauren McCarthy's account of how Russian law enforcement deals with human trafficking cases confirms that this would have been challenging, while also providing an impressive account of its feasibility. Lauren A. McCarthy, *Trafficking Justice: How Russian Police Enforce New Laws, from Crime to Courtroom* (Ithaca, NY: Cornell University Press, 2015).

of my data, I became progressively more convinced that I would be intercepted prior to departing – in the preceding days, then on the way to the airport, and, finally, while going through customs and boarding the plane. Rationally, I knew the likelihood that I would get into real trouble with the state was extremely low.[27] But fieldwork exhaustion increasingly crowded out my logical thinking, and the fact that poking around in an authoritarian regime comes with risks expanded to fill the space and take on an oversized life of its own.

Yet more than fear and anxiety, I often just felt awkward: I was out of my element both in China and in the sex industry. I took some comfort in the fact that others have described such feelings as a necessary part of the fieldwork process: I identified with the remark that, to carry out participant observation, "you have to be willing to be a horse's ass,"[28] and descriptions of how humbling the process is.[29] But the knowledge that I was in shared company did little in the moment to remedy feelings of discomfort, unease, or embarrassment that emerged in countless situations: when sexual transactions occurred in the room adjacent to me; when a barely clad client walked by me on his way to taking a shower; when karaoke rooms were particularly grimy, the air thick with cigarette smoke and the stench of alcohol, with music pounding and bright lights flashing around me; when my words offended or upset my interlocutors, including the sex worker rights activist who taught me how offensive the term *maiyin piaochang* (a formal term for "prostitution") sounds when talking to sex workers about their engagement in prostitution;[30] or when, over the course of a banquet or other gathering with police officers, public health officials, or other informants, the focus of conversation gradually veered away from me, transitioned toward shop talk I could not engage in, and might even shift to a local dialect, which left me sitting silent and self-conscious, counting the minutes until the meal would come to an end.

I also spent a lot of time feeling sad. I was constantly hearing about and bearing witness to hardship, violence, and abuse. Every day presented new embodiments and permutations of gender inequality,

[27] That calculus might look different now, under the more repressive climate of the Xi Jinping era.

[28] Erving Goffman, "On Fieldwork," *Journal of Contemporary Ethnography* 18, no. 2 (July 1, 1989): 128, https://doi.org/10.1177/089124189018002001.

[29] For discussions of humility, see Alice Goffman, *On the Run: Fugitive Life in an American City* (Chicago, IL: University of Chicago Press, 2014), 231; Hoang, *Dealing in Desire*, 22–23; Schatz, *Political Ethnography*, 11.

[30] In Chapter 10, I discuss the different terms used in Mandarin Chinese in reference to sex work, and their respective connotations.

poverty, as well as authoritarian state brutality. It was heart-wrenching. I felt powerless to address these injustices, and guilty that I was building my professional advancement upon them. More alarming was the realization, many months into my fieldwork, that all of those feelings had become muted within me. Early on, I would be emotionally drained after speaking with just one sex worker, and her life story might sit with me for days. Toward the end of my research, I sometimes felt like an automaton as I navigated much more labor-intensive data collection efforts, such as protracted stretches of ethnographic observation and multiple interviews in a day. The identities and personal narratives of individual respondents started blurring together in my mind. I felt numb, desensitized, and detached from the human suffering that I was witnessing. It was time for me to leave and commit to writing what I had learned through the kindness and generosity of everyone who opened doors for me and welcomed me into their lives.

APPENDIX B

INTERVIEW LIST

Interview 1. Foreign journalist. Beijing. August 28, 2008.

Interview 2. Group interview with one foreign employee and one Chinese employee of an international NGO, and one foreign employee of an international organization. Beijing. August 29, 2008.

Interview 3. Foreign researcher. Beijing. September 2, 2008.

Interview 4. Foreign professor. Beijing. September 5, 2008.

Interview 5. Chinese professor. Beijing. September 9, 2008.

Interview 6. Chinese NGO leader. Beijing. September 10, 2008.

Interview 7. Foreign embassy employee. Beijing. September 12, 2008.

Interview 8. Foreign independent researcher. Beijing. September 14, 2008.

Interview 9. Foreign independent researcher. Beijing. September 15, 2008.

Interview 10. Chinese public health official. Beijing. September 18, 2008.

Interview 11. Chinese government official. Beijing. September 21, 2008.

Interview 12. Chinese staff of Chinese NGO. Beijing. September 24, 2008.

Interview 13. Chinese NGO leader. Beijing. September 26, 2008.

Interview 14. Chinese NGO staff. Beijing. September 27, 2008.

Interview 15. Foreign researcher. Beijing. September 28, 2008.

Interview 16. Foreign researcher at Chinese government health agency. Beijing. September 28, 2008.

Interview 17. Group interview with two foreign researchers. Beijing. September 29, 2008.

Interview 18. Foreign head of foreign NGO. Beijing. October 2, 2008.

Interview 19. Chinese professor. Beijing. October 5, 2008.

Interview 20. Foreign businessperson. Beijing. October 7, 2008.

Interview 21. Foreign academic. Beijing. October 8, 2008.

Interview 22. Foreign head of foreign NGO. Beijing. October 8, 2008.
Interview 23. Chinese NGO employee. Beijing. October 9, 2008.
Interview 24. Sex Worker Interview 1. Beijing. October 13, 2008.
Interview 25. Chinese professor. Beijing. October 14, 2008.
Interview 26. Chinese public health official. Beijing. October 15, 2008.
Interview 27. Chinese public health official. Beijing. October 15, 2008.
Interview 28. Chinese NGO leader. Beijing. October 16, 2008.
Interview 29. Chinese journalist. Beijing. October 16, 2008.
Interview 30. Foreign journalist. Beijing. October 17, 2008.
Interview 31. Foreign researcher. Beijing. October 17, 2008.
Interview 32. Chinese NGO leader. Beijing. October 19, 2008.
Interview 33. Chinese NGO employee. Beijing. October 20, 2008.
Interview 34. Chinese NGO employee. Beijing. October 20, 2008.
Interview 35. Foreign employee of foreign foundation. Beijing. October 21, 2008.
Interview 36. Chinese NGO leader. Beijing. October 21, 2008. (Second interview with interviewee 28.)
Interview 37. Chinese journalist. Beijing. October 21, 2008. (Second interview with interviewee 29.)
Interview 38. Foreign head of foreign foundation. Beijing. October 22, 2008.
Interview 39. Foreign employee of foreign foundation. Beijing. October 22, 2008.
Interview 40. Chinese professor. Beijing. October 22, 2008.
Interview 41. Chinese professor. Beijing. October 23, 2008.
Interview 42. Client of sex worker. Beijing. October 23, 2008.
Interview 43. Foreign researcher. Beijing. October 24, 2008.
Interview 44. Law enforcement expert. Beijing. October 28, 2008.
Interview 45. Chinese researcher. Beijing. October 28, 2008.
Interview 46. Foreign employee of international organization. Beijing. October 30, 2008.
Interview 47. Chinese consultant. Beijing. October 30, 2008.
Interview 48. Foreign employee of foreign NGO. Beijing. October 30, 2008.
Interview 49. Chinese public health official. Hunan. November 3, 2008.
Interview 50. Chinese NGO leader. Harbin. November 7, 2008.
Interview 51. Chinese public health official. Harbin. November 7, 2008.
Interview 52. Chinese NGO leader. Shenyang. November 9, 2008.

Interview 53. Foreign professor. Beijing. March 20, 2009.
Interview 54. Foreign employee of foreign embassy. Beijing. March 31, 2009.
Interview 55. Chinese public health official. Beijing. April 1, 2009.
Interview 56. Chinese employee of Chinese NGO. Beijing. April 1, 2009.
Interview 57. Chinese public health official. Beijing. March 26, 2009. (Second interview with interviewee 26.)
Interview 58. Chinese public health official. Beijing. April 2, 2009.
Interview 59. Chinese professor. Beijing. April 3, 2009. (Second interview with interviewee 41.)
Interview 60. Chinese employee of Chinese NGO. Beijing. April 4, 2009.
Interview 61. Chinese professor. Beijing. April 13, 2009.
Interview 62.

a. Interview 62a. Chinese researcher. Beijing. April 14, 2009.
b. Interview 62b. Chinese journalist. Shanghai. April 16, 2009. (Due to a labeling error, I have two "Interview 62s" and am reproducing their labels as such here to maintain consistency with my fieldnotes.)

Interview 63. Chinese NGO employee. Shanghai. April 16, 2009.
Interview 64. Chinese researcher. Shanghai. April 16, 2009.
Interview 65. Chinese NGO employee. Shanghai. April 16, 2009.
Interview 66. Foreign journalist. Shanghai. April 17, 2009.
Interview 67. Chinese researcher. Shanghai. April 17, 2009.
Interview 68. Chinese researcher. Shanghai. April 17, 2009.
Interview 69. Chinese law enforcement official. Shanghai. April 18, 2009.
Interview 70. Chinese law enforcement official. Shanghai. April 18, 2009. (Informants 69 and 70 were interviewed together.)
Interview 71. Foreign professor. Hong Kong. April 22, 2009.
Interview 72. Chinese researcher. Hong Kong. April 22, 2009.
Interview 73. Hong Kong NGO. Hong Kong. April 27, 2009.
Interview 74. Foreign journalist. Hong Kong. April 27, 2009.
Interview 75. Chinese public health official. Shenzhen. April 28, 2009.
Interview 76. Chinese NGO leader. Shenzhen. April 29, 2009.
Interview 77. Chinese NGO staff members. Beijing. April 30, 2009.
Interview 78. Chinese NGO staff members. Beijing. May 1, 2009.
Interview 79. Foreign researcher. Shenzhen. May 2, 2009.
Interview 80. Chinese public health official. Shenzhen. May 4, 2009.

Interview 81. Two Chinese public health officials. Shenzhen. May 4, 2009.
Interview 82. Chinese NGO leader. Shenzhen. May 4, 2009.
Interview 83. Chinese NGO leader and their partner. Guangzhou. May 6, 2009.
Interview 84. Two Chinese professors. Guangzhou. May 6, 2009.
Interview 85. Chinese journalist. Guangzhou. May 7, 2009.
Interview 86. Chinese NGO leader. Guangzhou. May 7, 2009.
Interview 87. Chinese professor. Guangzhou. May 16, 2009.
Interview 88. Chinese professor. Guangzhou. May 16, 2009. (Second interview with one of interviewees 84.)
Interview 89. Law enforcement expert. Beijing. June 16, 2009. (Second interview with interviewee 44.)
Interview 90. Chinese employee of Chinese NGO. June 16, 2009. (Second interview with interviewee 60.)
Interview 91. Chinese leader of Chinese NGO. Beijing. June 16, 2009.
Interview 92. Chinese law enforcement official. Beijing. June 16, 2009.
Interview 93. Foreign professor. Hong Kong. July 27, 2009.
Interview 94. Foreign government employee. Beijing. August 4, 2009.
Interview 95. Hong Kong NGO employee. Hong Kong. January 15, 2009. (Included nonsequentially in this list due to a labeling error, to maintain consistency with my fieldnotes.)
Interview 96. Hong Kong professor. Hong Kong. January 19, 2009. (Included nonsequentially in this list due to a labeling error, to maintain consistency with my fieldnotes.)
Interview 97. Hong Kong professor. Hong Kong. January 19, 2009. (Included nonsequentially in this list due to a labeling error, to maintain consistency with my fieldnotes.)
Interview 98. Four Chinese law enforcement officials. Zhengti. August 5, 2009.
Interview 99. Two Chinese law enforcement officials. Zhengti. August 6, 2009.
Interview 100.

a. Interview 100a. Seven Chinese law enforcement officials. Zhengti. August 7, 2009.
b. Interview 100b. One Chinese public health official and one Chinese law enforcement official. Zhengti. August 7, 2009. (Due to a labeling error, I have two "Interview 100s" and am reproducing their labels as such here to maintain consistency with my fieldnotes.)

Interview 101. Six Chinese law enforcement officials. Zhengti. August 8, 2009.
Interview 102.
 a. Interview 102a. Madam. Zhengti. August 9, 2009.
 b. Interview 102b.Three law enforcement officials. Zhengti. August 9, 2009. (Due to a labeling error, I have notes from two "Interview 102s" and am reproducing their labels as such here to maintain consistency with my fieldnotes.)
Interview 103. Three law enforcement officials. Zhengti. August 10, 2009.
Interview 104. Chinese employee of international public health organization. Beijing. August 12, 2009.
Interview 105. Foreign employee of international public health organization. Beijing. August 13, 2009.
Interview 106. Chinese employee of international public health organization. Beijing. August 13, 2009.
Interview 107. Interview with two Chinese employees of Chinese NGO. Beijing. August 14, 2009. (This was the third interview for one of the two interviewees, who is also interviewee 60 and 90.)
Interview 108. Foreign employee of international public health organization. Beijing. August 14, 2009.
Interview 109. Madam Interview 1. Beijing. August 15, 2009.
Interview 110. Sex Worker Interview 1. Beijing. August 15, 2009.
Interview 111. Sex Worker Interview 2. Beijing. August 15, 2009.
Interview 112. Sex Worker Interview 3. Beijing. August 15, 2009.
Interview 113. Sex Worker Interview 4. Beijing. August 15, 2009.
Interview 114. Sex Worker Interview 1. Beijing. August 16, 2009.
Interview 115. Sex Worker Interview 2. Beijing. August 16, 2009.
Interview 116. Sex Worker Interview 3. Beijing. August 16, 2009.
Interview 117. Sex Worker Interview 4. Beijing. August 16, 2009.
Interview 118. Sex Worker Interview 5. Beijing. August 16, 2009.
Interview 119. Sex Worker Interview 1. Beijing. August 17, 2009.
Interview 120. Sex Worker Interview 2. Beijing. August 17, 2009.
Interview 121. Sex Worker Interview 3. Beijing. August 17, 2009.
Interview 122. Sex Worker Interview 4. Beijing. August 17, 2009.
Interview 123. Madam Interview 1. Beijing. August 17, 2009.
Interview 124. Sex Worker Interview 1. Beijing. August 18, 2009.
Interview 125. Sex Worker Interview 2. Beijing. August 18, 2009.
Interview 126. Sex Worker Interview 3. Beijing. August 18, 2009.
Interview 127. Sex Worker Interview 4. Beijing. August 18, 2009.

Interview 128. Sex Worker Interview 5. Beijing. August 18, 2009.
Interview 129. Madam Interview 1. Beijing. August 18, 2009.
Interview 130. Foreign head of international public health organization. Beijing. August 19, 2009.
Interview 131. Foreign professor. Beijing. August 19, 2009.
Interview 132. Sex Worker Interview 1. Beijing. August 20, 2009.
Interview 133. Sex Worker Interview 2. Beijing. August 20, 2009.
Interview 134. Sex Worker Interview 3. Beijing. August 20, 2009.
Interview 135. Sex Worker Interview 4. Beijing. August 20, 2009.
Interview 136. Sex Worker Interview 5. Beijing. August 20, 2009.
Interview 137. Sex Worker Interview 6. Beijing. August 20, 2009.
Interview 138. Sex Worker Interview 1. Beijing. August 21, 2009.
Interview 139. Sex Worker Interview 2. Beijing. August 21, 2009.
Interview 140. Sex Worker Interview 3. Beijing. August 21, 2009.
Interview 141. Madam Interview 1. Beijing. August 21, 2009.
Interview 142. Madam Interview 2. Beijing. August 21, 2009.
Interview 143. Sex Worker Interview 1. Beijing. August 22, 2009.
Interview 144. Sex Worker Interview 2. Beijing. August 22, 2009.
Interview 145. Sex Worker Interview 3. Beijing. August 22, 2009.
Interview 146. Sex Worker Interview 4. Beijing. August 22, 2009.
Interview 147. Sex Worker Interview 5. Beijing. August 22, 2009.
Interview 148. Sex Worker Interview 6. Beijing. August 22, 2009.
Interview 149. Sex Worker Interview 1. Beijing. August 23, 2009.
Interview 150. Sex Worker Interview 2. Beijing. August 23, 2009.
Interview 151. Sex Worker Interview 3. Beijing. August 23, 2009.
Interview 152. Sex Worker Interview 4. Beijing. August 23, 2009.
Interview 153. Sex Worker Interview 5. Beijing. August 23, 2009.
Interview 154. Sex Worker Interview 6. Beijing. August 23, 2009.
Interview 155. Sex Worker Interview 1. Beijing. August 24, 2009.
Interview 156. Sex Worker Interview 2. Beijing. August 24, 2009.
Interview 157. Sex Worker Interview 3. Beijing. August 24, 2009.
Interview 158. Sex Worker Interview 4. Beijing. August 24, 2009.
Interview 159. Sex Worker Interview 5. Beijing. August 24, 2009.
Interview 160. Sex Worker Interview 1. Beijing. August 25, 2009.
Interview 161. Sex Worker Interview 2. Beijing. August 25, 2009.
Interview 162. Sex Worker Interview 3. Beijing. August 25, 2009.
Interview 163. Sex Worker Interview 4. Beijing. August 25, 2009.
Interview 164. Sex Worker Interview 5. Beijing. August 25, 2009.
Interview 165. Sex Worker Interview 6. Beijing. August 25, 2009.
Interview 166. Sex Worker Interview 1. Beijing. August 26, 2009.

Interview 167. Sex Worker Interview 2. Beijing. August 26, 2009.
Interview 168. Sex Worker Interview 3. Beijing. August 26, 2009.
Interview 169. Sex Worker Interview 4. Beijing. August 26, 2009.
Interview 170. Sex Worker Interview 5. Beijing. August 26, 2009.
Interview 171. Venue Manager. Beijing. August 26, 2009.
Interview 172. Foreign employee of Chinese public health agency. September 2, 2009. Beijing.
Interview 173. Law enforcement officer. Hebei province. September 4, 2009.
Interview 174. Two foreign employees of foreign embassy. Beijing. September 5, 2009.
Interview 175. Chinese professor. Beijing. September 8, 2009.
Interview 176. Taxi driver. Beijing. April 1, 2009.
Interview 177. Taxi driver. Beijing. April 1, 2009.
Interview 178. Taxi driver. Beijing. March 25, 2009.
Interview 179. Taxi driver. Beijing. March 27, 2009.
Interview 180. Taxi driver. Beijing. March 27, 2009.
Interview 181. Taxi driver. Beijing. March 31, 2009.
Interview 182. Taxi driver. Beijing. March 31, 2009.
Interview 183. Taxi driver. Beijing. March 31, 2009.
Interview 184. Public health official. Guangzhou. September 26, 2009.
Interview 185. Foreign researcher. Hong Kong. January 14, 2009.
Interview 186. Sex Worker Interview 1. Shenzhen. November 5, 2009.
Interview 187. Sex Worker Interview 2. Shenzhen. November 5, 2009.
Interview 188. Madam Interview 1. Shenzhen. November 7, 2009.
Interview 189. Law enforcement officer interview. San Francisco, CA (USA). July 11, 2013.
Interview 190. Chinese employee of foreign NGO. Beijing. October 12, 2009.

APPENDIX C

THE SEX WORKER SURVEY

In the fall of 2009, I conducted an in-person survey of 568 female sex workers in one red-light district in Beijing. I carried it out in collaboration with a sex worker outreach community center located in that red-light district.

Staff at the center recruited all survey participants, using convenience sampling. Staff spread news, through word of mouth, that they were recruiting sex workers to participate in a study. They shared the information with sex workers who stopped by the community center and asked them to spread the word to their sex worker acquaintances. They also went to sex work venues and public spaces in the district to recruit participants. About 10 percent of the sample consisted in low-tier sex workers, and the remaining 90 percent consisted in middle-tier sex workers.

Six enumerators, all young, female university students, conducted the face-to-face interviews, either at the community center or at the sex work venues. The interviews were about thirty minutes long. The survey included questions about basic demographics, experiences in the sex industry, attitudes toward prostitution, attitudes toward and experiences with the state (including law enforcement and public health officials), and knowledge of prostitution laws.

In Chapter 7, I compare the attitudes of surveyed sex workers with those of the general population for four variables: importance of politics; interest in politics; trust in the central government; trust in the police. The sex worker survey was conducted in 2009, so I used data from both the 2007 and the 2012 World Values Survey for this comparison. Respondents were provided with four answer choices for these questions.[1] Data were condensed to code any form of agreement with

[1] For example, when asked "What is the importance of politics in your life," answer choices were: (1) very important; (2) important; (3) not very important; (4) not important at all.

a value of 1, and any form of disagreement with a value of 0.[2] The percentages represented in Figures 7.2 and 7.3 show the proportion of respondents in the sex worker survey and the World Values Survey who express agreement with each of the four variables.

I have included in this section the English-language wording of the sex worker survey questions that I discuss in this book. For the Chinese-language version of the survey questions, I used appropriately respectful euphemisms to refer to prostitution, sex work, and sex workers.

1. What year were you born?
2. What is your education level? [Answer choices: No education; Not graduated from primary; Graduated from primary; Not graduated from middle school; Graduated from middle school; Not graduated from high school; Graduated from high school; Technical school; University or higher.]
3. Are you currently married?
4. Who are you currently living with? [Answer choices: Husband; Boyfriend; Other sex workers; Other friends or family; Alone; Other.]
5. How many children do you have?
6. What province are you from?
7. Do you come from the city or the countryside?
8. How long have you lived in Beijing?
9. How old were you when you started engaging in prostitution?
10. What type of [prostitution] spaces do you work in now?
11. In the past, what types of [prostitution] spaces did you work in?
12. About how many clients do you have in a month?
13. How much did you earn last time you were with a client?
14. Do you currently do any work other than sex work?
15. What other types of work do you do?
16. Some people think that prostitution is harmful to society, for reasons tied to health, safety, or morality. Rank the harms that prostitution causes in society.
17. Do you think that selling sex is good or bad? [Answer choices: Very good; Good; Bad; Very bad.]
18. Is it appropriate or inappropriate for a man to solicit sex? [Answer choices: Very appropriate; Appropriate; Not appropriate; Very inappropriate.]

[2] For example, for the importance in politics question, "very important" and "important" were coded as "1," and "not very important" and "not important at all" were coded as "0."

19. For you, is being engaged in prostitution: [Answer choices: Very beneficial; Beneficial; Disadvantageous; Very disadvantageous]?
20. For the client, do you think that prostitution is: [Answer choices: Very beneficial; Beneficial; Disadvantageous; Very disadvantageous]?
21. Could you accept it if your husband solicits a sex worker? [Answer choices: Absolutely accept it; Accept it; Cannot accept it; Absolutely cannot accept it.]
22. Do you think prostitution policies are fair or unfair toward sex workers? [Answer choices: Very unfair; A little unfair; A little fair; Very fair.]
23. Do you think prostitution policies are fair or unfair toward clients? [Answer choices: Very unfair; A little unfair; A little fair; Very fair.]
24. What do you think is the main goal of China's prostitution policies?
25. Do you think that China's prostitution policies are effective or ineffective? [Ten-point scale.]
26. In the past six months, have police come to you as clients?
27. This profession helps reduce the rate of rape. [Answer choices: Strongly agree; Agree; Disagree; Strongly disagree.]
28. Do you trust the central government? [Answer choices: Trust a lot; Trust; Not really trust; Not trust at all.]
29. Do you trust the local government? [Answer choices: Trust a lot; Trust; Not really trust; Not trust at all.]
30. Do you trust the police? [Answer choices: Trust a lot; Trust; Not really trust; Not trust at all.]
31. In the past year, how many times did the police come to your place of work to inspect?
32. Have you ever been arrested by the police?
33. How many times have you been arrested by the police?
34. How were you punished?
35. How was the client punished?
36. If a client robs you and you know how to find him, what will you do? [Answer choices: Report to the police: Do nothing; Ask the madam for help; Ask the pimp for help; Ask friends for help; Other.]
37. If you are raped by a client and you know how to find him, what will you do? [Answer choices: Report to the police: Do nothing; Ask the madam for help; Ask the pimp for help; Ask friends for help; Other.]

38. If you enter into a conflict with people around you and you cannot resolve it yourself, would you call the police?
39. If someone robs you of your money, would you report to the police?
40. If your valuables are stolen, would you report to the police?
41. What is the importance of politics in your life? [Answer choices: Very important; important; Not very important; Not important at all.]
42. Are you interested in politics? [Answer choices: Very interested; A little interested; Not very interested; Not interested at all.]
43. Is prostitution legal or illegal in China?
44. What is your opinion toward the legalization of prostitution? [Answer choices: Strongly support; Support; Opposed; Strongly opposed.]
45. Have you gotten a health checkup in the past year?
46. How many times [have you gotten a health checkup]?
47. Have you ever heard of HIV and AIDS?
48. Have you ever done an HIV/AIDS test before?

APPENDIX D

THE POLICE SURVEY

In the spring of 2010, I carried out a survey of eighty-nine police officers in a city in southern China through a research center that conducts police trainings in China. The research center administered the survey as part of one of their trainings.[1] This was a convenience sample. Local police officials selected training participants, and I do not have information on the criteria used to select participants.

These were self-administered surveys that respondents completed at the training. The survey included questions about basic demographics, attitudes toward prostitution and prostitution policies, and experiences with anti-prostitution enforcement.

Most survey participants (82 percent) were male. Their mean age was thirty-eight. Most of them (95 percent) were either graduates of special police training academies or universities. They had spent an average of seventeen years in law enforcement. Of the five different official ranks within the police force, most were in the lowest third (警督) (35 percent) and fourth (警司) (63 percent).

I have included in this section the English-language wording of the police survey questions that I discuss in this book. For the Chinese-language version of the survey questions, I used appropriately respectful euphemisms to refer to prostitution, sex work, and sex workers.

1. What is your gender?
2. How old are you?
3. What is your education level? [Answer choices: Less than high school; High school; Specialty police training school; College undergraduate; More than college undergraduate.]
4. How many years have you been a police officer?
5. What is your police officer rank?

[1] In order to maintain the center's anonymity, I am not able to provide more information on the substance of the trainings.

6. The following places are all spaces where sex workers might work. According to you, and in this city, which are the three types of venues where sex workers are most likely to be found?
7. In your city, in which three types of venues are sex workers and clients most often caught?
8. In your city, which of the following three types of businesses are most frequently punished for harboring prostitution?
9. If the intensity of prostitution crackdowns varies over the course of a year in your city, what are the reasons for this?
10. How important are the following reasons in driving your own decision to crack down on prostitution in your city?
11. In your city, what is the frequency of the following types of punishments for sex workers? [Answer choices: Warning; Fine; Short-term detention; Reform through reeducation; Reeducation through labor.] [Ten-point scale for each answer choice.]
12. In your city, what is the frequency of the following types of punishments for clients? [Answer choices: Warning; Fine; Short-term detention; Reform through reeducation; Reeducation through labor.] [Ten-point scale for each answer choice.]
13. Do you think that China's prostitution policies are effective? [Answer choice: Ten-point scale, from very ineffective to very effective.]
14. As a police officer, what is your opinion with respect to the legalization of prostitution? [Answer choice: Ten-point scale, from strongly oppose to strongly support.]
15. Some people think that prostitution is harmful to society, for reasons tied to health, safety, or morality. Please rank the harms that prostitution causes in society.
16. Do you think it is appropriate for someone to be a sex worker? [Answer choices: Very appropriate; Appropriate; Not very appropriate; Extremely inappropriate.]
17. Do you think it is appropriate for someone to solicit a sex worker? [Answer choices: Very appropriate; Appropriate; Not very appropriate; Extremely inappropriate.]

BIBLIOGRAPHY

ARTICLES, BOOKS, AND REPORTS

"2021 Di Ershisan Jie Quanguo (Guangzhou) Xingwenhua Jie" 2021第二十三届全国 (广州) 性文化节 [The 23rd National (Guangzhou) Sex Culture Festival 2021]. Xingshang Wang 性商网. Accessed April 30, 2022. www.chinasexq.com/zh/2021/1174.shtml.

Agence France Presse. "China Province Admits Unlawful Detention Centres." February 14, 2014. www.capitalfm.co.ke/news/2014/02/china-province-admits-unlawful-detention-centres/.

Allison, Anne. *Nightwork: Sexuality, Pleasure, and Corporate Masculinity in a Tokyo Hostess Club*. Chicago, IL: University of Chicago Press, 1994.

Al-Riahi, Nada. "Prostitution in the Arab World: A Legal Study of Arab Legislation." Working Paper Prepared for the Middle East and North Africa Regional Consultation of the Global Commission on HIV and the Law, 2011. http://hivlawcommission.org/index.php/report-working-papers?task=document.viewdoc&id=97.

Amnesty International. "China's 'Re-Education through Labour' Camps: Replacing One System of Repression with Another?" December 17, 2013. www.amnesty.org/en/latest/news/2013/12/china-s-re-education-through-labour-camps-replacing-one-system-repression-another/.

"Harmfully Isolated: Criminalizing Sex Work in Hong Kong." 2016. www.amnesty.org/en/wp-content/uploads/2021/05/ASA1740322016ENGLISH.pdf.

Anonymous. "Wednesday-Day 27." *Beijing Haze* (blog), August 28, 2009. http://beijinghaze.blogspot.com/2009_08_01_archive.html.

Arditi, Lynn. "How R.I. Opened the Door to Prostitution." *Providence Journal*, May 31, 2009. www.providencejournal.com/story/news/2014/11/14/20141114-2009-opened-door-prostitution-broken-legal-barriers-made-public-nuisance-private-act-ece/35264827007/.

Asia Catalyst. "'Custody and Education': Arbitrary Detention for Female Sex Workers in China." December 2013. www.aidsdatahub.org/sites/default/files/resource/asia-catalyst-custody-education-arbitrary-detention-fsw-china.pdf.

"The Condom Quandary: A Study of the Impact of Law Enforcement Practices on Effective HIV Prevention among Male, Female, and Transgender Sex Workers in China." July 2016. https://asiacatalyst.org/wp-content/uploads/2014/09/The-Condom-Quandary-Report_en.pdf.

Asian Development Bank. "People's Republic of China Country Gender Assessment." December 2006. www.adb.org/documents/peoples-republic-china-country-gender-assessment.

Associated Press. "Police Detain China Activist for Sex Worker Rights." *The San Diego Union-Tribune*, August 2, 2010. www.sandiegouniontribune.com/sdut-police-detain-china-activist-for-sex-worker-rights-2010aug02-story.html.

Baculinao, Eric. "China Grapples with Legacy of Its 'Missing Girls': Disturbing Demographic Imbalance Spurs Drive to Change Age-Old Practices." *NBC News*, September 14, 2004. www.nbcnews.com/id/wbna5953508.

Barry, Kathleen. *Female Sexual Slavery*. New York: New York University Press, 1984.

Barton, Dominic, Yougang Chen, and Amy Jin. "Mapping China's Middle Class." *McKinsey Quarterly*, June 1, 2013. www.mckinsey.com/industries/retail/our-insights/mapping-chinas-middle-class.

Baum, Richard. "Modernization and Legal Reform in Post-Mao China: The Rebirth of Socialist Legality." *Studies in Comparative Communism* 19, no. 2 (June 1, 1986): 69–103. https://doi.org/10.1016/0039-3592(86)90007-4.

BBC News. "China Executes Female Gangland Prostitution Ringleader." December 7, 2011. www.bbc.com/news/world-asia-china-16077743.

"China NPC: Three-Child Policy Formally Passed into Law." August 20, 2021, sec. China. www.bbc.com/news/world-asia-china-58277473.

"Chinese Birth Rate Falls to Lowest in Seven Decades." January 17, 2020, sec. China. www.bbc.com/news/world-asia-china-51145251.

"Chinese Rail Official's Mistress Jailed over Bribery." March 12, 2014. www.bbc.com/news/world-asia-china-30305724.

"Profile: China's Fallen Security Chief Zhou Yongkang." July 29, 2014, sec. China. www.bbc.com/news/world-asia-china-26349305.

Beach, Sophie. "Chongqing Sex Scandal May Implicate Wang Lijun." *China Digital Times*, November 25, 2012. http://chinadigitaltimes.net/2012/11/chongqing-sex-scandal-may-implicate-wang-lijun/.

Bernhardt, Kathryn. "Women and the Law: Divorce in the Republican Period." In *Civil Law in Qing and Republican China*, edited by Kathryn Bernhardt and Philip C. Huang, 187–214. Stanford, CA: Stanford University Press, 1994.

Bernstein, Elizabeth. "The Sexual Politics of the 'New Abolitionism.'" *Differences* 18, no. 3 (December 1, 2007): 128–151. https://doi.org/10.1215/10407391-2007-013.

Temporarily Yours: Intimacy, Authenticity, and the Commerce of Sex. Chicago, IL: University of Chicago Press, 2007.

Bernstein, Laurie. *Sonia's Daughters: Prostitutes and Their Regulation in Imperial Russia*. Berkeley, CA: University of California Press, 1995.

Biddulph, Sarah. "Justice at the Margins: Notions of Justice in the Punishment of Prostitution." In *Justice: The China Experience*, edited by Flora Sapio, Susan Trevaskes, Sarah Biddulph, and Elisa Nesossi, 312–355. Cambridge: Cambridge University Press, 2017. https://doi.org/10.1017/9781108115919.012.

Legal Reform and Administrative Detention Powers in China. Cambridge: Cambridge University Press, 2007.

"Punishments in the Post Re-education through Labour World: Questions about Minor Crime in China." In *Chinese Legal Reform and the Global Legal Order: Adoption and Adaptation*, edited by Yun Zhao and Michael H. K. Ng, 15–43. Cambridge: Cambridge University Press, 2017.

Bikales, Bill. "Reflections on Poverty Reduction in China." 2021. www.eda.admin.ch/dam/countries/countries-content/china/en/20210608-Poverty-Reduction-China_EN.pdf.

Bloomberg News. "China's Two-Child Policy." January 20, 2020. www.bloomberg.com/quicktake/china-s-two-child-policy.

Blum, Susan D. *Lies That Bind: Chinese Truth, Other Truths*. New York: Rowman & Littlefield, 2007.

Boittin, Margaret L. "New Perspectives from the Oldest Profession: Abuse and the Legal Consciousness of Sex Workers in China." *Law & Society Review* 47, no. 2 (2013): 245–278.

"Out of Place When Studying China's Sex Industry." In *Out of Place: Fieldwork and Positionality in Law and Society*, edited by Lynette J. Chua and Mark Fathi Massoud, 84–101. Cambridge: Cambridge University Press, 2024. www.cambridge.org/core/books/out-of-place/DF0793FDF8D5F2638980268A06FF0145.

"Using Incentives to Increase HIV/AIDS Testing by Sex Workers: Evidence from a Randomized Field Experiment in China." *Law & Policy* 40, no. 4 (2018): 398–423. https://doi.org/10.1111/lapo.12114.

Bouey, Jennifer. "China's Health System Reform and Global Health Strategy in the Context of COVID-19." *RAND Corporation*, 2020. https://doi.org/10.7249/CTA321-1.

Bougon, François, and Brice Pedroletti. "Chine: Le Marxiste En Chef Tombe Pour Un Scandale Sexuel." *Le Monde*, January 19, 2013. www.lemonde.fr/chine/article/2013/01/19/chine-le-marxiste-en-chef-tombe-pour-un-scandale-sexuel_6005534_1667009.html.

Bradsher, Keith. "China's Anticorruption Commission Investigates Senior Official." *New York Times*, December 5, 2012, sec. World. www.nytime

s.com/2012/12/06/world/asia/early-target-of-chinas-anti-corruption-commission-identified.html.

"Jobs, Houses and Cows: China's Costly Drive to Erase Extreme Poverty." *New York Times*, December 31, 2020, sec. World. www.nytimes.com/2020/12/31/world/asia/china-poverty-xi-jinping.html.

Branigan, Tani. "China's Village of the Bachelors: No Wives in Sight in Remote Settlement." *Guardian*, September 2, 2011. www.theguardian.com/world/2011/sep/02/china-village-of-bachelors.

"Chinese Sex Workers Protest against Crackdown." *Guardian*, August 3, 2010. www.theguardian.com/world/2010/aug/03/china-prostitution-sex-workers-protest.

Brant, Robin. "The Lonely Men of China's 'Bachelor Village.'" *BBC News*, August 28, 2016. www.bbc.com/news/world-asia-china-37192818.

Brodeur, Jean-Paul. "High Policing and Low Policing: Remarks about the Policing of Political Activities." *Social Problems* 30, no. 5 (1983): 507–520. https://doi.org/10.2307/800268.

Brooks, Rob. "China's Biggest Problem? Too Many Men." CNN, March 4, 2013. www.cnn.com/2012/11/14/opinion/china-challenges-one-child-brooks/index.html.

Buckley, Chris. "China Aims to Abolish Goals for Arrests and Convictions." *New York Times*, January 21, 2015. www.nytimes.com/2015/01/22/world/asia/china-said-to-be-doing-away-with-goals-for-arrests-and-convictions.html.

"China Sex Theme Park Comes to Abrupt End." *Reuters*, May 18, 2009. www.reuters.com/article/worldNews/idUSTRE54H03N20090518.

Burris, Scott, and Guomei Xia. "The 'Risk Environment' for Commercial Sex Work in China: Considering the Role of Law and Law Enforcement Practices." In *Gender Policy and HIV in China*, Vol. 22, edited by Joseph Tucker and Dudley L. Poston, 179–188. The Springer Series on Demographic Methods and Population Analysis. Dordrecht: Springer, 2009.

Canaves, Sky. "Mistresses Enlisted in the Fight against Corruption." *WSJ Blogs – China Real Time Report* (blog), June 26, 2008. http://blogs.wsj.com/chinarealtime/2008/06/26/mistresses-enlisted-in-the-fight-against-corruption/.

Cao, Liqun, and Steven Stack. "Exploring Terra Incognita: Family Values and Prostitution Acceptance in China." *Journal of Criminal Justice* 38, no. 4 (July 1, 2010): 531–537. https://doi.org/10.1016/j.jcrimjus.2010.04.023.

Carter, Liz. "China's Latest Corruption Target Allegedly Embezzled Millions and Kept 46 Mistresses; Where's the Shock?" *Tea Leaf Nation*, April 9, 2013. www.tealeafnation.com/2013/04/chinas-latest-corruption-target-embezzled-millions-and-kept-46-mistresses-wheres-the-shock/.

Ch'u, T'ung-tsn. *Law and Society in Traditional China*. Paris: Mouton, 1965.

Chan, Alexsia T., and Kevin J. O'Brien. "Phantom Services: Deflecting Migrant Workers in China." *The China Journal* 81 (October 22, 2018): 103–122. https://doi.org/10.1086/699215.

Chapman-Schmidt, Ben. "'Sex Trafficking' as Epistemic Violence." *Anti-Trafficking Review*, no. 12 (April 29, 2019): 172–187. https://doi.org/10.14197/atr.2012191211.

Chen, Fei 陈菲, and Wu Jing 吴晶. "Zhongyang Zhengfa Wei Chutai Shouge Qieshi Fangzhi Yuanjia Cuoan De Zhidao Yijian" 中央政法委出台首个切实防止冤假错案的指导意见 [The First Guideline on Effective Prevention of Wrongful Convictions Published by the Committee of Political and Legal Affairs]. *Xinhua News Agency* 新华社, August 13, 2013. www.gov.cn/jrzg/2013-08/13/content_2466100.htm.

Chen, Xiang-Sheng, Guo-Jun Liang, Qian-Qiu Wang et al. "HIV Prevalence Varies between Female Sex Workers from Different Types of Venues in Southern China." *Sexually Transmitted Diseases* 39, no. 11 (November 2012): 868–870. https://doi.org/10.1097/OLQ.0b013e318264c3ba.

Chen, Xiang-Sheng, Xiang-Dong Gong, Guo-Jun Liang, and Guo-Cheng Zhang. "Epidemiologic Trends of Sexually Transmitted Diseases in China." *Sexually Transmitted Diseases* 27, no. 3 (March 2000): 138–142.

Chen, Xiang-Sheng, Yue-Ping Yin, and Ning Jiang. "Was the HIV Infection Burden in Female Sex Workers in China Overestimated?" *The Lancet Infectious Diseases* 13, no. 1 (January 2013): 13. https://doi.org/10.1016/S1473-3099(12)70298-0.

Chersich, Matthew. "Preventing HIV among Sex Workers in Sub-Saharan Africa: A Literature Review." *WHO*, 2011. https://apps.who.int/iris/handle/10665/44549.

Chin, Josh. "China Poised to Approve Crackdown on Foreign NGOs." *Wall Street Journal*, April 26, 2016, sec. World. www.wsj.com/articles/china-crackdown-on-foreign-ngos-about-to-become-law-1461674598.

"Chinese Officials Ousted over Alleged Sexual Exploits." *Wall Street Journal*, January 25, 2013. http://online.wsj.com/article/SB10001424127887323854904578263764051190022.html.

"Mistress-Driven Anticorruption: Study Says 15% of Accusers Are Lovers." *WSJ.Com* (blog), October 17, 2013. http://blogs.wsj.com/chinarealtime/2013/10/17/mistress-driven-anticorruption-study-says-15-of-accusers-are-lovers/.

Chin, Ko-lin, and Sheldon X. Zhang. *The Chinese Heroin Trade: Cross-Border Drug Trafficking in Southeast Asia and beyond*. New York: New York University Press, 2015.

China Power Team. "How Well-off Is China's Middle Class?" *China Power* (blog), April 26, 2017. https://chinapower.csis.org/china-middle-class/.

Chinese Center for Disease Control and Prevention 中国疾病预防控制中心. "Aizibing Xingbing Zonghe Jiance Zhinan Ji Fangan (Shixing)" 艾滋病

性病综合监测指南及方案（试行）[STD Comprehensive Surveillance Guidelines (For Trial Implementation)]. 2002. www.hfcdc.ah.cn/include/downloand.php?ID=247.

Choi, Susanne Y. P. "State Control, Female Prostitution and HIV Prevention in China." *The China Quarterly* 205 (March 2011): 96–114.

Choi, Susanne Y. P., and Eleanor Holroyd. "The Influence of Power, Poverty and Agency in the Negotiation of Condom Use for Female Sex Workers in Mainland China." *Culture, Health & Sexuality* 9, no. 5 (2007): 489–503.

Choi, Susanne Y. P., and Ruby Y. S. Lai. "Sex Work and Stigma Management in China and Hong Kong: The Role of State Policy and NGO Advocacy." *The China Quarterly* 247 (September 2021): 855–874. https://doi.org/10.1017/S0305741021000035.

Chow, Elaine. "First Sex Workers Protest in China Demands Legalization of Prostitution." *Shanghaiist*, August 4, 2010. https://web.archive.org/web/20171106003821/. http://shanghaiist.com/2010/08/04/first_sex_workers_protest_in_china.php.

Chuang, Julia. "Factory Girls after the Factory: Female Return Migrations in Rural China." *Gender & Society* 30, no. 3 (June 1, 2016): 467–489. https://doi.org/10.1177/0891243215621718.

City Weekend. "Beijing's First-Ever Sex Toy Fair Ends Today." April 6, 2009. www.cityweekend.com.cn/beijing/articles/blogs-beijing/cw-blog/beijings-first-ever-sex-toy-fair-ends-today/.

Clarke, Donald C. "Is China a Dual State?" GWU Legal Studies Research Paper No. 2022–74, GWU Law School Public Law Research Paper No. 2022–74, December 15, 2022. https://doi.org/10.2139/ssrn.4317126.

Congressional-Executive Commission on China. "Ministry of Public Security Launches Seven-Month Nationwide 'Strike Hard' Campaign." August 11, 2010. www.cecc.gov/publications/commission-analysis/ministry-of-public-security-launches-seven-month-nationwide-strike.

Corbin, Alain. *Women for Hire: Prostitution and Sexuality in France after 1850.* Cambridge, MA: Harvard University Press, 1990.

Credit Suisse Research Institute. "Global Wealth Report 2020." Accessed October 22, 2020. www.credit-suisse.com/about-us/en/reports-research/global-wealth-report.html.

Cui, Junjie 崔俊杰. "Gonggong Xingzheng Renwu Quxiang De Jibing Yufang Kongzhi Tixi Gaige" 公共行政任务取向的疾病预防控制体系改革 [Public Administrative Oriented Reforms of the Disease Prevention and Control System]. *Administrative Law Review* 行政法学研究, no. 5 (2020): 102–116. http://en.fzzfyjy.cupl.edu.cn/info/1096/1736.htm.

Cui, Wei. "Administrative Decentralization and Tax Compliance: A Transactional Cost Perspective." *The University of Toronto Law Journal* 65, no. 3 (2015): 186–238.

"What Is a 'Small and Micro-Profit Enterprise' in China?" *Centre for Asian Legal Studies Peter A. Allard School of Law at the University of British Columbia* (blog), December 5, 2019. https://blogs.ubc.ca/cals/what-is-a-small-and-micro-profit-enterprise-in-china/.

Cui, Yan, Cynthia X. Shi, and Zunyou Wu. "Epidemiology of HIV/AIDS in China: Recent Trends." *Global Health Journal* 1, no. 1 (June 1, 2017): 26–32. https://doi.org/10.1016/S2414-6447(19)30057-0.

Cui, Yan, Dongmin Li, and Elizabeth Pisani. "The National HIV Surveillance Program." In *HIV/AIDS in China: Epidemiology, Prevention and Treatment*, edited by Zunyou Wu, Yu Wang, Roger Detels, Marc Bulterys, and Jennifer M. McGoogan, 25–40. Singapore: Springer Singapore, 2019.

Cunningham, Scott, and Manisha Shah. "Decriminalizing Indoor Prostitution: Implications for Sexual Violence and Public Health." *The Review of Economic Studies* 85, no. 3 (July 1, 2018): 1683–1715. https://doi.org/10.1093/restud/rdx065.

Daofeng 1927 刀锋1927. "Butong Leixing Maiyingnü De Xinli Tezheng" 不同类型卖淫女的心理特征 [The Psychological Characteristics of Different Types of Female Sex Workers]. *Wangyi Hao* 网易号 [NetEase Accounts], February 8, 2021. https://web.archive.org/web/20210213161232/https://www.163.com/dy/article/G27VCRGJ0515DPP5.html (original webpage discontinued).

Davidson, Helen, and Vincent Ni. "Chinese Celebrities Warned over Morality in Cultural Crackdown." *Guardian*, September 8, 2021, sec. World news. www.theguardian.com/world/2021/sep/08/chinese-celebrities-warned-over-morality-in-cultural-crackdown.

Davis, Deborah, and Wang Feng, eds. *Creating Wealth and Poverty in Postsocialist China*. Redwood City, CA: Stanford University Press, 2008.

Daxue Consulting. "The Adult Toys Market in China: Untapped Economic Potential." March 4, 2020. https://daxueconsulting.com/adult-toys-market-in-china/.

de Certeau, Michel. *The Practice of Everyday Life*. Translated by Steven F. Rendall. 1st US ed. Berkeley, CA: University of California Press, 1984.

De, Rohit. *A People's Constitution: The Everyday Life of Law in the Indian Republic*. Princeton, NJ: Princeton University Press, 2018.

Della Giusta, Marina. "Simulating the Impact of Regulation Changes on the Market for Prostitution Services." In *Demanding Sex: Critical Reflections on the Regulation of Prostitution*, edited by Vanessa Munro and Marina Della Giusta, 121–135. London: Routledge, 2008.

den Boer, Andrea, and Valerie M. Hudson. "The Security Risks of China's Abnormal Demographics." *Washington Post*, April 30, 2014, sec. Monkey Cage. www.washingtonpost.com/news/monkey-cage/wp/2014/04/30/the-security-risks-of-chinas-abnormal-demographics/.

Denyer, Simon, and Annie Gowen. "Too Many Men: China and India Battle with the Consequences of Gender Imbalance." *South China Morning Post*, April 24, 2018. www.scmp.com/magazines/post-magazine/long-reads/article/2142658/too-many-men-china-and-india-battle-consequences.

Dep't of Diseases Control, National Health Commission 卫健委疾病预防控制局. "2019 Nian Quanguo Fading Chuanranbing Yiqing Gaikuang" 2019年全国法定传染病疫情概况 [The National Overview of Epidemiologic Features of Notifiable Diseases in 2019]. *National Health Commission* 国家卫生健康委员会, April 20, 2020. www.nhc.gov.cn/jkj/s6873/202004/b1519e1bc1a944fc8ec176db600f68d1.shtml.

Desmond, Matthew. *Evicted: Poverty and Profit in the American City*. 1st ed. New York: Crown, 2016.

Diamant, Neil J. *Revolutionizing the Family: Politics, Love, and Divorce in Urban and Rural China, 1949–1968*. 1st ed. Berkeley, CA: University of California Press, 2000.

Ding, Iza Yue. *The Performative State: Public Scrutiny and Environmental Governance in China*. Ithaca, NY: Cornell University Press, 2022. https://doi.org/10.1515/9781501760396.

Distelhorst, Greg. "The Power of Empty Promises: Quasi-Democratic Institutions and Activism in China." *Comparative Political Studies* 50, no. 4 (March 1, 2017): 464–498. https://doi.org/10.1177/0010414015617960.

Do*** 豆***. "Ruhe Kandai Sanpeinu Ne?" 如何看待三陪女呢? [How Do People Perceive Escort Girls?]. *Iask* 爱问知识人, 2007. https://iask.sina.com.cn/b/8966358.html.

Dong, Liu 董柳. "Guangdong Jieyang Fubaiwo An De Shenmi Nvzi 'Xu Xiaowan' Huoxing." 广东揭阳腐败窝案的神秘女子'许小婉'获刑 ["Xu Xiaowan" – Mysterious Woman in Guangdong Jieyang Corruption Case Receives Sentence]. *Yangcheng Evening News* 羊城晚报, April 26, 2016. www.chinacourt.org/article/detail/2016/04/id/1846584.shtml.

Dong, Madeleine Yue. *Republican Beijing: The City and Its Histories*. Berkeley, CA: University of California Press, 2003.

Dong, Xiao-yuan, and Lixin Colin Xu. "Labor Restructuring in China: Toward a Functioning Labor Market." *Journal of Comparative Economics* 37, no. 2 (June 2009): 287–305.

Dong, Xiao-yuan, and Manish Pandey. "Gender and Labor Retrenchment in Chinese State Owned Enterprises: Investigation Using Firm-Level Panel Data." *China Economic Review* 23, no. 2 (June 2012): 385–395.

Dui Hua Foundation. "Custody and Education Worse than Reeducation through Labor?" *Dui Hua Human Rights Journal* (blog), December 26, 2013.www.duihuahrjournal.org/2013/12/.

"Detained Actor Spotlights Custody and Education, Censors Intervene." *Dui Hua Human Rights Journal* (blog), June 10, 2014. Accessed

September 8, 2014. www.duihuahrjournal.org/2014/06/detained-actor-spotlights-custody-and.html.

"Detention House Rules Can't Accommodate Oversight." *Dui Hua Human Rights Journal* (blog), March 6, 2012. Accessed September 17, 2014. www.duihuahrjournal.org/2012/03/detention-house-rules-cant-accommodate.html.

"Is Detention Center Law Enough to Prevent Police Abuse?" *Dui Hua Human Rights Journal* (blog), July 2, 2014. Accessed September 17, 2014. www.duihuahrjournal.org/2014/07/is-detention-center-law-enough-to.html.

"MPS: China Has 116 Custody and Education Centers Nationwide." *Dui Hua Human Rights Journal* (blog), September 4, 2014. Accessed September 8, 2014. www.duihuahrjournal.org/2014/09/mps-china-has-116-custody-and-education.html.

"'Perp Walks' for Petty Thieves Should Cease." *Dui Hua Human Rights Journal* (blog), July 29, 2010. www.duihuahrjournal.org/2010/07/translation-perp-walks-for-petty.html.

Dworkin, Shari L. *Men at Risk: Masculinity, Heterosexuality and HIV Prevention.* New York: New York University Press, 2015.

EastSouthWestNorth. "Shenzhen Sex Worker Protest 2006." 2006. www.zonaeuropa.com/20060120_2.htm.

Ebenstein, Avraham Y., and Ethan Jennings. "Bare Branches, Prostitution, and HIV in China: A Demographic Analysis." In *Gender Policy and HIV in China: Catalyzing Policy Change*, 1st ed., 71–94. The Springer Series on Demographic Methods and Population Analysis, 22. Dordrecht: Springer Netherlands, 2009. https://doi.org/10.1007/978-1-4020-9900-7.

Economist. "Crackdown on Sex City." February 14, 2014. www.economist.com/analects/2014/02/14/crackdown-on-sex-city.

"Old Profession, New Debate: One Woman's Controversial Campaign to Legalise Prostitution." October 27, 2012. www.economist.com/news/china/21565275-one-woman%E2%80%99s-controversial-campaign-legalise-prostitution-old-profession-new-debate.

"Reported Cases of HIV in China Are Rising Rapidly." January 12, 2019. www.economist.com/china/2019/01/12/reported-cases-of-hiv-in-china-are-rising-rapidly.

"Sin City - in China, Sex Work Is Being Pushed Back into the Shadows." Accessed October 21, 2020. www.economist.com/china/2018/07/05/in-china-sex-work-is-being-pushed-back-into-the-shadows.

"Thirty More Days of Hell - Why China's Divorce Law Is So Controversial." Accessed October 16, 2020. www.economist.com/china/2020/08/06/why-chinas-divorce-law-is-so-controversial.

"Why Only 2% of Chinese Pay Any Income Tax." December 1, 2018. www.economist.com/china/2018/12/01/why-only-2-of-chinese-pay-any-income-tax.

Edin, Maria. "State Capacity and Local Agent Control in China: CCP Cadre Management from a Township Perspective." *The China Quarterly* 173 (March 2003): 35–52. https://doi.org/10.1017/S0009443903000044.

Edlund, Lena, and Evelyn Korn. "A Theory of Prostitution." *The Journal of Political Economy* 110, no. 1 (2002): 181–214.

Edlund, Lena, Hongbin Li, Junjian Yi, and Junsen Zhang. "Sex Ratios and Crime: Evidence from China." *Review of Economics and Statistics* 95, no. 5 (2013): 1520–1534.

Eklund, Lisa, and Isabelle Attané. "Marriage Squeeze and Mate Selection in China." In *Handbook on the Family and Marriage in China*, edited by Xiaowei Zang and Lucy Xia Zhao, 156–174. Cheltenham: Edward Elgar, 2017.

Erie, Matthew S. "Anticorruption as Transnational Law: The Foreign Corrupt Practices Act, PRC Law, and Party Rules in China." *The American Journal of Comparative Law* 67, no. 2 (July 31, 2019): 233–279. https://doi.org/10.1093/ajcl/avz018.

China and Islam: The Prophet, the Party, and Law. New York: Cambridge University Press, 2016.

Ewick, Patricia, and Susan S. Silbey. *The Common Place of Law: Stories from Everyday Life*. Chicago, IL: University of Chicago Press, 1998.

Fan, C. Cindy. *China on the Move: Migration, the State, and the Household.* London: Routledge, 2007.

Fan, Jiayang. "China's Mistress-Dispellers." *New Yorker*, June 19, 2017. www.newyorker.com/magazine/2017/06/26/chinas-mistress-dispellers.

Fan, Song Li, C. N. Xiao, Ying-Kui Zhang et al. "How Does the Two-Child Policy Affect the Sex Ratio at Birth in China? A Cross-Sectional Study." *BMC Public Health* 20, no. 1 (May 27, 2020): 1–11. https://doi.org/10.1186/s12889-020-08799-y.

Fang, Lin 方琳. "Shilun Xiandai Gonggong Zhengce De Jiazhi Chongtu" 试论现代公共政策的价值冲突 [On Value Confrontation in Modern Public Policy]. *Administrative Management in China* 中国行政管理 12 (1998): 66–69.

Farmer, Paul, Arthur Kleinman, Jim Kim, and Matthew Basilico, eds. *Reimagining Global Health: An Introduction*. Berkeley, CA: University of California Press, 2013.

Farquhar, Judith. *Appetites: Food and Sex in Postsocialist China*. Durham, NC: Duke University Press, 2002.

Farrer, James. *Opening up: Youth Sex Culture and Market Reform in Shanghai.* Chicago, IL: University of Chicago Press, 2002.

Farrer, James, and Sun Zhongxin. "Extramarital Love in Shanghai." *The China Journal* 50 (July 1, 2003): 1–36.

Feng, Emily, and Charlotte Yang. "China's Cheating Husbands Fuel an Industry of 'Mistress Dispellers'." *New York Times*, July 29, 2016, sec. Asia Pacific. www.nytimes.com/2016/07/30/world/asia/china-marriage-affair-mistress.html.

Feng, Wang, Baochang Gu, and Yong Cai. "The End of China's One-Child Policy." *Studies in Family Planning* 47, no. 1 (March 2016): 83–86.

Feng, Xiaoqing. "A Review of the Development of Marriage Law in the People's Republic of China." *University of Detroit Mercy Law Review* 79, no. 3 (2002): 331–398.

Feng, Xinrui, Yue Hou, and Mingxing Liu. "Underrepresented Outperformers: Female Legislators in the Chinese Congress." *The China Quarterly* 257 (March 2024): 59–74. https://doi.org/10.1017/S0305741023001157.

Ferguson, Michaele L. "Beyond Gender Politics? Mainstreaming the Study of Sex Work." *Perspectives on Politics* 13, no. 2 (June 2015): 437–445. https://doi.org/10.1017/S1537592715000250.

Fincher, Leta Hong. *Betraying Big Brother: The Feminist Awakening in China.* London: Verso Books, 2018.

Leftover Women: The Resurgence of Gender Inequality in China. London: Zed Books, 2014.

Fish, Eric. "The Lives of Sex Workers in Modern China (Interview with Zhang Lijia)." *Asia Society* (blog), February 7, 2017. https://asiasociety.org/blog/asia/lives-sex-workers-modern-china.

Foyle-Hunwick, Robert. "Guys and Sex Dolls–Scenes from the Guangzhou Sexpo." *Danwei* (blog), October 16, 2012. https://web.archive.org/web/20121021062323/http://www.danwei.com/guys-and-sex-dolls-scenes-from-the-guanzghou-sexpo/.

Fraenkel, Ernst. *The Dual State: A Contribution to the Theory of Dictatorship.* New York: Oxford University Press, 1941.

Fu, Diana. *Mobilizing without the Masses: Control and Contention in China.* New York: Cambridge University Press, 2017.

Fu, Hualing. "Duality and China's Struggle for Legal Autonomy." *China Perspectives* 166, no. 1 (2019): 3–10.

"Understanding the Evolving Relationship between the Party and the Law: The Case of China's National Supervision Commission." SSRN Scholarly Paper. Rochester, NY, December 6, 2020. https://doi.org/10.2139/ssrn.3743636.

"Zhou Yongkang and the Recent Police Reform in China." *Australian & New Zealand Journal of Criminology* 38, no. 2 (August 1, 2005): 241–253. https://doi.org/10.1375/acri.38.2.241.

Fu, Hualing, and D. W. Choy. "Administrative Detention of Prostitutes: The Legal Aspects." In *Gender Policy and HIV in China*, Vol. 22, edited by

Joseph Tucker and Dudley L. Poston, 189–199. The Springer Series on Demographic Methods and Population Analysis. Dordrecht: Springer Netherlands, 2009.

"Policing for Profit: Fiscal Crisis and Institutionalized Corruption of Chinese Police." In *Police Corruption: Paradigms, Models and Concepts–Challenges for Developing Countries*, edited by Stanley Einstein and Amir Menachem, 537–552. Huntsville, TX: Office of International Criminal Justice, 2003.

Fu, Hualing, and Weitseng Chen, eds. *Regime Type and beyond: The Transformation of Police in Asia*. Cambridge: Cambridge University Press, 2023. www.cambridge.org/core/books/regime-type-and-beyond/2D2A6A16D4A7EDEE9C28AAAF588A10D0.

Gaetano, Arianne M., and Tamara Jacka. *On the Move: Women and Rural-to-Urban Migration in Contemporary China*. New York: Columbia University Press, 2004.

Gallagher, Mary. *Authoritarian Legality in China: Law, Workers, and the State*. New York: Cambridge University Press, 2017.

Gamble, Sidney D. *Peking: A Social Survey*. New York: George H. Doran, 1921.

Gao, Yu Yang 高语阳, Dong Xin 董鑫, and Zhao Meng 赵萌. "San Wei Lushi Daibiao Weiyuan Jianyi Feizhi Maiyin Piaochang Shourong Jiaoyu" 三位律师代表委员建议废止'卖淫嫖娼收容教育' [Three Lawyer Representatives Recommend to Abolish Custody and Education of Prostitutes and Clients of Prostitutes]. *Beijing Youth Daily* 北京青年报, March 10, 2018. http://media.china.com.cn/cmyw/2018-03-10/1233840.html.

Ge, Lin 葛琳, Li Dongmin 李东民, Li Peilong 李培龙, Guo Wei 郭巍, and Cui Yan 崔岩. "2010–2015 Nian Zhongguo Aizibing Shaodian Jiance Renqun HIV, Meidu He HCV Ganran Zhuangkuang Fenxi" 2010–2015年中国艾滋病哨点监测人群HIV、梅毒和HCV感染状况分析 [Population Specific Sentinel Surveillance for HIV Infection, Syphilis and HCV Infection in China, during 2010–2015]. *Jibing Jiance* 疾病监测 [Disease Surveillance] 32, no. 2 (2017): 111–117.

Gieryn, Thomas F. "Boundary-Work and the Demarcation of Science from Non-Science: Strains and Interests in Professional Ideologies of Scientists." *American Sociological Review* 48, no. 6 (1983): 781–795. https://doi.org/10.2307/2095325.

Gilley, Bruce. "Legitimacy and Institutional Change: The Case of China." *Comparative Political Studies* 41, no. 3 (March 1, 2008): 259–284. https://doi.org/10.1177/0010414007308020.

Goffman, Alice. *On the Run: Fugitive Life in an American City*. Chicago, IL: University of Chicago Press, 2014.

"On the Run: Wanted Men in a Philadelphia Ghetto." *American Sociological Review* 74, no. 3 (2009): 339–357.

Goffman, Erving. "On Fieldwork." *Journal of Contemporary Ethnography* 18, no. 2 (July 1, 1989): 123–132. https://doi.org/10.1177/089124189018002001.

Gold, Thomas, Doug Guthrie, and David Wank, eds. *Social Connections in China: Institutions, Culture, and the Changing Nature of Guanxi*. Cambridge: Cambridge University Press, 2002.

Graham-Harrison, Emma, and Vincent Ni. "China's 'Piano Prince' Li Yundi Detained for Allegedly Hiring Sex Worker." *Guardian*, October 22, 2021, sec. World news. www.theguardian.com/world/2021/oct/22/china-piano-prince-li-yundi-detained-for-allegedly-hiring-sex-worker.

Grover, Anand. "*Report of the Special Rapporteur on the Right of Everyone to the Enjoyment of the Highest Attainable Standard of Physical and Mental Health*." UN Human Rights Council, 2010. www2.ohchr.org/english/bodies/hrcouncil/docs/14session/A.HRC.14.20.pdf.

Gu, Zexu 顾则徐. "Shanghai Pudong Diqu Mouzhen Falang Xingfuwu Zhuangkuang Diaocha" 上海浦东地区某镇发廊性服务状况调查 [Investigation on Sex Service Work Conditions in a Township in Shanghai Pudong District]. *Tianya Luntan* 天涯论坛 [Tianya Forum]. Accessed November 16, 2021. http://bbs.tianya.cn/post-no01-86555-1.shtml (webpage discontinued).

Guangdong People's Procuratorate 广东省人民检察院. "Guo Sheng Kun: Cong Zhongyang Zhengfa Danwei Zuoqi! Yanjin Xiada Pibu Lü Qisu Lü Jiean Lü Deng Zhibiao" 郭声琨:从中央政法单位做起!严禁下达批捕率起诉率结案率等指标 [Guo Shengkun: Central Political and Legal Affairs Authorities to Lead by Example! Quotas for Criminal Detention, Arrests, Prosecutions, Convictions and Case Closures are Strictly Forbidden]. *Yangguang Jianwu Wang* 阳光检务网, April 16, 2019. www.gd.jcy.gov.cn/xwzx/jcyw/201904/t20190416_2543600.shtml.

Guo, Yanli, Xiaoguo Xu, Gengfeng Fu et al. "Risk Behaviours and Prevalences of HIV and Sexually Transmitted Infections among Female Sex Workers in Various Venues in Changzhou, China." *International Journal of STD & AIDS* 28, no. 11 (October 1, 2017): 1135–1142. https://doi.org/10.1177/0956462416689763.

Hail-Jares, Katie, Sugy Choi, Lin Duo, Zhi Luo, and Z. Jennifer Huang. "Occupational and Demographic Factors Associated with Drug Use among Female Sex Workers at the China–Myanmar Border." *Drug and Alcohol Dependence* 161 (April 1, 2016): 42–49. https://doi.org/10.1016/j.drugalcdep.2016.01.026.

Halley, Janet, Prabha Kotiswaran, Hila Shamir, and Chantal Thomas. "From the International to the Local in Feminist Legal Responses to Rape, Prostitution/Sex Work, and Sex Trafficking: Four Studies in Contemporary Governance Feminism." *Harvard Journal of Law & Gender* 29, no. 2 (2006): 335–424.

He, Guojun, and Wenwei Peng. "Guns and Roses: Police Complicity in Organized Prostitution." *Journal of Public Economics* 207 (March 2022): 104599. https://doi.org/10.1016/j.jpubeco.2022.104599.

He, Haibo. "Why Should Custody and Education Be Abolished?" *Peking University Law Journal* 4, no. 1 (2016): 1–44. www.tandfonline.com/doi/full/10.1080/20517483.2016.1174426.

He, Huifeng. "Chongqing Official Wu Hong Latest to Become Embroiled in Sex Scandal." *South China Morning Post*, December 5, 2012.www.scmp.com/news/china/article/1097638/chongqing-official-wu-hong-latest-become-embroiled-sex-scandal.

"Da Xue Sheng Dang 'Er Nai' Kai Chu Xue Ji Re Zheng Yi" 大学生当'二奶'开除学籍惹争议 [College Student Dismissed for Being a 'Second Wife' Aroused Controversy]. *South China Morning Post*, August 7, 2010. http://edu.sina.com.cn/en/2010-08-10/094756998.shtml.

He, Na. "Research Progress in the Epidemiology of HIV/AIDS in China." *China CDC Weekly* 3, no. 48 (2021): 1022–1030.

He, Xin. *Divorce in China: Institutional Constraints and Gendered Outcomes*. New York: New York University Press, 2021.

Hendley, Kathryn. "Resisting Multiple Narratives of Law in Transition Countries: Russia and beyond." *Law & Social Inquiry* 40, no. 2 (2015): 531–552. https://doi.org/10.1111/lsi.12132.

Henochowicz, Anne. "Minitrue: Legal Basis for Custody and Education." *China Digital Times*, June 6, 2014. http://chinadigitaltimes.net/2014/06/minitrue-legal-basis-custody-education/.

Henriot, Christian. "'From a Throne of Glory to a Seat of Ignominy': Shanghai Prostitution Revisited (1849–1949)." *Modern China* 22, no. 2 (1996): 132–163.

"'La Fermeture': The Abolition of Prostitution in Shanghai, 1949–58." *The China Quarterly* 142 (1995): 467–486.

Prostitution and Sexuality in Shanghai: A Social History 1849–1949. Cambridge: Cambridge University Press, 2001.

Hershatter, Gail. *Dangerous Pleasures: Prostitution and Modernity in Twentieth-Century Shanghai*. Berkeley, CA: University of California Press, 1997.

"The Hierarchy of Shanghai Prostitution, 1870–1949." *Modern China* 15, no. 4 (1989): 463–498.

Hesketh, Therese, Li Lu, and Zhu Wei Xing. "The Consequences of Son Preference and Sex-Selective Abortion in China and Other Asian Countries." *CMAJ: Canadian Medical Association Journal* 183, no. 12 (September 6, 2011): 1374–1377. https://doi.org/10.1503/cmaj.101368.

Hildebrandt, Timothy. *Social Organizations and the Authoritarian State in China*. Cambridge: Cambridge University Press, 2013.

Ho, Petula Sik Ying, Stevi Jackson, Siyang Cao, and Chi Kwok. "Sex with Chinese Characteristics: Sexuality Research in/on 21st-Century China."

The Journal of Sex Research 55, no. 4–5 (2018): 486–521. https://doi.org/10.1080/00224499.2018.1437593.

Hoang, Kimberly Kay. *Dealing in Desire: Asian Ascendancy, Western Decline, and the Hidden Currencies of Global Sex Work*. 1st ed. Oakland, CA: University of California Press, 2015.

Hochschild, Arlie Russell. *The Managed Heart: Commercialization of Human Feeling*. Berkeley, CA: University of California Press, 1983.

Hofford, Alex. "A Sleazy 'Sexual Culture Festival' in Guangzhou, China." *Alex Hofford Photography* (blog), November 5, 2009. https://web.archive.org/web/20160513082456/http://www.alexhofford.com:80/node/2262.

Holland, Alisha C. "Forbearance." *American Political Science Review* 110, no. 2 (May 2016): 232–246. https://doi.org/10.1017/S0003055416000083.

Hong, Brendan. "China's Concubine Culture Lives on in Mistress Villages." *The Daily Beast* (blog), April 14, 2014. www.thedailybeast.com/articles/2014/04/14/china-s-concubine-culture-lives-on-in-mistress-villages.html.

Hong, Yan, and Xiaoming Li. "Behavioral Studies of Female Sex Workers in China: A Literature Review and Recommendation for Future Research." *AIDS and Behavior* 12, no. 4 (July 2008): 623–636.

Hong, Yan, Chen Zhang, Xiaoming Li et al. "HIV Testing Behaviors among Female Sex Workers in Southwest China." *AIDS and Behavior* 16, no. 1 (January 2012): 44–52. https://doi.org/10.1007/s10461-011-9960-8.

Horizon Market Research and Futures Group Europe. "2001 Behavioural Surveillance Survey in Yunnan and Sichuan. Adult Male Report." *Horizon Market Research*. Beijing, 2002.

Hou, Rui. "Maintaining Social Stability without Solving Problems: Emotional Repression in the Chinese Petition System." *The China Quarterly* 243 (2020): 635–654. https://doi.org/10.1017/S0305741019001528.

Hu, Hong, Guy Taylor, and Qingfeng Chen. "HIV Education: Raising Awareness and Increasing Knowledge." In *HIV/AIDS in China: Epidemiology, Prevention and Treatment*, edited by Zunyou Wu, Yu Wang, Roger Detels, Marc Bulterys, and Jennifer M. McGoogan, 225–249. Singapore: Springer Singapore, 2019. http://ebookcentral.proquest.com/lib/york/detail.action?docID=5940511.

Hu, Xiujie 胡秀洁. "Wanshan Woguo Seqing Wenti Lifa Han Zhifa De Sikao" 完善我国色情问题立法和执法的思考 [Reflections on How to Improve the Legalization and Law Enforcement of the Sex Industry]. *Journal of Zhangzhou Normal University* 漳州师范学院学报 2 (2011): 25–30.

Huang, Xiaoqing 黄晓晴. "Chen Hongping Qingfu Shousheng" 陈弘平情妇受审 [Chen Hongping's Mistress on Trial]. *Yangcheng Evening News* 羊城晚报, June 17, 2015. https://news.sina.com.cn/o/2015-06-17/140931960830.shtml.

Huang, Yingying. "Illegal 'Profession' Is Risky Business." *China Daily*, May 5, 2010. www.chinadaily.com.cn/opinion/2010-05/31/content_9909738.htm.

Huang, Yingying, and Suiming Pan. "Job Mobility of Brothel-Based Female Sex Workers in Current Northeast China: The Process from Xiagang (Lay-Offs) to Sex Worker." Institute of Sexuality and Gender, Renmin University of China, March 18, 2004. https://usiraq.procon.org/sourcefiles/job-mobility-of-brothel-based-female-sex-workers-in-current-northeast-china-the-process-from-xiagang-worker-lay-offs-to-sex-worker.pdf.

Huang, Yingying, Gail E. Henderson, Suiming Pan, and Myron S. Cohen. "HIV/AIDS Risk among Brothel-Based Female Sex Workers in China: Assessing the Terms, Content, and Knowledge of Sex Work." *Sexually Transmitted Diseases* 31, no. 11 (November 2004): 695–700.

Huang, Yingying, Laurie Abler, Pan Suiming et al. "Population-Based Sexual Behavior Surveys in China: Liuzhou Compared with Other Prefectural Cities." *AIDS and Behavior* 18, no. 2 (February 2014): 118–125. https://doi.org/10.1007/s10461-013-0645-3.

Hudson, Valerie M., and Andrea Den Boer. "A Surplus of Men, a Deficit of Peace: Security and Sex Ratios in Asia's Largest States." *International Security* 26, no. 4 (April 1, 2002): 5–38.

Human Rights Watch. "Locked Doors: The Human Rights of People Living with HIV/AIDS in China." September 3, 2003. www.hrw.org/report/2003/09/02/locked-doors/human-rights-people-living-hiv/aids-china.

"Sex Workers at Risk: Condoms as Evidence of Prostitution in Four US Cities." July 2012. https://www.hrw.org/report/2012/07/19/sex-workers-risk/condoms-evidence-prostitution-four-us-cities.

Hwang, Kwang-kuo. "Face and Favor: The Chinese Power Game." *American Journal of Sociology* 92, no. 4 (January 1987): 944–974.

Jacobs, Andrew. "China Pushes to End Public Shaming." *New York Times*, July 27, 2010. www.nytimes.com/2010/07/28/world/asia/28china.html.

Jeffreys, Elaine. *China, Sex and Prostitution*. London: Routledge Curzon, 2004.

"Debating the Legal Regulation of Sex-Related Bribery and Corruption in the People's Republic of China." In *Sex and Sexuality in China*, edited by Elaine Jeffreys, 159–178. London: Routledge, 2006.

"Exposing Police Corruption and Malfeasance: China's Virgin Prostitute Cases." *The China Journal* 63 (January 1, 2010): 127–149. https://doi.org/10.1086/tcj.63.20749197.

"Introduction: Talking Sex and Sexuality in China." In *Sex and Sexuality in China*, edited by Elaine Jeffreys, 1–20. Routledge Studies on China in Transition 26. London: Routledge, 2006.

Prostitution Scandals in China: Policing, Media and Society. London: Routledge, 2012.

Jeffreys, Elaine, and Gang Su. "China's 100 Per Cent Condom Use Program: Customising the Thai Experience." *Asian Studies Review* 35, no. 3 (2011): 315–333.

Jeffreys, Sheila. *The Industrial Vagina: The Political Economy of the Global Sex Trade*. United Kingdom: Routledge, 2008.

Jia, Yujiang, Fan Lu, Xinhua Sun, and Sten H. Vermund. "Sources of Data for Improved Surveillance of HIV/AIDS in China." *The Southeast Asian Journal of Tropical Medicine and Public Health* 38, no. 6 (November 2007): 1041–1052.

Jiang, Xinhui. "Gendered Pathways to the County-Level People's Congress in China." *The China Quarterly* 249 (March 2022): 68–90. https://doi.org/10.1017/S0305741021001156.

Jim, Clare, and Yimou Lee. "Anti-Vice Crackdown on China's 'Sin City' Takes Extra Toll as Economy Slows." *Reuters*, April 3, 2014, sec. Business News. www.reuters.com/article/cbusiness-us-china-economy-dongguan-idCABREA3223S20140403.

Kaufman, Joan. "Civil Society Involvement in National HIV/AIDS Programs." In *HIV/AIDS in China: Epidemiology, Prevention and Treatment*, edited by Zunyou Wu, Yu Wang, Roger Detels, Marc Bulterys, and Jennifer M. McGoogan, 427–440. Singapore: Springer, 2020. https://doi.org/10.1007/978-981-13-8518-6_22.

"HIV, Sex Work, and Civil Society in China." *Journal of Infectious Diseases* 204, no. suppl 5 (January 12, 2011): S1218–S1222. https://doi.org/10.1093/infdis/jir538.

Kaufman, Joan, Arthur Kleinman, and Tony Saich, eds. *AIDS and Social Policy in China*. Cambridge, MA: Harvard University Asia Center, 2006.

Kavemann, Barbara, Heike Rabe, and Claudia Fischer. "*The Act Regulating the Legal Situation of Prostitutes–Implementation, Impact, Current Developments: Findings of a Study on the Impact of the German Prostitution Act, Berlin.*" Berlin: Sozialwissenschaftliches FrauenForschungsInstitut an der Evangelischen Fachhochschule Freiburg, 2007. www.cahrv.uni-osnabrueck.de/reddot/BroschuereProstGenglisch.pdf.

Keen, David. "Opinion | When 'Do No Harm' Hurts." *New York Times*, November 6, 2013, sec. Opinion. www.nytimes.com/2013/11/07/opinion/when-fear-impedes-aid.html.

Kennedy, John. "China: Sex Workers Demand Legalization, Organizer Detained." *Global Voices*, August 1, 2010. https://globalvoices.org/2010/08/01/china-sex-workers-demand-legalization-organizer-detained/.

Kipnis, Andrew B. *Producing Guanxi: Sentiment, Self, and Subculture in a North China Village*. Durham, NC: Duke University Press, 1997.

Ko, Dorothy. *Teachers of the Inner Chambers: Women and Culture in Seventeenth-Century China*. Stanford, CA: Stanford University Press, 1994.

Kotiswaran, Prabha. *Dangerous Sex, Invisible Labor: Sex Work and the Law in India*. Princeton, NJ: Princeton University Press, 2011.

Kuo, Lily. "China Claims to Have Eliminated Poverty, but the Figures Mask Harsh Challenges." *Washington Post*, February 25, 2021. Accessed September 14, 2021. www.washingtonpost.com/world/asia_pacific/china-poverty-economy-growth/2021/02/25/9e92cb18-7722-11eb-9489-8f7dacd51e75_story.html.

Lafraniere, Sharon. "In Grant Dispute, AIDS Funds Frozen for China." *New York Times*, May 20, 2011. www.nytimes.com/2011/05/21/world/asia/21china.html.

Laliberté, André, and Marc Lanteigne. "The Issue of Challenges to the Legitimacy of CCP Rule." In *The Chinese Party-State in the 21st Century: Adaptation and the Reinvention of Legitimacy*, edited by André Laliberté and Marc Lanteigne, 1st ed., 1–21. London: Routledge, 2011.

Lam, Oiwan. "Mistresses – China's New Corruption Warriors." *Global Voices* (blog), November 27, 2012. http://globalvoicesonline.org/2012/11/27/china-mistresses-vs-corruption/.

Landry, Pierre F. *Decentralized Authoritarianism in China: The Communist Party's Control of Local Elites in the Post-Mao Era*. Cambridge: Cambridge University Press, 2008.

Lau, Mimi. "Activist Ye Haiyan Evicted from Home by Guangdong Police." *South China Morning Post*, July 7, 2013. www.scmp.com/news/china/article/1277003/activist-ye-haiyan-evicted-home-guangdong-police.

Lee, Ching Kwan. *Gender and the South China Miracle: Two Worlds of Factory Women*. Berkeley, CA: University of California Press, 1998.

"School Sexual Abuse Protester Ye Haiyan Beaten up in Her Own Home." *South China Morning Post*, May 31, 2013. www.scmp.com/news/china/article/1250041/school-sexual-abuse-protester-ye-haiyan-beaten.

Lee, Ching Kwan, and Yong Hong Zhang. "Seeing Like a Grassroots State: Producing Power and Instability in China's Bargained Authoritarianism." In *To Govern China: Evolving Practices of Power*, edited by Vivienne Shue and Patricia M. Thornton, 177–201. Cambridge: Cambridge University Press, 2017.

Lee, Deborah Jian, and Sushma Subramanian. "China's Bachelors: When Men Outnumber Women." *Pulitzer Center*, October 17, 2011. Accessed October 19, 2020. http://pulitzercenter.org/projects/china-population-women-bachelor-marriage.

Legal Daily 法制日報. "Ping Lun: Xiang Anmo Xiaojie Deng Shoushui Yu Zongrong Seqing Bingbu Xianggan" 评论:向按摩小姐等收税与纵容色情并不相干 [Commentary-It's Pointless in Comparing Taxing Parlor Girls to Indulging Sex Business]. *Sohu.Com* 搜狐, December 24, 2002. http://news.sohu.com/53/10/news205201053.shtml.

Legal Systems Times 法制时报. "'Xu Xiaowan' Fan Xinghuizui Huoxing Liunian" "许小婉"犯行贿罪获刑6年 ["Xu Xiaowan" Convicted for 6 Years for Accepting Bribery]. April 27, 2016.

Legislative Affairs Office of the State Council 国务院法制办公室. "Guowuyuan Fazhiban Jiaokewen Fazhisi Youguan Fuze Tongzhi Jiu 'Yule Changsuo Guanli Tiaoli' De Youguan Wenti Da 'Zhengfu Fazhi Xinxi Wang' Jizhe Wen" 国务院法制办教科文卫法制司有关负责同志就《娱乐场所管理条例》的有关问题答《政府法制信息网》记者问 [Legislative Affairs Office of the State Council's Reply for the Reporter from Government Legal Information Website on Questions Regarding the Measures for the Administration of Entertainment Venues]. December 4, 2006. www.moj.gov.cn/pub/sfbgw/zcjd/200612/t20061204_389810.html.

Leng, Sidney. "Coronavirus: China's Income Inequality Could Expand in 2020 as Outbreak Rattles World's No 2 Economy." *South China Morning Post*, March 17, 2020. www.scmp.com/economy/china-economy/article/3075497/coronavirus-chinas-income-inequality-could-expand-2020.

Levin, Dan. "China's New Wealth Spurs a Market for Mistresses." *New York Times*, August 9, 2011. www.nytimes.com/2011/08/10/world/asia/10mistress.html.

Levine, Jessica. "China's New Bachelor Class." *Atlantic*, February 11, 2013. www.theatlantic.com/international/archive/2013/02/chinas-new-bachelor-class/273040/

Levine, Philippa. *Prostitution, Race, and Politics: Policing Venereal Disease in the British Empire*. New York: Routledge, 2003. https://doi.org/10.4324/9780203881941.

Levitt, Peggy, and Sally Merry. "Vernacularization on the Ground: Local Uses of Global Women's Rights in Peru, China, India and the United States." *Global Networks* 9, no. 4 (October 1, 2009): 441–461.

Li, Amy. "China Activists Launch Campaign against Paedophiles: 'Call Me, Not Schoolchildren'." *South China Morning Post*, May 30, 2013. www.scmp.com/news/china/article/1249565/china-activists-launch-campaign-against-paedophiles-call-me-not.

Li, Clara. "Marriage Law Overhaul Bans 'Second Wives'." *South China Morning Post*, April 29, 2001. www.scmp.com/article/345532/marriage-law-overhaul-bans-second-wives.

Li, Hong Xun 李红汛, and Yin Yi 尹伊. "Gonganbu Fa Tongzhi Piping Dui Maiyin Piaochang Renyuan Youjie Shizhong" 公安部发通知批评对卖淫嫖娼人员游街示众 [The Ministry of Public Security Issued a Notice Criticizing Prostitution Shame Parades]. *Dahe Bao* 大河报, July 26, 2010. www.chinanews.com.cn/fz/2010/07-26/2424235.shtml.

Li, Ke. *Marriage Unbound: State Law, Power, and Inequality in Contemporary China*. Stanford, CA: Stanford University Press, 2022.

"'What He Did Was Lawful': Divorce Litigation and Gender Inequality in China." *Law & Policy* 37, no. 3 (2015): 153–179. https://doi.org/10.1111/lapo.12034.

Li, Yan, Roger Detels, Peng Lin et al. "Difference in Risk Behaviors and STD Prevalence between Street-Based and Establishment-Based FSWs in Guangdong Province, China." *AIDS and Behavior* 16, no. 4 (May 2012): 943–951. https://doi.org/10.1007/s10461-011-0102-0.

Li, Yunfang 李云芳. "Hangzhou Yi Paichusuo Saohuang Xiang 'Falangnu' Jiashu Fa Gaozhixin" 杭州一派出所扫黄向"发廊女"家属发告知信 [A Police Station in Hangzhou Cracks down on Prostitution by Notifying Families of Women Who Work in Hair Salons]. *Sichuan Zaixian* 四川在线, September 6, 2010. https://web.archive.org/web/20100909004044/http://news.163.com:80/10/0906/06/6FSKSU6O00011229.html.

Li, Zhisui. *The Private Life of Chairman Mao: The Memoirs of Mao's Personal Physician*. New York: Random House, 1994.

Liang, Lily. "No Room for Respectability: Boundary Work in Interaction at a Shanghai Rental." *Symbolic Interaction* 41, no. 2 (2018): 185–209. https://doi.org/10.1002/symb.325.

Liang, Zai, Zhen Li, and Zhongdong Ma. "Changing Patterns of the Floating Population in China during 2000–2010." *Population and Development Review* 40, no. 4 (December 2014): 695–716. https://doi.org/10.1111/j.1728-4457.2014.00007.x.

Lieberthal, Kenneth G., and David M. Lampton, eds. *Bureaucracy, Politics, and Decision Making in Post-Mao China*. Berkeley, CA: University of California Press, 1992.

Lieberthal, Kenneth, and Michel Oksenberg. *Policy Making in China: Leaders, Structures, and Processes*. Princeton, NJ: Princeton University Press, 1988.

Lin, Wen, Sanny Chen, Nicole Seguy et al. "Is the HIV Sentinel Surveillance System Adequate in China? Findings from an Evaluation of the National HIV Sentinel Surveillance System." *Western Pacific Surveillance and Response Journal* 3, no. 4 (2012): 76–85.

Ling, Bonny. "Prostitution and Female Trafficking in China: Between Phenomena and Discourse." *China Perspectives*, no. 1–2 (June 1, 2018): 65–74. https://doi.org/10.4000/chinaperspectives.7742.

Lipkin, Zwia. *Useless to the State: "Social Problems" and Social Engineering in Nationalist Nanjing, 1927–1937*. Cambridge, MA: Harvard University Press, 2006.

Lipsky, Michael. *Street-Level Bureaucracy: Dilemmas of the Individual in Public Services*. New York: Russell Sage Foundation, 1980.

Liu, Min. "Chinese Migrant Women in the Sex Industry: Exploring Their Paths to Prostitution." *Feminist Criminology* 7, no. 4 (2012): 327–349.

Liu, Sida. "Boundary Work and Exchange: The Formation of a Professional Service Market." *Symbolic Interaction* 38, no. 1 (2015): 1–21. https://doi.org/10.1002/symb.137.

Liu, Sida, and Terence C. Halliday. *Criminal Defense in China: The Politics of Lawyers at Work*. Cambridge: Cambridge University Press, 2016.

Long, Yan. "The Contradictory Impact of Transnational AIDS Institutions on State Repression in China, 1989–2013." *American Journal of Sociology* 124, no. 2 (September 1, 2018): 309–366. https://doi.org/10.1086/698466.

Lu, Fan, Peng Xu, Jennifer M. McGoogan, Wanying Chen, and Liping Ma. "Evolution of HIV/AIDS Policy." In *HIV/AIDS in China: Epidemiology, Prevention and Treatment*, edited by Zunyou Wu, Yu Wang, Roger Detels, Marc Bulterys, and Jennifer M. McGoogan, 359–374. Singapore: Springer Singapore, 2019.

Lu, Shen. "Pretty Lady Cadres." *ChinaFile*, December 21, 2020. www.chinafile.com/reporting-opinion/features/pretty-lady-cadres-china.

Lu, Yansi 陆妍思. "Xiang Anmou Nu Zhengshui De Shishi Feifei" 向按摩女征税的是是非非 [Pros and Cons on Taxing Massage Parlor Girls]. *Xin Kuai Bao* 新快报, November 20, 2002. http://news.sina.com.cn/c/2002-11-20/09422043s.html.

Lucky, Xue Molin 薛墨麟. "Ruhe Kandai KTV Li Peijiu De Nuren" 如何看待ktv里陪酒的女人 [How Do You See Women Who are Hostesses in KTVs?]." *Zhihu* 知乎, April 16, 2020. www.zhihu.com/question/264971299/answer/1157534765.

Luo, Chris. "Chongqing Authority to Examine Official's Alleged Sex Romp." *South China Morning Post*, November 21, 2012. www.scmp.com/news/china/article/1087580/chongqing-authority-examine-officials-alleged-sex-romp.

Luo, Congran 罗聪冉, and Wu Jie 武杰. "Li Yundi Piaochang Beiju Yansheng Pufa Xiaoketang: Ruohe Rending Zhengju? Huiyou Hezhong Yingxiang?" 李云迪嫖娼被拘衍生普法小课堂:如何认定证据？会有何种影响？ [A Popular Law Class on Li Yundi's Detention over Prostitution: How to Evaluate Evidence? What are the Consequences?]. *Legal Daily* 法治日报, October 21, 2021. https://new.qq.com/rain/a/20211021A0EHFW00.

Macfarlane, Rachel, Celene Fuller, Chris Wakefield, and Barbara Brents. "Sex Industry and Sex Workers in Nevada." *The Social Health of Nevada: Leading Indicators and Quality of Life in the Silver State*, January 1, 2017, 1–38. https://cdclv.unlv.edu/healthnv_2017/sexindustry.pdf.

MacKinnon, Catharine A. *Toward a Feminist Theory of the State*. Cambridge, MA: Harvard University Press, 1989.

Majic, Samantha. "'I'm Just a Woman. But I've Never Been a Victim': Re-Conceptualizing Prostitution Policy through Individual Narratives."

Journal of Women, Politics & Policy 36, no. 4 (October 2, 2015): 356–387. https://doi.org/10.1080/1554477X.2015.1082889.

Sex Work Politics: From Protest to Service Provision. Philadelphia, PA: University of Pennsylvania Press, 2013.

Maldonado, Camilo. "Credit Suisse: Top 1% Own Nearly 50% of Global Wealth and China's Wealthy Now Outnumber America's." *Forbes*, October 23, 2019. www.forbes.com/sites/camilomaldonado/2019/10/23/credit-suisse-top-1-own-nearly-50-of-global-wealth-and-chinas-wealthy-now-outnumber-americas/#16528512ede5.

Mann, Susan. *Precious Records: Women in China's Long Eighteenth Century*. Stanford, CA: Stanford University Press, 1997.

Mason, Katherine A. "Becoming Modern after SARS: Battling the H1N1 Pandemic and the Politics of Backwardness in China's Pearl River Delta." *Behemoth* 3, no. 3 (December 2010): 8–35.

"The Correct Secret: Discretion and Hypertransparency in Chinese Biosecurity." *Focaal* 2016, no. 75 (January 1, 2016). www.berghahnjournals.com/view/journals/focaal/2016/75/fcl750104.xml.

Infectious Change: Reinventing Chinese Public Health after an Epidemic. 1st ed. Stanford, CA: Stanford University Press, 2016.

"To Your Health! Toasting, Intoxication and Gendered Critique among Banqueting Women." *The China Journal* 69 (January 2013): 108–133.

Massoud, Mark Fathi. *Law's Fragile State: Colonial, Authoritarian, and Humanitarian Legacies in Sudan*. Cambridge: Cambridge University Press, 2013.

McCarthy, Lauren A. *Trafficking Justice: How Russian Police Enforce New Laws, from Crime to Courtroom*. Ithaca, NY: Cornell University Press, 2015.

McMillan, Jo. "Selling Sexual Health: China's Emerging Sex Shop Industry." In *Sex and Sexuality in China*, edited by Elaine Jeffreys, 124–138. London: Routledge, 2006.

Merry, Sally Engle. *Human Rights and Gender Violence: Translating International Law into Local Justice*. Chicago, IL: University of Chicago Press, 2006.

The Seductions of Quantification: Measuring Human Rights, Gender Violence, and Sex Trafficking. 1st ed. Chicago, IL: University of Chicago Press, 2016.

Merry, Sally Engle, and Rachel E. Stern. "The Female Inheritance Movement in Hong Kong: Theorizing the Local/Global Interface." *Current Anthropology* 46, no. 3 (2005): 387–409.

Mertha, Andrew C. *China's Water Warriors: Citizen Action and Policy Change*. 1st ed. Ithaca, NY: Cornell University Press, 2008.

"'Fragmented Authoritarianism 2.0': Political Pluralization in the Chinese Policy Process." *The China Quarterly* 200 (December 2009): 995–1012. https://doi.org/10.1017/S0305741009990592.

The Politics of Piracy: Intellectual Property in Contemporary China. Ithaca, NY: Cornell University Press, 2005.

Michelson, Ethan. *Decoupling: Gender Injustice in China's Divorce Courts*. New ed. Cambridge: Cambridge University Press, 2022.

"Justice from above or below? Popular Strategies for Resolving Grievances in Rural China." *The China Quarterly* 193 (2008): 43–64.

Micollier, Evelyne, ed. *Sexual Cultures in East Asia: The Social Construction of Sexuality and Sexual Risk in a Time of AIDS*. Routledge Curzon–IIAS Asian Studies Series. London: Routledge Curzon, 2004.

Migdal, Joel. "Foreword." In *The Everyday Life of the State: A State-in-Society Approach*, edited by Adam White, vii–xiv. Seattle, DC: University of Washington Press, 2013.

State in Society: Studying How States and Societies Transform and Constitute One Another. Later Printing. Used ed. Cambridge: Cambridge University Press, 2001.

Miller, Richard E., and Austin Sarat. "Grievances, Claims, and Disputes: Assessing the Adversary Culture." *Law & Society Review* 15, no. 3/4 (1980): 525–566. https://doi.org/10.2307/3053502.

Ministry of Foreign Affairs (BZ). "Dutch Policy on Prostitution. Questions and Answers 2012." Netherlands: Ministry of Foreign Affairs (BZ), 2012. AVT12/BZ106006. https://web.archive.org/web/20130903173702/http://www.minbuza.nl/binaries/content/assets/minbuza/en/import/en/you_and_the_netherlands/about_the_netherlands/ethical_issues/faq-prostitutie-pdf–engels.pdf-2012.pdf.

Ministry of Health of the People's Republic of China. "China 2010 UNGASS Country Progress Report." April 2, 2010. www.aidsdatahub.org/sites/default/files/resource/china-ungass-2010-country-progress-report-jan-2008-dec-2009.pdf.

Mo, Lian. "China's Store-Bought Sexual Revolution." *China Daily*, July 10, 2010. www.chinadaily.com.cn/business/2010-07/10/content_10090544.htm.

Munro, Vanessa, and Marina Della Giusta, eds. *Demanding Sex: Critical Reflections on the Regulation of Prostitution*. Aldershot: Ashgate, 2008.

National Bureau of Statistics 国家统计局. "2009 Nian Nongmin Gong Jiance Diaocha Baogao" 2009年农民工监测调查报告 [2009 Migrant Workers Survey Report]. March 22, 2010. http://cn.chinagate.cn/reports/2010-03/22/content_19655996.htm.

"2019 Nian Nongmin Gong Jiance Diaocha Baogao" 2019年农民工监测调查报告 [2019 Migrant Workers Survey Report]. April 30, 2020. www.stats.gov.cn/sj/zxfb/202302/t20230203_1900710.html.

National Center for AIDS/STD Control and Prevention 性病艾滋病预防控制中心. "Quanguo Aizibing Shaodian Jiance Shishi Fangan (Shixing) Caozuo Shouce" 全国艾滋病哨点监测实施方案(试行)操作手册 [Guidebook for Monitoring on the Implementation of National AIDS Checkpoints (for

Trial Implementation)]. March 2009. www.doc88.com/p-903997410407.html.

"Quanguo Aizibing Shaodian Jiance Shishi Fangan Caozuo Shouce" 全国艾滋病哨点监测实施方案操作手册 [Guidebook for Monitoring on the Implementation of National AIDS Checkpoints]. March, 2012.www.yascdc.com/Files/file/20160128/20160128111936643664.pdf.

"Quanguo Aizibing Shaodian Jiance Shishi Fangan Caozuo Shouce" (全国艾滋病哨点监测实施方案操作手册) [Guidebook for Monitoring on the Implementation of National AIDS Checkpoints]. March 2017. www.jygcdc.com/userfiles/files/%E5%85%A8%E5%9B%BD%E8%89%BE%E6%BB%8B%E7%97%85%E5%93%A8%E7%82%B9%E7%9B%91%E6%B5%8B%E5%AE%9E%E6%96%BD%E6%96%B9%E6%A1%88(2017%E7%89%88).pdf.

National Center for AIDS/STD Control and Prevention, and China CDC 性病艾滋病预防控制中心 中国疾病预防控制中心. "Yixing Xingchuanbo Gaowei Renqun Yufang Aizibing Ganyu Gongzuo Zhinan" 异性性传播高危人群预防艾滋病干预工作指南 [Working Guidelines on Intervention on High-Risk Populations for HIV/AIDS Heterosexual Sex Transmission]. May 2016. https://ncaids.chinacdc.cn/fzyw_10256/jsgf/201804/W020160913346815311893.pdf.

National Health Commission 国家卫生健康委员会. "Dui Shisanjie Quanguo Renda Yici Huiyi Di 4342 Hao Jianyi De Dafu" 对十三届全国人大一次会议第4342号建议的答复 [Reply to Proposal No. 4342 of the First Session of the Thirteenth National People's Congress]. September 27, 2018. www.nhc.gov.cn/wjw/jiany/201812/14726c604d3045469853ed5b12058b40.shtml.

National Public Radio. "Corruption Blurs the Lines of China's Mistress Culture." March 2, 2014. www.npr.org/2014/03/02/284905579/corruption-blurs-the-lines-of-chinas-mistress-culture.

New York Times. "Why Shaming Has Lost Power in China: Introduction." July 31, 2010. www.nytimes.com/roomfordebate/2010/07/31/china-shaming.

Ng, Hui Hsien. "Moral Order Underground: An Ethnography of the Geylang Sex Trade." Master's thesis, National University of Singapore, 2011. https://core.ac.uk/download/pdf/48648807.pdf.

Ni, Vincent and Helen Davidson. "China's Cultural Crackdown: Few Areas Untouched as Xi Reshapes Society." *Guardian*, September 10, 2021, sec. World news. www.theguardian.com/world/2021/sep/10/chinas-cultural-crackdown-few-areas-untouched-as-xi-reshapes-society.

Normile, Dennis. "China Overhauls Its Public Health Bureaucracy." *Science (New York, NY)* 372, no. 6544 (May 21, 2021): 779. https://doi.org/10.1126/science.372.6544.779.

O'Brien, Kevin J., and Lianjiang Li. *Rightful Resistance in Rural China*. 1st ed. Cambridge: Cambridge University Press, 2006.

"Selective Policy Implementation in Rural China." *Comparative Politics* 31, no. 2 (January 1, 1999): 167–186.

Ong, Jason J., Mingzhou Xiong, Joseph D. Tucker et al. "Sexualized Drug Use among Female Sex Workers from Eight Cities in China: A Cross-Sectional Study." *Archives of Sexual Behavior* 51, no. 5 (2022): 2689–2698. https://doi.org/10.1007/s10508-021-02117-2.

Open Society Foundations. "10 Reasons to Decriminalize Sex Work." Horizon Market Research, 2015. www.opensocietyfoundations.org/uploads/c24963af-78fd-4497-a79d-f824413182b4/10-reasons-to-decriminalize-sex-work-20150410.pdf.

Osburg, John. *Anxious Wealth: Money and Morality among China's New Rich*. Stanford, CA: Stanford University Press, 2013.

"Tough Love: Money and Mistresses in the Middle Kingdom." *Foreign Affairs*, June 12, 2014. www.foreignaffairs.com/articles/141562/john-osburg/tough-love.

Osnos, Evan. "Boss Rail." *New Yorker*, October 15, 2012. www.newyorker.com/magazine/2012/10/22/boss-rail.

Otis, Eileen M. "The Dignity of Working Women: Service, Sex, and the Labor Politics of Localization in China's City of Eternal Spring." *American Behavioral Scientist* 52, no. 3 (November 1, 2008): 356–376. https://doi.org/10.1177/0002764208325309.

Outshoorn, Joyce. "Introduction: Prostitution, Women's Movements and Democratic Politics." In *The Politics of Prostitution: Women's Movements, Democratic States, and the Globalisation of Sex Commerce*, edited by Joyce Outshoorn, 1–20. Cambridge: Cambridge University Press, 2004.

ed. *The Politics of Prostitution: Women's Movements, Democratic States, and the Globalisation of Sex Commerce*. Cambridge: Cambridge University Press, 2004.

Palmer, James. "The Bro Code." *ChinaFile*, February 4, 2015. www.chinafile.com/reporting-opinion/postcard/bro-code.

"How Young Women in China become Mistresses." *Aeon*, October 10, 2013. https://aeon.co/essays/why-do-young-rural-women-in-china-become-mistresses.

Pan, Suiming 潘绥铭. *Cunzai Yu Huangmiu: Zhongguo Dixia "Xingchanye" Kao Cha* 存在与荒谬: 中国地下"性产业"考察 [Existing in Falsehoods: An Investigation of China's Underground "Sex Industry"]. Beijing: Qunyan Press 群言出版社, 1999.

"The Realistic Response to China's Prostitution Problem." *Sixth Tone* (blog), November 30, 2017. www.sixthtone.com/news/1001266.

Sheng Cun Yu Ti Yan 生存与体验 [Survival and Experiences]. Beijing: Chinese Social Science Press 中国社会科学出版社, 2000.

"Transformations in the Primary Life Cycle: The Origins and Nature of China's Sexual Revolution." In *Sex and Sexuality in China*, edited by Elaine Jeffreys, 21–42. London: Routledge, 2006.

Pan, Suiming 潘绥铭, Huang Yingying 黄盈盈, and Liu Zhenying 刘振英. *Qingjing Yu Ganwu : Xinan Zhongguo Sange Hongdengqu Tansuo* 情境与感悟: 西南中国三个红灯区探索 [Situation and Inspiration: Study on Three Red Light Districts in Southwest China]. Kaohsiung: Wanyou Press 万有出版社, 2005.

Pan, Suiming 潘绥铭, Huang Yingying 黄盈盈, Wang Jie et al. *Chengxian Yu Biaoding: Zhongguo "Xiao Jie" Shen Yanjiu* 呈现与标定: 中国"小姐"深研究 [Performing and Labeling: In-Depth Study on Female Sex Workers in China]. Kaohsiung: Wanyou Press 万有出版社, 2005.

Xiaojie: Laodong De Quanli: Zhongguo Dongnan Yanhai Yu Dongbei Chengshi De Duizhao Kaocha 小姐: 劳动的权利: 中国东南沿海与东北城市的对照考察 [Female Sex Workers: The Rights of Labor: Comparative Study between Southeastern and Northeastern Chinese Cities]. Hong Kong: Hong Kong Dadao Press 香港大道出版社, 2005.

Pan, Suiming, William L. Parish, and Yingying Huang. "Clients of Female Sex Workers: A Population-Based Survey of China." *The Journal of Infectious Diseases* 204, no. suppl 5 (October 31, 2011): S1211–S1217.

Pang, Jingcheng 庞京城, and Shen Deli 沈德理. "Zhifa Tongyi Yu Guanli Youxiao: Ruhe Renshi Dui Yule (Baogua Shehuang) Changsuo Congye Renyuan De Shoushui Wenti" 执法统一与管理有效: 如何认识对娱乐(包括涉黄)场所从业人员的收税问题 [Effective and Unified Law Enforcement: How to Recognize the Problem of Taxing Employees in Entertainment Venues (Sex-Related Industries Included]. In *The 8th (2013) Annual Conference of Chinese Society for Management Modernization – Session Essays on a Study of Management Cases*. Beijing: Chinese Society for Management Modernization 中国管理学年会, 2013.

Parish, William L., Edward O. Laumann, and Sanyu A. Mojola. "Sexual Behavior in China: Trends and Comparisons." *Population and Development Review* 33, no. 4 (2007): 729–756.

Peerenboom, Randall. "Introduction." In *Judicial Independence in China: Lessons for Global Rule of Law Promotion*, edited by Randall Peerenboom, 1st ed., 1–22. Cambridge: Cambridge University Press, 2009.

People's Daily Online. "1 in 5 Marriage Age Chinese Men to Remain Bachelors within 10 Years." January 13, 2010. https://web.archive.org/web/20110203010722/http://english.peopledaily.com.cn:80/90001/90782/90872/6867770.html.

Pepinsky, Thomas B., Jan H. Pierskalla, and Audrey Sacks. "Bureaucracy and Service Delivery." *Annual Review of Political Science* 20, no. 1 (2017): 249–268. https://doi.org/10.1146/annurev-polisci-051215-022705.

Perry, Elizabeth J. *Rebels and Revolutionaries in North China, 1845–1945*. Stanford, CA: Stanford University Press, 1980.

Phillips, Tom. "Chinese Official Shamed over Adultery 'Contract' That Fines Bad Behaviour." *Telegraph*, November 18, 2013. www.telegraph.co.uk/news/worldnews/asia/china/10457027/Chinese-official-shamed-over-adultery-contract-that-fines-bad-behaviour.html. https://perma.cc/E9L9-WGPG.

Phoenix, Joanna. "Prostitute Identities: Men, Money and Violence." *The British Journal of Criminology* 40, no. 1 (2000): 37–55.

Piketty, Thomas, Li Yang, and Gabriel Zucman. "Capital Accumulation, Private Property, and Rising Inequality in China, 1978–2015." *American Economic Review* 109, no. 7 (July 2019): 2469–2496. https://doi.org/10.1257/aer.20170973.

Pils, Eva. *China's Human Rights Lawyers: Advocacy and Resistance*. London: Routledge, 2014.

Portillo, Shannon, and Danielle S. Rudes. "Construction of Justice at the Street Level." *Annual Review of Law and Social Science* 10, no. 1 (2014): 321–334. https://doi.org/10.1146/annurev-lawsocsci-102612-134046.

Prasso, Sheridan. "China's Divorce Spike Is a Warning to Rest of Locked-Down World." *Bloomberg*, March 31, 2020. www.bloomberg.com/news/articles/2020-03-31/divorces-spike-in-china-after-coronavirus-quarantines.

Rajagopalan, Megha, and Huang Yan. "China's Spurned Mistresses Can't Be Relied on to Bust Graft." *Reuters*, May 29, 2013. www.reuters.com/article/china-corruption/chinas-spurned-mistresses-cant-be-relied-on-to-bust-graft-paper-idINDEE94S04X20130529.

Rajah, Jothie. *Authoritarian Rule of Law: Legislation, Discourse and Legitimacy in Singapore*. Revised ed. Cambridge: Cambridge University Press, 2012.

Remick, Elizabeth J. "Police-Run Brothels in Republican Kunming." *Modern China* 33, no. 4 (2007): 423–461.

"Prostitution Taxes and Local State Building in Republican China." *Modern China* 29, no. 1 (2003): 38–70.

Regulating Prostitution in China: Gender and Local Statebuilding, 1900–1937. Stanford, CA: Stanford University Press, 2014.

Reuters. "Communist Party Expels Xu Jie, Former Petitions Bureau Deputy, over 'Bribery and Adultery'." June 27, 2014. www.scmp.com/news/china/article/1541599/ex-petitioning-bureau-chief-xu-jie-expelled-party-over-bribery-adultery.

Rojanapithayakorn, Wiwat. "The 100% Condom Use Programme in Asia." *Reproductive Health Matters* 14, no. 28 (2006): 41–52.

Rose, Dina R., and Todd R. Clear. "Incarceration, Social Capital, and Crime: Implications for Social Disorganization Theory." *Criminology* 36, no. 3 (1998): 441–480.

Rozelle, Scott, and Natalie Hell. *Invisible China: How the Urban-Rural Divide Threatens China's Rise*. 1st ed. Chicago, IL: University of Chicago Press, 2020.

Rubin, Herbert J., and Irene S. Rubin. *Qualitative Interviewing: The Art of Hearing Data*. 3rd ed. Thousand Oaks, CA: SAGE, 2011.

Saich, Tony. "Is SARS China's Chernobyl or Much Ado about Nothing?" In *SARS in China: Prelude to Pandemic?*, edited by Arthur Kleinman and James L. Watson, 71–104. Redwood City, CA: Stanford University Press, 2006.

"The Blind Man and the Elephant: Analysing the Local State in China." In *On the Roots of Growth and Crisis: Capitalism, State and Society in East Asia*, edited by Luigi Tomba, Vol. 36, 75–99. Annali Della Fondazione Feltrinelli, Milan: Annale Feltinelli, 2002.

Sapio, Flora. "Perp Parades." *Forgotten Archipelago* (blog), July 26, 2010. http://florasapio.blogspot.com/search/label/prostitution.

Sauer, Birgit. "Taxes, Rights and Regimentation: Discourses on Prostitution in Austria." In *The Politics of Prostitution: Women's Movements, Democratic States and the Globalisation of Sex Commerce*, edited by Joyce Outshoorn, 41–61. Cambridge: Cambridge University Press, 2004.

Schatz, Edward, ed. *Political Ethnography: What Immersion Contributes to the Study of Power*. Chicago, IL: University of Chicago Press, 2009.

Scoggins, Suzanne E. "Authoritarian Policing under Xi Jinping." *Journal of Chinese Political Science* 28, no. 2 (July 23, 2022): 251–271. https://doi.org/10.1007/s11366-022-09825-z.

Policing China: Street-Level Cops in the Shadow of Protest: Studies of the Weatherhead East Asian Institute, Columbia University. Ithaca, NY: Cornell University Press, 2021.

"Policing Modern China." *China Law and Society Review* 3, no. 2 (October 30, 2018): 79–117. https://doi.org/10.1163/25427466-00302001.

Scoggins, Suzanne E., and Kevin J. O'Brien. "China's Unhappy Police." *Asian Survey* 56, no. 2 (April 1, 2016): 225–242. https://doi.org/10.1525/as.2016.56.2.225.

Scott, James C. *Domination and the Arts of Resistance: Hidden Transcripts*. 1st ed. New Haven, CT: Yale University Press, 1990.

Scoular, Jane, and Maggie O'Neill. "Legal Incursions into Supply/Demand: Criminalising and Responsibilising the Buyers and Sellers of Sex in the UK." In *Demanding Sex: Critical Reflections on the Regulation of Prostitution*, edited by Vanessa Munro and Marina Della Giusta, 13–33. Aldershot: Ashgate, 2008.

Sea-ling, Cheng. "Assuming Manhood: Prostitution and Patriotic Passions in Korea." *East Asia* 18, no. 4 (2000): 40–78.

Seligsohn, Deborah. "The Rise and Fall of the US-China Health Relationship." *Asian Perspective* 45, no. 1 (2021): 203–224. https://doi.org/10.1353/apr.2021.0023.

SFGate. "Cities Shame Johns to Fight Prostitution." October 13, 2012. www.sfgate.com/crime/article/Cities-shame-johns-to-fight-prostitution-3946434.php.

Shah, Svati P. "Trafficking and the Conflation with Sex Work: Implications for HIV Control and Prevention." Working Paper for the Third Meeting of the Technical Advisory Group of the Global Commission on HIV and the Law, 2011. https://hivlawcommission.org/wp-content/uploads/2017/06/Sex-Work-Trafficking-and-HIV.pdf.

Shen, Linsong 沈林松, and Wang Zhiwen 王志文. "Maiyin Piaochang Huodong Zhong De Aizibing Chuanbo Yinhuan Ji Fangzhi Duice Chuyi" 卖淫嫖娼活动中的艾滋病传播隐患及防治对策刍议 [Comments on the HIV Risks in and Prevention Strategies Regarding Prostitution and Whoring Activities]. *Journal of Hunan Public Security College* 湖南公安高等专科学校学报 18, no. 1 (2006): 51–53.

Shen, Tingting. "A Rare Rights Victory in China." *The Diplomat*. Accessed April 21, 2020. https://thediplomat.com/2020/03/a-rare-rights-victory-in-china/.

Shen, Tingting, and Joanne Csete. "HIV, Sex Work, and Law Enforcement in China." *Health and Human Rights* 19, no. 2 (2017): 133–146.

Shi, Lingen, Weiming Tang, Haiyang Hu et al. "The Impact of COVID-19 Pandemic on HIV Care Continuum in Jiangsu, China." *BMC Infectious Diseases* 21, no. 1 (August 7, 2021): 1–9. https://doi.org/10.1186/s12879-021-06490-0.

Shih, Victor, Christopher Adolph, and Mingxing Liu. "Getting Ahead in the Communist Party: Explaining the Advancement of Central Committee Members in China." *American Political Science Review* 106, no. 1 (February 2012): 166–187. https://doi.org/10.1017/S0003055411000566.

Shirk, Susan L. "China in Xi's 'New Era': The Return to Personalistic Rule." *Journal of Democracy* 29, no. 2 (April 10, 2018): 22–36. https://doi.org/10.1353/jod.2018.0022.

Shively, Michael, Sarah Kuck Jalbert, William Rhodes et al. "Final Report on the Evaluation of the First Offender Prostitution Program." March 7, 2008. www.ncjrs. gov/pdffiles1/nij/grants/221894.pdf.

Sicular, Terry, Xiuna Yang, and Björn Gustafsson. "The Rise of China's Global Middle Class in International Perspective." IZA Institute of Labor Economics Discussion Paper Series, 2021. https://docs.iza.org/dp14531.pdf.

Sigley, Gary. "Sex, Politics and the Policing of Virtue in the People's Republic of China." In *Sex and Sexuality in China*, edited by Elaine Jeffreys, 43–61. Routledge Studies on China in Transition 26. London: Routledge, 2006.

Sigley, Gary, and Elaine Jeffreys. "On 'Sex' and 'Sexuality' in China: A Conversation with Pan Suiming." *Bulletin of Concerned Asian Scholars* 31, no. 1 (March 1999): 50–58. https://doi.org/10.1080/14672715.1999.10415730.

Sommer, Matthew Harvey. *Polyandry and Wife-Selling in Qing Dynasty China: Survival Strategies and Judicial Interventions*. 1st ed. Oakland, CA: University of California Press, 2015.

Sex, Law, and Society in Late Imperial China. Stanford, CA: Stanford University Press, 2000.

Song, Jianlin, and James Paul Gee. "Slogans with Chinese Characteristics: The Political Functions of a Discourse Form." *Discourse & Society* 31, no. 2 (March 1, 2020): 201–217. https://doi.org/10.1177/0957926519880033.

South China Morning Post. "Pictured: The Twin 'Mistresses' at the Centre of Xinjiang Police Official Scandal." December 10, 2012. www.scmp.com/news/china/article/1102123/pictured-twin-mistresses-centre-xinjiang-police-official-scandal.

Southern Weekly. "Gongan Bu: 'Maiyin Nu' Ke Gai Jiao 'Shizu Funu'" 公安部: '卖淫女'可改叫'失足妇女' [The Ministry of Public Security: 'Prostitutes' Should Be Termed 'Women Who Have Lost Their Way']. December 13, 2010. https://web.archive.org/web/20110216070125/http://www.infzm.com/content/53485.

Spires, Anthony J. "Regulation as Political Control: China's First Charity Law and Its Implications for Civil Society." *Nonprofit and Voluntary Sector Quarterly* 49, no. 3 (October 25, 2019): 571–588. https://doi.org/10.1177/0899764019883939.

Stern, Rachel E. *Environmental Litigation in China: A Study in Political Ambivalence*. Cambridge: Cambridge University Press, 2013.

"Unpacking Adaptation: The Female Inheritance Movement in Hong Kong." *Mobilization: An International Quarterly* 10, no. 3 (October 1, 2005): 421–439.

Stern, Rachel E., and Kevin J. O'Brien. "Politics at the Boundary: Mixed Signals and the Chinese State." *Modern China* 38, no. 2 (March 1, 2012): 174–198. https://doi.org/10.1177/0097700411421463.

Stevenson, Alexandra. "Leadership Changes Reveal That in China, Men Still Rule." *New York Times*, October 23, 2022, sec. World. www.nytimes.com/2022/10/23/world/asia/women-china-party-congress.html.

Stuart, Forrest. "Becoming 'Copwise': Policing, Culture, and the Collateral Consequences of Street-Level Criminalization." *Law & Society Review* 50, no. 2 (2016): 279–313. https://doi.org/10.1111/lasr.12201.

Sullivan, Barbara. “The Women’s Movement and Prostitution Politics in Australia.” In *The Politics of Prostitution: Women’s Movements, Democratic States and the Globalisation of Sex Commerce*, edited by Joyce Outshoorn, 21–40. Cambridge: Cambridge University Press, 2004.

“When (Some) Prostitution Is Legal: The Impact of Law Reform on Sex Work in Australia.” *Journal of Law and Society* 37, no. 1 (March 1, 2010): 85–104.

Sun, Jiangping, Duo Shan, Yiyun Hu, and Jonas Tillman. “International Cooperation Projects and the HIV/AIDS Response.” In *HIV/AIDS in China: Epidemiology, Prevention and Treatment*, edited by Zunyou Wu, Yu Wang, Roger Detels, Marc Bulterys, and Jennifer M. McGoogan, 393–404. Singapore: Springer Singapore, 2019.

Sun, Jiangping, Hui Liu, Hui Li et al. “Contributions of International Cooperation Projects to the HIV/AIDS Response in China.” *International Journal of Epidemiology* 39, no. suppl 2 (January 12, 2010): ii14–ii20. https://doi.org/10.1093/ije/dyq208.

Sun, Liangzi 孙良滋. “Zhang Shuguang Qingfu Luofei Beijianyi Jianxing Cengyin Shouhui Panxing Wunian” 张曙光情妇罗菲被建议减刑 曾因受贿判刑五年 [Reduced Sentence Recommended for Luo Fei, Mistress of Zhang Shuguang, Who Had Been Sentenced for Five Years for Accepting Bribery]. *Caixin News* 财新新闻, August 25, 2017. https://china.caixin.com/2017-08-25/101135561.html.

Sun, Xinhua, Ning Wang, Dongmin Li et al. “The Development of HIV/AIDS Surveillance in China.” *AIDS* 21, no. suppl 8 (December 2007): S33–S38.

Sun, Yan. *Corruption and Market in Contemporary China*. Ithaca, NY: Cornell University Press, 2004.

Tam, Fiona. “Crackdown Fails to Scare Dongguan’s Sex-Trade Veterans.” *South China Morning Post*, November 26, 2009. www.scmp.com/article/699410/crackdown-fails-scare-dongguans-sex-trade-veterans.

“Party Chief Vows to Crack down but Excessive Measures Will Be Avoided.” *South China Morning Post*, November 26, 2009. www.scmp.com/article/699448/party-chief-vows-crack-down-excessive-measures-will-be-avoided.

Tan, Kenneth. “The World’s Oldest Profession Gets a New Name in China and a Thumbs up from Li Yinhe.” *Shanghaiist*, December 18, 2010. http://shanghaiist.com/2010/12/18/prostitution-li-yinhe.php.

Tan, Shin Bin, and Alisha Gill. “Containing Commercial Sex to Designated Red Light Areas: An Idea Past Its Prime?” 2014. https://web.archive.org/web/20140912005614/http://lkyspp.nus.edu.sg/wp-content/uploads/2014/04/Containing-Commercial-Sex-to-Designated-Red-Light-Areas.pdf.

Tan, Yanzi. "Sex Theme Park Prepares to Open." *China Daily*, May 15, 2009. https://web.archive.org/web/20090722054446/http://www.chinadaily.com.cn/china/2009-05/15/content_7780762.htm.

Tan, Zhihong 谭志红. "Guangdong Dongguan Jingfang Shengqian Maiyinnu Youjie Re Zhengyi" 广东东莞警方绳牵卖淫女游街惹争议 [Controversy over Police from Dongguan, Guangdong Parading Prostitutes through the Streets on a Leash]. *Nanfang Daily* 南方日报, July 18, 2010. http://news.sohu.com/20100718/n273587691.shtml.

Taraud, Christelle. *La prostitution coloniale: Algérie, Tunisie, Maroc (1830–1962)*. Paris: Payot, 2003.

Tarrow, Sidney G. *The New Transnational Activism*. New York: Cambridge University Press, 2005.

Tatlow, Didi Kirsten. "Petition Seeks Closure of Extrajudicial Detention Centers." *Sinosphere Blog* (blog), May 5, 2014. https://archive.nytimes.com/sinosphere.blogs.nytimes.com/2014/05/05/petition-seeks-closure-of-extrajudicial-detention-centers/.

Telford, Ted A. "Family and State in Qing China: Marriage in the Tongcheng Lineages, 1650–1880." In *Family Process and Political Process in Modern Chinese History*, Vol. 2, 921–42. Taipei: Institute of Modern History, Academia Sinica, 1992.

The China Sex Worker Organization Network Forum 中国性工作者机构网络平台. "Research on the Impact of 2010 Crackdown on Sex Work and HIV Interventions in China 2010年严打对性工作与艾滋病防治影响研究." 2011. https://asiacatalyst.org/wp-content/uploads/2012/01/EN_Research_on_the_Impact_of_Crackdown_on_Sex_Work_and_HIV_Interventions_in_China.pdf.

"Zhong Guo Di Dang (Di Shou Ru) Nu Xing Xing Gong Zuo Zhe Ai Zi Bing Fang Zhi Xian Zhuang Yan Jiu Bao Gao" 中国低档(低收入)女性性工作者艾滋病防治现状研究报告 [Research on HIV/AIDS Prevention and Intervention among Chinese Low-Tier (Low-Income) Female Sex Workers]. September 18, 2013. https://groups.google.com/g/sex-worker/c/ijN082VYLfM.

The Global Fund. "The Global Fund to Fight AIDS, Tuberculosis and Malaria Sixth Call for Proposals Guidelines." 2006.

"Government Donors-China." *The Global Fund* (blog). Accessed November 23, 2019. www.theglobalfund.org/en/government/profiles/china/.

Tian, Yew Lun. "Chinese Professor Who Criticized Xi Seeks to Overturn Prostitution Charge, Lawyer Says." *Reuters*, July 29, 2020, sec. China. www.reuters.com/article/us-china-politics-professor-idUSKCN24U1L2.

Tran, Lisa. "The Concubine in Republican China: Social Perception and Legal Construction." *Etudes Chinoises* 28 (2008): 119–149.

Concubines in Court: Marriage and Monogamy in Twentieth-Century China. Lanham, MD: Rowman & Littlefield, 2015.

Trevaskes, Susan. *Policing Serious Crime in China: From "Strike Hard" to "Kill Fewer."* London: Routledge, 2010.

Trubek, David M. "Law and Development: Forty Years after 'Scholars in Self-Estrangement.'" *University of Toronto Law Journal* 66, no. 3 (May 19, 2016): 301–329. https://doi.org/10.3138/UTLJ.3671.

Tsang, Eileen Yuk-ha. *China's Commercial Sexscapes: Rethinking Intimacy, Masculinity, and Criminal Justice*. Toronto: University of Toronto Press, 2019.

UNAIDS. "Blind Spot: Reaching out to Men and Boys Addressing a Blind Spot in the Response to HIV." 2017. www.unaids.org/sites/default/files/media_asset/blind_spot_en.pdf.

"Guidance Note on HIV and Sex Work." 2012. www.unaids.org/sites/default/files/media_asset/JC2306_UNAIDS-guidance-note-HIV-sex-work_en_0.pdf.

"HIV and Sex Work." Human Rights Fact Sheet Series, 2021. www.unaids.org/sites/default/files/media_asset/05-hiv-human-rights-factsheet-sex-work_en.pdf.

"Intensifying HIV Prevention: A UNAIDS Policy Position Paper." 2005. https://data.unaids.org/publications/irc-pub06/jc1165-intensif_hiv-newstyle_en.pdf.

"International Guidelines on HIV/AIDS and Human Rights." 2006. www.ohchr.org/Documents/Issues/HIV/ConsolidatedGuidelinesHIV.pdf.

United Nations Development Program. "Access for All: Basic Public Services for 1.3 Billion People." 2008. www.undp.org/china/publications/china-human-development-report-2007/2008.

"Risks, Rights & Health." 2012. www.undp.org/sites/g/files/zskgke326/files/publications/Commissions%20report%20final-EN.pdf.

Uretsky, Elanah. "'Mobile Men with Money': The Socio-Cultural and Politico-Economic Context of 'High-Risk' Behaviour among Wealthy Businessmen and Government Officials in Urban China." *Culture, Health & Sexuality* 10, no. 8 (November 2008): 801–814.

"Mixing Business with Pleasure: Masculinity and Male Sexual Culture in Urban China in the Era of HIV/AIDS." PhD diss., Columbia University, 2007.

Occupational Hazards: Business, Sex, and HIV in Post-Mao China. Stanford, CA: Stanford University Press, 2016.

Wagenaar, Hendrik, and Sietske Altink. "Prostitution as Morality Politics or Why It Is Exceedingly Difficult to Design and Sustain Effective Prostitution Policy." *Sexuality Research and Social Policy* 9, no. 3 (September 2012): 279–292. https://doi.org/10.1007/s13178-012-0095-0.

Walsh, Matthew, and Danmeng Ma. "China Diagnoses 131,000 New HIV Cases This Year – Caixin Global." *Caixin Global*, December 5, 2019. www.caixinglobal.com/2019-12-05/china-diagnoses-131000-new-hiv-cases-this-year-101491090.html.

Wan, Xia, Sanghyuk S. Shin, Qian Wang et al. "Smoking among Young Rural to Urban Migrant Women in China: A Cross-Sectional Survey." *PLOS ONE* 6, no. 8 (August 4, 2011): e23028. https://doi.org/10.1371/journal.pone.0023028.

Wang, Haibo, Ray Y. Chen, Guowei Ding et al. "Prevalence and Predictors of HIV Infection among Female Sex Workers in Kaiyuan City, Yunnan Province, China." *International Journal of Infectious Diseases* 13, no. 2 (2009): 162–169.

Wang, Junrong 王军荣. "Gaicheng Shizu Funu Shi Dui Teshu Renqun De Zunzhong" 改称"失足妇女"是对特殊人群的尊重 [Be Renamed as 'Women Who Have Lost Their Way' Is to Show Respect for the Special Group]. *Eastday*, December 12, 2010. https://web.archive.org/web/20110106005550/http://pinglun.eastday.com/p/20101222/u1a5625940.html.

Wang, Lu, and Ning Wang. "HIV/AIDS Epidemic and the Development of Comprehensive Surveillance System in China with Challenges." *Chinese Medical Journal* 123, no. 23 (December 2010): 3495–3500.

Wang, Nanfu, dir. *Hooligan Sparrow* 流氓燕. San Francisco: Kino Lorber Edu, 2016.

Wang, Xing 王星. "Shoujiao Sanshi Nian" 收教三十年 [Detention Education for 30 Years]. *Southern Metropolis Daily* 南方都市报, July 2, 2014. http://news.ifeng.com/a/20140702/40979790_0.shtml.

Wang, Xinzi 王欣子. "Wuhan Jingfang Jietou Tie Gaoshi Shiming Puguang Maiyin Piaochang Renyuan" 武汉警方街头贴告示实名曝光卖淫嫖娼人员 [Wuhan Police Post Official Notices on the Street Revealing the Names of Individuals Who Engage in Prostitution]. *Changjiang Shangbao* 长江商报, July 17, 2010. https://web.archive.org/web/20100719150325/http://news.163.com/10/0717/02/6BOU3MNS00011229.html.

Watts, Jonathan. "Ai Weiwei Investigated over Nude Art." *Guardian*, November 18, 2011. www.theguardian.com/artanddesign/2011/nov/18/ai-weiwei-investigation-nude-art.

"Outrage at Chinese Prostitutes' Shame Parade." *Guardian*, December 6, 2006. www.theguardian.com/world/2006/dec/06/china.jonathanwatts.

Weaver, Vesla M., and Amy E. Lerman. "Political Consequences of the Carceral State." *American Political Science Review* 104, no. 4 (2010): 817–833.

Weitzer, Ronald John. *Legalizing Prostitution: From Illicit Vice to Lawful Business*. New York: New York University Press, 2012.

Westcott, Ben. "China Moves to End Two-Child Limit, Finishing Decades of Family Planning." *CNN*. Accessed October 19, 2020. www.cnn.com/2018/08/28/asia/china-family-planning-one-child-intl/index.html.

White, Tyrene. *China's Longest Campaign: Birth Planning in the People's Republic, 1949–2005*. Ithaca, NY: Cornell University Press, 2006.

Wong, Edward. "Chinese City Is Chilly to a Sex Theme Park." *New York Times*, May 18, 2009. www.nytimes.com/2009/05/19/world/asia/19china.html.

Wong, Gillian. "Global Fund Lifts China Grant Freeze." *Associated Press*, August 23, 2011. www.sandiegouniontribune.com/sdut-apnewsbreak-global-fund-lifts-china-grant-freeze-2011aug23-story.html.

Wong, Kam C. *Police Reform in China*. Boca Raton, FL: CRC Press, 2012.

Wong, Linda. "Chinese Migrant Workers: Rights Attainment Deficits, Rights Consciousness and Personal Strategies." *China Quarterly* 208 (2011): 870–892.

Woo, Margaret Y. K. "Contesting Citizenship: Marriage and Divorce in the People's Republic of China." In *Sex and Sexuality in China*, edited by Elaine Jeffreys, 62–81. Routledge Studies on China in Transition 26. London: Routledge, 2006.

World Health Organization, UNFPA, and UNAIDS. "Prevention and Treatment of HIV and Other Sexually Transmitted Infections for Sex Workers in Low and Middle-Income Countries." December 2012. www.unaids.org/en/resources/presscentre/featurestories/2012/december/20121212sexworkguidance/.

World Health Organization, United Nations Population Fund, UNAIDS, Global Network of Sex Work Projects, and The World Bank. *Implementing Comprehensive HIV/STI Programmes with Sex Workers: Practical Approaches from Collaborative Interventions*. Geneva: World Health Organization, 2013. https://apps.who.int/iris/rest/bitstreams/424844/retrieve.

Wright, Teresa. *Accepting Authoritarianism: State-Society Relations in China's Reform Era*. Stanford, CT: Stanford University Press, 2010.

Wu, Fengshi. "Double-Mobilization: Transnational Advocacy Networks for China's Environment and Public Health." PhD diss., University of Maryland, College Park, 2005.

Wu, Zunyou, Junfang Chen, Sarah Robbins Scott, and Jennifer M. McGoogan. "History of the HIV Epidemic in China." *Current HIV/AIDS Reports* 16, no. 6 (December 1, 2019): 458–466. https://doi.org/10.1007/s11904-019-00471-4.

Wu, Zunyou, Sheena G. Sullivan, Yu Wang, Mary Jane Rotheram-Borus, and Roger Detels. "Evolution of China's Response to HIV/AIDS." *The Lancet* 369, no. 9562 (February 2007): 679–690.

Wu, Zunyou, Yu Wang, Roger Detels, and Jennifer M. McGoogan. "Introduction." In *HIV/AIDS in China: Epidemiology, Prevention and Treatment*, edited by Zunyou Wu, Yu Wang, Roger Detels, Jennifer M. McGoogan, and Marc Butlerys, v–xiv. Singapore: Springer Singapore, 2019. http://ebookcentral.proquest.com/lib/york/detail.action?docID=5940511.

Xiao, Rong 肖荣. "'Shourong Jiaoyu' Falu Yiju Hezai?" '收容教育'法律依据何在? [What Is the Legal Basis for 'Custody and Education'?]. *Jiancha Ribao* 检察日报[Procuratorate Daily], June 4, 2014, sec. 01. http://newspaper.jcrb.com/html/2014-06/04/node_2.htm.

Xiao, Suowei. "China's New Concubines? The Contemporary Second-Wife Phenomenon." ProQuest Dissertations, 2009. www.proquest.com/docview/507467912/abstract/24DB5D6F920743BBPQ/1.

"The 'Second-Wife' Phenomenon and the Relational Construction of Class-Coded Masculinities in Contemporary China." *Men and Masculinities* 14, no. 5 (December 1, 2011): 607–627. https://doi.org/10.1177/1097184X11412171.

肖索未. *Yuwang Yu Zunyan: Zhuanxingqi Zhongguo De Jieceng, Xingbie Yu Qinmi Guanxi* 欲望与尊严：转型期中国的阶层，性别与亲密关系 [Desire and Dignity: Class, Gender and Intimacy in Transitional China]. Beijing: China Social Sciences Academic Press 社会科学文献出版社, 2018.

Xie, Yue. "The Political Logic of Weiwen in Contemporary China." *Issues & Studies* 48, no. 3 (September 2012): 1–41.

Xinhua News Agency 新华社. "Anti-AIDS Campaign Spotlights Sex Workers." *China.Org.Cn* 中国网, May 5, 2005. www.china.org.cn/english/Life/127807.htm.

"China Lifts 13.86 Mln Rural Poor out of Poverty in 2018." February 15, 2019. https://web.archive.org/web/20190219093034/http://www.xinhuanet.com/english/2019-02/15/c_137824705.htm.

"Li Keqiang Dui Aizibing Fangzhi Gongzuo Zuochu Zhongyao Pishi" 李克强对艾滋病防治工作作出重要批示 [Premier Li Keqiang Issues Major Comments on HIV Prevention and Treatment Work]. November 30, 2021. www.gov.cn/xinwen/2021-11/30/content_5654997.htm.

"Online Sex Video Leads to Dismissal of Chinese Official." August 6, 2011. www.wantchinatimes.com/news-subclass-cnt.aspx?id=20110806000032&cid=1303.

"Safe-Sex Education for Prostitutes Stirs Debate." *China.Org.Cn* 中国网, October 16, 2006. www.china.org.cn/english/2006/Oct/184130.htm.

"Xi Jinping Jiangshu De Gushi: Renlei Mianlin De Gongtong Tiaozhan" 习近平讲述的故事：人类面临的共同挑战 [Story Told by Xi Jinping: Common Challenges Faced by Humankind]. December 1, 2021. www.news.cn/politics/2021-12/01/c_1128119600.htm.

Xu, Jianhua. "Police Accountability and the Commodification of Policing in China: A Study of Police/Business Posters in Guangzhou." *The British Journal of Criminology* 53, no. 6 (2013): 1093–1117.

Xu, Junfang, Yu Shi, Feng Cheng, and Wannian Liang. "China's Public Health System: Time for Improvement." *The Lancet Public Health* 6, no. 12 (December 1, 2021): e869–e870. https://doi.org/10.1016/S2468-2667(21)00250-4.

Xu, Yuanfeng 徐元锋. "Shenyang Fenji Guanli Yule Changsuo" 沈阳分级管理娱乐场所 [Classification Management of the Entertainment Venues in Shenyang]. *Renminwang* 人民网, April 20, 2006. http://news.sohu.com/20060421/n242916929.shtml.

Yan, Yunxiang. *The Flow of Gifts: Reciprocity and Social Networks in a Chinese Village*. Stanford, CA: Stanford University Press, 1996.

Yang, Bo, Zheng Wu, Christoph M. Schimmele, and Shuzhuo Li. "HIV Knowledge among Male Labor Migrants in China." *BMC Public Health* 15, no. 1 (December 2015): 323. https://doi.org/10.1186/s12889-015-1653-1.

Yang, Dali L. *Remaking the Chinese Leviathan: Market Transition and the Politics of Governance in China*. Stanford, CA: Stanford University Press, 2004.

Yang, Jia Lynn. "Jilted Mistresses Expose Chinese Officials' Corruption." *Washington Post*, July 25, 2013. www.washingtonpost.com/world/ji-yingnan-and-other-jilted-mistresses-expose-chinese-officials-corruption/2013/07/25/8d8d35f6-eb02-11e2-aa9f-c03a72e2d342_story.html.

Yang, Mayfair Mei-hui. *Gifts, Favors, and Banquets: The Art of Social Relationships in China*. Ithaca, NY: Cornell University Press, 1994.

Yang, Wanli. "Sexologist Punished for Swindling Research Funds." *China Daily*, October 29, 2014. www.chinadaily.com.cn/china/2014-10/29/content_18818940.htm.

Yang, Xueying, Chengbo Zeng, Cheuk Chi Tam et al. "HIV Service Interruptions during the COVID-19 Pandemic in China: The Role of COVID-19 Challenges and Institutional Response from Healthcare Professional's Perspective." *AIDS and Behavior* 26, no. 4 (April 1, 2022): 1270–1278. https://doi.org/10.1007/s10461-021-03484-6.

Ye, Zhenmiao 叶振淼, Chen Sheng 陈晟, Yao Xiao-qiu 姚晓秋 et al. "Wenzhou Shi Nongcun Diqu ≥ 60 Sui Laonian Nanxing Piaoke Aizibing Zhishi Ji Xingxingwei Tezheng Diaocha" 温州市农村地区≥60岁老年男性嫖客艾滋病知识及性行为特征调查 [HIV/AIDS-Related Knowledge and Sexual Behavior Characteristics among Elderly Male Clients Aged 60 Years and above in Rural Areas of Wenzhou City]. *Practical Preventive Medicine* 实用预防医学 27, no. 1 (2020): 38–41. https://doi.org/10.3969/j.issn.1006-3110.2020.01.010.

Yi, Huso, Joanne E. Mantell, Rongrong Wu et al. "A Profile of HIV Risk Factors in the Context of Sex Work Environments among Migrant

Female Sex Workers in Beijing, China." *Psychology, Health & Medicine* 15, no. 2 (March 2010): 172–187. https://doi.org/10.1080/13548501003623914.

Yi, Huso, Tiantian Zheng, Yanhai Wan et al. "Occupational Safety and HIV Risk among Female Sex Workers in China: A Mixed-Methods Analysis of Sex-Work Harms and Mommies." *Global Public Health* 7, no. 8 (2012): 840–855. https://doi.org/10.1080/17441692.2012.662991.

Yu, Verna. "How China Is Using Criminal Detention in Place of Re-Education through Labour." *South China Morning Post*, April 21, 2014. www.scmp.com/news/china/article/1492192/china-using-criminal-detention-place-re-education-through-labour.

Yu, Yeon Jung. "Positional Embodiment: How Networks Shape the Lived Experiences of the Bodies of Female Sex Workers in Post-Socialist China." *Gender, Work & Organization* 29, no. 3 (2022): 953–970. https://doi.org/10.1111/gwao.12753.

Yuen, Samson. "Friend or Foe? The Diminishing Space of China's Civil Society." *China Perspectives; Wanchai* 2015, no. 3 (2015): 51–56.

Yule, Ergege 二哥哥娱乐. "Tashi Shean Liuyiduo De Zhengtingji Jutan, Beipan Sihuan, Erzi Pan Shijiunian, Qifu Huoxing Wunian" 他是涉案6亿多的正厅级巨贪，被判死缓，儿子判19年，情妇获刑5年 [He Is a Department-Level Corrupt Official Involved in a 600 Million CNY Case, Received Suspended Death Sentence; Son Received 19-Year Sentence, and Mistress 5-Year Sentence]. *Wangyi Hao* 网易号 [NetEast Accounts], June 22, 2021. www.163.com/dy/article/GD2L33I805373JOH.html.

Zang, Xiaowei, and Michael Musheno. "Exploring Frontline Work in China." *Public Administration* 95, no. 3 (2017): 842–855. https://doi.org/10.1111/padm.12340.

Zeng, Yi, and Therese Hesketh. "The Effects of China's Universal Two-Child Policy." *The Lancet* 388, no. 10054 (October 2016): 1930–1938. https://doi.org/10.1016/S0140-6736(16)31405-2.

Zhai, Keith. "Chongqing 21 Sentenced over Sex Scandal." *South China Morning Post*, May 8, 2013. www.scmp.com/news/china/article/1232551/chongqing-21-sentenced-over-scandal.

"Chongqing Cadre Lei Zhengfu, Taped Having Sex, Is Jailed 13 Years for Bribery." *South China Morning Post*, June 29, 2013. www.scmp.com/news/china/article/1270935/lei-zhengfu-receives-13-years-prison-bribery.

Zhan, Wei 詹伟. "Zhongguo Dui Maiyin Piaochang Renyuan Shourong Jiaoyu Zhidu De Yanjiu Baogao" 中国对卖淫嫖娼人员收容教育制度的研究报告 [A Study on China's Custody and Education System for Prostitutes]. In *Xianzhi Dui Renshen Ziyou De Xianzhi–Zhongguo Xingzhengxing Xianzhi Renshen Ziyou Falu Chufen De Fazhi Jianshe* 限制对人身自由的限制-中国行政性限制人身自由法律处分的法治建设 [To Refrain from the

Restrictions of Personal Freedom], edited by Guo Jianan 郭建安 and Zheng Xiaze 郑霞泽, 416–466. Beijing: China Law Press 法律出版社, 2005.

Zhang, Heqing. "Female Sex Sellers and Public Policy in the People's Republic of China." In *Sex and Sexuality in China*, edited by Elaine Jeffreys, 139–158. Routledge Studies on China in Transition 26. London: Routledge, 2006.

Zhang, Lei, Eric Pui Fung Chow, Jun Zhang, Jun Jing, and David P. Wilson. "Describing the Chinese HIV Surveillance System and the Influences of Political Structures and Social Stigma." *The Open AIDS Journal* 6 (2012): 163–168.

Zhang, Lijia. "China's Corrupt Officials Have More to Fear from Jilted Lover than Crackdown." *South China Morning Post*, August 16, 2013. www.scmp.com/comment/insight-opinion/article/1296922/chinas-corrupt-officials-have-more-fear-jilted-lover.

Zhang, Sheldon X., and Ko-lin Chin. "A People's War: China's Struggle to Contain Its Illicit Drug Problem." *Foreign Policy at Brookings*, 2016. www.brookings.edu/wp-content/uploads/2016/07/a-peoples-war-final.pdf.

Zhang, Songyun 张松筠. "Chu Zhichi Sheli Xingzhuanqu Wai! Yanse Bufen Lanlü Zhichi Xingzhuanqu Yanse Tian Shenjie Shoudu Gongkai Zhengzhi Qingxiang Pian Dupai: Wo Shi Taiwanpai, Tianran Tai!" 除支持設立性專區外!顏色不分藍綠支持性專區顏色田慎節首度公開政治傾向「偏獨派」:我是台灣派, 天然台! [Apart from Supporting Setting up Sex-Trade Zones, Colorblind Support-Sex-Trade Tian Shenjie Reveals Political Orientation for the First Time: I am Pro-Taiwan, Naturally Pro-Taiwan]. *Fount Media* 放言, December 27, 2022. Accessed January 31, 2023. www.fountmedia.io/article/164581.

Zhang, Ye, Joe Young, and Virginia A. Hulme. "Hope for China's Migrant Women Workers." *The China Business Review* 29, no. 3 (May, 2002): 30–36.

Zhao, Dingxin. "The Mandate of Heaven and Performance Legitimation in Historical and Contemporary China." *American Behavioral Scientist* 53, no. 3 (November 1, 2009): 416–433. https://doi.org/10.1177/0002764209338800.

Zhao, Jingyi 赵婧夷. "Gonganbu Youguan Bumen Bushu Gedi Yanda Shehuang Shedu Weifa Fanzui" 公安部有关部门部署各地严打涉黄涉毒违法犯罪 [Deploying the National Crackdown Plan on Drug and Sex-Related Crimes by the Relative Departments of the Ministry of Public Security]. *Zhongguo Zhengfu Wang* 中国政府网, November 25, 2015. www.gov.cn/xinwen/2015-11/25/content_5016400.htm.

Zhao, Jun 赵军. *Chengfa De Bianjie: Maiyin Xingshi Zhengce Shizheng Yanjiu* 惩罚的边界: 卖淫刑事政策实证研究 [The Limit for Punishment: The

Positive Research on Prostitution Criminal Policy]. Beijing: China Legal Publishing House 中国法制出版社, 2007.

"Falu Jingji Chengban Zhi Shizheng Fenxi–Yi 'Maiyin Fa' Weili" 法律经济成本之实证分析-以'卖淫法'为例 [Empirical Research on the Economic Cost of China's Prostitution Laws]. *Jiangxi Gongan Zhuanke Xuexiao Xuebao* 江西公安专科学校学报 1 (2006): 11–18.

Zheng, Tiantian. "Commodifying Romance and Searching for Love: Rural Migrant Bar Hostesses' Moral Vision in Post-Mao Dalian." *Modern China* 34, no. 4 (October 2008): 442–476. https://doi.org/10.1177/0097700408319493.

"The Plight of Sex Workers in China: From Criminalisation and Abuse to Activism." *Made in China Journal* (blog), April 18, 2019. https://madeinchinajournal.com/2019/04/18/the-plight-of-sex-workers-in-china-from-criminalisation-and-abuse-to-activism/.

Red Lights: The Lives of Sex Workers in Postsocialist China. Minneapolis, MN: University of Minnesota Press, 2009.

"Zheng Zhidaole" 郑知道了 [Zheng Knows]. SET News 三立新聞台, January 27, 2023, *YouTube*, Accessed January 31, 2023. www.youtube.com/watch?v=cL96Nw8IXFM&ab_channel=%E9%84%AD%E7%9F%A5%E9%81%93%E4%BA%86.

Zhi, Mo 至墨, and Ouyang Bin 欧阳斌. "Anfang Naxie Zai Zhongguo De Yang Jinv Men" 暗访那些在中国的'洋妓女'们 [A Discrete Investigation of Foreign Prostitutes in China]. *Phoenix Weekly* 凤凰周刊, September 8, 2003. www.chinaaffairs.org/gb/detail.asp?id=35936.

Zhong, Wei. "A Close Look at China's Sex Industry." *Lianhe Zaobao*, October 2, 2000. https://web.archive.org/web/20020421054050/http://www.usembassy-china.org.cn/sandt/sex-industry.html.

Zhou, Jinghao. "Chinese Prostitution: Consequences and Solutions in the Post-Mao Era." *China: An International Journal* 4, no. 2 (2006): 238–262.

Zhou, Yu 周羽, and Liao Kaidi 廖开迪. "Zhong Nanshan: Yao Tigao Woguo Jikong Zhongxing De Diwei" 钟南山：要提高我国疾控中心的地位 [Zhong Nanshan: We Need to Elevate the Position of Our CDCs]. *Yangguang News* 央广网, February 27, 2020. www.cnr.cn/gd/ygsy/20200227/t20200227_524994057.shtml.

Zhu, Bang-Yong, Jin Bu, Pei-Yong Huang et al. "Epidemiology of Sexually Transmitted Infections, HIV, and Related High-Risk Behaviors among Female Sex Workers in Guangxi Autonomous Region, China." *Japanese Journal of Infectious Diseases* 65, no. 1 (2012): 75–78.

Zhu, Guang Rong, Cheng Ye Ji, and Xing Hua Yang. "Relationship between Migration and HIV Risky Behavior: A Comparative Study of Returning Migrants and Non Migrants Based on Rural Out-of-School Youth in Jilin, China." *Biomedical and Environmental Sciences* 28, no. 6 (2015): 429–436. https://doi.org/10.3967/bes2015.060.

Zhu, Suli. "The Party and the Courts." In *Judicial Independence in China: Lessons for Global Rule of Law Promotion*, edited by Randall Peerenboom, 1st ed., 52–68. Cambridge: Cambridge University Press, 2009.

Zhu, Wei Xing, Li Lu, and Therese Hesketh. "China's Excess Males, Sex Selective Abortion, and One Child Policy: Analysis of Data from 2005 National Intercensus Survey." *BMJ* 338, no. 2 (April 18, 2009): 920–923.

Zhuang, Pinhui. "I Was Unfaithful to Wife Gu Kailai, Bo Xilai Admits in Court." *South China Morning Post*, August 25, 2013. www.scmp.com/news/china/article/1299253/i-was-unfaithful-wife-gu-kailai-bo-xilai-admits-court.

LAWS, RULES, REGULATIONS, AND POLICIES

110 Jiechu Jing Gongzuo Guize (110接处警工作规则) [Handling Policing Affairs by 110 Hotline] (promulgated by the Min. of Public Security, April 30, 2003, effective April 30, 2003).

2012 Jibing Yufang Kongzhi Gongzuo Jixiao Pinggu Biaozhun (疾病预防控制工作绩效评估标准（2012年版)) [2012 Performance Assessment Screening Criteria for Disease Control and Prevention] (promulgated by the Ministry of Health (dissolved), January 7, 2013, effective January 7, 2013).

Aizibing Fangzhi Tiaoli (艾滋病防治条例) [Regulation on the Prevention and Treatment of HIV/AIDS] (promulgated by the St. Council, January 18, 2006, effective March 6, 2006, rev'd March 2, 2019).

Beijing Shi Difang Shuiwuju Duiyu Benshi Yule Yinshi Fuwuye Bufen Congye Renyuan Shixing Dinge Zhengshou Geren Suodeshui De Zhanxing Banfa Buchong Guiding De Tongzhi (北京市地方税务局关于对本市娱乐、饮食服务业部分从业人员实行定额征收个人所得税的暂行办法补充规定的通知) [Notice of the Supplementary Regulations for Beijing Local Taxation Bureau's Provisional Measures on Collecting Personal Income Tax from Entertainment and Food Service Industry Employees] (promulgated by the Beijing Local Taxation Bureau, July 25, 2000, effective October 1, 2000).

Beijing Shi Wenhuaju Xingzheng Xuke Shixiang He Xingzheng Xuke Chengxu (北京市文化局行政许可事项和行政许可程序) [Beijing Municipal Bureau of Culture Administrative Licensing Items and Procedures] (promulgated by the Beijing Mun. Bureau of Culture, October 28, 2009, effective October 28, 2009).

Chuanranbing Fangzhifa (传染病防治法) [Law on Prevention and Treatment of Infectious Diseases] (promulgated by the Standing Comm. Nat'l People's Cong., February 21, 1989, rev'd August 28, 2004, amended June 29, 2013).

Gaowei Xingwei Ganyu Gongzuo Zhidao Fangan (Shixing) (高危行为干预工作指导方案（试行)) [Guidelines for Intervention Works on High-Risk

Behaviors (For Trial Implementation)] (promulgated by the Ministry of Health (dissolved), May 20, 2005, effective May 20, 2005).

Geti Gongshanghu Shuishou Dingqi Dinge Zhengshou Guanli Banfa (个体工商户税收定期定额征收管理办法) [Measures for the Administration of Regular and Fixed-Amount Taxation on Self-Employed Industrial and Commercial Households] (promulgated by the St. Admin. of Tax'n, August 30, 2006, effective January 1, 2007, amended June 15, 2018).

Gongan Jiguan Renmin Jingcha Guanli Tiaoling (公安机关人民警察纪律条令) [Ordinance on Disciplines for the People's Police of the Public Security Organs] (promulgated by the Ministry of Supervision, the Ministry of Human Res. & Soc. Sec. and the Ministry of Pub. Sec., April 21, 2010, effective June 1, 2010).

Gonggong Changsuo Weisheng Guanli Tiaoli (公共场所卫生管理条例) [Regulations on the Administration of Sanitation at Public Places] (promulgated by the St. Council., April 1, 1987, effective April 1, 1987, amended April 23, 2019).

Guanyu Chongxin Fabu "Guanyu Tezhong Xiaofei Hangye Linshi Shoupin Fuwu Renyuan Geren Suodeshui Zhengshou Guanli De Zanxing Guiding" Wenjian De Jueding (关于重新发布《特种消费行业临时受聘服务人员个人所得税征收管理的暂行规定》文件的决定) [Decision on Reissuing the Interim Provisions on the Collection of Individual Income Tax from Temporarily Employed Service Providers in the Special Services Industries] (promulgated by the Shenzhen Local Tax'n Bureau, November 6, 2003, effective November 6, 2003).

Juliu Suo Tiaoli (拘留所条例) [Regulation on Detention Facilities] (promulgated by the St. Council, February 15, 2012, effective April 1, 2012).

Maiyin Piaochang Renyuan Shourong Jiaoyu Banfa (卖淫嫖娼人员收容教育办法) [Measures for the Custody and Education of Persons Engaged in Prostitution and Whoring] (promulgated by the St. Council., September 4, 1993, effective September 4, 1993, amended January 8, 2011, repealed March 27, 2020).

Quanguo Aizibing Jiance Gongzuo Guifan (全国艾滋病监测工作规范) [Standards for HIV Surveillance and HIV/AIDS] (promulgated by the Ministry of Health (dissolved), March 20, 2002, effective March 20, 2002).

Quanguo Renmin Daibiao Dahui Changwu Weiyuanhui Guanyu Yanjin Maiyin Piaochang De Jueding (全国人民代表大会常务委员会关于严禁卖淫嫖娼的决定) [Decision of the Standing Committee of the National People's Congress on the Strict Prohibition against Prostitution and Whoring] (promulgated by the St. Council, September 4, 1991, effective September 4, 1991).

"Shisi Wu" Guomin Jiankang Guihua ("十四五"国民健康规划) [The 14th Five Year Plan on National Health Planning] (promulgated by the Gen. Office of the St. Council, April 27, 2022, effective April 27, 2022).

Shourong Jiaoyu Suo Guanli Banfa (收容教育所管理办法) [Measures for the Administration of the Custody and Education Centers] (promulgated by the Ministry of Pub. Sec., April 24, 2000, effective April 24, 2000, rev'd June 29, 2014, repealed August 6, 2020).

Weishengbu Bangongting Guanyu Zai Geji Jibing Yufang Kongzhi Zhongxin (Weisheng Fangyi Zhan) Jianli Gaowei Renqun Ganyu Gongzuodui De Tongzhi (卫生部办公厅关于在各级疾病预防控制中心(卫生防疫站)建立高危人群干预工作队的通知) [General Office of Ministry of Health's Notice for Setting up Intervention Working Group for High-Risk People at Health and Epidemic Prevention Centers at Every Administrative Level] (promulgated by the Ministry of Health(dissolved), August 20, 2004).

Weishengbu Gonganbu Guanyu Dui Maiyin Piaochang Renyuan Qiangzhi Jinxing Xingbing Jiancha Zhiliao Youguan Wenti De Tongzhi (卫生部、公安部关于对卖淫嫖娼人员强制进行性病检查治疗有关问题的通知) [Notice of the Ministry of Health and the Ministry of Public Security of Issues Concerning Compulsory STD Inspection and Treatment of Persons Engaging in Prostitution] (promulgated by the Min. of Health and the Min. of Public Security, December 16, 1991).

Yingyeshui Gaizheng Zengzhishui Shidian Shishi Banfa (营业税改征增值税试点实施办法) [Measures for Implementing the Pilot Program of Replacing Business Tax with Value-Added Tax] (promulgated by the Ministry of Fin. and St. Admin. of Tax'n, December 12, 2013, effective January 1, 2014).

Yule Changsuo Guanli Banfa (娱乐场所管理办法) [Measures for the Administration of Entertainment Venues] (promulgated by the St. Coun., January 25, 2013, effective March 11, 2013).

Yule Changsuo Guanli Tiaoli (娱乐场所管理条例) [Regulation on the Administration of Entertainment Venues] (promulgated by the St. Coun., January 18, 2006, effective March 6, 2006).

Yule Changsuo Xingzheng Shenpi Gongzuo Zhidao Yijian (娱乐场所行政审批工作指导意见) [Guiding Opinions on the Administrative Approval of Entertainment Venues] (promulgated by the Jiangsu Provincial Department of Culture, July 1, 2013, effective August 8, 2013).

Yule Changsuo Zhian Guanli Banfa (娱乐场所治安管理办法) [Measures for the Public Security of Entertainment Venues] (promulgated by the Min. of Public Security, April 21, 2008, effective October 1, 2008).

Zhongguo Ezhi Yu Fangzhi Aizibing Shierwu Xingdong Jihua (中国遏制与防治艾滋病'十二五'行动计划) [China's '12th Five-Year' Action Plan for Containment and Prevention of HIV/AIDS (2011–2015)] (promulgated by the General Office of the St. Council, January 13, 2012, effective January 13, 2012).

Zhongguo Ezhi Yu Fangzhi Aizibing Xingdong Jihua 2006-2010 (中国遏制与防治艾滋病行动计划 (2006–2010年)) [China's Action Plan for Containment and Prevention of HIV/AIDS (2006–2010)] (promulgated by the General Office of the St. Council, February 27, 2006, effective February 27, 2006, repealed November 27, 2015).

Zhonghua Renmin Gongheguo Gere Suodeshui Fa (中华人民共和国个人所得税法) [Individual Income Tax Law of the People's Republic of China] (promulgated by the Standing Comm. Nat'l People's Cong., September 10, 1980, amended August 31, 2018, effective January 1, 2019).

Zhonghua Renmin Gongheguo Lifa Fa (中华人民共和国立法法) [Legislation Law of the People's Republic of China] (promulgated by the Standing Comm. Nat'l People's Cong., March 15, 2000, effective July 1, 2000).

Zhonghua Renmin Gongheguo Qiye Suodeshui Fa (中华人民共和国企业所得税法) [Enterprise Income Tax Law of the People's Republic of China] (promulgated by the Standing Comm. Nat'l People's Cong., March 16, 2007, effective January 1, 2008, amended December 29, 2018).

Zhonghua Renmin Gongheguo Xianfa (中华人民共和国宪法) [Constitution of the People's Republic of China] (promulgated by the Standing Comm. Nat'l People's Cong., December 4, 1982, effective December 4, 1986, amended March 11, 2018).

Zhonghua Renmin Gongheguo Xingfa (中华人民共和国刑法) [Criminal Law of the People's Republic of China] (promulgated by the Standing Comm. Nat'l People's Cong., July 6, 1979, rev'd March 14, 1997, amended December 26, 2020, effective March 1, 2021).

Zhonghua Renmin Gongheguo Xingzheng Chufa Fa (中华人民共和国行政处罚法) [Administrative Penalty Law of the People's Republic of China] (promulgated by the Standing Comm. Nat'l People's Cong., March 17, 1996, effective October 1, 1996).

Zhonghua Renmin Gongheguo Yingyeshui Zanxing Tiaoli (中华人民共和国营业税暂行条例) [Provisional Regulations of the People's Republic of China on Business Tax] (promulgated by the St. Council, December 13, 1993, rev'd November 5, 2008, repealed November 19, 2017).

Zhonghua Renmin Gongheguo Zhian Guanli Chufa Fa (中华人民共和国治安管理处罚法) [Public Security Administration Punishments Law of the People's Republic of China] (promulgated by the Standing Comm. Nat'l People's Cong., August 28, 2005, effective March 1, 2006, amended October 26, 2012).

INDEX

CAMBRIDGE STUDIES IN LAW AND SOCIETY

Books in the Series

Diseases of the Will: Alcohol and the Dilemmas of Freedom
Mariana Valverde

The Politics of Truth and Reconciliation in South Africa: Legitimizing the Post-Apartheid State
Richard A. Wilson

Modernism and the Grounds of Law
Peter Fitzpatrick

Unemployment and Government: Genealogies of the Social
William Walters

Autonomy and Ethnicity: Negotiating Competing Claims in Multi-Ethnic States
Yash Ghai

Constituting Democracy: Law, Globalism and South Africa's Political Reconstruction
Heinz Klug

The Ritual of Rights in Japan: Law, Society, and Health Policy
Eric A. Feldman

Governing Morals: A Social History of Moral Regulation
Alan Hunt

The Colonies of Law: Colonialism, Zionism and Law in Early Mandate Palestine
Ronen Shamir

Law and Nature
David Delaney

Social Citizenship and Workfare in the United States and Western Europe: The Paradox of Inclusion
Joel F. Handler

Law, Anthropology, and the Constitution of the Social: Making Persons and Things
Edited by
Alain Pottage and Martha Mundy

Judicial Review and Bureaucratic Impact: International and Interdisciplinary Perspectives Edited by
Marc Hertogh and Simon Halliday

Immigrants at the Margins: Law, Race, and Exclusion in Southern Europe
Kitty Calavita

Lawyers and Regulation: The Politics of the Administrative Process
Patrick Schmidt

Law and Globalization from Below: Towards a Cosmopolitan Legality Edited by
Boaventura de Sousa Santos and César A. Rodríguez-Garavito

Public Accountability: Designs, Dilemmas and Experiences Edited by
Michael W. Dowdle

Law, Violence and Sovereignty among West Bank Palestinians
Tobias Kelly

Legal Reform and Administrative Detention Powers in China
Sarah Biddulph

The Practice of Human Rights: Tracking Law between the Global and the Local
Edited by
Mark Goodale and Sally Engle Merry

Judges beyond Politics in Democracy and Dictatorship: Lessons from Chile
Lisa Hilbink

Paths to International Justice: Social and Legal Perspectives Edited by
Marie-Bénédicte Dembour and Tobias Kelly

Law and Society in Vietnam: The Transition from Socialism in Comparative Perspective
Mark Sidel

Constitutionalizing Economic Globalization: Investment Rules and Democracy's Promise
David Schneiderman

The New World Trade Organization Knowledge Agreements: Second Edition
Christopher Arup

Justice and Reconciliation in Post-Apartheid South Africa Edited by
François du Bois and Antje du Bois-Pedain

Militarization and Violence against Women in Conflict Zones in the Middle East: A Palestinian Case-Study
Nadera Shalhoub-Kevorkian

Child Pornography and Sexual Grooming: Legal and Societal Responses
Suzanne Ost

Darfur and the Crime of Genocide
John Hagan and Wenona Rymond-Richmond

Fictions of Justice: The International Criminal Court and the Challenge of Legal Pluralism in Sub-Saharan Africa
Kamari Maxine Clarke

Conducting Law and Society Research: Reflections on Methods and Practices
Simon Halliday and Patrick Schmidt

Planted Flags: Trees, Land, and Law in Israel/Palestine
Irus Braverman

Culture under Cross-Examination: International Justice and the Special Court for Sierra Leone
Tim Kelsall

Cultures of Legality: Judicialization and Political Activism in Latin America
Javier Couso, Alexandra Huneeus, and Rachel Sieder

Courting Democracy in Bosnia and Herzegovina: The Hague Tribunal's Impact in a Postwar State
Lara J. Nettelfield

The Gacaca Courts, Post-Genocide Justice and Reconciliation in Rwanda: Justice without Lawyers
Phil Clark

Law, Society, and History: Themes in the Legal Sociology and Legal History of Lawrence M. Friedman Edited by
Robert W. Gordon and Morton J. Horwitz

After Abu Ghraib: Exploring Human Rights in America and the Middle East
Shadi Mokhtari

Adjudication in Religious Family Laws: Cultural Accommodation, Legal Pluralism, and Gender Equality in India
Gopika Solanki

Water on Tap: Rights and Regulation in the Transnational Governance of Urban Water Services
Bronwen Morgan

Elements of Moral Cognition: Rawls' Linguistic Analogy and the Cognitive Science of Moral and Legal Judgment
John Mikhail

Mitigation and Aggravation at Sentencing Edited by
Julian V. Roberts

Institutional Inequality and the Mobilization of the Family and Medical Leave Act: Rights on Leave
Catherine R. Albiston

Authoritarian Rule of Law: Legislation, Discourse and Legitimacy in Singapore
Jothie Rajah

Law and Development and the Global Discourses of Legal Transfers Edited by
John Gillespie and Pip Nicholson

Law against the State: Ethnographic Forays into Law's Transformations Edited by
Julia Eckert, Brian Donahoe, Christian Strümpell and Zerrin Özlem Biner

Transnational Legal Ordering and State Change Edited by
Gregory C. Shaffer

Legal Mobilization under Authoritarianism: The Case of Post-Colonial Hong Kong
Waikeung Tam

Complementarity in the Line of Fire: The Catalysing Effect of the International Criminal Court in Uganda and Sudan
Sarah M. H. Nouwen

Political and Legal Transformations of an Indonesian Polity: The Nagari from Colonisation to Decentralisation
Franz von Benda-Beckmann and Keebet von Benda-Beckmann

Pakistan's Experience with Formal Law: An Alien Justice
Osama Siddique

Human Rights under State-Enforced Religious Family Laws in Israel, Egypt, and India
Yüksel Sezgin

Why Prison? Edited by
David Scott

Law's Fragile State: Colonial, Authoritarian, and Humanitarian Legacies in Sudan
Mark Fathi Massoud

Rights for Others: The Slow Home-Coming of Human Rights in the Netherlands
Barbara Oomen

European States and Their Muslim Citizens: The Impact of Institutions on Perceptions and Boundaries Edited by
John R. Bowen, Christophe Bertossi, Jan Willem Duyvendak, and Mona Lena Krook

Environmental Litigation in China: A Study in Political Ambivalence
Rachel E. Stern

Indigeneity and Legal Pluralism in India: Claims, Histories, Meanings
Pooja Parmar

Paper Tiger: Law, Bureaucracy and the Developmental State in Himalayan India
Nayanika Mathur

Religion, Law and Society
Russell Sandberg

The Experiences of Face Veil Wearers in Europe and the Law Edited by
Eva Brems

The Contentious History of the International Bill of Human Rights
Christopher N. J. Roberts

Transnational Legal Orders Edited by
Terence C. Halliday and Gregory Shaffer

Lost in China? Law, Culture and Society in Post-1997 Hong Kong
Carol A. G. Jones

Security Theology, Surveillance and the Politics of Fear
Nadera Shalhoub-Kevorkian

Opposing the Rule of Law: How Myanmar's Courts Make Law and Order
Nick Cheesman

Ironies of Colonial Governance: Law, Custom and Justice in Colonial India
James Jaffe

The Clinic and the Court: Law, Medicine and Anthropology Edited by
Ian Harper, Tobias Kelly, and Akshay Khanna

The World of Indicators: The Making of Government Knowledge through Quantification Edited by
Richard Rottenburg, Sally E. Merry, Sung-Joon Park, and Johanna Mugler

Contesting Immigration Policy in Court: Legal Activism and Its Radiating Effects in the United States and France
Leila Kawar

The Quiet Power of Indicators: Measuring Governance, Corruption, and Rule of Law Edited by
Sally Engle Merry, Kevin E. Davis, and Benedict Kingsbury

Investing in Authoritarian Rule: Punishment and Patronage in Rwanda's Gacaca Courts for Genocide Crimes
Anuradha Chakravarty

Contractual Knowledge: One Hundred Years of Legal Experimentation in Global Markets Edited by
Grégoire Mallard and Jérôme Sgard

Iraq and the Crimes of Aggressive War: The Legal Cynicism of Criminal Militarism
John Hagan, Joshua Kaiser, and Anna Hanson

Culture in the Domains of Law Edited by
René Provost

China and Islam: The Prophet, the Party, and Law
Matthew S. Erie

Diversity in Practice: Race, Gender, and Class in Legal and Professional Careers Edited by
Spencer Headworth, Robert L. Nelson, Ronit Dinovitzer, and David B. Wilkins

A Sociology of Constitutions: Constitutions and State Legitimacy in Historical-Sociological Perspective
Chris Thornhill

A Sociology of Transnational Constitutions: Social Foundations of the Post-National Legal Structure
Chris Thornhill

Genocide Never Sleeps: Living Law at the International Criminal Tribunal for Rwanda
Nigel Eltringham

Shifting Legal Visions: Judicial Change and Human Rights Trials in Latin America
Ezequiel A. González-Ocantos

The Demographic Transformations of Citizenship
Heli Askola

Criminal Defense in China: The Politics of Lawyers at Work
Sida Liu and Terence C. Halliday

Contesting Economic and Social Rights in Ireland: Constitution, State and Society, 1848–2016
Thomas Murray

Buried in the Heart: Women, Complex Victimhood and the War in Northern Uganda
Erin Baines

Palaces of Hope: The Anthropology of Global Organizations Edited by
Ronald Niezen and Maria Sapignoli

The Politics of Bureaucratic Corruption in Post-Transitional Eastern Europe
Marina Zaloznaya

Revisiting the Law and Governance of Trafficking, Forced Labor and Modern Slavery Edited by
Prabha Kotiswaran

Incitement on Trial: Prosecuting International Speech Crimes
Richard Ashby Wilson

Criminalizing Children: Welfare and the State in Australia
David McCallum

Global Lawmakers: International Organizations in the Crafting of World Markets
Susan Block-Lieb and Terence C. Halliday

Duties to Care: Dementia, Relationality and Law
Rosie Harding

Insiders, Outsiders, Injuries, and Law: Revisiting "The Oven Bird's Song" Edited by
Mary Nell Trautner

Hunting Justice: Displacement, Law, and Activism in the Kalahari
Maria Sapignoli

Injury and Injustice: The Cultural Politics of Harm and Redress Edited by
Anne Bloom, David M. Engel, and Michael McCann

Ruling Before the Law: The Politics of Legal Regimes in China and Indonesia
William Hurst

The Powers of Law: A Comparative Analysis of Sociopolitical Legal Studies
Mauricio García-Villegas

A Sociology of Justice in Russia Edited by
Marina Kurkchiyan and Agnieszka Kubal

Constituting Religion: Islam, Liberal Rights, and the Malaysian State
Tamir Moustafa

The Invention of the Passport: Surveillance, Citizenship and the State, Second Edition
John C. Torpey

Law's Trials: The Performance of Legal Institutions in the US "War on Terror"
Richard L. Abel

Law's Wars: The Fate of the Rule of Law in the US "War on Terror"
Richard L. Abel

Transforming Gender Citizenship: The Irresistible Rise of Gender Quotas in Europe
Edited by
Eléonore Lépinard and Ruth Rubio-Marín

Muslim Women's Quest for Justice: Gender, Law and Activism in India
Mengia Hong Tschalaer

Children as 'Risk': Sexual Exploitation and Abuse by Children and Young People
Anne-Marie McAlinden

The Legal Process and the Promise of Justice: Studies Inspired by the Work of Malcolm Feeley
Jonathan Simon, Rosann Greenspan, Hadar Aviram

Gift Exchanges: The Transnational History of a Political Idea
Grégoire Mallard

Measuring Justice: Quantitative Accountability and the National Prosecuting Authority in South Africa
Johanna Mugler

Negotiating the Power of NGOs: Women's Legal Rights in South Africa
Reem Wael

Indigenous Water Rights in Law and Regulation: Lessons from Comparative Experience
Elizabeth Jane Macpherson

The Edge of Law: Legal Geographies of a War Crimes Court
Alex Jeffrey

Everyday Justice: Law, Ethnography, and Injustice
Sandra Brunnegger

The Uncounted: Politics of Data in Global Health
Sara L. M. Davis

Transnational Legal Ordering of Criminal Justice
Gregory Shaffer and Ely Aaronson

Five Republics and One Tradition
Pablo Ruiz-Tagle

The Law Multiple: Judgment and Knowledge in Practice
Irene van Oorschot

Health as a Human Right: The Politics and Judicialisation of Health in Brazil
Octávio Luiz Motta Ferraz

Shari'a, Inshallah: Finding God in Somali Legal Politics
Mark Fathi Massoud

Policing for Peace: Institutions, Expectations, and Security in Divided Societies
Matthew Nanes

Rule of Law Intermediaries: Brokering Influence in Myanmar
Kristina Simion

Lactation at Work: Expressed Milk, Expressing Beliefs, and the Expressive Value of Law
Elizabeth A. Hoffmann

The Archival Politics of International Courts
Henry Redwood

Global Pro Bono: Causes, Context, and Contestation Edited by
Scott L. Cummings, Fabio de Sa e Silva and Louise G. Trubek

The Practice and Problems of Transnational Counter-Terrorism
Fiona de Londras

Decoupling: Gender Injustice in China's Divorce Courts
Ethan Michelson

Anti-Constitutional Populism
Martin Krygier, Adam Czarnota and Wojciech Sadurski

Lawyers in Conflict and Transition
Kieran McEvoy, Louse Mallinder and Anna Bryson

The Ghostwriters: Lawyers and the Politics behind the Judicial Construction of Europe
Tommaso Pavone

The Sentimental Court: The Affective Life of International Criminal Justice
Jonas Bens

Practices of Reparations in International Criminal Justice
Christoph Sperfeldt

Seeking Supremacy: The Pursuit of Judicial Power in Pakistan
Yasser Kureshi

The Power of the Jury: Transforming Citizens into Jurors
Nancy S. Marder

Undue Process: Persecution and Punishment in Autocratic Courts
Fiona Feiang Shen-Bayh

Discounting Life: Necropolitical Law, Culture, and the Long War on Terror
Jothie Rajah

Clean Air at What Cost? The Rise of Blunt Force Regulation in China
Denise Sienli van der Kamp

Law and Precarity: Legal Consciousness and Daily Survival in Vietnam
Tu Phuong Nguyen

Prosecutors, Voters and The Criminalization of Corruption in Latin America: The Case of Lava Jato
Ezequiel A. Gonzalez-Ocantos and Paula Muñoz Chirinos

Entangled Domains: Empire, Law and Religion in Northern Nigeria
Rabiat Akande

The Social Constitution: Embedding Social Rights Through Legal Mobilization
Whitney K. Taylor

Out of Place: Fieldwork and Positionality in Law and Society Edited by
Lynette J. Chua and Mark Fathi Massoud

Negotiating Legality: Chinese Companies in the U.S. Legal System
Ji Li

For EU product safety concerns, contact us at Calle de José Abascal, 56–1°, 28003 Madrid, Spain or eugpsr@cambridge.org.

www.ingramcontent.com/pod-product-compliance
Lightning Source LLC
Chambersburg PA
CBHW071552020525
26092CB00004B/47
* 9 7 8 1 1 0 7 1 7 9 2 2 6 *